macroeconomics

A CONTEMPORARY INTRODUCTION

11e

William A. McEachern

University of Connecticut

CENGAGE
Learning®

Australia • Brazil • Mexico • Singapore • United Kingdom • United States

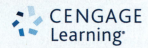
CENGAGE
Learning®

Macroeconomics: A Contemporary Introduction, 11e

William A. McEachern

Vice President, General Manager, Social Science & Qualitative Business: Erin Joyner

Product Director: Michael Worls

Senior Product Manager: Michael Parthenakis

Senior Content/Media Developer: Julia Chase

Executive Marketing Manager: John Carey

Senior Content Project Manager: Colleen A. Farmer

Manufacturing Planner: Kevin Kluck

Production Service: Cenveo Publisher Services

Sr. Art Director: Michelle Kunkler

Internal & Cover Designer: cmillerdesign

Cover Image: Sergey Nivens/Getty Images

Intellectual Property

    Analyst: Jen Nonemacher

    Project Manager: Sarah Swainwald

For product information and technology assistance, contact us at
Cengage Learning Customer & Sales Support, 1-800-354-9706

For permission to use material from this text or product,
submit all requests online at **www.cengage.com/permissions**
Further permissions questions can be emailed to
permissionrequest@cengage.com

Unless otherwise noted, all items © Cengage Learning.

Library of Congress Control Number: 2015953057

ISBN: 978-1-305-50549-0

Cengage Learning
20 Channel Center Street
Boston, MA 02210
USA

Cengage Learning is a leading provider of customized learning solutions with employees residing in nearly 40 different countries and sales in more than 125 countries around the world. Find your local representative at **www.cengage.com.**

Cengage Learning products are represented in Canada by Nelson Education, Ltd.

To learn more about Cengage Learning Solutions, visit **www.cengage.com**

Purchase any of our products at your local college store or at our preferred online store **www.cengagebrain.com**

Printed in the United States of America
Print Number: 01   Print Year: 2015

Will McEachern started teaching large sections of economic principles shortly after joining the University of Connecticut. Not long after that, he began offering teaching workshops around the country. And Will created *The Teaching Economist*, now in its third decade, a newsletter that focuses on making teaching more effective and more fun.

His research in public finance, public policy, and industrial organization has appeared in a variety of journals, including *Economic Inquiry, National Tax Journal, Journal of Industrial Economics, Quarterly Review of Economics and Finance, Southern Economic Journal,* and *Public Choice*. His books and monographs include *Managerial Control and Performance* (D.C. Heath), *School Finance Reform* (CREUES), and *Tax-Exempt Property and Tax Capitalization in Metropolitan Areas* (CREUES). He has also contributed chapters to edited volumes such as *Rethinking Economic Principles* (Irwin Publishing), *Impact Evaluations of Vertical Restraint Cases* (Federal Trade Commission), *Readings in Public Choice Economics* (University of Michigan Press), and *International Handbook on Teaching and Learning Economics* (Edward Elgar Publishing).

This principles textbook has been translated into Spanish, Chinese, and Bahasa Indonesia, and has been adapted for students in Australia and in India. Will has also written a high school principles textbook, now in its third edition.

Professor McEachern has been quoted in or written for the *Times* of London, *New York Times, Wall Street Journal, Christian Science Monitor, USA Today, Challenge Magazine,* and *Reader's Digest*.

Professor McEachern won the University of Connecticut Alumni Association's Faculty Award for Distinguished Public Service as well as the Association's Faculty Award for Excellence in Undergraduate Teaching. He is the only person in UConn history to be awarded both. He was born in Portsmouth, N.H., earned an undergraduate degree with honors from College of the Holy Cross, served three years as a U.S. Army officer, and earned an M.A. and Ph.D. from the University of Virginia.

To Pat

Brief Contents

Table of Contents

ix

PART 2   Fundamentals of Macroeconomics

Chapter 5

Chapter 6

Chapter 7

Chapter 8

Chapter 9

Chapter 10

Aggregate Supply   212

PART 3   Fiscal and Monetary Policy

Chapter 11

Fiscal Policy   233

Chapter 12

Federal Budgets and Public Policy   256

Chapter 13

Money and the Financial System   280

Economics has a short history but a long past. As a distinct discipline, economics has been around for only a few hundred years, yet civilizations have confronted the economic problem of scarce resources and unlimited wants for millennia. Economics, the discipline, may be centuries old, but it's new every day, with fresh evidence that refines and extends economic theory. For example, what could be newer than how technological change is reshaping the way we live? In this edition of *Economics: A Contemporary Introduction*, I draw on more than three decades of teaching and research to convey the vitality, timeliness, and relevance of economics.

Lead by Example

Remember the last time you were in unfamiliar parts and had to ask for directions? Along with the directions came the standard comment, "You can't miss it!" So how come you missed it? Because the "landmark," so obvious to locals, was invisible to you, a stranger. Writing a principles textbook is much like giving directions. Familiarity is a must, but that very familiarity can cloud the author's ability to see the material through the fresh eyes of a new student. One could revert to a tell-all approach, but that will bury students in information. An alternative is to opt for the minimalist approach, writing abstractly about good x and good y, units of labor and units of capital, or the proverbial widget. But that shorthand turns economics into a foreign language.

Good directions rely on landmarks familiar to us all—a stoplight, a fork in the road, a white picket fence. Likewise, a good textbook builds bridges from the familiar to the new. That's what I try to do—*lead by example*. By beginning with examples that draw on common experience, I try to create graphic images that need little explanation, thereby eliciting from the reader that light of recognition, that "Aha!" I believe that the shortest distance between an economic principle and student comprehension is a lively example. Examples should convey the point quickly and directly. Having to explain an example is like having to explain a joke—the point gets lost. Throughout the book, I try to provide just enough intuition and institutional detail to get the point across. But my emphasis is on economic ideas, not economic jargon.

Students show up the first day of class with at least 17 years of experience with economic choices, economic institutions, and economic events. Each grew up in a household—the most important economic institution in a market economy. As consumers, students become well acquainted with fast-food outlets, cineplexes, car dealerships, online retailers, and scores of stores at the mall. Most students have supplied labor to the job market—more than half had jobs in high school. Students also have interacted with government—they know about sales taxes, driver's licenses, speed limits, public schools, and laws about texting while driving. And students have a growing familiarity with the rest of the world. Thus, students have abundant experience with economics. This rich lode of personal experience offers a perfect starting point. Rather than try to create for students a new world of economics—a new way of thinking, my approach is to build on student experience—on what Alfred Marshall called "the ordinary business of life." I frequently remind students how much they already know.

This book starts with what students bring to the party. For example, to explain resource substitution, rather than rely on abstract units of labor and capital, I begin with washing a car, where the mix can vary from a drive-through car wash (much capital and little labor) to a Saturday morning charity car wash (much labor and little capital). Down-to-earth examples turn the abstract into the concrete to help students learn and remember. In this edition of *Macroeconomics: A Contemporary Introduction*, I add about 140 fresh examples to the exposition, bringing the total number of examples to about 300. Because instructors can cover only a portion of a textbook in the classroom, material should be self-contained and self-explanatory. This gives instructors the flexibility to emphasize in class topics of special interest.

What's New With the Eleventh Edition

If there is one overarching theme with this edition, it's the impact of technological change on all aspects of economic life. From Spotify, to smart apps, to Uber, to bitcoin, to interactive learning software, I underscore how technological change is affecting the way we work, learn, play, and live. This edition builds on previous success with additional examples, more questions along the way, and frequent summaries as a chapter unfolds. By making the material both more natural and more personal, I try to engage students in a collaborative discussion. Chapters have been streamlined for a clearer, more intuitive presentation, with fresh examples, new research findings, revised case studies, and additional exhibits to crystallize key points.

Recent research suggests that students learn best by trying to recall what they have just read. In that spirit, I pose "Checkpoint" questions after each section of a chapter. And to help students grasp the material, I also break down each chapter into at least four sections. As with the previous edition, each chapter includes a relevant case study integrated into the narrative flow, not isolated from the mainstream. New with this edition is an additional case study per chapter available on the companion site at www.cengagebrain.com. Questions at the end of each chapter and after each online case study aid student comprehension.

It goes without saying that I revised all data to reflect the most recent figures available. Time-sensitive examples and discussions have also been updated. To make economic principles richer and more interesting, this edition of *Macroeconomics: A Contemporary Introduction* places greater emphasis on recent research. I report on findings from 94 additional studies, nearly all appearing since my previous edition went to press. This brings the total number of studies cited and discussed in this edition to 174. In the following chapter-by-chapter summaries, I will note the number of fresh examples added and the number of new studies reported. I will then sample new material and outline changes to the coverage.

Introductory Chapters: 1–4

As with earlier editions, background material common to both macro- and microeconomics is covered in the first four chapters. Limiting introductory material to four chapters saves precious class time, particularly at those institutions where students may take macro and micro courses in either order (and so must cover introductory chapters twice). New or revised features in the introductory chapters include:

Ch. 1: *The Art and Science of Economic Analysis* I add nine fresh examples and report on three new studies. This chapter provides more detail on the implications of rational self-interest. For example, a physician who owns a pharmacy prescribes more medication than other physicians, and a physician who owns a nuclear scanner is seven times more likely to prescribe such a scan.

Ch. 2: *Economic Tools and Economic Systems* I add seven fresh examples and report on four new studies. I note that an economy's productive capacity depends not only on the *state of technology* but also on the *level of know-how*. Know-how can boost production even if technology and resources are unchanged. By improved know-how, a steel mini-mill, for example, doubled production with no change in technology or the work force. The significance of know-how carries throughout this revision.

Ch. 3: *Economic Decision Makers* I add four fresh examples and report on three new studies. Unlike other principles books, I discuss the role of cooperatives, such as Sunkist, and the not-for-profit sector more generally, such as the Texas Medical Center, which employs more than 100,000 people, exceeding employment at major corporations such as Apple, Google, and Chevron.

Ch. 4: *Demand, Supply, and Markets* I add eight fresh examples and report on two new studies. In explaining the effect of a price change on quantity demanded, I note that the more important the item is as a share of the consumer's budget, the bigger the income effect. That's why, for example, consumers increase other purchases when the price of gasoline plunges, as happened in 2015.

Macroeconomic Chapters: 5–16

Rather than focus on the differences among competing schools of thought, I use the aggregate demand and aggregate supply model to underscore the fundamental distinction between the *active approach*, which views the economy as unstable and in need of government intervention when it gets off track, and the *passive approach*, which views the economy as essentially stable and self-correcting. Again, all macro data have been updated to reflect the most recent figures available. Equilibrium values for real GDP and the price level used in theoretical models throughout the macro chapters match actual values prevailing in the U.S. economy.

Wherever possible, I rely on student experience and intuition to help explain macroeconomic abstractions such as aggregate demand and aggregate supply. For example, to explain how employment can temporarily exceed its natural rate, I note how students, as the term draws to a close, can temporarily shift into a higher gear, studying for exams and finishing term papers. To reinforce the link between income and consumption, I point out how easy it is to figure out the relative income of a neighborhood just by driving through it. And to offer students a feel for the size of the federal budget, I note that if all 4.6 thousand tons of gold stored in Fort Knox could be sold at prevailing prices, the proceeds would run the federal government for about two weeks.

Chapters in this edition follow the same order as in the previous edition. New or revised features in the macroeconomics chapters include:

Ch. 5: *Introduction to Macroeconomics* I add four fresh examples. A new section, "The Global Economy," discusses the interdependence among national economies over the last three decades.

Ch. 6: *Tracking the U.S. Economy* I add five fresh examples and report on a new study. I note that in 2014 the United Kingdom and Italy began counting spending on prostitution and illegal drugs in their GDP estimates. I also add a pie chart showing the composition of the CPI.

Ch. 7: *Unemployment and Inflation* I add six fresh examples and report on 13 new studies. I also add a bar chart showing that the unemployment rate declines as the level of education increases. (But graduating from college is key, because college dropouts have the same unemployment rate as high school graduates.)

Ch. 8: *Productivity and Growth* I add eight fresh examples and report on 15 new studies. As an example of technological progress, I note that putting an hour of video online cost about $400 in the late 1990s but less than two cents today. To elevate the importance of *social capital*, I move that discussion from the final chapter to this chapter.

Ch. 9: *Aggregate Demand* I add three fresh examples and report on five new studies. I simplify the chapter title from "Aggregate Expenditure and Aggregate Demand," to "Aggregate Demand," to reflect the content and match the title of the next chapter, "Aggregate Supply." I add "The Life-Cycle Hypothesis" as a new section and key term, but include evidence from behavioral economics at odds with this hypothesis.

Ch. 10: *Aggregate Supply* I add two fresh examples and report on a new study. "Hysteresis and the Natural Rate of Unemployment" is a new section, with *hysteresis* as a key term.

Ch. 11: *Fiscal Policy* I add two fresh examples and report on four new studies. "Fiscal Policy from 2007 to 2014" is a new section discussing the effects of federal spending and deficits on jobs and economic growth. This section includes a new exhibit showing deficit financing by year as a share of federal outlays by year. After the spike in federal spending in 2009, that spending remained flat over the next five years even in nominal dollars.

Ch. 12: *Federal Budgets and Public Policy* I add two fresh examples and report on three new studies. I have a new subsection on federal budget *sequestration* and include that as a key term.

Ch. 13: *Money and the Financial System* I add five fresh examples and report on six new studies. An exhibit shows that China is now home to four of the world's five largest banks. While the United States may have some financial institutions considered "too big to fail," only one U.S. bank ranks among the world's ten largest.

Ch. 14: *Banking and the Money Supply* I add three fresh examples and report on two new studies. Two new pie charts now show consumer payment systems in 2013 and projected in 2018. In keeping with an emphasis on technological change, I add a section entitled "Is Bitcoin Money?" examining this digital currency.

Ch. 15: *Monetary Theory and Policy* I add two fresh examples and report on a new study. I say more about quantitative easing and about the Fed's payment of interest on bank reserves held at the Fed.

Ch. 16: *Macro Policy Debate: Active or Passive* I add three fresh examples and report on three new studies. A new section discusses "Active Policies, Passive Policies, and Presidential Politics."

International Chapters: 17–19

This edition reflects the growing impact of the world economy on U.S. economic welfare. International issues are introduced early and discussed often. For example, the rest of the world is introduced in Chapter 1 and profiled in Chapter 3. Comparative advantage and the production possibilities frontier are discussed from a global perspective in Chapter 2. International coverage is woven throughout the text. By comparing the U.S. experience with that of other countries around the world, students gain a better perspective about such topics as unionization trends, antitrust policies, pollution, conservation, environmental laws, research and development, tax rates, the distribution of income, economic growth, productivity, unemployment, inflation, central bank independence, government spending, and federal debt. Exhibits show comparisons across countries of various economic measures—everything from the percentage of paper that gets recycled to public outlays relative to GDP. International references are scattered throughout the book, including a number of relevant case studies.

Again, every effort is made to give students a feel for the numbers. For example, to convey the importance of U.S. consumers in the world economy, I note that Americans represent less than 5 percent of the world's population but buy 38 percent of the diamond jewelry sold worldwide. New or revised features in the international chapters include:

Ch. 17: *International Trade* I add 12 fresh examples and report on eight new studies. People prefer having a choice of products, and international trade helps broaden that choice. Yet another benefit of international trade is that trading partners are less likely to go to war because war with trading partners would involve more economic loss. *Bilateral agreement, multilateral agreement,* and *common market* are upgraded to key terms.

Ch. 18: *International Finance* I add three fresh examples and report on two new studies. Foreigners find America an attractive place to invest because U.S. capital markets are the deepest and most liquid in the world. Fiscal problems in eurozone nations such as Greece have taken some of the shine off the euro. I note that arbitrage opportunities are short lived; most are available for less than a second. High-speed computers act on such opportunities instantly.

Ch. 19: *Economic Development* I add 12 fresh examples and report on 18 new studies. Education is valued more in some economies than in others. For example, some teachers in Mexico can legally sell their tenured positions or pass them on to their children.

Student-Friendly Features

In some principles textbooks, chapters are broken up by boxed material, qualifying footnotes, and other distractions that disrupt the flow of the material. Students aren't sure when or if they should read such segregated elements. But this book has a natural flow. Each chapter opens with a few off-beat questions and then follows with a logical narrative. Case studies appear in the natural sequence of the chapter. Students can thus read each chapter from the opening questions to the conclusion and summary. I also adhere to a "just-in-time" philosophy, introducing material just as it's needed to build an argument. Footnotes are used to cite sources, not to qualify or extend material in the text.

This edition is more visual than its predecessors, with more exhibits to reinforce key findings. Exhibit titles convey the central points, and more exhibits now have summary captions. Captions have been edited for clarity and brevity. The point is to make the exhibits more self-contained. Students learn more if concepts are presented both in words and in exhibits.

Additional summary paragraphs have been added throughout each chapter; these summaries begin with the bold-faced identifier "**To Review.**" As noted earlier, each section now is followed by "Checkpoint" questions. Economic jargon has been reduced. Although the number of terms defined in the margin has increased modestly, definitions have been pared to make them clearer and less like entries from a dictionary. In short, economic principles are now more transparent (a textbook should not be like some giant Easter egg hunt, where it's up to the student to figure out what the author is trying to say). Overall, the eleventh edition is a cleaner presentation, a straighter shot into the student's brain.

Color is used systematically within graphs, charts, and tables to ensure that students can easily see what's going on. Throughout the book, demand curves are blue and supply curves are red. Color shading distinguishes key areas of many graphs, and color identifies outcomes in others. For example, economic profit and welfare gains are always shaded blue and economic loss and welfare losses are always shaded pink. In short, color is more than mere eye candy—it is coordinated consistently and with forethought to help students learn (a dyslexic student once told me she found the book's color guide quite helpful). Students benefit from these visual cues.

The Support Package

The teaching and learning support package that accompanies *Economics: A Contemporary Introduction* provides instructors and students with focused, accurate, and innovative supplements to the textbook.

Instructor's Manual   The *Instructor's Manual* provides chapter outlines, teaching ideas, experiential exercises for many chapters, and solutions to all end-of-chapter problems.

Instructor Resources on the Product Support Web Site.   This site at www.cengagebrain.com features the essential resources for instructors, password protected, in downloadable format: the *Instructor's Manual in Word*, the *Teaching Assistance Manual* (discussed next), the online case studies, the test banks, and PowerPoint lecture and exhibit slides.

Teaching Assistance Manual   Written and revised by me, the *Teaching Assistance Manual* provides additional support beyond the *Instructor's Manual*. It is especially useful to new instructors, graduate assistants, and teachers interested in generating more class discussion. This manual offers (1) overviews and outlines of each chapter, (2) chapter objectives and quiz material, (3) material for class discussion, (4) topics warranting special attention, (5) supplementary examples, and (6) "What if?" discussion questions. Appendices provide guidance on (1) presenting material; (2) generating and sustaining class discussion; (3) preparing, administering, and grading quizzes; and (4) coping with the special problems confronting foreign graduate assistants.

Test Banks   Thoroughly revised for currency and accuracy, the microeconomics and macroeconomics test banks contain over 6,000 questions in multiple-choice and true-false formats. All multiple-choice questions are rated by degree of difficulty, and are labeled with learning outcomes tags.

Cengage Learning Testing Powered by Cognero.

This is a flexible, online system that allows you to:

- author, edit, and manage test bank content from multiple Cengage Learning solutions
- create multiple test versions in an instant
- deliver tests from your LMS, your classroom or wherever you want

Start right away!

Cengage Learning Testing Powered by Cognero works on any operating system or browser.

- No special installs or downloads needed
- Create tests from school, home, the coffee shop—anywhere with Internet access

What will you find?

- Simplicity at every step. A desktop-inspired interface features drop-down menus and familiar, intuitive tools that take you through content creation and management with ease.
- Full-featured test generator. Create ideal assessments with your choice of 15 question types (including true/false, multiple choice, opinion scale/Likert, and essay). Multi-language support, an equation editor, and unlimited metadata help ensure your tests are complete and compliant.
- Cross-compatible capability. Import and export content into other systems.

Microsoft PowerPoint Lecture Slides   Lecture slides contain tables and graphs from the textbook, and are intended to enhance lectures and help integrate technology into the classroom.

Microsoft PowerPoint Figure Slides   These PowerPoint slides contain key figures from the text. Instructors who prefer to prepare their own lecture slides can use these figures as an alternative to the text's PowerPoint lecture slides.

The Teaching Economist   Since 1990, I have edited *The Teaching Economist*, a newsletter aimed at making teaching more interesting and more fun. The newsletter discusses imaginative ways to present topics—for example, how to "sensationalize" economic concepts, useful resources on the Internet, economic applications from science fiction, recent research in teaching and learning, and more generally, ways to teach just for the fun of it. A regular feature of *The Teaching Economist*, "The Grapevine," offers teaching ideas suggested by colleagues from across the country. The latest issue—and back issues—of *The Teaching Economist* are available online at cengage.com/economics/mceachern/theteachingeconomist.

Additional Case Studies Online   As mentioned earlier, this edition's companion site now includes an additional case study for each chapter followed by a Checkpoint question. To access this material, log into www.cengagebrain.com, search for McEachern, then find the 11th edition.

Aplia   Started in 2000 by economist and instructor Paul Romer, more students are currently using an Aplia Integrated Textbook Solution for principles of economics than are using all other web-based learning programs combined. Because the assignments in Aplia are automatically graded, you can assign homework more frequently to ensure your students are putting forth a full effort and getting the most out of your class. Assignments are closely tied to the text and each McEachern Aplia course has a digital edition of the textbook embedded right in the Aplia program. This digital text is now in the Aplia Text format, which gives students the same interactive experience they get on Web sites they use in their personal lives.

MindTap for McEachern

- Personalized teaching becomes yours through a Learning Path built with key student objectives and your syllabus in mind. Control what students see and when they see it.
- Analytics and reports provide a snapshot of class progress, time in course, engagement and completion rates.
- An additional case study per chapter along with a Checkpoint question.
- Aplia generic homework and math and graphing tutorials.
- Homework; Concept Clips videos with assessment; online exercises; Checkpoint Q&A; end of chapter questions and problems.
- Adaptive Test Prep to help students master chapter concepts.

Custom Solutions   Create a text as unique as your course quickly, simply, and affordably. Custom Solutions allows you to add your personal touch to *Economics: A Contemporary Introduction* with a course-specific cover and up to 32 pages of your own content, at no additional cost. Contact your sales consultant to learn more about this and other custom options to fit your course.

Acknowledgments

Many people contributed to this book's development. I gratefully acknowledge the insights, comments, and criticisms of those who have reviewed the book for this and previous editions or provided feedback on particular points. Their remarks changed my thinking on many points and improved the book.

Steve Abid,
Grand Rapids Community College

Basil Al-Hashimi,
Mesa Community College–Red Mountain

Polly Reynolds Allen,
University of Connecticut

Mary Allender,
University of Portland

Jeffrey Alstete,
Iona College

Hassan Y. Aly,
Ohio State University

Ted Amato,
University of North Carolina, Charlotte

Donna Anderson,
University of Wisconsin, La Crosse

Richard Anderson,
Texas A&M University

Kyriacos Aristotelous,
Otterbein College

James Aylesworth,
Lakeland Community College

Mohsen Bahmani-Oskooee,
University of Wisconsin, Milwaukee

Dale Bails,
Christian Brothers College

Benjamin Balak,
Rollins College

A. Paul Ballantyne,
University of Colorado at Colorado Springs

Andy Barnett,
Auburn University

Bharati Basu,
Central Michigan University

Lauri J. Bates,
Bryant University

Lee Beard,
Southwest Indian Polytechnical Institute

Klaus Becker,
Texas Tech University

Getachew Begashaw,
Harper College

Charles Bennett,
Gannon University

John J. Bethune,
Barton College

Trisha L. Bezmen,
Old Dominion University

Jay Bhattacharya,
Okaloosa Walton Community College

Gerald W. Bialka,
University of North Florida

Roberta Biby,
Grand Valley State University

William Bogart,
Case Western Reserve University

Andrew A. Bonacic,
Adirondack College

Kenneth Boyer,
Michigan State University

David Brasfield,
Murray State University

Jurgen Brauer,
Augusta College

Taggert Brooks,
University of Wisconsin, La Crosse

Gardner Brown, Jr.,
University of Washington

Eric Brunner,
Morehead State University

Francine Butler,
Grand View College

Judy Butler,
Baylor University

Charles Callahan III,
SUNY College at Brockport

Giorgio Canarella,
California State University, Los Angeles

Shirley Cassing,
University of Pittsburgh

Shi-fan Chu,
University of Nevada–Reno

Ronald Cipcic,
Kalamazoo Valley Community College

Larry Clarke,
Brookhaven College

Rebecca Cline,
Middle Georgia College

Stephen Cobb,
Xavier University

Francis P. Connolly,
Nassau Community College

Doug Conway,
Mesa Community College

Mary E. Cookingham,
Michigan State University

James P. Cover,
University of Alabama

James Cox,
DeKalb College

Jerry Crawford,
Arkansas State University

Thomas Creahan,
Morehead State University

Carl Davidson,
Michigan State University

Elynor Davis,
Georgia Southern University

Susan Davis,
SUNY College at Buffalo

A. Edward Day,
University of Central Florida

David Dean,
University of Richmond

Janet Deans,
Chestnut Hill College

Dennis Debrecht,
Carroll College

David Denslow,
University of Florida

Kruti R. Dholakia,
Grayson County College

Albert Duncan,
Borough of Manhattan Community College of CUNY

Mary Sue DuPuy,
Arizona Western College

Gary Dymski,
University of California–Riverside

John Eastwood,
Northern Arizona University

John Edgren,
Eastern Michigan University

John C. Edward,
Bentley University

Ron D. Elkins,
Central Washington University

Kenneth G. Elzinga,
University of Virginia

Donald Elliott, Jr.,
Southern Illinois University

G. Rod Erfani,
Transylvania University

Gisela Meyer Escoe,
University of Cincinnati

Mark Evans,
California State University, Bakersfield

Jamie Falcon,
University of Maryland Baltimore County

Gregory Falls,
Central Michigan University

Eleanor Fapohunda,
SUNY College at Farmingdale

Mohsen Fardmanesh,
Temple University

Paul Farnham,
Georgia State University

Rudy Fichtenbaum,
Wright State University

T. Windsor Fields,
James Madison University

Fathali Firoozi,
University of Texas at San Antonio

Linda R. Fisher,
Quinnipiac University

Rodney Fort,
Washington State University

Richard Fowles,
University of Utah

Roger Frantz,
San Diego State University

Julie Gallaway,
Southwest Montana State University

Gary Galles,
Pepperdine University

Edward Gamber,
Lafayette College

Adam Gifford,
California State University, Northridge

J. P. Gilbert,
MiraCosta College

Robert Gillette,
University of Kentucky

Art Goldsmith,
Washington and Lee University

Rae Jean Goodman,
U.S. Naval Academy

Robert Gordon,
San Diego State University

Fred Graham,
American University

Philip Graves,
University of Colorado, Boulder

Gary Greene,
Manatee Community College

Harpal S. Grewal,
Claflin College

Carolyn Grin,
Grand Rapids Community College

Daniel Gropper,
Auburn University

Simon Hakim,
Temple University

Robert Halvorsen,
University of Washington

Nathan Eric Hampton,
St. Cloud State University

Mehdi Haririan,
Bloomsburg University

Oskar Harmon,
University of Connecticut

William Hart,
Miami University

Baban Hasnat,
SUNY College at Brockport

Travis Lee Hayes,
Chattanooga State Technical Community College

Julia Heath,
University of Memphis

James Heisler,
Hope College

James Henderson,
Baylor University

Michael Heslop,
Northern Virginia Community College

James R. Hill,
Central Michigan University

Jane Smith Himarios,
University of Texas, Arlington

Calvin Hoerneman,
Delta College

Tracy Hofer,
University of Wisconsin, Stevens Point

George E. Hoffer,
Virginia Commonwealth University

Dennis Hoffman,
Arizona State University

Bruce Horning,
Fordham University

Calvin Hoy,
County College of Morris

George Hughes,
University of Hartford

Jennifer Imazeki,
San Diego State University

Beth Ingram,
University of Iowa

Susan Iredale,
Cuesta College

Paul Isley,
Grand Valley State University

Joyce Jacobsen,
Wesleyan University

Nancy Jianakoplos,
Colorado State University

Claude Michael Jonnard,
Fairleigh Dickinson University

Nake Kamrany,
University of Southern California

Bryce Kanago,
Miami University

John Kane,
SUNY College at Oswego

David Kennett,
Vassar College

William Kern,
Western Michigan University

Robert Kleinhenz,
California State University, Fullerton

Faik Koray,
Louisiana State University

Joseph Kotaska,
Monroe Community College

Barry Kotlove,
Edmonds Community College

Marie Kratochvil,
Nassau Community College

Joseph Lammert,
Raymond Walters College

Philip J. Lane,
Fairfield University

Steven P. Lanza,
University of Connecticut

Christopher Lee,
Saint Ambrose University, Davenport

Jim Lee,
Fort Hays State University

Dennis Leyden,
University of North Carolina, Greensboro

Carl Liedholm,
Michigan State University

Hyoung-Seok Lim,
Ohio State University

C. Richard Long,
Georgia State University

Ken Long,
New River Community College

Michael Magura,
University of Toledo

Thomas Maloy,
Muskegon Community College

Gabriel Manrique,
Winona State University

Barbara Marcus,
Davenport College

Robert Margo,
Vanderbilt University

Nelson Mark,
Ohio State University

Richard Martin,
Agnes Scott College

Peter Mavrokordatos,
Tarrant County College

Wolfgang Mayer,
University of Cincinnati

Bruce McCrea,
Lansing Community College

John McDowell,
Arizona State University

KimMarie McGoldrick,
University of Richmond

David McKee,
Kent State University

James McLain,
University of New Orleans

Mark McNeil,
Irvine Valley College

Michael A. McPherson,
University of North Texas

Scott Eric Merryman,
University of Oregon

Michael Metzger,
University of Central Oklahoma

Art Meyer,
Lincoln Land Community College

Carrie Meyer,
George Mason University

Charles Meyrick,
Housatonic Community College

Martin Milkman,
Murray State University

Green R. Miller,
Morehead State University

Stephen M. Miller,
University of Nevada, Las Vegas

Bruce D. Mills,
Troy State University, Montgomery

Milton Mitchell,
University of Wisconsin, Oshkosh

Shannon Mitchell,
Virginia Commonwealth University

Brian Mock,
Indiana Wesleyan University

Barry Morris,
University of North Alabama

Tina Mosleh,
Ohlone College

Kathryn Nantz,
Fairfield University

Paul Natke,
Central Michigan University

Rick Nelson,
Lansing Community College

Heather Newsome,
Baylor University

Farrokh Nourzad,
Marquette University

Maureen O'Brien,
University of Minnesota, Duluth

Norman P. Obst,
Michigan State University

Patrick Olson,
Upper Iowa University

Joan Q. Osborne,
Palo Alto College

Jeffrey Phillips,
Thomas College

Miguel A. Pinzon,
Florida National University

Jeffrey D. Prager,
East Central College

Fernando Quijano,
Dickinson State University

Jaishankar Raman,
Valparaiso University

Reza Ramazani,
St. Michael's University

Carol Rankin,
Xavier University

Mitch Redlo,
Monroe Community College

Kevin Rogers,
Mississippi State University

Scanlon Romer,
Delta College

Duane Rosa,
West Texas A&M University

Robert Rossana,
Wayne State University

Mark Rush,
University of Florida

Richard Saba,
Auburn University

Simran Sahi,
University of Minnesota, Twin Cities

Richard Salvucci,
Trinity University

Rexford Santerre,
University of Connecticut

George D. Santopietro,
Radford University

Sue Lynn Sasser,
University of Central Oklahoma

Ward Sayre,
Kenyon College

Ted Scheinman,
Mt. Hood Community College

Peter Schwartz,
University of North Carolina, Charlotte

Carol A. Scotese,
Virginia Commonwealth University

Shahrokh Shahrokhi,
San Diego State University

Roger Sherman,
University of Houston

Michael Shields,
Central Michigan University

Alden Shiers,
California Polytechnic State University

Virginia Shingleton,
Valparaiso University

Frederica Shockley,
California State University, Chico

William Shughart II,
University of Mississippi

Paul Sicilian,
Grand Valley State University

Charles Sicotte,
Rock Valley College

Calvin Siebert,
University of Iowa

Michele Sims,
Arizona Western College

Gerald P. W. Simons,
Grand Valley State University

Brian W. Sloboda,
University of Phoenix

Phillip Smith,
DeKalb College

V. Kerry Smith,
Duke University

David Spencer,
Brigham Young University

Jane Speyrer,
University of New Orleans

Joanne Spitz,
University of Massachusetts

Denise Stanley
California State University, Fullerton

Mark Stegeman,
Virginia Polytechnic Institute

Houston Stokes,
University of Illinois, Chicago

Robert Stonebreaker,
Indiana University of Pennsylvania

Michael Stroup,
Stephen Austin State University

William Swift,
Pace University

James Swofford,
University of South Alabama

Linghui Tang,
Drexel University

Donna Thompson,
Brookdale Community College

Jill Trask,
Tarrant County College

John Tribble,
Russell Sage College

Steven Trost,
Virginia Polytechnic Institute

Lee J. Van Scyoc,
University of Wisconsin, Oshkosh

Percy Vera,
Sinclair Community College

Han X. Vo,
Winthrop University

Jin Wang,
University of Wisconsin, Stevens Point

Gregory Wassall,
Northeastern University

William Weber,
Eastern Illinois University

David Weinberg,
Xavier University

Bernard Weinrich,
St. Louis Community College

Donald Wells,
University of Arizona

Robert Whaples,
Wake Forest University

Mark Wheeler,
Western Michigan University

Michael White,
St. Cloud State University

Richard Winkelman,
Arizona State University

Stephan Woodbury,
Michigan State University

Kenneth Woodward,
Saddleback College

Patricia Wyatt,
Bossier Parish Community College

Peter Wyman,
Spokane Falls Community College

Mesghena Yasin,
Morehead State University

Edward Young,
University of Wisconsin, Eau Claire

Michael J. Youngblood,
Rock Valley College

William Zeis,
Bucks Community College

I also thank the many contributions and comments from the group of instructors who participated in the Online Survey of my book, or responded to our phone surveys:

John Abell,
Randolph College

Richard U. Agesa,
Marshall University

John Beck,
Gonzaga University

John Bellettiere IV,
San Diego State University

Randall Bennett,
Gonzaga University

Bettina Berch,
Borough of Manhattan Community College

Andrew M. Bonacic,
Adirondack College

Kathryn L. Brownell,
Jefferson Community College

Joseph Daniels,
Marquette University

Maria Davis,
Indian River State College

Mary Sue DePuy,
Arizona Western College

John C. Edward
Bentley University

Dennis S. Edwards,
Coastal Carolina University

Ali Erhan,
Aquinas College

Erwin F. Erhardt, III,
University of Cincinnati

Jeff Florea,
Madisonville Community College

Ronald Gunderson,
Northern Arizona University

George Hoffer,
Virginia Commonwealth University

Judy Hurtt,
East Central Community College

Charles James,
Washington State University

E.M. Jankovic,
Fairfield University

Leland Kempe,
CSU Fresno

Sunita Kumari,
St. Petersburg College

Nazma Latif-Zaman,
Providence College

J. Franklin Lee,
Pitt Community College

Harry Miley,
South Carolina State University

Martin Milkman,
Murray State University

Kaustav Misra,
Mississippi State University

Phillip Mixon,
Troy University

Paul Olmsted,
Moorpark College

John Rapczak,
Community College of Rhode Island

Richard Rouch,
Volunteer State Community College

Martin Sabo,
University of Colorado at Denver

Ahmad Saranjam,
Northeastern University

Michelle Sims,
Arizona Western College

Jeff Wiltzius,
Indian River State College

Sourushe Zandvakili,
University of Cincinnati

The talented professionals at Cengage Learning provided invaluable editorial, administrative, and sales support. I owe a special debt to Julia Chase, Senior Content/Media Developer, who nurtured the manuscript through reviews, revisions, editing, and production. She also helped with photography selection and coordinated the work of others who contributed to the publishing package. For the fresh look of the book, I owe a debt to Michelle Kunkler, Senior Art Director. I am also grateful to the Senior Content Product Manager, Colleen Farmer. The actual production of this book was expertly handled by Cenveo Publisher Services, especially Rajachitra Suresh, who coordinated the manuscript through its several stages. Her good cheer and steady guidance made things go smoothly. I would also like to thank Sarah Greber, Senior Marketing Communications Manager, who has been especially helpful with the publications of my newsletter, *The Teaching Economist*.

I am most grateful to Erin Joyner, VP, GM Social Science & Qualitative Business; Michael Worls, Product Director; Michael Parthenakis, Senior Product Manager and problem solver; Kasie Jean, Digital Content Designer; and John Carey, the Senior Marketing Manager whose knowledge of the book dates back to the beginning. As good as the book may be, all our efforts would be wasted unless students get to read it. To that end, I greatly appreciate the dedicated service and sales force of Cengage Learning, who have contributed in a substantial way to the book's success.

Finally, I owe an abiding debt to my wife, Pat, who provided abundant encouragement and support along the way.

William A. McEachern

The Art and Science of Economic Analysis

Bernd Vogel/AGE Fotostock

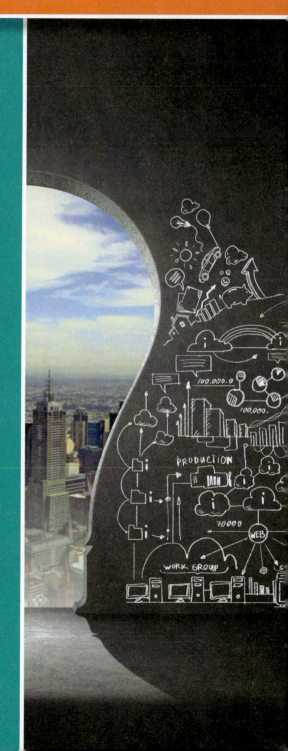

- *In what way are people who pound on vending machines relying on theory?*

- *Why are comic-strip and TV characters like those in* FoxTrot, The Simpsons, *and* Family Guy *missing a finger on each hand? And where is* Dilbert's *mouth?*

- *Which college majors pay the most?*

- *Why is a good theory like a California Closet?*

- *What's the big idea with economics?*

- *Finally, how can it be said that in economics "what goes around comes around"?*

These and other questions are answered in this chapter, which introduces the art and science of economic analysis.

You have been reading and hearing about economic issues for years—unemployment, inflation, poverty, recessions, federal deficits, college tuition, airfares, stock prices, computer prices, smartphone prices, gas prices. When explanations of such issues go into any depth, your eyes may glaze over and you may tune out, the same way you do when a weather forecaster tries to explain high-pressure fronts colliding with moisture carried in from the coast.

What many people fail to realize is that economics is livelier than the dry accounts offered by the news media. Economics is about making choices, and you make economic choices every day—choices about whether to get a part-time job or focus on your studies, live in a dorm or off campus, take a course in accounting or one in history, get married or stay single, pack a lunch or buy a sandwich. You already know much more about economics than you realize. You bring to the subject a rich personal experience, an experience that will be tapped throughout the book to reinforce your understanding of the basic ideas.

Topics discussed in this chapter include:

- The economic problem
- Marginal analysis
- Rational self-interest
- The scientific method
- Normative versus positive analysis
- Some pitfalls of economic thinking

1-1 The Economic Problem: Scarce Resources, Unlimited Wants

Would you like a new car, a nicer home, a smarter phone, tastier meals, more free time, a more interesting social life, more spending money, more leisure, more sleep? Who wouldn't? But even if you can satisfy some of these desires, others keep popping up. *The problem is that, although your wants, or desires, are virtually unlimited, the resources available to satisfy these wants are scarce.* A resource is *scarce* when it is not freely available—that is, when its price exceeds zero. Because resources are scarce, you must choose from among your many wants, and whenever you choose, you must forgo satisfying some other wants. The problem of scarce resources but unlimited wants exists to a greater or lesser extent for each of the 7.4 billion people on Earth. Everybody—cab driver, farmer, brain surgeon, dictator, shepherd, student, politician—faces the problem. For example, a cab driver uses time and other scarce resources, such as the taxi, knowledge of the city, driving skills, and gasoline, to earn income. That income, in turn, buys housing, groceries, clothing, trips to Disney World, and thousands of other goods and services that help satisfy some of the driver's unlimited wants. **Economics** examines how people use their scarce resources to satisfy their unlimited wants. Let's pick apart

economics
The study of how people use their scarce resources to satisfy their unlimited wants

the definition, beginning with resources, then goods and services, and finally focus on the heart of the matter—economic choice, which results from scarcity.

1-1a Resources

Resources are the inputs, or factors of production, used to produce the goods and services that people want. *Goods and services are scarce because resources are scarce.* Resources sort into four broad categories: labor, capital, natural resources, and entrepreneurial ability. **Labor** is human effort, both physical and mental. Labor includes the effort of the cab driver and the brain surgeon. Labor itself comes from a more fundamental resource: *time.* Without time we can accomplish nothing. We allocate our time to alternative uses: We can *sell* our time as labor, or we can *spend* our time doing other things, like sleeping, eating, studying, playing sports, going online, attending class, watching TV, or just relaxing with friends.

Capital includes all human creations used to produce goods and services. Economists often distinguish between physical capital and human capital. *Physical capital* consists of factories, tools, machines, computers, buildings, airports, highways, and other human creations used to produce goods and services. Physical capital includes the cab driver's taxi, the surgeon's scalpel, and the building where your economics class meets (or, if you are taking this course online, your computer and online connectors). *Human capital* consists of the knowledge and skill people acquire to increase their productivity, such as the cab driver's knowledge of city streets, the surgeon's knowledge of human anatomy, and your knowledge of economics.

Natural resources include all *gifts of nature,* such as bodies of water, trees, oil reserves, minerals, even animals. Natural resources can be divided into renewable resources and exhaustible resources. A *renewable resource* can be drawn on indefinitely if used conservatively. Thus, timber is a renewable resource if felled trees are replaced to regrow a steady supply. The air and rivers are renewable resources if they are allowed sufficient time to cleanse themselves of any pollutants. More generally, biological resources such as fish, game, livestock, forests, rivers, groundwater, grasslands, and soil are renewable if managed properly. An *exhaustible resource*—such as oil or coal—does not renew itself and so is available in a limited amount. Once burned, each barrel of oil or ton of coal is gone forever. The world's oil and coal deposits are exhaustible.

A special kind of human skill called **entrepreneurial ability** is the talent required to dream up a new product or find a better way to produce an existing one, organize production, and assume the risk of profit or loss. This special skill comes from an entrepreneur. An **entrepreneur** is a profit-seeking decision maker who starts with an idea, organizes an enterprise to bring that idea to life, and then assumes the risk of operation. An entrepreneur pays resource owners for the opportunity to employ their resources in the firm. Every firm in the world today, such as Ford, Microsoft, Google, and Facebook, began as an idea in the mind of an entrepreneur.

Resource owners are paid **wages** for their labor, **interest** for the use of their capital, and **rent** for the use of their natural resources. Entrepreneurial ability is rewarded by **profit**, which equals the *revenue* from items sold minus the *cost* of the resources employed to make those items. Sometimes the entrepreneur suffers a loss. Resource earnings are usually based on the *time* these resources are employed. Resource payments therefore have a time dimension, as in a wage of $10 *per hour,* interest of 6 percent *per year,* rent of $600 *per month,* or profit of $10,000 *per year.*

resources
The inputs, or factors of production, used to produce the goods and services that people want; consist of labor, capital, natural resources, and entrepreneurial ability

labor
The physical and mental effort used to produce goods and services

capital
The buildings, equipment, and human skills used to produce goods and services

natural resources
All gifts of nature used to produce goods and services; includes renewable and exhaustible resources

entrepreneurial ability
The imagination required to develop a new product or process, the skill needed to organize production, and the willingness to take the risk of profit or loss

entrepreneur
A profit-seeking decision maker who starts with an idea, organizes an enterprise to bring that idea to life, and assumes the risk of the operation

wages
Payment to resource owners for their labor

interest
Payment to resource owners for the use of their capital

rent
Payment to resource owners for the use of their natural resources

profit
Reward for entrepreneurial ability; sales revenue minus resource cost

1-1b Goods and Services

Resources are combined in a variety of ways to produce goods and services. A farmer, a tractor, 50 acres of land, seeds, and fertilizer combine to grow the good: corn. One hundred musicians, musical instruments, chairs, a conductor, a musical score, and a music hall combine to produce the service: Beethoven's *Fifth Symphony*. Corn is a **good** because it is something you can see, feel, and touch; it requires scarce resources to produce; and it satisfies human wants. The book you are now holding, the chair you are sitting in, the clothes you are wearing, and your next meal are all goods. The performance of the *Fifth Symphony* is a **service** because it is intangible, yet it uses scarce resources to satisfy human wants. Lectures, movies, concerts, phone service, wireless connections, yoga lessons, dry cleaning, and haircuts are all services.

Because goods and services are produced using scarce resources, they are themselves scarce. *A good or service is scarce if the amount people desire exceeds the amount available at a zero price.* Because we cannot have all the goods and services we would like, we must continually choose among them. We must choose among more pleasant living quarters, better meals, nicer clothes, more reliable transportation, faster computers, smarter phones, and so on. Making choices in a world of **scarcity** means we must pass up some goods and services. Exhibit 1 shows the options of one individual facing scarcity. But not everything is scarce. In fact, some things we would prefer to have less of. For example, we would prefer to have less garbage, less spam email, fewer telemarketing calls, and less pollution. Things we want none of even at a zero price are called *bads*, the opposite of goods.

good
A tangible product used to satisfy human wants

service
An activity, or intangible product, used to satisfy human wants

scarcity
Occurs when the amount people desire exceeds the amount available at a zero price

EXHIBIT 1	Scarcity Means You Must Choose Among Options

laola/Shutterstock.com, colia/Shutterstock.com, Utekhina Anna/Shutterstock.com, james weston/Shutterstock.com, Elena Elisseeva/Shutterstock.com, zimmytws/Shutterstock.com

A few goods and services seem *free* because the amount available at a zero price exceeds the amount people want. For example, air and seawater often seem free because we can breathe all the air we want and have all the seawater we can haul away. Yet, despite the old saying "The best things in life are free," most goods and services are scarce, not free, and even those that appear to be free come with strings attached. For example, *clean* air and *clean* seawater have become scarce. *Goods and services that are truly free are not the subject of economics. Without scarcity, there would be no economic problem and no need for prices.*

Sometimes we mistakenly think of certain goods as free because they involve no apparent cost to us. Napkins seem to be free at Starbucks. Nobody stops you from taking a fistful. Supplying napkins, however, costs the company millions each year and prices reflect that cost. Some restaurants make special efforts to keep napkin use down—such as packing them tightly into the dispenser or making you ask for them. And Starbucks recently reduced the thickness of its napkins.

You may have heard the expression "There is no such thing as a free lunch." *There is no free lunch because all goods and services involve a cost to someone.* The lunch may seem free to you, but it draws scarce resources away from the production of other goods and services, and whoever provides a free lunch often expects something in return. A Russian proverb makes a similar point but with a bit more bite: "The only place you find free cheese is in a mousetrap." Albert Einstein once observed, "Sometimes one pays the most for things one gets for nothing."

1-1c Economic Decision Makers and Markets

There are four types of decision makers in the economy: households, firms, governments, and the rest of the world. Their interaction determines how an economy's resources are allocated. *Households* play the starring role. As consumers, households demand the goods and services produced. As resource owners, households supply labor, capital, natural resources, and entrepreneurial ability to firms, governments, and the rest of the world. *Firms, governments,* and *the rest of the world* demand the resources that households supply and then use these resources to supply the goods and services that households demand. The rest of the world includes foreign households, foreign firms, and foreign governments that supply resources and products to U.S. demanders and demand resources and products from U.S. suppliers.

Markets are the means by which buyers and sellers carry out exchange at mutually agreeable terms. By bringing together the two sides of exchange, markets determine price, quantity, and quality. Markets are often physical places, such as supermarkets, department stores, shopping malls, yard sales, flea markets, and swap meets. But markets also include other mechanisms by which buyers and sellers communicate, such as classified ads, radio and television ads, telephones, bulletin boards, online sites, and face-to-face bargaining. These market mechanisms provide information about the quantity, quality, and price of products offered for sale. Goods and services are bought and sold in **product markets**. Resources are bought and sold in **resource markets**. The most important resource market is the labor, or job, market. Think about your own experience looking for a job, and you'll already have some idea of that market.

1-1d A Simple Circular-Flow Model

Now that you have learned a bit about economic decision makers and markets, consider how all these interact. Such a picture is conveyed by the **circular-flow model**, which describes the flow of resources, products, income, and revenue among economic

market
A set of arrangements by which buyers and sellers carry out exchange at mutually agreeable terms

product market
A market in which a good or service is bought and sold

resource market
A market in which a resource is bought and sold

circular-flow model
A diagram that traces the flow of resources, products, income, and revenue among economic decision makers

decision makers. The simple circular-flow model focuses on the primary interaction in a market economy—that between households and firms. Exhibit 2 shows households on the left and firms on the right; please take a look.

Households supply labor, capital, natural resources, and entrepreneurial ability to firms through resource markets, shown in the lower portion of the exhibit. In return, households demand goods and services from firms through product markets, shown on the upper portion of the exhibit. Viewed from the business end, firms demand labor, capital, natural resources, and entrepreneurial ability from households through resource markets, and firms supply goods and services to households through product markets.

The flows of resources and products are supported by the flows of income and expenditure—that is, by the flow of money. So let's add money. The demand and supply of resources come together in resource markets to determine what firms pay for

---

EXHIBIT   2   **The Simple Circular-Flow Model for Households and Firms**

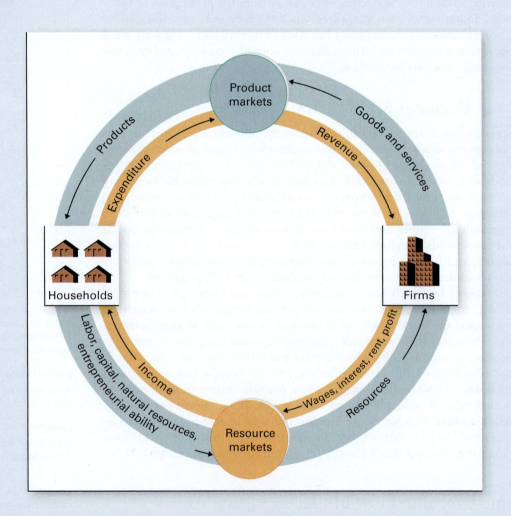

Households earn income by supplying resources to resource markets, as shown in the lower portion of the model. Firms demand these resources to produce goods and services, which they supply to product markets, as shown in the upper portion of the model. Households spend their income to demand these goods and services. This spending flows through product markets as revenue to firms.

resources. These resource prices—wages, interest, rent, and profit—flow as *income* to households. The demand and supply of products come together in product markets to determine what households pay for goods and services. This *expenditure* on goods and services flows as *revenue* to firms. Resources and products flow in one direction—in this case, counterclockwise—and the corresponding payments flow in the other direction—clockwise. What goes around comes around. Take a little time now to trace the logic of the circular flows.

CHECKPOINT

Identify and describe the movement of resources and products through the circular-flow model.

1-2 The Art of Economic Analysis

An economy results as millions of individuals attempt to satisfy their unlimited wants. Because their choices lie at the heart of the economic problem—coping with scarce resources but unlimited wants—these choices deserve a closer look. Learning about the forces that shape economic choices is the first step toward understanding the art of economic analysis.

1-2a Rational Self-Interest

A key economic assumption is that individuals, in making choices, rationally select what they perceive to be in their best interests. By *rational,* economists mean simply that people try to make the best choices they can, given the available time and information. People may not know with certainty which alternative will turn out to be the best. They simply select the alternatives they *expect* will yield the most satisfaction and happiness. In general, **rational self-interest** means that each individual tries to maximize the expected benefit achieved with a given cost or to minimize the expected cost of achieving a given benefit. Thus, economists begin with the assumption that people look out for their self-interest. For example, a physician who owns a pharmacy prescribes 8 percent more drugs on average than a physician who does not own a pharmacy.[1] A physician who owns a nuclear scanner (used to look inside the human body) is seven times more likely to recommend a scan than a physician who does not own a nuclear scanner.[2] And as one more example of self-interest, the *USA Today* weekly football poll asks coaches to list the top 25 teams in the country. It is no surprise that coaches distort their selections to favor their own teams and their own conferences. And, to make their own records look better, coaches inflate the rankings of teams they have beaten.[3]

Rational self-interest should not necessarily be viewed as blind materialism, pure selfishness, or greed. We all know people who are tuned to radio station WIIFM (What's In It For Me?). For most of us, however, self-interest often includes the welfare of our family, our friends, and perhaps the poor of the world. Even so, our concern for others

rational self-interest
Each individual tries to maximize the expected benefit achieved with a given cost or to minimize the expected cost of achieving a given benefit

[1] Brian Chen, Paul Gertler, and Chuh-Yuh Yang, "Moral Hazard and Economies of Scope in Physician Ownership of Complementary Medical Services," NBER Working Paper No. 19622 (November 2013).

[2] Sandeep Jouhar, *Doctored: The Disillusionment of an American Physician* (Farrar, Straus, and Giroux, 2014), p. 96.

[3] Matthew Kotchen and Matthew Potoski, "Conflicts of Interest Distort Public Evaluations: Evidence from the Top 25 Ballots of NCAA Football Coaches," *Journal of Economic Behavior & Organization*, 107 (November 2014): 51–63.

is influenced by our personal cost of that concern. We may readily volunteer to drive a friend to the airport on Saturday afternoon but are less likely to offer a ride if the flight leaves at 6:00 A.M. When we donate clothes to an organization such as Goodwill Industries, they are more likely to be old and worn than brand new. People tend to give more to charities when their contributions are tax deductible and when contributions garner social approval in the community (as when contributor names are made public or when big donors get buildings named after them).[4] Managers donate more company funds to charitable causes when they own less of the company (and, thus, when their personal cost of contributing is lower).[5] TV stations are more likely to donate airtime for public-service announcements during the dead of night than during prime time (which is why 80 percent of such announcements air between 11:00 P.M. and 7:00 A.M.). In Asia some people burn money to soothe the passage of a departed loved one. But they burn fake money, not real money.

The notion of self-interest does not rule out concern for others; it simply means that concern for others is influenced by the same economic forces that affect other economic choices. *The lower the personal cost of helping others, the more help we offer.* We don't like to think that our behavior reflects our self-interest, but it usually does. As Jane Austen wrote in *Pride and Prejudice*, "I have been a selfish being all my life, in practice, though not in principle."

1-2b Choice Requires Time and Information

Rational choice takes time and requires information, but time and information are themselves scarce and therefore valuable. If you have any doubts about the time and information needed to make choices, talk to someone who recently purchased a home, a car, or a personal computer. Talk to a corporate official trying to decide whether to introduce a new product, sell online, build a new factory, or buy another firm. Or think back to your own experience in choosing a college. You probably talked to friends, relatives, teachers, and guidance counselors. You likely used school catalogs, college guides, and Web sites. You may have even visited some campuses to meet the admissions staff and anyone else willing to talk. The decision took time and money, and it probably involved aggravation and anxiety.

Because information is costly to acquire, we are often willing to pay others to gather and digest it for us. College guidebooks, stock analysts, travel agents, real estate brokers, career counselors, restaurant critics, movie reviewers, specialized Web sites, and *Consumer Reports* magazine attest to our willingness to pay for information that improves our choices. As we'll see next, *rational decision makers continue to acquire information as long as the additional benefit expected from that information exceeds the additional cost of gathering it.*

1-2c Economic Analysis Is Marginal Analysis

Economic choice usually involves some adjustment to the existing situation, or status quo. Amazon.com must decide whether to add a new line of products. The school superintendent must decide whether to hire another teacher. Your favorite jeans are on sale, and you must decide whether to buy another pair. You are wondering whether to carry an extra course next term. You just finished lunch and are deciding whether to order dessert.

[4.] Dean Karlan and Margaret McConnell, "Hey Look at Me: The Effect of Giving Circles on Giving," *Journal of Economic Behavior & Organization* (forthcoming).

[5.] Ing-Haw Cheng, Harrison Hong, and Kelly Shue, "Do Managers Do Good with Other People's Money?" NBER Working Paper No. 19432 (September 2013).

Economic choice is based on a comparison of the *expected marginal benefit* and the *expected marginal cost* of the action under consideration. **Marginal** means incremental, additional, or extra. Marginal refers to a change in an economic variable, a change in the status quo. *A rational decision maker changes the status quo if the expected marginal benefit from the change exceeds the expected marginal cost.* For example, Amazon.com compares the marginal benefit expected from adding a new line of products (the additional sales revenue) with the marginal cost (the additional cost of the resources required). Likewise, you compare the marginal benefit you expect from eating dessert (the additional pleasure or satisfaction) with its marginal cost (the additional money, time, and calories).

Typically, the change under consideration is small, but a marginal choice can involve a major economic adjustment, as in the decision to quit school and find a job. For a firm, a marginal choice might mean building a plant in Mexico or even filing for bankruptcy. By focusing on the effect of a marginal adjustment to the status quo, the economist is able to cut the analysis of economic choice down to a manageable size. Rather than confront a bewildering economic reality head-on, the economist begins with a marginal choice to see how this choice affects a particular market and shapes the economic system as a whole. Incidentally, to the noneconomist, *marginal* usually means relatively inferior, as in "a movie of marginal quality." Forget that meaning for this course and instead think of *marginal* as meaning incremental, additional, or extra.

1-2d Microeconomics and Macroeconomics

Although you have made thousands of economic choices, you probably seldom think about your own economic behavior. For example, why are you reading this book right now rather than doing something else? **Microeconomics** is the study of your economic behavior and the economic behavior of others who make choices about such matters as how much to study and how much to party, how much to borrow and how much to save, what to buy and what to sell. Microeconomics examines individual economic choices and how markets coordinate the choices of various decision makers. Microeconomics explains how price and quantity are determined in individual markets—the market for breakfast cereal, sports equipment, or used cars, for instance.

You have probably given little thought to what influences your own economic choices. You have likely given even less thought to how your choices link up with those made by millions of others in the U.S. economy to determine economy-wide measures such as total production, employment, and economic growth. **Macroeconomics** studies the performance of the economy as a whole. Whereas microeconomics studies the individual pieces of the economic puzzle, as reflected in particular markets, macroeconomics puts all the pieces together to focus on the big picture. Macroeconomics sees the forest, not the trees; the beach, not the grains of sand; and the Rose Bowl parade float, not the individual flowers that shape and color that float.

The national economy usually grows over time, but along the way it sometimes stumbles, experiencing *recessions* in economic activity, as reflected by a decline in production, employment, and other aggregate measures. **Economic fluctuations** are the rise and fall of economic activity relative to the long-term growth trend of the economy. These fluctuations, or *business cycles,* vary in length and intensity, but they usually involve the entire nation and often other nations too. For example, the U.S. economy now produces more than four times as much as it did in 1960, despite experiencing eight recessions since then, including the Great Recession of 2007–2009.

To Review: The art of economic analysis focuses on how people use their scarce resources in an attempt to satisfy their unlimited wants. Rational self-interest guides individual choice. Choice requires time and information and involves a comparison of

marginal
Incremental, additional, or extra; used to describe a change in an economic variable

microeconomics
The study of the economic behavior in particular markets, such as that for computers or unskilled labor

macroeconomics
The study of the economic behavior of entire economies, as measured, for example, by total production and employment

economic fluctuations
The rise and fall of economic activity relative to the long-term growth trend of the economy; also called business cycles

the expected marginal benefit and the expected marginal cost of alternative actions. Microeconomics looks at the individual pieces of the economic puzzle; macroeconomics fits the pieces together to form the big picture.

CHECKPOINT

What two measures are compared when making an economic choice?

1-3 The Science of Economic Analysis

Economists use scientific analysis to develop theories, or models, that help explain economic behavior. An **economic theory**, or **economic model**, is a simplification of economic reality that *is used to make predictions about cause and effect in the real world*. A theory, or model, such as the circular-flow model, captures the important elements of the problem under study but need not spell out every detail and interrelation. In fact, adding more details may make a theory more unwieldy and, therefore, less useful. For example, a wristwatch is a model that tells time, but a watch festooned with extra features is harder to read at a glance and is therefore less useful as a time-telling model. The world is so complex that we must simplify it to make sense of things. Store mannequins simplify the human form (some even lack arms and heads). Comic strips and cartoons simplify a character's anatomy—leaving out fingers (in the case of *FoxTrot*, *The Simpsons*, and *Family Guy*) or a mouth (in the case of *Dilbert*), for instance. You might think of economic theory as a stripped-down, or streamlined, version of economic reality.

A good theory helps us understand a messy and confusing world. Lacking a theory of how things work, our thinking can become cluttered with facts, one piled on another, as in a messy closet. You could think of a good theory as a closet organizer for the mind, similar to the organizing service offered by California Closets. A good theory offers a helpful guide to sorting, saving, and understanding information.

economic theory, or economic model

A simplification of reality used to make predictions about cause and effect in the real world

1-3a The Role of Theory

Most people don't understand the role of theory. Perhaps you have heard, "Oh, that's fine in theory, but in practice it's another matter." The implication is that the theory in question provides little aid in practical matters. People who say this fail to realize that they are merely substituting their own theory for a theory they either do not believe or do not understand. They are really saying, "I have my own theory that works better."

All of us employ theories, however poorly defined or understood. Someone who pounds on the Pepsi machine that just ate a quarter has a crude theory about how that machine works. One version of that theory might be, "The quarter drops through a series of *whatchamacallits*, but sometimes it gets stuck. *If* I pound on the machine, *then* I can free up the quarter and send it on its way." Evidently, this theory is widespread enough that people continue to pound on machines that fail to perform (a real problem for the vending machine industry and one reason newer machines are fronted with glass). Yet, if you were to ask these mad pounders to explain their "theory" about how the machine works, they would look at you as if you were crazy.

Siri Stafford/Getty Images

1-3b The Scientific Method

To study economic problems, economists employ a process called the *scientific method,* which consists of four steps, as outlined in Exhibit 3.

Step One: Identify the Question and Define Relevant Variables

The scientific method begins with curiosity: Someone wants to answer a question. Thus, the first step is to identify the economic question and define the variables relevant to a solution. For example, the question might be, "What is the relationship between the price of Pepsi and the quantity of Pepsi purchased?" In this case, the relevant variables are price and quantity. A **variable** is a measure that can take on different values at different times. The variables of concern become the elements of the theory, so they must be selected with care.

Step Two: Specify Assumptions

The second step is to specify the assumptions under which the theory is to apply. One major category of assumptions is the **other-things-constant assumption**—in Latin, the

variable
A measure, such as price or quantity, that can take on different values at different times

other-things-constant assumption
The assumption, when focusing on the relation among key economic variables, that other variables remain unchanged; in Latin, *ceteris paribus*

EXHIBIT 3 The Scientific Method: Step by Step

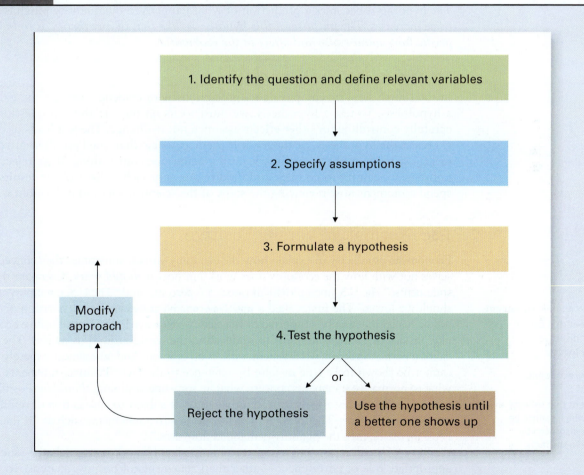

The steps of the scientific method are designed to develop and test hypotheses about how the world works. The objective is a theory that predicts outcomes more accurately than the best alternative theory.

A hypothesis is rejected if it does not predict as accurately as the best alternative. A rejected hypothesis can be modified or reworked in light of the test results.

ceteris paribus assumption. The idea is to identify the variables of interest and then focus exclusively on the relationships among them, assuming that nothing else important changes—that other things remain constant. Again, suppose we are interested in how the price of Pepsi influences the amount purchased. To isolate the relation between these two variables, we assume that there are no changes in other relevant variables such as consumer income, the average daytime temperature, or the price of Coke.

behavioral assumption
An assumption that describes the expected behavior of economic decision makers— what motivates them

We also make assumptions about how people behave; these are called **behavioral assumptions**. The primary behavioral assumption is rational self-interest. Earlier we assumed that each decision maker pursues self-interest rationally and makes choices accordingly. Rationality implies that each consumer buys the products expected to maximize his or her level of satisfaction. Rationality also implies that each firm supplies the products expected to maximize the firm's profit. These kinds of assumptions are called behavioral assumptions because they specify how we expect economic decision makers to behave—what makes them tick, so to speak.

Step Three: Formulate a Hypothesis

hypothesis
A theory about how key variables relate

The third step in the scientific method is to formulate a **hypothesis**, which is a theory about how key variables relate to each other. For example, one hypothesis holds that if the price of Pepsi goes up, other things constant, then the quantity purchased declines. The hypothesis becomes a prediction of what happens to the quantity purchased if the price increases. *The purpose of this hypothesis, like that of any theory, is to help make predictions about cause and effect in the real world.*

Step Four: Test the Hypothesis

In the fourth step, by comparing its predictions with evidence, we test the validity of a hypothesis. To test a hypothesis, we must focus on the variables in question, while carefully controlling for other effects assumed not to change. The test leads us either to (1) reject the hypothesis, or theory, if it predicts worse than the best alternative theory or (2) use the hypothesis, or theory, until a better one comes along. If we reject the hypothesis, we can try to go back and modify our approach in light of the results. Please spend a moment now reviewing the steps of the scientific method in Exhibit 3.

1-3c Normative Versus Positive

Economists usually try to explain how the economy works. Sometimes they concern themselves not with how the economy *does* work but how it *should* work. Compare these two statements: "The U.S. unemployment rate is 5.6 percent," and "The U.S. unemployment rate should be lower." The first, called a **positive economic statement**, is an assertion about economic reality that can be supported or rejected by reference to the facts. Positive economics, like physics or biology, attempts to understand the world around us as it is. The second, called a **normative economic statement**, reflects an opinion. And an opinion is merely that—it cannot be shown to be true or false by reference to the facts. Positive statements concern what *is;* normative statements concern what, in someone's opinion, *should be.* Positive statements need not necessarily be true, but they must be subject to verification or refutation by reference to the facts. Theories are expressed as positive statements such as "If the price of Pepsi increases, then the quantity demanded decreases."

positive economic statement
A statement that can be proved or disproved by reference to facts

normative economic statement
A statement that reflects an opinion, which cannot be proved or disproved by reference to the facts

Most of the disagreement among economists involves normative debates—such as the appropriate role of government—rather than statements of positive analysis. To be sure, many theoretical issues remain unresolved, but economists generally agree on most fundamental theoretical principles—that is, about positive economic analysis. For example, in a survey of 464 U.S. economists, only 6.5 percent disagreed with the statement "A ceiling on rents reduces the quantity and quality of housing available." This is a positive statement because it can be shown to be consistent or inconsistent with the evidence. In contrast, there was much less agreement on normative statements such as "The distribution of income in the United States should be more equal." Half the economists surveyed "generally agreed," a quarter "generally disagreed," and a quarter "agreed with provisos."[6]

Normative statements, or value judgments, have a place in a policy debate such as the proper role of government, provided that statements of opinion are distinguished from statements of fact. In such policy debates, you are entitled to your own opinion, but you are not entitled to your own facts.

1-3d Economists Tell Stories

Despite economists' reliance on the scientific method for developing and evaluating theories, economic analysis is as much art as science. Formulating a question, isolating the key variables, specifying the assumptions, proposing a theory to answer the question, and devising a way to test the predictions all involve more than simply an understanding of economics and the scientific method. Carrying out these steps requires good intuition and the imagination of a storyteller. Economists explain their theories by telling stories about how they think the economy works. To tell a compelling story, an economist relies on case studies, anecdotes, parables, the personal experience of the listener, and supporting data. Throughout this book, you'll hear stories that bring you closer to the ideas under consideration. These stories, such as the one about the Pepsi machine, breathe life into economic theory and help you personalize abstract ideas.

1-3e Predicting Average Behavior

Economic theory is used to predict the impact of an economic event on economic choices and, in turn, the effect of these choices on particular markets or on the economy as a whole. Does this mean that economists try to predict the behavior of particular consumers or producers? Not necessarily, because a specific individual may behave in an unpredictable way. But the unpredictable actions of numerous individuals tend to cancel one another out, so the *average behavior* of groups can be predicted more accurately. For example, if the federal government cuts personal income taxes, certain households might save the entire tax cut. On average, however, household spending would increase. Likewise, if Burger King cuts the price of Whoppers, the manager can better predict how much sales will increase than how a specific customer coming through the door will respond. *The random actions of individuals tend to offset one another, so the average behavior of a large group can be predicted more accurately than the behavior of a particular individual.* Consequently, economists tend to focus on the average, or typical, behavior of people in groups—for example, as average taxpayers or average Whopper consumers—rather than on the behavior of a specific individual.

1-3f Some Pitfalls of Faulty Economic Analysis

Economic analysis, like other forms of scientific inquiry, is subject to common mistakes in reasoning that can lead to faulty conclusions. Here are three sources of confusion.

The Fallacy That Association Is Causation

In the past two decades, the number of physicians specializing in cancer treatment increased sharply. At the same time, the incidence of some cancers increased. Can we

6. Richard M. Alston et al. "Is There a Consensus among Economists in the 1990s?" *American Economic Review*, 82 (May 1992): 203–209, Table 1.

association-is-causation fallacy
The incorrect idea that if two variables are associated in time, one must necessarily cause the other

conclude that physicians cause cancer? No. To assume that event A caused event B simply because the two are associated in time is to commit the **association-is-causation fallacy**, a common error. The fact that one event precedes another or that the two events occur simultaneously does not necessarily mean that one causes the other. Remember: Association is not necessarily causation.

The Fallacy of Composition

Perhaps you have been to a rock concert where everyone stands to get a better view. At some concerts, most people even stand on their chairs. But even standing on chairs does not improve your view if others do the same, unless you are quite tall. Likewise, arriving early to buy concert tickets does not work if many have the same idea. Earning a college degree to get a better job does not work as well if everyone earns a college degree. These are examples of the **fallacy of composition**, which is an erroneous belief that what is true for the individual, or the part, is also true for the group, or the whole.

fallacy of composition
The incorrect belief that what is true for the individual, or part, must necessarily be true for the group, or the whole

The Mistake of Ignoring the Secondary Effects

In many cities, public officials have imposed rent controls on apartments. The primary effect of this policy, the effect policy makers focus on, is to keep rents from rising. Over time, however, fewer new apartments get built because renting them becomes less profitable. Moreover, existing rental units deteriorate because owners have plenty of customers anyway. Thus, the quantity and quality of housing may decline as a result of what appears to be a reasonable measure to keep rents from rising. The mistake was to ignore the **secondary effects**, or the unintended consequences, of the policy. Economic actions have secondary effects that often turn out to be more important than the primary effects. Secondary effects may develop more slowly and may not be immediately obvious, but good economic analysis tries to anticipate them and take them into account.

secondary effects
Unintended consequences of economic actions that may develop slowly over time as people react to events

1-3g If Economists Are So Smart, Why Aren't They Rich?

Why aren't economists rich? Well, some are, earning over $25,000 per appearance on the lecture circuit. Others top $2 million a year as consultants and expert witnesses.[7] Economists have been appointed to federal cabinet posts, as secretaries of commerce, defense, labor, state, and treasury, for example, and to head the U.S. Federal Reserve System. Economics is the only social science and the only business discipline for which the prestigious Nobel Prize is awarded, and pronouncements by economists are reported in the media daily. A 2015 journal article argued that "the superiority of economists" gives them considerable influence over economic policy.[8] And *The Economist,* a widely respected news weekly from London, has argued that economic ideas have influenced policy "to a degree that would make other social scientists drool."[9]

The economics profession thrives because its models usually do a better job of making economic sense out of a confusing world than do alternative approaches. But not all economists are wealthy, nor is personal wealth the goal of the discipline. In a similar vein, not all doctors are healthy (some even smoke), not all carpenters live in perfectly built homes, not all marriage counselors are happily married, and not all child psychologists have well-adjusted children. Still, those who study economics do reap financial rewards, as discussed in this closing case study, which looks at the link between a college major and annual earnings.

7. As reported by George Anders, "An Economist's Courtroom Bonanza," *Wall Street Journal,* 19 March 2007.
8. Marion Fourcade, Etienne Ollion, and Yann Algan, "The Superiority of Economists," *Journal of Economic Perspectives,* 29 (Winter 2015): 89–114.
9. "The Puzzling Failure of Economics," *The Economist,* 23 August 1997, p. 11.

CASE STUDY

THE INFORMATION ECONOMY

COLLEGE MAJOR AND ANNUAL EARNINGS

Earlier in the chapter, you learned that economic choice involves comparing the expected marginal benefit and the expected marginal cost. Surveys show that students go to college because they believe a college diploma is the ticket to better jobs and higher pay. Put another way, for nearly two-thirds of U.S. high school graduates, the expected marginal benefit of college apparently exceeds the expected marginal cost. The cost of college will be discussed in the next chapter; the focus here is on the benefits of college, particularly expected earnings.

Among college graduates, all kinds of factors affect earnings, such as general ability, effort, occupation, college attended, college major, highest degree earned, appearance, and, yes, luck. PayScale.com collects real-time information on annual pay from its 10 million users. To isolate the effects of a college major on earnings, only workers with a bachelor's as their highest degree are included in the results. Exhibit 4 shows the median earnings in 2015 by major for two groups of college graduates: (1) those with 0 to 5 years of job experience and (2) those with 10 to 20 years of job experience. Majors are listed from the top down by the median annual pay of those with between 0 and 5 years of experience, identified by the light green bars. The top pay of $67,300 per year went to those who had majored in computer engineering; indeed, the top four slots went to engineering and computer majors. Nursing ranked fifth and economics ranked sixth out of the twenty majors listed. Economics had a median pay of $51,400, or 24 percent below the top pay. Elementary education majors held the bottom spot of $33,600, which was only half the top pay.

The dark green bars show the median pay by major for those with 10 to 20 years of job experience. Again, those who had majored in computer engineering led the field with $108,600, an increase of 61 percent over the pay of newer graduates with that degree. Economics majors with 10 to 20 years of job experience saw a 90 percent increase to $97,700. While economics majors with 0 to 5 years experience were paid 24 percent less than the top paying major, among those with at least a decade of job experience, the median pay for economics majors

moved up to within 10 percent of the top pay. In fact, economics majors saw their median pay grow more in dollar terms and in percentage terms than did any other major listed. This suggests that those who study economics acquire skills that appreciate with experience. The bump in median pay based on experience for the 19 other majors averaged 67 percent. Elementary education remained the lowest paying major among those with 10 to 20 years of experience. Note that the majors ranked toward the top of the list tend to be more quantitative and analytical. The selection of a relatively more challenging major such as engineering or economics may send a favorable signal to future employers. Nursing majors ranked high right out of school, thanks to strong demand for health care. But nurses with 10 to 20 years of experience earned only 29 percent more than those with only 0 to 5 years of experience. This was the slowest growth rate among the 20 majors.

Incidentally, Exhibit 4 ranks only 20 majors, but Payscale.com ranks 207 majors in all. Median pay for economics majors ranked them in the top 10 percent of that larger group of majors.

Remember, the survey was limited to those whose highest degree was the baccalaureate, so it excluded the many economics majors who went on to pursue graduate studies in law, business administration, economics, public administration, journalism, and other fields (a different study found that lawyers with undergraduate degrees

Bloomberg/Getty Images

continued

EXHIBIT 4   Median Annual Pay by College Major

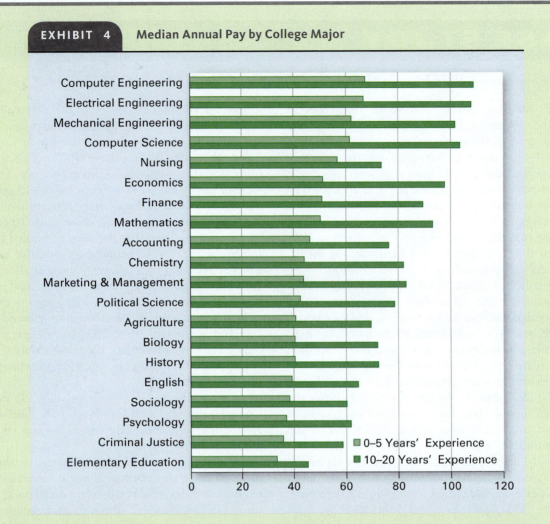

in economics earned more on average than lawyers with other majors).

A number of world leaders majored in economics, including three of the last seven U.S. presidents; Prime Minister Stephen Harper of Canada; billionaire and former president of Chile, Sebastian Pinera (who earned a Ph.D. in economics from Harvard); Turkey's first female prime minister, Tansu Ciller (who earned a Ph.D. in economics from the University of Connecticut); Italy's former prime minister, Mario Monti (who earned a Ph.D. in economics from Yale); Greece's former prime minister, Lucas Papademos (who earned a Ph.D. in economics from MIT); U.S. Supreme Court justices Stephen Breyer and Anthony Kennedy; and former justice Sandra Day

O'Connor. Other notable economics majors include billionaire Donald Trump, Hewlett-Packard president (and billionaire) Meg Whitman, former head of Microsoft (and billionaire) Steve Ballmer, CNN founder (and billionaire) Ted Turner, financial guru (and billionaire) Warren Buffett, Walmart founder (and billionaire) Sam Walton, and Scott Adams, creator of *Dilbert*, the mouthless wonder.

Sources: Median pay data for 2015 were found at http://www.payscale.com/best-colleges/degrees.asp; "The World's Billionaires," *Forbes*, 23 March 2015; and R. Kim Craft and Joe Baker, "Do Economists Make Better Lawyers?" *Journal of Economic Education*, 34 (Summer 2003): 263–281. For a survey of employment opportunities, go to the U.S. Labor Department's Occupational Outlook Handbook at http://www.bls.gov/oco/.

CHECKPOINT

What are the steps of the scientific method?

1-4 Conclusion

This textbook describes how economic factors affect individual choices and how all these choices come together to shape the economic system. Economics is not the whole story, and economic factors are not always the most important. But economic considerations have important and predictable effects on individual choices, and these choices affect the way we live.

Sure, economics is a challenging discipline, but it is also an exciting and rewarding one. The good news is that you already know a lot about economics. To use this knowledge, however, you must cultivate the art and science of economic analysis. You must be able to simplify the world to formulate questions, isolate the relevant variables, and then tell a persuasive story about how these variables relate.

An economic relation can be expressed in words, represented as a table of quantities, described by a mathematical equation, or illustrated as a graph. The appendix to this chapter introduces graphs. You may find a detailed reading of this unnecessary. If you are already familiar with relations among variables, slopes, tangents, and the like, you can probably just browse. But if you have little recent experience with graphs, you might benefit from a more careful reading with pencil and paper in hand.

The next chapter introduces key tools of economic analysis. Subsequent chapters use these tools to explore economic problems and to explain economic behavior that may otherwise seem puzzling. You must walk before you can run, however, and in the next chapter, you will take your first wobbly steps.

Summary

1. Economics is the study of how people choose to use their scarce resources to produce, exchange, and consume goods and services in an attempt to satisfy unlimited wants. The economic problem arises from the conflict between scarce resources and unlimited wants. If wants were limited or if resources were not scarce, there would be no need to study economics.

2. Economic resources are combined in a variety of ways to produce goods and services. Major categories of resources include labor, capital, natural resources, and entrepreneurial ability. Because economic resources are scarce, only a limited number of goods and services can be produced with them. Therefore, goods and services are also scarce so choices must be made.

3. Microeconomics focuses on choices made in households, firms, and governments and how these choices affect particular markets, such as the market for used cars. Choice is guided by rational self-interest. Choice typically requires time and information, both of which are scarce and valuable.

4. Whereas microeconomics examines the individual pieces of the puzzle, macroeconomics steps back to consider the big picture—the performance of the economy as a whole as reflected by such measures as total production, employment, the price level, and economic growth.

5. Economists use theories, or models, to help understand the effects of an economic change, such as a change in price or income, on individual choices and how these choices affect particular markets and the economy as a whole. Economists employ the scientific method to study an economic problem by (a) formulating the question and identifying relevant variables, (b) specifying the assumptions under which the theory operates, (c) developing a theory, or hypothesis, about how the variables relate, and (d) testing that theory by comparing its predictions with the evidence. A theory might not work perfectly, but it is useful as long as it predicts better than competing theories do.

6. Positive economics aims to discover how the economy works. Normative economics is concerned more with how, in someone's opinion, the economy should work. Those who are not careful can fall victim to the fallacy that association is causation, to the fallacy of composition, and to the mistake of ignoring secondary effects.

Key Concepts

Economics 2	Good 4	Economic fluctuations 9
Resources 3	Service 4	Economic theory, or economic model 10
Labor 3	Scarcity 4	Variable 11
Capital 3	Market 5	Other-things-constant assumption 11
Natural resources 3	Product market 5	Behavioral assumption 12
Entrepreneurial ability 3	Resource market 5	Hypothesis 12
Entrepreneur 3	Circular-flow model 5	Positive economic statement 12
Wages 3	Rational self-interest 7	Normative economic statement 12
Interest 3	Marginal 9	Association-is-causation fallacy 14
Rent 3	Microeconomics 9	Fallacy of composition 14
Profit 3	Macroeconomics 9	Secondary effects 14

Questions for Review

1. **Definition of Economics** What determines whether or not a resource is scarce? Why is the concept of scarcity important to the definition of economics?

2. **Resources** To which category of resources does each of the following belong?

   a. A taxi
   b. Computer software
   c. One hour of legal counsel
   d. A parking lot
   e. A forest
   f. The Mississippi River
   g. An individual introducing a new way to market products on the Internet

3. **Goods and Services** Explain why each of the following would *not* be considered "free" for the economy as a whole:

   a. Food vouchers
   b. U.S. aid to developing countries
   c. Corporate charitable contributions
   d. Noncable television programs
   e. Public high school education

4. **Economic Decision Makers** Which group of economic decision makers plays the leading role in the economic system?

Which groups play supporting roles? In what sense are they supporting actors?

5. **Micro Versus Macro** Determine whether each of the following is primarily a microeconomic or a macroeconomic issue:

   a. What price to charge for an automobile
   b. Measuring the impact of tax policies on consumer spending in the economy
   c. Your family's decisions about what to buy
   d. A worker deciding how much to work each week
   e. Designing a government policy to increase total employment

6. **Micro Versus Macro** Some economists believe that to understand macroeconomics, you must first understand microeconomics. How does microeconomics relate to macroeconomics?

7. **Normative Versus Positive Analysis** Determine whether each of the following statements is normative or positive:

   a. The U.S. unemployment rate was 6.2 percent in 2014.
   b. The inflation rate in the United States is too high.
   c. The U.S. government should increase the minimum wage.
   d. U.S. trade restrictions cost consumers $100 billion annually.

8. **Role of Theory** What good is economic theory if it can't predict the behavior of a specific individual?

Problems and Exercises

9. **Rational Self-Interest** Discuss the impact of rational self-interest on each of the following decisions:

   a. Whether to attend college full time or enter the workforce full time
   b. Whether to buy a new textbook or a used one
   c. Whether to attend a local college or an out-of-town college

10. **Rational Self-Interest** If behavior is governed by rational self-interest, why do people make charitable contributions of time and money?

11. **Marginal Analysis** The owner of a small pizzeria is deciding whether to increase the radius of delivery area by one mile. What considerations must be taken into account if such a decision is to increase profitability?

12. **Time and Information** It is often costly to obtain the information necessary to make good decisions. Yet your own interests can be best served by rationally weighing all options available to you. This requires informed decision making. Does this mean that making uninformed decisions is irrational? How do you determine how much information is the right amount?

13. **Pitfalls of Economic Analysis** Review the discussion of pitfalls in economic thinking in this chapter. Then identify the fallacy, or mistake in thinking, in each of the following statements:

    a. Raising taxes always increases government revenues.
    b. Whenever there is a recession, imports decrease. Therefore, to stop a recession, we should increase imports.
    c. Raising the tariff on imported steel helps the U.S. steel industry. Therefore, the entire economy is helped.
    d. Gold sells for about $1,200 per ounce. Therefore, the U.S. government could sell all the gold in Fort Knox at $1,200 per ounce to reduce the national debt.

14. **Association Versus Causation** Suppose I observe that communities with lots of doctors tend to have relatively high rates of illness. I conclude that doctors cause illness. What's wrong with this reasoning?

15. **Case Study: College Major and Annual Earnings** Because some college majors pay nearly twice as much as others, why would students pursuing their rational self-interest choose a lower paying major?

Understanding Graphs

Take out a pencil and a blank piece of paper. Go ahead. Put a point in the middle of the paper. This is your point of departure, called the **origin**. With your pencil at the origin, draw a straight line off to the right. This line is called the **horizontal axis**. The value of the variable *x* measured along the horizontal axis increases as you move to the right of the origin. Now mark off this line from 0 to 20, in increments of 5 units each. Returning to the origin, draw another line, this one straight north. This line is called the **vertical axis**. The value of the variable *y* measured along the vertical axis increases as you move north of the origin. Mark off this line from 0 to 20, in increments of 5 units each.

Within the space framed by the two axes, you can plot possible combinations of the variables measured along each axis. Each point identifies a value measured along the horizontal, or *x*, axis *and* a value measured along the vertical, or *y*, axis. For example, place point *a* in your graph to reflect the combination where *x* equals 5 units and *y* equals 15 units. Likewise, place point *b* in your graph to reflect 10 units of *x* and 5 units of *y*. Now compare your results with points shown in Exhibit 5.

A **graph** is a picture showing how variables relate, and a picture can be worth a thousand words. Take a look at Exhibit 6, which shows the U.S. annual unemployment rate since 1900. The year is measured along the horizontal axis and the unemployment rate is measured as a percentage along the vertical axis. Exhibit 6 is a *time-series graph,* which shows the value of a variable, in this case the percent of the labor force unemployed, over time. If you had to describe the information presented in Exhibit 6, the explanation could take many words. The picture shows not only how one year compares to the next but also how one decade compares to another and how the unemployment rate trends over time. The sharply higher unemployment rate during the Great Depression of the 1930s is unmistakable. *Graphs convey information in a compact and efficient way.*

This appendix shows how graphs express a variety of possible relations among variables. Most graphs of interest in this book reflect the relationship between two economic variables, such as the unemployment rate and

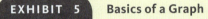

EXHIBIT 5 **Basics of a Graph**

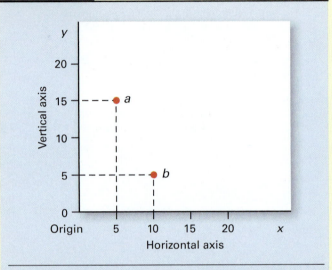

Any point on a graph represents a combination of values of two variables. Here point *a* represents the combination of 5 units of variable *x* (measured on the horizontal axis) and 15 units of variable *y* (measured on the vertical axis). Point *b* represents 10 units of *x* and 5 units of *y*.

the year, the price of a product and the quantity demanded, or the price of production and the quantity supplied. Because we focus on just two variables at a time, we usually assume that other relevant variables remain constant.

One variable often depends on another. The time it takes you to drive home depends on your average speed. Your weight depends on how much you eat. The amount of Pepsi you buy depends on the price. A *functional relation* exists between two variables when the value of one variable *depends* on the value of another variable. The value of the **dependent variable** depends on the value of the **independent variable**. The task of the economist is to isolate economic relations and determine the direction of causality, if any. Recall that one of the pitfalls of economic thinking is the erroneous belief that association is causation. We cannot conclude that, simply because two events relate in time, one causes the other. There may be no relation between the two events.

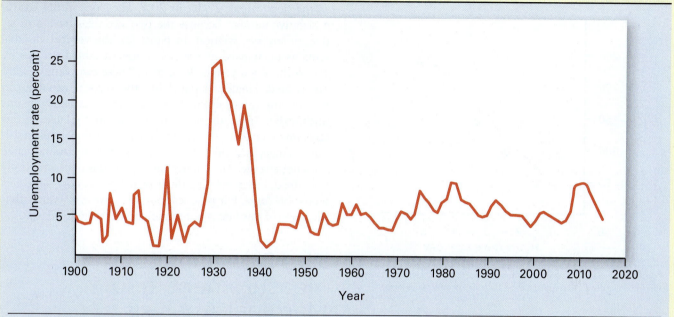

EXHIBIT 6   **U.S. Unemployment Rate Since 1900**

A time-series graph depicts the behavior of some economic variable over time. Shown here are U.S. unemployment rates since 1900.

Source: Historical Statistics of the United States, 1970; and *Economic Report of the President*, February 2015.

Drawing Graphs

Let's begin with a simple relation. Suppose you are planning to drive across the country and want to figure out how far you will travel each day. You plan to average 50 miles per hour. Possible combinations of driving time and distance traveled per day appear in Exhibit 7. One column lists the hours driven per day, and the next column lists the number of miles traveled per day, assuming an average speed of 50 miles per hour. The distance traveled, the *dependent* variable, depends on the number of hours

EXHIBIT 7   **Schedule Relating Distance Traveled to Hours Driven**

	Hours Driven per Day	Distance Traveled per Day (miles)
a	1	50
b	2	100
c	3	150
d	4	200
e	5	250

The distance traveled per day depends on the hours driven per day, assuming an average speed of 50 miles per hour. This table shows combinations of hours driven and distance traveled. These combinations are shown as points in Exhibit 8.

driven, the *independent* variable. Combinations of hours driven and distance traveled are shown as *a, b, c, d,* and *e.* Each combination is represented by a point in Exhibit 8. For example, point *a* shows that if you drive for 1 hour, you travel 50 miles. Point *b* indicates that if you drive for 2 hours, you travel 100 miles. By connecting the points, or possible combinations, we create a line running upward and to the right. This makes sense because, the longer you drive, the farther you travel. Assumed constant along this line is your average speed of 50 miles per hour.

Types of relations between variables include the following:

1. As one variable increases, the other increases—as in Exhibit 8; this is called a **positive,** or **direct, relation** between the variables.
2. As one variable increases, the other decreases; this is called a **negative,** or **inverse, relation**.
3. As one variable increases, the other remains unchanged; the two variables are said to be *independent,* or *unrelated.*

One of the advantages of graphs is that they easily convey the relation between variables. We do not need to examine the particular combinations of numbers; we need only focus on the shape of the curve.

EXHIBIT 8 — Graph Relating Distance Traveled to Hours Driven

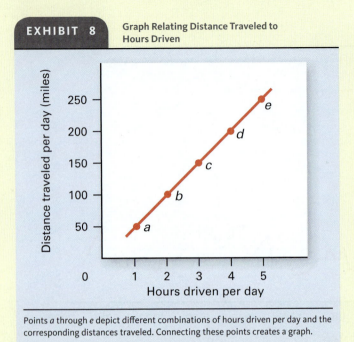

Points *a* through *e* depict different combinations of hours driven per day and the corresponding distances traveled. Connecting these points creates a graph.

The Slope of a Straight Line

A more precise way to describe the shape of a curve is to measure its slope. The **slope of a line** indicates how much the vertical variable changes for a given increase in the horizontal variable. Specifically, the slope between any two points along any straight line is the vertical change between these two points divided by the horizontal increase, or

$$\text{Slope} = \frac{\text{Change in the vertical distance}}{\text{Increase in the horizontal distance}}$$

Each of the four panels in Exhibit 9 indicates a vertical change, given a 10-unit increase in the horizontal variable. In panel (a), the vertical distance increases by 5 units when the horizontal distance increases by 10 units. The slope of the line is therefore 5/10, or 0.5. Notice that the slope in this case is a positive number because the relation between the two variables is positive, or direct. This slope indicates that for every 1-unit increase in the horizontal variable, the vertical variable increases by 0.5 units. The slope, incidentally, does not imply causality; the increase in the horizontal variable does not necessarily *cause* the increase in the vertical variable. The slope simply measures the relation between an increase in the horizontal variable and the associated change in the vertical variable.

In panel (b) of Exhibit 9, the vertical distance declines by 7 units when the horizontal distance increases by 10 units, so the slope equals 27/10, or 20.7. The slope in this case is a negative number because the two variables have a negative, or inverse, relation. In panel (c), the vertical variable remains unchanged as the horizontal variable increases by 10, so the slope equals 0/10, or 0. These two variables are not related. Finally, in panel (d), the vertical variable can take on any value, although the horizontal variable remains unchanged. Again, the two variables are not related. In this case, any change in the vertical measure, for example a 10-unit change, is divided by 0, because the horizontal value does not change. Any change divided by 0 is mathematically undefined, but as the line tilts toward vertical, its slope gets incredibly large. For practical purposes, we will assume that the slope of this line is not undefined but infinitely large.

The Slope, Units of Measurement, and Marginal Analysis

The mathematical value of the slope depends on the units measured on the graph. For example, suppose copper tubing costs $1 a foot. Graphs depicting the relation between total cost and quantity purchased are shown in Exhibit 10. In panel (a), the total cost increases by $1 for each 1-foot increase in the amount of tubing purchased. Thus, the slope equals 1/1, or 1. If the cost per foot remains the same but units are measured not in *feet* but in *yards*, the relation between total cost and quantity purchased is as depicted in panel (b). Now total cost increases by $3 for each 1-*yard* increase in output, so the slope equals 3/1, or 3. Because different units are used to measure the copper tubing, the two panels reflect different slopes, even though the cost is $1 per foot in each panel. Keep in mind that *the slope depends in part on the units of measurement.*

Economic analysis usually involves *marginal analysis,* such as the marginal cost of one more unit of output. The slope is a convenient device for measuring marginal effects because it reflects the change in total cost, measured along the vertical axis, for each 1-unit change in output, measured along the horizontal axis. For example, in panel (a) of Exhibit 10, the marginal cost of another *foot* of copper tubing is $1, which also equals the slope of the line. In panel (b), the marginal cost of another *yard* of tubing is $3, which again is the slope of that line. Because of its applicability to marginal analysis, the slope has special relevance in economics.

EXHIBIT 9   **Alternative Slopes for Straight Lines**

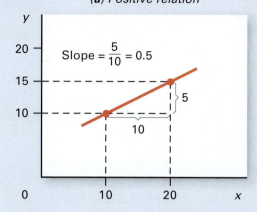

(a) Positive relation

$$\text{Slope} = \frac{5}{10} = 0.5$$

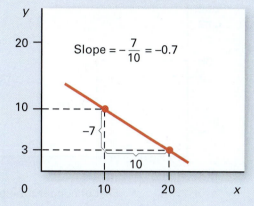

(b) Negative relation

$$\text{Slope} = -\frac{7}{10} = -0.7$$

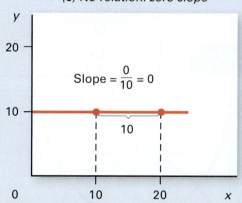

(c) No relation: zero slope

$$\text{Slope} = \frac{0}{10} = 0$$

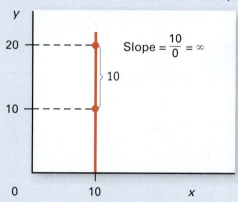

(d) No relation: assumed infinite slope

$$\text{Slope} = \frac{10}{0} = \infty$$

The slope of a line indicates how much the vertically measured variable changes for a given increase in the variable measured along the horizontal axis. Panel (a) shows a positive relation between two variables; the slope is 0.5, a positive number. Panel (b) depicts a negative, or inverse, relation. When the x variable increases, the y variable decreases; the slope is 20.7, a negative number.

Panels (c) and (d) represent situations in which two variables are unrelated. In panel (c), the y variable always takes on the same value; the slope is 0. In panel (d), the x variable always takes on the same value; the slope is mathematically undefined but we simplify by assuming the slope is infinite.

The Slopes of Curved Lines

The slope of a straight line is the same everywhere along the line, but the slope of a curved line differs along the curve, as shown in Exhibit 11. To find the slope of a curved line at a particular point, draw a straight line that just touches the curve at that point but does not cut or cross the curve. Such a line is called a tangent to the curve at that point. The slope of the **tangent** gives the slope of the curve at that point. Look at line *A*, which is tangent to the curve at point *a*. As the horizontal value increases from 0 to 10, the vertical value drops along *A* from 40 to 0. Thus, the vertical change divided by the horizontal change equals 240/10, or 24, which is the slope of the curve at point *a*. This slope is negative because the vertical value decreases as the horizontal value increases. Line *B*, a line tangent to the curve at point *b*, has the slope 210/30, or 20.33. As you can see, the curve depicted in Exhibit 11 gets flatter as the horizontal variable increases, so the value of its slope approaches zero.

Other curves, of course, will reflect different slopes as well as different changes in the slope along the curve.

EXHIBIT 10   **Slope Depends on the Unit of Measure**

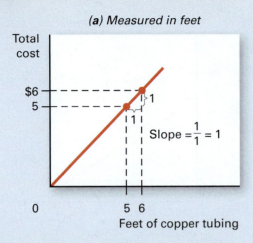

(a) *Measured in feet*

Total cost

$6
5

Slope $= \dfrac{1}{1} = 1$

0   5 6
Feet of copper tubing

(b) *Measured in yards*

Total cost

$6

3

Slope $= \dfrac{3}{1} = 3$

0   1 2
Yards of copper tubing

The value of the slope depends on the units of measure. In panel (a), output is measured in feet of copper tubing; in panel (b), output is measured in yards.

Although the cost is $1 per foot in each panel, the slope is different in the two panels because copper tubing is measured using different units.

EXHIBIT 11   **Slopes at Different Points on a Curved Line**

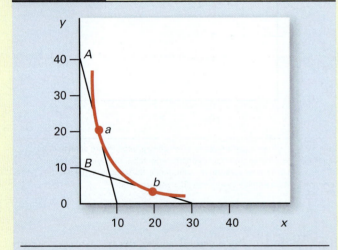

y

40 — A

30 —

20 — a

10 — B
                    b
0 —

      10   20   30   40   x

The slope of a curved line varies from point to point. At a given point, such as *a* or *b*, the slope of the curve is equal to the slope of the straight line that is tangent to the curve at the point.

EXHIBIT 12   **Curves with Both Positive and Negative Slopes**

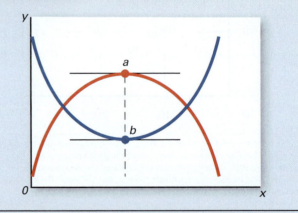

y

a

b

0   x

Some curves have both positive and negative slopes. The hill-shaped curve (in red) has a positive slope to the left of point *a*, a slope of 0 at point *a*, and a negative slope to the right of that point. The U-shaped curve (in blue) starts off with a negative slope, has a slope of 0 at point *b*, and has a positive slope to the right of that point.

Downward-sloping curves have negative slopes, and upward-sloping curves, positive slopes. Sometimes curves, such as those in Exhibit 12, are more complex, having both positive and negative ranges, depending on the horizontal value. In the hill-shaped curve, for small values of *x*, there is a positive relation between *x* and *y*, so the slope is positive. As the value of *x* increases, however, the slope declines and eventually becomes negative. We can divide the curve into two segments: (1) the segment between the origin and point *a*, where the slope is positive; and (2) the segment of the curve to the right of point *a*, where the slope is negative. The slope of the curve at point *a* is 0. The U-shaped curve in Exhibit 12 represents the opposite relation: *x* and *y* are negatively related until point *b* is reached; thereafter, they are positively related. The slope equals 0 at point *b*.

Line Shifts

Let's go back to the example of your cross-country trip, where we were trying to determine how many miles you would travel per day. Recall that we measured hours driven per day on the horizontal axis and miles traveled per day on the vertical axis, assuming an average speed of 50 miles per hour. That same relation is shown as line T in Exhibit 13. What happens if the average speed is 40 miles per hour? The entire relation between hours driven and distance traveled would change, as shown by the shift to the right of line T to T'. With a slower average speed, any distance traveled per day now requires more driving time. For example, 200 miles traveled requires 4 hours of driving when the average speed is 50 miles per hour (as shown by point d on curve T), but 200 miles takes 5 hours when your speed averages 40 miles per hour (as shown by point f on curve T'). Thus, *a change in the assumption about average speed changes the relationship between the two variables observed.* This changed relationship is expressed by a shift of the line that shows how the two variables relate.

That ends our once-over of graphs. Return to this appendix when you need a review.

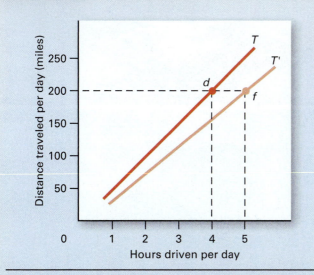

EXHIBIT 13   Shift of Line Relating Distance Traveled to Hours Driven

Line T appeared originally in Exhibit 8 to show the relation between hours driven and distance traveled per day, assuming an average speed of 50 miles per hour. If the speed averages only 40 miles per hour, the entire relation shifts to the right to T', indicating that any given distance traveled requires more driving time. For example, 200 miles traveled takes 4 hours at 50 miles per hour but 5 hours at 40 miles per hour. This figure shows how a change in assumptions, in this case, the average speed, can shift the entire relationship between two variables.

Appendix Questions

1. **Understanding Graphs** Look at Exhibit 6 and answer the following questions:

   a. In what year (approximately) was the unemployment rate the highest? In what year was it the lowest?
   b. In what decade, on average, was the unemployment rate highest? In what decade was it lowest?
   c. Between 1950 and 1980, did the unemployment rate generally increase, decrease, or remain about the same?

2. **Drawing Graphs**   Sketch a graph to illustrate your idea of each of the following relationships. Be sure to label each axis appropriately. For each relationship, explain under what circumstances, if any, the curve could shift:

   a. The relationship between a person's age and height
   b. Average monthly temperature in your hometown over the course of a year
   c. A person's income and the number of hamburgers consumed per month
   d. The amount of fertilizer added to an acre and the amount of corn grown on that land in one growing season
   e. An automobile's horsepower and its gasoline mileage (in miles per gallon)

3. **Slope**   Suppose you are given the following data on wage rates and number of hours worked:

Point	Hourly Wage	Hours Worked per Week
a	$0	0
b	5	0
c	10	30
d	15	35
e	20	45
f	25	50

   a. Construct and label a set of axes and plot these six points. Label each point a, b, c, and so on. Which variable do you think should be measured on the vertical axis, and which variable should be measured on the horizontal axis?
   b. Connect the points. Describe the resulting curve. Does it make sense to you?
   c. Compute the slope of the curve between points a and b. Between points b and c. Between points c and d. Between points d and e. Between points e and f. What happens to the slope as you move from point a to point f?

2 Economic Tools and Economic Systems

Digital Vision/Jupiter Images

- *Why are you reading this book right now rather than doing something else?*
- *What is college costing you?*
- *Why will you eventually major in one subject rather than continue to take courses in various subjects?*
- *Why is fast food so fast?*
- *Why is there no point crying over spilled milk?*
- *Why does common ownership often lead to common neglect?*

These and other questions are addressed in this chapter, which introduces some tools of economic analysis—some tools of the trade.

Chapter 1 introduced the idea that scarcity forces us to make choices, but the chapter said little about how to make economic choices. This chapter develops a framework for evaluating economic alternatives. First, we consider the cost involved in selecting one alternative over others. Next, we develop tools to explore the choices available to individuals and to the economy as a whole. Finally, we examine the questions that different economies must answer—questions about what goods and services to produce, how to produce them, and for whom to produce them.

Topics discussed in this chapter include:

- Opportunity cost
- Comparative advantage
- Specialization
- Division of labor

- Production possibilities frontier
- Economic systems
- Three economic questions
- Capitalism, command systems, and in between

2-1 Choice and Opportunity Cost

Think about a choice you just made: the decision to begin reading this chapter right now rather than use your time to study for another course, play sports, watch TV, play video games, go online, get some sleep, hang with friends, or do something else. Suppose it's late and your best alternative to reading right now is getting some sleep. The cost of reading is passing up the opportunity of sleep. Because of scarcity, whenever you make a choice, you must pass up another opportunity; you must incur an *opportunity cost*.

2-1a Opportunity Cost

What do we mean when we talk about the cost of something? Isn't it what we must give up—must forgo—to get that thing? The **opportunity cost** of the chosen item or activity is *the value of the best alternative that is forgone*. You can think of opportunity cost as the *opportunity lost*. Sometimes opportunity cost can be measured in terms of money, although, as we shall see, money is usually only part of opportunity cost.

How many times have you heard people say they did something because they "had nothing better to do"? They actually mean they had nothing else going on. Yet, according to the idea of opportunity cost, people *always* do what they do because they have nothing better to do. The choice selected seems, at the time, preferable to any other possible alternative. You are reading this chapter right now because you have nothing better to do. In fact, you are attending college for the same reason: College appears more attractive than your best alternative, as discussed in the following case study.

opportunity cost
The value of the best alternative forgone when an item or activity is chosen

CASE STUDY

BRINGING THEORY TO LIFE

THE OPPORTUNITY COST OF COLLEGE What is your opportunity cost of attending college full time this year? What was the best alternative you gave up? If you held a full-time job, you would have some idea of the income you gave up to attend college. Suppose you expected to earn $20,000 a year, after taxes, from a full-time job. As a full-time college student, you plan to work part time during the academic year and full time during the summer, earning a total of $10,000 after taxes (about 40 percent of college students hold jobs during the academic year). Thus, by attending college this year, you gave up after-tax earnings of $10,000 (= $20,000 − $10,000).

What about the direct cost of college itself? Suppose you are paying $12,000 this year for in-state tuition, fees, and books at a public college (paying out-of-state rates would cost $24,000 and attending a private college would cost $32,000). *The opportunity cost of paying for tuition, fees, and books is what you and your family could otherwise have purchased with that money.*

How about room and board? Expenses for room and board are not necessarily an opportunity cost because, even if you were not attending college, you would still need to live somewhere and eat something, though these could differ from your college costs. Likewise, whether or not you attended college, you would still buy goods such as a smartphone, clothes, and toiletries, and services such as cell service, laundry, and haircuts. Your spending for such products is not an opportunity cost of attending college but personal-upkeep costs that arise regardless of

what you do. So for simplicity, assume that room, board, and personal expenses are the same whether or not you attend college. Your forgone earnings of $10,000 plus the $12,000 for tuition, fees, and books yield an opportunity cost of $22,000 this year for a student paying in-state rates at a public college. Opportunity cost jumps to about $34,000 for students paying out-of-state rates and to about $42,000 for those at private colleges. Scholarships, but not loans, would reduce your opportunity cost (why not loans?).

This analysis assumes that other things remain constant. But if, in your view, attending college is more of a pain than you expected your best alternative to be, then the opportunity cost of college is even higher. In other words, if you are one of those people who find college difficult, often boring, and in most ways more unpleasant than a full-time job, then the money cost understates your opportunity cost, because your best alternative offers a more enjoyable quality of life. If, on the other hand, you believe the wild and crazy life of a college student is more enjoyable than a full-time job would be, then the dollar figures overstate your opportunity cost, because your best alternative involves a less satisfying quality of life.

Apparently, you view college as a good investment in your future, even though it's costly and perhaps even painful. College graduates on average earn about twice as much per year as high school graduates, a difference that exceeds $1 million over a lifetime. These pay-gains from college prompt some college students to pile up debts to finance their education. Seven in ten 2014 graduates finished with college debt, and that debt averaged more than $33,000. Loans taken out by their parents increased that total by about $10,000.

Still, college is not for everyone. Some find the opportunity cost too high. For example, Bill Gates and Paul Allen dropped out of college to cofound Microsoft (both are now among the richest people on Earth). Mark Zuckerberg dropped out to found Facebook. Tiger Woods, once an economics major at Stanford, dropped out after two years to earn a fortune in professional golf. And Paula Creamer, who skipped college to play golf, won her first $1 million sooner than any other LPGA player in tour history. High school basketball players who believed they were ready for the pros,

Chris Schmidt/Getty Images

continued

such as Kobe Bryant and LeBron James, also skipped college (now players can't enter the pros until they reach 19 years of age and are out of high school at least a year, which usually means only one year of college), as do most tennis pros. Many actors even dropped out of high school to follow their dreams, including Jim Carrey, Nicolas Cage, Johnny Depp, Cameron Diaz, Robert Downey Jr., Colin Farrell, Ryan Gosling, Nicole Kidman, Lindsay Lohan, Demi Moore, Keanu Reeves, Seth Rogen, Charlie Sheen, Kiefer Sutherland, Hilary Swank and Kate Winslet.

Sources: Kevin Carey, "A Quiet Revolution in Helping Lift the Burden of Student Debt," *New York Times*, 25 January 2015; Mitchell E. Daniels, "How Student Debt Harms the Economy," *Wall Street Journal*, 27 January 2015; "The World's Billionaires," *Forbes*, 23 March 2015; and "College Board Connect to College Success" at http://www.collegeboard.com/.

2-1b Opportunity Cost Is Subjective

Like beauty, opportunity cost is in the eye of the beholder. It is subjective. Only the individual making the choice can identify the most attractive alternative. But the chooser seldom knows the actual value of what was passed up, because that alternative is "the road not taken." If you give up an evening of pizza and conversation with friends to work on a research paper, you will never know exactly what you gave up. You know only what you *expected*. Evidently, you expected the benefit of working on that paper to exceed the benefit of the best alternative. (Incidentally, focusing on the best alternative forgone makes all other alternatives irrelevant.)

Calculating Opportunity Cost Requires Time and Information

Economists assume that people rationally choose the most valued alternative. This does not mean you exhaustively assess the value of all possibilities. You assess alternatives as long as the expected marginal benefit of gathering more information about your options exceeds the expected marginal cost (even if you are not aware of making such conscious calculations). In other words, you do the best you can for yourself.

Because learning about alternatives is costly and time consuming, some choices are based on limited or even wrong information. Indeed, some choices may turn out badly (you went for a picnic but it rained; the movie that cost $10 stunk; your new shoes pinched; your new exercise equipment gets no exercise; the stock you bought tanked). Regret about lost opportunities is captured in the common expression "coulda, woulda, shoulda." At the time you made the selection, however, you believed you were making the best use of all your scarce resources, including the time required to gather and evaluate information about your choices.

Time: The Ultimate Constraint

The Sultan of Brunei is among the richest people on Earth, worth billions based on huge oil revenues that flow into his tiny country. He and his royal family (which has ruled since 1405) live in a palace with 1,788 rooms, including 257 bathrooms and a throne room the size of a football field. The family owns hundreds of cars, including dozens of Rolls-Royces; he can drive any of these or pilot one of his seven planes, including the 747 with gold-plated furniture. Supported by such wealth, the Sultan would appear to have overcome the economic problem of scarcity. Yet, though he can buy just about anything he wants, he lacks the time to enjoy all his stuff. If he pursues one activity, he cannot at the same time do something else. Each activity involves an opportunity cost. Consequently, the Sultan must choose from among the competing uses of his scarcest resource, time. Although your alternatives are less exotic, you too face a time constraint, especially as the college term winds down.

Opportunity Cost Varies With Circumstance

Opportunity cost depends on your alternatives. This is why you are more likely to study on a Tuesday night than on a Saturday night. The opportunity cost of studying is lower on a Tuesday night, because your alternatives are less attractive than on a Saturday night, when more is going on. Suppose you go to a movie on Saturday night. Your opportunity cost is the value of your best alternative forgone, which might be attending a college game. For some of you, studying on Saturday night may rank well down the list of alternatives—perhaps ahead of reorganizing your closet but behind doing your laundry.

Opportunity cost is subjective, but in some cases, money paid for goods and services is a reasonable approximation. For example, the opportunity cost of the new smartphone you bought is the benefit from spending that $300 on the best forgone alternative. The money measure may leave out some important elements, however, particularly the value of the time involved. For example, watching the latest hit movie costs you not only the $10 admission price but also the time needed to get there, watch the movie, and return home.

Even religious practices are subject to opportunity cost. For example, about half the U.S. population attends religious services at least once a month. In some states, so-called blue laws prohibit retail activity on Sunday. Some states have repealed these laws in recent years, thus raising the opportunity cost of church attendance. Researchers have found that when a state repeals its blue laws, religious attendance declines, as do church donations. These results do not seem to be linked to any decline in religiosity before the repeal.[1]

2-1c Sunk Cost and Choice

sunk cost
A cost that has already been incurred, cannot be recovered, and thus is irrelevant for present and future economic decisions

Suppose you have just finished grocery shopping and are wheeling your cart toward the checkout counters. How do you decide which line to join? Easy. You pick the one with the shortest expected wait. Suppose that line has barely moved for 10 minutes, when you notice that a cashier has opened a new one and invites you to check out. Do you switch to the open cashier, or do you think, "Since I've already spent 10 minutes in this line, I'm staying put"? The 10 minutes you waited represents a **sunk cost**, which is a cost that has already been incurred and cannot be recovered, regardless of what you do next. Sunk cost is like a sunken ship—it's gone. You should ignore sunk costs in making economic choices. Hence, you should switch lines. *Economic decision makers should consider only those costs that are affected by the choice. Sunk costs have already been incurred and are not affected by the choice, so they are irrelevant.* Likewise, you should walk out on a bad movie, even if you spent $10 to get in. Your $10 is gone, and sitting through that stinker only makes you worse off. The irrelevance of sunk costs is underscored by proverbs such as "Don't throw good money after bad," "Let bygones be bygones," "That's water over the dam," and "There's no point crying over spilled milk." The milk has already spilled, so whatever you do now cannot change that. Or, as Shakespeare's Lady Macbeth put it, "Things without all remedy should be without regard: what's done is done." In other words, forget about it.

Now that you have some idea about opportunity cost, let's see how it helps solve the economic problem.

 **CHECKPOINT**

What is the opportunity cost of an activity, and why is that cost sometimes difficult to estimate?

---

[1] Jonathan Gruber and Daniel Hungerman, "The Church vs. the Mall: What Happens When Religion Faces Increased Secular Competition?" *Quarterly Journal of Economics*, 123 (May 2008): 831–862.

2-2 Comparative Advantage, Specialization, and Exchange

Suppose you live in a dormitory. You and your roommate have such tight schedules that you each can spare only about an hour a week for mundane tasks like ironing shirts and typing papers (granted, in reality you may not iron shirts or type papers, but this example will help you understand some important principles). Each of you must turn in a typed three-page paper every week, and you each prefer ironed shirts when you have the time. Let's say it takes you a half hour to type a handwritten paper. Your roommate is from the hunt-and-peck school and takes about an hour. But your roommate is a talented ironer and can iron a shirt in 5 minutes flat (or should that be, iron it flat in 5 minutes?). You take twice as long, or 10 minutes, to iron a shirt.

During the hour set aside each week for typing and ironing, typing takes priority. If you each do your own typing and ironing, you type your paper in a half hour and iron three shirts in the remaining half hour. Your roommate spends the entire hour typing the paper, leaving no time for ironing. Thus, if you each do your own tasks, the combined output is two typed papers and three ironed shirts.

2-2a The Law of Comparative Advantage

Before long, you each realize that total output would increase if you did all the typing and your roommate did all the ironing. In the hour available for these tasks, you type both papers and your roommate irons 12 shirts. As a result of specialization, total output increases by 9 shirts! You strike a deal to exchange your typing for your roommate's ironing, so you each end up with a typed paper and 6 ironed shirts. Thus, *each of you is better off as a result of specialization and exchange*. By specializing in the task that you each do better, you rely on the **law of comparative advantage**, which states that the individual with the lower opportunity cost of producing a particular output should specialize in that output. You face a lower opportunity cost of typing than does your roommate, because in the time it takes to type a paper, you could iron 3 shirts whereas your roommate could iron 12 shirts. And if you face a lower opportunity cost of typing, your roommate must face a lower opportunity cost of ironing (try working that out).

law of comparative advantage

The individual, firm, region, or country with the lowest opportunity cost of producing a particular good should specialize in that good

2-2b Absolute Advantage Versus Comparative Advantage

The gains from specialization and exchange so far are obvious. A more interesting case is if you are faster at both tasks. Suppose the example changes only in one respect: Your roommate takes 12 minutes to iron a shirt compared with your 10 minutes. You now have an *absolute* advantage in both tasks, meaning each task takes you less time than it does your roommate. More generally, having an **absolute advantage** means making something using fewer resources than other producers require.

Does your absolute advantage in both activities mean specialization is no longer a good idea? Recall that the law of comparative advantage states that the individual with *the lower opportunity cost* of producing a particular good should specialize in that good. You still take 30 minutes to type a paper and 10 minutes to iron a shirt, so your opportunity cost of typing the paper remains at three ironed shirts. Your roommate takes an hour to type a paper and 12 minutes to iron a shirt, so your roommate could iron five shirts in the time it takes to type a paper. *Because your opportunity cost of typing is lower than your roommate's, you still have a comparative advantage in typing.* Consequently, your roommate must have a comparative advantage in ironing (again, try working this out to your satisfaction). Therefore, you should do all the typing and your roommate, all the ironing. Although you have an absolute advantage in both

absolute advantage

The ability to make something using fewer resources than other producers use

comparative advantage
The ability to make something at a lower opportunity cost than other producers face

tasks, your **comparative advantage** calls for specializing in the task for which you have the lower opportunity cost—in this case, typing.

If neither of you specialized, you could type one paper and iron three shirts. Your roommate could still type just the one paper. Your combined output would be two papers and three shirts. If you each specialized according to comparative advantage, in an hour you could type both papers and your roommate could iron five shirts. Thus, specialization increases total output by two ironed shirts. Even though you are better at both tasks than your roommate, you are comparatively better at typing. Put another way, your roommate, although worse at both tasks, is not quite as bad at ironing as at typing.

Don't think that this is just common sense. Common sense would lead you to do your own ironing and typing, because you are better at both. *Absolute advantage focuses on who uses the fewest resources, but comparative advantage focuses on what else those resources could produce—that is, on the opportunity cost of those resources.* Comparative advantage is the better guide to who should do what.

The law of comparative advantage applies not only to individuals but also to firms, regions of a country, and entire nations. Individuals, firms, regions, or countries with the lowest opportunity cost of producing a particular good should specialize in producing that good. Because of such factors as climate, workforce skills, natural resources, and capital stock, certain parts of the country and certain parts of the world have a comparative advantage in producing particular goods. From Washington State apples to Florida oranges, from software in India to hardware in Taiwan—*resources are allocated most efficiently across the country and around the world when production and trade conform to the law of comparative advantage.*

2-2c Specialization and Exchange

barter
The direct exchange of one product for another without using money

In the previous example, you and your roommate specialized and then exchanged output. No money was involved. In other words, you engaged in **barter**, where products are traded directly for other products. Barter works best in simple economies with little specialization and few traded goods. But for economies with greater specialization, *money* facilitates exchange. Money—coins, bills, checks, and debit cards—is a *medium of exchange* because it is the one thing that everyone accepts in return for goods and services.

Because of specialization and comparative advantage, most people consume little of what they produce and produce little of what they consume. Each individual specializes, then exchanges that product for money, which in turn is exchanged for other products. Did you make anything you are wearing? Probably not. Think about the degree of specialization that went into your cotton shirt. A farmer in a warm climate grew the cotton and sold it to someone who spun it into thread, who sold it to someone who wove it into fabric, who sold it to someone who sewed the shirt, who sold it to a wholesaler, who sold it to a retailer, who sold it to you. Many specialists in the chain of production created that shirt. Exhibit 1 traces these steps. *Specialization and exchange create more interdependence in an economy.*

Evidence of specialization is all around us. Shops at the mall specialize in products ranging from luggage to lingerie. Restaurants range from subs to sushi. Or let your fingers do the walking through the help-wanted ads or Craigslist, where you will find thousands of specializations. Without moving a muscle, you can observe the division of labor within a single industry by watching the credits roll at the end of a movie. The credits list scores of specialists—from gaffer (lighting electrician) to assistant location scout. As an extreme example, more than 3,000 specialists helped create the movie *Avatar*.[2] Even TV dramas, such as *NCIS* or *The Walking Dead*, require hundreds of specialists.

[2.] As reported in Hendrik Hertzberg, "And the Oscar Goes To," *The New Yorker*, 15 & 22 February 2010.

EXHIBIT 1	Specialization in the Production of Cotton Shirts

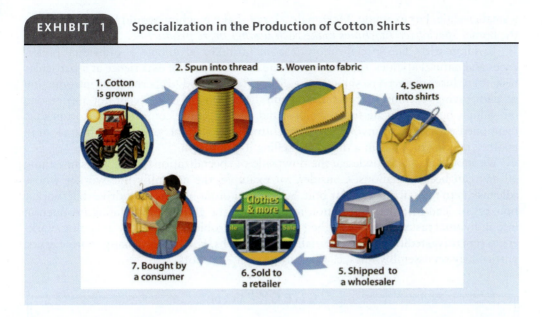

Some specialties may seem odd. For example, professional mourners in Taiwan are hired by grieving families to scream, wail, and otherwise demonstrate the deep grief befitting a proper funeral. The sharp degree of specialization is perhaps most obvious online, where the pool of potential customers is so vast that individual sites become finely focused. For example, you can find sites specializing in musical bowls, tongue studs, toe rings, brass knuckles, mouth harps, ferret toys, and cat bandannas—just to name a few of the hundreds of thousands of specialty sites. You won't find such precise specialization at the mall. Adam Smith (1723–1790), who is considered the father of economics, said the degree of specialization is limited by the extent of the market. Online sellers draw on the broadest customer base in the world to find a market niche.

2-2d Division of Labor and Gains From Specialization

Picture a visit to McDonald's: "Let's see, I'll have a Big Mac, an order of fries, and a chocolate shake." In minutes your order is ready. It would take you much longer to make a homemade version of this meal. Why is the McDonald's meal faster, cheaper, and—for some people—tastier than one you could make yourself? Why is fast food so fast? McDonald's takes advantage of the gains resulting from the **division of labor**. Each worker, rather than preparing an entire meal, specializes in separate tasks. This division of labor allows the group to produce much more.

division of labor
Breaking down the production of a good into separate tasks

How is this increase in productivity possible? First, the manager can assign tasks according to *individual preferences and abilities*—that is, according to the law of comparative advantage. The worker with the friendly smile and pleasant personality can handle the customers up front; the one with the strong back but few social graces can handle the heavy lifting out back. Second, a worker who performs the same task again and again gets better at it (experience is a good teacher). The worker filling orders at the drive-through, for example, learns to deal with special problems that arise. As another example, consider the experience gained by someone screening bags at airport security. Experience helps the screener distinguish the harmful from the harmless. Third, specialization means no time is lost moving from one task to another. Finally, and perhaps most importantly, the **specialization of labor** allows for the introduction of more sophisticated production techniques—techniques that would not make sense on

specialization of labor
Focusing work effort on a particular product or a single task

a smaller scale. For example, McDonald's large shake machine would be impractical in the home. *Specialized machines make each worker more productive.*

To summarize: The specialization of labor (a) takes advantage of individual preferences and natural abilities, (b) allows workers to develop more experience at a particular task, (c) reduces the need to shift among different tasks, and (d) permits the introduction of labor-saving machinery. Specialization and the division of labor occur not only among individuals but also among firms, regions, and, indeed, entire countries. The cotton shirt mentioned earlier might involve growing cotton in one country, turning it into cloth in another, making the shirt in a third, and selling it in a fourth.

We should also acknowledge the downside of specialization. Doing the same thing all day can become tedious. Consider, for example, the assembly line worker whose sole task is to tighten a particular bolt. Such a monotonous job could drive that worker bonkers or lead to repetitive motion injury. Thus, the gains from dividing production into individual tasks must be weighed against any problems caused by assigning workers to repetitive, tedious, and potentially harmful jobs. Fortunately, many routine tasks, particularly on assembly lines, can be turned over to robots.

CHECKPOINT

What is the difference between absolute advantage and comparative advantage, and which is more relevant in deciding who should do what?

2-3 The Economy's Production Possibilities

The focus, up to this point, has been on how individuals choose to use their scarce resources to satisfy their unlimited wants or, more specifically, how they specialize based on comparative advantage. This emphasis on the individual has been appropriate because the economy is shaped by the choices of individual decision makers, whether they are consumers, producers, or public officials. Just as resources are scarce for the individual, they are also scarce for the economy as a whole (no fallacy of composition here). An economy has millions of different resources that can be combined in all kinds of ways to produce millions of different goods and services. This section steps back from the immense complexity of the real economy to develop another simple model, which explores the economy's production options.

2-3a Efficiency and the Production Possibilities Frontier, or PPF

To get an idea of how well the economy works, you need some perspective; you need a place to stand. Let's develop a model to get some idea of how much an economy can produce with the resources available. What are the economy's production capabilities? Here are the model's assumptions:

1. To simplify matters, output is limited to just two broad classes of products: consumer goods and capital goods.
2. The focus is on production during a given period—in this case, a year.
3. The economy's resources are fixed in both quantity and quality during that period.

4. Society's knowledge about how these resources combine to produce output—that is, the available *technology and know-how*—does not change during the year.
5. Also assumed fixed during the period are the "rules of the game" that facilitate production and exchange. These include such things as the legal system, property rights, tax laws, patent laws, and the manners, customs, and conventions of the market.

The point of these simplifying assumptions is to freeze in time the economy's resources, technology and know-how, and rules of the game so we can focus on the economy's production options. Otherwise, the production possibilities of the economy would be a moving target.

Given the resources, technology and know-how, and rules of the game available in the economy, the **production possibilities frontier**, or **PPF**, identifies possible combinations of the two types of goods that can be produced when available resources are employed efficiently. *Resources are employed efficiently when there is no change that could increase the production of one good without decreasing the production of the other good.* **Efficiency** involves getting the most from available resources.

The economy's PPF for consumer goods and capital goods is shown by the curve *AF* in Exhibit 2. Point *A* identifies the amount produced per year if all the economy's resources are used efficiently to produce consumer goods. Point *F* identifies the amount produced per year if all the economy's resources are used efficiently to produce capital goods. Points along the curve between *A* and *F* identify possible combinations of the two goods that can be produced when all the economy's resources are used efficiently.

2-3b Inefficient and Unattainable Production

Points inside the PPF, such as *I* in Exhibit 2, identify combinations that do not employ resources efficiently. Note that *C* yields more consumer goods and no fewer capital goods than *I*. And *E* yields more capital goods and no fewer consumer goods than *I*. Indeed, any point along the PPF between *C* and *E*, such as *D,* yields both more consumer goods and more capital goods than *I*. Hence, combination *I* is *inefficient*. By using resources more efficiently, the economy can produce more of at least one good without reducing the production of the other good. Points outside the PPF, such as *U* in Exhibit 2, identify *unattainable* combinations, given the availability of resources, technology and know-how, and rules of the game. Thus, *the PPF not only shows efficient combinations of production but also serves as the boundary between inefficient combinations inside the frontier and unattainable combinations outside the frontier.*

2-3c The Shape of the PPF

Any movement along the PPF involves producing less of one good to produce more of the other. Movements down along the curve indicate that the opportunity cost of more capital goods is fewer consumer goods. For example, moving from point *A* to point *B* *increases* capital production from none to 10 million units but *reduces* consumer units from 50 million to 48 million. Increasing capital goods by 10 million reduces consumer goods only a little. Capital production initially employs resources (such as heavy machinery used to build factories) that produce few consumer goods but are quite productive in making capital.

As shown by the dashed lines in Exhibit 2, each additional 10 million units of capital produced reduce consumer goods by successively larger amounts. The resources used to produce more capital are increasingly better suited to producing consumer goods. *The opportunity cost of making more capital goods increases, because not all*

production possibilities frontier (PPF)
A curve showing alternative combinations of goods that can be produced when available resources are used efficiently; a boundary line between inefficient and unattainable combinations

efficiency
The condition that exists when there is no way resources can be reallocated to increase the production of one good without decreasing the production of another; getting the most from available resources

EXHIBIT 2   **The Economy's Production Possibilities Frontier**

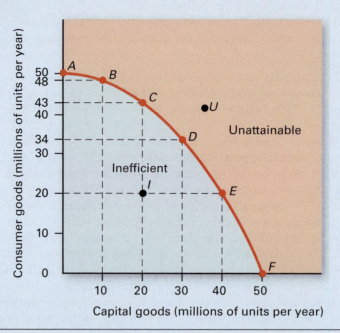

If the economy uses its available resources and its technology and know-how efficiently to produce consumer goods and capital goods, that economy is on its production possibilities frontier, *AF*. The PPF is bowed out to reflect the law of increasing opportunity cost; the economy must sacrifice more and more units of consumer goods to produce each additional increment of capital goods. Note that more consumer goods must be given up in moving from *E* to *F* than in moving from *A* to *B*, although in each case the gain in capital goods is 10 million units. Points inside the PPF, such as *I*, represent inefficient use of resources. Points outside the PPF, such as *U*, represent unattainable combinations.

law of increasing opportunity cost

To produce more of one good, a successively larger amount of the other good must be sacrificed

resources in the economy are perfectly adaptable to the production of both types of goods. The shape of the production possibilities frontier reflects the **law of increasing opportunity cost**. If the economy uses resources efficiently, the law of increasing opportunity cost states that each additional increment of one good requires the economy to sacrifice successively larger and larger increments of the other good.

The PPF derives its bowed-out shape from the law of increasing opportunity cost. For example, whereas the first 10 million units of capital have an opportunity cost of only 2 million consumer units, the final 10 million units of capital—that is, the increase from *E* to *F*—have an opportunity cost of 20 million consumer units. Notice that the slope of the PPF shows the opportunity cost of an increment of capital. As the economy moves down the curve, the curve becomes steeper, reflecting the higher opportunity cost of capital goods in terms of forgone consumer goods. The law of increasing opportunity cost also applies when moving from capital goods to consumer goods. Incidentally, if resources were perfectly adaptable to the production of both consumer goods and capital goods, the PPF would be a straight line, reflecting a constant opportunity cost along the PPF.

2-3d What Can Shift the PPF?

Any production possibilities frontier assumes the economy's resources, technology and know-how, and rules of the game are fixed during the period under consideration. Over time, however, the PPF may shift if resources, technology and know-how, or the rules of the game change. **Economic growth** is an expansion in the economy's production possibilities as reflected by an outward shift of the PPF.

Changes in Resource Availability

If people decide to work longer hours, the PPF shifts outward, as shown in panel (a) of Exhibit 3. An increase in the size or health of the labor force, an increase in the skills of the labor force, or an increase in the availability of other resources, such as new oil discoveries, also shifts the PPF outward. In contrast, a decrease of resources shifts the PPF inward, as depicted in panel (b). For example, in 1990 Iraq invaded Kuwait, setting oil fields ablaze and destroying much of Kuwait's physical capital. In West Africa, the encroaching sands of the Sahara destroy thousands of square miles of farmland each year. And in northwest China, a rising tide of wind-blown sand has claimed grasslands, lakes, and forests, and swallowed entire villages, forcing tens of thousands of people to flee.

The new PPFs in panels (a) and (b) appear to be parallel to the original ones, indicating that the resources that changed could produce both capital goods and consumer goods. For example, an increase in electrical power can enhance the production of both, as shown in panel (a). If a resource such as farmland benefits just consumer goods, then increased availability or productivity of that resource shifts the PPF more along the consumer goods axis, as shown in panel (c). Panel (d) shows the effect of an increase in a resource such as construction equipment that is suited only to capital goods.

Increases in the Capital Stock

An economy's PPF depends in part on the stock of human and physical capital. The more capital an economy produces in one period, the more output can be produced in the next period. Thus, producing more capital goods during this period (for example, more machines in the case of physical capital or more education in the case of human capital) shifts the economy's PPF outward the next period.

Technological Change and More Know-How

A technological discovery that employs resources more efficiently could shift the economy's PPF outward. Some discoveries enhance the production of both consumer goods and capital goods, as shown in panel (a) of Exhibit 3. For example, the Internet has increased each firm's ability to find available resources. A technological discovery that benefits consumer goods only, such as more disease-resistant crops, is reflected by a rotation outward of the PPF along the consumer goods axis, as shown in panel (c). Note that point *F* remains unchanged because the breakthrough does not affect the production of capital goods. Panel (d) shows a technological advance in the production of capital goods, such as better software for designing heavy machinery. But even for a given level of technology and a given number of workers, output can increase over time with more know-how. For example, researchers have documented a doubling of steel production at a mini-mill even though the technology did not change nor did the number of workers. Through experimentation, workers developed more know-how.[3]

Improvements in the Rules of the Game

The **rules of the game** are the formal and informal institutions that support the economy—the laws, customs, manners, conventions, and other institutional underpinnings that encourage people to pursue productive activity. A more stable political

economic growth
An increase in the economy's ability to produce goods and services; reflected by an outward shift of the economy's production possibilities frontier

[3.] Igal Hendel and Yossi Spiegel, "Small Steps for Workers, a Giant Leap for Productivity," *American Economic Journal: Applied Economics*, 6 (February 2014): 73–90.

Shifts of the Economy's Production Possibilities Frontier

(a) Increase in available resources, better technology, more know-how, or improvement in the rules of the game

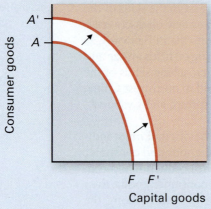

(b) Decrease in available resources or greater uncertainty in the rules of the game

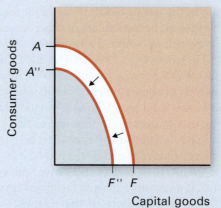

(c) Change in resources, technology, know-how, or rules that benefits consumer goods

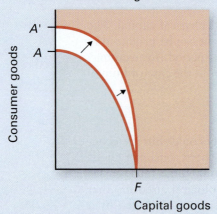

(d) Change in resources, technology, know-how, or rules that benefits capital goods

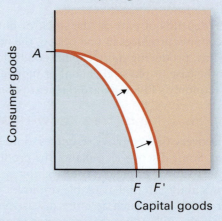

When the resources available to an economy change, the PPF shifts. If more resources become available, if technology and know-how improve, or if the rules of the game create greater stability, the PPF shifts outward, as in panel (a), indicating that more output can be produced. A decrease in available resources or an upheaval in the rules causes the PPF to shift inward, as in panel (b). Panel (c) shows a change affecting consumer goods. More consumer goods can now be produced at any given level of capital goods. Panel (d) shows a change affecting the production of capital goods.

environment and more reliable property rights increase the incentive to work and to invest, and thus help the economy grow. For example, people have more incentive to work if taxes claim less of their paychecks. People have more incentive to invest if they are confident that their investment will not be appropriated by government, stolen by thieves, destroyed by civil unrest, or blown up by terrorists. Greater certainty and stability in the rules of the game shift the economy's PPF outward. On the other hand, greater uncertainty about the rules of the game reduces the economy's productive capacity, as reflected by an inward shift of the PPF. For example, during the Great Recession of 2007–2009, trust in U.S. institutions such as banks, newspapers, Congress, and big corporations declined and this reduced the economy's productive ability.[4]

2-3e What We Learn From the PPF

The PPF demonstrates several ideas introduced so far. The first is *efficiency:* The PPF describes efficient combinations of output, given the economy's resources, technology and know-how, and rules of the game. The second idea is *scarcity:* Given the resources, technology and know-how, and rules of the game, the economy can produce only so much output per period. The PPF slopes downward, because more of one good means less of the other good, thus demonstrating *opportunity cost.* The PPF's bowed-out shape reflects the *law of increasing opportunity cost*, which arises because some resources are not perfectly adaptable to the production of each type of good. And a shift outward in the PPF reflects *economic growth*.

Finally, because society must somehow select a specific combination of output—a single point—along the PPF, the PPF also underscores the need for *choice*. Selecting a particular combination determines not only the consumer goods available in this period, but also the capital stock available in the next period. One thing the PPF does not tell us is which combination to choose. The PPF tells us only about the costs, not the benefits, of the two goods. To make a selection, we need to know about both costs *and* benefits. How society goes about choosing a particular combination depends on the nature of the economic system, as you will see next.

CHECKPOINT

List the assumptions used to develop the PPF, and identify six economic ideas demonstrated by the PPF.

2-4 Economic Systems

Each point along the economy's production possibilities frontier is an efficient combination of outputs. Whether the economy produces efficiently and how the economy selects the most preferred combination depends on the decision-making rules employed. But regardless of how decisions are made, each economy must answer three fundamental questions.

2-4a Three Questions Every Economic System Must Answer

What goods and services are to be produced? How are they to be produced? And for whom are they to be produced? An **economic system** is the set of mechanisms and institutions that resolve the *what, how,* and *for whom* questions. Some criteria used to distinguish among economic systems are (1) who owns the resources, (2) what decision-making process is used to allocate resources and products, and (3) what types of incentives guide economic decision makers.

economic system

The set of mechanisms and institutions that resolve the what, how, and for whom questions

---

[4.] Betsey Stevenson and Justin Wolfers, "Trust in Public Institutions Over the Business Cycle," *American Economic Review*, 101 (May 2011): 281–287.

What Goods and Services Are to Be Produced?

Most of us take for granted the incredible number of choices that go into deciding what gets produced—everything from which new kitchen appliances are introduced and which roads get built, to which of the 10,000 movie scripts purchased by U.S. studios each year get to be among the 650 or so movies made. Although different economies resolve these and millions of other questions using different decision-making rules and mechanisms, all economies must somehow make such choices.

How Are Goods and Services to Be Produced?

The economic system must determine how output gets produced. Which resources should be used, and how should they be combined to make stuff? How much labor should be used and at what skill levels? What kinds of machines should be used? What new technology should be incorporated into the latest video games? Should the office complex be built in the city or closer to the interstate highway? Millions of individual decisions determine which resources are employed and how these resources are combined.

For Whom Are Goods and Services to Be Produced?

Who will actually consume the goods and services produced? The economic system must determine how to allocate the fruits of production among the population. Should everyone receive equal shares? Should the weak and the sick get more? Should it be "first come, first served," so that those willing to wait in line get more? Should goods be allocated according to height? Weight? Religion? Age? Gender? Race? Looks? Strength? Political connections? Lottery? Majority rule? The value of resources supplied? The question "For whom are goods and services to be produced?" is often referred to as the *distribution question*.

Although the three economic questions were discussed separately, they are closely related. The answer to one depends on the answers to the others. For example, an economy that distributes goods and services uniformly to everyone will, no doubt, answer the what-will-be-produced question differently than an economy that somehow allows more personal choice. As we have seen, laws about resource ownership and the role of government determine the "rules of the game"—the set of conditions that shape individual incentives and constraints. Along a spectrum ranging from the freest to the most regimented types of economic systems, *pure capitalism* would be at one end and the *pure command system* at the other.

2-4b Pure Capitalism

pure capitalism
An economic system characterized by the private ownership of resources and the use of prices to coordinate economic activity in unregulated markets

private property rights
An owner's right to use, rent, or sell resources or property

Under **pure capitalism**, there is no government. The rules of the game include the private ownership of resources and the market distribution of products. Owners have *property rights* to the use of their resources and are therefore free to supply those resources to the highest bidder. **Private property rights** allow individual owners to use resources or to charge others for their use. Any income from supplying labor, capital, natural resources, or entrepreneurial ability goes to the individual resource owners. Producers are free to make and sell whatever they think will be profitable. Consumers are free to buy whatever goods they can afford. All this voluntary buying and selling is coordinated by unrestricted markets, where buyers and sellers make their intentions known. Market prices guide resources to their most productive use and channel goods and services to the consumers who value them the most.

Under pure capitalism, markets answer the what, how, and for whom questions. That's why capitalism is also referred to as a *market system*. Markets transmit information about relative scarcity, provide individual incentives, and distribute income among resource suppliers. No individual or small group coordinates these activities. Rather, it is the voluntary choices of many buyers and sellers responding only to their individual incentives and constraints that direct resources and products to those who value them the most.

According to Adam Smith, market forces allocate resources as if by an "invisible hand"—an unseen force that harnesses the pursuit of self-interest to direct resources where they earn the greatest reward. According to Smith, *although each individual pursues his or her self-interest, the "invisible hand" of market forces promotes the general welfare.* Capitalism is sometimes called *laissez-faire;* translated from the French, this phrase means "to let do," or to let people do as they choose without government intervention. Thus, under capitalism, voluntary choices based on rational self-interest are made in unrestricted markets to answer the questions what, how, and for whom.

As we will see in later chapters, pure capitalism has its flaws. The most notable market failures are these:

1. No central authority protects property rights, enforces contracts, and otherwise ensures that the rules of the game are followed.
2. People with no resources to sell could starve.
3. Some producers may try to monopolize markets by eliminating the competition.
4. The production or consumption of some goods involves side effects that can harm or benefit people not involved in the market transaction.
5. Firms have no incentive to produce so-called *public goods,* such as national defense, because private firms cannot prevent nonpayers from enjoying the benefits of public goods.
6. Market economies experience *economic fluctuations,* which are alternating periods of expansions and recessions in their level of economic activity, especially in employment and production.

Because of these limitations, countries have modified pure capitalism to allow some role for government. Even Adam Smith believed government should play a role. The United States is among the most market-oriented economies in the world today.

2-4c Pure Command System

In a **pure command system**, resources are directed and production is coordinated not by market forces but by the "command," or central plan, of government. In theory at least, instead of private property, there is public, or *communal,* ownership of property. That's why central planning is sometimes called *communism.* Government planners, as representatives of all the people, answer the three questions through *central plans* spelling out how much steel, how many cars, and how much housing to produce. They also decide how to produce these goods and who gets them.

In theory, the pure command system incorporates individual choices into collective choices, which, in turn, are reflected in the central plans. Command economies often have names that focus on collective choice, such as the People's Republic of China and the Democratic People's Republic of Korea (North Korea). In practice, the pure command system also has flaws, most notably the following:

1. Running an economy is so complicated and requires so much information that some resources are used inefficiently.
2. Because nobody in particular owns resources, each person has less incentive to employ them in their highest-valued use, so some resources are wasted.

pure command system
An economic system characterized by the public ownership of resources and centralized planning

KCNA/Xinhua Press/Corbis

3. Central plans may reflect more the preferences of central planners, who in many cases are unelected dictators, than the preferences of society.
4. Because government is responsible for all production, the variety of products tends to be more limited than in a capitalist economy.
5. Each individual has less personal freedom in making economic choices.
6. Because profit has no place in a command economy, people have less incentive to invent new and better products or find more efficient ways to make existing products.

Because of these limitations, countries have modified the pure command system to allow a role for markets. North Korea, a country run for decades by three generations of dictators, is perhaps the most centrally planned economy in the world today.

2-4d Mixed and Transitional Economies

mixed system

An economic system characterized by the private ownership of some resources and the public ownership of other resources; some markets are regulated by government

No country on Earth exemplifies either type of economic system in its pure form. Economic systems have grown more alike over time, with the role of government increasing in capitalist economies and the role of markets increasing in command economies. The United States represents a **mixed system**, with government directly accounting for a little more than one-third of all economic activity. What's more, governments at all levels in the United States regulate the private sector in a variety of ways. For example, local zoning boards determine lot sizes, home sizes, and the types of industries allowed. Federal bodies regulate workplace safety, environmental quality, competitive fairness, food and drug quality, and many other activities.

Although both ends of the spectrum have moved toward the center, capitalism has gained the most converts in recent decades. Perhaps the benefits of markets are no better illustrated than where a country, as a result of war or political upheaval, became divided by ideology into a capitalist economy and a command economy, such as with Taiwan and China or South Korea and North Korea. In each case, the economies began with similar human and physical resources, but once they went their separate ways, economic growth diverged sharply, with the capitalist economies outperforming the command economies. For example, Taiwan's production per capita in 2015 was four times that of China's, and South Korea's production per capita was 18 times that of North Korea's.

Consider the experience of the pilgrims in 1620 while establishing Plymouth Colony. They first tried communal ownership of the land. That turned out badly. Crops were neglected and food shortages developed. After three years of near starvation, the system was changed so that each family was assigned a plot of land and granted the fruits of that plot. Yields increased sharply. The pilgrims learned that people take better care of what they own individually; by contrast, common ownership often leads to common neglect.

Recognizing the incentive power of property rights and markets, some of the most die-hard central planners are now allowing a role for markets. For example, about one-fifth of the world's population lives in China, which grows more market oriented each day, even going so far as to give private property constitutional protection on a par with state property. In a poll of Chinese citizens, 74 percent agreed that "the free enterprise system is the best system on which to base the future of the world." Among Americans polled, 71 percent agreed with that statement.[5] A quarter-century

---

[5.] As reported in "Capitalism, Comrade," *Wall Street Journal*, 18 January 2006.

ago, the former Soviet Union dissolved into 15 independent republics; most converted state-owned enterprises into private firms. From Moscow to Beijing, from Hungary to Mongolia, the transition to mixed economies now underway in former command economies will shape the world for decades to come.

Note that nations with freer markets tend to rely more on democratic political systems. Recent research finds that democracy increases economic growth by encouraging investment, increasing schooling, promoting economic reforms, and reducing social unrest.[6]

2-4e Economies Based on Custom or Religion

Finally, some economic systems are molded largely by custom or religion. For example, caste systems in India and elsewhere restrict occupational choices. Charging interest is banned under Islamic law. Family relations also play significant roles in organizing and coordinating economic activity. In some countries, businesses are reluctant to hire anyone outside the family because outsiders are less trusted. This limits business growth. Even in the United States, some occupations are still dominated by women, and others by men, largely because of tradition. Your own pattern of consumption and choice of occupation may be influenced by some of these considerations.

CHECKPOINT

What three questions must every economic system answer?

2-5 Conclusion

Although economies can answer the three economic questions in a variety of ways, this book focuses primarily on the mixed market system, such as exists in the United States. This type of economy blends *private choices,* guided by the price system in competitive markets, with *public choices,* guided by democracy in political markets. The study of mixed market systems grows more relevant as former command economies try to develop markets. The next chapter focuses on the economic actors in a mixed economy and explains why and how government gets into the act.

Summary

1. Resources are scarce, but human wants are unlimited. That's the economic problem. Because you cannot satisfy all your wants, you must choose, and whenever you choose, you must forgo something. Choice involves an opportunity cost. The opportunity cost of the chosen option is the value of the best alternative forgone.

2. The law of comparative advantage says that the individual, firm, region, or country with the lowest opportunity cost of producing a particular good should specialize in that good.

Specialization according to the law of comparative advantage promotes the most efficient use of resources.

3. The specialization of labor in a particular task increases efficiency by (a) taking advantage of individual preferences and natural abilities, (b) allowing each worker to develop expertise and experience at a particular task, (c) reducing the need to switch tasks, and (d) allowing for the introduction of more specialized machines and large-scale production techniques.

6. Daron Acemoglu, et al. "Democracy Does Cause Growth," American Economic Association annual meetings, 3 January 2015.

4. The production possibilities frontier, or PPF, shows the productive capabilities of an economy when all resources are used efficiently. The frontier's bowed-out shape reflects the law of increasing opportunity cost, which arises because some resources are not perfectly adaptable to the production of different goods. Over time, the PPF can shift in or out as a result of changes in the availability of resources, in technology and know-how, or in the rules of the game. The PPF demonstrates several economic concepts, including efficiency, scarcity, opportunity cost, the law of increasing opportunity cost, economic growth, and the need for choice.

5. All economic systems, regardless of their decision-making processes, must answer three basic questions: What is to be produced? How is it to be produced? And for whom is it to be produced? Economies answer the questions differently, depending on who owns the resources and how economic activity is coordinated. Economies can be directed by market forces, by the central plans of government officials, or, in most cases, by a mix of the two.

Key Concepts

Opportunity cost 27	Division of labor 33	Economic system 39
Sunk cost 30	Specialization of labor 33	Pure capitalism 40
Law of comparative advantage 31	Production possibilities frontier (PPF) 35	Private property rights 40
Absolute advantage 31	Efficiency 35	Pure command system 41
Comparative advantage 32	Law of increasing opportunity cost 36	Mixed system 42
Barter 32	Economic growth 37	

Questions for Review

1. **Opportunity Cost** Discuss the ways in which the following conditions might affect the opportunity cost of going to a movie tonight:

   a. You have a final exam tomorrow.
   b. School will be out for one month starting tomorrow.
   c. The same movie will be on TV next week.
   d. The Super Bowl is on TV tonight.

2. **Opportunity Cost** Determine whether each of the following statements is true, false, or uncertain. Explain your answers:

   a. The opportunity cost of an activity is the total value of all the alternatives passed up.
   b. Opportunity cost is an objective measure of cost.
   c. When making choices, people carefully gather all available information about the costs and benefits of alternative choices.
   d. A decision maker seldom knows the actual value of forgone alternatives and therefore must make decisions based on expected values.

3. **Comparative Advantage** "You should never buy precooked frozen foods because the price you pay includes the labor costs of preparing food." Is this conclusion always valid, or can it be invalidated by the law of comparative advantage?

4. **Specialization and Exchange** Explain how the specialization of labor can increase productivity.

5. **Production Possibilities** Under what conditions is it possible to increase production of one good without decreasing production of another good?

6. **Production Possibilities** Under what conditions would an economy be operating inside its PPF? On its PPF? Outside its PPF?

7. **Shifting Production Possibilities** In response to an influx of undocumented workers, Congress made it a federal offense to hire them. How do you think this measure affected the U.S. production possibilities frontier? Do you think all industries were affected equally?

8. **Production Possibilities** "If society decides to use its resources efficiently (that is, to produce *on* its production possibilities frontier), then future generations will be worse off because they will not be able to use these resources." If this assertion is true, full employment of resources may not be a good thing. Comment on the validity of this assertion.

9. **Economic Questions** What basic economic questions must be answered in a barter economy? In a primitive economy? In a capitalist economy? In a command economy?

10. **Economic Systems** What are the major differences between a pure capitalist system and a pure command system? Is the United States closer to a pure capitalist system or to a pure command system?

Problems and Exercises

11. **Case Study: The Opportunity Cost of College** During the Vietnam War, colleges and universities were overflowing with students. Was this bumper crop of students caused by a greater expected return on a college education or by a change in the opportunity cost of attending college? Explain.

12. **Sunk Cost and Choice** Suppose you go to a restaurant and buy an expensive meal. Halfway through, despite feeling quite full, you decide to clean your plate. After all, you think, you paid for the meal, so you are going to eat all of it. What's wrong with this thinking?

13. **Opportunity Cost** You can spend spring break either working at home for $100 per day for five days or go to Florida for the week. If you stay home, your personal expenses will total about $120. If you go to Florida, the airfare, hotel, food, and miscellaneous expenses will total about $1,000. What's your opportunity cost of going to Florida?

14. **Absolute and Comparative Advantage** You have the following information concerning the production of wheat and cloth in the United States and the United Kingdom:

Labor Hours Required to Produce One Unit

	United Kingdom	United States
Wheat	2	1
Cloth	6	5

   a. What is the opportunity cost of producing a unit of wheat in the United Kingdom? In the United States?
   b. Which country has an absolute advantage in producing wheat? In producing cloth?
   c. Which country has a comparative advantage in producing wheat? In producing cloth?
   d. Which country should specialize in producing wheat? In producing cloth?

15. **Specialization** Provide some examples of specialized markets or retail outlets. What makes the Web so conducive to specialization?

16. **Shape of the PPF** Suppose a production possibilities frontier includes the following combinations:

Cars	Washing Machines
0	1,000
100	600
200	0

   a. Graph the PPF, assuming that it has no curved segments.
   b. What is the cost of producing an additional car when 50 cars are being produced?
   c. What is the cost of producing an additional car when 150 cars are being produced?
   d. What is the cost of producing an additional washing machine when 50 cars are being produced? When 150 cars are being produced?
   e. What do your answers tell you about opportunity costs?

17. **Production Possibilities** Suppose an economy uses two resources (labor and capital) to produce two goods (wheat and cloth). Capital is relatively more useful in producing cloth, and labor is relatively more useful in producing wheat. If the supply of capital falls by 10 percent and the supply of labor increases by 10 percent, how will the PPF for wheat and cloth change?

18. **Production Possibilities** There's no reason why a production possibilities frontier could not be used to represent the situation facing an individual. Imagine your own PPF. Right now—today—you have certain resources—your time, your skills, perhaps some capital. And you can produce various outputs. Suppose you can produce combinations of two outputs, call them studying and partying.

   a. Draw your PPF for studying and partying. Be sure to label the axes of the diagram appropriately. Label the points where the PPF intersects the axes, as well as several other points along the frontier.
   b. Explain what it would mean for you to move upward and to the left along your personal PPF. What kinds of adjustments would you have to make in your life to make such a movement along the frontier?
   c. Under what circumstances would your personal PPF shift outward? Do you think the shift would be a "parallel" one? Why, or why not?

19. **Shifting Production Possibilities** Determine whether each of the following would cause the economy's PPF to shift inward, outward, or not at all:

   a. An increase in average length of annual vacations
   b. An increase in immigration
   c. A decrease in the average retirement age
   d. The migration of skilled workers to other countries

20. **Economic Systems** The United States is best described as having a mixed economy. What are some elements of command in the U.S. economy? What are some elements of tradition?

3 Economic Decision Makers

©Africa Studio/Shutterstock.com

- *If we live in the age of specialization, then why haven't specialists taken over all production?*

- *For example, why do most of us still do our own laundry and perform dozens of other tasks for ourselves?*

- *Why is the value of some products such as Facebook created mostly by users rather than by the suppliers?*

- *If the "invisible hand" of competitive markets is so efficient, why does government get into the act?*

- *And if specialization based on comparative advantage is such a good idea, why do most nations try to restrict imports?*

Answers to these and other questions are addressed in this chapter, which discusses the four economic decision makers: households, firms, governments, and the rest of the world.

T o develop a better feel for how the economy works, you must become more acquainted with the key players. You already know more about them than you may realize. You grew up in a household. You have dealt with firms all your life, from Sony to Subway. You know much about governments, from taxes to public schools. And you have a growing awareness of the rest of the world, from online sites, to imported goods, to foreign travel. This chapter draws on your abundant personal experience with economic decision makers to consider their makeup and objectives.

Topics discussed in this chapter include:

- Evolution of the household
- Evolution of the firm
- Types of firms

- Role of government
- Taxing and public spending
- International trade and finance

3-1 The Household

Households play the starring role in a market economy. Their demand for goods and services determines what gets produced. And their supply of labor, capital, natural resources, and entrepreneurial ability produces that output. As demanders of goods and services and suppliers of resources, households make all kinds of choices, such as what to buy, how much to save, where to live, and where to work. Although a household usually consists of several individuals, we will view each household as a single decision maker.

3-1a The Evolution of the Household

In earlier times, when the economy was primarily agricultural, a farm household was largely self-sufficient. Each family member often specialized in a specific farm task—cooking meals, making clothes, tending livestock, planting crops, mending fences, and so on. These early households produced what they consumed and consumed what they produced. With the introduction of new seed varieties, better fertilizers, and labor-saving machinery, farm productivity increased sharply. Fewer farmers were needed to grow enough food to feed a nation. At the same time, the growth of urban factories increased the demand for factory labor. As a result, many workers moved from farms to urban factories, where they became more specialized but less self-sufficient.

Households evolved in other ways. For example, in 1950, only about 15 percent of married women with young children were in the labor force. Since then, higher levels of education among women and a growing demand for their labor have increased women's earnings, thus raising their opportunity cost of working in the home. This higher opportunity cost contributed to their growing labor force participation. Today about 70 percent of women with children under 18 are in the labor force.

The rise of two-earner households has reduced specialization in household production—a central feature of the farm family. Households now produce less for themselves and demand more from the market. For example, child-care services and fast-food restaurants have displaced some household production (Americans now consume at least one-third of their calories away from home). Nonetheless, some production still occurs in the home, as we'll explore later.

3-1b Households Maximize Utility

There are about 120 million U.S. households. All those who live together under one roof are considered part of the same household. What exactly do households attempt to accomplish in making decisions? Economists assume that people try to maximize their level of satisfaction, sense of well-being, happiness, and overall welfare. In short, households attempt to maximize **utility**. Households, like other economic decision makers, are viewed as rational, meaning that they try to act in their best interests and do not deliberately try to make themselves less happy. Utility maximization depends on each household's subjective goals, not on some objective standard. For example, some households maintain neat homes with well-groomed lawns; others pay little attention to their homes and use their lawns as junkyards.

utility
The satisfaction received from consumption; sense of well-being

3-1c Households as Resource Suppliers

Households use their limited resources—labor, capital, natural resources, and entrepreneurial ability—in an attempt to satisfy their unlimited wants. They can use these resources to produce goods and services in their homes. For example, they can cook, wash, sew, dust, iron, sweep, vacuum, mop, mow, paint, and fix a leaky faucet. They can also sell these resources in resource markets and use the income to buy goods and services in product markets. The most valuable resource sold by most households is labor.

Panel (a) of Exhibit 1 shows the sources of personal income received by U.S. households in 2014. As you can see, 62 percent of personal income came from wages

---

EXHIBIT 1   **Where U.S. Personal Income Comes From and Where It Goes**

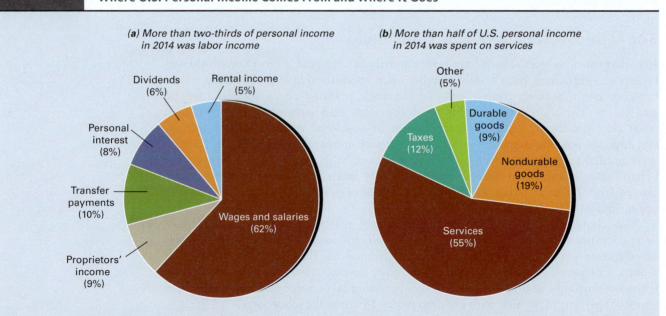

(a) *More than two-thirds of personal income in 2014 was labor income*

Dividends (6%)
Rental income (5%)
Personal interest (8%)
Transfer payments (10%)
Proprietors' income (9%)
Wages and salaries (62%)

(b) *More than half of U.S. personal income in 2014 was spent on services*

Other (5%)
Durable goods (9%)
Taxes (12%)
Nondurable goods (19%)
Services (55%)

Source: Based on figures from *Survey of Current Business*, Bureau of Economic Analysis, February 2015, Tables 1.5.5 and 2.1. For the latest figures, go to http://www.bea.gov/scb/index.htm.

and salaries. A distant second was transfer payments (to be discussed shortly), at 10 percent of personal income, followed by proprietors' income at 9 percent. *Proprietors* are people who work for themselves rather than for employers; farmers, plumbers, and doctors are often self-employed. Proprietors' income should also be considered a form of labor income. *Thus, more than two-thirds of personal income in the United States comes from labor earnings rather than from the ownership of other resources such as capital or natural resources.*

Because of a limited education, disability, discrimination, poor health, caring for small children, limited job opportunities, or just bad luck, some households have few resources that are valued in the market. Society has made the political decision that individuals in such circumstances should receive short-term public assistance. Consequently, the government gives some households **transfer payments**. *Cash transfers* are monetary payments, such as welfare benefits, Social Security, unemployment compensation, and disability benefits. *In-kind transfers* provide for specific goods and services, such as food, health care, and housing.

transfer payments
Cash or in-kind benefits given to individuals by the government

3-1d Households as Demanders of Goods and Services

What happens to personal income once it comes into the household? Most goes to personal consumption, which sorts into three broad spending categories: (1) *durable goods*—that is, goods expected to last three or more years—such as an automobile or a refrigerator; (2) *nondurable goods*, such as food, clothing, and gasoline; and (3) *services*, such as haircuts, air travel, and medical care. As you can see from panel (b) of Exhibit 1, spending on durable goods in 2014 claimed 9 percent of U.S. personal income; nondurables, 19 percent; and services, 55 percent. Taxes claimed 12 percent, and all other categories, including saving, claimed just 5 percent. So more than half of all personal income went for services—the fastest growing sector, because many services, such as child care, are shifting from do-it-yourself home production to market purchases.

CHECKPOINT

What is the biggest source of household income, and what is the biggest household expenditure?

3-2 The Firm

Household members once built their own homes, made their own clothes and furniture, grew their own food, and amused themselves with books, games, and hobbies. Over time, however, the efficiency arising from comparative advantage resulted in a greater specialization among resource suppliers. This section takes a look at firms, beginning with their evolution.

3-2a The Evolution of the Firm

Specialization and comparative advantage explain why households are no longer self-sufficient. But why is a firm the natural result? For example, rather than make a woolen sweater from scratch, couldn't a consumer take advantage of specialization by negotiating with someone who produced the wool, another who spun the wool into yarn, and a third who knit the yarn into a sweater? Here's the problem with that model: If the consumer had to visit each of these specialists and reach an agreement, the resulting *transaction costs* could easily erase the gains from specialization. Instead of visiting and bargaining with each specialist, the consumer can pay someone to do the bargaining—an entrepreneur, who hires all the resources necessary to make the sweater. *An entrepreneur, by contracting for many sweaters rather than just one, is able to reduce the transaction costs per sweater.*

For about 200 years, profit-seeking entrepreneurs relied on "putting out" raw material, like wool and cotton, to rural households that turned this into finished products, like woolen goods made from yarn. The system developed in the British Isles, where workers' cottages served as tiny factories, especially during winter months, when farming chores were few (so the opportunity cost was low). This approach, which came to be known as the *cottage industry system*, still exists in some parts of the world today. You might think of this system as partway between household self-sufficiency and the modern firm.

As the British economy expanded in the 18th century, entrepreneurs began organizing the stages of production under one factory roof. Technological developments, such as waterpower and later steam power, increased the productivity of each worker and helped shift employment from rural areas to urban factories. *Work, therefore, became organized in large, centrally powered factories that (1) promoted a more efficient division of labor, (2) allowed for the direct supervision of production, (3) reduced transportation costs, and (4) facilitated the use of machines far bigger than anything used in the home.* The development of large-scale factory production, known as the **Industrial Revolution**, began in Great Britain around 1750 and spread to the rest of Europe, North America, and Australia.

Production, then, evolved from self-sufficient rural households to the cottage industry system, where specialized production occurred in the household, to production in a firm. Today, entrepreneurs combine resources in firms such as factories, mills, offices, stores, and restaurants. **Firms** are economic units formed by profit-seeking entrepreneurs who combine labor, capital, and natural resources to produce goods and services. Just as we assume that households try to maximize utility, we assume that firms try to *maximize profit*. Profit, the entrepreneur's reward, equals sales revenue minus the cost of production, including the opportunity cost of the entrepreneur's time. Thus,

$$\text{Profit} = \text{Revenue} - \text{Cost}$$

3-2b Types of Firms

There are more than 30 million for-profit businesses in the United States. Two-thirds are small retail businesses, small service operations, part-time home-based businesses, and small farms. Each year more than a million new businesses start up and many fail. A firm is organized in one of three ways: as a sole proprietorship, as a partnership, or as a corporation.

Sole Proprietorships

The simplest form of business organization is the **sole proprietorship**, a single-owner firm. Examples include self-employed plumbers, farmers, and dentists. Most sole proprietorships consist of just the self-employed proprietor—there are no hired employees. To organize a sole proprietorship, the owner simply opens for business by, for example, taking out a classified ad offering plumbing services or whatever. The owner is in complete control. But he or she faces unlimited liability and could lose everything, including

Industrial Revolution
Development of large-scale factory production that began in Great Britain around 1750 and spread to the rest of Europe, North America, and Australia

firms
Economic units formed by profit-seeking entrepreneurs who employ resources to produce goods and services for sale

sole proprietorship
A firm with a single owner who has the right to all profits but who also bears unlimited liability for the firm's losses and debts

a home and other personal assets, to settle business debts or other claims against the business. Also, because the sole proprietor has no partners or other investors, raising enough money to get the business up and running and keep it going can be a challenge. One final disadvantage is that a sole proprietorship usually goes out of business when the proprietor dies or leaves the business. Still, a sole proprietorship is the most common type of business, accounting most recently for 71 percent of all U.S. businesses. Nonetheless, because this type of firm is typically small, proprietorships generate just a tiny portion of all U.S. business sales—only 4 percent. But keep in mind that many of the largest businesses in the world today began as an idea of a sole proprietor.

Partnerships

A more complicated form of business is the **partnership**, which involves two or more individuals who agree to combine their funds and efforts in return for a share of any profit or loss. Law, accounting, and medical partnerships typify this business form. Partners have strength in numbers and often find it easier than sole proprietors to raise enough funds to get the business going. But partners may not always agree on what's best for the business. Also, each partner usually faces unlimited liability for any debts or claims against the partnership, so one partner could lose everything because of another partner's mistake. Finally, the death or departure of one partner can disrupt the firm's continuity and require a complete reorganization. The partnership is the least common form of U.S. business, making up only 10 percent of all firms and 15 percent of all business sales.

partnership
A firm with multiple owners who share the profits and bear unlimited liability for the firm's losses and debts

Corporations

By far the most influential form of business is the corporation. A **corporation** is a legal entity established through articles of incorporation. Shares of stock confer corporate ownership, thereby entitling stockholders to a claim on any profit. A major advantage of the corporate form is that many investors—hundreds, thousands, even millions—can pool their funds, so incorporating represents the easiest way to amass large sums to get a business off the ground. Also, stockholders' liability for any loss is limited to the value of their stock, meaning stockholders enjoy *limited liability*. A final advantage of this form of organization is that the corporation has a life apart from its owners. The corporation survives even if ownership changes hands, and it can be taxed, sued, and even charged with a crime as if it were a person.

corporation
A legal entity owned by stockholders who share any profit but whose liability is limited to the value of their stock ownership

The corporate form has some disadvantages as well. A stockholder's ability to influence corporate policy is limited to voting for a board of directors, which oversees the operation of the firm. Each share of stock usually carries with it one vote. The typical stockholder of a large corporation owns only a tiny fraction of the shares and thus has little say. Whereas the income from sole proprietorships and partnerships is taxed only once, corporate income gets whacked twice—first as corporate profits and second as stockholder income, either as corporate dividends or as realized capital gains. A *realized capital gain* is any increase in the market price of a share that occurs between the time the share is purchased and the time it is sold.

A hybrid type of corporation has evolved to take advantage of the limited liability feature of the corporate structure while reducing the impact of double taxation. The *S corporation* provides owners with limited liability, but profits are taxed only once—as income on each shareholder's personal income tax return. To qualify as an S corporation, a firm must have no more than 100 stockholders and no foreign stockholders.

Corporations make up only 19 percent of all U.S. businesses, but because they tend to be much larger than the other two business forms, corporations account for 81 percent of all business sales. Exhibit 2 shows, by business type, the percentage of U.S. firms and

EXHIBIT 2   **Percent Distribution by Type of Firm Based on Number of Firms and Firm Sales**

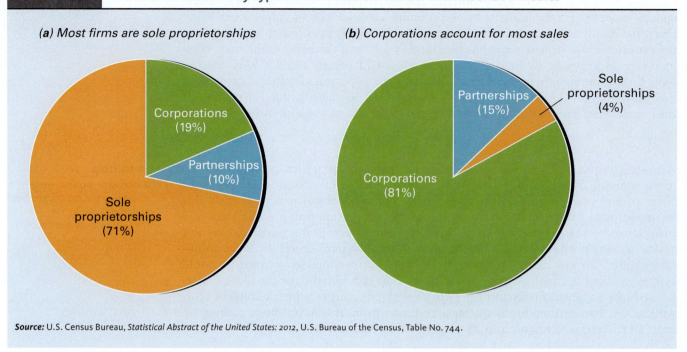

(a) *Most firms are sole proprietorships*

Corporations
(19%)

Partnerships
(10%)

Sole
proprietorships
(71%)

(b) *Corporations account for most sales*

Partnerships
(15%)

Sole
proprietorships
(4%)

Corporations
(81%)

Source: U.S. Census Bureau, *Statistical Abstract of the United States: 2012*, U.S. Bureau of the Census, Table No. 744.

the percentage of U.S. sales. *The sole proprietorship is the most important in sheer numbers, but the corporation is the most important in total sales.*

3-2c Cooperatives

cooperative

An organization consisting of people who pool their resources to buy and sell more efficiently than they could individually

A **cooperative**, or "co-op" for short, is a group of people who cooperate by pooling their resources to buy and sell more efficiently than they could independently. Cooperatives try to minimize costs and operate with limited liability of members. The government grants most cooperatives tax-exempt status. There are two types: consumer cooperatives and producer cooperatives.

Consumer Cooperatives

A *consumer cooperative* is a retail business owned and operated by some or all of its customers in order to reduce costs. Some cooperatives require members to pay an annual fee and others require them to work a certain number of hours each year in the business. Members sometimes pay lower prices than other customers or may share in any revenues that exceed costs. In the United States, consumer cooperatives operate college bookstores, credit unions, electric-power facilities, health plans, apartment buildings, and grocery stores.

Producer Cooperatives

In a *producer cooperative,* producers join forces to buy supplies and equipment and to market their output. Each producer's objective is to reduce costs and increase profits. Federal legislation allows farmers to cooperate without violating antitrust laws (to be discussed later in the chapter). Firms in other industries could not do this legally. Farmers pool their funds to purchase machinery and supplies, provide storage and processing facilities, and transport products to market. Sunkist, for example, is a farm cooperative owned and operated by about 6,000 citrus growers in California and Arizona.

3-2d Not-for-Profit Organizations

So far, you have learned about organizations that try to maximize profits or, in the case of cooperatives, to minimize costs. Some organizations have neither as a goal. **Not-for-profit organizations** engage in charitable, educational, humanitarian, cultural, professional, and other activities, often with a social purpose. Any revenue exceeding cost is plowed back into the organization. Government agencies do not have profit as a goal either, but governments are not included in this definition of not-for-profit organizations.

Like businesses, not-for-profit organizations evolved to help people accomplish their goals. Examples include nonprofit hospitals, private schools and colleges, religious organizations, the Red Cross, Greenpeace, charitable foundations, soup kitchens, orchestras, museums, labor unions, and professional organizations. There are about 1.6 million not-for-profit organizations in the United States, and they employ about 12 million workers, or about 8 percent of the U.S. workforce. Not-for-profit hospitals are the largest employers. For example, the Texas Medical Center employs more than 100,000 people, surpassing employment at major corporations such as Apple, Chevron, or Google. But even not-for-profit organizations must somehow pay the bills. Revenue typically includes some combination of voluntary contributions and service charges, such as college tuition and hospital charges. In the United States, not-for-profit organizations are usually exempt from taxes.

Thus far we have discussed a variety of profit and nonprofit institutions that help people accomplish their goals. With greater frequency, some products are being created and improved by the users of those products, as discussed in the following case study.

not-for-profit organizations
Groups that do not pursue profit as a goal; they engage in charitable, educational, humanitarian, cultural, professional, or other activities, often with a social purpose

THE INFORMATION ECONOMY

USER-GENERATED PRODUCTS In a market economy, new products and processes are usually developed by profit-seeking entrepreneurs, but sometimes sheer curiosity and the challenge of solving difficult problems lead to new and better ways of doing things. For example, loose communities of computer programmers have been collaborating for decades. By the early 1990s, they formed a grass-roots movement known as "open source," which was fueled by the Internet. In 1991, Linus Torvalds, a student at the University of Helsinki in Finland, wrote the core program for what would become known as the Linux operating system. He posted his program online and invited anyone to tinker with the coding. Word spread, and computer aficionados around the world began spending their free time making Linux better; Linux is now the most popular operating system on supercomputers.

Other software has developed in the open-source arena. For example, from the University of Illinois came Apache, now the most widely used Web server. The *Free Software Directory* lists more than 5,000 free software packages. The term *free* refers not only to the dollar cost of the software, which is zero, but to what you can do with the software—you are free to examine it, modify it, and redistribute it to anyone. Free user-generated software also includes the second most popular Web browser (Firefox) and office suite (LibreOffice).

Other user-generated products include some familiar names—Wikipedia, Facebook, YouTube, and Twitter. Wikipedia is a free online encyclopedia written and edited by volunteers. The idea is that collaboration over time will improve content much the way that open-source software has evolved. Wikipedia claims to be one of the most visited online sites. Founder Jimmy Wales

continued

says he spent a half million dollars getting Wikipedia going, but now the project relies on volunteers and donations.

As you well know, Facebook is a social-networking site that allows users to post personal profiles, blogs, photos, music, videos, and more. The main attraction is the material provided by users. The company simply provides the software and hardware backbone to support the network. Facebook was started by a college sophomore in 2004; the company had 1.4 billion active users by 2015 and an estimated market value of more than $200 billion.

YouTube is an online site that allows users to post their own videos and view those posted by others. Searching is easy. For example, "comparative advantage" turned up more than 13,000 videos. When sold to Google in 2006, YouTube had only 67 employees and no profit. Still, because visitors at the time were viewing more than 100 million videos a day, all those eyeballs offered tremendous advertising potential. Google paid $1.7 billion for a company with no profit.

Finally, Twitter is a social networking and microblogging service that allows users to send and receive "tweets," which are messages limited to 140 characters. Delivery can be online via the Twitter Web site, by cell phones, or by using other applications. The company in 2015 had more than 300 million active users sending more than 500 million tweets a day.

User-generated products are not new. Radio call-in shows have been making money off callers for decades. But new technology has increased opportunities for users to create new products and to improve existing products. Most of the users are just having fun. The more users involved, the more attractive that product is to each user (and to advertisers). That's why networking and video sites try to dominate their markets.

Sources: Jaron Lanier, *You Are Not a Gadget* (Knopf, 2010); "Professor Facebook," *The Economist*, 11 February 2012; and Justus Haucap and Ulrich Heimeschoff, "Google, Facebook, Amazon, eBay: Is the Internet Driving Competition of Market Monopolization?" *International Economics and Economic Policy*, 11 (February 2014): 49–61. The *Free Software Directory* is found at http://directory.fsf.org/.

3-2e   Why Does Household Production Still Exist?

If firms are so efficient at reducing transaction and production costs, why don't they make everything? Why do households still perform some tasks, such as cooking and cleaning? *If a household's opportunity cost of performing a task is below the market price, then the household usually performs that task.* People with a lower opportunity cost of time do more for themselves. For example, janitors are more likely to mow their lawns than are physicians. Let's look at some reasons for household production.

No Skills or Special Resources Are Required

Some activities require so few skills or special resources that householders find it cheaper to do the jobs themselves. Sweeping the kitchen floor requires only a broom and some time so it's usually performed by household members. Sanding a wooden floor, however, involves special machinery and expertise, so households hire professionals. Similarly, although you wouldn't hire someone to brush your teeth, dental work is not for amateurs. *Households usually perform domestic chores that demand neither expertise nor special machinery.*

Household Production Avoids Taxes

Suppose you are deciding whether to pay someone $3,000 to paint your house or do it yourself. If the income tax rate is one-third, you must earn $4,500 before taxes to have the $3,000 after taxes to pay for the job. And the painter who charges you $3,000 nets only $2,000 after paying $1,000 in taxes. Thus, you must earn $4,500 so that the painter can take home $2,000. If you paint the house yourself, no taxes are involved. The tax-free nature of do-it-yourself activity favors household production over market transactions.

Household Production Reduces Transaction Costs

Getting estimates, hiring a contractor, negotiating terms, and monitoring job performance all take time and require information. Doing the job yourself reduces these transaction costs. Household production also allows for more personal control over the final product than is usually available through the market. For example, some people prefer home cooking, because they can prepare home-cooked meals to individual tastes.

Household production often grows during hard times. The economic recession of 2007–2009 prompted some families to shift from market purchases to household production to save money. For example, sales of hair clippers used for home haircuts increased 10 percent in 2008 and 11 percent in 2009.[1]

Technological Advances Increase Household Productivity

Technological breakthroughs are not confined to market production. Vacuum cleaners, washers and dryers, dishwashers, microwave ovens, and other modern appliances reduce the time and often the skill required to perform household tasks. Also, new technologies such as DVRs, HDTVs, broadband downloads, and computer games enhance home entertainment. The **Information Revolution** spawned by the microchip and the Internet has also enhanced the acquisition, analysis, and transmission of information. Indeed, microchip-based technologies have shifted some production from the firm back to the household. Because of technological change, more people can work from their homes.

Information Revolution
Technological change spawned by the microchip and the Internet that enhanced the acquisition, analysis, and transmission of information

CHECKPOINT

Trace the evolution of production over the centuries from the household to the modern corporation.

3-3 The Government

You might think that production by households and firms could satisfy all consumer wants. Why must yet another economic decision maker get into the act? After all, governments play some role in every nation on Earth.

3-3a The Role of Government

Sometimes the unrestrained operation of markets yields undesirable results. Too many of some goods and too few of other goods get produced. This section discusses the sources of **market failure** and how society's overall welfare may be improved through government intervention in the market.

market failure
A condition that arises when the unregulated operation of markets yields socially undesirable results

---

[1.] Mary Pilon, "Per Capita Saving: Home Barbering Grows in Recession," *Wall Street Journal*, 31 August 2009.

Establishing and Enforcing the Rules of the Game

Market efficiency depends on people like you using your resources to maximize your utility. But what if you were repeatedly robbed of your paycheck on your way home from work? Or what if, after you worked two weeks in a new job, your boss called you a sucker and said you wouldn't get paid? Why bother working? The market system would break down if you could not safeguard your private property or if you could not enforce contracts. Governments safeguard private property through police protection and enforce contracts through a judicial system. More generally, governments try to make sure that market participants abide by the rules of the game—that is, play fair. These rules are established through government laws and regulations and also through the customs and conventions of the marketplace. For example, the U.S. Bureau of Weights and Measures regulates the uniformity of measuring devices to promote confidence in market transactions and to ensure fairness between buyers and sellers.

Promoting Competition

Although the "invisible hand" of competition usually promotes an efficient allocation of resources, some firms try to avoid competition through *collusion*, which is an agreement among firms to fix the price and carve up the market. Or an individual firm may try to eliminate the competition by using unfair business practices. For example, to drive out local competitors, a large firm may temporarily sell at a price below cost. Government **antitrust laws** try to promote competition by prohibiting collusion and other anticompetitive practices.

antitrust laws
Prohibitions against price fixing and other anticompetitive practices

monopoly
A sole supplier of a product with no close substitutes

Regulating Natural Monopolies

Competition usually keeps the product price below the price charged by a **monopoly**, a sole supplier to the market. In rare instances, however, a monopoly can produce and sell the product for less than could competing firms. For example, electricity is delivered more efficiently by a single firm that wires the community than by competing firms each stringing their own wires. When it is cheaper for one firm to serve the market than for two or more firms to do so, that one firm is called a **natural monopoly**. Because a natural monopoly faces no competition, it maximizes profit by charging a higher price than would be optimal from society's point of view. A lower price and greater output would improve social welfare. Therefore, the government usually regulates a natural monopoly, forcing it to lower its price and increase output.

natural monopoly
One firm that can supply the entire market at a lower per-unit cost than could two or more firms

Providing Public Goods

So far this book has been talking about private goods, which have two important features. First, private goods are *rival* in consumption, meaning that the amount consumed by one person is unavailable for others to consume. For example, when you and some friends share a pizza, each slice they eat is no longer available for you. Second, the supplier of a private good can easily exclude those who fail to pay. Only paying customers get pizza. Thus, private goods are said to be *exclusive*. So **private goods**, such as pizza, are both rival in consumption and exclusive. In contrast, **public goods** are *nonrival* in consumption. For example, your family's benefit from a safer neighborhood does not reduce your neighbor's benefit. What's more, once produced, public goods are available to all. Suppliers cannot easily prevent consumption by those who fail to pay. For example, reducing terrorism is *nonexclusive*. It benefits all in the community, regardless of who pays to reduce terrorism and who doesn't. Because public goods are *nonrival* and *nonexclusive*, private firms cannot sell them profitably. The government, however, has the authority to enforce tax collections for public goods. Thus, the government provides public goods and funds them with taxes.

private good
A good, such as pizza, that is both rival in consumption and exclusive

public good
A good that, once produced, is available for all to consume, regardless of who pays and who doesn't; such a good is nonrival and nonexclusive, such as a safer community

Dealing With Externalities

Market prices reflect the private costs and private benefits of producers and consumers. But sometimes production or consumption imposes costs or benefits on third parties—on those who are neither suppliers nor demanders in a market transaction. For example, a paper mill fouls the air breathed by nearby residents, but the price of paper usually fails to reflect such costs. Because these pollution costs are outside, or external to, the market, they are called *externalities*. An **externality** is a cost or a benefit that falls on a third party. A negative externality imposes an external cost, such as factory pollution, auto emissions, or traffic congestion. A positive externality confers an external benefit, such as getting a good education, getting inoculated against a disease (thus reducing the possibility of infecting others), or driving carefully. Because market prices usually do not reflect externalities, governments often use taxes, subsidies, and regulations to discourage negative externalities and encourage positive externalities. For example, a polluting factory may face taxes and regulations aimed at curbing that pollution. And because more educated people can read road signs and have options that pay better than crime, governments try to encourage education with free public schools, subsidized higher education, and by keeping people in school until their 16th birthdays.

externality
A cost or a benefit that affects neither the buyer nor seller, but instead affects people not involved in the market transaction

A More Equal Distribution of Income

As mentioned earlier, some people, because of poor education, mental or physical disabilities, bad luck, or perhaps the need to care for small children, are unable to support themselves and their families. Because resource markets do not guarantee even a minimum level of income, transfer payments reflect society's willingness to ensure a basic standard of living to all households. Most Americans agree that government should redistribute income to the poor (note the normative nature of this statement). Opinions differ about who should receive benefits, how much they should get, what form benefits should take, and how long benefits should last.

Full Employment, Price Stability, and Economic Growth

Perhaps the most important responsibility of government is fostering a healthy economy, which benefits just about everyone. The government—through its ability to tax, to spend, and to control the money supply—attempts to promote full employment, price stability, and economic growth. Pursuing these objectives by taxing and spending is called **fiscal policy**. Pursuing them by regulating the money supply is called **monetary policy**. Macroeconomics examines both policies.

fiscal policy
The use of government purchases, transfer payments, taxes, and borrowing to influence economy-wide variables such as inflation, employment, and economic growth

3-3b Government's Structure and Objectives

The United States has a *federal system* of government, meaning that responsibilities are shared across levels of government. State governments grant some powers to local governments and surrender some powers to the national, or federal, government. As the system has evolved, the federal government has primary responsibility for national security, economic stability, and promoting market competition. State governments fund public higher education, prisons, and—with aid from the federal government—highways and welfare. Local governments provide primary and secondary education with aid from the state, plus police and fire protection. Here are some distinguishing features of government.

monetary policy
Regulation of the money supply to influence economy-wide variables such as inflation, employment, and economic growth

Difficulty in Defining Government Objectives

We assume that households try to maximize utility and firms try to maximize profit, but what about governments—or, more specifically, what about government decision makers? What do they try to maximize? One problem is that our federal system consists of not one but many governments—about 89,150 separate jurisdictions in all, including 1 nation, 50 states, 3,000 counties, 36,000 cities and towns, 12,900 school districts, and 37,200 special districts. What's more, because the federal government relies on offsetting, or countervailing, powers across the executive, legislative, and judicial branches, government does not act as a single, consistent decision maker. Even within the federal executive branch, there are so many agencies and bureaus that at times they seem to work at cross-purposes. For example, at the same time as the U.S. Surgeon General required health warnings on cigarette packages, the U.S. Department of Agriculture pursued policies to benefit tobacco growers. Given this thicket of jurisdictions, branches, and bureaus, one useful theory of government behavior is that elected officials try to maximize the number of votes they get in the next election. So let's assume that elected officials are vote maximizers. In this theory, vote maximization guides the decisions of elected officials who, in turn, oversee government employees.

Voluntary Exchange Versus Coercion

Market exchange relies on the voluntary behavior of buyers and sellers. Don't like tofu? No problem—don't buy any. But in political markets, the situation is different. Any voting rule except unanimous consent must involve some government coercion. Public choices are enforced by the police power of the state. Those who don't pay their taxes could go to prison, even though they may object to some programs those taxes support, such as capital punishment or war in the Middle East.

No Market Prices

Another distinguishing feature of governments is that public output is usually offered at either a zero price or at some price below the cost of providing it. If you now pay in-state tuition at a public college or university, your tuition probably covers only about half the state's cost of providing your education. Because the revenue side of the government budget is usually separate from the expenditure side, there is no necessary link between the cost of a program and the benefit. In the private sector, the expected marginal benefit of a product is at least as great as its price; otherwise, nobody would buy it.

3-3c The Size and Growth of Government

One way to track the impact of government over time is by measuring government outlays relative to the U.S. *gross domestic product,* or *GDP,* which is the total value of all final goods and services produced in the United States. In 1929, the year the Great Depression began, all government outlays, mostly by state and local governments, totaled about 10 percent of GDP. At the time, the federal government played a minor role. In fact, during the nation's first 150 years, federal outlays, except during war years, never exceeded 3 percent relative to GDP.

The Great Depression, World War II, a change in macroeconomic thinking, and extraordinary measures following the financial crisis of 2008 boosted the share of government outlays to 38 percent of GDP in 2016, with about two-thirds of that by the federal government. In comparison, government outlays relative to GDP that year were 39 percent in Canada and Japan, 41 percent in the United Kingdom, 44 percent in Germany, 50 percent in Italy, and 56 percent in France. Government outlays by 31 advanced

EXHIBIT 3   Redistribution Has Grown and Defense Has Declined as Share of Federal Outlays: 1960–2016

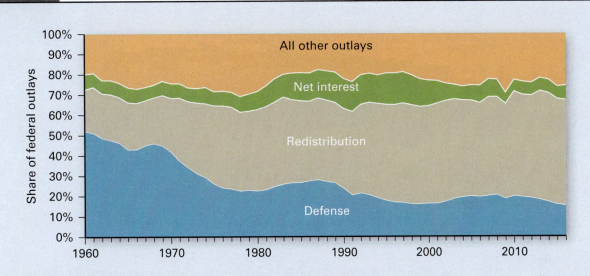

Source: Computed based on figures from the *Economic Report of the President*, February 2015, Table B-21. Figures for 2015 and 2016 are estimates based on the president's budget. For the latest figures, go to http://www.whitehouse.gov/administration/eop/cea/economic-report-of-the-President.

industrial economies averaged 40 percent of GDP in 2016.[2] Thus, government outlays in the United States relative to GDP are slightly below the average of advanced economies.

Let's look briefly at the composition of federal outlays. Since 1960, defense spending has declined from over half of federal outlays to less than one-fifth by 2016, as shown in Exhibit 3. Redistribution—Social Security, Medicare, and welfare programs—has been the mirror image of defense spending, jumping from only about one-fifth of federal outlays in 1960 to more than half by 2016.

3-3d Sources of Government Revenue

Taxes provide the bulk of revenue at all levels of government. The federal government relies primarily on the individual income tax, state governments rely on income and sales taxes, and local governments rely on the property tax. Other revenue sources include user charges, such as highway tolls and college tuition, and borrowing. For additional revenue, some states also act as monopolies in certain markets, such as selling lottery tickets and liquor.

Exhibit 4 focuses on the composition of federal revenue since 1960. The share made up by the individual income tax has remained relatively steady, ranging from a low of 42 percent in the mid-1960s to a high of 50 percent in 2001, before averaging about 47 percent from 2011 to 2016. The share from payroll taxes doubled from 16 percent in 1960 to 32 percent in 2016. *Payroll taxes* are deducted from paychecks to support Social Security and Medicare, which fund retirement income and medical care for the elderly. Corporate taxes and revenue from other sources, such as excise (sales) taxes and user charges, have declined as a share of federal revenue since 1960.

[2.] The Organization of Economic Cooperation and Development, *OECD Economic Outlook*, 97 (May 2015), Total Disbursements, General Government, as a Percent of GDP, at http://stats.oecd.org/index.aspx?queryid=51396.

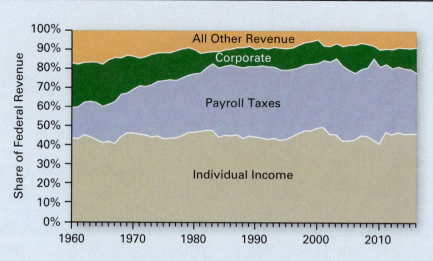

EXHIBIT 4   Composition of Federal Revenue Between 1960 and 2016

Source: Computed based on figures from the *Economic Report of the President*, February 2015, Table B-21. Figures for 2015 and 2016 are projections based on the president's budget. For the latest figures, go to http://www.whitehouse.gov/administration/eop/cea/economic-report-of-the-President.

3-3e Tax Principles and Tax Incidence

ability-to-pay tax principle
Those with a greater ability to pay, such as those earning higher incomes or those owning more property, should pay more taxes

benefits-received tax principle
Those who get more benefits from the government program funded by the tax should pay more of that tax

tax incidence
The distribution of tax burden among taxpayers; who ultimately pays the tax

proportional taxation
The tax as a percentage of income remains constant as income increases; also called a flat tax

progressive taxation
The tax as a percentage of income increases as income increases

marginal tax rate
The percentage of each additional dollar of income that goes to the tax

The structure of a tax is often justified on the basis of one of two general principles. First, a tax could relate to the individual's ability to pay, so those with a greater ability pay more taxes. Income or property taxes often rely on this **ability-to-pay tax principle**. Alternatively, the **benefits-received tax principle** relates taxes to the benefits taxpayers receive from the government activity funded by the tax. For example, the tax on gasoline funds highway construction and maintenance, thereby linking tax payment to road use, since those who drive more, pay more gas taxes.

Tax incidence indicates who actually bears the burden of the tax. One way to evaluate tax incidence is by measuring the tax as a percentage of income. Under **proportional taxation**, taxpayers at all income levels pay the same percentage of their income in taxes. A proportional income tax is also called a *flat tax*, since the tax as a percentage of income remains constant, or flat, as income increases. Note that under proportional taxation, although taxes remain constant as a percentage of income, the dollar amount of taxes increases proportionately as income increases.

Under **progressive taxation**, the percentage of income paid in taxes increases as income increases. The **marginal tax rate** indicates the percentage of each additional dollar of income that goes to taxes. Because high marginal rates reduce the after-tax return from working or investing, high marginal rates can reduce people's incentives to work and invest. The seven marginal rates applied to the U.S. personal income in 2015 tax ranged from 10 to 39.6 percent.

The top marginal tax bracket each year during the history of the personal income tax is shown by Exhibit 5. Although the top rate is now lower than it was during most other years, high-income households still pay most of the federal income tax collected. More than 40 percent of U.S. households pay no federal income taxes; these are low-income households. According to the U.S. Internal Revenue Service, the top 1 percent of tax filers, based on income, paid 38 percent of all income taxes collected in 2012. Their average tax rate was 23.5 percent. And the top 10 percent of tax filers paid 70 percent of all income taxes collected. Their average tax rate was 18.7 percent. In contrast, the bottom 50 percent of tax

| EXHIBIT 5 | Top Marginal Rate on Federal Personal Income Tax Since 1913 |

Source: U.S. Internal Revenue Service. For the latest figures on the personal income tax go to http://www.irs.gov/individuals/index.html.

filers paid only 2.8 percent of all income taxes collected. Their tax rate averaged only 3.0 percent. Whether we look at marginal tax rates or average tax rates, the U.S. income tax is progressive. High-income filers pay the overwhelming share of federal income taxes.

Finally, under **regressive taxation**, the percentage of income paid in taxes decreases as income increases, so the marginal tax rate declines as income increases. Most U.S. *payroll taxes* are regressive, because they impose a flat rate up to a certain level of income, above which the marginal rate drops to zero. For example, Social Security taxes were levied on the first $118,500 of workers' pay in 2015. Employers pay 6.2 percent and employees pay 6.2 percent (the self-employed pay the entire 12.4 percent).

Taxes often do more than fund public programs. Some taxes discourage certain activity. For example, a pollution tax can help clean the air. A tax on gasoline can encourage people to work at home, car pool, or use public transportation. Some taxes have unintended consequences. For example, in Egypt a property tax is not imposed until a new building is completed. To avoid such taxes, builders never finish the job; multistory dwellings are usually missing the top floor. As another example of how taxes can distort the allocation of resources, property taxes in Amsterdam and Vietnam were originally based on the width of the building. As a result, buildings there are extremely narrow. As a final example, in 1696 England levied a property tax based on a dwelling's number of windows. As a consequence, property owners boarded up existing windows and new dwellings had fewer windows. These actions cut ventilation and light, creating health hazards, yet the tax persisted for more than 150 years.[3] Such taxes have unintended consequences that distort the efficient allocation of resources.

This discussion of revenue sources brings to a close, for now, our examination of the role of government in the U.S. economy. Government has a pervasive influence on the economy, and its role is discussed throughout the book.

regressive taxation
The tax as a percentage of income decreases as income increases

[3.] Wallace E. Oates and Robert M. Schwab, "The Window Tax: A Case of Excess Burden," *Journal of Economic Perspectives*, 29 (Winter 2015): 163–180.

Identify seven roles of government.

3-4 The Rest of the World

So far, the focus has been on institutions within the United States—that is, on *domestic* households, firms, and governments. This focus is appropriate because our primary objective is to understand the workings of the U.S. economy. But the rest of the world affects what U.S. households consume and what U.S. firms produce. For example, Japan and China supply all kinds of manufactured goods to America, thereby affecting U.S. prices, wages, and profits. Likewise, political events in the Middle East can affect what Americans pay for oil. Foreign decision makers, therefore, influence the U.S. economy—what we produce and what we consume. The *rest of the world* consists of the households, firms, and governments in the other 200 or so sovereign nations throughout the world.

3-4a International Trade

In the previous chapter, you learned about comparative advantage and the gains from specialization. These gains explain why householders stopped doing everything for themselves and began to specialize. International trade arises for the same reasons. *International trade occurs because the opportunity cost of producing specific goods differs across countries.* Americans import raw materials like crude oil, bauxite (aluminum ore), and coffee beans and finished goods like cameras, computers, and cut diamonds. U.S. producers export sophisticated products like computer software, aircraft, and movies, as well as agricultural products like wheat, corn, and cotton. Farm exports are why America has long been called the "breadbasket of the world."

Trade between the United States and the rest of the world has increased in recent decades. In 1970, U.S. exports of goods and services amounted to only 6 percent of the gross domestic product. That has increased to about 14 percent today. The top 10 destinations for U.S. exports in order of importance are Canada, Mexico, China, Japan, United Kingdom, Germany, Netherlands, South Korea, France, and Brazil.

The **merchandise trade balance** equals the value of exported goods minus the value of imported goods. Goods in this case are distinguished from services, which show up in another trade account. For the last quarter century, the United States has imported more goods than it has exported, resulting in a merchandise trade deficit. Just as a household must pay for its spending, so too must a nation. The merchandise trade deficit must be offset by a surplus in one or more of the other *balance-of-payments* accounts. A nation's **balance of payments** is the record of all economic transactions between its residents and residents of the rest of the world.

3-4b Exchange Rates

The lack of a common currency complicates trade between countries. How many U.S. dollars buy a Porsche? An American buyer cares only about the dollar cost; the German carmaker cares only about the *euros* received (the common currency of 19 European

merchandise trade balance
The value during a given period of a country's exported goods minus the value of its imported goods

balance of payments
A record of all economic transactions during a given period between residents of one country and residents of the rest of the world

countries). To facilitate trade funded by different currencies, a market for foreign exchange has developed. **Foreign exchange** is foreign currency needed to carry out international transactions. The supply and demand for foreign exchange comes together in *foreign exchange markets* to determine the exchange rate. The *exchange rate* measures the price of one currency in terms of another. For example, the exchange rate between the euro and the dollar might indicate that one euro exchanges for $1.10. At that exchange rate, a Porsche selling for €100,000 costs $110,000. The exchange rate affects the prices of imports and exports and thus helps shape the flow of foreign trade.

foreign exchange

Foreign money needed to carry out international transactions

3-4c Trade Restrictions

Despite clear gains from international specialization and exchange, nearly all nations restrict trade to some extent. These restrictions can take the form of (1) **tariffs**, which are taxes on imports; (2) **quotas**, which are limits on the quantity of a particular good that can be imported or exported; and (3) other trade restrictions. If specialization according to comparative advantage is so beneficial, why do most countries restrict trade? Restrictions benefit certain domestic producers that lobby governments for these benefits. For example, U.S. growers of sugarcane have benefited from legislation restricting sugar imports, thereby raising U.S. sugar prices. These higher prices hurt domestic consumers, but consumers are usually unaware of this harm. Trade restrictions interfere with the free flow of products across borders and tend to hurt the overall economy.

tariff

A tax on imports

quota

A legal limit on the quantity of a particular product that can be imported or exported

**CHECKPOINT**

Why do countries trade with each other?

3-5 Conclusion

This chapter examined the four economic decision makers: households, firms, governments, and the rest of the world. Domestic households are by far the most important, for they supply resources and demand goods and services.

If you were to stop reading right now, you would already know more economics than most people. But to understand market economies, you must learn how markets work. The next chapter introduces demand and supply.

Summary

1. Most household income arises from the sale of labor, and most household income is spent on personal consumption, primarily services.

2. Household members once built their own homes, made their own clothes and furniture, grew their own food, and supplied their own entertainment. Over time, however, the efficiency arising from comparative advantage resulted in a greater specialization among resource suppliers.

3. Firms bring together specialized resources and in the process reduce the transaction costs of bargaining with all these resource suppliers. U.S. firms can be organized in three different ways: as sole proprietorships, partnerships, or corporations. Because corporations are typically large, they account for the bulk of sales.

4. When resource and product markets yield undesirable results, government may intervene to address these market failures. Government programs are designed to (a) protect private property

and enforce contracts; (b) promote competition; (c) regulate natural monopolies; (d) provide public goods; (e) discourage negative externalities and encourage positive externalities; (f) promote a more even distribution of income; and (g) promote full employment, price stability, and economic growth.

5. In the United States, the federal government has primary responsibility for providing national defense, ensuring market competition, and promoting stability of the economy. State governments provide public higher education, prisons, and—with aid from the federal government—highways and welfare. And local governments provide police and fire protection, and, with help from the state, local schools.

6. The federal government relies primarily on the personal income tax, states rely on income and sales taxes, and localities rely on the property tax. A tax is often justified based on (a) the individual's ability to pay or (b) the benefits the taxpayer receives from the activities financed by the tax.

7. The rest of the world is also populated by households, firms, and governments. International trade creates gains that arise from comparative advantage. The balance of payments summarizes transactions between the residents of one country and the residents of the rest of the world. Although consumers gain from comparative advantage, nearly all countries impose trade restrictions to protect specific domestic industries.

Key Concepts

Utility 48	Antitrust laws 56	Proportional taxation 60
Transfer payments 49	Monopoly 56	Progressive taxation 60
Industrial Revolution 50	Natural monopoly 56	Marginal tax rate 60
Firms 50	Private good 56	Regressive taxation 61
Sole proprietorship 50	Public good 56	Merchandise trade balance 62
Partnership 51	Externality 57	Balance of payments 62
Corporation 51	Fiscal policy 57	Foreign exchange 63
Cooperative 52	Monetary policy 57	Tariff 63
Not-for-profit organizations 53	Ability-to-pay tax principle 60	Quota 63
Information Revolution 55	Benefits-received tax principle 60	
Market failure 55	Tax incidence 60	

Questions for Review

1. **Households as Demanders of Goods and Services** Classify each of the following as a durable good, a nondurable good, or a service:v
   a. A gallon of milk
   b. A lawn mower
   c. A smartphone
   d. A manicure
   e. A pair of shoes
   f. An eye exam
   g. A personal computer
   h. A neighborhood teenager mowing your lawn

2. **Evolution of the Firm** Explain how production after the Industrial Revolution differed from production under the cottage industry system.

3. **Household Production** What factors does a householder consider when deciding whether to produce a good or service at home or buy it in the marketplace?

4. **Corporations** How did the institution of the firm get a boost from the advent of the Industrial Revolution? What type of business organization existed before this?

5. **Sole Proprietorships** What are the disadvantages of the sole proprietorship form of business?

6. **Cooperatives** How do cooperatives differ from typical businesses?

7. **Case Study: User-Generated Products** Why are users willing to help create certain products even though few, if any, users are paid for their efforts?

8. **Government** Often it is said that government is necessary when private markets fail to work effectively and fairly. Based on your reading of the text, discuss how private markets might break down.

9. **Externalities** Suppose there is an external cost, or negative externality, associated with production of a certain good. What's wrong with letting the market determine how much of this good will be produced?

10. **Government Revenue** What are the sources of government revenue in the United States? Which types of taxes are most important at each level of government? Which two taxes provide the most revenue to the federal government?

11. **Objectives of the Economic Decision Makers** In economic analysis, what are the assumed objectives of households, firms, and the government?

12. **International Trade** Why does international trade occur? What does it mean to run a deficit in the merchandise trade balance?

13. **International Trade** Distinguish between a tariff and a quota. Who benefits from and who is harmed by such restrictions on imports?

Problems and Exercises

14. **Evolution of the Household** Determine whether each of the following would increase or decrease the opportunity costs for mothers who decide not to work outside the home. Explain your answers.

    a. Higher levels of education for women
    b. Higher unemployment rates for women
    c. Higher average pay levels for women
    d. Lower demand for labor in industries that traditionally employ women

15. **Household Production** Many households supplement their food budget by cultivating small vegetable gardens. Explain how each of the following might influence this kind of household production:

    a. Both husband and wife are professionals who earn high salaries.
    b. The household is located in a city rather than in a rural area.
    c. The household is located in a region with a high sales tax on food.
    d. The household is located in a region with a high property tax rate.

16. **Government** Complete each of the following sentences:

    a. Goods that are nonrival and nonexclusive are known as _____.
    b. _____ are cash or in-kind benefits given to individuals as outright grants from the government.
    c. A(n) _____ confers an external benefit on third parties that are not directly involved in a market transaction.
    d. _____ refers to the government's pursuit of full employment and price stability through variations in taxes and government spending.

17. **Tax Rates** Suppose taxes are related to income level as follows:

Income	Taxes
$1,000	$200
$2,000	$350
$3,000	$450

    a. What percentage of income is paid in taxes at each level?
    b. Is the tax rate progressive, proportional, or regressive?
    c. What is the marginal tax rate on the first $1,000 of income? The second $1,000? The third $1,000?

4 Demand, Supply, and Markets

©MJTH/Shutterstock.com

- *Why do roses cost more on Valentine's Day than during the rest of the year?*
- *Why do TV ads cost more during the Super Bowl ($4.5 million for 30 seconds in 2015) than during Nick at Nite reruns?*
- *Why do hotel room rates double in the host city during Super Bowl weekend?*
- *Why do surgeons earn more than butchers?*
- *Why do economics majors earn more than most other majors?*

Answers to these and most other economic questions boil down to the workings of demand and supply—the subject of this chapter.

This chapter introduces demand and supply and shows how they interact in competitive markets. Demand and supply are the most fundamental and the most powerful of all economic tools—important enough to warrant a chapter. Indeed, some believe that if you program a computer to answer "demand and supply" to every economic question, you could put many economists out of work. An understanding of the two ideas will take you far in mastering the art and science of economic analysis. Because of the subject matter, this chapter uses lots of graphs, so you may need to review the Chapter 1 appendix as a refresher.

Topics discussed in this chapter include:

- Demand and quantity demanded
- Movement along a demand curve
- Shift of a demand curve
- Supply and quantity supplied

- Movement along a supply curve
- Shift of a supply curve
- Markets and equilibrium
- Disequilibrium

4-1 Demand

How many six-packs of Pepsi will people buy each month at a price of $4? What if the price is $3? What if it's $5? The answers reveal the relationship between the price of a six-pack and the quantity of Pepsi demanded. Such a relationship is called the *demand* for Pepsi. **Demand** indicates the quantity consumers are both *willing and able* to buy at each price during a given time period, other things constant. Because demand pertains to a specific period—a day, a week, a month—think of demand as the *amount purchased per period* at each price. Also, notice the emphasis on *willing and able*. You may be *able* to buy a new Harley-Davidson Sportster Forty-Eight that lists for $10,749 because you can afford one, but you may not be *willing* to buy one if motorcycles just don't interest you.

demand
A relation between the price of a good and the quantity that consumers are willing and able to buy per period, other things constant

4-1a Law of Demand

In 1962, Sam Walton opened his first store in Rogers, Arkansas, with a sign that read: "Wal-Mart Discount City. We sell for less." Now called Walmart, this store chain sells more than any other retailer in the world because prices there are among the lowest around. As a consumer, you understand why people buy more at a lower price. Sell for less, and the world will beat a path to your door. Walmart, for example, sells on average over 20,000 pairs of shoes *an hour*. This relation between the price and the quantity demanded is an economic law. The **law of demand** says that the quantity of a good that consumers are willing and able to buy per period varies inversely, or negatively, with the price, other things constant. Thus, the higher the price, the smaller the quantity demanded; the lower the price, the greater the quantity demanded.

law of demand
The quantity of a good that consumers are willing and able to buy per period relates inversely, or negatively, to the price, other things constant

Demand, Wants, and Needs

Consumer demand and consumer wants are not the same. As we have seen, wants are unlimited. You may want a new Mercedes-Benz SL65 Roadster convertible, but the $215,250 price tag is likely beyond your budget (that is, the quantity you demand at that price is zero). Nor is demand the same as need. You may need a new muffler for your car, but a price of $300 is just too high for you right now. If, however, the price drops enough—say, to $200—then you may be both willing and able to buy one.

Substitution Effect of a Price Change

What explains the law of demand? Why, for example, does the quantity demanded increase as the price declines? The explanation begins with unlimited wants confronting scarce resources. Many goods and services can help satisfy particular wants. For example, you can satisfy your hunger with pizza, tacos, burgers, chicken, or hundreds of other foods. Similarly, you can satisfy your desire for warmth in the winter with warm clothing, a home-heating system, a trip to Hawaii, or in many other ways. Clearly, some alternatives are more appealing than others (a trip to Hawaii is more fun than warm clothing). In a world without scarcity, everything would be free, so you would always choose the most attractive alternative. Scarcity, however, is the reality, and the degree of scarcity of one good relative to another helps determine each good's relative price.

Notice that the definition of *demand* includes the other-things-constant assumption. Among the "other things" assumed to remain constant are the prices of other goods. For example, if the price of pizza declines while other prices remain constant, pizza becomes relatively cheaper. Consumers are more *willing* to purchase pizza when its relative price falls; they substitute pizza for other goods. This idea is called the **substitution effect of a price change**. On the other hand, an increase in the price of pizza, other things constant, increases the opportunity cost of pizza—that is, the amount of other goods you must give up to buy pizza. This higher opportunity cost causes some consumers to substitute other goods for the now higher-priced pizza, thus reducing their quantity of pizza demanded. Remember that *it is the change in the relative price—the price of one good relative to the prices of other goods—that causes the substitution effect*. If all prices changed by the same percentage, there would be no change in relative prices and no substitution effect.

Income Effect of a Price Change

A fall in the price of a good increases the quantity demanded for a second reason. Suppose you earn $30 a week from a part-time job, so $30 is your money income. **Money income** is simply the number of dollars received per period, in this case, $30 per week. Suppose you spend all that on pizza, buying three a week at $10 each. What if the price drops to $6? At that lower price, you can now afford five pizzas a week. Your money income remains at $30 per week, but the price drop increases your **real income**—that is, your income measured by what it can buy. The price reduction, other things constant, increases the purchasing power of your income, thereby increasing your *ability* to buy pizza. The quantity you demand will likely increase because of the **income effect of a price change**. You may not increase your quantity demanded to five pizzas, but you could. If you decide to purchase four pizzas a week when the price drops to $6, you would still have $6 remaining to buy other stuff. Thus, the income effect of a lower price increases your real income and thereby increases your ability to buy pizza and other goods, making you better off. The income effect is reflected in Walmart's slogan, which trumpets low prices: "Save money. Live better." Because of the income effect, consumers typically increase their quantity demanded when the price declines.

---

substitution effect of a price change
When the price of a good falls, that good becomes cheaper compared to other goods, making consumers more willing to substitute that good for other goods

money income
The number of dollars a person receives per period, such as $400 per week

real income
Income measured by the goods and services it can buy; real income changes when the price changes

income effect of a price change
A fall in the price of a good increases consumers' real income, making consumers more able to purchase goods; for a normal good, the quantity demanded increases

Conversely, an increase in the price of pizza, other things constant, reduces real income, thereby reducing your ability to buy pizza and other goods. Because of the income effect, consumers typically reduce their quantity demanded when the price increases. The more important the item is as a share of your budget, the bigger the income effect. That's why, for example, consumers cut back on a variety of purchases when the price of gasoline spikes, as it did in 2012. And that's why consumers increase a variety of purchases when the price of gasoline plunges, as it did in late 2014 and early 2015. Again, note that money income, not real income, is assumed to remain constant along a demand curve. Because a change in price changes your real income, real income varies along a demand curve. The lower the price, the greater your real income.

4-1b Demand Schedule and Demand Curve

Demand can be expressed as a *demand schedule* or as a *demand curve*. Panel (a) of Exhibit 1 shows a hypothetical demand schedule for pizza. In describing demand, we must specify the units measured and the period considered. In our example, the unit is a 12-inch regular pizza and the period is a week. The schedule lists possible prices, along with the quantity demanded at each price. At a price of $15, for example, consumers demand 8 million pizzas per week. As you can see, the lower the price, other things constant, the greater the quantity demanded. Consumers substitute pizza for other foods. And as the price falls, real income increases, causing consumers to increase the quantity of pizza they demand. If the price drops as low as $3, consumers demand 32 million per week.

The demand schedule in panel (a) appears as a **demand curve** in panel (b), with price measured on the vertical axis and the quantity demanded per week on the horizontal axis. Each price–quantity combination listed in the demand schedule in the left panel

demand curve
A curve showing the relation between the price of a good and the quantity consumers are willing and able to buy per period, other things constant

EXHIBIT 1 **Market Demand Schedule and Market Demand Curve for Pizza**

(a) Market demand schedule

	Price per Pizza	Quantity Demanded per Week (millions)
a	$15	8
b	12	14
c	9	20
d	6	26
e	3	32

(b) Market demand curve

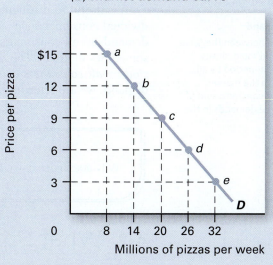

The market demand curve D shows the quantity of pizza demanded, at various prices, by all consumers. Price and quantity demanded are inversely related other things constant, reflecting the law of demand.

becomes a point in the right panel. Point *a*, for example, indicates that if the price is $15, consumers demand 8 million pizzas per week. Connecting points forms the demand curve for pizza, labeled *D*. (By the way, some demand curves are straight lines, some are curved lines, and some are even crooked lines, but for simplicity they all are called demand *curves*.)

A demand curve slopes downward, reflecting the *law of demand*: Price and quantity demanded are inversely related, other things constant. Besides money income, also assumed constant along the demand curve are the prices of other goods. Thus, along the demand curve, the price of pizza changes *relative to the prices of other goods*. The demand curve therefore shows the effect of a change in the *relative price* of pizza—that is, relative to other prices, which do not change.

Take care to distinguish between *demand* and *quantity demanded*. The *demand* for pizza is not a specific amount, but rather the *entire relationship* between price and quantity demanded—represented by the demand schedule or the demand curve. An individual point on the demand curve indicates the **quantity demanded** at a particular price. For example, at a price of $12, the quantity demanded is 14 million pizzas per week. If the price drops from $12 to, say, $9, this is shown in Exhibit 1 by *a movement along the demand curve*—in this case from point *b* to point *c*. Any movement along a demand curve reflects a *change in quantity demanded*, not a change in demand. Got that?

The law of demand applies to the millions of products sold by grocery stores, department stores, clothing stores, shoe stores, drugstores, music stores, bookstores, hardware stores, other retailers, travel agencies, and restaurants, as well as through mail-order catalogs, Craigslist, classified ads, online sites, stock markets, real estate markets, job markets, flea markets, yard sales, and all other markets. The law of demand applies even to choices that seem more personal than economic, such as whether or not to own a pet. For example, after New York City passed an anti-dog-litter law, law-abiding owners had to follow their dogs around the city with scoopers, plastic bags—whatever would do the job. Because the law in effect raised the personal cost of owning a dog, the quantity of dogs demanded decreased. Some dogs were abandoned, increasing strays in the city. The number of dogs left at animal shelters doubled. The law of demand predicts this inverse relation between cost, or price, and quantity demanded.

It is useful to distinguish between **individual demand**, which is the demand of an individual consumer such as you, and **market demand**, which is the sum of the individual demands of all consumers in the market. In most markets, there are many consumers, sometimes millions. *The market demand curve shows the quantities demanded per period by all consumers at various prices.* Unless otherwise noted, when we talk about demand, we are referring to market demand, as shown in Exhibit 1.

quantity demanded

The amount of a good consumers are willing and able to buy per period at a particular price, as reflected by a point on a demand curve

individual demand

The relation between the price of a good and the quantity purchased per period by an individual consumer, other things constant

market demand

The relation between the price of a good and the quantity purchased per period by all consumers in the market, other things constant; sum of the individual demands in the market

CHECKPOINT

Why does a demand curve slope downward?

4-2 What Shifts a Demand Curve?

A demand curve isolates the relation between the price of a good and quantity demanded when other factors that could affect demand remain unchanged. What are those other factors? Variables that can affect market demand are (1) the money income of consumers, (2) the prices of other goods, (3) consumer expectations, (4) the number or composition of consumers in the market, and (5) consumer tastes. How could changes in each affect demand?

4-2a Consumer Income

Exhibit 2 shows the market demand curve *D* for pizza. This demand curve assumes a given money income. Suppose consumer income increases. Some consumers are then willing and able to buy more pizza at each price, so market demand increases. The demand curve shifts to the right from *D* to *D'*. For example, at a price of $12, the amount of pizza demanded increases from 14 million to 20 million per week, as indicated by the movement from point *b* on demand curve *D* to point *f* on demand curve *D'*. In short, *an increase in demand—that is, a rightward shift of the demand curve—means that consumers are willing and able to buy more pizza at each price.*

Goods are classified into two broad categories, depending on how consumers respond to changes in money income. The demand for a **normal good** increases as money income increases. Because pizza is a normal good, its demand curve shifts rightward when money income increases. Most goods are normal. In contrast, demand for an **inferior good** actually decreases as money income increases, so the demand curve shifts leftward. Examples of inferior goods include bologna sandwiches, used furniture, and used clothes. As money income increases, consumers tend to switch from these inferior goods to normal goods (such as roast beef sandwiches, new furniture, and new clothes).

normal good
A good, such as new clothes, for which demand increases, or shifts rightward, as consumer income rises

inferior good
A good, such as used clothes, for which demand decreases, or shifts leftward, as consumer income rises

4-2b Prices of Other Goods

Again, the prices of other goods are assumed to remain constant along a given demand curve. Now let's bring these other prices into play. Consumers have various ways of

EXHIBIT 2 **An Increase in the Market Demand for Pizza**

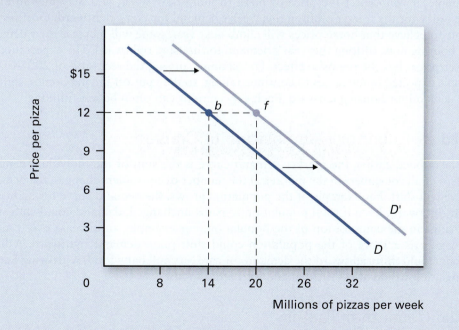

An increase of the market demand for pizza is shown by a rightward shift of the curve, indicating that the quantity demanded increases at each price. For example, at a price of $12, quantity demanded increases from 14 million (point *b*) to 20 million (point *f*).

trying to satisfy any particular want. Consumers choose among substitutes based on relative prices. For example, pizza and tacos are substitutes, though not perfect ones. An increase in the price of tacos, other things constant, reduces the quantity of tacos demanded along a given taco demand curve. An increase in the price of tacos also increases the demand for pizza, shifting the demand curve for pizza to the right. Two goods are considered **substitutes** if an increase in the price of one shifts the demand for the other rightward.

Goods used in combination are called complements. Examples include Pepsi and pizza, milk and cookies, hot dogs and hot-dog buns, cars and gasoline, computer software and hardware, and airline tickets and rental cars. Two goods are considered **complements** if an increase in the price of one decreases the demand for the other, shifting that demand curve leftward. For example, an increase in the price of Pepsi shifts the demand curve for pizza leftward. But most pairs of goods selected at random are *unrelated*—for example, pizza and housing, or milk and gasoline. Still, an increase in the price of an unrelated good reduces the consumers' real income and can thereby reduce the demand for pizza and other goods. For example, a sharp increase in housing prices reduces the income left over for other goods, such as pizza.

4-2c Consumer Expectations

Another factor assumed constant along a given demand curve is consumer expectations about factors that influence demand, such as incomes or prices. A change in consumers' *income expectations* can shift the demand curve. For example, a consumer who learns about a pay raise might increase demand well before the raise takes effect. A college senior who lands that first full-time job may buy a new car even before graduation. Likewise, a change in consumers' *price expectations* can shift the demand curve. For example, if you expect the price of pizza to jump next week, you may buy an extra one today for the freezer, shifting this week's demand for pizza rightward. Or if people come to believe that home prices will climb next year, some will increase their demand for housing now, shifting this year's demand for housing rightward. The expectation of lower prices has the opposite effect. For example, during the recession of 2007–2009, people expected home prices to continue falling, so they put off buying homes, shifting the demand for housing leftward. Such expectations can often be self-fulfilling.

4-2d Number or Composition of Consumers

As mentioned earlier, the market demand curve is the sum of the individual demand curves of all consumers in the market. If the number of consumers changes, the demand curve will shift. For example, if the population grows, the demand curve for pizza will shift rightward. Even if total population remains unchanged, demand could shift with a change in the composition of the population. For example, an increase over time in teenagers as a share of the population could shift pizza demand rightward. A baby boom would shift rightward the demand for car seats and baby food. A growing Latino population would affect the demand for Latino foods.

4-2e Consumer Tastes

Do you like anchovies on your pizza? How about sauerkraut on your hot dogs? Are you into tattoos and body piercings? Is music to your ears more likely to be rock, country, hip-hop, reggae, R&B, jazz, funk, Latin, gospel, new age, or classical? Choices in food, body art, music, sports, clothing, books, movies, TV shows—indeed, all consumer choices—are

---

substitutes

Goods, such as tacos and pizza, that relate in such a way that an increase in the price of one shifts the demand for the other rightward

complements

Goods, such as Pepsi and pizza, that relate in such a way that an increase in the price of one shifts the demand for the other leftward influenced by consumer tastes. **Tastes** are nothing more than your likes and dislikes as a consumer. What determines tastes? Your desires for food when hungry and drink when thirsty are largely biological. So too is your desire for comfort, rest, shelter, friendship, love, status, personal safety, and a pleasant environment. Your family background affects some of your tastes—your taste in food, for example, has been shaped by years of home cooking. Other influences include the surrounding culture, peer pressure, and religious convictions. So economists can say a little about the origin of tastes, but they claim no special expertise in understanding how tastes develop and change over time. Economists recognize, however, that tastes have an important impact on demand. For example, although pizza is popular, some people just don't like it and those who are lactose intolerant can't stomach the cheese topping. Thus, most people like pizza but some don't.

In our analysis of consumer demand, *we will assume that tastes are given and are relatively stable.* Tastes are assumed to remain constant along a given demand curve. A change in the tastes for a particular good would shift that good's demand curve. For example, a discovery that the tomato sauce and cheese combination on pizza promotes overall health could change consumer tastes, shifting the demand curve for pizza to the right. But because a change in tastes is so difficult to isolate from changes in other determinants of demand, we should be reluctant to attribute a shift of the demand curve to a change in tastes. We therefore try to rule out other possible reasons for a shift of the demand curve before accepting a change in tastes as the explanation.

That wraps up our look at changes in demand. Before we turn to supply, you should remember the distinction between a **movement along a given demand curve** and a **shift of a demand curve**. A change in *price,* other things constant, causes a *movement along a demand curve,* changing the quantity demanded. A change in one of the determinants of demand other than price causes a *shift of a demand curve,* changing demand.

**CHECKPOINT**

Identify five changes that could shift a market demand curve to the right.

4-3 Supply

Just as demand is a relation between price and quantity demanded, supply is a relation between price and quantity supplied. **Supply** indicates how much producers are *willing and able* to offer for sale per period at each possible price, other things constant. The **law of supply** states that the quantity supplied is usually directly related to its price, other things constant. Thus, the lower the price, the smaller the quantity supplied; the higher the price, the greater the quantity supplied.

4-3a Supply Schedule and Supply Curve

Exhibit 3 presents the market *supply schedule* and the market **supply curve** *S* for pizza. Both show the quantities supplied per week at various possible prices by the thousands of pizza makers in the economy. As you can see, price and quantity supplied are directly, or positively, related. Producers have a profit incentive to offer more at a higher price than at a lower price, so the supply curve slopes upward.

Here are two reasons why producers offer more for sale when the price rises. First, as the price increases, other things constant, a producer becomes more *willing* to supply

tastes
Consumer preferences; likes and dislikes in consumption; assumed to remain constant along a given demand curve

movement along a demand curve
A change in quantity demanded resulting from a change in the price of the good, other things constant

shift of a demand curve
Movement of a demand curve right or left resulting from a change in one of the determinants of demand other than the price of the good

supply
A relation between the price of a good and the quantity that producers are willing and able to sell per period, other things constant

law of supply
The amount of a good that producers are willing and able to sell per period is usually directly related to its price, other things constant

supply curve
A curve showing the relation between price of a good and the quantity producers are willing and able to sell per period other things constant

EXHIBIT 3	The Market Supply Schedule and Market Supply Curve for Pizza

(a) *Market supply schedule*

Price per Pizza	Quantity Supplied per Week (millions)
$15	28
12	24
9	20
6	16
3	12

(b) *Market supply curve*

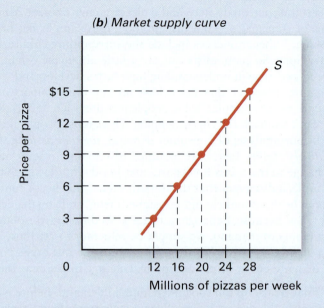

The market supply curve S shows the quantities of pizza supplied, at various prices, by all pizza makers. Price and quantity supplied are directly related.

the good. Prices act as signals to existing and potential suppliers about the rewards for producing various goods. A higher pizza price attracts resources from lower-valued uses. *A higher price makes producers more willing to increase quantity supplied.*

Second, higher prices also increase the producer's *ability* to supply the good. The law of increasing opportunity cost, as noted in Chapter 2, states that the opportunity cost of producing more of a particular good rises as output increases—that is, the *marginal cost* of production increases as output increases. Because producers face a higher marginal cost for additional output, they need to get a higher price for that output to be *able* to increase the quantity supplied. *A higher price makes producers more able to increase quantity supplied.* As a case in point, a higher price for gasoline increases a producer's ability to extract oil from tar sands, to drill deeper, and to explore in less accessible areas, such as the remote jungles of the Amazon, the stormy waters of the North Sea, or the frozen tundra above the Arctic Circle. For example, at a market price of $45 per barrel, extracting oil from tar sands is unprofitable, but at a price of $50 per barrel, such production is profitable.

Thus, a higher price makes producers more *willing* and more *able* to increase quantity supplied. Producers are more *willing* because production becomes more attractive than other uses of the resources involved. Producers are more *able* because they can afford to cover the higher marginal cost that typically results from increasing output.

On the other hand, a lower price makes production less attractive, so suppliers are less willing and less able to offer the good. For example, a mining company "reacted quickly to steep copper price declines in 2008 by curbing production at its North American sites and implementing layoffs at its mines and corporate headquarters."[1]

---

[1] Andrew Johnson, "Freeport Outsourcing Will Cut 60 Valley Jobs," *Arizona Republic*, 23 February 2010.

As with demand, we distinguish between *supply* and *quantity supplied*. *Supply* is the entire relationship between prices and quantities supplied, as reflected by the supply schedule or supply curve. **Quantity supplied** refers to a particular amount offered for sale at a particular price, as reflected by a point on a supply curve. We also distinguish between **individual supply**, which is the supply of an individual producer, and **market supply**, which is the sum of individual supplies of all producers in the market. Unless otherwise noted, the term *supply* refers to market supply.

 **CHECKPOINT**

Why does the supply curve usually slope upward?

quantity supplied
The amount offered for sale per period at a particular price, as reflected by a point on a supply curve

individual supply
The relation between the price of a good and the quantity an individual producer is willing and able to sell per period, other things constant

market supply
The relation between the price of a good and the quantity all producers in the market are willing and able to sell per period, other things constant

4-4 What Shifts a Supply Curve?

The supply curve isolates the relation between the price of a good and the quantity supplied, other things constant. Assumed constant along a supply curve are the determinants of supply other than the price of the good, including (1) the state of technology and know-how, (2) the prices of resources, (3) the prices of other goods, (4) producer expectations, and (5) the number of producers in the market. Let's see how a change in each affects the supply curve.

4-4a State of Technology and Know-How

Recall from Chapter 2 that the state of technology and know-how represents the economy's knowledge about how to combine resources efficiently. Along a given supply curve, technology and know-how are assumed to remain unchanged. If a better technology or a better production process is discovered, production costs will fall; so suppliers will be more willing and able to supply the good at each price. For example, new techniques helped Marathon Oil cut drilling time for a new well from 56 days in 2006 to only 24 days in 2009.[2] Consequently, supply will increase, as reflected by a rightward shift of the supply curve. In our pizza example, suppose a new, high-tech oven that costs the same as existing ovens can bake pizza in half the time. Such a breakthrough would shift the market supply curve rightward, as from *S* to *S'* in Exhibit 4, indicating that more is supplied at each possible price. For example, at a price of $12, the amount supplied increases from 24 million to 28 million pizzas per week, as shown in Exhibit 4 by the movement from point *g* to point *h*. In short, *an increase in supply—that is, a rightward shift of the supply curve—means that producers are willing and able to sell more pizza at each price.*

4-4b Resource Prices

The prices of resources employed to make the good affect the cost of production and therefore the supply of the good. For example, suppose the price of mozzarella cheese falls. This reduces the cost of making pizza, so producers are more willing and better able to supply pizza. The supply curve for pizza shifts rightward, as shown in Exhibit 4. On the other hand, an increase in the price of a resource reduces supply, meaning a shift of the supply curve leftward. For example, a higher price of mozzarella increases the cost of making pizza. Higher production costs decrease supply, as reflected by a leftward shift of the supply curve.

[2] Ben Casselman, "Oil Industry Boom—in North Dakota," *Wall Street Journal*, 26 February 2010.

4-4c Prices of Other Goods

Nearly all resources have alternative uses. The labor, building, machinery, ingredients, and knowledge needed to run a pizza business could produce other goods instead. A drop in the price of one of these other goods, with the price of pizza unchanged, makes pizza production more attractive. For example, if the price of Italian bread declines, some bread makers become pizza makers so the supply of pizza increases, shifting the supply curve of pizza rightward as in Exhibit 4. On the other hand, if the price of Italian bread increases, supplying pizza becomes relatively less attractive compared to supplying Italian bread. The opportunity cost of supplying pizza increases. As resources shift from pizza to bread, the supply of pizza decreases, or shifts to the left.

4-4d Producer Expectations

Changes in producer expectations can shift the supply curve. For example, if pizza makers expect higher pizza prices in the future, some will expand operations now, thereby shifting the supply curve rightward. If, however, a good can be easily stored (crude oil, for example, can be left in the ground), expecting higher prices in the future might prompt some producers to *reduce* their current supply while awaiting the higher price. Thus, an expectation of higher prices in the future could either increase or decrease current supply, depending on the good. More generally, any change affecting future profitability, such as a change in business taxes, could shift the supply curve now.

EXHIBIT 4	An Increase in the Market Supply of Pizza

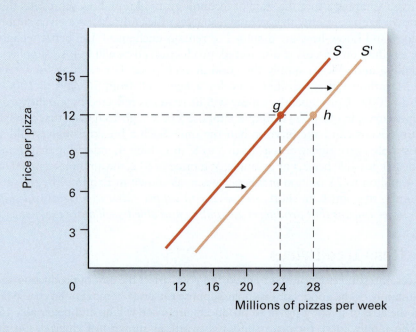

An increase in the market supply of pizza is reflected by a rightward shift of the supply curve, from S to S'. Quantity supplied increases at each price. For example, at a price of $12, the quantity supplied increases from 24 million pizzas (point g) to 28 million pizzas (point h).

4-4e Number of Producers in the Market

Because market supply sums the amounts supplied at each price by all producers in that market, market supply depends on the number of producers in that market. If that number increases, the supply will increase, shifting the supply curve to the right. If the number of producers decreases, supply will decrease, shifting the supply curve to the left. As an example of increased supply, the number of gourmet coffee bars has more than quadrupled in the United States since 1990 (think Starbucks), shifting the supply curve of gourmet coffee to the right.

Finally, note again the distinction between a **movement along a supply curve** and a **shift of a supply curve**. A change in *price*, other things constant, causes *a movement along a supply curve*, changing the quantity supplied. A change in one of the determinants of supply other than price causes a *shift of a supply curve*, changing supply.

You are now ready to bring demand and supply together.

CHECKPOINT

Identify five changes that could shift a market supply curve to the right.

4-5 Demand and Supply Create a Market

Demanders and suppliers have different views of price. Demanders pay the price and suppliers receive it. Thus, a higher price is bad news for consumers but good news for producers. As the price rises, consumers reduce their quantity demanded along the demand curve and producers increase their quantity supplied along the supply curve. How is this conflict between producers and consumers resolved?

4-5a Markets

Markets sort out differences between demanders and suppliers. A *market*, as you know from Chapter 1, includes all the arrangements used to buy and sell a particular good or service. Markets reduce **transaction costs**—the costs of time and information required for exchange. For example, suppose you are looking for a summer job. One approach might be to go from employer to employer looking for openings. But this could have you running around for days or weeks. A more efficient strategy would be to pick up a copy of the local newspaper or go online and look for job openings. Classified ads and Web sites, which are elements of the job market, reduce the transaction costs of bringing workers and employers together.

The coordination that occurs through markets takes place not because of some central plan but because of Adam Smith's "invisible hand." For example, auto dealers in your community tend to locate together, usually on the outskirts of town, where land is cheaper. The dealers congregate not because they all took an economics course or because they like one another's company but because grouped together they become a more attractive destination for car buyers. A dealer who makes the mistake of locating away from the others misses out on a lot of business. Similarly, stores locate together so that more shoppers will be attracted by the call of the mall. From Orlando theme parks to Broadway theaters to Las Vegas casinos, suppliers in a particular market tend to congregate to attract demanders. Some groupings can be quite specialized. For example, shops in Hong Kong that sell dress mannequins cluster along Austin Road. And diamond merchants in New York City congregate within the same few blocks.

movement along a supply curve

Change in quantity supplied resulting from a change in the price of the good, other things constant

shift of a supply curve

Movement of a supply curve left or right resulting from a change in one of the determinants of supply other than the price of the good

transaction costs

The costs of time and information required to carry out market exchange

4-5b Market Equilibrium

To see how a market works, let's bring together market demand and market supply. Exhibit 5 shows the market for pizza, using schedules in panel (a) and curves in panel (b). Please take a look now. Suppose the price initially is $12. At that price, producers supply 24 million pizzas per week, but consumers demand only 14 million, resulting in an *excess quantity supplied*, or a **surplus**, of 10 million pizzas per week. Producers compete by dropping the price. Suppliers don't like getting stuck with unsold pizzas. Competition among producers puts downward pressure on the price, as shown by the

surplus

At a given price, the amount by which quantity supplied exceeds quantity demanded; a surplus usually forces the price down

---

EXHIBIT 5   **Equilibrium in the Pizza Market**

(a) Market schedules

Millions of Pizzas per Week

Price per Pizza	Quantity Demanded	Quantity Supplied	Surplus or Shortage	Effect on Price
$15	8	28	Surplus of 20	Falls
12	14	24	Surplus of 10	Falls
9	20	20	Equilibrium	Remains the same
6	26	16	Shortage of 10	Rises
3	32	12	Shortage of 20	Rises

(b) Market curves

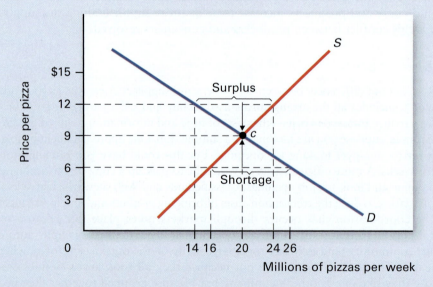

Market equilibrium occurs at the price where quantity demanded equals quantity supplied. This is shown at point *c*, where the price is $9 and the quantity is 20 million pizzas per week. Above the equilibrium price, quantity supplied exceeds quantity demanded. This creates a surplus, which puts downward pressure on the price. Below the equilibrium price, quantity demanded exceeds quantity supplied. The resulting shortage puts upward pressure on the price.

arrow pointing down in the graph. As the price falls, producers reduce their quantity supplied and consumers increase their quantity demanded. The price continues to fall as long as quantity supplied exceeds quantity demanded.

Alternatively, suppose the price initially is $6. You can see from Exhibit 5 that at that price consumers demand 26 million pizzas but producers supply only 16 million, resulting in an *excess quantity demanded*, or a **shortage**, of 10 million pizzas per week. Consumers compete to buy pizza, which is in short supply. Consumer competition forces the price higher. Profit-maximizing producers and eager consumers create market pressure for a higher price, as shown by the arrow pointing up in the graph. As the price rises, producers increase their quantity supplied and consumers reduce their quantity demanded. The price continues to rise as long as quantity demanded exceeds quantity supplied.

shortage
At a given price, the amount by which quantity demanded exceeds quantity supplied; a shortage usually forces the price up

Thus, *a surplus creates downward pressure on the price, and a shortage creates upward pressure*. As long as quantity demanded differs from quantity supplied, this difference forces a price change. Note that a shortage or a surplus depends on the price. There is no such thing as a general shortage or a general surplus, only a shortage or a surplus at a particular price.

To repeat, buyers prefer a lower price and sellers prefer a higher price. A market reaches equilibrium when the quantity demanded equals quantity supplied. In **equilibrium**, the independent plans of buyers and sellers exactly match, so market forces exert no pressure for change. In Exhibit 5, the demand and supply curves intersect at the *equilibrium point,* identified as point *c*. The *equilibrium price* is $9 per pizza, and the *equilibrium quantity* is 20 million per week. At that price and quantity, the market *clears*. Because there is no shortage or surplus, there is no pressure for the price to change. The demand and supply curves form an "x" at the intersection. You could say that the equilibrium point is found where "x" marks the spot.

equilibrium
The condition that exists in a market when the plans of buyers match those of sellers, so quantity demanded equals quantity supplied and the market clears

Markets indicate the price, quantity, and variety of goods available to you—from the latest social network to the smartest phone. You should be interested in equilibrium prices because they are what you usually pay for the thousands of goods and services you consume.

A market finds equilibrium through the independent actions of thousands, or even millions, of buyers and sellers. In one sense, the market is personal because each consumer and each producer makes a personal decision about how much to buy or sell at a given price. In another sense, the market is impersonal because it requires no conscious communication or coordination among consumers or producers. The price does all the talking. *Impersonal market forces synchronize the personal and independent decisions of many individual buyers and sellers to achieve equilibrium price and quantity*. Prices reflect relative scarcity. For example, to rent a 26-foot truck one-way from San Francisco to Austin, U-Haul recently charged $3,236. Its one-way charge for that same truck from Austin to San Francisco was just $399. Why the difference? Far more people wanted to move from San Francisco to Austin than vice versa, so U-Haul had to pay its own employees to drive the empty trucks back from Texas. Rental rates reflected that extra cost.

 **CHECKPOINT**

What forces the price down if it is above equilibrium? What forces the price up if it is below equilibrium?

4-6 Changes in Equilibrium Price and Quantity

Equilibrium occurs when the plans of demanders and suppliers exactly match. Once a market reaches equilibrium, that price and quantity remain stable until something affects demand or supply. A change in any non-price determinant of demand or supply usually changes equilibrium price and quantity in a predictable way, as you'll see.

4-6a Shifts of the Demand Curve

In Exhibit 6, demand curve D and supply curve S intersect at point c to yield the initial equilibrium price of $9 and the initial equilibrium quantity of 20 million 12-inch regular pizzas per week. Now suppose that one of the determinants of demand changes in a way that increases demand, shifting the demand curve to the right from D to D'. Any of the following could shift the demand for pizza rightward: (1) an increase in the money income of consumers (because pizza is a normal good); (2) an increase in the price of a substitute, such as tacos, or a decrease in the price of a complement, such as Pepsi; (3) a change in consumer expectations that causes people to demand more pizzas now; (4) a growth in the number of pizza consumers; or (5) a change in consumer tastes—based, for example, on a discovery that the tomato sauce on pizza has antioxidant properties that improve overall health.

After the demand curve shifts rightward to D' in Exhibit 6, the amount demanded at the initial price of $9 is 30 million pizzas, which exceeds the amount supplied of 20 million by 10 million pizzas. Competition among consumers for the limited quantity supplied puts

EXHIBIT 6   **Effects of an Increase in Market Demand**

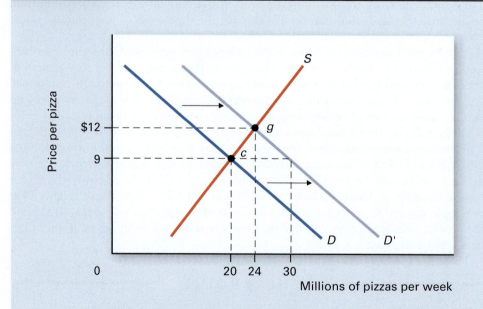

An increase in demand is shown by a shift of the demand curve rightward from D to D'. Quantity demanded exceeds quantity supplied at the original price of $9 per pizza; this shortage puts upward pressure on the price. As the price rises, quantity supplied increases along supply curve S, and quantity demanded decreases along demand curve D'. When the new equilibrium price of $12 is reached at point g, quantity demanded once again equals quantity supplied.

upward pressure on the price. As the price increases, the quantity demanded decreases along the new demand curve D', and the quantity supplied increases along the existing supply curve S until the two quantities are equal once again at equilibrium point g. The new equilibrium price is $12, and the new equilibrium quantity is 24 million pizzas per week. Thus, given an upward-sloping supply curve, an increase in demand increases both equilibrium price and quantity. For example, an increase in demand explains why roses cost more on Valentine's Day, why TV ads cost more on the Super Bowl broadcast, and why hotel rooms cost more in the host city during Super Bowl weekend.

A decrease in demand would initially create a surplus. Competition among producers to sell pizzas would lower both equilibrium price and quantity. These results can be summarized as follows: *Given an upward-sloping supply curve, a rightward shift of the demand curve increases both equilibrium price and quantity and a leftward shift decreases both equilibrium price and quantity.*

beyond foto/Getty Images

4-6b Shifts of the Supply Curve

Let's now consider shifts of the supply curve. In Exhibit 7, as before, we begin with demand curve D and supply curve S intersecting at point c to yield an equilibrium price

EXHIBIT 7 **Effects of an Increase in Market Supply**

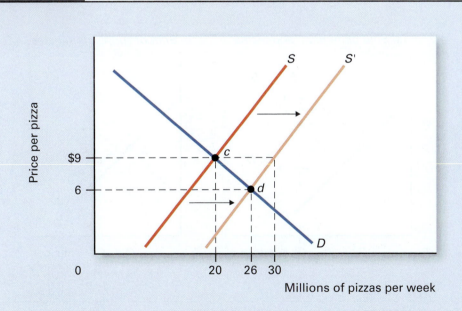

An increase in supply is shown by a shift of the supply curve rightward, from S to S'. Quantity supplied exceeds quantity demanded at the original price of $9 per pizza, putting downward pressure on the price. As the price falls, quantity supplied decreases along supply curve S', and quantity demanded increases along demand curve D. The new equilibrium price of $6 is reached at point d, where quantity demanded once again equals quantity supplied.

of $9 and an equilibrium quantity of 20 million pizzas per week. Suppose one of the determinants of supply changes, increasing supply from *S* to *S′*. Changes that could shift the supply curve rightward include (1) a technological breakthrough in pizza ovens; (2) a reduction in the price of a resource such as mozzarella cheese; (3) a decline in the price of another good such as Italian bread; (4) a change in expectations that encourages pizza makers to expand production now; or (5) an increase in the number of pizzerias.

After the supply curve shifts rightward in Exhibit 7, the amount supplied at the initial price of $9 increases from 20 million to 30 million, so producers now supply 10 million more pizzas than consumers demand. Pizza makers compete to sell the surplus by lowering the price. As the price falls, the quantity supplied declines along the new supply curve and the quantity demanded increases along the existing demand curve until a new equilibrium point *d* is established. The new equilibrium price is $6, and the new equilibrium quantity is 26 million pizzas per week. In short, an increase in supply reduces the price and increases the quantity. This recent *Wall Street Journal* headline captures the idea: "Global Oil Glut Sends Prices Plunging."[3] On the other hand, a decrease in supply increases the price but decreases the quantity. As a case in point, a recent worldwide shortage of baby eels, an Asian delicacy, rocketed the price to more than $2,000 per pound.[4] Thus, *given a downward-sloping demand curve, a rightward shift of the supply curve decreases price but increases quantity, and a leftward shift increases price but decreases quantity.*

4-6c Simultaneous Shifts of Demand and Supply Curves

As long as only one curve shifts, we can say how equilibrium price and quantity will change. If both curves shift, however, the outcome is less obvious. For example, suppose

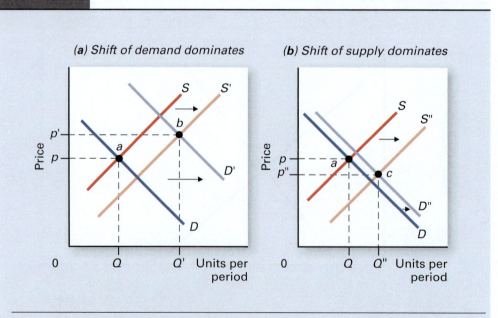

EXHIBIT 8   **Effects of an Increase in Both Demand and Supply**

(a) Shift of demand dominates   **(b)** Shift of supply dominates

When both demand and supply increase, the equilibrium quantity also increases. The effect on price depends on which curve shifts more. In panel (a), the demand curve shifts more, so the price rises. In panel (b), the supply curve shifts more, so the price falls.

[3.] Written by Russell Gold, this story appeared October 14, 2014.
[4.] Clark Canfield, "Candia Man Cited for 41 Pounds of Illegal Eels in Maine," *Concord Monitor*, 9 April 2013.

both demand and supply increase, or shift rightward, as in Exhibit 8. Note that in panel (a), demand shifts more than supply, and in panel (b), supply shifts more than demand. In both panels, equilibrium quantity increases. The change in equilibrium price, however, depends on which curve shifts more. If demand shifts more, as in panel (a), equilibrium price increases. For example, between 1995 and 2005, the demand for housing increased more than the supply, so both price and quantity increased. But if supply shifts more, as in panel (b), equilibrium price decreases. For example, in the last decade, the supply of personal computers has increased more than the demand, so price has decreased and quantity has increased.

Conversely, if both demand and supply decrease, or shift leftward, equilibrium quantity decreases. But, again, we cannot say what will happen to equilibrium price unless we examine relative shifts. (You can use Exhibit 8 to consider decreases in demand and supply by viewing D' and S' as the initial curves.) If demand shifts more, the price will fall. If supply shifts more, the price will rise.

If demand and supply shift in opposite directions, we can say what will happen to equilibrium price. Equilibrium price will increase if demand increases and supply decreases. Equilibrium price will decrease if demand decreases and supply increases. Without reference to particular shifts, however, we cannot say what will happen to equilibrium quantity.

These results are no doubt confusing, but Exhibit 9 summarizes the four possible combinations of changes. Using Exhibit 9 as a reference, please take the time right now to work through some changes in demand and supply to develop a feel for the results.

EXHIBIT 9   **Effects of Shifts of Both Demand and Supply**

Shift of demand

	Demand increases	Demand decreases
Supply increases	Equilibrium price change is indeterminate. Equilibrium quantity increases.	Equilibrium price falls. Equilibrium quantity change is indeterminate.
Supply decreases	Equilibrium price rises. Equilibrium quantity change is indeterminate.	Equilibrium price change is indeterminate. Equilibrium quantity decreases.

Shift of supply

When the demand and supply curves shift in the same direction, equilibrium quantity also shifts in that direction. The effect on equilibrium price depends on which curve shifts more. If the curves shift in opposite directions, equilibrium price will move in the same direction as demand. The effect on equilibrium quantity depends on which curve shifts more.

What happens to equilibrium price and quantity if demand and supply both increase?

4-7 Disequilibrium

disequilibrium
The condition that exists in a market when the plans of buyers do not match those of sellers; a temporary mismatch between quantity supplied and quantity demanded as the market seeks equilibrium

A surplus exerts downward pressure on the price, and a shortage exerts upward pressure. Markets, however, don't always reach equilibrium quickly. During the time required to adjust, the market is said to be in disequilibrium. **Disequilibrium** is usually temporary as market forces push toward equilibrium. But sometimes, often as a result of government intervention, when market forces are suppressed, disequilibrium can last a while, perhaps decades, as we will see next.

4-7a Price Floors

price floor
A minimum legal price below which a product cannot be sold; to have an impact, a price floor must be set above the equilibrium price

Sometimes public officials force a price above the equilibrium level. For example, the federal government regulates some agriculture prices in an attempt to ensure farmers a higher and more stable income than they would otherwise earn. To achieve a higher price, the government imposes a **price floor**, or a *minimum* selling price that is above the equilibrium price. Panel (a) of Exhibit 10 shows the effect of a $2.50 per gallon price floor for milk.

EXHIBIT 10   **Effects of Price Floors and Price Ceilings**

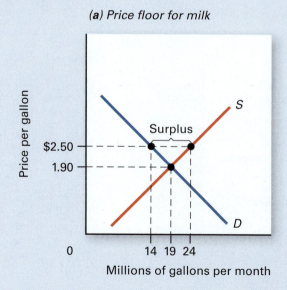

(a) Price floor for milk

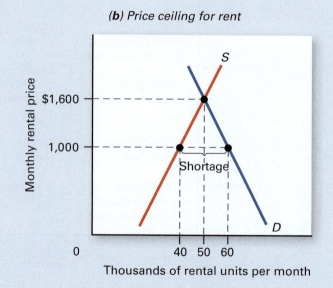

(b) Price ceiling for rent

A price floor set above the equilibrium price results in a surplus, as shown in panel (a). A price floor set at or below the equilibrium price has no effect. A price ceiling set below the equilibrium price results in a shortage, as shown in panel (b). A price ceiling set at or above the equilibrium price has no effect.

At that price, farmers supply 24 million gallons per week, but consumers demand only 14 million gallons, yielding a surplus of 10 million gallons. This surplus milk will pile up on store shelves, eventually souring. To take it off the market, the government usually agrees to buy the surplus milk. The federal government, in fact, has spent billions buying and storing surplus agricultural products over the years. Note, to have an impact, a price floor must be set *above* the equilibrium price. A price floor set at or below the equilibrium price wouldn't matter (how come?). Price floors distort markets and reduce economic welfare.

4-7b Price Ceilings

Sometimes public officials try to keep a price below the equilibrium level by setting a **price ceiling**, or a *maximum* selling price. Concern about the rising cost of rental housing in some cities prompted city officials to impose rent ceilings. Panel (b) of Exhibit 10 depicts the demand and supply of rental housing. The vertical axis shows monthly rent, and the horizontal axis shows the quantity of rental units. The equilibrium, or market-clearing, rent is $1,600 per month, and the equilibrium quantity is 50,000 housing units. Suppose city officials set a maximum rent of $1,000 per month. At that ceiling price, 60,000 rental units are demanded, but only 40,000 supplied, resulting in a housing shortage of 20,000 units. Because of the price ceiling, the rental price no longer rations housing to those who value it the most. Other devices emerge to ration housing, such as long waiting lists, personal connections, and the willingness to make under-the-table payments, such as "key fees," "finder's fees," high security deposits, and the like. To have an impact, a price ceiling must be set *below* the equilibrium price. A price ceiling set at or above equilibrium wouldn't matter. (Again, why not?) Price floors and price ceilings distort markets and reduce economic welfare. Let's take a closer look at rent ceilings in New York City in the following case study.

price ceiling
A maximum legal price above which a product cannot be sold; to have an impact, a price ceiling must be set below the equilibrium price

BRINGING THEORY TO LIFE

RENT CEILINGS IN NEW YORK CITY New York City rent controls began after World War I, when greater demand for rental housing threatened to push rents higher. To keep rents from rising to their equilibrium levels, city officials imposed rent ceilings. Because the quantity demanded at the ceiling rent exceeded the quantity supplied, a housing shortage resulted, as was sketched out in panel (b) of Exhibit 10. Thus, the perverse response to a tight housing market was a policy that reduced the quantity of rental housing over time. Rent controls during World War II created such shortages of rental housing that many families decided to become homeowners.

Prior to rent controls, builders in New York City completed about 30,000 housing units a year and 90,000 units in the peak year. After rent controls, new construction dropped sharply. To stimulate supply, the city periodically promised rent-ceiling exemptions for new construction. But three times the city broke that promise after the housing was built. So builders remain understandably wary. During the peak year of the last decade only about 10,000 new housing units were built.

The excess demand for housing in the rent-controlled sector spilled into the free-market sector, increasing demand there. This greater demand raised rents in the free-market sector, making a rent-controlled apartment that much more attractive. New York City rent regulations now cover nearly half of the 2.1 million rental apartments in the city.

Tenants in rent-controlled apartments can stay until they die, and with a little planning, they can pass the apartment to their heirs. They can even leave the apartment to a friend who has lived with them at least

continued

two years. Rent control forces tenants into housing choices they would not otherwise make. After the kids have grown and one spouse has died, the last parent standing usually remains in an apartment too big for one person but too much of a bargain to give up. An heir or a friend will often stay for the same reason. Some people keep rent-controlled apartments as weekend retreats for decades after they have moved out of New York City. All this wastes valuable resources, worsens the city's housing shortage, and raises rents in the unregulated market.

Because there is excess quantity demanded for rent-controlled apartments, landlords have less incentive to keep apartments in good shape. A survey found that about 30 percent of rent-controlled housing in the United States was deteriorating versus only 8 percent of free-market housing. Similar results have been found for England and France. Sometimes the rent is so low that owners simply abandon their property. During one decade, owners abandoned a third of a million units in New York City. So rent controls reduce both the quality and the quantity of housing available.

You would think that rent control benefits the poor most, but it hasn't worked out that way. Henry Pollakowski, an MIT housing economist, concludes that tenants in low- and moderate-income areas get little or no benefit from rent control. But some rich people living in a rent-controlled apartment in the nicest part of town get a substantial windfall. Someone renting in upscale sections of Manhattan might pay only $1,000 a month for a three-bedroom apartment that would rent for $12,000 a month on the open market. According to a recent study, more than 87,000 New York City households with incomes exceeding $100,000 a year benefited from rent control by paying below-market rents.

Once a tenant leaves a rent-controlled apartment, landlords can raise the rent on the next tenant and under some circumstances can escape rent controls entirely. With so much at stake, landlords under rent control have a strong incentive to oust tenants. Some landlords have been known to pay $5,000 bounties to doormen who report tenants violating their lease (for example, the apartment is not the tenant's primary residence or the tenant is illegally subletting). Landlords also hire private detectives to identify lease violators. And landlords use professional "facilitators" to negotiate with tenants about moving out. Many tenants end up getting paid hundreds of thousands of dollars for agreeing to move. Some have been paid more than $1 million. Facilitators can often find tenants a better apartment in the free-market sector along with enough cash to cover the higher rent for, say, 10 years. Since the rental market is in disequilibrium, other markets, such as the market for buying out tenants, kick in.

Sources: David Autor, Christopher Palmer, and Parag Pathak, "Housing Market Spillovers: Evidence from Rent Control in Cambridge Massachusetts," *Journal of Political Economy*, 122 (June 2014): 661–717; Daniel Fetter, "The Home Front: Rent Control and the Rapid Wartime Increase in Home Ownership," NBER Working Paper No. 19604 (October 2013); Edward Glaeser and Erzo Luttmer, "The Misallocation of Housing Under Rent Control," *American Economic Review*, 93 (September 1993): 1027–1046; Henry Pollakowski, "Who Really Benefits from New York City's Rent Regulation System?" Manhattan Institute, Civic Report 34 (March 2003) at http://manhattan-institute.org/pdf/cr_34.pdf; and Jacob Gershman, "1 BR, $1,000: Rent Control in Court Test," *Wall Street Journal*, 5 March 2012. The New York City Rent Guideline Board's Web site is at http://www.nycrgb.org/.

Government intervention is not the only source of market disequilibrium. Sometimes, when new products are introduced or when demand suddenly changes, it takes a while to reach equilibrium. For example, popular toys and best-selling books sometimes sell out. On the other hand, some products attract few customers and pile up unsold on store shelves, awaiting a "clearance sale."

CHECKPOINT

How does a product get allocated if government fixes a price below its equilibrium level?

4-8 Conclusion

Demand and supply are the building blocks of a market economy. Although a market usually involves the interaction of many buyers and sellers, few markets are consciously designed. Just as the law of gravity works whether or not we understand Newton's principles, market forces operate whether or not participants understand demand and supply. These forces arise naturally, much the way car dealers cluster on the outskirts of town to attract more customers.

Markets have their critics. Some observers may be troubled, for example, that Boston Patriots quarterback Tom Brady earns a salary that could pay 675 new schoolteachers $40,000 a year; or that corporate head Ralph Lauren earned enough in a recent year to pay for 1,600 new schoolteachers; or that U.S. consumers spend more than $60 billion a year on their pets.[5] On your next trip to the supermarket, notice how much shelf space goes to pet products—often an entire aisle. PetSmart, a chain store, sells over 12,000 different pet items. Veterinarians offer cancer treatment, cataract removal, root canals, kidney transplants, even acupuncture. Kidney dialysis for a pet can cost over $75,000 per year.

In a market economy, consumers are kings and queens. Consumer sovereignty rules, deciding what gets produced. Those who don't like the market outcome usually look to government for a solution through price ceilings and price floors, regulations, income redistribution, and public finance more generally.

Summary

1. Demand is a relationship between the price of a product and the quantity consumers are willing and able to buy per period, other things constant. According to the law of demand, quantity demanded varies negatively, or inversely, with the price, so the demand curve slopes downward.

2. A demand curve slopes downward for two reasons. A lower price makes consumers (a) more *willing* to substitute this good for other goods and (b) more *able* to buy the good because the lower price increases their real income.

3. Assumed constant along a demand curve are (a) money income, (b) prices of other goods, (c) consumer expectations, (d) the number or composition of consumers in the market, and (e) consumer tastes. A change in any of these could shift, or change, the demand curve.

4. Supply is a relationship between the price of a good and the quantity producers are willing and able to sell per period, other things constant. According to the law of supply, price and quantity supplied are usually positively, or directly, related, so the supply curve typically slopes upward.

[5] Arlene Weintraub, "The Rising Cost of Health Care—for Cats and Dogs," *Bloomberg Business,* 17 February 2015 at http://www.bloomberg.com/news/articles/2015-02-17/the-rising-costs-of-health-care-for-cats-and-dogs.

5. The supply curve slopes upward because higher prices make producers (a) more *willing* to supply this good rather than supply other goods that use many of the same resources and (b) more *able* to cover the higher marginal cost associated with greater output rates.

6. Assumed to remain constant along a supply curve are (a) the state of technology and know-how; (b) prices of resources used to produce the good; (c) prices of other goods that could be produced with these resources; (d) supplier expectations; and (e) the number of producers in this market. A change in any of these could shift, or change, the supply curve.

7. Demand and supply come together in the market for the good. A market provides information about the price, quantity, and quality of the good. In doing so, a market reduces the transaction costs of exchange—the costs of time and information required for buyers and sellers to make a deal. The interaction of demand and supply guides resources and products to their highest-valued use.

8. Impersonal market forces reconcile the personal and independent plans of buyers and sellers. Market equilibrium, once established, will continue unless there is a change in a determinant that shapes demand or supply. Disequilibrium is usually temporary while markets seek equilibrium, but sometimes disequilibrium lasts a while, such as when government regulates the price.

9. A price floor is the minimum legal price below which a particular good or service cannot be sold. The federal government imposes price floors on some agricultural products to help farmers achieve a higher and more stable income than would be possible with freer markets. If the floor price is set above the market clearing price, quantity supplied exceeds quantity demanded. Policy makers must figure out some way to prevent this surplus from pushing the price down.

10. A price ceiling is a maximum legal price above which a particular good or service cannot be sold. Governments sometimes impose price ceilings to reduce the price of some consumer goods such as rental housing. If the ceiling price is below the market clearing price, quantity demanded exceeds the quantity supplied, creating a shortage. Because the price system is not allowed to clear the market, other mechanisms arise to ration the product among demanders.

Key Concepts

Demand 67	Inferior good 71	Market supply 75
Law of demand 67	Substitutes 72	Movement along a supply curve 77
Substitution effect of a price change 68	Complements 72	Shift of a supply curve 77
Money income 68	Tastes 73	Transaction costs 77
Real income 68	Movement along a demand curve 73	Surplus 78
Income effect of a price change 68	Shift of a demand curve 73	Shortage 79
Demand curve 69	Supply 73	Equilibrium 79
Quantity demanded 70	Law of supply 73	Disequilibrium 84
Individual demand 70	Supply curve 73	Price floor 84
Market demand 70	Quantity supplied 75	Price ceiling 85
Normal good 71	Individual supply 75	

Questions for Review

1. **Law of Demand** What is the law of demand? Give two examples of how you have observed the law of demand at work in the "real world." How is the law of demand related to the demand curve?

2. **Changes in Demand** What variables influence the demand for a normal good? Explain why a reduction in the price of a normal good does not increase the demand for that good.

3. **Substitution and Income Effects** Distinguish between the substitution effect and income effect of a price change. If a good's price increases, does each effect have a positive or a negative impact on the quantity demanded?

4. **Demand** Explain the effect of an increase in consumer income on the demand for a good.

5. **Income Effects** When moving along the demand curve, income must be assumed constant. Yet one factor that can cause a change in the quantity demanded is the "income effect." Reconcile these seemingly contradictory facts.

6. **Demand** If chocolate is found to have positive health benefits, would this lead to a shift of the demand curve or a movement along the demand curve?

7. **Supply** What is the law of supply? Give an example of how you have observed the law of supply at work. What is the relationship between the law of supply and the supply curve?

8. **Changes in Supply** What kinds of changes in underlying conditions can cause the supply curve to shift? Give some examples and explain the direction in which the curve shifts.

9. **Supply**   If a severe frost destroys some of Florida's citrus crop, would this lead to a shift of the supply curve or a movement along the supply curve?

10. **Markets**   How do markets coordinate the independent decisions of buyers and sellers?

11. **Income Definitions**   What's the difference between money income and real income?

Problems and Exercises

12. **Shifting Demand**   Using demand and supply curves, show the effect of each of the following on the market for cigarettes:
    a. A cure for lung cancer is found.
    b. The price of cigars increases.
    c. Wages increase substantially in states that grow tobacco.
    d. A fertilizer that increases the yield per acre of tobacco is discovered.
    e. There is a sharp increase in the price of matches, lighters, and lighter fluid.
    f. More states pass laws restricting smoking in restaurants and public places.

13. **Substitutes and Complements**   For each of the following pair of goods, determine whether the goods are substitutes, complements, or unrelated:
    a. Peanut butter and jelly
    b. Private and public transportation
    c. Coke and Pepsi
    d. Alarm clocks and automobiles
    e. Golf clubs and golf balls

14. **Equilibrium**   "If a price is not an equilibrium price, there is a tendency for it to move to its equilibrium level. Regardless of whether the price is too high or too low to begin with, the adjustment process will increase the quantity of the good purchased." Explain, using a demand and supply diagram.

15. **Equilibrium**   Assume the market for corn is depicted as in the table that appears below.
    a. Complete the table below.
    b. What market pressure occurs when quantity demanded exceeds quantity supplied? Explain.
    c. What market pressure occurs when quantity supplied exceeds quantity demanded? Explain.
    d. What is the equilibrium price?
    e. What could change the equilibrium price?
    f. At each price in the first column of the table, how much is sold?

16. **Market Equilibrium**   Determine whether each of the following statements is true, false, or uncertain. Then briefly explain each answer.
    a. In equilibrium, all sellers can find buyers.
    b. In equilibrium, there is no pressure on the market to produce or consume more than is being sold.
    c. At prices above equilibrium, the quantity exchanged exceeds the quantity demanded.
    d. At prices below equilibrium, the quantity exchanged is equal to the quantity supplied.

17. **Demand and Supply**   How do you think each of the following affected the world price of oil? (Use demand and supply analysis.)
    a. Tax credits were offered for expenditures on home insulation.
    b. The Alaskan oil pipeline was completed.
    c. The ceiling on the price of oil was removed.
    d. Oil was discovered in the North Sea.
    e. Sport utility vehicles and minivans became popular.
    f. The use of nuclear power declined.

18. **Demand and Supply**   What happens to the equilibrium price and quantity of ice cream in response to each of the following? Explain your answers.
    a. The price of dairy cow fodder increases.
    b. The price of beef decreases.
    c. Concerns arise about the high fat content of ice cream. Simultaneously, the price of sugar (used to produce ice cream) increases.

19. **Equilibrium**   Consider the graph on the next page, where demand and supply are initially D and S. What are the equilibrium price and quantity? If demand increases to D', what are the new equilibrium price and quantity? What happens if the government does not allow the price to change when demand increases?

Price per Bushel ($)	Quantity Demanded (millions of bushels)	Quantity Supplied (millions of bushels)	Surplus/ Shortage	Will Price Rise or Fall?
1.80	320	200	_____	_____
2.00	300	230	_____	_____
2.20	270	270	_____	_____
2.40	230	300	_____	_____
2.60	200	330	_____	_____
2.80	180	350	_____	_____

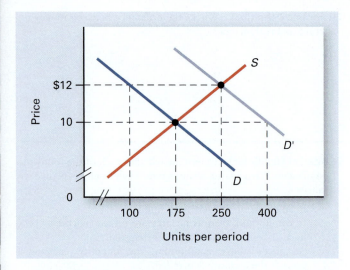

21. **Price Floor** There is considerable interest in whether the minimum wage rate contributes to teenage unemployment. Draw a demand and supply diagram for the unskilled labor market, and discuss the effects of a minimum wage. Who is helped and who is hurt by the minimum wage?

22. **Case Study: Rent Ceilings in New York City** Suppose the demand and supply curves for rental housing units have the typical shapes and that the rental housing market is in equilibrium. Then, government establishes a rent ceiling below the equilibrium level.

    a. What happens to the quantity of housing available?
    b. What happens to the quality of housing and why?
    c. Who benefits from rent control?
    d. Who loses from rent control?
    e. How do landlords of rent-controlled apartments try to get tenants to leave?

20. **Changes in Equilibrium** What are the effects on the equilibrium price and quantity of steel if the wages of steelworkers rise and, simultaneously, the price of aluminum rises?

Introduction to Macroeconomics

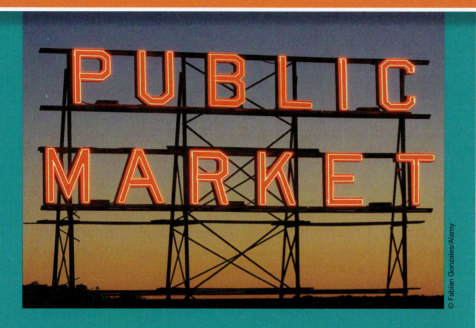

© Fabian Gonzales/Alamy

- *What's the big idea with macroeconomics?*
- *Why is its focus the national economy?*
- *How do we measure the economy's performance over time?*
- *Which has more impact on your standard of living, the economy's short-term ups and downs or the long-term growth trend?*
- *What's the difference between demand-side economics and supply-side economics?*
- *How has the economic role of government evolved during the last century?*
- *How is learning about the macroeconomy like learning about the weather?*

Answers to these and other questions are addressed in this chapter, which introduces macroeconomics.

Macroeconomics looks at the big picture—not the demand for Apple Watches but the demand for everything produced in the economy; not the price of gasoline but the average price of all goods and services produced in the economy; not consumption by the Martinez household but consumption by all households; not investment by Google but investment by all firms in the economy.

Macroeconomists develop and test theories about how the economy as a whole works—theories that can help predict the impact of economic policies and events. Macroeconomists are concerned not only with what determines such big-picture indicators as production, employment, and the price level but also with understanding how and why they change over time. Macroeconomists are especially interested in what makes an economy grow, because a growing economy creates more jobs and more goods and services—in short, more growth means a rising standard of living. What determines the economy's ability to use resources productively, to adapt, to grow? This chapter begins exploring such questions.

Topics discussed in this chapter include:

- The national economy
- Economic fluctuations
- Aggregate demand
- Aggregate supply
- Equilibrium price level and aggregate output

- Brief history of the U.S. economy
- Demand-side economics
- Stagflation
- Supply-side economics
- The Great Recession of 2007–2009

5-1 The National Economy

economy
The structure of economic activity in a community, a region, a country, a group of countries, or the world

gross domestic product (GDP)
The market value of all final goods and services produced in the nation during a particular period, usually a year

Macroeconomics concerns the overall performance of the *economy*. The term **economy** describes the structure of economic activity, in a community, a region, a country, a group of countries, or the world. We could talk about the Chicago economy, the Illinois economy, the Midwest economy, the U.S. economy, the North American economy, or the world economy. We measure an economy in different ways, such as the amount produced, the number of people working, or their total income. The most common yardstick is *gross product,* which measures the market value of all final goods and services produced in a particular geographical region during a given period, usually one year.

If the focus is the Illinois economy, we consider the *gross state product*. If the focus is the U.S. economy, we consider the **gross domestic product**, or **GDP**, which measures the market value of all final goods and services produced in the United States during a given period, usually a year. GDP adds up production of the economy's incredible variety of goods and services, from trail bikes to pedicures. We can use the gross domestic product to compare different economies at the same time or to track the same economy over time.

We could also consider the **gross world product**, which measures the value of all final goods and services produced in the world during a given period, usually a year. Just as a point of reference, the gross world product was estimated to be about $105 trillion in 2014, up 3.3 percent from the year before.[1] The United States, with 4.5 percent of the world's population in 2014, accounted for 17 percent of gross world product. The focus of macroeconomics is usually the national economy

gross world product
The market value of all final goods and services produced in the world during a given period, usually a year

5-1a What's Special About the National Economy?

The national economy deserves special attention. Here's why: If you were to drive west on Interstate 10 in Texas, you would hardly notice crossing into New Mexico. But if, instead, you took the Juarez exit south into Mexico, you would be stopped at the border and asked for identification, and you and your vehicle could be searched. You would become quite aware of crossing an international border. Like most other countries, the United States and Mexico usually allow people and goods to move more freely *within* their borders than *across* their borders.

The differences between the United States and Mexico are far greater than the differences between Texas and New Mexico. For example, each country has its own standard of living and currency, its own culture and language, its own communication and transportation system, its own system of government, and its own "rules of the game"—that is, its own laws, regulations, customs, manners, and ways of doing business both within and across its borders.

Macroeconomics typically focuses on the performance of the national economy, including how the national economy interacts with other national economies around the world. The U.S. economy is one of the largest and most complex in world history, with about 120 million households, more than 30 million for-profit businesses, and about 89,150 government jurisdictions. The world economy includes about 200 sovereign nations, ranging in population from tiny Liechtenstein, with only 37,000 people, to China, with 1.4 billion, or about 38,000 Liechtensteins. These numbers offer snapshots, but the economy is a motion picture, a work in progress—too complex to capture in snapshots. That's why we use theoretical models to focus on key relationships. To help you get your mind around the economy, let's begin with a simple analogy.

5-1b The Human Body and the U.S. Economy

Consider the similarities and differences between the human body and the economy. The body consists of millions of cells, each performing particular functions yet each linked to the entire body. Similarly, the U.S. economy is composed of millions of decision makers, each acting with some independence yet each connected with the economy as a whole. The economy, like the body, is continually renewing itself, with new households, new businesses, a changing cast of public officials, and new foreign competitors and customers. Blood circulates throughout the body, facilitating the exchange of oxygen and vital nutrients among cells. Similarly, *money* circulates throughout the economy, facilitating the exchange of resources and products among individual economic units. In fact, blood and money are each called a *medium of exchange*. In Chapter 1 we saw that the movement of money, products, and resources throughout the economy follows a *circular flow,* as does the movement of blood, oxygen, and nutrients throughout the body.

[1.] Central Intelligence Agency, *World Factbook*, at https://www.cia.gov/library/publications/the-world-factbook/geos/xx.html; and The World Bank at http://data.worldbank.org/.

Flow and Stock Variables

Just as the same blood recirculates as a medium of exchange in the body, the same dollars recirculate as a medium of exchange in the economy to finance transactions. The dollars you spend on bagels are spent by the baker on butter and then spent by the dairy farmer on work boots. Dollars *flow* through the economy. To measure a flow, we use a **flow variable**, which is an amount per period of time, such as your average spending per week or your heartbeats per minute. In contrast, a **stock variable** is an amount measured at a particular point in time, such as the amount of money you have with you right now or your current weight.

Testing New Theories

Physicians and other natural scientists test their theories using controlled experiments. Macroeconomists, however, have no laboratories and little ability to run economy-wide experiments of any kind. Granted, they can study different economies around the world, but each economy is unique, so comparisons are tricky. Controlled experiments also provide the natural sciences with something seldom available to economists—the chance, or serendipitous, discovery (such as penicillin). Macroeconomists studying the U.S. economy have only one patient, so they can't introduce particular policies in a variety of alternative settings. You can't squeeze economies into a test tube. Cries of "Eureka!" are seldom heard from macroeconomists. An economy consisting of hundreds of millions of individual actors is a complicated thing. As Nobel Prize–winning physicist Murray Gell-Mann once observed, "Think how hard physics would be if particles could think."

5-1c Knowledge and Performance

Throughout much of history, little was known about how the human body works, yet many people still enjoyed good health. For example, the fact that blood circulates in the body was not established until 1638; it took scientists another 150 years to figure out why. Similarly, over the millennia, various complex economies developed and flourished, although at the time there was little understanding about how an economy worked.

The economy is much like the body: As long as it functions smoothly, policy makers need not understand how it works. But if a problem arises—severe unemployment, high inflation, or sluggish growth, for example—we must know how a healthy economy works before we can consider whether anything can be done. We need not know every detail of the economy, just as we need not know every detail of the body. But we must understand essential relationships among key variables. For example, does the economy work well on its own, or does it often perform poorly? If it performs poorly, are there public-policy remedies? Can we be sure that a proposed remedy would not do more harm than good? When doctors didn't understand how the human body worked, their attempted "cures" were often worse than the diseases. Much of the history of medicine describes misguided efforts to deal with disease. For example, when George Washington became ill in 1799, doctors drained half his blood, believing that this bloodletting would cure him. Instead, he died. The best doctors in the land couldn't help Washington because they did not understand how the human body works.

Even today, medical care is based on less scientific evidence than you might think. According to one study, only one in seven medical interventions was supported by reliable scientific evidence.[2] For example, acetaminophen (e.g., Tylenol) is a popular pain

---

[2.] As reported by Sherwin B. Nuland, "Medical Fads: Bran, Midwives and Leeches," *New York Times*, 25 January 1995.

reliever, but nobody really knows how it works. According to an old saying, "Nature heals and the doctor collects the fee." Or as Voltaire wrote, "The art of medicine consists of amusing the patient while nature cures the disease."

Likewise, policy makers may adopt the wrong prescription because of a flawed theory about how the economy works. At one time, for example, a nation's economic vitality was thought to spring from the stock of precious metals accumulated in the public treasury. This theory spawned a policy called **mercantilism**, which held that, as a way of accumulating gold and silver, a nation should try to export more than it imports. To pursue this, nations restricted imports by such barriers as tariffs and quotas. But these restrictions led to retaliations by other countries, reducing international trade and the gains from specialization. Another flawed economic theory prompted President Herbert Hoover to introduce a major tax *increase* during the Great Depression. Economists have since learned that such a policy does more harm than good. Debates about the effectiveness of government policies were widespread as officials reacted to the crushing recession of 2007–2009, now known as the Great Recession.

We turn now to the performance of the U.S. economy.

mercantilism
The incorrect theory that a nation's economic objective should be to accumulate precious metals in the public treasury; this theory prompted trade barriers, which cut imports, but other countries retaliated, reducing trade and the gains from specialization

 **CHECKPOINT**

What's special about a national economy compared to regional, state, or local economies?

5-2 Economic Fluctuations and Growth

The U.S. economy and other industrial market economies historically have experienced alternating periods of expansion and contraction in economic activity. As noted in Chapter 1, *economic fluctuations* are the rise and fall of economic activity relative to the long-term growth trend of the economy. These fluctuations, or *business cycles,* vary in length and intensity, yet some features appear common to all. The ups and downs usually involve the entire nation and often many other economies around the world, and they affect nearly all dimensions of economic activity, not just production and employment.

5-2a U.S. Economic Fluctuations

Perhaps the easiest way to understand the business cycle is to examine its components. During the 1920s and 1930s, Wesley C. Mitchell, director of the National Bureau of Economic Research (NBER), analyzed business cycles, noting that the economy has two phases: *expansions* and *contractions*. During an **expansion**, the economy grows as reflected by rising output, employment, income, and other aggregate measures. During a **contraction**, the economy declines as reflected by falling output, employment, income, and other aggregate measures. A contraction might be so sharp as to be called a **depression**, which is a severe and prolonged reduction in the nation's economic activity, as occurred during the 1930s. A milder contraction is called a **recession**, which is a period of decline in economic activity lasting more than a few months, as reflected by falling output employment, income, and other aggregate measures. The U.S. economy experienced both recessions and depressions before World War II. Since then, there have been recessions but no depressions, so things have improved.

expansion
A period during which the economy grows as reflected by rising output, employment, income, and other aggregate measures

contraction
A period during which the economy declines as reflected by falling output, employment, income, and other aggregate measures

depression
A severe and prolonged reduction in economic activity, as occurred during the 1930s

recession
A period of decline in economic activity lasting more than a few months, as reflected by falling output, employment, income, and other aggregate measures

inflation

An increase in the economy's average price level

Despite these ups and downs, the U.S. economy has grown dramatically over the long term. Although economic activity is measured in a variety of ways, if we had to settle on a single indicator, *output* best captures what's going on. The economy in 2014 produced 15 times more output than it did in 1929. Output is measured by real GDP, the value of final goods and services after stripping away changes due to **inflation**, which is an increase in the economy's average price level. Production increased because of (1) increases in the amount and quality of resources, especially labor and capital; (2) better technology and know-how; and (3) improvements in the *rules of the game* that facilitate production and exchange, such as property rights, patent laws, the legal system, and market practices.

Exhibit 1 shows the long-term growth trend in economic activity as an upward-sloping straight line. Economic fluctuations reflect movements around this growth trend. A contraction begins after the previous expansion has reached a *peak,* or high point, and continues until the economy reaches a *trough,* or low point. The period between a peak and trough is a *contraction,* and the period between a trough and subsequent peak is an *expansion.* Note that expansions last longer than contractions, but the length of the full cycle varies.

Analysts at the NBER have tracked the U.S. economy back to 1854. Since then, the nation has experienced 33 peak-to-trough-to-peak cycles. No two have been exactly alike. During the 22 business cycles prior to 1945, expansions averaged 29 months and contractions 21 months. During the 11 cycles since 1945, expansions stretched twice as long to 57 months, and recessions fell by nearly half to 11 months—so expansions averaged nearly five years and recessions nearly one year. Thus, since 1945 expansions are longer and recessions are shorter. Both developments have been hugely beneficial

EXHIBIT 1	**Hypothetical Business Cycles**

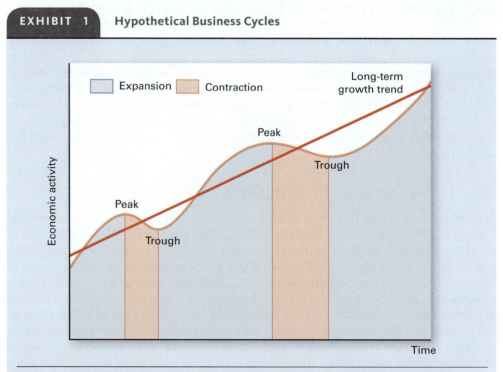

Business cycles reflect movements of economic activity around a trend line that shows long-term growth. An expansion (shaded in blue) begins when the economy starts to grow and continues until the economy reaches a peak. After an expansion has peaked, a contraction (shaded in pink) begins and continues until the economy reaches a trough.

for economic growth and the U.S. standard of living. The longest expansion on record lasted ten years, from March 1991 to March 2001. The longest contraction lasted five and a half years, from 1873 to 1879.

Exhibit 2 shows annual percentage changes in real GDP since 1929. Years of declining real GDP are shown as red bars and years of increasing real GDP as blue bars. The big decline during the Great Depression of the early 1930s and the sharp jump during World War II stand in stark contrast. Growth since 1929 has averaged 3.3 percent a year.

The intensity of U.S. economic fluctuations varies across regions. A recession hits hardest those regions that produce more capital goods, such as heavy machinery, and durable goods, such as appliances, furniture, and automobiles. The demand for these goods falls more during hard times than does the demand for other goods and services, such as breakfast cereal, electricity, and haircuts. Recessions also hit hardest those states that rely more on housing construction such as Arizona, California, Florida, and Nevada.

Because of seasonal fluctuations and random disturbances, the economy does not move smoothly through phases of the business cycle. Economists can't always distinguish a temporary drop in economic activity from the beginning of a downturn. A drop in economic activity may result from a temporary slowdown, such as a snowstorm or a poor growing season. Turning points—peaks and troughs—are thus identified by the NBER only after the fact. Because a recession means economic activity declines for more than a few months (two quarters, or six months, is sometimes used as a rule of thumb), and because the official announcement that a recession has begun is not made until months after that, we sometimes don't know for sure when a recession starts until a year later (as was the case with the recession that began in December 2007).

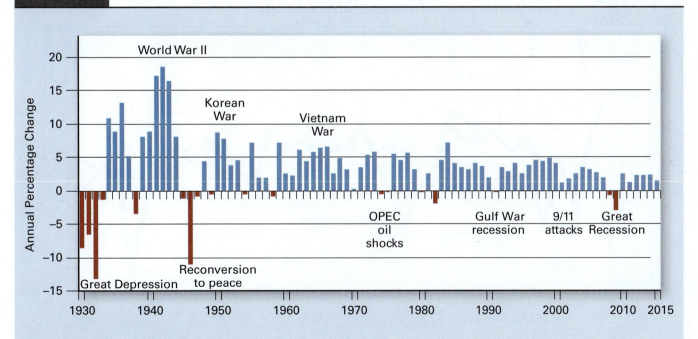

EXHIBIT 2 | **Annual Percentage Change in U.S. Real GDP Since 1929**

Years of declining real GDP are shown as red bars and years of growth as blue bars. Note that the year-to-year swings in output became less pronounced after World War II.

Source: Bureau of Economic Analysis, U.S. Dept. of Commerce. For the latest data, go to http://bea.gov/national/index.htm#gdp. The growth rate for 2015 is based on official quarterly estimates through the first half of the year.

Likewise, a recession's end is sometimes not announced until a year or more after it's over (for example, the Great Recession ended in June 2009, but the official announcement of that fact did not come until 15 months later).

5-2b The Global Economy

As noted, fluctuations usually involve the entire nation. Indeed, major economies around the world often fluctuate together. Though business cycles are not perfectly synchronized across countries, a link is usually apparent. Economies are related through international trade, finance, and migration, and ties grow stronger each year. For example, U.S. exports as a share of U.S. output are now double what they were four decades ago. Consider the experience of two leading economies—the United States and the United Kingdom, nations separated by the Atlantic Ocean. Exhibit 3 shows for each country the year-to-year percentage changes in real GDP since 1978. Again, *real* means that the effects of inflation have been erased, so remaining changes reflect *real* changes in the total value of goods and services produced each year.

If you spend a minute looking at the annual changes, you will notice the similarities. For example, both economies went into recession in the early 1980s, grew strongly for the rest of the decade, entered another recession in 1991, then recovered for the rest of that decade. After a short recession in 2001, both economies grew until the Great Recession of 2007–2009, when they both took a dive. After that, both economies recovered.

EXHIBIT 3	U.S. and U.K. Annual Growth Rates in Output Are Similar

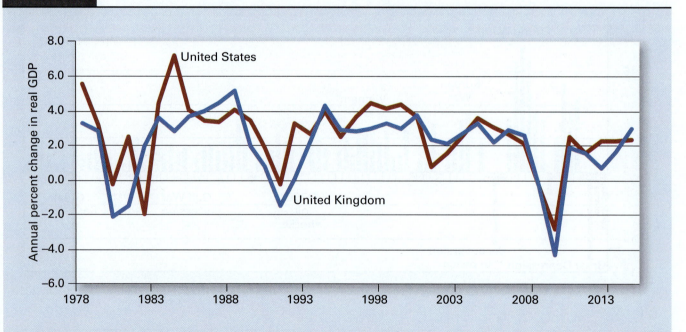

Source: Bureau of Economic Analysis, U.S. Dept. of Commerce. For the latest data, go to http://bea.gov/national/index.htm#gdp. And *OECD Economic Outlook*, 97 (May 2015), Annex Table 1.

One problem with the linkage across economies is that a slump in another major economy can worsen a recession in the United States and vice versa. For example, the Great Recession of 2007–2009 affected economies around the world, increasing unemployment and cutting production. Trouble in seemingly minor economies, such as Greece, can sometimes spill over and drag down other economies with them. On the brighter side, economic strength abroad can give the U.S. economy a lift, as reflected by the recent headline "IMF Says Asia to Lead Growth in 2015."[3] The point is that the U.S. economy depends more and more on what's going on with the rest of the world and vice versa.

5-2c Leading Economic Indicators

Certain events foreshadow a turning point in economic activity. Months before a recession is fully under way, changes in leading economic indicators point to the coming storm. In the early stages of a recession, business slows down, orders for machinery and computers slip, and the stock market, anticipating lower profits, turns down. Consumer confidence in the economy also begins to sag, so households spend less, especially on big-ticket items like homes and automobiles. Unsold goods start piling up. All these signs are called **leading economic indicators** because they usually predict, or *lead to*, a downturn. Likewise, upturns in leading indicators point to an economic recovery. But leading indicators cannot predict precisely *when* a turning point will occur, or even *whether* one will occur. Sometimes leading indicators sound a false alarm.

Some economic indicators measure what's going on in the economy right now. **Coincident economic indicators** are those measures that reflect expansions, contractions, peaks, and troughs as they occur. Coincident indicators include total employment, personal income, and industrial production. And some economic indicators measure what has already happened. **Lagging economic indicators** follow, or trail, changes in overall economic activity. Lagging indicators, which look at the economy through the rearview mirror, include interest rates, the unemployment rate, and how long people remain unemployed.

Our introduction to business cycles has been largely mechanical, focusing on the history and measurement of these fluctuations. We have not discussed why economies fluctuate, in part because such a discussion requires firmer footing in macroeconomic theory and in part because the causes remain in dispute. In the next section, we begin to build a macroeconomic framework by introducing a key model of analysis.

leading economic indicators
Variables that predict, or *lead to*, a recession or recovery; examples include consumer confidence, stock market prices, business investment, and big-ticket purchases, such as automobiles and homes

coincident economic indicators
Variables that reflect peaks and troughs in economic activity as they occur; examples include employment, personal income, and industrial production

lagging economic indicators
Variables that follow, or trail, changes in overall economic activity; examples include the interest rate, the unemployment rate, and the average duration of unemployment

CHECKPOINT

Describe the phases of the business cycle.

5-3 Aggregate Demand and Aggregate Supply

The economy is so complex that we need to simplify matters, or to abstract from the millions of relationships to isolate the important ones. We must step back from all the individual economic transactions to survey the resulting mosaic.

[3.] This headline appeared above a story written by Elaine Kurtenbach in *The Arizona Republic*, 8 May 2015.

5-3a Aggregate Output and the Price Level

Let's begin with something you already know. Picture a pizza. Now picture food more generally. Food, of course, includes not just pizza but thousands of other items. Although food is more general than pizza, you probably have no difficulty picturing food. Now make the leap from food to all goods and services produced in the economy—food, housing, clothing, entertainment, transportation, health care, and so on. Economists call this **aggregate output**. Because *aggregate* means total, aggregate output is the total amount of goods and services produced in the economy during a given period. Because output is measured per period, it's a flow measure. The best measure of aggregate output is *real GDP*, which you'll soon learn more about.

Just as we can talk about the demand for pizza, or the demand for food, we can talk about the demand for aggregate output. **Aggregate demand** is the relationship between the average price of aggregate output in the economy and the quantity of aggregate output demanded. The average price of aggregate output is called the economy's **price level**. You are more familiar with these aggregate measures than you may think. Headlines refer to the growth of aggregate output—as in "Growth Slows in Second Quarter." News accounts also report on changes in the "cost of living," reflecting movements in the economy's price level—as in "Prices Jump in June."

In a later chapter, you learn how the economy's price level is computed. All you need to know now is that the price level in any year is an *index number,* or a reference number, comparing average prices that year with average prices in some base, or reference, year. If we say that the price level is higher, we mean compared with where it was. In Chapter 4, we talked about the price of a particular product, such as pizza, *relative to the prices of other products*. Now we talk about the *average price* of all goods and services produced in the economy *relative to the price level in some base year*.

The price level in the *base year* is standardized to a benchmark value of 100, and price levels in other years are expressed relative to the base-year price level. For example, in 2014, the U.S. price level, or price index, was 108.3, indicating that the price level that year was 8.3 percent higher than its value of 100 in the base year of 2009. The price level, or price index, is used not only to compare prices over time but also to compare real aggregate output over time. Economists use the *price index* to eliminate year-to-year changes in GDP due solely to changes in the price level. What's left is the change in real output—the change in the amount of goods and services produced. After adjusting GDP for price level changes, we end up with what is called the **real gross domestic product**, or **real GDP**. So the price index (1) shows how the economy's price level changes over time and (2) is used to figure out real GDP each year. You'll get a better idea of these two roles as we discuss the U.S. economy.

5-3b Aggregate Demand Curve

In Chapter 4, you learned about the demand for a particular product, such as pizza. Now let's talk about the demand for our composite measure of output—aggregate output, or real GDP. The **aggregate demand curve** shows the relationship between the price level in the economy and real GDP demanded, other things constant. Exhibit 4 shows a hypothetical aggregate demand curve, *AD*. The vertical axis measures an index of the economy's price level relative to a 2009 base-year price level of 100. The horizontal axis shows real GDP, which measures output in dollars of constant purchasing power (here we use 2009 prices).

The aggregate demand curve in Exhibit 4 reflects an inverse relationship between the price level in the U.S. economy and real GDP demanded. Aggregate demand sums demands of the four economic decision makers: households, firms, governments, and

---

aggregate output

A composite measure of all final goods and services produced in an economy during a given period; real GDP

aggregate demand

The relationship between the economy's price level and aggregate output demanded, with other things constant

price level

A composite measure reflecting the prices of all goods and services in the economy relative to prices in a base year

real gross domestic product (real GDP)

The economy's aggregate output measured in dollars of constant purchasing power

aggregate demand curve

A curve representing the relationship between the economy's price level and real GDP demanded per period, with other things constant

EXHIBIT 4 **U.S. Aggregate Demand Curve**

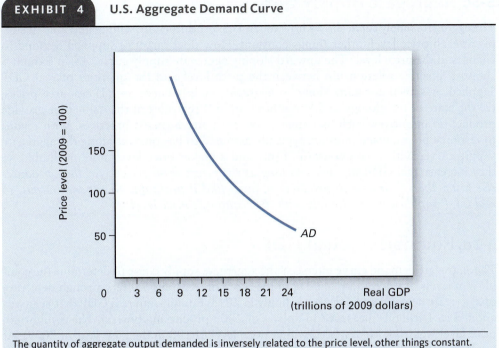

The quantity of aggregate output demanded is inversely related to the price level, other things constant. This inverse relationship is reflected by the aggregate demand curve *AD*.

the rest of the world. As the price level increases, other things constant, households demand less housing and furniture, firms demand fewer trucks and tools, governments demand less computer software and military hardware, and the rest of the world demands less U.S. grain and U.S. aircraft.

The reasons behind this inverse relationship get a closer look in later chapters, but here's a quick summary. Real GDP demanded depends in part on household *wealth*. Some wealth is usually held in bank accounts and in currency. An increase in the price level, other things constant, decreases the purchasing power of bank accounts and currency. Households are therefore poorer when the price level increases, so the quantity of real GDP they demand decreases. Conversely, a reduction in the price level increases the purchasing power of bank accounts and currency. Because households are richer as the price level decreases, the quantity of real GDP they demand increases.

Factors held constant along a given aggregate demand curve include the price levels in other countries as well as the exchange rates between the U.S. dollar and foreign currencies. When the U.S. price level increases, U.S. products become more expensive relative to foreign products. Consequently, households, firms, and governments both here and abroad decrease the quantity of U.S. products demanded. On the other hand, a lower U.S. price level makes U.S. products cheaper relative to foreign products, so the quantity of U.S. products demanded increases.

Consider the demand for a particular product versus aggregate demand. If the price of a particular product, such as pizza, increases, quantity demanded declines in part because pizza becomes more costly compared to substitutes. If the U.S. economy's price level increases, the quantity of U.S. real GDP demanded declines in part because U.S. products become more costly compared to foreign products.

5-3c Aggregate Supply Curve

aggregate supply curve
A curve representing the relationship between the economy's price level and real GDP supplied per period, with other things constant

The **aggregate supply curve** shows how much U.S. producers are willing and able to supply at each price level, other things constant. How does quantity supplied respond to changes in the price level? The upward-sloping aggregate supply curve, *AS*, in Exhibit 5 shows a positive relationship between the price level and the quantity of real GDP supplied. Assumed constant along an aggregate supply curve are (1) resource prices, (2) the state of technology and know-how, and (3) the rules of the game that provide production incentives, such as patents, tax rates, and business practices. With regard to resource prices, wage rates are typically assumed to be constant along the aggregate supply curve. With wages constant, firms find a higher price level more profitable, so they increase real GDP supplied. *As long as the prices firms receive for their products rise faster than their cost of production, firms find it profitable to expand output, so real GDP supplied varies directly with the economy's price level.*

5-3d Equilibrium Real GDP

The aggregate demand curve intersects the aggregate supply curve to determine the equilibrium levels of price and real GDP in the economy. Exhibit 5 offers a rough depiction of aggregate demand and aggregate supply in 2014. Equilibrium real GDP that year was about $16.1 trillion (measured in dollars of 2009 purchasing power). The equilibrium price level was 108.3 (compared with a price level of 100 in the base year of 2009). At any other price level, quantity demanded would not match quantity supplied.

Incidentally, although employment is not measured directly along the horizontal axis, firms usually must hire more workers to produce more output. So higher levels of real GDP can be beneficial because (1) more goods and services become available in

---

EXHIBIT 5 **U.S. Aggregate Demand and Aggregate Supply in 2014**

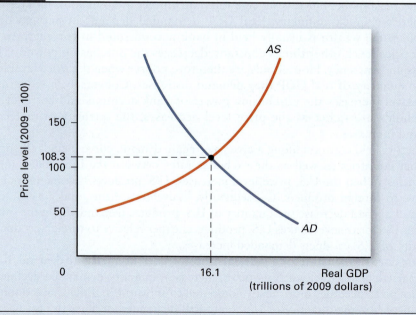

The total output of the economy and its price level are determined at the intersection of the aggregate demand and aggregate supply curves. This point reflects real GDP and the price level for 2014, using 2009 as the base year.

the economy, and (2) more people are employed. Perhaps the best way to understand aggregate demand and aggregate supply is to apply these tools to the U.S. economy. The following section simplifies U.S. economic history to review changes in the price and output levels over time.

CHECKPOINT

Explain the shapes of the aggregate demand curve and the aggregate supply curve.

5-4 A Brief History of the U.S. Economy

The history of the U.S. economy can be divided roughly into five economic eras: (a) before and during the Great Depression, (b) after the Great Depression to the early 1970s, (c) from the early 1970s to the early 1980s, (d) from the early 1980s to 2007, and (e) the Great Recession of 2007–2009 and beyond. The first era suffered from recessions and depressions, culminating in the Great Depression of the 1930s. These depressions were often accompanied by a falling price level. The second era was one of generally strong economic growth, with only moderate increases in the price level. The third era saw both high unemployment and high inflation at the same time, a troubling combination. The fourth era was more like the second, with good economic growth on average and only moderate increases in the price level. And the fifth era brought us the worst recession since the Great Depression. It remains to be seen whether the Great Recession turns out to be just a temporary setback or has long-term consequences for the United States and the world.

5-4a The Great Depression and Before

Before World War II, the U.S. economy alternated between hard times and prosperity. As noted earlier, the longest contraction on record occurred between 1873 and 1879, when 80 railroads went bankrupt and most of the nation's steel mills shut down. During the 1890s, the economy contracted about half the time, and the unemployment rate topped 18 percent. In October 1929, the stock market crash began what was to become the deepest, though not the longest, economic contraction in our nation's history, the Great Depression of the 1930s.

In terms of aggregate demand and aggregate supply, the Great Depression can be viewed as a shift to the left of the aggregate demand curve, as shown in Exhibit 6. AD_{1929} depicts the aggregate demand curve in 1929, before the onset of the depression. Real GDP in 1929 was $1,057 billion (measured in dollars of 2009 purchasing power), and the price level was 9.9 (relative to a 2009 base-year price level of 100). By 1933, aggregate demand shifted leftward, decreasing to AD_{1933}. Why did aggregate demand decline? Though economists still debate the exact causes, most agree that the stock market crash of 1929 was the trigger. From there, grim business expectations cut investment, consumer spending fell, banks failed, the nation's

Russell Kord / Alamy

EXHIBIT 6   **The Decrease in U.S. Aggregate Demand From 1929 to 1933**

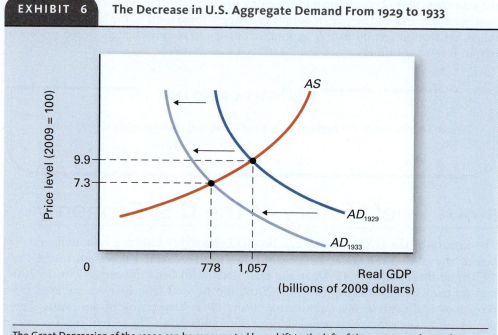

The Great Depression of the 1930s can be represented by a shift to the left of the aggregate demand curve, from AD_{1929} to AD_{1933}. In the resulting depression, real GDP fell from $1,057 billion to $778 billion, and the price level dropped from 9.9 to 7.3, measured relative to a price level of 100 in the base year 2009.

money supply shrank by one-third, and world trade was severely restricted by high tariffs. All this contributed to a big decline in aggregate demand. The aggregate supply curve probably also shifted somewhat during this period, but the drop in aggregate demand was the dominant force.

Because of the decline in aggregate demand, both the price level and real GDP dropped. Real GDP fell 27 percent, from $1,057 billion in 1929 to $778 billion in 1933, and the price level fell 26 percent, from 9.9 to 7.3. As real GDP declined, unemployment soared from only 3 percent of the labor force in 1929 to 25 percent in 1933, the highest U.S. rate ever recorded.

Before the Great Depression, macroeconomic policy was based primarily on the *laissez-faire* philosophy of Adam Smith. Smith, you may recall, argued in his famous book, *The Wealth of Nations*, that if people are allowed to pursue their self-interest in free markets, resources would be guided as if by an "invisible hand" to produce the most efficient and most valued level of aggregate output. Although the U.S. economy suffered many sharp contractions even before the Great Depression, most economists of the day viewed these as a natural phase of the economy—unfortunate for those who lost jobs and savings but ultimately therapeutic and self-correcting.

5-4b The Age of Keynes: After the Great Depression to the Early 1970s

The Great Depression was so deep that it stimulated new thinking about how the economy worked (or didn't work). In 1936, John Maynard Keynes (1883–1946) published *The General Theory of Employment, Interest, and Money*, the most famous economics book of the 20th century. In it, he argued that aggregate demand was inherently unstable, in part because investment decisions were often guided by the unpredictable "animal spirits" of business expectations. If businesses grew pessimistic about the economy, they would invest less, which would reduce aggregate demand, output, and employment. For example, investment spending dropped more than 80 percent between 1929 and 1933. Keynes saw no natural market forces operating to ensure that the economy, even if allowed a reasonable time to adjust, would get output and employment growing again.

Keynes proposed that the government jolt the economy out of its depression by increasing aggregate demand. He recommended an expansionary fiscal policy to help offset a contraction. The government could achieve this stimulus either directly by increasing its own spending, or indirectly by cutting taxes to stimulate consumption and investment. But either action would likely create a federal budget deficit. A **federal budget deficit** is a flow variable that measures, for a particular period, the amount by which federal outlays exceed federal revenues.

To understand what Keynes had in mind, imagine federal budget policies that would increase aggregate demand in Exhibit 6, shifting the aggregate demand curve to the right, back to its original position. Such a shift would raise real GDP, which would increase employment. According to the Keynesian prescription, the miracle drug of fiscal policy—changes in government spending and taxes—could compensate for what he viewed as the instability of private-sector spending, especially investment. If demand in the private sector declined, Keynes said the government should pick up the slack. We can think of the Keynesian approach as **demand-side economics** because it focused on how changes in aggregate demand might promote full employment. Keynes argued that government stimulus could shock the economy out of its depression. Once investment returned to normal levels, and the economy started growing on its own, the government's shock treatment would no longer be necessary.

The U.S. economy bounced back beginning in 1933, growing four years in a row (see Exhibit 2 again). The outbreak of World War II boosted employment to fight for the country and to make tanks, ships, aircraft, and the like. Federal government spending increased from 7 percent of GDP in 1940 to 46 percent in 1944. The explosion of output and sharp drop in unemployment seemed to confirm the powerful role government spending could play in the economy. But the increase in government spending, with no significant increase in tax rates, created large federal deficits during the war.

Immediately after the war, memories of the Great Depression were still vivid. Trying to avoid another depression, Congress approved the *Employment Act of 1946,* which imposed a clear responsibility on the federal government to promote "maximum employment, production, and purchasing power." The act also required the president to appoint a *Council of Economic Advisers,* a three-member team of economists to provide economic advice and report on the economy.

The economy seemed to prosper during the 1950s largely without added stimulus from fiscal policy. The 1960s, however, proved to be the *golden age of Keynesian economics,* a period when fiscal policy makers thought they could "fine-tune" the economy for top performance—just as a mechanic fine-tunes a racecar. During the early 1960s, nearly all advanced economies around the world enjoyed low unemployment and healthy growth with only modest inflation.

The U.S. economy was on such a roll that toward the end of the 1960s some economists believed the business cycle was history. As a sign of the times, the name of a federal publication, *Business Cycle Developments,* was changed to *Business Conditions Digest.* In the early 1970s, however, the business cycle returned with a fury. Worse yet, the problems of recession were compounded by higher inflation, which increased during the recessions of 1973–1975 and 1980. Prior to that, high inflation had been limited primarily to periods of expansion—that is, to boom times. Confidence in demand-side policies was shaken, and the expression "fine-tuning" dropped from the economic vocabulary. What ended the golden age of Keynesian economics?

federal budget deficit
A flow variable measuring the amount by which federal government outlays exceed federal government revenues in a particular period, usually a year

demand-side economics
Macroeconomic policy that focuses on shifting the aggregate demand curve as a way of promoting full employment and price stability

5-4c Stagflation: 1973–1975 and 1979–1980

During the late 1960s, federal spending increased on both the war in Vietnam and social programs at home. This combined stimulus increased aggregate demand enough that in 1968 the *inflation rate,* the annual percentage increase in the price level, rose to 4.4 percent, after averaging only 2.0 percent during the previous decade. Inflation climbed to 4.9 percent in 1969 and to 5.3 percent in 1970. These rates were so alarming at the time that in 1971, President Richard Nixon imposed ceilings on prices and wages. Those ceilings were eliminated in 1973, about the time that crop failures around the world caused grain prices to soar. To compound these problems, the Organization of Petroleum Exporting Countries (OPEC) cut its supply of oil to world markets, so oil prices jumped. Crop failures plus the OPEC action reduced aggregate supply, shown in Exhibit 7 by the leftward shift of the aggregate supply curve from AS_{1973} to AS_{1975}. This resulted in **stagflation**, meaning a *stag*nation, or a contraction, in the economy's aggregate output and in*flation*, or increase, in the economy's price level. Real GDP declined between 1973 and 1975, and unemployment climbed from 4.9 percent to 8.5 percent. During the same two-year period, the price level jumped by 19 percent.

stagflation

A contraction, or *stagnation,* of a nation's output accompanied by in*flation* in the price level

Stagflation hit again five years later, stoked again by more OPEC cutbacks. Between 1979 and 1980, real GDP declined but the price level increased by 9.1 percent. Macroeconomics has not been the same since. Because stagflation was on the supply side, not on the demand side, the demand-management prescriptions of Keynes seemed ineffective. Increasing aggregate demand might reduce unemployment but would worsen inflation.

EXHIBIT 7   **U.S. Stagflation From 1973 to 1975**

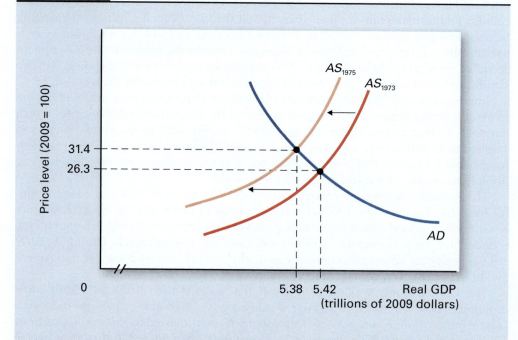

The stagflation of the mid-1970s can be represented as a leftward shift of the aggregate supply curve from AS_{1973} to AS_{1975}. Aggregate output fell from $5.42 trillion in 1973 to $5.38 trillion in 1975, for a decline of about $40 billion (*stagnation*). The price level rose from 26.3 to 31.4, for an increase of 19 percent (*inflation*).

5-4d Somewhat Normal Times: 1980 to 2007

Increasing aggregate supply seemed an appropriate way to combat stagflation, for such a move would both lower the price level and increase output and employment. Attention thus turned from aggregate demand to aggregate supply. A key idea behind **supply-side economics** was that the federal government, by lowering tax rates, would increase after-tax wages, which would provide incentives to increase the supply of labor and other resources. According to advocates of the supply-side approach, the resulting increase in aggregate supply would achieve the happy result of expanding real GDP and reducing the price level. You can get the idea behind supply-side economics in Exhibit 7 by picturing the aggregate supply curve as shifting back to the right from AS_{1975} to AS_{1973}. Such a move would increase real GDP while lowering the price level. But this was easier said than done.

In 1981, to provide economic incentives to increase aggregate supply, President Ronald Reagan and Congress cut personal income tax rates by an average of 23 percent to be phased in over three years. They believed that lower tax rates would increase aggregate supply, thereby expanding output and employment. They hoped that higher tax revenue from a larger economy would more than make up for the revenue lost by the cut in tax rates. In other words, the tax cutters hoped that the government's smaller share of a bigger pie would exceed what had been its larger share of a smaller pie.

But even before the tax cut took effect, recession hit, contracting output and pushing the unemployment rate up to 10 percent. Once the recession ended in late 1982, the economy began to grow, and this growth continued for the rest of the decade. Between 1982 and 1990 employment grew 19 percent and real GDP grew 38 percent, an indication that each worker was producing more. But the growth in federal spending exceeded the growth in federal tax revenues during this period, so federal budget deficits increased. Deficits worsened with the onset of a recession in 1990–1991, which was brought on by the first war in the Persian Gulf. Annual deficits accumulated as a growing federal debt. The **federal debt** is a stock variable that measures the net accumulation of prior federal deficits. But robust economic growth during the 1990s boosted employment by 15 percent and real GDP by 40 percent, again an indication that output per worker was growing nicely. The expanding economy combined with a booming stock market to increase tax revenue enough to yield a federal budget surplus by the end of the 1990s.

By early 2001, the U.S. economic expansion had lasted ten years to become the longest on record. Then the economy slipped into a short recession aggravated by the terrorist attacks of September 11, 2001. The recession lasted only eight months, but the recovery was slow and uneven. President George W. Bush pushed through tax cuts "to get the economy moving again." But the tax cuts and spending programs increased the federal budget deficit, which exceeded $400 billion in 2004. Still, employment grew 7 percent between 2000 and 2007, and real GDP grew 18 percent. That growth helped cut the budget deficit to $161 billion by 2007. In fact, during the quarter century between 1982 and 2007, employment grew 47 percent and real GDP grew 128 percent, quite an impressive performance and the envy of the world. Then things went bad.

5-4e The Great Recession of 2007–2009 and Beyond

By late 2007, the expansion that began in late 2001 had lasted six years, about average for expansions since World War II. So it was not that surprising when the

supply-side economics
Macroeconomic policy that focuses on a rightward shift of the aggregate supply curve through tax cuts or other changes to increase production incentives

federal debt
A stock variable that measures the net accumulation of annual federal deficits

expansion peaked in December 2007; then the recession began, this time precipitated by declining home prices and rising foreclosures, as more borrowers failed to make their mortgage payments. With home prices falling, fewer were getting built, meaning fewer jobs in residential construction, furnishings, and other industries that rely on the housing sector. During the first eight months of the recession, U.S. job losses averaged 151,000 a month, in line with monthly losses during the prior two recessions. In early 2008, Washington tried to stimulate aggregate demand with a $117 billion tax rebate, but the result was disappointing. The softer economy and tax cuts nearly tripled the federal deficit from $161 billion in 2007 to $459 billion in 2008; at the time this deficit seemed huge.

Fears about the effect of rising home foreclosures on the banking system fed into a full-scale global financial panic in September 2008, triggered by the collapse of Lehman Brothers, a Wall Street investment bank. An *investment bank* is a financial institution that helps businesses raise financial capital. Because Lehman Brothers was the largest bankruptcy in U.S. history, financial institutions grew reluctant to lend, so credit dried up—a major problem for an economy that relies a lot on credit. Businesses cut investments sharply. Consumers cut their spending in the face of sliding home prices, mounting job losses, and a collapsing stock market. You could picture all this as a leftward shift of the aggregate demand curve. These events unfolded against the backdrop of a presidential election. Is it any wonder that voters in 2008 went for "hope and change"?

After the collapse of Lehman Brothers and the freezing up of financial flows around the world, policy makers were emboldened to enact some extraordinary measures to shore up confidence in financial institutions, open up the flow of credit, and stimulate consumer spending. These included two huge programs: (1) the $700 billion Troubled Asset Relief Program, or TARP, aimed at stabilizing financial institutions, and (2) the $787 billion American Recovery and Reinvestment Act, or the stimulus bill, aimed at increasing aggregate demand (the estimated cost would rise to $831 billion). The effects of these programs are still being debated today and will be discussed in later chapters. One point to underscore now is just how extraordinary these measures were. What we know for sure is that these rescue programs tripled the federal deficit from $459 billion in 2008 to $1.4 trillion in 2009.

We also know that during the 12 months following the failure of Lehman Brothers, job losses averaged 565,000 a month, nearly four times the average during the two prior recessions and during the first eight months of 2008. Job losses on that scale had not been experienced since the Great Depression. Altogether, employment fell by 8.4 million between December 2007 and December 2009, a drop of 6.1 percent. Despite the sizable job losses, real GDP didn't fall that much. Because those who still had jobs were more productive, output dropped only about 2 percent between 2007 and 2009, and the price level hardly budged. The recession ended in June 2009. By the third quarter of 2009, real GDP was growing again, though the unemployment rate remained stubbornly high deep into 2012. Events during the recession of 2007–2009 traumatized the economy. Lasting 18 months, what has come to be called the Great Recession was the longest of the 11 recessions since World War II. This recession will be discussed in the course of these macroeconomic chapters.

Focusing on the ups and downs of the economy can miss the point that the U.S. economy over the long run has been an incredible creator of jobs and output—one of the most productive economies in the world. To underscore that point, we close with a case study that tracks U.S. economic growth since 1929.

PUBLIC POLICY

U.S. ECONOMIC GROWTH SINCE 1929 Points in Exhibit 8 trace the U.S. real GDP and price level for each year since 1929. Aggregate demand and aggregate supply curves are shown for 2014, but all points in the series reflect such intersections. Years of growing GDP are indicated as blue points and years of declining GDP as red ones. Despite the Great Depression of the 1930s and the 11 recessions since World War II, the long-term growth in output is unmistakable. Real GDP, measured along the horizontal axis in 2009 constant dollars, grew from about $1.1 trillion in 1929 to about $16.1 trillion

in 2014 — a fifteenfold increase and an average annual growth rate of 3.3 percent. The price index also rose, but not quite as fast, rising from 9.9 in 1929 to 108.3 in 2014 an elevenfold increase and an average inflation rate of 2.9 percent per year. Note that what matters here is the growth in real GDP, because that nets out the effects of inflation (inflation is mostly troublesome noise in the economy). Since 1982, annual output declined only three times—in 1991, in 2008, and in 2009.

Because the U.S. population is growing all the time, the economy must create more jobs just to employ the

EXHIBIT 8   **Tracking U.S. Real GDP and Price Level Since 1929**

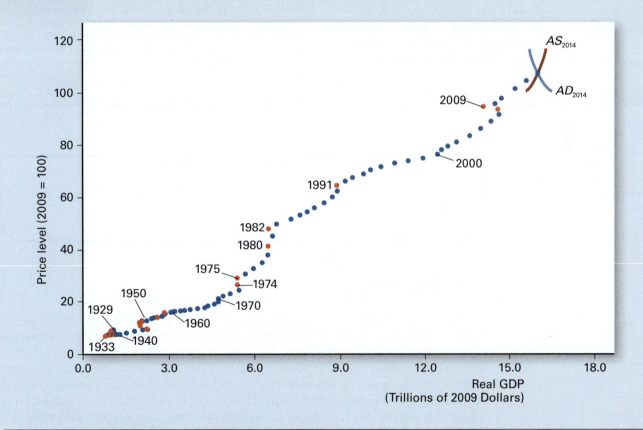

As you can see, both real GDP and the price level trended higher since 1929. Blue points indicate years of growing real GDP, and red points are years of declining real GDP. Real GDP in 2014 was 15 times greater than in 1929.

continued

Not only did the number employed more than triple since 1929, the average education of workers increased as well. Other resources, especially capital, also rose sharply. What's more, the level of technology and know-how improved steadily, thanks to breakthroughs such as the personal computer and the Internet. The availability of more and higher-quality human capital and physical capital increased the productivity of each worker, contributing to the fifteen fold jump in real GDP since 1929.

Real GDP is important, but the best measure of the average standard of living is an economy's **real GDP per capita**, which tells us how much an economy produces on average per resident. Because real GDP grew much faster than the population, real GDP *per capita* jumped nearly sixfold between 1929 and 2014. The United States is one of the largest economies in the world and a leader among major economies in output per capita.

Sources: "GDP and the Economy," *Survey of Current Business* 95 (April 2015); *Economic Report of the President*, February 2015; *Economic Report of the President*, January 1980; and *OECD Economic Outlook* 97 (May 2015). For the latest real GDP and price level data, go to http://bea.gov/. For the latest population data, go to http://www.census.gov. For the latest employment data, go to http://www.bls.gov.

additional people entering the workforce. For example, the U.S. population grew from 122 million in 1929 to 319 million in 2014, a rise of 162 percent. Fortunately, employment grew even faster, from 47 million in 1929 to 146 million in 2014, for a growth of 211 percent. So, since 1929, employment grew more than enough to keep up with a rising population. Despite the recessions, the United States has been an impressive job machine over the long run.

real GDP per capita
Real GDP divided by the population; the best measure of an economy's standard of living

 **CHECKPOINT**

Identify the five eras of the U.S. economy, and describe briefly what was going on during each.

5-5 Conclusion

Because macroeconomists have no test subjects and cannot rely on luck, they hone their craft by developing models of the economy and then searching for evidence to support or reject these models. In this sense, macroeconomics is retrospective, always looking at recent developments for hints about which model works best. The macroeconomist is like a traveler who can see only the road behind and must find the way ahead using a collection of poorly drawn maps. The traveler must continually check each map (or model) against the landmarks to see whether one map is more consistent with the terrain than the others. Each new batch of information about the economy causes macroeconomists to shuffle through their "maps" to check their models.

Macroeconomics often emphasizes what can go wrong with the economy. Sagging output, high unemployment, and rising inflation capture much of the attention, and we'll examine those problems in the next two chapters. But perhaps the most important performance measure is economic growth, and we'll devote a chapter to that after you learn more about real GDP, unemployment, and inflation.

Finally, learning about the macro economy is like learning about the weather. You may not be able to change the weather, but knowing what's coming will help you cope with it better—for example, by bringing an umbrella if rain is on the way. Likewise, you may not be able to change macroeconomic conditions, but knowing what's coming will help you adapt to them better—for example, by deciding to pursue graduate studies rather than dive into a poor job market. A knowledge of macroeconomics will give you an edge in coping with a complex economic environment.

Summary

1. Macroeconomics focuses on the national economy. A standard measure of performance is the growth of real gross domestic product, or real GDP, the value of all final goods and services produced in the nation during the year.

2. The economy has two phases: periods of expansion and periods of contraction. No two business cycles are the same. Before 1945, expansions averaged 29 months and contractions 21 months. Since 1945, expansions have averaged 57 months and contractions 11 months. Despite the Great Depression and later recessions, the economy's output has grown fifteenfold since 1929 and employment has grown faster than the population.

3. The aggregate demand curve slopes downward, reflecting a negative, or inverse, relationship between the price level and real GDP demanded. The aggregate supply curve slopes upward, reflecting a positive, or direct, relationship between the price level and real GDP supplied. The intersection of the two curves determines the economy's real GDP and price level.

4. The Great Depression and earlier depressions prompted John Maynard Keynes to argue that the economy can be unstable, largely because business investment is erratic. Keynes did not believe that contractions were self-correcting. He argued that whenever aggregate demand sagged, the federal government should spend more or tax less to stimulate aggregate demand. His demand-side policies dominated macroeconomic thinking between World War II and the late 1960s.

5. During the 1970s, higher oil prices and global crop failures reduced aggregate supply. The result was stagflation, the troublesome combination of declining real GDP and rising inflation. Demand-side policies appeared less effective in an economy suffering from a reduction in aggregate supply, because stimulating aggregate demand would worsen inflation.

6. Supply-side tax cuts in the early 1980s were aimed at increasing aggregate supply, thereby increasing output while dampening inflation. Output and employment grew nicely during the 1980s, but federal spending increased faster than federal tax revenue, resulting in budget deficits that grew into the early 1990s. Output and employment also grew nicely during the 1990s. The expanding economy increased federal revenues enough to create a federal budget surplus by the end of the decade. But after the longest expansion on record, the economy experienced an eight-month recession in 2001. The economy started growing again, and that expansion lasted until the end of 2007.

7. After peaking in December 2007, the economy entered a recession because of falling home prices and rising foreclosure rates. The collapse of a Wall Street bank in September 2008 panicked financial markets around the world, cutting investment and consumption. Monthly job losses during this Great Recession were the highest since the Great Depression. Massive federal programs aimed at stabilizing the economy resulted in gigantic federal deficits. Economic growth returned in the second half of 2009, but the unemployment rate remained stubbornly high for years.

Key Concepts

Questions for Review

1. **The National Economy** Why do economists pay more attention to national economies (for example, the U.S. or Canadian economies) than to state or provincial economies (such as California or Ontario)?

2. **The Human Body and the U.S. Economy** Based on your own experiences, extend the list of analogies between the human body and the economy as outlined in this chapter. Then, determine which variables in your list are stocks and which are flows.

3. **Stocks and Flows** Differentiate between stock and flow variables. Give an example of each.

4. **Economic Fluctuations** Describe fluctuations in economic activity over time. Because economic activity fluctuates, how is long-term growth possible?

5. **Economic Fluctuations** Why doesn't the National Bureau of Economic Research identify the turning points in economic activity until months or even a year after they occur?

6. **The Great Recession** The recession of 2007–2009 was made worse by a global financial crisis. Show the effect of the Great Recession on the economy by shifting aggregate demand and/or aggregate supply curves as appropriate.

7. **The Global Economy** How are economic fluctuations linked across national economies? How could a recession in the United States trigger a recession abroad or vice-versa?

8. **Leading Economic Indicators** Define *leading economic indicators* and give some examples. You may wish to take a look at the Conference Board's index of leading economic indicators at http://www.conference-board.org/data/.

9. **Aggregate Demand and Aggregate Supply** Why does a decrease of the aggregate demand curve result in less employment, given an aggregate supply curve?

10. **Aggregate Demand and Aggregate Supply** Is it possible for the price level to fall while production and employment both rise? If it is possible, how could this happen? If it is not possible, explain why not.

11. **Aggregate Demand Curve** Describe the relationship illustrated by the aggregate demand curve. Why does this relationship exist?

12. **Demand-Side Economics** What is the relationship between demand-side economics and the federal budget deficit?

13. **Stagflation** What were some of the causes of the stagflations of 1973 and 1979? In what ways were these episodes of stagflation different from the Great Depression of the 1930s?

14. **Great Recession of 2007–2009** Discuss the role of the housing sector as a contributing factor in this recession.

15. **Case Study: U.S. Economic Growth Since 1929** The price level grew slightly faster than real GDP between 1947 and 2014. Does this mean that the rising price level masked an actual decline in output? Why or why not?

Problems and Exercises

16. **Aggregate Demand and Supply** Review the information on demand and supply curves in Chapter 4. How do the aggregate demand and aggregate supply curves presented in this chapter differ from the market curves of Chapter 4?

17. **Aggregate Demand and Supply** Determine whether each of the following would cause a shift of the aggregate demand curve, a shift of the aggregate supply curve, neither, or both. Which curve would shift, and in which direction? What happens to aggregate output and the price level in each case?

a. The price level changes
b. Consumer confidence declines
c. The supply of resources increases
d. The wage rate increases

18. **Supply-Side Economics** One supply-side measure introduced by the Reagan administration was a cut in income tax rates. Use an aggregate demand/aggregate supply diagram to show what effect was intended. What might happen if such a tax cut also shifted the aggregate demand curve?

Tracking the U.S. Economy

6

- *How do we track one of the most complex economies in world history?*
- *What's gross about the gross domestic product?*
- *What's domestic about it?*
- *If you make yourself a tuna sandwich, how much does your effort add to the gross domestic product?*
- *Because prices change over time, how can we compare the economy's production in one year with that in other years?*

Answers to these and other questions are addressed in this chapter, which introduces an economic scorecard for one of the largest economies in world history. That scorecard is the national income accounting system, which reduces a huge network of economic activity to a few aggregate measures.

As you will see, aggregate output is measured either by the spending on that output or by the income derived from producing it. In this chapter, we examine each approach and learn why they are equivalent. The major components and important equalities built into the national income accounts are offered here as another way of understanding how the economy works—not as a foreign language to be mastered before the next exam. The emphasis is more on economic intuition than on accounting precision. The body of the chapter provides the background you need for later chapters. More details about the national income accounts are offered in the appendix.

Topics discussed in this chapter include:

- National income accounts
- Expenditure approach to GDP
- Income approach to GDP
- Circular flow of income and expenditure
- Leakages and injections
- Limitations of national income accounting
- Consumer price index
- GDP price index

6-1 The Product of a Nation

How do we measure the economy's performance? During much of the 17th and 18th centuries, when the dominant economic policy was mercantilism, many thought that economic prosperity was best measured by the *stock* of precious metals a nation accumulated in the public treasury. Mercantilism led to restrictions on international trade, with the unintended consequence of reducing the gains from comparative advantage. In the latter half of the 18th century, François Quesnay became the first to measure economic activity as a *flow*. In 1758 he published his *Tableau Économique*, which described the *circular flow* of output and income through different sectors of the economy. His insight was likely inspired by his knowledge of blood's circular flow in the body—Quesnay was court physician to King Louis XV of France.

Rough measures of national income were developed in England two centuries ago, but detailed calculations built up from microeconomic data were refined in the United States during the Great Depression. The resulting *national income accounting system* organizes huge quantities of data collected from a variety of sources across America. These data are summarized, assembled into a coherent framework, and reported by the federal government. The conception and implementation of these accounts have been hailed as one of the greatest achievements of the 20th century. The U.S. national income accounts are the most widely copied and most highly regarded in the world and earned their developer, Simon Kuznets, the Nobel Prize in 1971 for "giving quantitative precision to economic entities."

6-1a National Income Accounts

How do the national income accounts keep track of the economy's incredible variety of goods and services, from hiking boots to Pilates classes? The *gross domestic product*, or GDP, measures the market value of all final goods and services produced during a year by resources located in the United States, regardless of who owns the resources. For example, GDP includes production in the United States by foreign firms, such as a Toyota plant in Kentucky, but excludes foreign production by U.S. firms, such as a Ford plant in Mexico.

GDP estimates are computed each quarter by the Bureau of Economic Analysis in Washington, D.C. On computation day, staff members follow a process that dates back half a century. The office is in "lockup." Communications with the outside are shut down—no cell phones or land lines can be used. Office drapes are drawn. Only certain people are allowed in and out. To estimate GDP, the staff draws on more than 10,000 streams of data describing economic activity. Nobody speaks the final GDP estimate aloud for fear that it could be overheard and exploited in securities markets. Once they estimate GDP and its components, they write a press release, make hundreds of copies, then lock all but one in a safe for distribution to the media the next morning at 8:30 a.m. Eastern Time. The single copy not locked away is delivered to the head of the president's Council of Economic Advisers, so he or she can give the president a heads-up. But despite all the security and formality, we should keep in mind that the GDP reported is still just an estimate, one that will be revised twice more each quarter as more data become available.

The national income accounts are based on the simple fact that *one person's spending is another person's income*. GDP can be measured either by total spending on U.S. production or by total income received from that production. The **expenditure approach** adds up spending on all final goods and services produced in the United States during the year. The **income approach** adds up earnings during the year by those who produce all that output. In the *double-entry bookkeeping system* used to track the economy, spending on aggregate output is recorded on one side of the ledger and income from producing that aggregate output is recorded on the other side.

Gross domestic product includes only **final goods and services**, which are goods and services sold to the final, or end, user. A toothbrush, a pair of contact lenses, and a bus ride are examples of final goods and services. Whether a sale is to the final user depends on who buys the product. When you buy chicken for dinner, that's reflected in GDP. When KFC buys chicken, however, that's not counted in GDP because KFC is not the final consumer. Only after the chicken is prepared, fried, and sold by KFC is the transaction counted in GDP.

Intermediate goods and services are those purchased for additional processing and resale, like KFC's chicken purchase. This change may be imperceptible, as when a grocer buys canned goods to restock shelves. Or the intermediate goods can be dramatically altered, as when an artist transforms a $100 canvas and $30 in oil paints into a work of art that sells for $5,000. Sales of intermediate goods and services are excluded from GDP to avoid the mistake of **double counting**, which is counting an item's value more than once. For example, suppose the grocer buys a can of tuna for $1.00 and sells it for $1.50. If GDP counted both the intermediate transaction of $1.00 and the final transaction of $1.50, the recorded value of $2.50 would exceed its final value by $1.00. Hence, GDP counts only the market value of the final sale. As another example, in a recent year Walmart paid $287 billion for products it sold for $375 billion. If GDP counted both Walmart's intermediate transactions and final transactions, Walmart's impact on GDP would be $287 billion too high. GDP also ignores most of the secondhand value of used goods, such as existing homes, used cars, and

expenditure approach to GDP
Calculating GDP by adding up spending on all final goods and services produced in the nation during the year

income approach to GDP
Calculating GDP by adding up all earnings from resources used to produce output in the nation during the year

final goods and services
Goods and services sold to final, or end, users

intermediate goods and services
Goods and services purchased by firms for further reprocessing and resale

double counting
The mistake of including both the value of intermediate products and the value of final products in calculating gross domestic product; counting the same production more than once

used books. These goods were counted in GDP when they were produced. But just as the services provided by the grocer and by Walmart are captured in GDP, so are the services provided by real estate agents, used-car dealers, and used-book sellers.

6-1b GDP Based on the Expenditure Approach

As noted already, one way to measure GDP is to add up spending on all final goods and services produced in the economy during the year. The easiest way to understand the spending approach is to sort aggregate expenditure into its components: consumption, investment, government purchases, and net exports. **Consumption**, or more specifically, *personal consumption expenditures*, consists of purchases of final goods and services by households during the year. Consumption is the largest spending category, averaging 68 percent of U.S. GDP during this past decade. Along with *services*, such as dry cleaning, haircuts, and air travel, consumption includes *nondurable goods*, such as soap and soup, and *durable goods*, such as furniture and kitchen appliances. Durable goods are expected to last at least three years.

Investment, or more specifically, *gross private domestic investment*, consists of spending on new construction, new capital goods, new software, and on net additions to inventories. The most important investment is **physical capital**, such as new buildings and new machinery. Investment also includes new **residential construction**. Although it fluctuates a lot from year to year, investment averaged 16 percent of U.S. GDP this past decade. More generally, investment consists of spending on current production that is not used for current consumption. A firm's net increase in inventories also counts as investment because it represents current production not used for current consumption. **Inventories** are stocks of goods in process, such as computer parts, and stocks of finished goods, such as new computers awaiting sale. Inventories help manufacturers cope with unexpected changes in the supply of their resources or in the demand for their products.

Although investment includes purchasing a new residence, it excludes purchases of *existing* buildings and machines and purchases of financial assets, such as stocks and bonds. Existing buildings and machines were counted in GDP when they were produced. Stocks and bonds are not investments themselves but simply indications of ownership.

Government purchases, or more specifically, *government consumption and gross investment*, include government spending for goods and services—from clearing snowy roads to clearing court dockets, from buying library books to paying teachers. Government purchases averaged 20 percent of U.S. GDP during the last decade. Government purchases, and therefore GDP, exclude transfer payments, such as Social Security, welfare benefits, and unemployment insurance. Such payments are not true purchases by the government or true earnings by the recipients.

The final spending component, net exports, reflects international trade in goods and services. Goods, or *merchandise*, include physical items such as wheat and machinery (stuff you can load on a ship). Services, or so-called *invisibles*, include intangible items, such as international travel and education. Foreign purchases of U.S. goods and services are counted as part of U.S. GDP. But U.S. purchases of foreign goods and services are subtracted from U.S. GDP. **Net exports** equal the value of U.S. exports of goods and services minus the value of U.S. imports of goods and services. U.S. imports have exceeded U.S. exports nearly every year since the 1960s, meaning U.S. net exports have been negative. During the last decade, net exports averaged a negative 4 percent of GDP.

Aggregate expenditure is total spending on final goods and services in an economy during a given period, usually a year. With the expenditure approach, the nation's aggregate expenditure sums consumption, *C;* investment, *I;* government

---

consumption

Household purchases of final goods and services, except for new residences, which count as investment

investment

The purchase of new plants, new equipment, new software, new buildings, and new residences, plus net additions to inventories

physical capital

Manufactured items used to produce goods and services; includes new plants and new equipment

residential construction

Building new homes or dwelling places

inventories

Producers' stocks of finished and in-process goods

government purchases

Spending for goods and services by all levels of government; government outlays minus transfer payments

net exports

The value of a country's exports minus the value of its imports

aggregate expenditure

Total spending on final goods and services in an economy during a given period, usually a year; the sum of consumption, investment, government purchases, and net exports purchases, *G;* and net exports, which is the value of exports, *X,* minus the value of imports, *M,* or ($X - M$). Summing these yields aggregate expenditure, or GDP:

$$C + I + G + (X - M) = \text{Aggregate expenditure} = \text{GDP}$$

6-1c Composition of Aggregate Expenditure

Now that we have introduced each component of aggregate spending, let's get a better idea of spending over time. Exhibit 1 shows the composition of spending in the United States since 1959. As you can see, consumption's share of GDP appears stable from year to year, but the long-term trend shows an increase from an average of 62 percent during the 1960s to 68 percent during the most recent decade. Investment fluctuates more year to year but with little long-term trend up or down; investment averaged 15 percent of GDP during the 1960s and 16 percent during the most recent decade. But, as you can see in the exhibit, investment's share of GDP dropped sharply during the recession of 2007–2009.

Government purchases declined from an average of 22 percent of GDP during the 1960s to an average of 20 percent during the last decade, due primarily to decreases in defense spending. Remember, government purchases do not include transfer payments, which have grown faster than government purchases.

EXHIBIT 1   **U.S. Spending Components as Percent of GDP Since 1959**

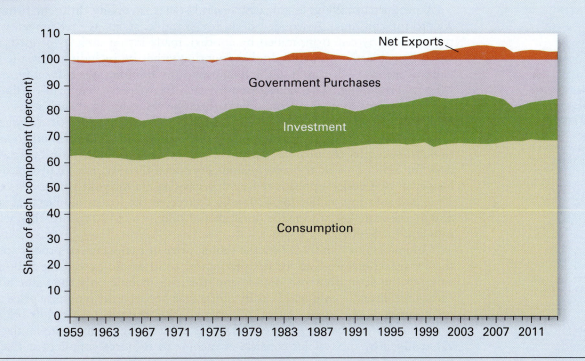

The composition of U.S. GDP has not changed that much since 1959. Consumption's share edged up from an average of 62 percent during the 1960s to 68 percent during the most recent decade. Investment has fluctuated from year to year but with no clear long-term trend up or down. Government purchases declined slightly from an average of 22 percent of GDP during the 1960s to an average of 20 percent in the most recent decade. And net exports have become more negative, expressed in red by that portion exceeding 100 percent of GDP.

Source: Bureau of Economic Analysis, U.S. Department of Commerce. For the latest data, go to http://bea.gov/national/nipaweb/index.asp and select Table 1.1.1.

Net exports averaged a surplus of 1 percent in the 1960s but were in deficit nearly every year since then, averaging a minus 4 percent of GDP during the last decade. Negative net exports mean that the sum of consumption, investment, and government purchases exceeds GDP, the amount produced in the U.S. economy. Americans are spending more than they make, and they are covering the difference by borrowing from abroad. U.S. spending exceeds U.S. GDP by the amount shown as negative net exports. Because the spending components must sum to GDP, *negative* net exports are expressed in Exhibit 1 by the red portion of spending that exceeds 100 percent of GDP. Thus, during the last five-and-one-half decades, consumption's share of total spending increased and government purchases decreased. Investment's share bounced around and net exports' share turned negative, meaning that imports exceeded exports.

6-1d GDP Based on the Income Approach

aggregate income

All earnings of resource suppliers in an economy during a given period, usually a year

The expenditure approach sums, or aggregates, spending on production. The income approach sums, or aggregates, income arising from that production. Again, double-entry bookkeeping ensures that the value of aggregate output equals the aggregate income paid for resources used to produce that output: the wages, interest, rent, and profit arising from production. The price of a Hershey's candy bar reflects the income earned by resource suppliers along the way. **Aggregate income** equals the sum of all the income earned by resource suppliers in the economy. Thus, we can say that

$$\text{Aggregate expenditure} = \text{GDP} = \text{Aggregate income}$$

value added

At each stage of production, the selling price of a product minus the cost of intermediate goods purchased from other firms

A product usually goes through several stages involving different firms on its way to the consumer. A wooden desk, for example, starts as raw timber, which is typically cut by one firm, milled by another, made into a desk by a third, and retailed by a fourth. We avoid double counting either by including only the market value of the desk when sold to the final user or by *summing the value added at each stage of production*. The **value added** by each firm equals that firm's selling price minus payments for inputs from other firms. The value added at each stage is the income earned by resource suppliers at that stage. *The value added at all stages sums to the market value of the final good, and the value added for all final goods sums to GDP based on the income approach.* For example, suppose you buy a wooden desk for $200. This final market value gets added directly into GDP. Consider the history of that desk. Suppose the tree that gave its life for your studies was cut into a log and sold to a miller for $20, who converted the log to lumber that sold for $50 to a desk maker, who made the desk and sold it for $120 to a retailer, who sold it to you for $200.

Column (1) of Exhibit 2 lists the selling price at each stage of production. If all these transactions were added up, the sum of $390 would exceed the $200 market value of the desk. To avoid double counting, we include only the value added at each stage, listed in column (3) as the difference between the purchase price and the selling price at that stage. Again, *the value added at each stage equals the income earned by those who supply their resources at that stage.* For example, the $80 in value added by the retailer consists of income to resource suppliers at that stage, from the salesperson to the janitor who cleaned the showroom to the trucker who provided "free delivery" of your desk. The value added at all stages totals $200, which is both the final market value of the desk and the total income earned by all resource suppliers along the way.

To reinforce your understanding of the equality of income and spending, let's return to something introduced in Chapter 1, the circular-flow model.

EXHIBIT 2	Computing Value Added for a New Desk

Stage of Production	(1) Sale Value	(2) Cost of Intermediate Goods	(3) Value Added (3) = (1) − (2)
Logger	$ 20	——	$ 20
Miller	50	$ 20	30
Manufacturer	120	50	70
Retailer	100	120	80
		Market value of final good	**$200**

The value added at each stage of production is the sale price at that stage minus the cost of intermediate goods purchased from other firms, or column (1) minus column (2). The value added at each stage sums to the market value of the final good, shown at the bottom of column (3).

✓ CHECKPOINT

Describe the two ways of computing GDP and explain why they are equivalent.

6-2 Circular Flow of Income and Expenditure

The model in Exhibit 3 outlines the circular flow of income and spending in the economy for not only households and firms, as was the case in Chapter 1, but governments and the rest of the world. The main stream flows clockwise around the circle, first as income from firms to households (in the lower half of the circle), and then as spending from households back to firms (in the upper half of the circle). For each flow of money, there is an equal and opposite flow of products or resources. Here we follow the money.

6-2a Income Half of the Circular Flow

To develop a circular flow of income and spending, we must make some simplifying assumptions. Specifically, by assuming that physical capital does not wear out (i.e., no capital depreciation occurs) and that firms pay out all profits to firm owners (i.e., firms retain no earnings), we can say that *GDP equals aggregate income*. The circular flow is a continuous process, but the logic of the model is clearest if we begin at juncture (1) in Exhibit 3, where U.S. firms make production decisions. After all, production must occur before output can be sold and income earned. As Henry Ford explained, "It is not the employer who pays the wages—the employer only handles the money. It is the product that pays wages." Households supply their labor, capital, natural resources, and entrepreneurial ability to make products that firms sell to pay wages, interest, rent, and profit. Production of aggregate output, or GDP, gives rise to an equal amount of aggregate income.

Thus, at juncture (1), aggregate output equals aggregate income. But not all that income is available to spend. At juncture (2), governments collect taxes. Some of these tax dollars return as transfer payments to the income stream at juncture (3). By

disposable income (*DI*)

The income households have available to spend or to save after paying taxes and receiving transfer payments

net taxes (*NT*)

Taxes minus transfer payments

subtracting taxes and adding transfers, we transform aggregate income into **disposable income, *DI***, which flows to households at juncture (4). Disposable income is take-home pay, which households can spend or save.

The bottom half of this circular flow is the *income half* because it focuses on the income arising from production. Aggregate income is the total income from producing GDP, and disposable income is the income remaining after taxes are subtracted and transfers added. To simplify the discussion, we define **net taxes, *NT***, as taxes minus transfer payments. So *disposable income equals GDP minus net taxes*. Put another way, we can say that aggregate income equals disposable income plus net taxes:

$$\text{GDP} = \text{Aggregate income} = DI + NT$$

At juncture (4), firms have produced output and have paid resource suppliers; governments have collected taxes and made transfer payments. With the resulting disposable income in hand, households now decide how much to spend and how much to save. Because firms have already produced the output and have paid resource suppliers, firms wait to see how much consumers want to spend. Any unsold production gets added to firm inventories.

6-2b Expenditure Half of the Circular Flow

Disposable income splits at juncture (5). Part is spent on consumption, *C*, and the rest is saved, *S*. Thus,

$$DI = C + S$$

financial markets

Banks and other financial institutions that facilitate the flow of funds from savers to borrowers

Consumption remains in the circular flow and is the biggest aggregate expenditure, about 68 percent of the total. Household saving flows to **financial markets**, which consist of banks and other financial institutions that link savers to borrowers. For simplicity, Exhibit 3 shows households as the only savers, though governments, firms, and the rest of the world could save as well (for example, savings from China finance U.S. borrowers). The primary borrowers are firms and governments, but households borrow too, particularly for new homes, and the rest of the world also borrows. In reality, financial markets should be connected to all four economic decision makers, but we have simplified the flows to keep the model from looking like a plate of spaghetti.

In our simplified model, firms pay resource suppliers an amount equal to the entire value of output. With nothing left for investment—that is, with no retained earnings—firms must borrow to finance purchases of physical capital plus any increases in their inventories. Households also borrow to purchase new homes. Therefore, investment, *I*, consists of spending on new capital by firms, including inventory changes, plus spending on residential construction. Investment enters the circular flow at juncture (6), so aggregate spending at that point totals *C* + *I*.

Governments must also borrow whenever they incur deficits, that is, whenever their total *outlays*—transfer payments plus purchases of goods and services—exceed their revenues. Government purchases of goods and services, represented by *G*, enter the spending stream in the upper half of the circular flow at juncture (7). Remember that *G excludes* transfer payments, which already entered the stream as income at juncture (3).

Some spending by households, firms, and governments goes for imports. Because spending on imports flows to foreign producers, spending on imports, *M*, leaks from the circular flow at juncture (8). But the rest of the world buys U.S. products, so foreign spending on U.S. exports, *X*, enters the spending flow at juncture (9). Net exports, the impact of the *rest of the world* on aggregate expenditure, equal exports minus imports, *X* − *M*, which can be positive, negative, or zero. In recent decades, net exports have been negative.

EXHIBIT 3 | **Circular Flow of Income and Expenditure**

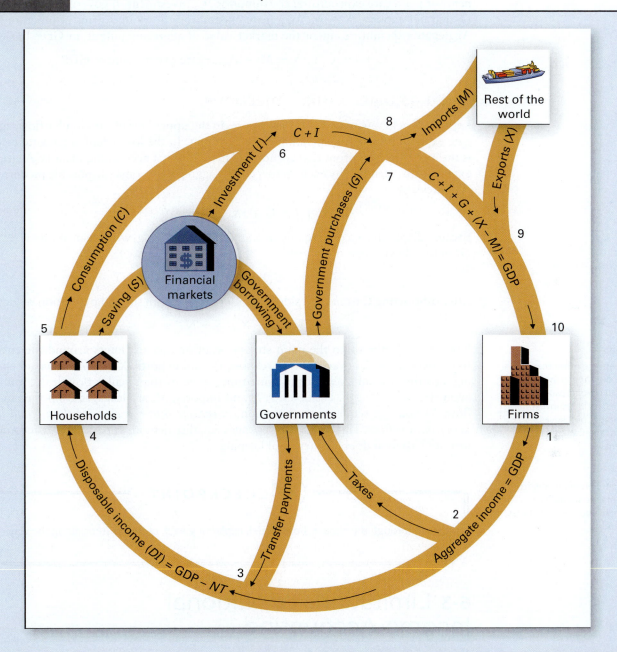

The circular-flow model captures important relationships in the economy. The bottom half depicts the income arising from production. At juncture (1), GDP equals aggregate income. Taxes leak from the flow at (2), but transfer payments enter the flow at (3). Taxes minus transfers equal net taxes, *NT*. Aggregate income minus net taxes equals disposable income, *DI*, which flows to households at juncture (4). The top half of the model shows the flow of expenditure. At (5), households either spend disposable income or save it. Consumption enters the spending flow directly. Saving leaks from the spending flow into financial markets, where it is channeled to borrowers. At (6), investment enters the spending flow. At (7), government purchases enter the spending flow. At (8), imports leak from the spending flow, and at (9), exports enter the spending flow. Consumption plus investment plus government purchases plus net exports add up to the aggregate expenditure on GDP received by firms at (10).

The upper half of the circular flow, the *expenditure half*, tracks the four components of aggregate expenditure: consumption, *C*; investment, *I*; government purchases, *G*; and net exports, *X − M*. Aggregate expenditure flows into firms at juncture (10). Aggregate expenditure equals the market value of aggregate output, or GDP. In short,

$$C + I + G + (X - M) = \text{Aggregate expenditure} = \text{GDP}$$

6-2c Leakages Equal Injections

Let's step back now to view the big picture. In the upper half of the circular flow, aggregate expenditure is total spending on U.S. output. In the lower half, aggregate income is the income arising from that spending. This is the first accounting identity. Aggregate expenditure (spending by each sector) equals aggregate income (disposable income plus net taxes), or

$$C + I + G + (X - M) = DI + NT$$

Because disposable income equals consumption plus saving, we can substitute *C + S* for *DI* in the above equation to yield

$$C + I + G + (X - M) = C + S + NT$$

After subtracting *C* from both sides and adding *M* to both sides, the equation reduces to

$$I + G + X = S + NT + M$$

injection
Any spending other than by households or any income other than from resource earnings; includes investment, government purchases, exports, and transfer payments

leakage
Any diversion of income from the domestic spending stream; includes saving, taxes, and imports

Note that **injections** into the main stream occur at various points around the circular flow. Investment, *I*, government purchases, *G*, and exports, *X*, are *injections* of spending into the circular flow. At the same time, some of the circular flow leaks from the main stream. Saving, *S*, net taxes, *NT*, and imports, *M*, are **leakages** from the circular flow. As you can see from the equation, *injections into the circular flow equal leakages from the flow*. This injections–leakages equality demonstrates a second accounting identity based on double-entry bookkeeping.

 **CHECKPOINT**

Trace through the circular flow model, explaining each of the 10 steps along the way.

6-3 Limitations of National Income Accounting

Imagine the difficulty of developing an accounting system that must capture such a complex and dynamic economy. In the interest of clarity and simplicity, certain features get neglected. In this section, we examine some limitations of the national income accounting system, beginning with production not captured by GDP.

6-3a Some Production Is Not Counted in GDP

With some minor exceptions, the official measure of GDP includes only those products that are sold in markets. This ignores all do-it-yourself production—child care, meal preparation, house-cleaning, family laundry, and home maintenance and repair. Thus, an economy in which householders are largely self-sufficient has a lower GDP than an otherwise similar economy in which households specialize and sell products to one another. During the 1950s, more than 80 percent of American mothers with small children remained at home caring for the family, but all this care added not one cent to GDP. Today most mothers are in the workforce, where their labor gets counted in GDP. Meals, child care, and the like are now often purchased in markets and thus get reflected in GDP. In less developed economies, more economic activity is do-it-yourself.

GDP also ignores off-the-books production. The term **underground economy** describes market activity that goes unreported because either it's illegal or because people want to evade taxes on otherwise legal activity. Although there is no official measure of the underground economy, most economists agree that it is substantial. A federal study suggests the equivalent of 15 percent of U.S. GDP is underground production; this amounted to about $2.7 trillion in 2015. Incidentally, in 2014, Britain and Italy began including spending on prostitution and illegal drugs in their GDP estimates.[1]

underground economy
Market transactions that go unreported either because they are illegal or because people involved want to evade taxes

For some economic activity, income must be *imputed*, or assigned a value, because market exchange does not occur. For example, included in GDP is an *imputed rental income* from home ownership, even though no rent is actually paid or received by those in owner-occupied housing. Also included in GDP is an imputed dollar amount for (1) wages paid *in kind*, such as an employer's payment for employees' medical insurance, and (2) food produced by a farm family for its own consumption. *GDP therefore includes some economic production that does not involve market exchange.*

6-3b Leisure, Quality, and Variety

The average U.S. workweek is much shorter now than it was a century ago, so people work less to produce today's output. People also retire earlier and live longer after retirement. As a result of a shorter workweek and earlier retirement, more leisure is available. But leisure is not reflected in GDP because it is not directly bought and sold in a market. The quality and variety of products available have also improved on average over the years because of technological advances and greater competition. For example, the magazine *Consumer Reports* has found a consistent improvement in the quality of automobiles over time. Yet most of these improvements are not reflected in GDP. Recording systems, computers, tires, running shoes, cell phones, and hundreds of other products have gotten better over the years. Also, new products are being introduced all the time, such as smartphones, e-readers, social networks, and energy drinks. *The gross domestic product fails to capture changes in the availability of leisure time and often fails to reflect changes in the quality of products or in the availability of new products.*

Brand X Pictures/Jupiter Images

6-3c What's Gross About Gross Domestic Product?

Again, a nation's physical capital consists of its buildings, machines, vehicles, computers, and all the other equipment used to produce GDP. In the course of producing

---

[1] Ricardo Lopez, "Britain, Italy Count Prostitution, Drugs in GDP Estimates," *Los Angeles Times*, 30 May 2014.

GDP, some capital wears out, such as the delivery truck that finally dies, and some capital becomes obsolete, such as an aging computer that no longer runs the latest software. A new truck that logs 100,000 miles its first year has been subject to wear and tear, and therefore has a diminished value as a resource. A truer picture of the *net* production that actually occurs during a year is found by subtracting this capital *depreciation* from GDP. **Depreciation** measures the value of the capital stock that is used up or becomes obsolete in the production process. Gross domestic product is called "gross" because it fails to take into account this depreciation. **Net domestic product** equals gross domestic product minus depreciation, the capital stock used up in the production process.

We now have two measures of investment. *Gross investment* is the value of all investment during a year and is used in computing GDP. *Net investment* equals gross investment minus depreciation. The economy's production possibilities depend on what happens to net investment. If net investment is positive—that is, if gross investment exceeds depreciation—the economy's capital stock increases, so its contribution to output increases as well. If net investment is zero, the capital stock remains constant, as does its contribution to output. And if net investment is negative, the capital stock declines, as does its contribution to output.

As the names imply, *gross* domestic product reflects gross investment and *net* domestic product reflects net investment. But estimating depreciation involves some guesswork. For example, what is the appropriate measure of depreciation for the roller coasters at Six Flags, the metal display shelves at Target, or the parking lots at the Mall of America in Minnesota?

depreciation

The value of capital stock used up to produce GDP or that becomes obsolete during the year

net domestic product

Gross domestic product minus depreciation

6-3d GDP Does Not Reflect All Costs

Some production and consumption degrades the quality of our environment. Trucks and automobiles pump pollution into the atmosphere, which could contribute to climate change. Housing developments displace scenic open space and forests. Paper mills foul the lungs and burn the eyes. Oil spills foul the coastline. Coal-fired electric plants pollute the air. More generally, U.S. mortality rates increase during economic expansion, in part, because of the increased air pollution that comes with more traffic and greater output.[2] These negative externalities—costs that fall on those not directly involved in the transactions—are mostly ignored in GDP calculations, even though they diminish the quality of life now and in the future. Recent research suggests that the external costs of some production, such as oil- and coal-fired electricity generation, could exceed the value added by these firms.[3] To the extent that growth in GDP generates negative externalities, a rising GDP may not be as attractive as it would first appear.

Although the national income accounts reflect the depreciation of buildings, machinery, vehicles, and other manufactured capital, this accounting ignores the depletion of natural resources, such as standing timber, oil reserves, fish stocks, and soil fertility. So national income accounts reflect depreciation of the physical capital stock but not the natural capital stock. For example, intensive farming may raise productivity and boost GDP temporarily, but this depletes soil fertility. Worse still, some production may speed the extinction of certain plants and animals. The U.S. Commerce Department is now in the process of developing so-called *green accounting*, or *green GDP*, trying to register the impact of production on air pollution, water pollution, soil depletion, and the loss of other natural resources.

[2] Garth Heutel and Christopher J. Ruhm, "Air Pollution and Procyclical Mortality," *Journal of the Association of Environmental and Resource Economists* (forthcoming).

[3] Nicholas Z. Muller, Robert Mendelsohn, and William Nordhaus, "Environmental Accounting for Pollution in the United States Economy," *American Economic Review*, 101 (August 2011): 1649–1675.

6-3e GDP and Economic Welfare

In computing GDP, the market price of output is the measure of its value. Therefore, each dollar spent on handguns or cigarettes is counted in GDP the same as each dollar spent on baby formula or preventive health care. Positive economic analysis tries to avoid making value judgments about *how* people spend their money. Because GDP, as a number, provides no information about its composition, some economists question whether GDP is the best measure of the nation's economic welfare.

Despite the limitations of official GDP estimates, GDP offers a useful snapshot of the U.S. economy at a point in time. Inflation, however, clouds comparability over time. In the next section, we discuss how to adjust GDP for changes in the economy's price level.

CHECKPOINT

Identify the limitations of the national income accounting system.

6-4 Accounting for Price Changes

As noted earlier, the national income accounts are based on the market values of final goods and services produced in a particular year. Initially, gross domestic product measures the value of output in *nominal dollars*—that is, in the dollar values at the time production occurs. When GDP is based on nominal dollars, the national income accounts measure the *nominal value* of national output. Thus, **nominal GDP** is based on the prices prevailing when production takes place. National income accounts based on nominal dollars allow for comparisons among income or expenditure components in a particular year. Because the economy's average price level changes over time, however, nominal-dollar comparisons across years can be misleading. For example, between 1979 and 1980, nominal GDP increased by about 9 percent. That sounds impressive, but the economy's average price level rose more than 9 percent. So the growth in nominal GDP came entirely from inflation. Real GDP, or GDP measured in terms of the goods and services produced, in fact declined. If nominal GDP increases in a given year, part of this increase may simply reflect inflation—pure hot air. To make meaningful comparisons of GDP across years, we must take out the hot air, or *deflate* nominal GDP. We focus on *real* changes in production by eliminating changes due solely to inflation.

nominal GDP
GDP based on prices prevailing at the time of production

6-4a Price Indexes

To compare the price level over time, let's first establish a point of reference, a base year to which prices in other years can be compared. An *index number* compares the value of some variable in a particular year to its value in a base year, or reference year. Think about the simplest of index numbers. Suppose bread is the only good produced in an economy. As a reference point, let's look at its price in some specific year. The year selected is called the **base year**; prices in other years are expressed relative to the base-year price.

Suppose the base year is 2014, when a loaf of bread in our simple economy sold for $2.50. Let's say the price of bread increased to $2.60 in 2015 and to $2.80 in 2016. We construct a **price index** by dividing each year's price by the price in the base year

base year
The year with which other years are compared when constructing an index; the index equals 100 in the base year

price index
A number that shows the average price of products; changes in a price index over time show changes in the economy's average price level

EXHIBIT 4 | **Hypothetical Example of a Price Index (base year = 2014)**

Year	(1) Price of Bread in Current Year	(2) Price of Bread in Base Year	(3) Price Index (3) = [(1)/(2)] × 100
2014	$2.50	$2.50	100
2015	2.60	2.50	104
2016	2.80	2.50	112

The price index equals the price in the current year divided by the price in the base year, all multiplied by 100.

and then multiplying by 100, as shown in Exhibit 4. For 2014, the base year, we divide the base price of bread by itself, $2.50/$2.50, or 1, so the price index in 2014 equals 1 × 100 = 100. *The price index in the base period is always 100.* The price index in 2015 is $2.60/$2.50, or 1.04, which when multiplied by 100 equals 104. In 2016, the index is $2.80/$2.50, or 1.12, which when multiplied by 100 equals 112. Thus, the index is 4 percent higher in 2015 than in the base year and 12 percent higher in 2016 than in the base year. The price index permits comparisons across years. For example, what if you were provided the indexes for 2015 and 2016 and asked what happened to the price level between the two years? By dividing the 2016 price index by the 2015 price index, 112/104, you find that the price level rose 7.7 percent.

This section has shown how to develop a price index assuming we already know the price level each year. Determining the price level is a bit more involved, as we'll now see.

6-4b Consumer Price Index

consumer price index, or CPI

A measure of inflation based on the cost of a fixed market basket of goods and services

The price index most familiar to you is the **consumer price index**, or **CPI**, which measures changes over time in the cost of buying a "market basket" of goods and services purchased by a typical family. For simplicity, suppose a typical family's market basket for the year includes 365 packages of Twinkies, 500 gallons of heating oil, and 12 months of cable TV. Prices in the base year are listed in column (2) of Exhibit 5. The total cost of each product in the base year is found by multiplying price by quantity, as shown in column (3). The cost of the market basket in the base year is shown at the bottom of column (3) to be $2,574.50.

Prices in the current year are listed in column (4). Notice that not all prices changed by the same percentage since the base year. The price of fuel oil increased, but the price of Twinkies declined. The cost of that same basket in the current year is $2,663.00 shown as the sum of column (5). To compute the consumer price index for the current year, we simply divide the cost in the current year by the cost of that same basket in the base year, $2,663.00/$2,574.50, and then multiply by 100. This yields a price index of 103.4. We could say that between the base period and the current year, the "cost of living" increased by 3.4 percent.

The federal government uses the 36 months of 1982, 1983, and 1984 as the base period for calculating the CPI for a market basket consisting of hundreds of goods and services. The CPI is reported monthly based on prices collected from about 23,000 sellers across the country in 87 metropolitan areas. In reality, each household consumes a unique market basket, so we could theoretically develop about 120 million CPIs—one for each household.

EXHIBIT 5	Hypothetical Market Basket Used to Develop the Consumer Price Index				

Product	(1) Quantity in Market Basket	(2) Prices in Base Year	(3) Cost of Basket in Base Year (3) = (1) × (2)	(4) Prices in Current Year	(5) Cost of Basket in Current Year (5) = (1) × (4)
Twinkies	365 packages	$ 1.30/package	$474.50	$ 1.20	$438.00
Fuel oil	500 gallons	3.00/gallon	1,500.00	3.25	1,625.00
Cable TV	12 months	50.00/month	600.00	50.00	600.00
			$2,574.50		$2,663.00

The cost of a market basket in the current year, shown at the bottom of column (5), sums the quantities of each item in the basket, shown in column (1), times the price of each item in the current year, shown in column (4).

Exhibit 6 shows the relative importance of major spending categories in the CPI market basket in 2015. As you can see, housing claimed the largest share, accounting for 33.0 percent of all consumer spending. Next was food, at 14.4 percent. Your market basket would likely differ from the official CPI mix. For example, you probably spend more than 3.1 percent of your budget on education.

6-4c Problems With the CPI

There is no perfect way to measure changes in the price level. As we have already seen, the quality and variety of some products are improving all the time, so some price increases may be as much a reflection of improved quality as of inflation. The CPI does not account very well for new products with more and better features than the products they replace. A price index that properly accounts for product upgrades could shave an average of 0.8 percentage points from the current CPI

EXHIBIT 6	Relative Importance of Items in CPI Market Basket

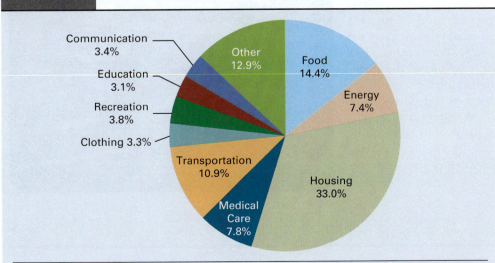

Source: "Consumer Price Index–February 2015," Bureau of Labor Statistics, 24 March 2015, at http://www. bls.gov/news.release/pdf/cpi.pdf.

measure.[4] Thus, there is a *quality bias* in the CPI, because it assumes that the quality of the market basket remains relatively constant over time. *To the extent that the CPI ignores quality improvements, it overstates the true extent of inflation.* Those who come up with the CPI each month try to make some quality adjustments, as discussed in the following case study.

CASE STUDY

PUBLIC POLICY

PRICE CHECK ON AISLE 2   The U.S. economy is one of the most dynamic in the world, marked by rapid technological change. The Bureau of Labor Statistics (BLS), the federal agency that calculates the CPI each month, employs dozens of economists to analyze the impact of any quality changes to products in the CPI market basket. Each month 400 data collectors visit stores to record about 85,000 prices for 211 item categories in the CPI basket. About a week before the CPI is released, the BLS office is locked down with bright red "restricted area" signs on all the doors. A total of 90 people, including product specialists and the other economists working on the CPI, compute the basic indexes in each category. Results are released at 8:30 a.m., Eastern Time, about two weeks after the end of the month in question. This release is a big deal.

Most price adjustments are straightforward. For example, if a candy bar shrinks but its price doesn't, the CPI shows that as a price increase. But sometimes a product changed in a more complicated way. Each economist at BLS specializes in particular products, such as televisions, automobiles, kitchen appliances, and so on. One of their greatest challenges is to identify substitutes for products that are no longer available. For example, data collectors find the model of TV they priced the previous month is missing about one-fifth of the time. When a particular product is missing, a four-page checklist of features such as screen size and the type of remote control guides the data collector to the nearest comparable model. That price is reported and the product specialist in Washington must then decide whether it's an acceptable substitute.

For example, the TV specialist decided that the newer version of the 42-inch model had some important improvements. A complex computer model estimated that the improvements alone would be valued by consumers as worth $135 more. After factoring improvements into the price of the $330 set, the analyst determined that the price of the TV had actually declined 29 percent [= 135/(330 + 135)]. In another example, the price of a 57-inch TV dropped from $2,239 to $1,910, for an apparent decline of 15 percent. But on closer inspection, the analyst found that the new model lacked an HDTV tuner that had been included in the model it replaced. This tuner would be valued by consumers at $514. So, instead of declining 15 percent, the price of the 57-inch TV actually rose 11 percent [= 1,910/(2,239 − 514)].

The TV analyst is applying the *hedonic method*, which breaks down the product into its characteristics, and then estimates the dollar value of each characteristic.

Richard Levine/Alamy

continued

[4] Christian Broda and David E. Weinstein, "Product Creation and Destruction: Evidence and Price Implications," *American Economic Review*, 100 (June 2010): 691–723.

This is a way of capturing the impact of a change in product quality on any price change. Otherwise, price changes would not reflect the fact that consumers are getting more or less for their money as product features change over time.

Sources: Min Zeng, "Inflation Expectations Tick Up," *Wall Street Journal*, 5 May 2015; Binyamin Appelbaum, "2% Inflation Rate Target Is Questioned as Fed Policy Panel Prepares to Meet," *New York Times*, 28 April 2015; and Mary Kokoski, Keith Waehrer, and Patricia Rozaklis, "Using Hedonic Methods for Quality Adjustment in the CPI," U.S. Bureau of Labor Statistics Working Paper (2000), at http://www. bls.gov/cpi/cpiaudio.htm.

But the CPI tends to overstate inflation for another reason. Recall that the CPI holds constant over time the kind and amount of goods and services in the typical market basket. Because not all items in the basket experience the same rate of price change, relative prices change over time. A rational household would respond to changes in relative prices by buying less of the more expensive products and more of the cheaper products. The CPI allows for some substitution within narrow categories (for example shoppers in Chicago can switch among choices of ground beef based on price), but consumers can't easily switch across categories because the point of the CPI is to look at price changes over time for a given market basket. Because the CPI holds the market basket constant for long periods, the CPI is slow to incorporate consumer responses to changes in relative prices. *The CPI calculations, by not allowing households to shift away from goods that have become more costly, overestimate the true extent of inflation experienced by the typical household.*

The CPI has also failed to keep up with the consumer shift toward discount stores such as Walmart, Costco, and Home Depot. Government statisticians consider goods sold by discounters as different from goods sold by regular retailers. Hence, the discounter's lower price does not necessarily translate into a reduction in the cost of living, but simply as a different consumer purchase decision.

Finally, the CPI overstates inflation because it includes an item in the market basket only after the product becomes widely used. By that time, the major price drops have already occurred. For example, the first portable video recorder and camera, the Ampex VR-3000 Backpack, weighed over 40 pounds and sold for $65,000 when it was introduced in 1967 (or about $465,000 in 2015 dollars). Now, for less than $100, you can buy a high-definition video camera that fits in a vest pocket. The CPI captured few of the major price drops. The same is true for all kinds of new products, such as the cell phone, which began as big as a brick and priced north of $1,000. Only after the price of cell phones fell far enough for wider adoption did they make it into the CPI basket.

Experts conclude that the CPI has overestimated inflation by more than 1 percentage point per year. This problem is of more than academic concern because changes in the CPI determine changes in tax brackets and in an array of payments, including wage agreements that include a cost-of-living adjustment, Social Security benefits totaling about $900 billion annually, welfare benefits, even alimony. In fact, about one-third of federal outlays are tied to changes in the CPI. Just a 1 percentage point correction each year in the upward bias of the CPI would save the federal budget about $100 billion annually by 2020.

Overstating the CPI also distorts other measures, such as wages, that use the CPI to adjust for inflation. For example, based on the official CPI, the average real wage in the U.S. economy fell by a total of about 2 percent in the last two decades. But if the CPI overstated inflation by at least 1 percent per year, as many researchers now believe, then the average real wage, instead of dropping by 2 percent, actually increased by about 20 percent. The Bureau of Labor Statistics, the group that estimates the CPI, is now working on these problems and has introduced an experimental version of the CPI that would reduce measured inflation. One experiment uses scanner data at supermarkets to find out how consumers respond, for example, to a rise in the price of romaine lettuce relative to iceberg lettuce, two products assumed to be reasonable substitutes.

6-4d The GDP Price Index

GDP price index

A comprehensive inflation measure of all goods and services included in the gross domestic product

A price index is a weighted sum of various prices. Whereas the CPI focuses on just a sample of consumer purchases, a more complex and more comprehensive price index, the **GDP price index,** measures the average price of all goods and services produced in the economy. To calculate the GDP price index, we use the formula

$$\text{GDP price index} = \frac{\text{Nominal GDP} \times 100}{\text{Real GDP}}$$

where nominal GDP is the dollar value of GDP in a particular year measured in prices of that same year, and real GDP is the dollar value of GDP in a particular year measured in base-year prices. The challenge is finding real GDP in a particular year. Any measure of real GDP is constructed as the weighted sum of thousands of different goods and services produced in the economy. The question is what weights, or prices, to use. Prior to 1995, the Bureau of Economic Analysis (BEA) used prices for a particular base year (most recently 1987) to estimate real GDP. In this case, the quantity of each output in a particular year was valued by using the 1987 price of each output. So real GDP in, say, 1994 was the sum of 1994 output valued at 1987 prices.

6-4e Moving From Fixed Weights to Chain Weights

chain-weighted system

An inflation measure that adjusts the weights from year to year in calculating a price index, thereby reducing the bias caused by a fixed-price weighting system

Estimating real GDP by using prices from a base year yields an accurate measure of real GDP as long as the year in question is close to the base year. But BEA used prices that prevailed in 1987 to value production from 1929 to 1995. In early 1996, BEA switched from a fixed-price weighting system to a **chain-weighted system**, using a complicated process that changes price weights from year to year. All you need to know is that the chain-weighted real GDP adjusts the weights more or less continuously from year to year, reducing the bias caused by a fixed-price weighting system.

Even though the chain-type index adjusts the weights from year to year, any index, by definition, must still use some year as an anchor, or reference point—that is, any index must answer the question, "Compared to what?" To provide such a reference point, BEA measures U.S. real GDP and its components in *chained (2009) dollars*. Exhibit 7 presents nominal-dollar estimates of GDP as well as chained (2009) dollar estimates of real GDP. The blue line indicates nominal-dollar GDP since 1929. The red line indicates real GDP since 1929, or GDP measured in chained (2009) dollars. The two lines intersect in 2009, because that's when real GDP equaled nominal GDP. Nominal GDP is below real GDP in years prior to 2009 because real GDP is based on chained (2009) prices, which on average are higher than prices prior to 2009. Nominal GDP reflects growth in real GDP and in the price level. Chained-dollar GDP reflects growth only in real GDP. So nominal-dollar GDP grows faster than chained-dollar GDP.

✓ CHECKPOINT

What is a price index and why is it useful?

| EXHIBIT 7 | U.S. Gross Domestic Product in Nominal Dollars and Chained (2009) Dollars Since 1929 |

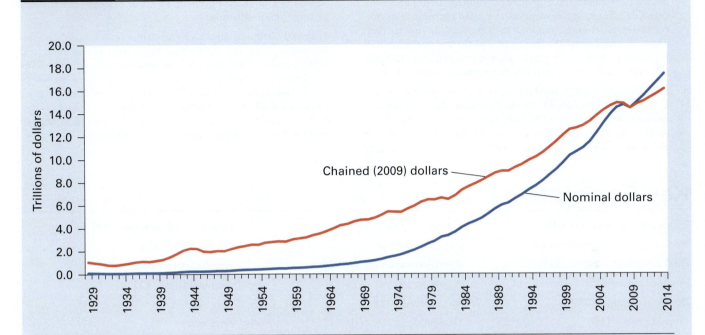

Real GDP, the red line, shows the value of output measured in chained (2009) dollars. The blue line measures GDP in nominal dollars of each year shown. The two lines intersect in 2009, when real GDP equaled nominal GDP. Year-to-year changes in nominal-dollar GDP reflect changes in both real GDP and in the price level. Year-to-year changes in chained-dollar GDP reflect changes in real GDP only. Nominal-dollar GDP grows faster than chained-dollar GDP. Prior to 2009, nominal-dollar prices are less than chained-dollar prices, so nominal-dollar GDP is less than chained-dollar GDP.

Source: Based on annual estimates from the Bureau of Economic Analysis, U.S. Department of Commerce. For the latest data, go to http://bea.gov/national/index.htm#gdp.

6-5 Conclusion

This chapter discussed how GDP is measured and how it's adjusted for changes in the price level over time. The national income accounts have limitations, but they offer a reasonably accurate picture of the economy at a point in time as well as year-to-year movements in the economy. Subsequent chapters will refer to the distinction between real and nominal values. The national income accounts are published in much greater detail than this chapter indicates. The appendix provides some flavor of the additional detail available.

Summary

1. Gross domestic product, or GDP, measures the market value of all final goods and services produced during the year by resources located in the United States, regardless of who owns those resources.

2. The expenditure approach to GDP adds up the market value of all final goods and services produced in the economy during the year. The income approach to GDP adds up all the income generated as a result of that production.

3. Consumption's share of GDP increased from an average of 62 percent during the 1960s to 68 percent during the most recent decade. Government purchases fell from 22 percent to 20 percent. Investment bounced around but averaged 15 percent of GDP during the 1960s and 16 percent during the most recent decade. Net exports averaged a surplus of 1 percent of GDP during the 1960s, but turned negative after that, meaning that imports exceeded exports, with an average deficit of 4 percent of GDP during the most recent decade.

4. The circular-flow model summarizes the flow of income and spending through the economy. The aggregate income from producing GDP equals the aggregate expenditure from purchasing that GDP. Thus, aggregate income equals aggregate expenditure. Saving, net taxes, and imports leak from the circular flow. These leakages equal the injections into the circular flow from investment, government purchases, and exports. Thus, leakages from the circular flow equal injections into the circular flow.

5. GDP reflects market production in a given period, usually a year. Most household production and the underground economy are not captured by GDP. Improvements in the quality and variety of products also are not fully reflected in GDP. Nor are changes in leisure captured in GDP. In other ways GDP may overstate the value of production. GDP fails to subtract for the depreciation of the capital stock or for the depletion of natural resources and fails to account for most negative externalities arising from production.

6. Nominal GDP in a particular year values output based on market prices when the output was produced. To determine real GDP, nominal GDP must be adjusted for price changes. The consumer price index, or CPI, tracks prices for a basket of goods and services over time. The GDP price index tracks price changes for all output. No adjustment for price changes is perfect, but current approaches offer a reasonably good estimate of real GDP both at a point in time and over time.

Key Concepts

Expenditure approach to GDP   115

Income approach to GDP   115

Final goods and services   115

Intermediate goods and services   115

Double counting   115

Consumption   116

Investment   116

Physical capital   116

Residential construction   116

Inventories   116

Government purchases   116

Net exports   116

Aggregate expenditure   116

Aggregate income   118

Value added   118

Disposable income (*DI*)   120

Net taxes (*NT*)   120

Financial markets   120

Injection   122

Leakage   122

Underground economy   123

Depreciation   124

Net domestic product   124

Nominal GDP   125

Base year   125

Price index   125

Consumer price index, or
  CPI   126

GDP price index   130

Chain-weighted system   130

Questions for Review

1. **National Income Accounting** Identify the component of aggregate expenditure to which each of the following belongs:

   a. A U.S. resident buys a new automobile manufactured in Japan
   b. A household's purchase of one hour of legal advice
   c. Construction of a new house
   d. An increase in semiconductor inventories over last year's level
   e. A city government's purchase of 10 new police cars

2. **National Income Accounting** Define gross domestic product. Determine which of the following would be included in the 2016 U.S. gross domestic product:

   a. Profits earned by Ford Motor Company in 2016 on automobile production in Ireland
   b. Automobile parts manufactured in the United States in 2016 but not used until 2017
   c. Social Security benefits paid by the U.S. government in 2016
   d. Ground beef purchased by McDonald's U.S. operations in 2016
   e. Ground beef purchased by a private U.S. household in 2016
   f. Goods and services purchased in the United States in 2016 by a Canadian tourist

3. **National Income Accounting** Explain why intermediate goods and services usually are not included directly in GDP.

4. **Leakages and Injections** What are the leakages from and injections into the circular flow? How are leakages and injections related in the circular flow?

5. **Investment** In national income accounting, one component of investment is net changes in inventories. Last year's inventories are subtracted from this year's inventories to get the net change. Explain why net inventory increases are counted as part of GDP. Also, discuss why it is not sufficient to measure the level of inventories only for the current year. (Remember the difference between stocks and flows.)

6. **Limitations of National Income Accounting** Explain why each of the following should be taken into account when GDP data are used to compare the "level of well-being" in different countries:

   a. Population levels
   b. The distribution of income
   c. The amount of production that takes place outside of markets
   d. The length of the average workweek
   e. The level of environmental pollution

7. **Nominal GDP** Which of the following is a necessary condition—something that must occur—for nominal GDP to rise? Explain your answers.

    a. Actual production must increase.
    b. The price level must increase.
    c. Real GDP must increase.
    d. Either the price level or real GDP must increase as long as the other does not decrease.
    e. Either the price level or real GDP must increase.

8. **Price Indexes** E-readers and HDTVs have not been part of the U.S. economy for very long. Both goods have been decreasing in price and improving in quality. What problems does this pose for people responsible for calculating a price index?

9. **GDP and Depreciation** What is gross about gross domestic product? Could an economy enjoy a constant—or growing—GDP while not replacing worn-out capital?

10. **Consumer Price Index** One form of the CPI that has been advocated by lobbying groups is a "CPI for the elderly." The Bureau of Labor Statistics currently produces indexes only for "all urban households" and "urban wage earners and clerical workers." Should the BLS produce such an index for the elderly?

11. **GDP Price Index** The health expenditure component of the GDP price index has been rising steadily. How might this index be biased by quality and substitution effects? Are there any substitutes for health care?

12. **Chain-Weighted Price Index** How does this approach help compensate for the distortion caused by a price index using fixed weights?

13. **Case Study: Price Check on Aisle 2** What is the hedonic method and why is it sometimes used to track changes in the consumer price index?

Problems and Exercises

14. **Income Approach to GDP** How does the income approach to measuring GDP differ from the expenditure approach? Explain the meaning of *value added* and its importance in the income approach. Consider the following data for the selling price at each stage in the production of a 5-pound bag of flour sold by your local grocer. Use the value-added approach to calculate the final market value of the flour.

Stage of Production	Sale Price
Farmer	$0.30
Miller	0.50
Wholesaler	1.00
Grocer	1.50

15. **Expenditure Approach to GDP** Given the following annual information about a hypothetical country, answer questions a through d.

	Billions of Dollars
Personal consumption expenditures	$200
Personal taxes	50
Exports	30
Depreciation	10
Government purchases	50
Gross private domestic investment	40
Imports	40
Government transfer payments	20

    a. What is the value of GDP?
    b. What is the value of net domestic product?
    c. What is the value of net investment?
    d. What is the value of net exports?

16. **Investment** Given the following data, answer questions a through c.

	Billions of Dollars
New residential construction	$500
Purchases of existing homes	250
Sales value of newly issued stocks and bonds	600
New physical capital	800
Depreciation	200
Net change in firms' inventories	100
Production of new intermediate goods	700

    a. What is the value of gross private domestic investment?
    b. What is the value of net investment?
    c. Are any intermediate goods counted in gross investment?

17. **Consumer Price Index** Calculate a new consumer price index for the data in Exhibit 5 in this chapter. Assume that current-year prices of Twinkies, fuel oil, and cable TV are $1.50/package, $3.15/gallon, and $25.00/month, respectively. Calculate the current year's cost of the market basket and the value of the current year's price index. What is this year's percentage change in the price level compared to the base year?

18. **Consumer Price Index** Given the following data, what was the value of the consumer price index in the base year? Calculate the annual rate of consumer price inflation in 2015 in each of the following situations:

    a. The CPI equals 200 in 2014 and 240 in 2015.
    b. The CPI equals 150 in 2014 and 175 in 2015.
    c. The CPI equals 325 in 2014 and 340 in 2015.
    d. The CPI equals 325 in 2014 and 315 in 2015.

National Income Accounts

This chapter has focused on gross domestic product, or GDP, the measure of output of most interest in subsequent chapters. Other economic aggregates also convey useful information and get media attention. In this appendix we examine those other aggregate measures for 2014.

National Income

So far, we have been talking about the value of production from resources located in the United States, regardless of who owns them. Sometimes we want to focus on how much American resources produce. The **gross national product**, or **GNP**, measures the market value of all final goods and services produced by resources supplied by U.S. residents and firms, regardless of where those resources are located. For example, GNP includes profits from a Ford plant in Europe but excludes profits from a Toyota plant in the United States. We find GNP by adding to GDP the net earnings of American resources abroad, as shown in Exhibit 8. To get the net earnings of American resources abroad, we add income earned by American resources abroad and subtract income earned by resources in the United States owned by those outside the country. After subtracting depreciation from gross national product, we get *net national product*. And after accounting for any statistical discrepancy created by

noise in the accounting system, we get national income, which captures all income earned by American-owned resources, whether those resources are located in the United States or abroad.

National income therefore equals net national product plus any statistical discrepancy. Exhibit 8 shows how to go from gross domestic product to gross national product to net national product to national income. Next we peel back another layer from the onion to arrive at personal income, the income people actually receive.

Personal and Disposable Income

Some of the income received this year was not earned this year and some of the income earned this year was not received this year by those who earned it. By adding to national income the income received but not earned and subtracting the income earned but not received, we move from national income to the income *received* by individuals, which is called **personal income**, a widely reported measure of economic welfare. The federal government estimates and reports personal income monthly.

EXHIBIT 8	Deriving Net Domestic Product and National Income in 2014 (trillions)
Gross domestic product (GDP)	$ 17.42
Plus net earnings of American resources abroad	+0.21
Gross national product (GNP)	17.63
Minus depreciation	−2.74
Net national product	14.89
Statistical discrepancy	+0.18
National income	$ 15.07

Source: Figures are nominal estimates for 2014 from the Bureau of Economic Analysis, U.S. Department of Commerce. For the latest figures, go to http://bea.gov/national/index.htm.

EXHIBIT 9	Deriving Personal Income and Disposable Income in 2014 (trillions)
National income	$ 15.07
Income received but not earned minus income earned but not received	−0.34
Personal income	14.73
Minus personal taxes and nontax charges	−1.74
Disposable income	$ 12.99

Source: Figures are nominal estimates for 2014 from the Bureau of Economic Analysis, U.S. Department of Commerce. For the latest figures, go to http://bea.gov/national/index.htm.

The adjustment from national income to personal income for 2014 is shown in Exhibit 9. Income *earned but not received* in 2014 includes the employer's share of Social Security taxes, taxes on production (e.g., sales and property taxes) net of subsidies, corporate income taxes, and undistributed corporate profits, which are profits the firm retains rather than pays out as dividends. Income *received but not earned* in 2014 includes government transfer payments, receipts from private pension plans, and interest paid by government and by consumers.

Although business taxes have been considered so far, we have not yet discussed personal taxes, which consist mainly of federal, state, and local personal income taxes and the employee's share of the Social Security tax. Subtracting personal taxes and other government charges from personal income yields *disposable income*, which is the amount available to spend or save—the amount that can be "disposed of" by the household. Think of disposable income as take-home pay. Exhibit 9 shows that personal income minus personal taxes and other government charges yields disposable income.

Summary of National Income Accounts

Let's summarize the income side of national income accounts. We begin with *gross domestic product*, or *GDP*, the market value of all final goods and services produced during the year by resources located in the United States. To gross domestic product we add net earnings from American resources abroad to get gross national product. We subtract depreciation from gross national product to get *net national product*. After accounting for any statistical discrepancy, we arrive at *national income*. We obtain *personal income* in 2014 by subtracting from national income all income earned that year but not received that year (for example, undistributed corporate profits) and by adding all income received that year but not earned that year (for example, transfer payments). By subtracting personal taxes and other government charges from personal income, we arrive at the bottom line: *disposable income*, the amount people can either spend or save.

Summary Income Statement of the Economy

Exhibit 10 presents an annual income statement for the entire economy. The upper portion lists aggregate

EXHIBIT 10	Expenditure and Income Statement for the U.S. Economy in 2014 (trillions)

Aggregate Expenditure	
Consumption (C)	$ 11.93
Gross investment (I)	2.85
Government purchases (G)	3.18
Net exports (X − M)	−0.54
GDP	$ 17.42

Aggregatet Income	
Depreciation	$ 2.74
Net taxes on production	1.15
Statistical discrepancy	0.18
Compensation of employees	9.22
Proprietors' income	1.10
Corporate profits	2.09
Net interest	0.49
Rental income of persons	0.45
GDP	$ 17.42

Source: Figures are nominal estimates for 2014 from the Bureau of Economic Analysis, U.S. Department of Commerce. For the latest figures, go to http://bea.gov/national/index.htm.

expenditure, which consists of consumption, gross investment, government purchases, and net exports. Because imports exceeded exports, net exports are negative. The aggregate income from this expenditure is allocated as shown in the lower portion of Exhibit 10. Some spending goes to cover depreciation, net taxes on production, and the statistical discrepancy; and so it's not received as income by anyone. What remains are five income sources: employee compensation, proprietors' income, corporate profits, net interest, and rental income of persons. *Employee compensation*, by far the largest income source, includes both money wages and employer contributions to cover Social Security taxes, medical insurance, and other fringe benefits. *Proprietors' income* includes the earnings of unincorporated businesses. *Corporate profits* are the net revenues received by incorporated businesses but before subtracting corporate income taxes. *Net interest* is the interest received by individuals, excluding interest paid by consumers to businesses and interest paid by government.

Each family that owns a home is viewed as a tiny firm that rents that home to itself. Because homeowners do not, in fact, rent homes to themselves, an imputed rental value is based on an estimate of market rent. *Rental income of persons* consists primarily of the imputed rental value of owner-occupied housing minus the cost of owning that property (such as property taxes, insurance, depreciation, and interest paid on the mortgage). From the totals in Exhibit 10, you can see that aggregate spending in the economy equals the income generated by that spending, thus satisfying the accounting identity.

Appendix Questions

1. **National Income Accounting**   Use the following data to answer the questions below:

	Billions of Dollars ($)
Net investment	$110
Depreciation	30
Exports	50
Imports	30
Government purchases	150
Consumption	400
Production taxes (net of subsidies)	35
Income earned but not received	60
Income received but not earned	70
Personal income taxes	50
Employee compensation	455
Corporate profits	60
Rental income	20
Net interest	30
Proprietor's income	40
Net earnings of U.S. resources abroad	40
Statistical discrepancy	10

a. Calculate GDP using the income and the expenditure methods.
b. Calculate gross investment.
c. Calculate gross national product, net national product, national income, personal income, and disposable income.

2. **National Income Accounting**   According to Exhibit 10 in this appendix, GDP can be calculated either by adding expenditures on final goods or by adding the allocations of these expenditures to the resources used to produce these goods. Why do you suppose the portion of final goods expenditures that goes to pay for intermediate goods or raw materials is excluded from the income method of calculation?

Unemployment and Inflation

7

- *What's so bad about unemployment?*
- *Who among the following would be counted as unemployed: a college student who is not working, a bank teller displaced by an automatic teller machine, Jennifer Lawrence between movies, and baseball slugger Miguel Cabrera in the off-season?*
- *What type of unemployment might be healthy for the economy?*
- *Why is the unemployment rate for young adults much higher than for other age groups?*
- *What's so bad about inflation?*
- *Why is anticipated inflation less of a problem than unanticipated inflation?*

These and other questions are answered in this chapter, where we explore two macroeconomic problems: unemployment and inflation.

To be sure, unemployment and inflation are not the only problems an economy could face. Sluggish growth and widespread poverty are others. But low unemployment and low inflation go a long way toward reducing other economic ills. Although unemployment and inflation are often related, each is discussed separately. The causes of each and the relationship between the two will become clearer as you learn more about how the economy works.

This chapter shows that not all unemployment or all inflation harms the economy. Even in a healthy economy, a certain amount of unemployment reflects the voluntary choices of workers and employers seeking their best options. And moderate inflation that is fully anticipated creates fewer distortions than does unanticipated inflation.

Topics discussed in this chapter include:

- Measuring unemployment
- Frictional, structural, seasonal, and cyclical unemployment
- Full employment
- Sources and consequences of inflation
- Relative price changes
- Nominal and real interest rates

7-1 Unemployment: Its Measure and Sources

"They scampered about looking for work. . . . They swarmed on the highways. The movement changed them; the highways, the camps along the road, the fear of hunger and the hunger itself, changed them. The children without dinner changed them, the endless moving changed them."[1] There is no question, as John Steinbeck wrote in *The Grapes of Wrath*, a novel set in the Great Depression, that a long stretch of unemployment profoundly affects the jobless and their families. The most obvious loss is a steady paycheck, but the unemployed often lose self-esteem and part of their identity as well. Losing a job also means losing connections to coworkers. According to psychologists, in terms of stressful events, the loss of a good job ranks only slightly below a divorce or the death of a loved one.

Even some economists argue that the other effects of unemployment can have a more serious impact on an individual's well-being than the loss of income itself.[2] Job losses worsen health in both men and women, in part because those out of work tend to smoke more cigarettes.[3] More generally, unemployment appears to be linked to a

[1] John Steinbeck, *The Grapes of Wrath* (Viking, 1939), p. 293.
[2] See, for example, John F. Helliwell and Haifang Huang, "New Measures of the Costs of Unemployment: Evidence From the Subjective Well-Being of 3.3 Million Americans," *Economic Inquiry*, 52 (October 2014): 1485–1502.
[3] Sandra E. Black, Paul J. Devereux, and Kjell G. Salvanes, "Losing Heart? The Effect of Job Displacement on Health," *ILR Review*, 68 (August 2015): 833–861.

greater incidence of crime and to a variety of afflictions, including heart disease, suicide, and clinical depression.[4] People out of work also report a greater level of sadness, which decreases dramatically if they find jobs.[5] And U.S. workers who experience a national economic recession in their 50s have a shorter lifespan because of long spells of unemployment and lost health insurance.[6] No matter how often people complain about their jobs, they rely on those same jobs not only for their livelihood but for part of their personal identity. When strangers meet, one of the first questions asked is "What do you do for a living?" Alfred Marshall, the most famous economist of the 19th century, wrote that a job is often the main object of our thoughts and intellectual development.

In addition to the personal costs, unemployment imposes a cost on the economy as a whole because fewer goods and services are produced. When those who are willing and able to work can't find jobs, their labor is lost forever. *This lost income and output coupled with the economic and psychological cost of unemployment on the individual and the family are the real costs of unemployment.* As we begin our analysis, keep in mind that the national unemployment rate reflects millions of individuals with their own stories. As President Harry Truman once remarked, "It's a recession when your neighbor loses his job; it's a depression when you lose your own." For some lucky people, unemployment is a brief vacation between jobs. For some others, a long stretch can have a lasting effect on family stability, economic welfare, self-esteem, and personal identity. Because young adults have higher unemployment rates than others in the labor force, this section should be of special interest to some of you.

7-1a Measuring Unemployment

The unemployment rate is the most widely reported measure of the nation's economic health. What does the unemployment rate measure? What are the sources of unemployment? How has unemployment changed over time? These are some of the questions explored in this section. Let's first see how to measure unemployment.

We begin with the U.S. *civilian noninstitutional adult population*, which consists of all civilians 16 years of age and older, except those in prison, in mental hospitals, or in homes for the aged. The adjective *civilian* means the definition excludes those in the military. From here on, references to the *adult population* will mean the civilian noninstitutional adult population. The **labor force** consists of the people in the adult population who are either working or looking for work. *Those who want a job but can't find one are unemployed.* The Bureau of Labor Statistics interviews 60,000 households monthly (which translates into about 110,000 individuals) and counts people as unemployed if they have no job but want one *and* have looked for work at least once during the preceding four weeks. Thus, the college student, the displaced bank teller, actress Jennifer Lawrence, and baseball slugger Miguel Cabrera in the off-season would all be counted as unemployed if they wanted a job and looked for work in the previous month. The **unemployment rate** measures the percentage of those in the labor force who are unemployed. Hence, the unemployment rate, which is reported monthly, equals the number unemployed—that is, people without jobs who are looking for work—divided by the number in the labor force.

labor force
Those 16 years of age and older who are either working or looking for work

unemployment rate
The number unemployed as a percentage of the labor force

---

4. For a study linking a higher incidence of suicides to recessions, see Christopher J. Ruhm, "Are Recessions Good for Your Health?" *Quarterly Journal of Economics*, 115 (May 2000): 617–650. Clinical depression is also higher among the unemployed, as demonstrated in Frederick J. Zimmerman and Wayne Katon, "Socioeconomic Status, Depression Disparities, and Financial Strain: What Lies Behind the Income-Depression Relationship," *Health Economics*, 14 (December 2005): 1197–1215.

5. Alan B. Krueger and Andreas I. Miller, "Time Use, Emotional Well-Being, and Unemployment: Evidence From Longitudinal Data," *American Economic Review*, 102 (May 2012): 594–599.

6. Courtney C. Coile, Phillip B. Levine, and Robin McKnight, "Recessions, Older Workers, and Longevity: How Long Are Recessions Good for Your Health?" *American Economic Journal: Economic Policy*, 6 (August 2014): 92–119.

Only a fraction of adults who are not working are considered unemployed. The others may have retired, are students, are caring for children at home, or simply don't want to work. Others may be unable to work because of long-term illness or disability. Some may have become so discouraged by a long, unfruitful job search that they have given up in frustration. These **discouraged workers** have, in effect, dropped out of the labor force, so they are not counted as unemployed. Finally, about one-third of those working part time would prefer to work full time, yet all part-timers are counted as employed. Because the official unemployment rate does not include discouraged workers and counts all part-time workers as employed, it may underestimate the true extent of unemployment in the economy. Later we'll consider some reasons why the unemployment rate may exaggerate the true extent of unemployment.

These definitions are illustrated in Exhibit 1, where circles represent the various groups, and the numbers (in millions) of individuals in each category and subcategory are shown in parentheses. The circle on the left depicts the entire U.S. labor force in February 2015, including both employed and unemployed people. The circle on the right represents those in the adult population who, for whatever reason, are not working. These two circles combine to show the adult population. The overlapping area identifies the number of *unemployed* workers—that is, people in the labor force who are not working. The unemployment rate is found by dividing the number unemployed by the number in the labor force. In February 2015, 8.7 million people were unemployed in a labor force of 157.0 million, yielding an unemployment rate of 5.5 percent (= 8.7/157.0).

discouraged workers
Those who drop out of the labor force in frustration because they can't find work

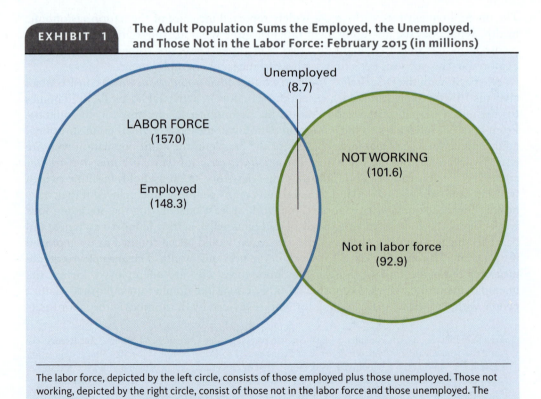

| EXHIBIT 1 | The Adult Population Sums the Employed, the Unemployed, and Those Not in the Labor Force: February 2015 (in millions) |

The labor force, depicted by the left circle, consists of those employed plus those unemployed. Those not working, depicted by the right circle, consist of those not in the labor force and those unemployed. The adult population sums the employed, the unemployed, and those not in the labor force.

Source: Figures are for February 2015 from the U.S. Bureau of Labor Statistics. For the latest data, go to http://www.bls.gov/news.release/empsit.toc.htm.

7-1b Labor Force Participation Rate

The productive capability of any economy depends in part on the proportion of adults in the labor force, measured as the *labor force participation rate*. In Exhibit 1, the U.S. adult population equals those in the labor force (157.0 million) plus those not in the labor force (92.9 million)—a total of 249.9 million people. The **labor force participation rate** therefore equals the number in the labor force divided by the adult population, or 62.8 percent (= 157.0/249.9). So, on average, one out of three adults is not in the labor force. The labor force participation rate increased from 60 percent in 1970 to 67 percent in 1990, but declined after the Great Recession, as many dropped out of the labor market because jobs were hard to find. In fact, the labor force participation rate in February 2015 was among the lowest in decades.

labor force participation rate The labor force as a percentage of the adult population

One striking development since World War II has been the convergence in the labor force participation rates of men and women. In 1950, only 34 percent of adult women were in the labor force. Today, 57 percent are, with the greatest increase among younger women. The labor force participation rate among men has declined from 86 percent in 1950 to 69 percent today, primarily because of earlier retirement. The participation rate is higher among white males, at 72 percent, than black males, at 67 percent, but higher among black females, at 62 percent, than white females, at 57 percent. Finally, the participation rate climbs with education—from only 45 percent for those lacking a high school diploma to 75 percent among those with at least a bachelor's degree.

7-1c Unemployment Over Time

Exhibit 2 shows the U.S. unemployment rate since 1900, with shaded bars to indicate periods of recession or depression. As you can see, rates rise during contractions and fall during expansions. Most striking is the jump during the Great Depression of the 1930s, when the rate topped 25 percent. Note that the rate trended upward from the end of World War II in the mid-1940s until the early 1980s; then it backed down, from a high of 10 percent in 1982 to a low of 4 percent in 2000. With the recession of 2001, the rate gradually increased to 6 percent by 2003, then declined into 2007. But the global financial crisis of 2008 and sharp U.S. recession boosted the rate to 10 percent by the end of 2009.

Let's examine some of the broad trends over the last three decades. Why did the unemployment rate trend down from 9.7 percent in 1982 to only 4.0 percent in 2000? First, the overall economy was on a roll during that period, interrupted by only a brief recession in the early 1990s triggered by the first war in Iraq. The number employed increased by 37 million between 1982 and 2000, making the U.S. economy an incredible job machine and the envy of the world. The unemployment rate also trended down because there were fewer teenagers in the workforce. Teenagers have an unemployment rate about three times that of adults, so the declining share of teenage workers helped cut the overall unemployment rate.

But job growth between 2000 and 2015 was hobbled by a mild recession in 2001 and the Great Recession of 2007–2009, when unemployment exceeded 10.0 percent. That rate gradually came down to 5.5 percent by early 2015. More troubling was that the labor force participation rate dropped from 66.3 percent in February 2007 to 62.8 percent in February 2015. If the labor force participation rate had remained constant, the labor force in early 2015 would have been 5.7 million workers greater than it turned out to be.

7-1d Duration of Unemployment

A given unemployment rate tells us little about how long people have been unemployed. In February 2015, with the unemployment rate at 5.5 percent, the average duration of

EXHIBIT 2	The U.S. Unemployment Rate Since 1900

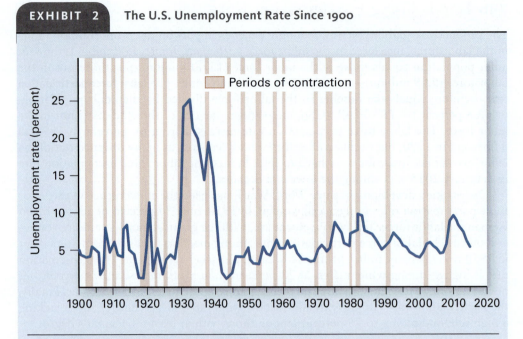

Since 1900, the unemployment rate has fluctuated widely, rising during contractions and falling during expansions. During the Great Depression of the 1930s, the rate spiked to 25 percent.

Sources: U.S. Census Bureau, *Historical Statistics of the United States: Colonial Times to 1970* (U.S. Government Printing Office, 1975); *Economic Report of the President*, February 2015; and U.S. Bureau of Labor Statistics. Figure for 2015 is estimated. For the latest unemployment rate, go to http://www.bls.gov/news.release/empsit.toc.htm.

unemployment was 32 weeks, down from 39 weeks in 2012, which had been the longest since the Great Depression. The 32-week average in early 2015 was still double the average of the previous three decades. Some people were unemployed longer than others in February 2015: 28 percent were unemployed less than 5 weeks, 26 percent 5–14 weeks, 15 percent 15–26 weeks, and 31 percent 27 weeks or longer. Those out of work 27 weeks or longer are called the **long-term unemployed**, and are of special concern to policy makers. Thus, about three in ten of those looking for work in February 2015 were long-term unemployed. Reported another way, that month, 1.7 percent of the labor force consisted of the long-term unemployed. In 2007, prior to the financial crisis and Great Recession, only 0.8 percent of the labor force were long-term unemployed. Researchers have found that the longer someone remains unemployed the more difficult it becomes to find work. Thus, a long stretch of unemployment reduces the chances of finding a job.[7]

long-term unemployed
Those looking for work for 27 weeks or longer

7-1e Unemployment Among Various Groups

The unemployment rate also says nothing about who is unemployed. The overall rate masks wide differences in the labor force based on education, race, gender, and age. Exhibit 3 shows the unemployment rate in 2014 based on educational attainment for people age 25 and older. For example, the unemployment rate for those with less than a high school diploma was 9.0 percent. From there, the rate drops as education increases. The lowest rate was 1.9 percent, for those with a professional degree. Note that the rate among those with some college but no degree was 6.0 percent, the same as those with just a high school diploma. So education provides some insurance against

[7] Kory Kroft, Fabian Lange, and Matthew J. Notowidigdo, "Duration Dependence and Labor Market Conditions: Evidence from a Field Experiment," *Quarterly Journal of Economics*, 128 (August 2013): 1123–1167.

unemployment, especially if you finish college. (But timing is important, even for college graduates. Not only do those who graduate from college during a recession have a harder time finding that first job, but their job opportunities can be limited for years.)[8]

Unemployment also differs based on race and ethnicity; in February 2015, the rate was 4.7 percent among white workers, 10.4 percent among African Americans, 6.6 percent among those of Hispanic ethnicity, and 4.0 percent among Asian workers. (According to the 2010 Census, half of those over 25 years of age who identified themselves as Asian had at least a bachelor's degree, compared to only 28 percent for the entire U.S. population over 25.) Finally, the unemployment rate in February 2015 was 5.2 percent among males 20 and older and 4.9 percent among females 20 and older, but 17.1 percent among workers 16 to 19 years of age.

Why is the unemployment rate among teenage workers so much higher than among other workers? Teenagers enter the labor force with little education or job experience, so they take unskilled jobs and are first to be laid off if the economy slows down (last hired, first fired). Teenagers also move in and out of the labor force more frequently as they juggle school demands. Even those who have left school often shop around more than workers 20 and older, quitting one job in search of a better one.[9]

| EXHIBIT 3 | Unemployment Rates and Educational Attainment |

Source: Bureau of Labor Statistics at http://www.bls.gov/emp/ep_chart_001.htm. Rates are for 2014 for persons age 25 and over.

---

8. Philip Oreopoulos, Till von Wachter, and Andrew Heisz, "The Short- and Long-Term Career Effects of Graduating in a Recession," *American Economic Journal: Applied Economics*, 4 (January 2012): 1–29.
9. Martin Gervais et al. "What Should I Be When I Grow Up? Occupation and Unemployment Over the Life Cycle," NBER Working Paper No. 20628 (October 2014).

The unemployment rate is higher among black workers for several reasons. The black workforce is on average younger, and younger workers tend to experience higher unemployment rates. A smaller than average percentage of black workers graduated from college. Black workers tend to live in areas harder hit by recessions. And racial discrimination is also a contributing factor.

Unemployment rates for different groups appear in Exhibit 4. Each panel shows the rate by race and by gender since 1972. Panel (a) shows the rates for workers 20 and older, and panel (b) the rates for 16- to 19-year-old workers. Periods of recession are shaded pink. As you can see, rates are higher among black workers than among white

EXHIBIT 4   **Unemployment Rates for Various Groups**

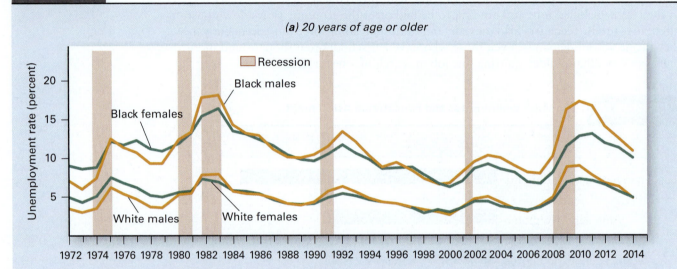

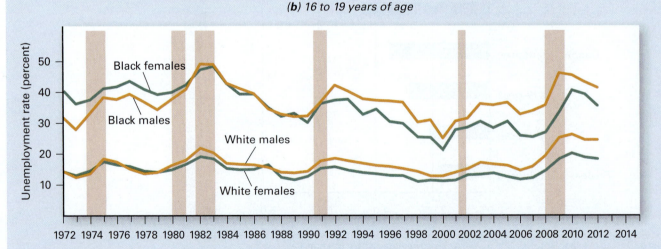

Different groups face different unemployment rates. The unemployment rate is higher for black workers than for white workers and higher for teenagers than for those age 20 years and older.

Source: *Economic Report of the President*, February 2013, Table B-43 for historical data; and U.S. Bureau of Labor Statistics for recent years. For the latest data, go to http://www.bls.gov/news.release/empsit.toc.htm. A breakout by race was not available for teenagers in 2013 and 2014.

workers, and rates are higher among teenage workers than among those 20 and older. During recessions, rates climbed for all groups. Rates peaked during the recession of 1982 and then trended down to 2000. The rate rose with the recession of 2001 and more sharply with the Great Recession of 2007–2009. Exhibit 4 shows that the unemployment rate among black men was more than double that among white men.

7-1f Unemployment Varies Across Occupations and Regions

The unemployment rate varies by occupation. Professional and technical workers experience lower unemployment rates than blue-collar workers. Construction workers at times face high rates because that occupation is both seasonal and subject to wide swings over the business cycle.

Partly because certain occupations dominate labor markets in certain regions, unemployment rates also vary by region. For example, the unemployment rates in New Jersey, Rhode Island, and West Virginia in February 2015 were double those in the upper Midwest farm states of Nebraska, North Dakota, and South Dakota. Even within a state, unemployment can vary widely. For example, the California city of El Centro had an unemployment rate of 20.0 percent, more than four times that of San Francisco.

Exhibit 5 shows unemployment rates for 27 major metropolitan areas in February 2015. As you can see, Washington, D.C. had the highest unemployment rate, at 8.1 percent. This was more than double the rate for Minneapolis and Honolulu. The point is that *the national unemployment rate masks differences across states and even within an individual state*. Still, most cities in Exhibit 5 had rates between 4.0 percent and 6.0 percent.

7-1g International Comparisons of Unemployment

How do U.S. unemployment rates compare with those around the world? Exhibit 6 shows rates since 1980 for the United States, Japan, and the average of four major European economies (France, Germany, Italy, and the United Kingdom). During the decades before the Great Recession, unemployment trended down in the United States, trended up in Japan, and remained high in Europe. During the Great Recession of 2007–2009, the unemployment rate spiked in the United States, even briefly exceeding the average in Europe. The rate in Japan remained relatively low. In recent years, the U.S. rate has dropped.

Since 1980 the unemployment rate in Europe has averaged 8.3 percent versus a U.S. average of 6.4 percent. Why have rates averaged higher in Europe? The ratio of unemployment benefits to average pay is higher in Europe than in the United States, and unemployment benefits last longer there, sometimes years. So those collecting unemployment benefits have less incentive to find work. What's more, government regulations have made European employers more reluctant to hire new workers because firing them can be difficult.

Historically, unemployment has been low in Japan, averaging only 3.5 percent since 1980, because many firms there offer job security for life. In a system called *shukatsu*, Japanese companies typically hire most workers right out of school and expect them to stay until retirement. Both labor laws and social norms limit layoffs in Japan. As a result, some employees who do little or no work are still carried on company payrolls. Unemployment has increased there since the early 1990s because more Japanese firms went bankrupt.

EXHIBIT 5 | **Unemployment Rates Differ Across U.S. Metropolitan Areas**

Source: Based on figures for February 2015 from the U.S. Bureau of Labor Statistics. For the latest figures, go to http://www.bls.gov/lau/home.htm.

7-1h Sources of Unemployment

Pick up any metropolitan newspaper and thumb through the classifieds. The help-wanted section may include hundreds of jobs, from accountants to X-ray technicians. Online job sites such as Monster.com list hundreds of thousands of openings. Why, when millions are unemployed, are so many jobs available? To understand this, we must think about all the reasons why people are unemployed. They may be looking for a first job, or they may be reentering the labor force after an absence. They may have quit or been fired from

| EXHIBIT 6 | **Unemployment Rates Increased After the Global Financial Crisis of 2008** |

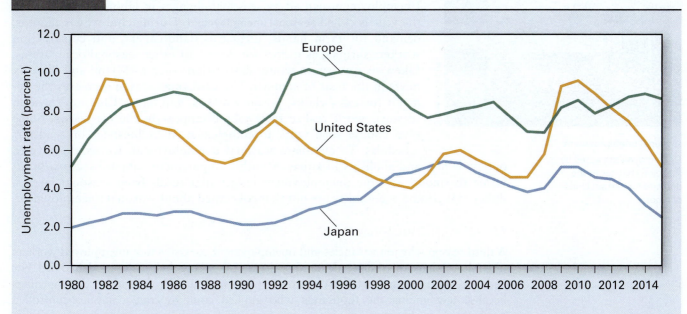

Source: Based on standardized rates in *OECD Economic Outlook*, 97 (May 2015); and *Economic Report of the President*, February 2015. Figures for Europe are the averages for France, Germany, Italy, and the United Kingdom. Figures for 2015 are projections. For the latest international data, go to http://www.bls.gov/fls/home.htm.

their last job. Fifty-two percent of those unemployed in February 2015 lost their previous job, 8 percent quit, 12 percent entered the labor market for the first time, and 28 percent reentered the labor market. *Thus, 48 percent were unemployed either because they quit jobs or because they were just joining or rejoining the labor force.*

More generally, there are four sources of unemployment: frictional, seasonal, structural, and cyclical.

Frictional Unemployment

Just as employers do not always hire the first applicant who comes through the door, job seekers do not always accept the first offer. Both employers and job seekers need time to explore the job market. Employers need time to learn about the talent available, and job seekers need time to learn about employment opportunities. The time required to bring together employers and job seekers is the source of **frictional unemployment**. Although unemployment often creates economic and psychological hardships, not all unemployment is necessarily bad. Frictional unemployment does not usually last long and it results in a better match between workers and jobs, so the entire economy works more efficiently. Workers switch jobs to find better fits; the resulting *churn* makes the labor market more efficient. Policy makers and economists are not that concerned about frictional unemployment. In recent years, however, there has been less job switching. This reduces frictional unemployment but makes for a less dynamic and less flexible economy.[10]

frictional unemployment
Unemployment that occurs because job seekers and employers need time to find each other

[10.] Ryan Decker et al. "The Role of Entrepreneurship in U.S. Job Creation and Economic Dynamism," *Journal of Economic Perspectives*, 28 (Summer 2014): 3–24.

AP Images/Gary He

seasonal unemployment
Unemployment caused by seasonal changes in the demand for certain kinds of labor

Seasonal Unemployment

Unemployment caused by seasonal changes in labor demand during the year is called **seasonal unemployment**. During cold winter months, demand for farm hands, lifeguards, landscapers, and construction workers shrinks, as it does for dozens of other seasonal occupations. Likewise, tourism in winter destinations such as Miami and Phoenix melts in the heat of summer. The Christmas season increases the demand for sales clerks, postal workers, and Santa Clauses. Those in seasonal work realize their jobs disappear in the off-season. Some even choose such work to complement their lifestyles or academic schedules. To eliminate seasonal unemployment, we would have to outlaw winter and abolish Christmas. Monthly employment data are *seasonally adjusted* to smooth out the unemployment bulges that result from seasonal factors. Policy makers and economists are not that concerned about seasonal unemployment.

Structural Unemployment

A third reason why job vacancies and unemployment coexist is that unemployed workers often do not have the skills in demand or do not live where their skills are demanded. For example, the Lincoln Electric Company in Ohio took a long time filling 200 openings because few among the thousands who applied could operate computer-controlled machines. Unemployment arising from a mismatch of skills or geographic location is called **structural unemployment**. *Structural unemployment occurs because changes in tastes, technology, taxes, and competition reduce the demand for certain skills and increase the demand for other skills.* In our dynamic economy, some workers, such as coal miners in West Virginia, are stuck with skills no longer demanded. Likewise, golf carts replaced caddies, ATMs replaced bank tellers, and office technology is replacing clerical staff. For example, because of email, voice mail, text messages, word processors, smartphones, and other electronic devices, the number of secretaries, typists, and administrative assistants in the United States has fallen by more than half over the past two decades. Structural unemployment may also arise from a change in tastes and preferences. For example, because Americans smoke less, some tobacco farmers had to grow other crops or find other work. And because Americans buy fewer newspapers, employment in that industry and in the paper industry has declined.

structural unemployment
Unemployment because (1) the skills demanded by employers do not match those of the unemployed, or (2) the unemployed do not live where the jobs are

Whereas most frictional unemployment is short term and voluntary, structural unemployment poses more of a problem because workers must either develop the skills demanded in the local job market or look elsewhere. Moving is not easy. Most people out of work prefer to remain near friends and relatives. Those laid off from good jobs hang around in hopes of getting rehired. Married couples with one spouse still employed may not want to give up that job to look for two jobs elsewhere. Finally, available jobs may be in regions where the living cost is much higher. So those structurally unemployed often stay put. U.S. interstate migration has slowed since the 1980s, which could worsen structural unemployment.[11] Some researchers concluded that, as a result of the Great Recession, structural unemployment in the U.S. economy between 2006 and 2010 increased by 1.75 percentage points.[12] Some federal retraining programs aim to reduce structural unemployment. Policy makers and economists are very much concerned about structural unemployment.

[11.] Raven Molloy, Christopher L. Smith, and Abigail Wozniak, "Internal Migration in the United States," *Journal of Economic Perspectives*, 25 (Summer 2011): 173–196.
[12.] Marcello Estevao and Evridiki Tsounta, "Has the Great Recession Raised U.S. Structural Unemployment?" IMF Working Paper (May 2011); and Aysegul Sahin et al. "Mismatch Unemployment," *American Economic Review*, 104 (November 2014): 3529–3564.

Cyclical Unemployment

As output declines during recessions, firms reduce their demand for nearly all resources, including labor. **Cyclical unemployment** increases during recessions and decreases during expansions. Between 1932 and 1934, when unemployment averaged about 24 percent because of the Great Depression, there was clearly much cyclical unemployment. Between 1942 and 1945, when unemployment averaged less than 2 percent because of the demands of World War II, there was no cyclical unemployment. Cyclical unemployment means the economy is operating inside its production possibilities frontier. Government policies that stimulate aggregate demand aim to reduce cyclical unemployment. Policy makers and economists worry about cyclical unemployment.

cyclical unemployment
Unemployment that fluctuates with the business cycle, increasing during recessions and decreasing during expansions

> ### ✔ CHECKPOINT
>
> What does the unemployment rate measure, and what are four sources of unemployment?

7-2 Other Unemployment Issues

Thus far we have discussed measures of unemployment, rates among various demographic groups, and sources of unemployment. Now we'll consider some other issues of unemployment.

7-2a The Meaning of Full Employment

In a dynamic economy such as ours, changes in product demand and in technology continually alter the supply and demand for particular types of labor. Thus, even in a healthy economy, there is some frictional, structural, and seasonal unemployment. The economy is viewed as operating at *full employment* if there is no cyclical unemployment. When economists talk about "full employment," they do not mean zero unemployment but low unemployment, with estimates ranging from 4 to 6 percent. Even when the economy is at **full employment**, there is some frictional, structural, and seasonal unemployment. As noted earlier, nearly half of those unemployed in February 2015 had quit their previous job or were new entrants or reentrants into the labor force. We can't expect people to find jobs overnight. Many in this group would be considered frictionally unemployed.

full employment
Employment level when there is no cyclical unemployment

7-2b Unemployment Compensation

As noted at the outset, unemployment often involves an economic and psychological hardship. For a variety of reasons, however, the burden of unemployment on the individual and the family may not be as severe today as it was during the Great Depression. Today, many households have two or more workers in the labor force, so if one loses a job, another may still have one—a job that could provide health insurance and other benefits for the family. *Having more than one family member in the labor force cushions the shock of unemployment.* And those just out of school who can't find work can usually move back home, an option that helps cushion unemployment.[13]

[13.] Greg Kaplan, "Moving Back Home: Insurance Against Labor Market Risk," *Journal of Political Economy*, 120 (June 2014): 446–512.

unemployment benefits
Cash transfers to those who lose their jobs and actively seek employment

Moreover, unlike the experience during the Great Depression, most who lose jobs now collect unemployment benefits. In response to the Great Depression, Congress passed the Social Security Act of 1935, which provided unemployment insurance financed by a tax on employers. Unemployed workers who meet certain qualifications can receive **unemployment benefits** for up to six months, provided they actively look for work. During recessions, benefits usually extend beyond six months in states with especially high unemployment. During and following the Great Recession of 2007–2009, the extension of benefits was nationwide, and many states offered benefits for up to two years. Benefits go primarily to people who have lost jobs. Those just entering or reentering the labor force are not covered, nor are those who quit their last job or those fired for just cause, such as excessive absenteeism or theft. In 2014 only 27 percent of the unemployed received benefits. Why so low? Recall that nearly a third of the unemployed most recently were out of work for 27 weeks or longer. This group would have run out of unemployment benefits, which typically last six months. And nearly half of the unemployed were not eligible in the first place because they either quit their job or were just entering or reentering the labor force.

Unemployment benefits replace on average about half of a person's take-home pay, with a higher percentage for those who lost lower-paying jobs. Benefits vary by state but averaged about $340 per week in 2015. That year, Massachusetts had the highest maximum benefits, at $700 per week, and Mississippi, the lowest, at $235 per week. Because these benefits reduce the opportunity cost of remaining unemployed, they may reduce the incentives to find work. For example, if faced with a choice between washing dishes for $350 per week and collecting $250 per week in unemployment benefits, which would you choose? Evidence suggests that those collecting unemployment benefits remain out of work weeks longer than those without benefits. Many leave the labor force once their benefits run out.[14] In a 2014 Harris Survey of 1,500 unemployed Americans, 82 percent said they would "search harder and wider" once their unemployment compensation ran out. Forty-eight percent said they "haven't had to look for work as hard" because of their unemployment benefits, and 62 percent agreed that those benefits "allowed me to take time for myself."[15]

There is also evidence that after receiving government-provided health insurance, people reduced their labor supply.[16] And unemployment spells are longer after receiving an Earned Income Tax Credit refund (based on work the previous year) than unemployment spells during other times of the year.[17] So unemployment insurance and other safety-net programs reduce the urgency of finding work, thereby increasing unemployment.[18] There is also the possibility of fraud, with some collecting unemployment benefits who are, in fact, working.[19] On the plus side, because beneficiaries need not take the first job that comes along, unemployment insurance allows for a higher-quality job search. As a result of a higher-quality search, there is a better match between job skills and job requirements, and this promotes economic efficiency.

[14.] See, for example, David Card, Raj Chetty, and Andrea Weber, "Cash-on-Hand and Competing Models of Intertemporal Behavior: New Evidence from the Labor Markets," *Quarterly Journal of Economics*, 122 (November 2007): 1511–1560; and Kory Kroft and Matthew J. Notowidigdo, "Should Unemployment Insurance Vary With the Unemployment Rate? Theory and Evidence," *Review of Economic Studies* (forthcoming).

[15.] Bob Funk, "Clear Evidence on Disincentives to Work," *Wall Street Journal*, 9 November 2014.

[16.] Laura Dague, Thomas DeLeire, and Lindsey Leininger, "The Effect of Public Insurance Coverage for Childless Adults on Labor Supply," NBER Working Paper No. 20111 (May 2014).

[17.] Sara LaLumia, "The EITC, Tax Refunds, and Unemployment Spells," *American Economic Journal: Economic Policy*, 5 (May 2013): 190–221.

[18.] Kurt Mitman and Stanislav Rabinovich, "Do Changes in Unemployment Insurance Explain the Emergence of Jobless Recoveries," American Economic Association annual meetings, 3 January 2014.

[19.] David L. Fuller, B. Ravikumar, and Yuzhe Zhang, "Unemployment Insurance Fraud and Optimal Monitoring," *American Economic Journal: Macroeconomics*, 7 (April 2015): 249–290.

7-2c Problems With Official Unemployment Figures

Official unemployment statistics are not problem free. We already discussed discouraged workers, those who have dropped out of the labor force in frustration. The U.S. Labor Department also keeps track of a second group of people who wanted a job but did not look for work in the prior four weeks. This group faced transportation problems, family problems, or other snags that kept them from looking for work. It wasn't that they were frustrated with their search; they just got sidetracked with some personal issues. Discouraged workers and this group that got sidetracked are considered *marginally attached to the labor force*. Not counting discouraged workers and others marginally attached to the labor force as unemployed understates unemployment. Official employment data also ignore the problem of **underemployment**, which arises because people are counted as employed even if they can find only part-time work or are overqualified for their jobs, as when someone with a Ph.D. in literature can find only a clerk's position. Counting overqualified and part-time workers as employed tends to understate the actual amount of unemployment. The federal government has another measure of unemployment, called *U-6*, which counts as unemployed those marginally attached to the labor force and those working part time who would prefer to work full time. In February 2015, the U-6 unemployment rate was 11 percent, or double the official unemployment rate that month.

underemployment
Workers are overqualified for their jobs or work fewer hours than they would prefer

On the other hand, because unemployment insurance benefits and most welfare programs require recipients to seek work, some people may go through the motions of looking for a job just to qualify for these benefits. If they do not in fact want a job, counting them as unemployed overstates actual unemployment. Likewise, some people who would prefer to work part time can find only full-time jobs, and some forced to work overtime and weekends would prefer to work less. To the extent that people must work more than they would prefer, the official unemployment rate overstates the actual rate. Finally, people in the underground economy may not admit they have jobs because they are breaking the law. For example, someone working off the books or someone selling illegal drugs may not admit to being employed.

On net, because discouraged workers and others marginally attached to the labor force aren't counted as unemployed and because underemployed workers are counted as employed, *most experts agree that the official U.S. unemployment rate underestimates unemployment.*

Despite these qualifications and limitations, the U.S. unemployment rate is a useful measure of trends across demographic groups, across regions, and over time.

We turn next to inflation.

CHECKPOINT

What are the pros and cons of unemployment insurance?

7-3 Inflation: Its Measure and Sources

As noted already, *inflation* is a sustained increase in the economy's average price level. Let's begin with a case study that underscores the problem of high inflation.

CASE STUDY

BRINGING THEORY TO LIFE

HYPERINFLATION IN ZIMBABWE In the troubled nation of Zimbabwe in southern Africa, the Zimbabwean dollar (ZD) was once worth about 1.59 U.S. dollars. But the collapse of the economy in the early 2000s severely devalued the ZD. The government tried paying its bills by printing huge amounts of money, and the result was inflation on an epic scale—hyperinflation. Consider this: The price level at the end of 2008 was *150 million times* higher than at the beginning of that year. To put that in perspective, with such inflation in the United States, a gallon of gasoline that sold for $2.75 at the beginning of the year would cost $412.5 million by year-end. Jeans that sold for $25 would cost $3.8 billion at year-end. With the value of the ZD cheapening by the hour, nobody wanted to hold any for long. Those fortunate enough to have jobs in this wreck of an economy wanted to get paid at least daily; they then immediately spent their pay before prices climbed further.

With such wild inflation, everyone, including merchants, had trouble keeping up with prices. Different price increases among sellers of the same product encouraged buyers to shop around more. Even though the government was printing money at an astounding rate, the huge spike in prices meant that it took mountains of cash to buy anything, an amount both difficult to round up and onerous to carry. For months, the maximum amount people could withdraw daily from their bank had the purchasing power of just one U.S. dollar. Because carrying enough money for even small purchases became physically impossible, currency in Zimbabwe was issued in ever higher denominations, with the highest being a $100 trillion dollar note;

that's $100,000,000,000,000. In addition to issuing these higher denominations, three times the central bank issued an entirely new series of notes, each a huge multiple of the previous one, while doing away with the old series. For example, the new ZD issued in February 2009 exchanged for 1,000,000,000,000 of the dollars it replaced. Larger denominations and new series of notes facilitated transactions but fed inflation, which raged all the more.

Many merchants would accept only stable currencies such as the U.S. dollar or the South African rand, and would rather barter than accept Zimbabwean currency. No question, the country had all kinds of other problems, but hyperinflation made everything worse. For example, Zimbabwe's real GDP plunged 75 percent between 2006 and 2009, and the unemployment rate reached 90 percent.

As a way out of the mess, by mid-2009 the government allowed all transactions to be carried out in foreign currencies, something that was already happening. The local currency, already worthless (a $100 trillion note was worth only U.S. pennies), mostly disappeared. Thus, Zimbabwe is now under what it calls a "multiple currency system," with the U.S. dollar the preferred currency (official government finances are reported in U.S. dollars). The country plans to operate that way for years. Annual inflation has been in single digits since 2009. One problem that foreign nations have with relying on U.S. money is a chronic shortage of cash in the economy. There are so few U.S. coins in Zimbabwe that merchants give change in pieces of candy or other low priced items. The coin shortage has prompted Zimbabwe's government to mint its own coins denominated in U.S. cents.

Although Zimbabwe ended its inflation nightmare, hyperinflation is usually flaring up somewhere in the world, as yet another country looks to print money as a "free lunch" solution to budget problems. For example, inflation in Venezuela was averaging 77 percent in 2015.

Sources: "Economic and Financial Indicators," *The Economist*, 10 July 2015; Patrick McGroarty, "Zimbabwe's Mugabe Seeks Investment from South Africa," *Wall Street Journal*, 8 April 2015; "Zimbabwe: Reaching Rock Bottom," *The Economist*, 8 December 2008; "Zimbabwe's Economy: Nothing for Money," *The Economist*, 14 February 2015; and Zimbabwe's Federal Reserve Bank, at http://www.rbz.co.zw/. This case study also drew on the author's visit to Zimbabwe in September 2008.

ppart/Shutterstock.com

We have already discussed inflation in different contexts. If the price level bounces around—moving up one month, falling back the next month—any particular increase in the price level would not necessarily be called inflation in a meaningful sense. We typically measure inflation on an annual basis. The annual *inflation rate* is the percentage increase in the average price level from one year to the next. Extremely high inflation, as in Zimbabwe, is called **hyperinflation**. A sustained *decrease* in the average price level is called **deflation**, as occurred in the United States during the Great Depression and in 2009. Japan, Hong Kong, and Taiwan have also experienced deflation in recent years. And a reduction in the rate of inflation is called **disinflation**, as occurred in the United States from 1981 to 1986, 1991 to 1994, 2000 to 2002, and 2011 to 2015.

In this section, we first consider two sources of inflation. Then, we examine the extent and consequences of inflation in the United States and around the world.

hyperinflation
A very high rate of inflation

deflation
A sustained decrease in the price level

disinflation
A reduction in the rate of inflation

7-3a Two Sources of Inflation

Inflation is a sustained increase in the economy's price level. Inflation results from an increase in aggregate demand, a decrease in aggregate supply, or both. Panel (a) of Exhibit 7 shows that an increase in aggregate demand raises the economy's price level from P to P'. In such cases, a shift to the right of the aggregate demand curve *pulls up* the price level. Inflation resulting from increases in aggregate demand is called **demand-pull inflation**. To generate continuous demand-pull inflation, the aggregate demand curve would have to keep shifting out along a given aggregate supply curve. Rising U.S. inflation during the late 1960s came from demand-pull inflation, when federal spending for the Vietnam War and for expanded social programs boosted aggregate demand.

demand-pull inflation
A sustained rise in the price level caused by a rightward shift of the aggregate demand curve

---

EXHIBIT 7   **Inflation Caused by Shifts of Aggregate Demand and Aggregate Supply Curves**

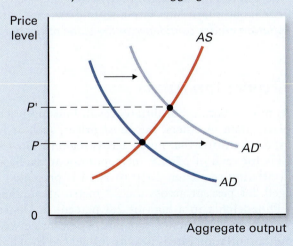

(a) Demand-pull inflation: inflation caused by an increase of aggregate demand

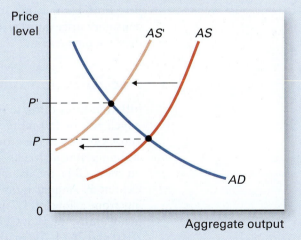

(b) Cost-push inflation: inflation caused by a decrease of aggregate supply

Panel (a) illustrates demand-pull inflation. An outward shift of the aggregate demand to AD' "pulls" the price level up from P to P'. Panel (b) shows cost-push inflation. A decrease of aggregate supply to AS' "pushes" the price level up from P to P'.

Alternatively, inflation can arise from reductions in aggregate supply, as shown in panel (b) of Exhibit 7, where a leftward shift of the aggregate supply curve raises the price level. For example, crop failures and OPEC price hikes reduced aggregate supply between 1973 and 1975, thereby raising the price level in the economy. Inflation stemming from decreases in aggregate supply is called **cost-push inflation**, suggesting that increases in the cost of production *push up* the price level. Prices increase and real GDP decreases, a combination identified earlier as *stagflation*. Again, to generate sustained and continuous cost-push inflation, the aggregate supply curve would have to keep shifting left along a given aggregate demand curve.

cost-push inflation
A sustained rise in the price level caused by a leftward shift of the aggregate supply curve

7-3b Historical Look at Inflation and the Price Level

The consumer price index is the inflation measure you most often encounter, so it gets the most attention here. As you learned in the previous chapter, the *consumer price index*, or *CPI*, measures the cost of a market basket of consumer goods and services over time. Exhibit 8 shows prices in the United States since 1913, using the consumer price index. Panel (a) shows the price *level*, measured by an index number relative to the base period of 1982 to 1984. As you can see, the price level was lower in 1940 than in 1920. Since 1940, however, it has risen steadily, especially during the 1970s.

People are concerned less about the price level and more about year-to-year changes in that level. The lower panel shows the annual *rate of change* in the CPI, or the annual rate of *inflation* or *deflation*. The 1970s and early 1980s were not the only periods of high inflation. Inflation exceeded 10 percent from 1916 to 1919 and in 1947—periods associated with world wars. Prior to the 1950s, high inflation was war related and was usually followed by deflation. Such an inflation-deflation cycle stretches back over the last two centuries. In fact, between the Revolutionary War and World War II, the price level fell in about as many years as it rose. At the end of World War II, the price level was about where it stood at the end of the Civil War.

So fluctuations in the price level are nothing new. But prior to World War II, years of inflation and deflation balanced out over the long run. Therefore, people had good reason to believe the dollar would retain its purchasing power over the long term. Since the end of World War II, however, the CPI has increased by an average of 3.5 percent per year. That may not sound like much, but it translates into a tenfold increase in the consumer price index since 1947. *Inflation erodes confidence in the value of the dollar over the long term.*

7-3c Inflation Across Metropolitan Areas

Inflation rates differ across regions mostly because of differences in housing prices, which rise or fall more in some places than in others. But most prices, such as for automobiles, refrigerators, or jeans, do not differ that much across regions. The federal government tracks separate CPIs for each of 27 U.S. metropolitan areas. Based on these CPIs, the average annual inflation rate from 2010 to 2014 is presented in Exhibit 9. Annual inflation averaged 2.1 percent across the 27 metro areas, ranging from a low of 1.7 percent in Philadelphia to a high of 2.8 percent in Denver. Incidentally, the U.S. CPI also grew at an average annual rate of 2.1 percent between 2010 and 2014. Again, the metropolitan inflation rate is heavily influenced by what's happening in the local housing market. Housing markets were strong throughout the United States during the years observed, but they were stronger in Denver than in Philadelphia.

| EXHIBIT 8 | Consumer Price Index Since 1913 |

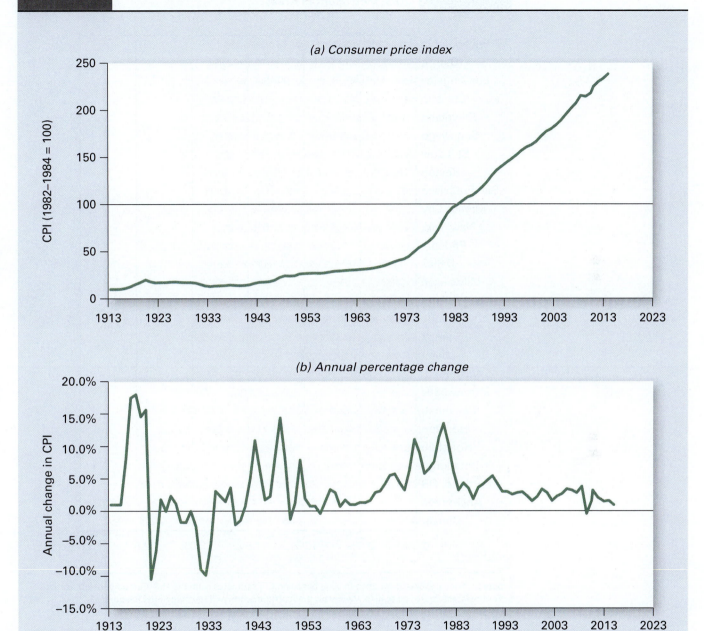

(a) Consumer price index

(b) Annual percentage change

Panel (a) shows that, despite fluctuations, the price level, as measured by the consumer price index, was lower in 1940 than in 1920. The price level began rising in the 1940s. Panel (b) shows the annual rate of change in the price level.

Source: The CPI home page of the U.S. Bureau of Labor Statistics is at http://www.bls.gov/cpi/home.htm. Go there for the latest figures.

7-3d International Comparisons of Inflation

Exhibit 10 shows annual inflation based on the GDP price index since 1981 in the United States, Japan, and Europe, represented here as the average of four major nations (France, Germany, Italy, and the United Kingdom). All three economies show a

| EXHIBIT 9 | Average Annual Inflation from 2010 to 2014 Differed Across U.S. Metropolitan Areas |

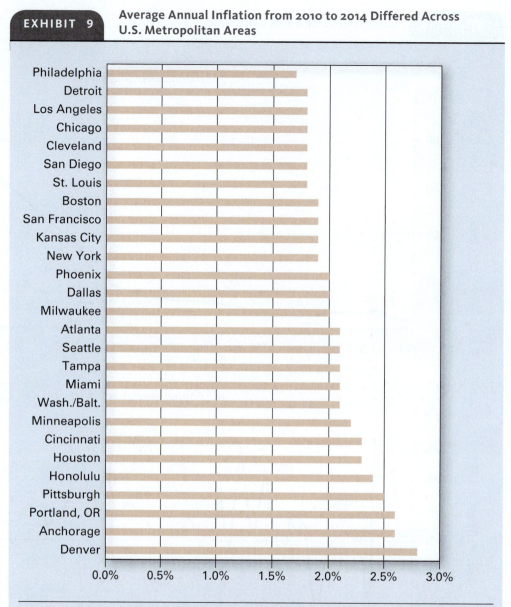

Source: Annual averages for 2010 to 2014 based on CPI estimates from the U.S. Bureau of Labor Statistics. For the latest figures go to http://www.bls.gov/cpi/home.htm and find "Regional Resources."

similar trend, with declining inflation, or disinflation, during the first half of the 1980s, rising inflation during the second half of the 1980s to a peak in the early 1990s, and then another trend lower. The overall trend since 1980 has been toward lower inflation. Inflation rates in Europe were similar to those in the United States. Rates in Japan were consistently lower, even dipping into deflation from 2005 to 2011. In recent years, inflation in the United States and Europe was low because of slack aggregate demand from the global recession. Inflation since 1981 has averaged 3.5 percent in Europe, 3.2 percent in the United States, and 0.7 percent in Japan.

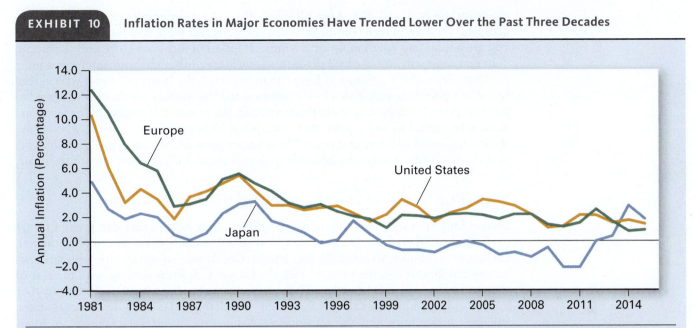

EXHIBIT 10 **Inflation Rates in Major Economies Have Trended Lower Over the Past Three Decades**

Source: Developed from CPI inflation reported in *OECD Economic Outlook*, 97 (May 2015). Figures for Europe are the averages for France, Germany, Italy, and the United Kingdom. Figures for 2015 are projections. For the latest data, go to http://www.bls.gov/fls/home.htm.

The quantity and quality of data used to measure inflation vary across countries. Governments in less-developed countries sample fewer products and measure prices only in the capital city. Whereas thousands of items are sampled to determine the U.S. consumer price index, as few as 30 might be sampled in some developing countries.

CHECKPOINT

What is inflation and what are two sources of inflation?

7-4 Effects of Inflation

We have defined inflation, considered sources of inflation, traced the record of inflation over the last century, and examined inflation both across metropolitan areas and across countries. Now let's consider some effects of inflation.

7-4a Anticipated Versus Unanticipated Inflation

What is the effect of inflation on the economy? *Unanticipated inflation* creates more problems than *anticipated inflation*. To the extent that inflation is higher or lower than anticipated, it arbitrarily creates winners and losers in the economy. For example, suppose inflation is expected to be 3 percent next year, and you and your employer agree to a 4 percent increase in your nominal, or money, wage. You both expect your *real* wage—that is, your wage measured in dollars of constant purchasing power—to increase by 1 percent. If inflation turns out to be 3 percent, as expected, you and your employer are both satisfied. After all, that's the wage your employer offered and you accepted. If inflation turns out to be 5 percent, your real wage will fall by 1 percent, so you are a loser and your employer a winner. If inflation turns out to be only 1 percent, your real wage will increase by 3 percent, so you are a winner and your employer a loser.

More generally, if inflation is higher than expected, the losers are those who agreed to sell at a price that anticipated lower inflation and the winners are those who agreed to pay that price. If inflation is lower than expected, the situation is reversed: The losers are those who agreed to pay a price that anticipated higher inflation, and the winners are those who agreed to sell at that price. *The arbitrary gains and losses arising from unanticipated inflation are partly why inflation is so unpopular.* Inflation just doesn't seem fair.

7-4b The Transaction Costs of Variable Inflation

During long periods of price stability, people correctly believe they can predict future prices and can therefore plan accordingly. If inflation changes unexpectedly, however, the future is cloudier, so planning gets harder. Uncertainty about inflation undermines money's ability to link the present with the future. U.S. firms dealing with the rest of the world face an added burden. They must not only anticipate U.S. inflation; they must also guess how the value of the dollar will change relative to foreign currencies. Inflation uncertainty and the resulting exchange-rate uncertainty complicate international transactions. In this more uncertain environment, companies with international ties must shift attention from production decisions to anticipating the effects of inflation and exchange-rate changes on the firm's finances. Market transactions, particularly long-term contracts, become more complicated as inflation becomes more unpredictable. Some economists believe that the high and variable U.S. inflation during the 1970s and early 1980s cut economic growth during those periods.

7-4c Inflation Obscures Relative Price Changes

Even with no inflation, some prices would increase and some would decrease, reflecting normal activity in particular markets. For example, since the mid-1980s the U.S. price level has more than doubled, yet the prices of flat-screen TVs, computers, long-distance phone service, and many other products have declined sharply. Prices for education and for hospital care increased more than fivefold. Because the prices of various goods change by different amounts, *relative prices* change. Consider price changes over a longer period. In the last hundred years, consumer prices overall increased about 2000 percent, but the price of a hotel room in New York City jumped 7500 percent, while the price of a three-minute phone call from New York to Chicago dropped 99 percent. Whereas the economy's price level describes the exchange rate between a market basket and *money*, relative prices describe the exchange rate among goods—that is, how much one good costs compared to another.

Inflation does not necessarily cause a change in relative prices, but it can obscure that change. During periods of volatile inflation, there is greater uncertainty about the price of one good relative to another—that is, about relative prices. But relative price changes are important signals for allocating the economy's resources efficiently. If all prices moved together, suppliers could link the selling prices of their goods to the overall inflation rate. Because prices usually do not move in unison, however, tying a particular product's price to the overall inflation rate may result in a price that is too high or too low based on market conditions. The same is true of agreements to link wages with inflation. If the price of an employer's product grows more slowly than the rate of inflation in the economy, the employer may be hard-pressed to increase wages by the rate of inflation. Consider the problem confronting oil refiners who signed labor contracts agreeing to pay their workers cost-of-living wage increases. In some years, those employers had to increase wages at a time when the price of oil was falling like a rock.

7-4d Inflation and Interest Rates

No discussion of inflation would be complete without some mention of the interest rate. **Interest** is the dollar amount paid by borrowers to lenders. Lenders must be rewarded for forgoing present consumption, and borrowers are willing to pay a premium to spend now. The **interest rate** is the amount paid per year as a percentage of the amount borrowed. For example, an interest rate of 5 percent means $5 per year on a $100 loan. The greater the interest rate, other things constant, the greater the reward for lending money. The amount of money people are willing to lend, called *loanable funds*, increases as the interest rate rises, other things constant. The supply curve for loanable funds therefore slopes upward, as indicated by curve S in Exhibit 11.

These funds are demanded by households, firms, and governments to finance homes, buildings, machinery, college, and other major purchases. The lower the interest rate, other things constant, the cheaper the cost of borrowing. So the quantity of loanable funds demanded increases as the interest rate decreases, other things constant. That is, the interest rate and the quantity of loanable funds demanded are inversely related. The demand curve therefore slopes downward, as indicated by curve D in Exhibit 11. The downward-sloping demand curve and the upward-sloping supply curve intersect to yield the equilibrium nominal rate of interest, i.

The **nominal interest rate** measures interest in terms of the current dollars paid. The nominal rate is the one that appears on the loan agreement; it is the rate discussed in the news media and is often of political significance. The **real interest rate** equals the nominal rate minus the inflation rate:

$$\text{Real interest rate} = \text{Nominal interest rate} - \text{Inflation rate}$$

interest
The dollar amount paid by borrowers to lenders

interest rate
Interest per year as a percentage of the amount loaned

nominal interest rate
The interest rate expressed in dollars of current value (that is, not adjusted for inflation) as a percentage of the amount loaned; the interest rate specified on the loan agreement

real interest rate
The interest rate expressed in dollars of constant purchasing power as a percentage of the amount loaned; the nominal interest rate minus the inflation rate

---

EXHIBIT 11   **The Market for Loanable Funds**

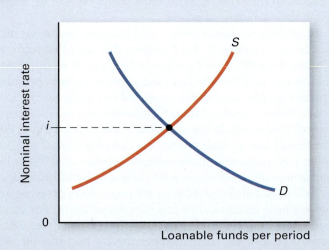

The upward-sloping supply curve, *S*, shows that more loanable funds are supplied at higher interest rates. The downward-sloping demand curve, *D*, shows that the quantity of loanable funds demanded is greater at lower interest rates. The two curves intersect to determine the market interest rate, *i*.

For example, if the nominal interest rate is 5 percent and the inflation rate is 3 percent, the real interest rate is 2 percent. With no inflation, the nominal rate and the real rate would be identical. But with inflation, the nominal rate exceeds the real rate. If inflation is unexpectedly high—higher, for example, than the nominal interest rate—then the real interest rate would be negative. In this case, the nominal interest earned for lending money would not even cover the loss of spending power caused by inflation. Lenders would lose purchasing power. This is why lenders and borrowers are concerned more with the real rate than with the nominal rate. The real interest rate, however, is known only after the fact—that is, only after inflation actually occurs.

Because the future is uncertain, lenders and borrowers must form expectations about inflation, and they base their willingness to lend and borrow on those expectations. The higher the *expected* inflation, the higher the nominal rate of interest that lenders require and that borrowers are willing to pay. Lenders and borrowers base their decisions on the *expected* real interest rate, which equals the nominal rate minus the expected inflation rate.

Although the discussion has implied that there is only one market rate of interest, there are many rates. Rates differ depending on such factors as the duration of the loan, tax treatment of interest, and the risk the loan will not be repaid.

7-4e Why Is Inflation So Unpopular?

Whenever the price level increases, spending must increase just to buy the same amount of goods and services. If you think of inflation only in terms of spending, you consider only the problem of paying those higher prices. But if you think of inflation in terms of the higher money income that results, you see that higher prices mean higher receipts for resource suppliers, usually including higher nominal wages for workers. When viewed from the income side, inflation is not so bad.

If every higher price is received by some resource supplier, why are people so troubled by inflation? People view their higher incomes as well-deserved rewards for their labor, but they see inflation as a penalty that unjustly robs them of purchasing power. Most people do not stop to realize that unless they are producing more with each hour of labor, higher wages *must* result in higher prices. Prices and wages are simply two sides of the same coin. To the extent that nominal wages on average keep up with inflation, workers retain their purchasing power.

Presidents Ford and Carter could not control inflation and were turned out of office. Inflation slowed significantly during President Reagan's first term, and he won reelection easily. During the 1988 election, George H. W. Bush won in part by reminding voters what inflation was in 1980, the last time a Democrat was president. But he lost his bid at reelection in part because inflation spiked to 6.0 percent in 1990, the highest in nearly a decade. Inflation remained under 3.0 percent during President Clinton's first term, and he was reelected easily. In the presidential elections of 2000, 2004, 2008, and 2012, inflation remained low enough not to be a campaign issue.

As noted earlier, unanticipated inflation creates winners and losers in the economy. The perceived unfairness and arbitrariness of these gains and losses are more reasons why people hate inflation. Finally, although inflation affects everyone to some extent, it hits hardest those whose incomes are fixed in nominal terms. For example, pensions are often fixed amounts and are eroded by inflation. And retirees who rely on fixed nominal interest income also see their incomes shrunk by inflation. But the benefits paid by the largest pension program, Social Security, are adjusted annually for changes in the CPI. Thus, Social Security recipients get a cost-of-living adjustment, or a **COLA**.

COLA
Cost-of-living adjustment; an increase in wages or transfer payments tied to increases in the price level

To Review: anticipated inflation is less of a problem than unanticipated inflation. Unanticipated inflation arbitrarily redistributes income and wealth from one group to another, reduces the ability to make long-term plans, and forces people to focus more on money and prices. The more unpredictable inflation becomes the harder it is to negotiate long-term contracts. Productivity suffers because people must spend more time coping with inflation, leaving less time for production.

CHECKPOINT

How does unanticipated inflation harm some individuals and harm the economy as a whole?

7-5 Conclusion

This chapter has focused on unemployment and inflation. Although we have discussed them separately, they are related in ways that will unfold in later chapters. Politicians sometimes add the unemployment rate to the inflation rate to come up with what they refer to as the "misery index." In 1980, for example, an unemployment rate of 7.1 percent combined with a CPI increase of 12.5 percent to yield a misery index of 19.6—a number that helps explain why President Carter was not reelected. By 1984 the misery index dropped to 11.8, and by 1988 to 9.6; Republicans retained the White House in both elections. In 1992, the index climbed slightly to 10.4 percent, spelling trouble for President George H. W. Bush. And in 1996, the index fell back to 8.4 percent, helping President Clinton's reelection. During the election of 2000, the misery index was down to 7.7, which should have helped Al Gore, the candidate of the incumbent party. But during the campaign, Gore distanced himself from President Clinton and thus was not able to capitalize on the strong economy. In the 2004 election, the misery index remained about the same as in 2000, which helps explain why challenger John Kerry had difficulty making much of an issue of the economy. A misery index of 10.4 right before the 2008 election helped defeat the incumbent party and put Barack Obama in office. The misery index showed no improvement in 2012, and this made President Obama's reelection more of a challenge.

Summary

1. The unemployment rate is the number of people looking for work divided by the number in the labor force. The unemployment rate masks differences among particular groups and across regions. The rate is lowest among white adults and highest among black teenagers.

2. There are four sources of unemployment. Frictional unemployment arises because employers and qualified job seekers need time to find one another. Seasonal unemployment stems from the effects of weather and the seasons on certain industries, such as construction, agriculture, and tourism. Structural unemployment arises because changes in tastes, technology, taxes, and competition reduce the demand for certain skills and increase the demand for other skills. And cyclical unemployment results from fluctuations in economic activity caused by the business cycle. Policy makers and economists are less concerned with frictional and seasonal unemployment. Full employment occurs when cyclical unemployment is zero.

3. Unemployment often creates both an economic and a psychological hardship. For some, this burden is reduced by an employed spouse and by unemployment insurance. Unemployment insurance provides a safety net and time to find another job, and that's good. But it may also reduce incentives to find work, as is the case in Europe, and that's an unintended consequence.

4. Inflation is a sustained rise in the average price level. An increase in aggregate demand can cause demand-pull inflation. A decrease in aggregate supply can cause cost-push inflation. Prior to World War II, both inflation and deflation were common and the combination kept the price level relatively stable

over time, but since World War II the price level has increased nearly every year.

5. Anticipated inflation causes fewer distortions in the economy than unanticipated inflation. Unanticipated inflation arbitrarily creates winners and losers, and forces people to spend more time and energy coping with the effects of inflation. The negative effects of high and variable inflation on productivity can be observed most dramatically in countries that have experienced hyperinflation, such as Zimbabwe.

6. Because not all prices change by the same amount during inflationary periods, people have trouble keeping track of the changes in relative prices. Unexpected inflation makes long-term planning more difficult and more risky.

7. The intersection of the demand and supply curves for loanable funds yields the market interest rate. The real interest rate is the nominal interest rate minus the inflation rate. Borrowers and lenders base decisions on the expected real interest rate.

Key Concepts

Labor force   139

Unemployment rate   139

Discouraged workers   140

Labor force participation rate   141

Long-term unemployed   142

Frictional unemployment   147

Seasonal unemployment   148

Structural unemployment   148

Cyclical unemployment   149

Full employment   149

Unemployment benefits   150

Underemployment   151

Hyperinflation   153

Deflation   153

Disinflation   153

Demand-pull inflation   153

Cost-push inflation   154

Interest   159

Interest rate   159

Nominal interest rate   159

Real interest rate   159

COLA   160

Questions for Review

1. **Labor Force**   Refer to Exhibit 1 in the chapter to determine whether each of the following statements is true or false.

   a. Some people who are officially unemployed are not in the labor force.
   b. Some people in the labor force are not working.
   c. Everyone who is not unemployed is in the labor force.
   d. Some people who are not working are not unemployed.

2. **Unemployment in Various Groups**   Does the overall unemployment rate offer an accurate picture of the impact of unemployment on each U.S. population group?

3. **Unemployment Rate**   If people dropped out of the labor force because they could not find work, what would this do to the unemployment rate? Why?

4. **The Meaning of Full Employment**   When the economy is at full employment, is the unemployment rate at zero percent? Why or why not? How would a more generous unemployment insurance system affect the full employment figure?

5. **International Comparisons of Unemployment**   How has the U.S. unemployment rate compared with rates in other major economies? Can you offer any reasons why rates on average have differed across major economies since 1981.

6. **Official Unemployment Figures**   Explain why most experts believe that official U.S. data underestimate the actual rate of

unemployment. What factors could make the official rate overstate the actual unemployment rate?

7. **Case Study: Hyperinflation in Zimbabwe**   In countries such as Zimbabwe, which had problems with high inflation, the increased use of another country's currency (such as the U.S. dollar) became common. Why do you suppose this occurred?

8. **Sources of Inflation**   What are the two sources of inflation? Illustrate them graphically.

9. **Anticipated Versus Unanticipated Inflation**   If actual inflation exceeds anticipated inflation, who will lose purchasing power and who will gain?

10. **Inflation and Relative Price Changes**   What does the consumer price index measure? Does the index measure changes in relative prices? Why, or why not?

11. **Inflation and Interest Rates**   Explain as carefully as you can why borrowers would be willing to pay a higher interest rate if they expected the inflation rate to increase in the future.

12. **Inflation**   Why is a relatively constant and predictable inflation rate less harmful to an economy than a rate that fluctuates unpredictably?

13. **Inflation**   Why do people dislike inflation?

Problems and Exercises

14. **Measuring Unemployment** Determine the impact on each of the following if 2 million unemployed workers decide to return to school full time and stop looking for work:

    a. The labor force participation rate
    b. The size of the labor force
    c. The unemployment rate

15. **Measuring Unemployment** Suppose that the U.S. noninstitutional adult population is 230 million and the labor force participation rate is 67 percent.

    a. What would be the size of the U.S. labor force?
    b. If 85 million adults are not working, what is the unemployment rate?

16. **Types of Unemployment** Determine whether each of the following would be considered frictional, structural, seasonal, or cyclical unemployment:

    a. A UPS employee who was hired for the Christmas season is laid off after Christmas.
    b. A worker is laid off due to reduced aggregate demand in the economy.
    c. A worker in a DVD rental store becomes unemployed as video-on-demand service becomes more popular.
    d. A new college graduate is looking for employment.

17. **Inflation** Here are some recent data on the U.S. consumer price index:

Year	CPI	Year	CPI	Year	CPI
1997	160.5	2003	184.0	2009	214.5
1998	163.0	2004	188.9	2010	218.1
1999	166.6	2005	195.3	2011	226.3
2000	172.2	2006	201.6	2012	230.3
2001	177.1	2007	207.3	2013	233.5
2002	179.9	2008	215.3	2014	237.1

Compute the inflation rate for each year 1998–2014 and determine which years were years of inflation. In which years did deflation occur? In which years did disinflation occur? Was there hyperinflation in any year?

18. **Sources of Inflation** Using the concepts of aggregate supply and aggregate demand, explain why inflation usually increases during wartime.

19. **Inflation and Interest Rates** Using a demand-supply diagram for loanable funds (like Exhibit 11), show what happens to the nominal interest rate and the equilibrium quantity of loans when both borrowers and lenders increase their estimates of the expected inflation rate from 2 percent to 4 percent.

8 Productivity and Growth

- *Why is the standard of living so much higher in some countries than in others?*

- *How does an economy increase its living standard?*

- *Why is the long-term growth rate more important than short-term fluctuations in economic activity?*

- *What's labor productivity, why is it important, and why has it varied so much over time?*

- *What's been the impact of computers and the Internet on labor productivity?*

Answers to these and other questions are addressed in this chapter, which focuses on arguably the most important criteria for judging an economy's performance—productivity and growth.

The single most important determinant of a nation's standard of living in the long run is the productivity of its resources. Even seemingly low growth in productivity, if sustained for years, can have a substantial effect on the standard of living—that is, on the availability of goods and services per capita. Growing productivity is therefore critical to a rising standard of living and has kept the U.S. economy a world leader.

You may not realize it, but you now live in one of the most technologically innovative times in human history. Each day brings faster computers, smarter phones, higher-definition video, more sophisticated social media, more effective medicines, more automated machines, and other breakthroughs that raise your productivity and your standard of living.

Economic growth is a complicated process, one that even experts do not yet fully understand. Since before Adam Smith wrote about *The Wealth of Nations*, economists have puzzled over what makes some economies thrive while others founder. Because a market economy is not the product of conscious design, it does not reveal its secrets readily, nor can it be easily manipulated in pursuit of growth. We can't simply push here and pull there to achieve the desired result. Changing the economy is not like remodeling a home by knocking out a wall to expand the kitchen. Because we have no clear blueprint of the economy, we cannot make changes to specifications.

Still, there is much economists do know. In this chapter, we first develop a few simple models to examine productivity and growth. Then, we use these models to help explain why some nations are rich and some poor. U.S. performance gets special attention, particularly compared with other major economies around the world. We close with some controversies of technology and growth.

Topics discussed in this chapter include:

- Labor productivity
- The production function
- U.S. productivity and growth
- Rules of the game
- Technological change and unemployment
- Research and development
- Industrial policy
- Income and happiness

8-1 Theory of Productivity and Growth

Two centuries ago, 90 percent of the American workforce was in agriculture, where the hours were long and rewards unpredictable. Other workers had it no better, toiling from sunrise to sunset for a wage that bought just the bare necessities. Most people had little intellectual stimulation and little contact with the outside world. A skilled worker's home in 1800 was described as follows: "Sand sprinkled on the floor did duty as a carpet. . . . What a stove was he did not know. Coal he had never seen. Matches he had never heard of. . . . He rarely tasted fresh meat. . . . If the food of a [skilled worker] would now be thought coarse, his clothes would be thought abominable."[1]

Over the last two centuries, there has been an incredible increase in the U.S. *standard of living* as measured by the amount of goods and services available on average per person. Note that economic progress was unusual during the long sweep of history. For example, people of Shakespearean England had a living standard little better than those of ancient Greece, who lived nearly two thousand years earlier.

An economy's standard of living grows over the long run because of (1) increases in the amount and quality of resources, especially labor and capital, (2) better technology and know-how, and (3) improvements in the *rules of the game* that facilitate production and exchange, such as tax laws, property rights, patent laws, the legal system, and the manners, customs, and conventions of the market. Perhaps the easiest way to introduce economic growth is by beginning with something you have already read about, the production possibilities frontier.

8-1a Growth and the Production Possibilities Frontier

The *production possibilities frontier,* or *PPF,* first introduced in Chapter 2, shows what the economy can produce if available resources are used efficiently. Let's briefly review the assumptions made in developing the frontier shown in Exhibit 1. During the period under consideration, usually a year, the quantity of resources in the economy and the level of technology and know-how are assumed to be fixed. Also assumed fixed during the

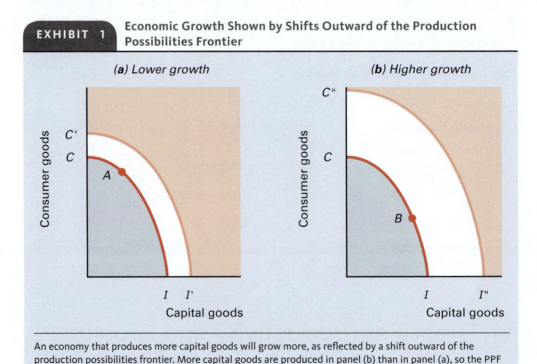

| EXHIBIT 1 | Economic Growth Shown by Shifts Outward of the Production Possibilities Frontier |

(a) Lower growth　　　　　　**(b) Higher growth**

An economy that produces more capital goods will grow more, as reflected by a shift outward of the production possibilities frontier. More capital goods are produced in panel (b) than in panel (a), so the PPF shifts out more in panel (b).

[1] E. L. Bogart, *The Economic History of the United States* (Longmans Green, 1912), pp. 157–158.

period are the rules of the game that facilitate production and exchange. We classify all production into two broad categories—in this case, consumer goods and capital goods. Capital goods are used to produce other goods. For example, the economy can bake pizzas and make pizza ovens. Pizzas are consumer goods, and ovens are capital goods.

When resources are employed efficiently, the production possibilities frontier *CI* in each panel of Exhibit 1 shows the possible combinations of consumer goods and capital goods that can be produced in a given year. Point *C* depicts the quantity of consumer goods produced if all the economy's resources are employed efficiently to produce them. Point *I* depicts the same for capital goods. Points inside the frontier are inefficient combinations, and points outside the frontier are unattainable combinations, given the resources, technology and know-how, and rules of the game. The production possibilities frontier is bowed out because resources are not perfectly adaptable to the production of both goods; some resources are specialized.

Economic growth is shown by an outward shift of the production possibilities frontier, as reflected in each panel of Exhibit 1. What can cause growth? An increase in resources, such as a growth in the labor supply or in the capital stock, shifts the frontier outward from one period to the next. Labor supply can increase either because of population growth or because the existing population works more. The capital stock increases if the economy produces more capital this year than it uses up. The more capital produced this year, on net, the more the economy grows, as reflected by an outward shift of the production frontier next year.

Breakthroughs in technology also shift out the frontier by making more efficient use of resources. Technological change often improves the quality of capital, but it can enhance the productivity of any resource. And technological change can free up resources for other uses. For example, the development of synthetic dyes in the 19th century freed up millions of acres of agricultural land around the world that had been growing dye crops such as madder (red) and indigo (blue). The development of fiber-optic cable and cellular technology freed up the world's largest stock of copper in the form of existing telephone wires strung on poles.

Finally, any improvement in the rules of the game that nurtures production and exchange promotes growth and expands the frontier. For example, the economy can grow as a result of improved patent laws that encourage more inventions[2] or legal reforms that reduce transaction costs. Extending the length of patent protection could lead to more R&D, more inventions, and more innovations.

Thus, *the economy grows because of a greater availability of resources, an improvement in the quality of resources, technological change that makes better use of resources, or improvements in the rules of the game that enhance production.*

The amount of capital produced this year shapes the PPF next year. For example, in panel (a) of Exhibit 1, the economy has chosen point *A* from possible points along *CI*. The capital produced this year shifts the PPF out to *C'I'* next year. But if more capital goods are produced this year, as reflected by point *B* in panel (b), the PPF shifts farther out next year, to *C"I"*. An economy that produces more capital this year is said to *invest* more in capital. As you can see, to invest more, people must give up some consumer goods this year. Thus, the opportunity cost of producing more capital goods this year is producing fewer consumer goods. More generally, we can say that people must *save* more now— that is, forgo some current consumption—to invest in capital. *Investment cannot occur without saving.* Economies that save more can invest more, as we'll see later. But let's get back to production.

[2.] For evidence how the greater protection of intellectual property stimulates technological change, see Sunil Kanwar and Robert Evenson, "Does Intellectual Property Protection Spur Technological Change?" *Oxford Economic Papers*, 55 (April 2003): 235–264.

production

A process that transforms resources into goods and services

productivity

The ratio of a specific measure of output, such as real GDP, to a specific measure of input, such as labor; in this case productivity measures real GDP per hour of labor

labor productivity

Output per unit of labor; measured as real GDP divided by the hours of labor employed to produce that output

8-1b What Is Productivity?

Production *is a process that transforms resources into goods and services.* Resources coupled with technology and know-how produce output. Productivity measures how efficiently resources are turned into goods and services. In simplest terms, the greater the productivity, the more can be produced from a given amount of resources, and the farther out the production possibilities frontier. Economies that use resources more efficiently create a higher standard of living, meaning that more goods and services are produced per capita.

Productivity is defined as the ratio of total output to a specific measure of input. Productivity usually reflects an average, expressing total output divided by the amount of a particular kind of resource employed to produce that output. For example, **labor productivity** is the output per unit of labor and measures total output divided by the hours of labor employed to produce that output.

We can talk about the productivity of any resource, such as labor, capital, or natural resources. When agriculture accounted for most output in the economy, land productivity, such as bushels of grain per acre, was a key measure of economic welfare. Where soil was rocky and barren, people were poorer than where soil was fertile and fruitful. Even today, soil productivity determines the standard of living in some economies. Industrialization and trade, however, have liberated many from dependence on soil fertility. Today, some of the world's most productive economies have little land or have land of poor fertility. For example, Japan has only 2 percent as much land per capita as Russia, but Japan's GDP per capita is 50 percent higher than Russia's.

8-1c Labor Productivity

Labor is the resource most commonly used to measure productivity. Why labor? First, labor accounts for most production cost—about 70 percent on average. Second, labor is more easily measured than other inputs, whether we speak of hours per week or full-

time workers per year. Statistics about employment and hours worked are more readily available and more reliable than those about other resources.

But the resource most responsible for increasing labor productivity is capital. As introduced in Chapter 1, the two broad categories are human capital and physical capital. *Human capital* is the accumulated knowledge, skill, and experience of the labor force. As workers acquire more human capital, their productivity and their incomes grow. That's why surgeons earn more than butchers and accountants earn more than file clerks. You are reading this book right now to enhance your human capital. *Physical capital* includes the machines, buildings, roads, airports, communication networks, and other human creations used to produce goods and services. Think about digging a ditch with bare hands versus using a shovel. Now switch the shovel for a backhoe. More physical capital obviously makes diggers more productive. Or consider picking oranges with bare hands versus using a picking machine that combs the trees with steel bristles. In less than 15 minutes that machine can pick 18 tons of oranges from 100 trees, catch the fruit, and drop it into storage carts. Without the machine, that job would take four workers all day.[3] The operator of the picking machine is at least 128 times more productive than someone picking oranges by hand.

[3.] Eduardo Porter, "In Florida Groves, Cheap Labor Means Machines," *New York Times*, 22 March 2004.

In poorer countries labor is cheap and capital dear, so producers substitute labor for capital. For example, in India a beverage truck makes its rounds festooned with workers so as to minimize the time the truck, the valuable resource, spends at each stop. In the United States, where labor is more costly (compared with capital), the truck makes its rounds with just the driver. As another example, in Haiti, the poorest country in the Western Hemisphere, a ferry service could not afford to rebuild a dock, so it hired workers to carry passengers on their shoulders through the water to and from the ferry.[4]

As an economy accumulates more capital per worker, labor productivity increases and the standard of living grows. The most productive combination of all is human capital combined with physical capital. For example, one certified public accountant with a computer and specialized software can sort out a company's finances more quickly and more accurately than could a thousand high-school-educated file clerks using just pencils and paper.

8-1d Per-Worker Production Function

We can express the relationship between the amount of capital per worker and the output per worker as an economy's **per-worker production function**. Exhibit 2 shows the amount of capital per worker, measured along the horizontal axis, and average output per worker, or labor productivity, measured along the vertical axis, other things constant—including the amount of labor, the level of technology and know-how, and rules of the game. Any point on the production function, *PF*, shows the average output per worker on the vertical axis for each level of capital per worker on the horizontal axis. For example, with *k* units of capital per worker, the average output per worker in the economy is *y*. The curve slopes upward from left to right because an increase in capital per worker helps each worker produce more output. For example, bigger trucks make truck drivers more productive.

per-worker production function

The relationship between the amount of capital per worker in the economy and average output per worker

---

EXHIBIT 2 **Per-Worker Production Function**

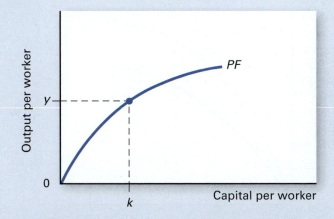

The per-worker production function, *PF*, shows a direct relationship between the amount of capital per worker, *k*, and the output per worker, *y*. The bowed shape of *PF* reflects the law of diminishing marginal returns from capital, which holds that as more capital is added to a given number of workers, output per worker increases but at a diminishing rate and eventually could turn negative.

[4.] This example was noted by Tyler Cowen in "The Ricardo Effect in Haiti," 23 February 2004, http://www.marginalrevolution.com.

capital deepening
An increase in the amount of capital per worker; one source of rising labor productivity

An increase in the amount of capital per worker is called **capital deepening** and is one source of rising productivity. *Capital deepening contributes to labor productivity and economic growth.* As the quantity of capital per worker increases, output per worker increases but at a diminishing rate, as reflected by the shape of the per-worker production function. The diminishing slope of this curve reflects the *law of diminishing marginal returns from capital*, which says that beyond some level of capital per worker, increases in capital add less and less to output per worker. For example, increasing the size of trucks beyond some point has diminishing returns as trucks become too large to negotiate some public roads. Thus, given the amount of labor, the level of technology and know-how, and the rules of the game, additional gains from more capital per worker eventually diminish and could turn negative.

8-1e Technological Change and Know-How

Held constant along a per-worker production function is the economy's level of technology and know-how. Technological change and better know-how usually improve the *quality* of capital and represent additional sources of increased productivity. For example, a tractor is more productive than a horse-drawn plow, a word processor more productive than a typewriter, and an Excel spreadsheet more productive than pencil and paper. Bill Gates, founder of Microsoft, noted that putting an hour of video online cost about $400 in the late 1990s but only two cents in 2013.[5] Better technology and know-how are reflected in Exhibit 3 by an upward rotation of the per-worker production function from *PF* to *PF'*. As a result of a technological breakthrough, more is produced at each level of capital per worker. For example, if there

EXHIBIT 3	Impact of a Technological Breakthrough on the Per-Worker Production Function

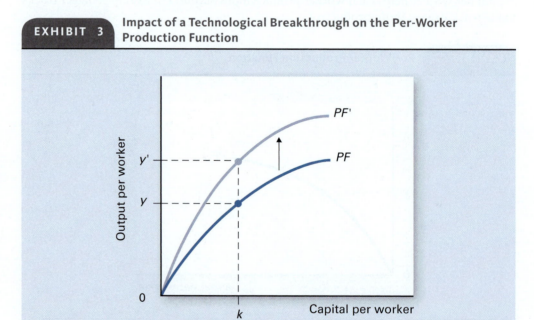

A technological breakthrough increases output per worker at each level of capital per worker. Better technology makes workers more productive. This is shown by an upward rotation of the per-worker production function from *PF* to *PF'*. An improvement in know-how or the rules of the game would have a similar effect.

[5.] "Catching On At Last," *The Economist*, 29 June 2013, pp. 24–25.

are k units of capital per worker, a major breakthrough in technology increases the output per worker in the economy from y to y'.

Simon Kuznets, who won a Nobel Prize in part for his analysis of economic growth, claimed that technological change and the ability to apply such breakthroughs to all aspects of production are the driving forces behind economic growth in market economies. Kuznets argued that changes in the *quantities* of labor and capital account for only one-tenth of the increase in economic growth. Nine-tenths came from improvements in the *quality* of these inputs. For example, by manipulating metallic structures at the nanometer level (a billionth of a meter), scientists are developing material that has the strength and lightness of titanium but at a tenth of the cost.[6] As technological breakthroughs become *embodied* in new capital, resources are combined more efficiently, increasing total output. *From the wheel to the assembly-line robot, capital embodies the fruits of discovery and drives economic growth.*

But even for a given level of technology and a given number of workers, output can increase over time by improved know-how. As mentioned in Chapter 2, researchers have documented a doubling of steel production at a mini-mill with no change in technology or in the number of workers. Through experimentation, workers collectively developed more know-how and thereby became more productive.[7]

Thus, two kinds of changes in capital improve worker productivity: (1) an increase in the *quantity* of capital per worker, as reflected by a movement along the per-worker production function, and (2) an improvement in the *quality* of capital per worker, as reflected by technological change and know-how that rotates the curve upward. More capital per worker and better capital per worker result in more output per worker, which, over time, translates into more output per capita, meaning a higher standard of living.

8-1f Rules of the Game

Perhaps the most elusive ingredients for productivity and growth are the **rules of the game**, the formal and informal institutions that promote economic activity: the laws, customs, manners, conventions, and other institutional elements that encourage people to undertake productive activity. A stable political environment and a system of well-defined property rights are important. It's been said that capital goes where it's welcome and remains where it is well treated. Less is invested in human and physical capital if people believe the fruits of their investment could be seized by the government, stolen by thieves, destroyed by civil unrest, or blown up by terrorists. For example, countries whose colonizers established strong property rights hundreds of years ago have, on average, much higher incomes today than countries whose colonizers did not.[8] And recent research finds that economies grow faster if people are more trusting and more trustworthy.[9] After all, one sign of an advanced economy is a willingness to participate in impersonal market exchange. More generally, some countries are more inviting to talented people than other countries. For example, one recent study found that 38 percent of scientists working in the United States came from abroad (China and India are the two biggest sources of scientists). On the other hand, only 5 percent of the scientists in Japan came from abroad.[10]

rules of the game
The laws, customs, manners, conventions, and other institutional elements that determine transaction costs and thereby affect people's incentive to undertake production and exchange

[6.] "Wings of Steel," *The Economist*, 7 February 2015, p. 77.

[7.] Igal Hendel and Yossi Spiegel, "Small Steps for Workers, a Giant Leap for Productivity," *American Economic Journal: Applied Economics*, 6 (January 2014): 73–90.

[8.] Daron Acemoglu, Simon Johnson, and James A. Robinson, "The Colonial Origins of Comparative Development," *American Economic Review*, 91(December 2001): 1369–1401.

[9.] Yann Algan and Pierre Cahuc, "Inherited Trust and Growth," *American Economic Review*, 100 (December 2010): 2060–2092.

[10.] Chiara Franzoni, Giuseppe Scellato, and Paula Stephan, "Foreign Born Scientists: Mobility Patterns for 16 Countries," *Nature Biotechnology*, 30 (December 2012): 1250–1253, at http://www.nature.com/nbt/journal/v30/n12/pdf/nbt.2449.pdf.

Improvements in the rules of the game could result in more output for each level of capital per worker, thus reflected by a rotation up in the per-worker production function as shown in Exhibit 3. On the other hand, a deterioration in the rules of the game would rotate down the per-worker production function. As an example, "Capital flight out of Russia has been high, blamed in part on a lack of confidence in the country's respect for property rights and on persistent, rampant corruption."[11]

We tend to think that laws are the backbone of market exchange, but we should not underestimate the role of manners, customs, and conventions. According to the 18th-century British philosopher Edmund Burke, "Manners are of more importance than law. . . . The law touches us but here and there and now and then. Manners are what vex or soothe, corrupt or purify, exalt or debase, barbarize or refine us, by a constant, steady, uniform and insensible operation like that of the air we breathe in."[12] The Russian proverb, "Custom is stronger than law," makes a similar point.

Simply put, a more stable political climate could benefit productivity just like a technological improvement could. Conversely, events that foster instability can harm an economy's productivity and rotate the per-worker production function downward. The terrorist attacks on the World Trade Center and Pentagon were such destabilizing events. According to Alberto Abadie, a Harvard economist, the attack affected "the spinal cord of any favorable business environment"—the ability of business and workers "to meet and communicate effectively without incurring risks."[13] The 9/11 attacks increased the vacancy rates of tall buildings even in cities other than New York, such as Chicago's Sears Tower, making that capital less productive.[14] As other examples, a greater threat to airport security adds to the time and cost of flying. Shops in countries plagued by suicide bombers must hire security guards to deter such horror, and this increases the cost of doing business. And the mortgage meltdown of 2007–2009 reduced the trust that one bank had in another, thereby freezing up credit markets and increasing the cost of borrowing.

Advanced economies have developed a reliable and respected system of property rights, customs, and conventions that nurture productive activity. These successful economies have also cultivated the social capital that helps an economy run more smoothly. **Social capital** consists of the shared values and trust that promote cooperation in the economy. At the national level, social capital could be reflected in a sense of common purpose. For example, despite the Great Recession, polls show that Americans remain among the most patriotic people in the world. In a recent survey, 83 percent said they were "extremely" or "very" proud to be Americans.[15] At the local level, social capital could be expressed by a neighborhood crime watch, and there is evidence that such efforts help reduce property crime.[16]

Low-income economies typically have poorly defined property rights, less social capital, and in the extreme, customs and conventions where violence, bribery, and government corruption are common. Worse still, civil wars have ravaged some of the poorest countries on Earth. Such violence and uncertainty make people less willing to invest in their own future or in the future of their country. In short, as the Nobel Prize winner

social capital
The shared values and trust that promote cooperation in the economy

---

[11.] Megan Davies and Melissa Akins, "Russian Risks Bear Down on Oligarch Fridman," *Reuters*, 6 June 2012.

[12.] Edmund Burke, *Letters to Parliament*, 2nd ed. (Rivington, 1796), p. 105.

[13.] As quoted in Greg Ip and John McKinnon, "Economy Likely Won't See Gain From War Against Terrorism," *Wall Street Journal*, 25 September 2001.

[14.] Alberto Abadie and Sofia Dermisi, "Is Terrorism Eroding Agglomeration Economies in Central Business Districts? Lessons From the Office Real Estate Market in Downtown Chicago," *Journal of Urban Economics*, 64 (September 2008): 451–463.

[15.] Lexington, "Where Has All the Greatness Gone?" *The Economist*, 17 July 2010.

[16.] Paolo Buonanno, Daniel Montolio, and Paolo Vanin, "Does Social Capital Reduce Crime?" *Journal of Law & Economics*, 52 (February 2009): 145–170.

Kenneth Arrow noted, "Virtually every commercial transaction has within itself an element of trust, certainly any transaction conducted over a period of time."[17] Economies do not work as well where there is less trust, less social capital.

Now that you have some idea about the theory of productivity and growth, let's look at them in practice, beginning with the vast difference in performance among economies around the world. Then we will turn to the United States.

CHECKPOINT

What's labor productivity, and why is it important for a nation's standard of living?

8-2 Productivity and Growth in Practice

Differences in the standard of living among countries are vast. To give you some idea, per capita output in the United States, a world leader among major economies, is about 90 times that of the world's poorest countries. Poor countries are poor because they experience low labor productivity. We can sort the world's economies into two broad groups. **Industrial market countries**, or *developed countries*, make up about 18 percent of the world's population. They consist of the economically advanced capitalist countries of Western Europe, North America, Australia, New Zealand, and Japan, plus the newly industrialized Asian countries of Taiwan, South Korea, Hong Kong, and Singapore. Industrial market countries were usually the first to experience long-term economic growth during the 19th century, and today have the world's highest standards of living based on abundant human and physical capital. Industrial market countries produce more than half the world's output. The rest of the world, the remaining 82 percent of the world's population, consists of **developing countries**, which have a lower standard of living because they have less human and physical capital. Many workers in developing countries are farmers. Because farming methods there are often primitive, labor productivity is low and most people barely subsist, much like Americans two centuries ago.

industrial market countries
Economically advanced capitalist countries of Western Europe, North America, Australia, New Zealand, and Japan, plus the newly industrialized Asian economies of Taiwan, South Korea, Hong Kong, and Singapore

developing countries
Countries with a lower living standard because of less human and physical capital per worker

8-2a Education and Economic Development

Another important source of productivity is human capital—the skill, experience, and education of workers. If knowledge is lacking, other resources may not be used efficiently. *Education makes workers aware of the latest production techniques and more receptive to new approaches and methods.* Exhibit 4 shows the percentage of the population ages 25 to 64 who have at least a degree beyond high school. Figures are presented for the United States and six other industrial market economies, together called the *Group of Seven*, or *G-7* (sometimes Russia is added to form the G-8, but Russia is not yet an industrial market economy). In 1998, 35 percent of the U.S. adult population had at least a degree beyond high school, ranking second behind Canada. The U.S. percentage grew to 42 by 2012, though America slipped to third behind Canada and Japan.

Not shown in Exhibit 4 are developing countries, which have far lower education levels. For example, only 13 percent of those in Brazil between the ages of 25 and 64

17. Kenneth Arrow, "Gifts and Exchanges," *Philosophy & Public Affairs*, 1 (Summer 1972): 343–362.

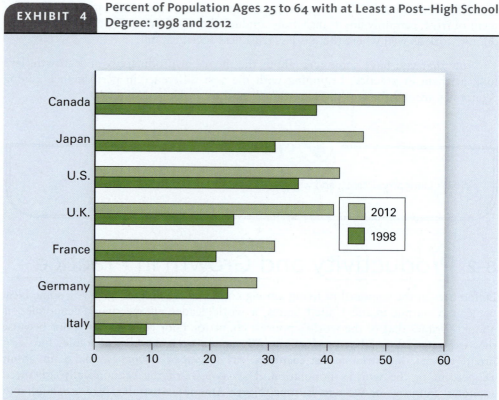

EXHIBIT 4 Percent of Population Ages 25 to 64 with at Least a Post–High School Degree: 1998 and 2012

The share of the U.S. population ages 25 to 64 with at least a degree beyond high school increased from 35 percent in 1998 to 42 percent in 2012. The United States slipped from second among the seven major industrial market economies in 1998 to third in 2012.

Source: Based on figures in OECD, *Education at a Glance: 2014*, at http://www.oecd.org/edu/Education-at-a-Glance-2014.pdf.

had a degree beyond high school in 2012. And while the literacy rate exceeds 95 percent in industrial market economies, nearly half the adults in the world's poorest countries can't read or write.

8-2b U.S. Labor Productivity

What has been the record of labor productivity in the United States? Exhibit 5 offers a long-run perspective, showing growth in real output per work hour for the last 145 years. Annual productivity growth is averaged by decade (except for the most recent period, which averages 2010 to 2015). The huge dip during the Great Depression and the strong rebound during World War II are unmistakable. Growth slowed during the 1970s and 1980s but recovered somewhat during the 1990s and 2000s. However, during the most recent period, 2010 to 2015, labor productivity growth dropped to just 1.0 percent, among the slowest on record. Labor productivity has grown an average of 2.1 percent per year since 1870. This may not impress you, but because of the power of compounding, output per hour has jumped more than 1,900 percent during the period. To put this in perspective, if a roofer in 1870 could shingle one roof in a day, today's roofer could shingle more than 20 roofs in a day.

Over long periods, small differences in productivity can make huge differences in the economy's ability to produce and therefore in the standard of living. For example, if

| EXHIBIT 5 | Long-Term Trend in U.S. Labor Productivity Growth: Annual Average by Decade |

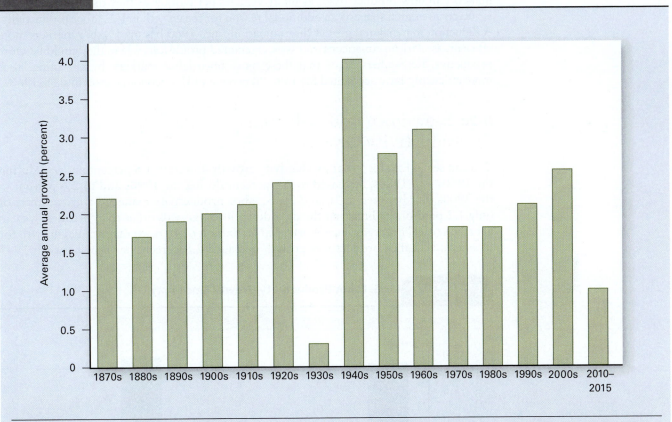

Annual productivity growth, measured as the growth in real output per work hour, is averaged by decade. For the entire period since 1870, labor productivity grew an average of 2.1 percent per year. Note the big dip during the Great Depression of the 1930s and the big bounce back during World War II. Productivity growth slowed during the 1970s and 1980s but recovered slightly during the 1990s and 2000s before dropping more recently.

Sources: Angus Maddison, *Phases of Capitalist Development* (Oxford University Press, 1982); and U.S. Bureau of Labor Statistics. The average for "2010–2015" goes through first half of 2015. For the latest data, go to http://www.bls.gov/lpc/.

productivity grew only 1.0 percent per year instead of 2.1 percent, output per work hour since 1870 would have increased by only 323 percent, not 1,936 percent. On the other hand, if productivity grew 2.6 percent per year (the average from 2000 to 2010), output per work hour since 1870 would have jumped about 4000 percent! The wheels of progress seem to grind slowly but they grind very fine, and the cumulative effect is powerful.

So far, we have averaged productivity growth for all workers. Productivity has grown more in some industries than in others. In ocean shipping, for example, cargo carried per worker hour is about 100 times greater now than in 1900, for an average annual growth of 4.1 percent. On the other hand, makers of wooden office furniture are only about three times more productive today than in 1900, for an average annual growth in productivity of only 1.0 percent. Consider productivity gains in TV journalism. Not long ago, a TV reporter covering a story would need a camera operator, a sound technician, and a broadcast editor. Now, because of technological advances in the size, quality, and ease of use of equipment, most TV reporters set up their own cameras on the scene, shoot their own footage, and do their own editing. One person can do what used to take four to accomplish. And because of technological advances in car manufacturing, some automakers can now produce twice as many vehicles per worker as they did a decade ago.[18]

Recent research suggests an additional reason for the growth in U.S. labor productivity: A reduction in racial and gender discrimination since 1960 has made labor markets more efficient, as African Americans and women entered professions where they could be more productive. Researchers argue that these more open labor markets, by allocating labor more efficiently, have accounted for 15 to 20 percent of U.S. economic growth since 1960.[19]

8-2c Slowdown and Rebound in Productivity Growth

You can see in Exhibit 5 that productivity growth slowed to 1.8 percent per year during the 1970s and 1980s, increased to 2.1 percent during the 1990s and to 2.6 percent in the 2000s. But between 2010 and 2015, labor productivity managed a growth rate of only 1.2 percent. By breaking the data down into intervals other than decades, we can get a better feel for years since World War II. Exhibit 6 offers average annual growth for five periods. Labor productivity growth averaged 2.8 percent per year between 1947

EXHIBIT 6   **U.S. Labor Productivity Growth Since 1947**

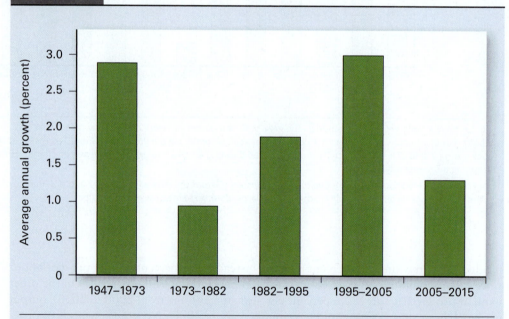

The growth in labor productivity declined from an average of 2.8 percent per year between 1947 and 1973 to only 0.9 percent between 1973 and 1982. A jump in the price of oil contributed to three recessions during that stretch, and new environmental and workplace regulations, though necessary and beneficial, slowed down productivity growth temporarily. The information revolution powered by the computer chip and the Internet boosted productivity between 1982 and 2005.

Source: Averages based on annual estimates from the U.S. Bureau of Labor Statistics. For the latest data go to http://www.bls.gov/lpc/home.htm. Average for 2005–2015 is through the first half of 2015.

[18.] "The Third Industrial Revolution," *The Economist*, 21 April 2012.
[19.] Chang-Tai Hsieh et al. "The Allocation of Talent and U.S. Economic Growth," American Economic Association annual meetings, 4 January 2013.

and 1973; these could be called the golden years of productivity growth. But, between 1973 and 1982, productivity growth slowed to only about a third of that, averaging just 0.9 percent. Why the slowdown? First, as a result of OPEC actions, oil prices jumped between 1973 and 1974 and again between 1979 and 1980, boosting inflation and contributing to stagflation and three recessions. Second, federal legislation in the early 1970s necessary to protect the environment and improve workplace safety slowed the growth of labor productivity.

Fortunately, productivity rebounded off the 1973–1982 low, averaging 1.8 percent from 1982 to 1995 and 3.0 percent from 1995 to 2005. Why the rebound? The information revolution powered by the computer chip and the Internet started paying off. One study of industrial economies found that the greater the penetration of broadband Internet service, the higher the economic growth per capita.[20] The U.S. dominance in computer technology carries over to U.S. multinational firms, which experienced higher productivity growth after 1995 than did multinationals from other countries.[21]

Unfortunately, between 2005 and 2015, U.S. labor productivity growth averaged just 1.3 percent, or less than half the average for 1995 to 2005. Some economists argue that the boost to productivity provided by information technology was just temporary, and the recent slowdown indicates that boost has now run its course.[22]

Higher labor productivity growth can make up for output lost from most recessions. For example, if over the next decade U.S. labor productivity grows an average of 3.0 percent per year (the average from 1995 to 2005) instead of 1.3 percent (the average from 2005 to 2015), that higher growth would add about $3.3 trillion to real GDP in the tenth year—more than enough to make up for the output lost during the worst recession since the Great Depression. *This cumulative power of productivity growth is why economists pay so much attention to long-term growth.*

One final point before we move on: The U.S. Bureau of Labor Statistics measures labor productivity in only about 60 percent of all industries, leaving out some of the newest ones. For example, many new apps make life easier and more enjoyable, but little of this is captured in productivity measures. So labor productivity is not a foolproof measure of what's going on throughout the economy.

8-2d Output per Capita

As noted earlier, the best measure of an economy's standard of living is output per capita. *Output per capita*, or GDP divided by the population, indicates how much an economy produces on average per resident. How does U.S. output per capita compare with that of other industrial countries? Exhibit 7 compares GDP per capita in 2014 for the United States and the six other G-7 countries plus China. Local currencies have been converted to U.S. dollars of 2014 purchasing power. With GDP per capita of $54,800 in 2014, the United States stood alone at the top, with a per capita GDP 23 percent above second-ranked Germany. Thus, the United States produced more per capita than any other major economy. GDP per capita for the world was about $16,100 in 2014. Hence, U.S. per capita income was more than three times the world average.

---

[20] Nina Czernich et al. "Broadband Infrastructure and Economic Growth," *Economic Journal*, 121 (May 2011): 505–532.

[21] Nicholas Bloom, Raffaella Sadun, and John Van Reenen, "Americans Do IT Better: U.S. Multinationals and the Productivity Miracle," *American Economic Review*, 102 (March 2012): 167–201.

[22] John Fernald and Bing Wang, "The Recent Rise and Fall of Rapid Productivity Growth," *FRBSF Economic Letter*, 9 February 2015, http://www.frbsf.org/economic-research/publications/economic-letter/2015/february/economic-growth-information-technology-factor-productivity/.

EXHIBIT 7   **U.S. GDP Per Capita in 2014 Was Highest of G-7 Economies and Four Times China's**

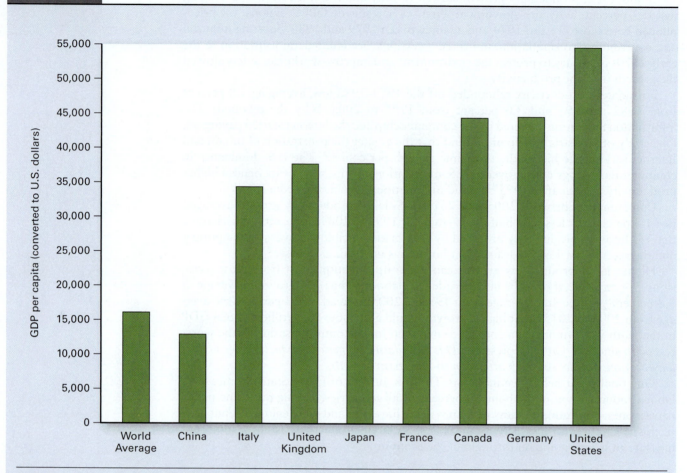

Source: Based on 2014 dollar estimates from the OECD at http://www.oecd.org/home/; and *The World Factbook 2015*, at https://www.cia.gov/library/publications/the-world-factbook/index.html. Estimates have been adjusted across countries using the purchasing power of the local currency in 2014.

Of course, U.S. output per capita is far greater than in less developed economies. For example, U.S. output per capita is more than four times that of China and more than nine times that of India. The United States has an open and competitive economy, where successful firms can thrive. Firms in less developed countries often remain small because of government regulations and a fear of hiring anyone outside the family for lack of trust. One economist joked that if Walmart's founder, Sam Walton, had started in India, he would have only five stores by now, they would all be called "Sam Walton's Family Market," and each store would be managed by one of his sons or sons-in-law.[23]

To Review: U.S. labor productivity growth has averaged 2.1 percent per year since 1870. Productivity growth slowed between 1973 and 1982, because of spikes in energy prices and the implementation of necessary but costly environmental and

[23.] Drawn from an "Interview with Nicholas Bloom," *Econ Focus: Federal Reserve Bank of Richmond*, 18 (Second Quarter 2014): 22–26.

workplace regulations. After 1982 labor productivity growth picked up, especially between 1995 and 2005, due primarily to breakthroughs in information technology. But the boost from information technology seemed to wane during the 2005 to 2015 decade, when the rate averaged less than half that of the decade from 1995 to 2005. Still, in 2014, U.S. GDP per capita was the highest among major economies, was more than three times the world average, and was four times that of China.

 **CHECKPOINT**

What was happening to U.S. labor productivity during each of the five periods since World War II identified in Exhibit 6, and why does it matter?

8-3 Other Issues of Technology and Growth

In this section we consider some other issues of technology and growth, beginning with the question whether technological change creates unemployment.

8-3a Does Technological Change Lead to Unemployment?

Because technological change usually reduces the labor needed to produce a given amount of output, some observers fear technological change increases unemployment. True, technological change can create dislocations as displaced workers try to find jobs elsewhere. But technological change can also create new products and job opportunities and make existing products more affordable. For example, the assembly line cut the cost of automobiles, making them more affordable for the average household. This increased the quantity of automobiles demanded, boosting production and employment. Even in industries where machines displace some workers, those who keep their jobs become more productive, so they earn more. And *because human wants are unlimited, displaced workers usually find jobs producing other goods and services demanded in a growing economy.*

Although job data from the 19th century are sketchy, there is no evidence that the unemployment rate is any higher today than it was in 1870. Since then, worker productivity per hour has increased more than 1,900 percent, and the length of the average workweek has been cut nearly in half. Although technological change may displace some workers in the short run, long-run benefits include higher real incomes and more leisure—in short, a higher standard of living.

If technological change causes unemployment, then the spurt in productivity growth from 1995 to 2005 should have increased unemployment compared to the slow-growth years from 1973 to 1982. But the unemployment rate, the share of the workforce looking for jobs, averaged 7.0 percent during 1973 to 1982, compared to only 5.1 percent from 1995 to 2005. What's more, the unemployment rate increased during the slowdown in labor productivity growth after 2005. And if technological change causes unemployment, then unemployment rates should be lower in economies where the latest technology has not yet been adopted, such as in developing countries. But unemployment is far worse there, and those fortunate enough to find work earn little because they are not very productive.

Again, there is no question that technological change sometimes creates job dislocations and hardships in the short run, as workers scramble to adjust to a changing world. Because of technological progress, labor is becoming less important in some types of production. For example, the $499 charged for the first-generation iPad included only about $33 of manufacturing labor. And the final assembly in China accounted for just $8 of that $33.[24] Some workers with specialized skills made obsolete by technology may be unable to find jobs that pay as well as the ones they lost. These dislocations are one price of progress. Over time, however, most displaced workers find other jobs, often in new industries created by technological change. In a typical month of expansion, the U.S. economy sheds about 3.8 million jobs but creates about 4 million new ones.

Although unemployment may not have increased because of technological change, researchers have found that advances in information technology during the last three decades have reduced the cost of investment goods, encouraging some firms to substitute capital for labor. The lower cost of investment goods has contributed to a decline in labor's share of total income in most countries and in most industries.[25] Because of the broad advances in technology, some companies can become successful with few workers. For example, Oculus VR, makers of virtual reality headsets, had only 75 employees in 2014, when it was purchased by Facebook for $2 billion.[26]

8-3b Research and Development

As noted several times already, a prime contributor to labor productivity growth has been an improvement in the quality of human and physical capital. Human capital has benefited from better education, better health care, and more job training. Better technology embodied in physical capital has also helped labor productivity. For example, because of extensive investments in cellular transmission, new satellites, and fiber-optic technology, labor productivity in the telecommunications industry has increased by an average of 5.5 percent per year during the past three decades.

basic research
The search for knowledge without regard to how that knowledge will be used

applied research
Research that seeks answers to particular questions or to apply scientific discoveries to develop specific products

Improvements in technology arise from scientific discovery, which is the fruit of research. We can distinguish between basic research and applied research. **Basic research,** the search for knowledge without regard to how that knowledge will be used, is a first step toward technological advancement. In terms of economic growth, however, scientific discoveries are of little value until they are implemented, which requires applied research. **Applied research** seeks to answer particular questions or to apply scientific discoveries to the development of specific products. Because technological breakthroughs may or may not have commercial possibilities, the payoff is less immediate with basic research than with applied research. *Yet basic research yields a higher return to society as a whole than does applied research.*

Because technological change is the fruit of research and development (R&D), investment in R&D improves productivity through technological discovery. One way to track R&D spending is to measure it relative to gross domestic product, or GDP. Exhibit 8 shows R&D spending as a share of GDP for the United States and the six other G-7 economies. Overall R&D spending in the United States has remained relatively constant, averaging 2.7 percent of GDP in the 1980s and 1990s, and 2.8 percent in 2013. During the 1990s, the United States ranked second among the major economies, behind Japan; in 2013 the United States tied with Germany for second place behind Japan.

[24.] "The Third Industrial Revolution," *The Economist*, 21 April 2012.

[25.] Loukas Karabarbounis and Brent Neiman, "The Global Decline of the Labor Share," *Quarterly Journal of Economics*, 129 (February 2014): 61–103.

[26.] Simon Parkin, "What Zuckerberg Sees in Oculus Rift," *MIT Technology Review*, 26 March 2014, at http://www.technologyreview.com/news/525881/what-zuckerberg-sees-in-oculus-rift/.

EXHIBIT 8   R&D Spending as a Percentage of GDP for G-7 Economies During the 1980s, 1990s, and in 2013

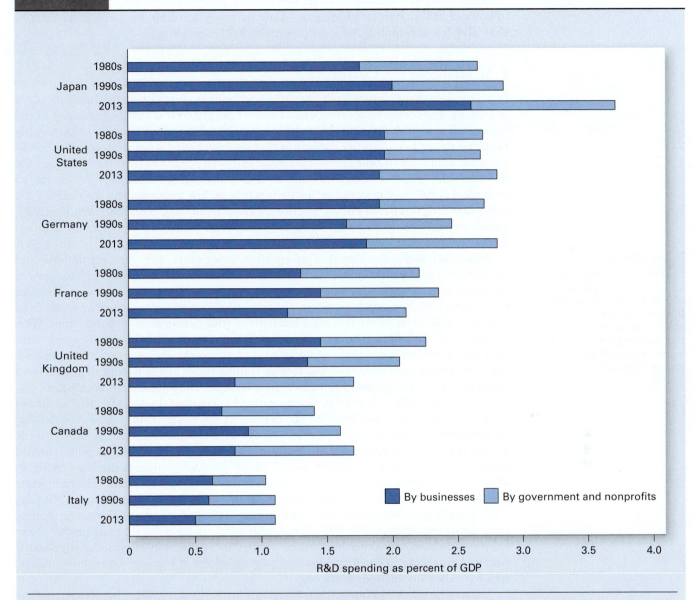

R&D spending as percent of GDP

■ By businesses □ By government and nonprofits

Source: Calculated from figures provided by the OECD at http://www.oecd.org/innovation/inno/researchanddevelopmentstatisticsrds.htm.

Bar segments in the chart distinguish between R&D by businesses (shown as dark blue segments) and R&D by governments and nonprofit institutions (shown as light blue segments). Business R&D is more likely to target applied research and innovations. R&D spending by governments and nonprofits, such as universities, may generate basic knowledge that has applications in the long run (for example, the Internet sprang from R&D spending on national defense). R&D by U.S. businesses was about 1.9 percent of GDP in all three periods. Again, only Japan had higher business R&D than the United States in the 1990s and in 2013. In short, the United States devotes more resources to R&D than most other advanced economies, and this helps America maintain a higher standard of living. Incidentally, manufacturers undertake more R&D than most other types of producers. Manufacturing accounts for only 11 percent of U.S. GDP but is responsible for 68 percent of R&D spending.[27]

8-3c Industrial Policy

Policy makers have debated whether the government should become more involved in shaping an economy's technological future. One concern is that technologies of the future will require huge sums to develop, sums that an individual firm cannot easily raise and put at risk. Another concern is that the benefits of some technological break-throughs spill over to other firms and other industries, but the firm that develops the breakthrough may not be in a position to reap benefits from these spillover effects, so individual firms may underinvest in such research. For example, the majority of the important drug discoveries in the last decade came from basic research.[28] Yet drug companies are often reluctant to invest in these long-term projects.[29] One possible solution is more government involvement in economic planning.

industrial policy

The view that government—using taxes, subsidies, and regulations—should nurture the industries and technologies of the future, thereby giving these domestic industries an advantage over foreign competition

Industrial policy is the idea that government, using taxes, subsidies, regulations, and coordination of the private sector, could help nurture the industries and technologies of the future to give domestic industries an advantage over foreign competitors. The idea is to secure a leading role for domestic industry in the world economy. One example of European industrial policy is Airbus Industrie, a four-nation aircraft consortium. With an estimated $20 billion in government aid, the aircraft maker has become Boeing's main rival. When Airbus seeks aircraft orders around the world, it can draw on government backing to promise favorable terms, such as landing rights at key European airports and an easing of regulatory constraints. U.S. producers get less government backing.

For decades, U.S. industrial policy was aimed at creating the world's most advanced military production capacity. With the demise of the Soviet Union, however, defense technologies became less important, but wars in Iraq and Afghanistan shifted some attention back to military applications. Some argue that U.S. industrial policy should shift from a military to a civilian focus. Many state governments are also trying to identify what industries to support. Economists have long recognized that firms in some industries gain a performance advantage by *clustering*—that is, by locating in a region already thick with firms in the same industry or in related industries. For example, new entrants to an industry can hire experienced workers from established firms.[30] New entrants can also buy other specialized factors of production from local suppliers.[31] And new entrants can benefit from local knowledge about industry know-how, such as which production methods work best.[32]

Clusters such as Hollywood studios, Wall Street brokers, Broadway theaters, Las Vegas casinos, Boston colleges, Orlando theme parks, and Silicon Valley software makers facilitate communication and promote healthy competition among cluster members.

[27] "Manufacturing and Innovation: Back to Making Stuff," *The Economist*, 21 April 2012.

[28] Dan Hurley, "Why Are So Few Block Buster Drugs Invented Today?" *New York Times*, 13 November 2014.

[29] Eric Budish, Benjamin N. Roin, and Heidi Williams, "Do Firms Underinvest in Long-Term Research? Evidence from Cancer Clinical Trials," *American Economic Review* (forthcoming).

[30] Andrey Stoyonov and Nikolay Zubanov, "Productivity Spillovers Across Firms Through Worker Mobility," *American Economic Journal: Applied Economics*, 4 (April 2012): 168–198.

[31] Ejaz Ghani, William R. Kerr, and Stephen D. O'Connell, "Spatial Determinants of Entrepreneurship in India," *Regional Studies*, 48 (June 2014): 1071–1089.

[32] Glenn Ellison, Edward L. Glaeser, and William R. Kerr, "What Causes Agglomeration? Evidence From Coagglomeration Patterns," *American Economic Review*, 100 (June 2010): 1195–1213.

The flow of information and cooperation between firms, as well as the competition among firms in close proximity, stimulates regional innovation and propels growth. Thus, by locating in a region already settled with similar firms, a firm can also tap into established local markets for specialized labor and for other inputs. Research into patent activity suggests that know-how in one firm spills over to other firms in the locality.[33] And there is some evidence that an industrial policy that nurtures younger and more productive enterprises can boost productivity growth in the economy.[34]

But skeptics wonder whether the government should be trusted to identify productive enterprises and to pick the industry clusters that will lead the way. Critics of industrial policy believe that markets allocate scarce resources better than governments do. For example, European governments' costly attempt to develop the supersonic transport Concorde never became cost efficient. Airbus also ran into financial difficulties, and sponsoring governments tried to distance themselves from the company. As a U.S. example, in the early 1980s, the U.S. government spent $1 billion to help military contractors develop a high-speed computer circuit. But Intel, a company getting no federal aid, was the first to develop the circuit. The 2009 federal stimulus program included funds to promote green energy, such as a $527 million loan to Solyndra, a California maker of solar panels. In 2011, that company went bankrupt, leaving taxpayers on the hook for the loan. Some other green energy companies getting federal aid also went bankrupt. The federal government's promotion of green energy sources such as solar panels and biofuels is an example of industrial policy.

There is also concern that an industrial policy could evolve into a government giveaway program. Rather than going to the most promising technologies, the money and the competitive advantages would go to the most politically connected. Critics also wonder why government should sponsor corporate research when beneficiaries may share their expertise with foreign companies or even build factories abroad. Most economists would prefer to let Microsoft, General Electric, Google, Apple, or some start-up bet its own money on the important technologies of the future. Note that the advantages of clustering create an economic impetus for firms in certain industries to group together. Most clusters form on their own, without government direction or support.

Some argue that the focus should be less on a nation's production and income and more on the happiness of the population. The link between income and happiness is discussed in this closing case study.

PUBLIC POLICY

INCOME AND HAPPINESS In 1776 the Declaration of Independence identified "certain unalienable Rights, that among these are Life, Liberty, and the Pursuit of Happiness." This did not guarantee happiness but did establish the pursuit of happiness as an "unalienable" right, meaning that right cannot be taken away, given away, or sold. Eighteenth-century philosopher and social reformer Jeremy Bentham argued that government policy should promote the greatest happiness for the greatest number of people.

Many people today apparently agree. In recent polls, 77 percent of Australians and 81 percent of Brits believed that a government's prime objective should be promoting the greatest happiness rather than the greatest wealth. The

continued

33. Yasusada Murata et al. "Localized Knowledge Spillovers and Patent Citations: A Distance-Based Approach," *Review of Economics and Statistics*, 96 (December 2014): 967–983.
34. Philippe Aghion et al. "Industrial Policy and Competition," *American Economics Journal: Macroeconomics* (forthcoming).

© iStockphoto.com/Skynesher

United Nations sponsored an international conference on "Happiness and Public Policy." Thailand now compiles a monthly Gross Domestic Happiness Index. Even China has joined in the fun, reporting a happiness index based on polling results about living conditions, income, the environment, social welfare, and employment. Australia, Canada, Germany and the United Kingdom are also developing indexes of happiness or well-being. For example, the Canadian Index of Wellbeing contains a measure of social connectedness, among other things.

Economists have long shied away from asking people how they feel, preferring instead to observe their behavior. But more economists now see some value in asking questions. In the most extensive of polls, the Gallup organization asked people in 130 countries: "How satisfied are you with your life, on a scale of zero to ten?" The results are not surprising. Most people in the high-income areas, such as the United States, Europe, and Japan, said they are happy. Most people in the low-income areas, especially in Africa, said they are not. Also, within a given country, income and happiness are positively related. After evaluating all the results of the Gallup world poll, Angus Deaton of Princeton concluded: "The very strong global relationship between per capita GDP and life satisfaction suggests that on average people have a good idea of how income, or the lack of it, affects their lives." Using this approach, the *World Happiness Report* began ranking countries each year based on happiness. For example, of the 156 countries ranked in the 2015 *Report*, the three happiest countries were Switzerland, Iceland,

and Denmark. The United States ranked 15th. The bottom three were Syria, Burundi, and Togo.

So these results are no surprise. What does puzzle economists is that other surveys suggest that Americans on average do not seem any happier over time even though each generation became richer than the last. The proportion of Americans who say they are happy has stayed about the same despite 60 years of economic growth.

The United States is unusual in that regard. Surveys in Europe and Japan do find an increase in happiness with increases in income over time. Here's a possible explanation. Americans begin taking for granted those luxuries they most desired. For example, two generations ago color TVs, automobiles, and major appliances were luxuries, but now they are must-have items for most households. Smartphones and HDTVs will soon move from luxuries to necessities. As each generation attains a higher standard of living, people become less sensitive to the benefits, they take them for granted, and thus they say they are no happier. And this adaptation may not take a generation. For example, researchers found that when housing for poor people in Brazil was dramatically upgraded, their subjective well-being initially improved substantially. But after only eight months, 60 percent of that gain had disappeared. Apparently, as they grew more accustomed to their new housing, they began taking it for granted and thus appreciated it less.

While there may have been no increase in the level of aggregate happiness in the United States, inequality in happiness has fallen substantially since the 1970s. Blacks have closed two-thirds of the happiness gap they had with whites, and women are no longer less happy than men.

Sources: Jorn-Steffen Pischke, "Money and Happiness: Evidence From the Industry Wage Structure," NBER Working Paper 17056, (May 2011); Daniel J. Benjamin et al. "Beyond Happiness and Satisfaction: Toward Well-Being Indices Based on Stated Preferences," *American Economic Review*, 104 (September 2014): 2698–2735. Angus Deaton, "Income, Health, and Well-Being Around the World: Evidence From the Gallup World Poll," *Journal of Economic Perspectives*, 22 (Spring 2008): 53–72; Sebastian Galiani, Paul J. Gertler, and Raimundo Undurraga, "The Half-Life of Happiness: Hedonic Adaptation in the Subjective Well-Being of Poor Slum Dwellers to a Large Improvement in Housing," NBER Working Paper No. 21098 (April 2015); Betsey Stevenson and Justin Wolfers, "Subjective Well-Being and Income: Is There Any Evidence of Satiation?" *American Economic Review*, 103 (May 2013): 598–604; and *World Happiness Report: 2015*, John Helliwell, Richard Layard, and Jeffrey Sachs, eds. Sustainable Development Solutions Network at http://worldhappiness.report/.

CHECKPOINT

Evaluate the evidence that technological change increases the unemployment rate.

8-4 Conclusion

Productivity and growth depend on the supply and quality of resources, the level of technology and know-how, and the rules of the game that nurture production and exchange. These elements tend to be correlated with one another. An economy with an unskilled and poorly educated workforce usually is deficient in physical capital, in the latest technology and know-how, and in the institutional support that promotes production and exchange, including social capital. Similarly, an economy with a high-quality workforce likely excels in the other sources of productivity and growth.

We should distinguish between an economy's standard of living, as measured by output per capita, and improvements in that standard of living, as measured by the growth in output per capita. Growth in output per capita can occur when labor productivity increases or when the number of workers in the economy grows faster than the population. *In the long run, productivity growth and the growth in workers relative to the growth in population will determine whether or not the United States continues to enjoy one of the world's highest standards of living.*

Summary

1. If the population is continually increasing, an economy must produce more goods and services just to maintain its standard of living, as measured by output per capita. If output grows faster than the population, the standard of living rises.

2. An economy's standard of living grows over the long run because of (a) increases in the amount and quality of resources, especially labor and capital, (b) better technology and know-how, and (c) improvements in the rules of the game that facilitate production and exchange, such as tax laws, property rights, patent laws, the legal system, and customs of the market.

3. The per-worker production function shows the relationship between the amount of capital per worker in the economy and the output per worker. As capital per worker increases, so does output per worker but at a decreasing rate. Technological change, more know-how, and improvements in the rules of the game shift the per-worker production function upward, so more is produced for each ratio of capital per worker.

4. Since 1870, U.S. labor productivity growth has averaged 2.1 percent per year. The *quality* of labor and capital is much more important than the *quantity* of these resources. Labor

productivity growth slowed between 1973 and 1982, in part because of spikes in energy prices and the implementation of costly but necessary environmental and workplace regulations. After 1982 productivity growth picked up, especially between 1995 and 2005, due primarily to information technology. But since 2005, productivity growth has slowed down perhaps because the boost from information technology tailed off.

5. Among the seven major industrial market economies, the United States most recently produced the highest real GDP per capita.

6. Technological change sometimes costs jobs and imposes hardships in the short run, as workers scramble to adapt to a changing world. Over time, however, most displaced workers find other jobs, sometimes in new industries created by technological change. There is no evidence that, in the long run, technological change increases unemployment in the economy.

7. Some governments use industrial policy in an effort to nurture the industries and technologies of the future, trying to give domestic industries an advantage over foreign competitors. But critics are wary of the government's ability to pick the winning technologies.

Key Concepts

Questions for Review

1. **Productivity**   As discussed in the text, per capita GDP in many developing countries depends on the fertility of land. However, many richer economies have little land or land of poor quality. How can a country with little land or unproductive land prosper?

2. **Labor Productivity**   What two kinds of changes in the capital stock can improve labor productivity? How can each type be illustrated with a per-worker production function? What determines the slope of the per-worker production function?

3. **Slowdown in Labor Productivity Growth**   What slowed the rate of growth of labor productivity during the 1973–1982 period?

4. **Output per Capita**   Explain how output per capita can grow faster than labor productivity. Is it possible for labor productivity to grow faster than output per capita? If so, how?

5. **Technology and Productivity**   What measures can government take to promote the development of practical technologies?

6. **Basic and Applied Research**   What is the difference between basic research and applied research? Relate this to the human genome project—research aimed at developing a complete map of human chromosomes, showing the location of every gene.

7. **Rules of the Game**   How do "rules of the game" affect productivity and growth? What types of "rules" should a government establish to encourage growth?

8. **Research and Development**   What's the relevance of research and development to an economy's productivity? Among major economies, how does the United States rank in R&D spending as a share of GDP?

9. **International Productivity Comparisons**   How does output per capita in the United States compare with output per capita in other major industrial economies? How does U.S. output per capita compare with the world average and with China?

10. **Industrial Policy**   Define industrial policy. What are some arguments for and against industrial policy?

11. **Technological Change and Unemployment**   Explain how technological change can lead to unemployment in certain industries. How can it increase employment?

12. **Productivity**   What factors might contribute to a low *level* of labor productivity in an economy? Regardless of the level of labor productivity, what impact does *growth* in labor productivity have on the economy's standard of living?

13. **Case Study: Income and Happiness**   How would you explain the finding that people in high-income economies seem happier than people in low-income economies, but, over generations, Americans do not say they are happier even though the nation grew richer?

Problems and Exercises

14. **Growth and the PPF**   Use the production possibilities frontier (PPF) to demonstrate economic growth.

    a. With consumption goods on one axis and capital goods on the other, show how the combination of goods selected this period affects the PPF in the next period.

    b. Extend this comparison by choosing a different point on this period's PPF and determining whether that combination leads to more or less growth.

15. **Long-Term Productivity Growth**   Suppose that two nations start out in 2016 with identical levels of output per work hour—say, $100 per hour. In the first nation, labor productivity grows by one percent per year in real terms. In the second,

it grows by two percent per year in real terms. Use a calculator or a spreadsheet to determine how much output per hour each nation will be producing 20 years later. Then, determine how much each will be producing per hour 100 years later. What do your results tell you about the effects of small differences in productivity growth rates?

16. **Technological Change and Unemployment**   What are some examples of technological changes that have caused unemployment? And what are some examples of new technologies that have created jobs? How do you think you might measure the net impact of technological change on overall employment and GDP in the United States?

Aggregate Demand

9

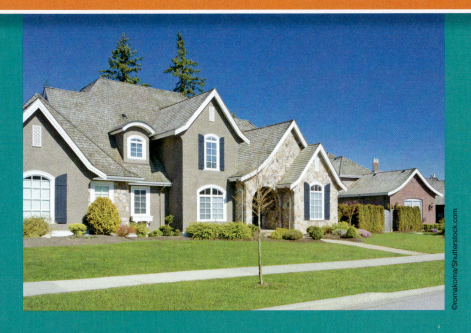

©romakoma/Shutterstock.com

- *When driving through a neighborhood new to you, how can you guess the income of the residents?*

- *What's one of the most predictable and useful relationships in macroeconomics?*

- *Why are consumer confidence and business confidence in the economy so important?*

- *How is spending linked to income?*

- *Why did Americans spend less and save more after the financial crisis of 2008?*

Answers to these and other questions are addressed in this chapter, which focuses on the makeup of aggregate spending, especially consumption, to develop the aggregate demand curve.

Your economic success depends in part on the overall performance of the economy. When the economy grows, job opportunities expand, so your chances of finding a good job increase. When the economy contracts, job opportunities shrink, and so do your job prospects. Thus, you have a personal stake in the economy's success.

Consumption is the most important component of aggregate expenditure, accounting for about 68 percent of the total. We discuss how consumption and the other spending components relate to income in the economy. We then see how a change in the economy's price level affects aggregate spending. All this is aimed at getting to the economy's aggregate demand curve. In the next chapter, we develop the aggregate supply curve and see how the two curves interact to determine the economy's equilibrium levels of price and output.

Topics discussed in this chapter include:

- Consumption and income
- The consumption function
- Marginal propensity to consume

- Marginal propensity to save
- Life-cycle model of consumption and saving
- Income-expenditure model

- Aggregate expenditure line
- Simple spending multiplier
- Aggregate demand curve

9-1 Consumption

What if a college friend invited you home for the weekend? On your first visit, you would get some idea of the family's standard of living. Is their house a mansion, a modest rental, or in between? Do they drive a new BMW or take the bus? The simple fact is that consumption tends to reflect income. Although some people can temporarily live beyond their means and others still have the first nickel they ever earned, in general, consumption depends on income. *The positive and stable relationship between consumption and income, both for the household and for the economy as a whole, is a fundamental point of this chapter.*

A key decision in the circular-flow model developed three chapters back was how much households spent and how much they saved. Consumption depends primarily on income. Although this relationship seems obvious, the link between consumption and income will help you understand how the economy works. Let's look at this link in the U.S. economy over time.

9-1a Consumption and Income

Exhibit 1 shows the relationship between consumption and income in the United States since 1959; disposable income is measured along the horizontal axis and consumption along the vertical axis. Notice that each axis measures the same units: trillions of

EXHIBIT 1 **U.S. Consumption and Disposable Income Since 1959**

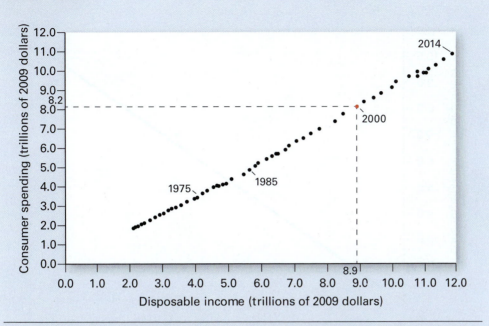

Consumption is on the vertical axis and disposable income on the horizontal axis. Notice that each axis measures trillions of 2009 dollars. For example, in 2000, identified by the red point, disposable income was $8.9 trillion and consumption $8.2 trillion. There is a clear and direct relationship over time between disposable income and consumption. As disposable income increases, so does consumption.

Source: Based on estimates from the Bureau of Economic Analysis, U.S. Department of Commerce. For the latest data, go to http://bea.gov/.

2009 dollars. Each year is depicted by a point that reflects two flow variables: disposable income and consumption. For example, the combination for 2000, identified by the red point, shows that when disposable income (measured along the horizontal axis) was $8.9 trillion, consumption (measured along the vertical axis) was $8.2 trillion.

As you can see, there is a clear and direct relationship between consumption and disposable income. You need little imagination to figure out that by connecting the dots, you could trace a line relating consumption to income. This relationship has special significance in macroeconomics.

9-1b The Consumption Function

After examining the link between consumption and income, we found it to be quite stable. Based on their disposable income, households decide how much to consume and how much to save. Scarcity prevents you from both spending and saving the same dollar. So consumption depends on disposable income. *Consumption is the dependent variable and disposable income is the independent variable.* Because consumption depends on income, we say that consumption is a *function* of income. Exhibit 2 presents for the economy a hypothetical **consumption function**, which shows that consumption increases with disposable income, assuming other determinants of consumption remain constant.

consumption function
The relationship in the economy between consumption and income, other things constant

EXHIBIT   2   **The Consumption Function**

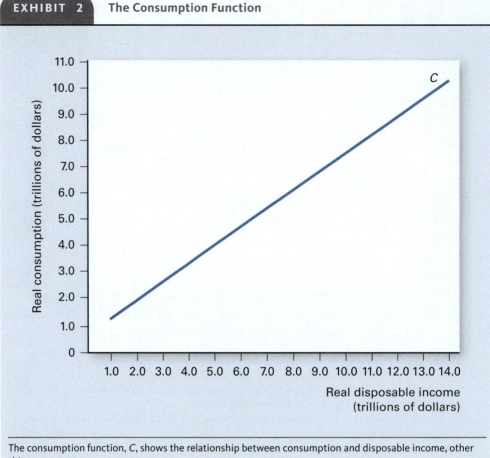

The consumption function, *C*, shows the relationship between consumption and disposable income, other things constant.

Again, both consumption and disposable income are in real terms, or in inflation-adjusted dollars. Notice that this hypothetical consumption function reflects the historical relationship between consumption and income shown in Exhibit 1.

9-1c Marginal Propensities to Consume and to Save

marginal propensity to consume (MPC)

The fraction of a change in income that is spent on consumption; the change in consumption divided by the change in income that caused it

marginal propensity to save (MPS)

The fraction of a change in income that is saved; the change in saving divided by the change in income that caused it

In Chapter 1, you learned that economic analysis focuses on activity at the margin. For example, what happens to consumption if income changes by a certain amount? Suppose U.S. households receive another billion dollars in disposable income. Some is spent on consumption, and the rest is saved. The fraction of the additional income that is spent is called the marginal propensity to consume. More precisely, the **marginal propensity to consume**, or **MPC**, equals the change in consumption divided by the change in income. Likewise, the fraction of that additional income that is saved is called the marginal propensity to save. More precisely, the **marginal propensity to save**, or **MPS**, equals the change in saving divided by the change in income.

For example, if U.S. income increases by $0.5 trillion, suppose consumption increases by $0.4 trillion and saving increases by $0.1 trillion. The marginal propensity to consume equals the change in consumption divided by the change in income. In this case, the change in consumption is $0.4 trillion and the change in income is $0.5 trillion, so the marginal propensity to consume is 0.4/0.5, or 4/5. Income not spent is saved. Saving increases by $0.1 trillion as a result of the $0.5 trillion increase in income, so the marginal propensity to save equals 0.1/0.5, or 1/5. Because disposable income is either spent or saved, the marginal propensity to consume plus the marginal propensity to save must sum to 1. In our example, 4/5 + 1/5 = 1. We can say more generally that $MPC + MPS = 1$.

9-1d The MPC Is the Slope of the Consumption Function

You may recall from the appendix to Chapter 1 that the slope of a straight line is the vertical distance between any two points divided by the horizontal distance between those same two points. Consider, for example, the slope between points *a* and *b* on the consumption function in Exhibit 3, where the delta symbol (Δ) means "change in." The horizontal distance between these points shows the change in disposable income, denoted as Δ*DI*—in this case, $0.5 trillion. The vertical distance shows the change in consumption, denoted as Δ*C*—in this case, $0.4 trillion. The slope equals the vertical distance divided by the horizontal distance, or 0.4/0.5, which equals the marginal propensity to consume of 4/5.

Thus, the marginal propensity to consume is measured graphically by the slope of the consumption function. After all, the slope is nothing more than the increase in consumption divided by the increase in income. Because the slope of any straight line is constant everywhere along the line, the MPC for any linear, or straight-line, consumption function is constant at all incomes. We assume here for convenience that the consumption function is a straight line, though it need not be.

| EXHIBIT 3 | The Marginal Propensity to Consume and the Consumption Function |

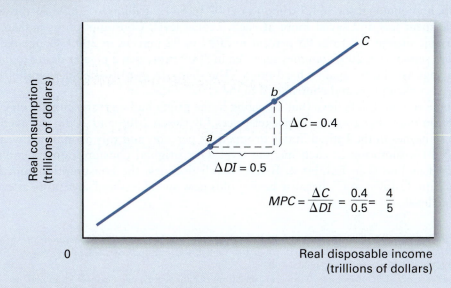

The slope of the consumption function equals the marginal propensity to consume. For the straight-line consumption function, the slope is the same at all levels of income and is given by the change in consumption divided by the change in disposable income that causes it. Thus, the marginal propensity to consume equals Δ*C*/Δ*DI*, or 0.4/0.5 = 4/5.

CHECKPOINT

What is a consumption function and what is its slope?

9-2 Nonincome Determinants of Consumption

Along a given consumption function, consumer spending depends on disposable income in the economy, other things constant. Now let's see what factors are held constant and how changes in them could shift the entire consumption function up or down.

9-2a Net Wealth

net wealth
The value of assets minus liabilities

Given the economy's income, an important influence on consumption is each household's **net wealth**—that is, the value of all assets that each household owns minus any liabilities, or debts. Net wealth is a *stock* variable. Consumption and income are *flow* variables. Your family's assets may include a home, furnishings, automobiles, bank accounts, corporate stocks and bonds, cash, and the value of any pensions. Your family's liabilities, or debts, may include a mortgage, car loans, student loans, credit card balances, and the like.

Net wealth is assumed to be constant along a given consumption function. A decrease in net wealth would make consumers less inclined to spend and more inclined to save at each income level. To see why, suppose prices fall sharply on the stock market. Stockholders are poorer than they were, so they spend less. For example, the stock market crash of 2008 combined with the slide in home prices to cut the net wealth of U.S. households from $64.5 trillion in 2007 to $54.5 trillion in 2009.[1] As a result, people spent less and saved more at each income level. Consumption as a share of disposable income fell from 95 percent in 2007 to 92 percent in 2009. Compared to families surveyed in 2007, families surveyed in 2009 expressed a greater desire to build up savings as a buffer against hard times.[2] The sharp drop in stockholder wealth thus reduced consumption and contributed to the Great Recession.[3]

Some economists believe that changing home prices had a greater impact on consumption than changing stock market prices.[4] Between 2006 and 2008, the average price of homes in the United States dropped 22 percent, and this drop in net wealth reduced consumption at each income level. Our original consumption function is depicted as line C in Exhibit 4. If net wealth declines, the consumption function shifts from C down to C', because households now spend less and save more at every income level.

1. Figures are from Board of Governors of the Federal Reserve System, *Flow of Funds Accounts of the United States: 2005 to 2009* (March 11, 2010), Table B.100, at http://www.federalreserve.gov/RELEASES/z1/Current/annuals/a2005–2009.
2. Jesse Bricker et al. "Drowning or Weathering the Storm? Changes in Family Finances From 2007 to 2009," Chapter 10 in *Measuring Wealth and Financial Intermediation and Their Links to the Real World*, Charles R. Hulten and Marshall B. Reinsdorf, eds. (University of Chicago Press, 2015).
3. Roger E. A. Farmer, "The Stock Market Crash of 2008 Caused the Great Recession: Theory and Evidence," *Journal of Economic Dynamics and Control*, 36 (May 2012): 693–707.
4. Karl E. Case, John M. Quigley, and Robert J. Shiller, "Wealth Effects Revisited 1975–2012," *Critical Finance Review*, 2 (July 2013): 101–128.

EXHIBIT 4   **Shifts of the Consumption Function**

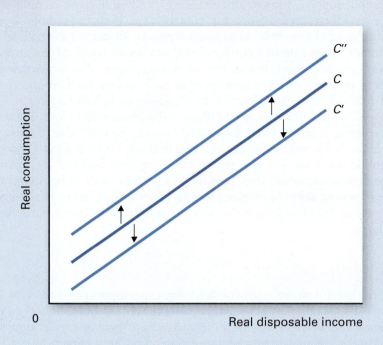

A downward shift of the consumption function, such as from *C* to *C'*, can be caused by a decrease in net wealth, an increase in the price level, an unfavorable change in consumer expectations, or an increase in the interest rate. An upward shift, such as from *C* to *C"*, can be caused by an increase in net wealth, a decrease in the price level, a favorable change in expectations, or a decrease in the interest rate.

Conversely, suppose stock prices increase sharply. This increase in net wealth increases the desire to spend. For example, stock prices surged in 1999, increasing stockholders' net wealth. Consumers spent 93 percent of disposable income that year compared with an average of about 90 percent during the first half of the decade. Purchases of homes and cars soared. Because of an increase in net wealth, the consumption function in Exhibit 4 shifts from C up to C", reflecting households' desire to spend more at each income level. Research by the Federal Reserve indicates that consumer spending eventually rises or falls between three to five cents for every dollar rise or fall in the value of stock market holdings.

Again, it is a change in net wealth, not a change in disposable income, that shifts the consumption function. A change in disposable income, other things constant, means a movement along a given consumption function, not a shift of that function. Be mindful of the difference between a movement along the consumption function, which results from a change in income, and a shift of the consumption function, which results from a change in one of the nonincome determinants of consumption, such as net wealth.

9-2b The Price Level

Another variable that affects the consumption function is the price level prevailing in the economy. As we have seen, net wealth is an important determinant of consumption. The greater the net wealth, other things constant, the greater the consumption at each income level. Some household wealth is held as money, such as cash and bank accounts. When the price level changes, so does the real value of cash and bank accounts.

For example, suppose your wealth consists of a $20,000 bank account. If the economy's price level increases by 5 percent, your bank account buys about 5 percent less in real terms. You feel poorer because you are poorer. To rebuild the real value of your money holdings to some desired comfort level, you decide to spend less and save more. *An increase in the price level reduces the purchasing power of money holdings, causing households to consume less and save more at each income level.* So the consumption function would shift downward from C to C′, as shown in Exhibit 4.

Conversely, should the price level fall, as it did frequently before World War II, in 2009, and recently in Japan, Hong Kong, and Taiwan, the real value of money holdings increases. Households would be wealthier, so they decide to consume more and save less at each income level. For example, if the price level declined by 5 percent, your $20,000 bank account would then buy about 5 percent more in real terms. A drop in the price level would shift the consumption function from C up to C″. *At each income level, a change in the price level influences consumption by affecting the real value of money holdings.*

9-2c The Interest Rate

Interest is the reward savers earn for deferring consumption and the cost borrowers pay for current spending power. When graphing the consumption function, we assume a given interest rate in the economy. If the interest rate increases, other things constant, savers or lenders are rewarded more, and borrowers are charged more. The higher the interest rate, the less is spent on those items typically purchased on credit, such as cars and major appliances. Thus, at a higher interest rate, households save more, borrow less, and spend less. Greater saving at each income level means less consumption. Simply put, *a higher interest rate, other things constant, shifts the consumption function downward.* Conversely, *a lower interest rate, other things constant, shifts the consumption function upward.*

9-2d Consumer Expectations

Expectations influence economic behavior in a variety of ways. For example, suppose as a college senior you land a good job that starts after graduation. Your consumption probably jumps long before the job actually begins because you expect an increase in your income. You might buy a car, for example. On the other hand, a worker who gets a layoff notice to take effect at the end of the year likely reduces consumption immediately, well before the actual layoff. More generally, if people grow more concerned about their job security, they reduce consumption at each income level.

A change in expectations about price levels or interest rates also affects consumption. For example, any change that leads householders to expect higher car prices or higher borrowing costs in the future prompts some to buy a new car now. On the other hand, any change leading householders to expect lower car prices or lower borrowing costs in the future causes some to defer a car purchase. Thus, expectations affect spending, and a change in expectations can shift the consumption function. This is why economic forecasters monitor consumer confidence so closely.

Sometimes people find they need to save more for the future. For example, each Chinese household now is more personally responsible for housing, education, and health care—items that in the past were more of a government responsibility. What's more, China's "one-child policy" meant that parents would have to rely less on their offspring for support in old age.[5] This increased the need to save. As a consequence, the average saving rate as a percentage of income among urban households in China jumped from 7 percent in 1995 to 25 percent in 2005.[6]

To Review: Keep in mind the distinction between *a movement along a given consumption function*, which results from a change in income, and a *shift of the consumption function,* which results from a change in one of the factors assumed to remain constant along the consumption function.

9-2e The Life-Cycle Model of Consumption and Saving

Do people with high income save a larger fraction of their income than those with low income? Both theory and evidence suggest they do. The easier it is to make ends meet, the more income is left over to save. Does it follow from this that richer economies save more than poorer ones—that economies save a larger fraction of total disposable income as they grow? In his famous book, *The General Theory of Employment, Interest, and Money*, published in 1936, John Maynard Keynes drew that conclusion. But as later economists studied the data—such as that presented earlier in Exhibit 1—it became clear that Keynes was wrong. The *fraction of disposable income saved in an economy seems to stay constant as the economy grows.*

So how can it be that richer people save more than poorer people, yet richer countries do not necessarily save more than poorer ones? Several answers have been proposed. One of the most important is the **life-cycle model of consumption and saving**. According to this model, young people tend to borrow to finance education and home purchases. In middle age, people pay off debts and save more. In old age, they draw down their savings, or *dissave*. Some people still have substantial wealth at death, because they are not sure when death will occur and because some parents want to bequeath wealth to their children. And some people die in debt. But on average net savings over a person's lifetime tend to be small. The life-cycle hypothesis suggests that the saving rate for an economy as a whole depends on, among other things, the relative number of savers and dissavers in the population.

A problem with the life-cycle hypothesis is that the elderly do not seem to draw down their assets as much as the theory predicts. One reason, already mentioned, is that some want to leave bequests to children. Another reason is that the elderly seem particularly concerned about covering unpredictable expenses such as divorce, health problems, and living much longer than average. Because of such uncertainty, many elderly spend less and save more than the life-cycle theory predicts. Researchers have found that those elderly who have not experienced a divorce or health problems continue to build their net wealth well into old age.[7]

Other evidence that seems at odds with the life-cycle hypothesis comes from a study of National Football League players. The theory predicts that players should save during their peak earning years in the NFL to help them get by when they can no longer play. But a high bankruptcy rate among former players suggests they saved little during their years of high pay.[8] Still, the life-cycle hypothesis offers an interesting theory about consumption patterns over a lifetime.

life-cycle model of consumption and saving
Young people borrow, middle agers pay off debt and save, and older people draw down their savings; on average, net savings over a lifetime is usually little or nothing

[5.] Dennis Tao Yang, Junsen Zhang, and Shaojie Zhou, "Why Are Saving Rates So High in China?" in *Capitalizing China*, Joseph P. H. Fan and Randall Morck, eds.(University of Chicago Press, 2012): 249-278; and Chadwick C. Curtis, Steven Lugauer, and Nelson C. Mark, "Demographic Patterns and Household Saving in China," *American Economic Journal: Macroeconomics*, 7 (April 2015): 58–94.

[6.] Marcos D. Chamon and Eswar S. Prasad, "Why Are Saving Rates of Urban Households in China Rising?" *American Economic Journal: Macroeconomics*, 2 (January 2010): 93–130.

[7.] James Poterba, Steven Venti, and David Wise, "The Composition and Drawdown of Wealth in Retirement," *Journal of Economic Perspectives*, 25 (Fall 2011): 95–118.

[8.] Kyle Carlson et al. "Bankruptcy Rates Among NFL Players with Short-Lived Income Spikes," *American Economic Review*, 105 (May 2015): 381–384.

We turn next to the other component of aggregate expenditure, with a special emphasis on investment. Keep in mind that our immediate goal is to understand the relationship between aggregate expenditure and income.

CHECKPOINT

What changes can shift the consumption function up or down?

9-3 Other Spending Components

While consumption is the most important spending component and the one that gets the most attention here, aggregate spending also includes investment, government purchases, and net exports. Here we look briefly at how each relates to income.

9-3a Investment

The second component of aggregate expenditure is investment, or, more precisely, *gross private domestic investment*. Again, by *investment* we do not mean buying stocks, bonds, or other financial assets. Investment consists of spending on (1) new factories, office buildings, malls, and new equipment, such as computers and software; (2) new housing; and (3) net increases to inventories. People invest now expecting a future return. Because the return is in the future, a would-be investor must estimate how much a particular investment will yield this year, next year, the year after, and in all years during the productive life of the investment. *Firms buy new capital goods only if they expect this investment to yield a higher return than other possible uses of their funds.*

Investment Demand Curve

The market interest rate is the opportunity cost of investing in capital. More is invested when the opportunity cost of borrowing is lower, other things constant. A downward-sloping investment demand curve for the entire economy can be derived, with some qualifications, from a horizontal summation of each firm's downward-sloping investment demand curve. The economy's *investment demand curve* is depicted as D_I in Exhibit 5, which shows the inverse relationship between the quantity of investment demanded and the market interest rate, other things—including business expectations—held constant. For example, in Exhibit 5, when the market rate of interest is 8 percent, the quantity of investment demanded is $1.0 trillion. If the interest rate rises to 10 percent, investment declines to $0.9 trillion, and if the rate falls to 6 percent, investment increases to $1.1 trillion.

Assumed constant along the investment demand curve are business expectations about the economy. If firms grow more optimistic about profit prospects, the demand for investment increases, so the investment demand curve shifts to the right. Investment demand depends primarily on what Keynes called the "animal spirits" of business. Examples of factors that could affect business expectations, and thus investment demand, include wars, technological changes, tax changes, and destabilizing events such as terrorist attacks or financial crises.

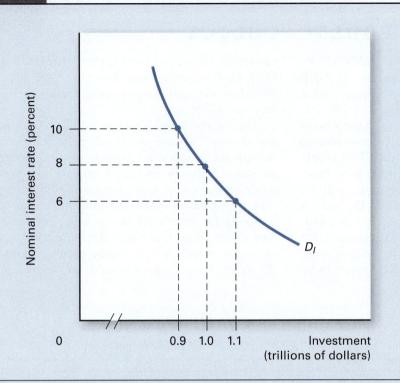

EXHIBIT 5 Investment Demand Curve for the Economy

The investment demand curve for the economy sums the investment demanded by each firm at each interest rate. At lower interest rates, other things constant, more investment projects become profitable for individual firms, so total investment in the economy increases.

Investment and Income

To integrate the discussion of investment with our earlier analysis of consumption, we need to know if and how investment varies with income in the economy. Whereas we were able to present evidence relating consumption to income over time, the link between investment and income is weaker. Investment in a particular year shows little relation to income that year. *Investment depends more on interest rates and on business expectations than on the current income level.* One reason investment is less related to income is that some investments, such as a new power plant or an oil pipeline, take years to build. And investment, once in place, is expected to last for years, sometimes decades. The investment decision is thus said to be *forward looking*, based more on expected profit than on current income in the economy.

So how does the amount firms plan to invest relate to income? The simplest assumption is that *investment* is unrelated to income. For example, suppose that, given current business expectations and a market interest rate of 8 percent, firms plan to invest $1.0 trillion per year, regardless of the economy's income level.

Now that we have examined consumption and investment, let's take a look at their year-to-year variability in the following case study.

CASE STUDY

PUBLIC POLICY

INVESTMENT VARIES MORE THAN CONSUMPTION   Consumption averaged 68 percent of GDP during the most recent decade, and investment varied from year to year, averaging 16 percent of GDP during the most recent decade. Exhibit 6 shows the annual percentage changes since 1959 in GDP, consumption, and investment, all measured in real terms. Two points are obvious. First, investment fluctuates much more than either consumption or GDP. For example, in 2009, GDP declined 2.8 percent and consumption slipped 1.6 percent, but investment plunged 21.6 percent. In 2010, GDP rose 2.5 percent and consumption increased 1.9 percent, but investment climbed 12.9 percent. Second, fluctuations in consumption and in GDP appear to be entwined, although consumption varies a bit less than GDP. Consumption varies less than GDP because consumption depends on disposable income, which varies less than GDP.

During the seven years of falling GDP since 1959, the decline in GDP averaged only 0.9 percent, but investment dropped an average of 12.5 percent. Consumption actually increased slightly on average. So *while consumption is the largest spending component, investment varies much more than consumption and accounts for nearly all the year-to-year variability in real GDP.* Note that GDP does not always fall during years in which a recession occurs. That's because the economy is not necessarily in recession for the

| EXHIBIT 6 | Annual Percentage Changes in U.S. Real GDP, Consumption, and Investment |

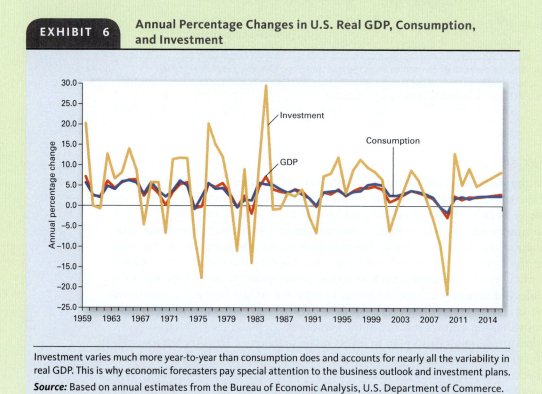

Investment varies much more year-to-year than consumption does and accounts for nearly all the variability in real GDP. This is why economic forecasters pay special attention to the business outlook and investment plans.

Source: Based on annual estimates from the Bureau of Economic Analysis, U.S. Department of Commerce. For the latest data, go to http://bea.gov/.

continued

entire year. For example, because the recession of 2001 lasted only eight months, GDP managed a small gain for the year of 1.0 percent and consumption grew 2.6 percent. It was the 6.1 percent drop in investment that caused the recession. That's why economic forecasters pay special attention to business expectations and investment plans.

Sources: *Economic Report of the President*, February 2015; *Survey of Current Business 95*, various months for 2015; and *OECD Economic Outlook 97* (May 2015). For data and articles about economic aggregates, go to the Bureau of Economic Analysis site at http://bea.gov/.

9-3b Government Purchases

The third component of aggregate expenditure is government purchases of goods and services. Federal, state, and local governments buy thousands of goods and services, ranging from weapon systems to traffic lights to education. During the most recent decade, government purchases in the United States accounted for 20 percent of GDP, most of that by state and local governments. Decisions about government purchases are largely under the control of public officials, such as the decision to build an interstate highway, boost military spending, or hire more teachers. These spending decisions do not depend directly on income in the economy. We therefore assume that *government purchases* are independent of income.

As noted earlier, government purchases represent only one of the two government outlays; the other is *transfer payments,* such as for Social Security, welfare benefits, and unemployment insurance. Government outlays equal government purchases plus transfer payments. Transfer payments, which make up more than a third of government outlays, are outright grants from governments to households and are thus not considered part of aggregate expenditure. Transfer payments vary inversely with income—as income increases, transfer payments decline.

To fund government outlays, governments impose taxes. Taxes vary directly with income; as income increases, so do taxes. *Net taxes* equal taxes minus transfers. Because taxes tend to increase with income but transfers tend to decrease with income, for simplicity, let's assume that net taxes do not vary with income. Thus, we assume that *net taxes* are independent of income.

Net taxes affect aggregate spending indirectly by changing disposable income, which in turn changes consumption. We saw from the discussion of the circular flow that by subtracting net taxes, we transform real GDP into *disposable income.* Disposable income is take-home pay—the income households can spend or save. We examine the impact of net taxes in the next few chapters.

9-3c Net Exports

The rest of the world affects aggregate expenditure through imports and exports and has a growing influence on the U.S. economy. The United States, with less than one-twentieth of the world's population, accounts for about one-eighth of the world's imports and one-ninth of the world's exports. How do imports and exports relate to the economy's income? When incomes rise, Americans spend more on all normal goods, including imports. Higher incomes lead to more spending on Persian rugs, French wine, German cars, Chinese toys, European vacations, African safaris, and thousands of other foreign goods and services.

How do U.S. exports relate to the economy's income? U.S. exports depend on the income of foreigners, not on U.S. income. U.S. disposable income does not affect Europe's purchases of U.S. smartphones or Africa's purchases of U.S. grain. Because our exports are insensitive to U.S. income but our imports tend to increase with income, *net exports,* which equal the value of exports minus the value of imports, tend to decline as U.S. incomes increase. For simplicity, we will assume that net exports are independent of income.

If exports exceed imports, net exports are positive; if imports exceed exports, net exports are negative; and if exports equal imports, net exports are zero. U.S. net exports have been negative nearly every year during the past three decades.

CHECKPOINT

Why does investment vary more than consumption from year to year?

9-4 Aggregate Expenditure and Income

The big idea so far in this chapter is that consumption depends on income, other things constant; this link is one of the most stable in all of macroeconomics. Let's build on that connection to learn how total spending in the economy changes with income. If we try to confront the economy head-on, it soon becomes a bewildering maze, which is why we make progress by starting with simple models. We continue to assume, as we did in developing the circular-flow model, that there is no capital depreciation and no business saving. Thus, we can say that *each dollar of spending translates directly into a dollar of income.* Therefore, gross domestic product, or GDP, equals aggregate income.

9-4a Components of Aggregate Expenditure

When income increases, consumption increases. As noted already, the marginal propensity to consume indicates the fraction of each additional dollar of income that is spent on consumption. For example, if the marginal propensity to consume is 4/5 (four-fifths), spending increases by $4 for every $5 increase in income. The consumption function shows how much consumption increases with income.

For simplicity, we continue to assume that investment, government purchases, and net exports are independent of the economy's income level.

Peter Adams/The Image Bank/Getty Images

If we add to the consumption function, investment, government purchases, and net exports, we get the aggregate expenditure line presented in Exhibit 7 as $C + I + G + (X − M)$. Real GDP is measured on the horizontal axis, and aggregate expenditure is measured on the vertical axis. The **aggregate expenditure line** shows how much households, firms, governments, and the rest of the world plan to spend on U.S. output at each level of real GDP, or real income, assuming a given price level in the economy. Again, the only spending component that varies with real GDP is consumption. Because only consumption varies with income, the slope of the aggregate expenditure line equals the marginal propensity to consume. Please give that a little thought.

aggregate expenditure line
A relationship tracing, for a given price level, spending at each level of income, or real GDP; the total of $C + I + G + (X − M)$ at each level of income, or real GDP

9-4b Real GDP Demanded

Let's begin developing the aggregate demand curve by asking how much aggregate output would be demanded at a given price level. By finding the quantity demanded at a given price level, we'll end up identifying a single point on the aggregate demand curve. We begin by considering the relationship between aggregate spending in the economy and aggregate income. To get us started, suppose that the price level in the economy is 110, or 10 percent higher than in the base-year price level. We want to find out how much is spent at various levels of real income, or real GDP. By *real* GDP, we mean GDP measured in terms of real goods and services produced. Exhibit 7 combines the relationships introduced earlier—consumption, investment, government purchases, and net exports. Although the entries are hypothetical, they bear some relation to current levels in the U.S. economy.

EXHIBIT 7 **Deriving the Real GDP Demanded for a Given Price Level**

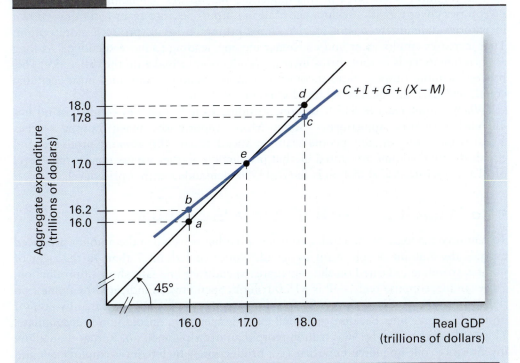

Real GDP demanded for a given price level is found where aggregate expenditure equals aggregate output—that is, where spending equals the amount produced, or real GDP. This occurs at point *e*, where the aggregate expenditure line intersects the 45-degree line.

Real GDP, measured along the horizontal axis in Exhibit 7, can be viewed in two ways—as the value of *aggregate output* and as the *aggregate income* generated by that output. Because real GDP or aggregate income is measured on the horizontal axis, and aggregate expenditure is measured on the vertical axis, this graph is often called the **income-expenditure model**. To gain perspective on the relationship between income and expenditure, we use a handy analytical tool: the 45-degree ray from the origin. The special feature of this line is that any point along it is the same distance from each axis. Thus, the 45-degree line identifies all points where spending equals real GDP. *Aggregate output demanded at a given price level occurs where aggregate expenditure, measured along the vertical axis, equals real GDP, measured along the horizontal axis.* In Exhibit 7, this occurs at point *e,* where the aggregate expenditure line intersects the 45-degree line. At point *e,* the amount people spend equals the amount produced. We conclude that, at a price level of 110, the quantity of real GDP demanded equals $17.0 trillion.

> **income-expenditure model**
> A relationship that shows how much people plan to spend at each income level; this model identifies, for a given price level, where the amount people plan to spend equals the amount produced in the economy

9-4c What if Spending Exceeds Real GDP?

To find the real GDP demanded at the given price level, consider what happens if real GDP is initially less than $17.0 trillion. As you can see from Exhibit 7, when real GDP is less than $17.0 trillion, the aggregate expenditure line is above the 45-degree line, indicating that spending exceeds the amount produced (again, give this a little thought). For example, if real GDP is $16.0 trillion, spending is $16.2 trillion, as indicated by point *b* on the aggregate expenditure line, so spending exceeds output by $0.2 trillion. When the amount people want to spend exceeds the amount produced, something has to give. Ordinarily what gives is the price, but remember that we are seeking the real GDP demanded for a given price level, so the price level is assumed to remain constant, at least for now. What gives in this model are *inventories.* Unplanned reductions in inventories cover the $0.2 trillion shortfall in output. Because firms can't draw down inventories indefinitely, *inventory reductions* prompt firms to produce more output. That increases employment and consumer income, leading to more spending. As long as spending exceeds output, firms increase production to make up the difference. This process of more output, more income, and more spending continues until spending equals real GDP, an equality achieved at point *e* in Exhibit 7.

When output reaches $17.0 trillion, spending exactly matches output, so no unintended inventory adjustments occur. More importantly, when output reaches $17.0 trillion, the amount people want to spend equals the amount produced and equals the total income generated by that production. Earlier we assumed a price level of 110. Therefore, $17.0 trillion is the real GDP demanded at that price level.

9-4d What if Real GDP Exceeds Spending?

To reinforce the logic of the model, consider what happens when the amount produced exceeds the amount people want to spend. Notice in Exhibit 7 that, to the right of point *e,* spending indicated on the aggregate expenditure line falls short of production. For example, suppose real GDP is $18.0 trillion. Spending, as indicated by point *c* on the aggregate expenditure line, is $0.2 trillion less than real GDP, indicated by point *d* on the 45-degree line. Because real GDP exceeds spending, unsold goods accumulate. This swells inventories by $0.2 trillion more than firms planned on. Rather than allow inventories to pile up indefinitely, firms cut production, which reduces employment and income. As an example of such behavior, a recent news account read, "General Motors will idle two assembly plants in a move to trim inventories in the wake of slowing sales." *Unplanned inventory buildups* cause firms to cut production until the amount they produce equals aggregate spending, which occurs, again, where real GDP is $17.0 trillion. Given the price level, real GDP demanded is found where the amount people spend equals the amount produced. *For a given price level, there is only one point along the aggregate expenditure line at which spending equals real GDP.*

We have now discussed the forces that determine real GDP demanded for a given price level. In the next section, we examine changes that can alter spending plans.

CHECKPOINT

How does the aggregate expenditure line determine the quantity of aggregate output demanded?

9-5 The Simple Spending Multiplier

We just used the aggregate expenditure line to find real GDP demanded for a particular price level. In this section, we continue to assume that the price level stays the same as we trace the effects of other changes that could affect spending plans. Like a stone thrown into a still pond, the effects of any change in spending ripple through the economy, generating changes in aggregate output that could exceed the initial change in spending.

9-5a An Increase in Spending

Let's consider the effect of an increase in one of the components of spending. Suppose that firms become more optimistic about profit prospects and decide to increase their investment from $1.0 trillion to $1.1 trillion per year, other things constant.

What happens to real GDP demanded? An instinctive response is to say that real GDP demanded increases by $0.1 trillion as well. The idea of the circular flow is central to an understanding of the adjustment process. Recall that production yields income, which generates spending. We can think of each trip around the circular flow as a "round" of income and spending.

Round One

OK, so planned spending now exceeds the amount produced by $0.1 trillion, or $100 billion. Initially, firms supply this increased investment spending by drawing down their inventories. John Deere, for example, satisfies the increased demand for tractors by drawing down tractor inventories. But reduced inventories prompt firms to expand production by $100 billion. This generates $100 billion more income. The income-generating process does not stop there, however, because those who earn this additional income spend some of it and save the rest, leading to round two of spending and income.

Round Two

Given a marginal propensity to consume of 0.8, those who earn the additional $100 billion spend $80 billion on toasters, backpacks, gasoline, restaurant meals, and thousands of other goods and services. They save the other $20 billion. Firms respond by increasing their output by $80 billion. Thus, the $100 billion in new income increases real GDP by $80 billion during round two.

Round Three and Beyond

We assume that four-fifths of the $80 billion earned during round two gets spent during round three and one-fifth gets saved. Thus, $64 billion is spent during round three on still more goods and services. The remaining $16 billion gets saved. The added spending causes firms to increase output by $64 billion. Round three's additional production generated $64 billion more income, which sets up subsequent rounds of spending, output, and income. *As long as spending exceeds output, production increases, thereby creating more income, which generates still more spending.*

Exhibit 8 summarizes the multiplier process, showing the first three rounds, round 10, and the cumulative effect of all rounds. The new spending from each round is shown in the second column, and the accumulation of new spending appears in the third column. For example, the cumulative new spending as of the third round totals $244 billion—the sum of the first three rounds of spending ($100 billion + $80 billion + $64 billion). The new saving from each round appears in the fourth column, and the accumulation of new saving appears in the final column. All this develops with the price level assumed to remain unchanged.

9-5b Using the Simple Spending Multiplier

In our model, consumers spend four-fifths of the change in income each round, with each fresh round equal to the change in spending from the previous round times the marginal propensity to consume, or the MPC. This goes on round after round, leaving less and less to fuel more spending and income. At some point, the new rounds of income and spending become so small that they disappear and the process stops. The question is, by how much does total spending increase? We can get some idea of the total by working through a limited number of rounds. For example, as shown in Exhibit 8, total new spending after 10 rounds sums to $446.3 billion. But calculating the exact total for all rounds would require us to work through an infinite number of rounds—an impossible task.

Fortunately, we can borrow a shortcut from mathematicians, who have shown that the sum of an infinite number of rounds, each of which is MPC times the previous round, equals $1/(1 - MPC)$ times the initial change. Translated, the cumulative spending change equals $1/(1 - MPC)$, which, in our example, was 1/0.2, or 5, times the initial increase in spending, which was $100 billion. In short, the increase in investment eventually boosts real GDP demanded by 5 times $100 billion, or $500 billion—and again, all this happens with the price level assumed to remain unchanged.

EXHIBIT 8	Tracking the Rounds of Spending Following a $100 Billion Increase in Investment (billions of dollars)

Round	New Spending This Round	Cumulative New Spending	New Saving This Round	Cumulative New Saving
1	100	100	—	—
2	80	180	20	20
3	64	244	16	36
⋮	⋮	⋮	⋮	⋮
10	13.4	446.3	3.35	86.6
⋮	⋮	⋮	⋮	⋮
∞	0	500	0	100

The simple spending multiplier is the factor by which real GDP demanded changes for a given initial change in spending.

$$\text{Simple spending multiplier} = \frac{1}{1 - MPC}$$

The simple spending multiplier provides a shortcut to the total change in real GDP demanded. This multiplier depends on the MPC. The larger the MPC, the larger the simple spending multiplier. That makes sense—the more people spend from each dollar of fresh income, the more total spending increases. For example, if the MPC was 0.9 instead of 0.8, the denominator of the multiplier formula would equal 1.0 minus 0.9, or 0.1, so the multiplier would be 1/0.1, or 10. With an MPC of 0.9, a $0.1 trillion investment increase would boost real GDP demanded by $1.0 trillion. On the other hand, an MPC of 0.5 would yield a denominator of 0.5 and a multiplier of 2. So a $0.1 trillion investment increase would raise real GDP demanded by $0.2 trillion.

Let's return to what started all this. The $0.1 trillion rise in investment raised real GDP demanded by $0.5 trillion. Note that real GDP demanded would have increased by the same amount if consumers had decided to spend $0.1 trillion more at each income level. Aggregate demand likewise would have increased if government purchases or net exports increased $0.1 trillion at each income level. *The change in aggregate output demanded depends on how much the aggregate expenditure line shifts, not on which spending component causes the shift.*

In our example, investment increased by $0.1 trillion in the year in question. *If this greater investment is not sustained the following year, real GDP demanded would fall back.* For example, if investment returns to its initial level, other things constant, real GDP demanded would return to $17.0 trillion. Finally, recall from the earlier discussion that the MPC and the MPS sum to 1, so 1 minus the MPC equals the MPS. With this information, we can define the simple spending multiplier in terms of the MPS as follows:

$$\text{Simple spending multiplier} = \frac{1}{1 - MPC} = \frac{1}{MPS}$$

We can see that the smaller the MPS, the less leaks from the spending stream as saving. Because less is saved, more gets spent each round, so the spending multiplier is greater. Incidentally, this spending multiplier is called "simple" because consumption is the only spending component that varies with income.

CHECKPOINT

What is the simple spending multiplier?

9-6 The Aggregate Demand Curve

In this chapter, we have identified the quantity demanded *for a given price level*. But what happens if the price level changes? As you will see, for each price level, there is a unique aggregate expenditure line, which yields a unique real GDP demanded. By altering the price level, we find a different real GDP demanded. By pairing a price level with the real GDP demanded at that price level, we can derive the aggregate demand curve.

9-6a A Higher Price Level

What is the effect of a higher price level on the quantity of real GDP demanded? Recall that consumers hold many assets that are fixed in dollar terms, such as currency and bank accounts. A higher price level decreases the real value of these money holdings. This cuts consumer wealth, making people less willing to spend at each income level. For reasons that will be explained in a later chapter, a higher price level also tends to increase the market interest rate, and a higher interest rate reduces investment. Finally, a higher U.S. price level, other things constant, means that foreign goods become relatively cheaper for U.S. consumers, and U.S. goods become more expensive abroad. So imports rise and exports fall, decreasing net exports. Therefore, *a higher price level reduces consumption, investment, and net exports, which all reduce aggregate spending.* This decrease in spending reduces real GDP demanded.

Exhibit 9 represents two different ways of expressing the effects of a change in the price level on real GDP demanded. Panel (a) offers the income-expenditure model, and panel (b) offers the aggregate demand curve, showing the inverse relationship between the price level and real GDP demanded. The idea is to find the real GDP demanded for a given price level in panel (a), and then show that price–quantity combination as a point on the aggregate demand curve in panel (b). The two panels measure real GDP on the horizontal axes. At the initial price level of 110 in panel (a), the aggregate expenditure line, now denoted simply as *AE*, intersects the 45-degree line at point *e* to yield real GDP demanded of $17.0 trillion. Panel (b) shows more directly the link between real GDP demanded and the price level. As you can see, when the price level is 110, the quantity of real GDP demanded is $17.0 trillion. This combination is identified by point *e* on the aggregate demand curve.

What if the price level increases from 110 to, say, 120? As you've just learned, an increase in the price level reduces consumption, investment, and net exports. This reduction in spending is reflected in panel (a) by a downward shift of the aggregate expenditure line from *AE* to *AE'*. As a result, real GDP demanded declines from $17.0 trillion to $16.5 trillion. Panel (b) shows that an increase in the price level from 110 to 120 decreases real GDP demanded from $17.0 trillion to $16.5 trillion, as reflected by the movement from point *e* to point *e'*.

9-6b A Lower Price Level

The opposite occurs if the price level falls. At a lower price level, the value of bank accounts, currency, and other money holdings increases. Consumers on average are wealthier and thus spend more at each income level. A lower price level also tends to decrease the market interest rate, which increases investment. Finally, a lower U.S. price level, other things constant, makes U.S. products cheaper abroad and foreign products relatively more expensive here, so exports increase and imports decrease. *Because of a decline in the price level, consumption, investment, and net exports increase at each income level.*

Refer again to Exhibit 9 and suppose the price level declines from 110 to, say, 100. This increases spending at each income level, as reflected by an upward shift of the spending line from *AE* to *AE''* in panel (a). An increase in spending increases real GDP demanded from $17.0 trillion to $17.5 trillion, as indicated by the intersection of the top aggregate expenditure line with the 45-degree line at point *e''*. This same price decrease can be viewed more directly in panel (b). As you can see, when the price level decreases to 100, real GDP demanded increases to $17.5 trillion.

The aggregate expenditure line and the aggregate demand curve present real output from different perspectives. The aggregate expenditure line shows, for a given price level, how spending relates to income, or the amount produced in the economy. Real GDP demanded is found where spending equals income, or the amount produced. The aggregate demand curve shows, for various price levels, the quantities of real GDP demanded.

EXHIBIT 9 Changing the Price Level to Find the Aggregate Demand Curve

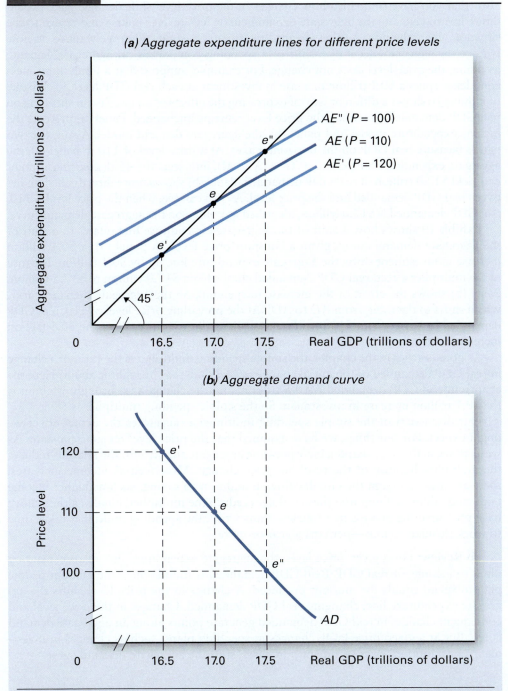

(a) Aggregate expenditure lines for different price levels

- AE'' ($P = 100$)
- AE ($P = 110$)
- AE' ($P = 120$)

Aggregate expenditure (trillions of dollars)

45°

Real GDP (trillions of dollars)

0   16.5   17.0   17.5

(b) Aggregate demand curve

Price level

120 — e'
110 — e
100 — e''

AD

0   16.5   17.0   17.5   Real GDP (trillions of dollars)

At the initial price level of 110, the aggregate expenditure line is AE, which identifies real GDP demanded of $17.0 trillion. This combination of a price level of 110 and a real GDP demanded of $17.0 trillion determines one combination (point e) on the aggregate demand curve in panel (b). At the higher price level of 120, the aggregate expenditure line shifts down to AE', and real GDP demanded falls to $16.5 trillion. This price–quantity combination is identified as point e' in panel (b). At the lower price level of 100, the aggregate expenditure line shifts up to AE'', which increases real GDP demanded. This combination is plotted as point e'' in panel (b). Connecting points e, e', and e'' in panel (b) yields the downward-sloping aggregate demand curve AD, which shows the inverse relation between the price level and real GDP demanded.

9-6c The Multiplier and Shifts in Aggregate Demand

Now that you have some idea how changes in the price level shift the aggregate expenditure line to generate the aggregate demand curve, let's reverse course and return to the situation where the price level is assumed to remain constant. What we want to do now is trace through the effects of a shift of a spending component on aggregate demand, assuming the price level does not change. For example, suppose that a jump in business confidence spurs a $0.1 trillion increase in investment at each real GDP level. Each panel of Exhibit 10 shows a different way of expressing the effects of an increase in spending on real GDP demanded, assuming the price level remains unchanged. Panel (a) presents the income-expenditure model and panel (b), the aggregate demand model. Again, the two panels measure real GDP on the horizontal axes. At a price level of 110 in panel (a), the aggregate expenditure line, $C + I + G + (X - M)$, intersects the 45-degree line at point e to yield $17.0 trillion in real GDP demanded. Panel (b) shows more directly the link between real GDP demanded and the price level. As you can see, when the price level is 110, real GDP demanded is $17.0 trillion, identified as point e on the aggregate demand curve.

Exhibit 10 shows how a shift of the aggregate expenditure line relates to a shift of the aggregate demand curve, given a constant price level. In panel (a), a $0.1 trillion increase in investment shifts the aggregate expenditure line up by $0.1 trillion. Because of the multiplier effect, real GDP demanded climbs from $17.0 trillion to $17.5 trillion. Panel (b) shows the effect of the increase in spending on the aggregate demand curve, which shifts to the right, from AD to AD'. At the prevailing price level of 110, real GDP demanded increases from $17.0 trillion to $17.5 trillion as a result of the $0.1 trillion increase in investment.

As noted earlier in the chapter, the simple spending multiplier is the ratio of a change in real GDP demanded to the initial change in spending that brought it about. Here the change in real GDP demanded is $0.5 trillion, and the change that brought it about is the $0.1 trillion increase in investment. So the simple spending multiplier is 5.

Our discussion of the simple spending multiplier exaggerates the actual effect we might expect. For one thing, we have assumed that the price level remains constant. As we shall see in the next chapter, incorporating aggregate supply into the analysis reduces the multiplier because of the resulting price change. Moreover, as income increases, there are leakages from the circular flow in addition to saving, such as higher income taxes and additional imports; these leakages reduce the multiplier. Finally, although we have presented the process in a timeless framework, the spending multiplier takes time to work through rounds—perhaps a year or more.

To Review: For a given price level, the aggregate expenditure line relates spending plans to income, or real GDP. Real GDP demanded is found where the amount people plan to spend equals the amount produced. A change in the price level shifts the aggregate expenditure line, changing real GDP demanded. Changes in the price level and consequent changes in real GDP demanded generate points along an aggregate demand curve. But at a given price level, changes in spending plans, such as changes in investment, consumption, or government purchases, shift the aggregate demand curve.

 **CHECKPOINT**

What's the relationship between the aggregate expenditure line and the aggregate demand curve?

EXHIBIT 10	A Shift of the Aggregate Expenditure Line That Shifts the Aggregate Demand Curve

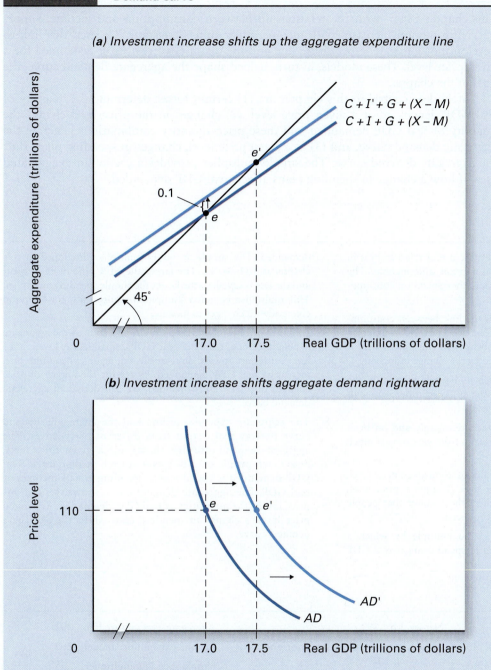

(a) *Investment increase shifts up the aggregate expenditure line*

Aggregate expenditure (trillions of dollars)

$C + I' + G + (X - M)$
$C + I + G + (X - M)$

0.1

e'

e

45°

0   17.0   17.5   Real GDP (trillions of dollars)

(b) *Investment increase shifts aggregate demand rightward*

Price level

110

e   e'

AD'

AD

0   17.0   17.5   Real GDP (trillions of dollars)

A shift of the aggregate expenditure line at a given price level shifts the aggregate demand curve. In panel (a), an increase in investment of $0.1 trillion, with the price level constant at 110, causes the aggregate expenditure line to increase from $C + I + G + (X - M)$ to $C + I' + G + (X - M)$. As a result, real GDP demanded increases from $17.0 trillion to $17.5 trillion. In panel (b), the aggregate demand curve has shifted from AD out to AD'. At the prevailing price level of 110, real GDP demanded has increased by $0.5 trillion.

9-7 Conclusion

This chapter began with the relationship between consumption and income. Simply put, consumption increases with income, other things constant. We used this link to develop the aggregate expenditure line and the quantity of real GDP demanded for a given price level. These models, in turn, helped shape the aggregate demand curve, the goal of the chapter.

Three ideas central to this chapter are (1) certain forces determine the quantity of real GDP demanded at a given price level, (2) changes in the price level change the quantity of real GDP demanded and these price–quantity combinations generate the aggregate demand curve, and (3) at a given price level, changes in spending plans shift the aggregate demand curve. The simple multiplier provides a crude but exaggerated idea of how a change in spending plans affects real GDP demanded.

Summary

1. One of the most predictable and most useful relationships in macroeconomics is between consumption and income. The more people have to spend, the more they spend on consumption, other things constant.

2. The consumption function shows the link between consumption and income in the economy. The slope of the consumption function reflects the marginal propensity to consume, which is the change in consumption divided by the change in income.

3. Changes in certain variables, such as household wealth, the price level, interest rates, and consumer expectations, can shift the consumption function up or down.

4. Investment depends on the market interest rate and on business expectations. Investment fluctuates from year to year much more than does consumption.

5. The aggregate expenditure line indicates, for a given price level, planned spending at each income level. At a given price level, real GDP demanded is found where the amount that people plan to spend equals the amount produced.

6. The spending multiplier indicates the multiple by which a change in the amount people plan to spend changes real GDP demanded. The simple spending multiplier developed in this chapter is $1/(1-MPC)$. The larger the MPC, the more is spent and the less is saved, so the larger the simple spending multiplier. This multiplier is called "simple" because only consumption changes with changes in income.

7. A higher price level causes a downward shift of the aggregate expenditure line, reducing real GDP demanded. A lower price level causes an upward shift of the aggregate expenditure line, increasing real GDP demanded. By tracing the impact of price changes on real GDP demanded, we can derive an aggregate demand curve.

8. The aggregate expenditure line and the aggregate demand curve portray real output from different perspectives. The aggregate expenditure line shows, for a given price level, how much people plan to spend at each income level. Real GDP demanded is found where spending equals income, or real GDP. The aggregate demand curve shows, for various price levels, the quantities of real GDP demanded. At a given price level, a change in spending plans shifts the aggregate demand curve.

Key Concepts

Consumption function 189	Net wealth 192	Aggregate expenditure line 201
Marginal propensity to consume (MPC) 190	Life-cycle model of consumption and saving 195	Income-expenditure model 202
Marginal propensity to save (MPS) 190		Simple spending multiplier 205

Questions for Review

1. **Consumption Function**   How would an increase in each of the following affect the consumption function?

   a. Net taxes
   b. The interest rate
   c. Consumer optimism, or confidence
   d. The price level
   e. Consumers' net wealth
   f. Disposable income

2. **Consumption Function**   What factors can cause the consumption function to shift?

3. **Life-Cycle Hypothesis** According to the life-cycle hypothesis, what is the typical pattern of saving and spending for an individual over his or her lifetime? What impact does this pattern have on the saving rate in the overall economy?

4. **Investment** Why would the following investments increase as the interest rate declines?

    a. Purchases of a new plant and equipment
    b. Construction of new housing
    c. Inventories

5. **Case Study: Investment Varies More Than Consumption** Why do economic forecasters pay special attention to investment plans? Take a look at the Conference Board's index of leading economic indicators at http://www.conference-board .org/. Which of those indicators might affect investment?

6. **Aggregate Expenditure** What are the components of aggregate expenditure? In the model developed in this chapter, which components vary with changes in the level of income? What determines the slope of the aggregate expenditure line?

7. **Real GDP Demanded** In your own words, explain the logic of the income-expenditure model. What determines the amount of real GDP demanded?

8. **Real GDP Demanded** What equalities hold at the level of real GDP demanded? When determining real GDP demanded, what do we assume about the price level? What do we assume about inventories?

9. **When Output and Spending Differ** What role do inventories play in determining real GDP demanded? In answering this question, suppose initially that firms are either producing more than people plan to spend, or producing less than people plan to spend.

10. **The Aggregate Demand Curve** What is the effect of a lower price level, other things constant, on the aggregate expenditure line and on real GDP demanded?

Problems and Exercises

11. **Consumption** Use the following data to answer the questions below:

Real Disposable Income (billions $)	Consumption Expenditures (billions $)	Saving (billions $)
100	150	_____
200	200	_____
300	250	_____
400	300	_____

    a. Graph the consumption function, with consumption spending on the vertical axis and disposable income on the horizontal axis.
    b. If the consumption function is a straight line, what is its slope?
    c. Fill in the saving column at each level of income.

12. **MPC and MPS** If consumption increases by $12 billion when disposable income increases by $15 billion, what is the value of the MPC? What is the relationship between the MPC and the MPS? If the MPC increases, what must happen to the MPS? How is the MPC related to the consumption function?

13. **Simple Spending Multiplier** For each of the following values for the MPC, determine the size of the simple spending multiplier and the total change in real GDP demanded following a $10 billion decrease in spending:

    a. $MPC = 0.9$
    b. $MPC = 0.75$
    c. $MPC = 0.6$

14. **Simple Spending Multiplier** Suppose that the MPC is 0.8 and that $17 trillion of real GDP is currently being demanded. The government wants to increase real GDP demanded to $18 trillion at the given price level. By how much would it have to increase government purchases to achieve this goal?

15. **Investment and the Multiplier** This chapter assumes that investment is independent of the income level in the economy. What would happen to the size of the multiplier if investment increases as real GDP increases? Explain.

10 Aggregate Supply

©06photo/Shutterstock.com

- *How do producers react when the economy's price level increases?*
- *If the economy is already operating at full employment, how can it produce more?*
- *What's your normal capacity for academic work, and when do you exceed that effort?*
- *What valuable piece of information do employers and workers lack when they negotiate wages?*
- *Why do employers and workers fail to agree on pay cuts that could save jobs?*

These and other questions are answered in this chapter, which develops the aggregate supply curve in the short run and in the long run.

Up to this point, we have focused on aggregate demand. We have not yet examined in any detail aggregate supply, a much-debated topic. The debate involves the shape of the aggregate supply curve and the reasons for that shape. This chapter develops a single, coherent approach to aggregate supply. Although the focus continues to be on economic aggregates, you should keep in mind that aggregate supply reflects billions of production decisions made by millions of individual resource suppliers and firms in the economy. Each firm operates in its own little world, dealing with its own suppliers and customers, and keeping a watchful eye on existing and potential competitors.

Yet each firm recognizes that success also depends on the performance of the economy as a whole. The theory of aggregate supply described here must be consistent with both the microeconomic behavior of individual suppliers and the macroeconomic behavior of the economy as a whole.

Topics discussed in this chapter include:

- Expected price level and long-term contracts
- Potential output
- Short-run aggregate supply curve
- Long-run aggregate supply curve
- Expansionary gap
- Recessionary gap
- Changes in aggregate supply
- Beneficial supply shocks
- Adverse supply shocks

10-1 Aggregate Supply in the Short Run

Aggregate supply is the relationship between the economy's price level and the amount of output firms are willing and able to supply, with other things constant. Assumed constant along a given aggregate supply curve are resource prices, the state of technology and know-how, and the rules of the game—the formal and informal institutions that structure production incentives, such as the system of property rights, patent laws, tax systems, respect for laws, and the customs and conventions of the marketplace. The greater the supply of resources, the better the technology and know-how, and the more effective the rules of the game, the greater the aggregate supply. Let's begin with the key resource—labor.

10-1a Labor and Aggregate Supply

Labor is the most important resource, accounting for about 70 percent of production costs. The supply of labor in an economy depends on the size and abilities of the adult population and their preferences for work versus leisure. Along a given labor supply curve—that is, for a given adult population with given abilities and preferences for work and leisure—the quantity of labor supplied depends on the wage. The higher the wage, other things constant, the more labor supplied.

So far, so good. But things start getting complicated once we recognize that the purchasing power of any given nominal wage depends on the economy's price level. *The higher the price level, the less any given money wage purchases, so the less attractive that wage is to workers.* Consider wages and the price level over time. Suppose a worker in 1970 was offered a job paying $20,000 per year. That salary may not impress you today, but its real purchasing power back then would exceed $80,000 in today's dollars. Because the price level matters, we must distinguish between the **nominal wage**, or money wage, which measures the wage in dollars of the year in question (such as 1970), and the **real wage**, which measures the wage in constant dollars—that is, dollars measured by the goods and services they buy. A higher real wage means workers can buy more goods and services.

Both workers and employers care more about the real wage than about the nominal wage. The problem is that nobody knows for sure how the price level will change during the life of the wage agreement, so labor contracts must be negotiated in terms of nominal wages, not real wages. Some resource prices, such as wages set by long-term contracts, remain in force for extended periods, often for two or three years. Workers as well as other resource suppliers must therefore negotiate based on the *expected* price level.

Even where there are no explicit labor contracts, there is often an implicit agreement that the wage, once negotiated, will not change for a while. For example, in many firms the standard practice is to revise wages annually. So wage agreements may be either *explicit* (based on a labor contract) or *implicit* (based on labor market practices). These explicit and implicit agreements are difficult to renegotiate while still in effect, even if the price level in the economy turns out to be higher or lower than expected.

10-1b Potential Output and the Natural Rate of Unemployment

Here's how resource owners and firms negotiate resource price agreements for a particular period, say, a year. Firms and resource suppliers expect a certain price level to prevail in the economy during the year. You could think of this as the *consensus* view for the upcoming year. Based on consensus expectations, firms and resource suppliers reach agreements on resource prices, such as wages. For example, firms and workers may expect the price level to increase 3 percent next year, so they agree on a nominal wage increase of 4 percent, which would increase the real wage by 1 percent. If these price-level expectations are realized, the agreed-on nominal wage translates into the expected real wage, so everyone is satisfied with the way things work out—after all, that's what they willingly negotiated. When the actual price level turns out as expected, we call the result the economy's potential output. *Potential output is the amount produced when there are no surprises about the price level.* So, at the agreed-on real wage, workers are supplying the quantity of labor they want and firms are hiring the quantity of labor they want. Both sides are content with the outcome.

We can think of **potential output** as the economy's maximum sustainable output, given the supply of resources, the state of technology and know-how, and the formal and informal production incentives offered by the rules of the game. Potential output is also referred to by other terms, including the *natural rate of output* and the *full-employment rate of output*.

The unemployment rate that occurs when the economy produces its potential GDP is called the **natural rate of unemployment**. That rate prevails when cyclical unemployment is zero. When the economy produces its potential output, the number of job openings equals the number of people unemployed for frictional, structural, and seasonal reasons. Widely accepted estimates of the natural rate range from about 4 percent to about 6 percent of the labor force. Some economists believe that, in the aftermath of the Great Recession, the

nominal wage
The wage measured in dollars of the year in question; the dollar amount on a paycheck

real wage
The wage measured in dollars of constant purchasing power; the wage measured in terms of the quantity of goods and services it buys

potential output
The economy's maximum sustainable output, given the supply of resources, technology and know-how, and rules of the game; the output level when there are no surprises about the price level

natural rate of unemployment
The unemployment rate when the economy produces its potential output

natural rate of unemployment increased toward the higher end of that range.[1] The Federal Reserve estimated the natural rate in 2015 as between 5.0 and 5.2 percent.

Potential output provides a reference point, an anchor, for the analysis in this chapter. *When the price-level expectations of both workers and firms are fulfilled, the economy produces its potential output.* Complications arise, however, when the actual price level differs from expectations, as we'll see next.

10-1c What If the Actual Price Level Is Higher Than Expected?

As you know, each firm's goal is to maximize profit. Profit equals total revenue minus total cost. Suppose workers and firms agree on a wage. What if the economy's price level turns out to be higher than expected? What happens *in the short run* to real GDP supplied? The **short run** in macroeconomics is a period during which some resource prices remain fixed by explicit or implicit agreements. Does output in the short run exceed the economy's potential, fall short of that potential, or equal that potential?

Because the prices of many resources are fixed for the duration of contracts, firms welcome a higher than expected price level. After all, the selling prices of their products, on average, are higher than expected, while the costs of at least some of the resources they employ remain constant. *A price level that is higher than expected results in a higher profit per unit, so firms have a profit incentive in the short run to increase production beyond the economy's potential level.*

At first it might appear odd to talk about producing beyond the economy's potential, but remember that potential output means not zero unemployment but the natural rate of unemployment. Even in an economy producing its potential output, there is some unemployed labor and some unused production capacity. If you think of potential GDP as the economy's *normal capacity*, you get a better idea of how production can temporarily exceed that capacity. For example, during World War II, the United States pulled out all the stops to win the war. Factories operated around the clock. Overtime was common. The unemployment rate dropped below 2 percent—well under its natural rate. People worked longer and harder for the war effort than they normally would have.

Think about your own study habits. During most of the term, you display your normal capacity for academic work. As the end of the term draws near, however, you may shift into a higher gear, finishing term papers, studying late into the night for final exams, and generally running yourself ragged trying to pull things together. During those final frenzied days of the term, you study beyond your normal capacity, beyond the schedule you follow on a regular or sustained basis. We often observe workers exceeding their normal capacity for short bursts: fireworks technicians around the Fourth of July, accountants at tax time, farmers at harvest time, and elected officials toward the end of a campaign or legislative session. Similarly, firms and their workers are able, *in the short run*, to push output beyond the economy's potential. But that higher rate of output is not normal and not sustainable in the long run.

10-1d Why Costs Rise When Output Exceeds Potential

The economy is flexible enough to expand output beyond potential GDP, but as output expands, the cost of additional output increases. Although many workers are bound by contracts, wage agreements may require overtime pay for extra hours or weekends.

short run

In macroeconomics, a period during which some resource prices, especially those for labor, remain fixed by explicit or implicit agreements

---

[1] See, for example, Murat Tasci and Saeed Zaman, "Unemployment After the Recession: A New Natural Rate?" *Economic Commentary*, September 2010, at http://www.clevelandfed.org/research/commentary/2010/2010-11.cfm.

As the economy expands and the unemployment rate declines, additional workers are harder to find. Retirees, homemakers, and students may require extra pay to draw them into the labor force. If few additional workers are available or if workers require additional pay for overtime, the nominal cost of labor increases as output expands in the short run, even though most wages remain fixed by implicit or explicit agreements.

As production increases, the demand for nonlabor resources increases too, so the prices of those resources in markets where prices are flexible—such as the market for oil—will increase, reflecting their greater scarcity. Also, as production increases, firms use their machines and trucks more intensively, so equipment wears out faster and is more prone to breakdowns. Thus, the nominal cost per unit of output rises when production is pushed beyond the economy's potential output. But *because some resource prices are fixed by contracts, the economy's price level rises faster than the per-unit production cost, so firms still find it profitable to increase the quantity supplied.*

When the economy's actual price level exceeds the expected price level, the real value of an agreed-on nominal wage declines. We might ask why workers would be willing to increase the quantity of labor they supply when the price level is higher than expected. One answer is that labor agreements require workers to do so, at least until workers have a chance to renegotiate.

In summary: If the price level is higher than expected, firms have a profit incentive to increase the quantity of goods and services supplied. At higher rates of output, however, the per-unit cost of additional output increases. Firms expand output as long as the revenue from additional production exceeds the cost of that production.

10-1e What If the Actual Price Level Is Lower Than Expected?

We have learned that if the price level is greater than expected, firms expand output in the short run, but as they do, the marginal cost of production increases. Now let's look at the effects of a price level that turns out to be lower than expected. Again, suppose that firms and resource suppliers have reached an agreement based on an expected price level. If the price level turns out to be lower than expected, firms find production less profitable, as reflected in the headline, "Consumer Price Drop Squeezes Profits."[2] The prices firms receive for their output are on average lower than they expected, yet many of their production costs, such as nominal wages, do not fall.

Because production is less profitable when prices are lower than expected, firms reduce their quantity supplied, so the economy's output is below its potential. As a result, some workers are laid off, some work fewer hours, and unemployment exceeds the natural rate. Not only is less labor employed, but machines go unused, delivery trucks sit idle, and entire plants may shut down—for example, automakers sometimes halt production for weeks. Cyclical unemployment increases.

Just as some costs increase in the short run when output is pushed beyond the economy's potential, some costs decline when output falls below that potential. As resources become unemployed, resource prices decline in markets where prices are flexible.

To Review: If the economy's price level turns out to be higher than expected, firms maximize profit by increasing the quantity supplied beyond the economy's potential output. As output expands, the per-unit cost of additional production increases, but firms expand production as long as prices rise more than costs. If the economy's price level turns out to be lower than expected, firms produce less than the economy's

[2.] Sudeep Reddy and Dana Mattioli, "Consumer Price Drop Squeezes Profits," *Wall Street Journal*, 18 June 2010.

potential output because prices fall more than costs. All of this is a long way of saying that *there is a direct relationship in the short run between the actual price level and real GDP supplied.*

10-1f The Short-Run Aggregate Supply Curve

What we have been describing so far traces out the **short-run aggregate supply (SRAS) curve**, which shows the relationship between the actual price level and real GDP supplied, other things constant. Again, the *short run* in this context is the period during which some resource prices, especially those for labor, are fixed by implicit or explicit agreements. For simplicity, we can think of the short run as the duration of labor contracts, which are based on the expected price level.

Suppose the expected price level is 110. The short-run aggregate supply curve in Exhibit 1, $SRAS_{110}$, is based on that expected price level (hence the subscript 110). If the price level turns out as expected, producers supply the economy's *potential output*, which in Exhibit 1 is $17.0 trillion. Although not shown in the exhibit, the aggregate demand curve would intersect the aggregate supply curve at point *a*. If the economy

short-run aggregate supply (SRAS) curve

A curve that shows a direct relationship between the actual price level and real GDP supplied in the short run, other things constant, including the expected price level

---

EXHIBIT 1 Short-Run Aggregate Supply Curve

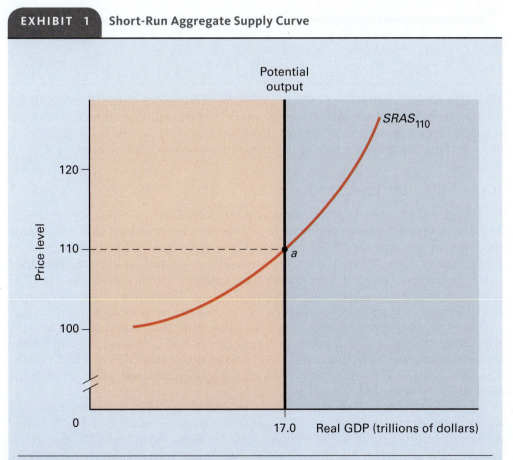

The short-run aggregate supply curve is based on a given expected price level, in this case, 110. Point *a* shows that if the actual price level equals the expected price level of 110, firms supply potential output. If the actual price level exceeds 110, quantity supplied exceeds potential. If the actual price level is below 110, quantity supplied is less than potential. Output levels that fall short of the economy's potential are shaded pink; output levels that exceed the economy's potential are shaded blue.

produces its potential output, unemployment is at the *natural rate*. Nobody is surprised, and all are content with the outcome. There is no tendency to move away from point *a* even if workers and firms could renegotiate wages.

In Exhibit 1, output levels that fall short of the economy's potential are shaded pink, and output levels that exceed the economy's potential are shaded blue. The slope of the short-run aggregate supply curve depends on how sharply the marginal cost of production rises as real GDP expands. If costs increase modestly as output expands, the supply curve is relatively flat. If these costs increase sharply as output expands, the supply curve is relatively steep. Much of the controversy about the short-run aggregate supply curve involves its shape. Shapes range from flat to steep. Notice that the short-run aggregate supply curve becomes steeper as output increases, because some resources become scarcer and thus more costly as output increases.

CHECKPOINT

What determines the shape and position of the short-run aggregate supply curve?

10-2 From the Short Run to the Long Run

This section begins with the price level exceeding expectations in the short run to see what happens in the long run. The long run is long enough that firms and resource suppliers can renegotiate all agreements based on knowledge of the actual price level. *So in the long run, there are no surprises about the economy's price level.*

10-2a Closing an Expansionary Gap

Let's begin our look at the long-run adjustment in Exhibit 2 with an expected price level of 110. The short-run aggregate supply curve for that expected price level is $SRAS_{110}$. Given this short-run aggregate supply curve, the equilibrium price level and real GDP depend on the aggregate demand curve. The actual price level would equal the expected price level only if the aggregate demand curve intersects the aggregate supply curve at point *a*—that is, where the short-run quantity equals potential output. Point *a* reflects potential output of $17.0 trillion and a price level of 110, which is the expected price level.

But what if aggregate demand turns out to be greater than expected, such as *AD'*, which intersects the short-run aggregate supply curve $SRAS_{110}$ at point *b*? Point *b* is the **short-run equilibrium**, reflecting a price level of 115 and a real GDP of $17.2 trillion. The actual price level in the short run is higher than expected, and output exceeds the economy's potential of $17.0 trillion.

The amount by which short-run output exceeds the economy's potential is called an **expansionary gap**. In Exhibit 2, that gap is the short-run output of $17.2 trillion minus potential output of $17.0 trillion, or $0.2 trillion. When real GDP exceeds its potential, the unemployment rate is less than its natural rate. Employees are working overtime, machines are being pushed to their limits, and farmers are sandwiching extra crops between usual plantings. Remember that the nominal wage was negotiated based on an expected price level of 110; because the actual price level is higher, that nominal wage translates into a lower-than-expected real wage. As we will see, output exceeding the economy's potential creates inflationary pressure. *The more that short-run output*

short-run equilibrium

The price level and real GDP that result when the aggregate demand curve intersects the short-run aggregate supply curve

expansionary gap

The amount by which actual output in the short run exceeds the economy's potential output

EXHIBIT 2   **Long-Run Adjustment When the Price Level Exceeds Expectations**

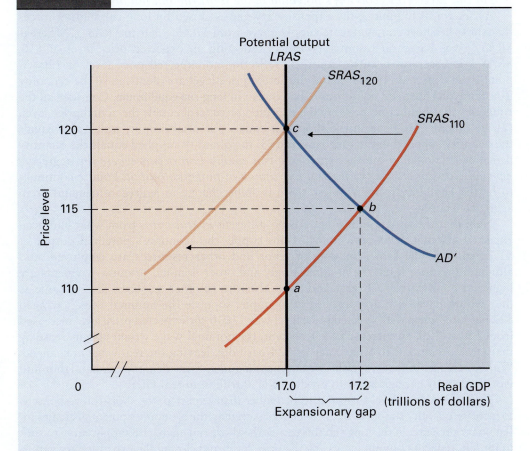

If the expected price level is 110, the short-run aggregate supply curve is $SRAS_{110}$. If the actual price level turns out as expected, the quantity supplied is the potential output of $17.0 trillion. But here the price level ends up higher than expected, and output exceeds potential, as shown by the short-run equilibrium at point b. The amount by which actual output exceeds the economy's potential output is called the expansionary gap. In the long run, price-level expectations and nominal wages will be revised upward. Costs will rise and the short-run aggregate supply curve will shift leftward to $SRAS_{120}$. Eventually, the economy will move to long-run equilibrium at point c, thus closing the expansionary gap.

exceeds the economy's potential, the larger the expansionary gap and the greater the upward pressure on the price level.

What happens in the long run? The **long run** is a period during which firms and resource suppliers know all about market conditions, particularly aggregate demand and the actual price level, and have the time to renegotiate resource payments based on that knowledge. Because the higher-than-expected price level cuts the real value of the nominal wage originally agreed to, workers try to negotiate a higher nominal wage at their earliest opportunity. Workers and other resource suppliers negotiate higher nominal payments, raising production costs for firms, so the short-run aggregate supply curve shifts leftward, resulting in cost-push inflation. In the long run, the expansionary gap causes the short-run aggregate supply curve to shift leftward to $SRAS_{120}$, which results in an expected price level of 120. Notice that the short-run aggregate supply

long run

In macroeconomics, a period during which wage contracts and resource price agreements can be renegotiated; there are no surprises about the economy's actual price level curve shifts until the equilibrium output equals the economy's potential output. *Actual output can exceed the economy's potential in the short run but not in the long run.*

As shown in Exhibit 2, the expansionary gap is closed by long-run market forces that shift the short-run aggregate supply curve from $SRAS_{110}$ left to $SRAS_{120}$. Whereas $SRAS_{110}$ was based on resource contracts reflecting an expected price level of 110, $SRAS_{120}$ is based on resource contracts reflecting an expected price level of 120. At point *c* the expected price level and the actual price level are identical, so the economy is not only in short-run equilibrium, but is also in **long-run equilibrium**. Consider all the equalities that hold at point *c:* (1) the expected price level equals the actual price level; (2) the quantity supplied in the short run equals potential output, which also equals the quantity supplied in the long run; and (3) the quantity supplied equals the quantity demanded. Looked at another way, *long-run equilibrium occurs where the aggregate demand curve intersects the vertical line drawn at potential output.* Point *c* continues to be the equilibrium point unless there is some change in aggregate demand or in aggregate supply.

Note that the situation at point *c* is no different *in real terms* from what had been expected at point *a*. At both points, firms supply the economy's potential output of $17.0 trillion. The same amounts of labor and other resources are employed, and although the price level, the nominal wage, and other nominal resource payments are higher at point *c*, the real wage and the real return to other resources are the same as they would have been at point *a*. For example, suppose the nominal wage averaged $22 per hour when the expected price level was 110. If the expected price level increased from 110 to 120, an increase of 9.1 percent, the nominal wage would also increase by that same percentage to an average of $24 per hour, leaving the real wage unchanged. With no change in real wages between points *a* and *c*, firms demand enough labor and workers supply enough labor to produce $17.0 trillion in real GDP.

Thus, if the price level turns out to be higher than expected, the short-run response is to increase quantity supplied. But production exceeding the economy's potential creates inflationary pressure. In the long run this causes the short-run aggregate supply curve to shift to the left, reducing output, increasing the price level, and closing the expansionary gap.

If an increase in the price level were predicted accurately year after year, firms and resource suppliers would build these expectations into their long-term agreements. The price level would move up each year by the expected amount, but the economy's output would remain at potential GDP, thereby skipping the round-trip beyond the economy's potential and back.

10-2b Closing a Recessionary Gap

Let's begin again with an expected price level of 110 as presented in Exhibit 3, where blue shading indicates output exceeding potential and pink shading indicates output below potential. If the price level turned out as expected, the resulting equilibrium combination would occur at *a*, which would be both a short-run and a long-run equilibrium. Suppose this time that the aggregate demand curve intersects the short-run aggregate supply curve to the left of potential output, yielding a price level below that expected. The intersection of the aggregate demand curve, AD'', with $SRAS_{110}$ yields the short-run equilibrium at point *d*, where the price level is below expectations and production is less than the economy's potential. The amount by which actual output falls short of potential GDP is called a **recessionary gap**. In this case, the recessionary gap is $0.2 trillion, and unemployment exceeds its natural rate.

Because the price level is less than expected, the nominal wage, which was based on the expected price level of 110 and not the actual price level of 105, translates into a higher real wage in the short run. What happens in the long run? With the price

---

long-run equilibrium
The price level and real GDP that occur when (1) the actual price level equals the expected price level, (2) real GDP supplied equals potential output, and (3) real GDP supplied equals real GDP demanded

recessionary gap
The amount by which actual output in the short run falls short of the economy's potential output

EXHIBIT 3 Long-Run Adjustment When the Price Level Is Below Expectations

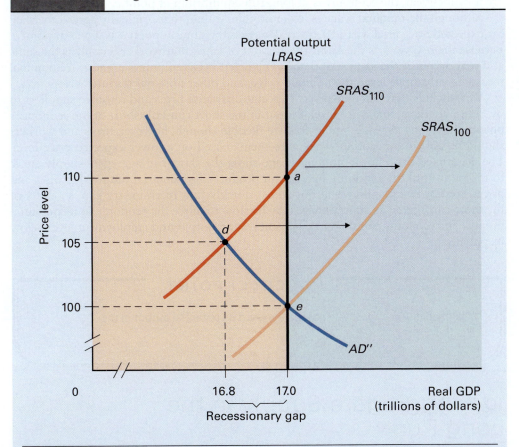

When the actual price level is below expectations, as indicated by the intersection of the aggregate demand curve AD'' with the short-run aggregate supply curve $SRAS_{110}$, short-run equilibrium occurs at point d. Production below the economy's potential opens a recessionary gap of $0.2 trillion. If prices and wages are flexible enough in the long run, nominal wages will be renegotiated lower. As resource costs fall, the short-run aggregate supply curve eventually shifts rightward to $SRAS_{100}$ and the economy moves to long-run equilibrium at point e, with output increasing to the potential level of $17.0 trillion.

level lower than expected, employers are no longer willing to pay as high a nominal wage. And with the unemployment rate higher than the natural rate, more workers are competing for jobs, putting downward pressure on the nominal wage. If the price level and the nominal wage are flexible enough, the combination of a lower price level and a pool of unemployed workers competing for jobs should make workers more willing to accept lower nominal wages next time wage agreements are negotiated.

If firms and workers negotiate lower nominal wages, the cost of production decreases, shifting the short-run aggregate supply curve rightward, leading to price deflation and greater output. The short-run supply curve continues to shift rightward until it intersects the aggregate demand curve where the economy produces its potential output. This is reflected in Exhibit 3 by a rightward shift of the short-run aggregate supply curve from $SRAS_{110}$ to $SRAS_{100}$. *If the price level and nominal wage are flexible enough, the short-run aggregate supply curve shifts rightward until the economy produces its potential output.* The new short-run aggregate supply curve is based on an expected price level of 100. Because the expected price level and the actual price level are now identical, the economy is in long-run equilibrium at point *e*.

Although the nominal wage is lower at point *e* than that originally agreed to when the expected price level was 110, the real wage is the same at point *e* as it was at point *a*. Because the real wage is the same, the amount of labor that workers supply is the same and real output is the same. All that has changed between points *a* and *e* are nominal measures—the price level, the nominal wage, and other nominal resource prices.

We conclude that when incorrect expectations cause firms and resource suppliers to overestimate the actual price level, output in the short run falls short of the economy's potential. As long as wages and prices are flexible enough, however, firms and workers should be able to renegotiate wage agreements based on a lower expected price level. The negotiated drop in the nominal wage shifts the short-run aggregate supply curve to the right until the economy once again produces its potential output. If wages and prices are not flexible, they will not adjust quickly to a recessionary gap, so shifts of the short-run aggregate supply curve may be slow to move the economy to its potential output. The economy can therefore get stuck at an output and employment level below its potential.

CHECKPOINT

What market forces push the economy toward its potential output in the long run?

10-3 Aggregate Supply in the Long Run

We are now in a position to provide an additional interpretation of the pink- and blue-shaded areas of our exhibits. If a short-run equilibrium occurs in the blue-shaded area, that is, to the right of potential output, then market forces in the long run increase nominal resource costs, shifting the short-run aggregate supply to the left. If a short-run equilibrium occurs in the pink-shaded area, then market forces in the long run reduce nominal resource costs, shifting the short-run aggregate supply curve to the right. *Closing an expansionary gap involves inflation and closing a recessionary gap involves deflation.*

10-3a Tracing Potential Output

long-run aggregate supply (LRAS) curve

A vertical line at the economy's potential output; aggregate supply when there are no surprises about the price level and all resource contracts can be renegotiated

If wages and prices are flexible enough, the economy produces its potential output in the long run, as indicated in Exhibit 4 by the vertical line drawn at the economy's potential GDP of $17.0 trillion. This vertical line is called the economy's **long-run aggregate supply (LRAS) curve**. *The long-run aggregate supply curve depends on the supply of resources in the economy, the level of technology and know-how, and the production incentives provided by the formal and informal institutions of the economic system.*

In Exhibit 4, the initial price level of 110 is determined by the intersection of *AD* with the long-run aggregate supply curve. If the aggregate demand curve shifts out to *AD'*, then in the long run, the equilibrium price level increases to 120 but equilibrium output remains at $17.0 trillion, the economy's potential GDP. Conversely, a decline in aggregate demand from *AD* to *AD''*, in the long run, leads only to a fall in the price level from

EXHIBIT 4 Long-Run Aggregate Supply Curve

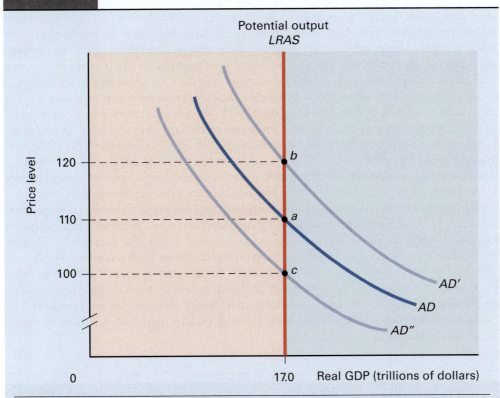

In the long run, when the actual price level equals the expected price level, the economy produces its potential. In the long run, $17.0 trillion in real GDP is supplied regardless of the actual price level. As long as wages and prices are flexible enough, the economy's potential GDP is consistent with any price level. Thus, shifts of the aggregate demand curve, in the long run, do not affect potential output. The long-run aggregate supply curve, *LRAS*, is a vertical line at potential GDP.

110 to 100, with no change in output. Note that these long-run movements are more like tendencies than smooth and timely adjustments. It may take a long time for resource prices to adjust, particularly when the economy faces a recessionary gap. But as long as wages and prices are flexible, the economy's potential GDP is consistent with any price level. *In the long run, equilibrium output equals long-run aggregate supply, which is also potential output. The equilibrium price level depends on the aggregate demand curve.*

10-3b Wage Flexibility and Employment

What evidence is there that a vertical line drawn at the economy's potential GDP depicts the long-run aggregate supply curve? Except during the Great Depression, unemployment over the last century has varied from year to year but typically has returned to what would be viewed as a natural rate of unemployment—again, estimates range from 4 percent to 6 percent.

An *expansionary* gap creates a labor shortage that eventually results in a higher nominal wage and a higher price level. But a *recessionary* gap does not necessarily generate enough downward pressure to lower the nominal wage. Studies indicate that nominal wages are slow to adjust to high unemployment. Nominal wages have declined in particular industries; during the 1980s, for example, nominal wages fell in airlines, steel, and trucking. But seldom have we observed actual declines in nominal wages across the economy, especially since World War II. Nominal wages do not adjust downward as quickly or as substantially as they adjust upward, and the downward response that does occur tends to be slow and modest. Consequently, we say that nominal wages tend to be "sticky" in the downward direction.[3] *Because nominal wages fall slowly, if at all, the supply-side adjustments needed to close a recessionary gap may take so long as to seem ineffective.* What, in fact, usually closes a recessionary gap is an increase in aggregate demand as the economy pulls out of its funk. For example, consider the U.S. economy's recovery from the Great Recession of 2007-2009. Here's how *The Wall Street Journal* reported events: "U.S. factories that were idled during the recession are now humming with activity. Office and apartment buildings have less empty space. Unemployment is falling, while wages and benefits are growing slowly."[4]

Although the nominal wage seldom falls, an actual decline in the nominal wage is not necessary to close a recessionary gap. All that's needed is a fall in the real wage. And *the real wage falls if the prices increase more than nominal wages.* For example, if the price level increases by 4 percent and the nominal wage increases by 3 percent, the real wage falls by 1 percent. If the real wage falls enough, firms demand enough additional labor to produce the economy's potential output. More generally, total compensation falls if employers cut back on employee benefits such as health insurance or paid time off.

In the following case study, we look more at output gaps and discuss why wages aren't more flexible downward.

PUBLIC POLICY

U.S. OUTPUT GAPS AND WAGE FLEXIBILITY   Let's look at estimates of actual and potential GDP. Exhibit 5 measures actual GDP minus potential GDP as a percentage of potential GDP for the United States. When actual output exceeds potential output, the output gap is positive and the economy has an expansionary gap. For example, actual output in 2000 was 3.4 percent above potential output, amounting to an expansionary gap that year of about $410 billion (in 2009 dollars). When actual output falls short of potential output, the output gap is negative and the economy suffers a recessionary gap. For example, actual output in 2009 was 4.7 percent below potential output, amounting to a recessionary gap

of about $710 billion (in 2009 dollars). If actual output equals potential output, there is no output gap, as was the case in 2008. Note that the economy need not be in recession for actual output to fall short of potential output. For example, from 2010 to 2015, real GDP expanded, yet actual output was below potential output. As long as unemployment exceeds its natural rate, the economy suffers a recessionary gap.

Employers and employees would have been better off if these recessionary gaps had been reduced or eliminated. After all, more people would have jobs to produce more goods and services, thereby increasing the nation's standard of living. If workers and employers fail to reach

continued

[3.] For evidence on sticky wages, see Alessandro Barattieri, Susanto Basu, and Peter Gottschalk, "Some Evidence on the Importance of Sticky Wages," *American Economic Journal: Macroeconomics*, 6 (January 2014): 70–101.

[4.] Pedro Nicolaci da Costa, "Decline in 'Slack' Helps Fed Gauge Recovery," *Wall Street Journal*, 10 August 2014.

EXHIBIT 5	The U.S. Output Gap: Red Bars Show Actual Output Below Potential Output and Blue Bars Show Actual Output Exceeding Potential Output

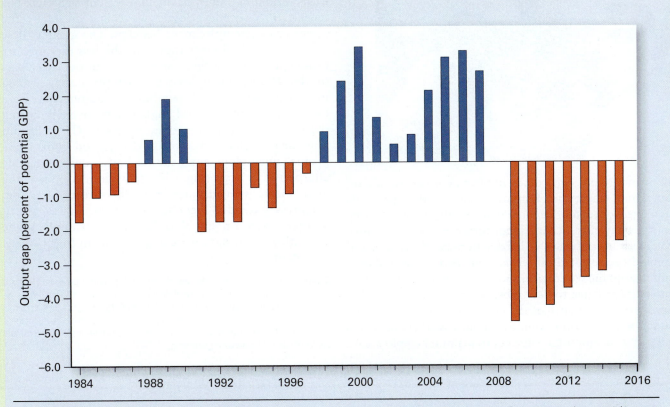

The output gap each year equals actual GDP minus potential GDP as a percentage of potential GDP. When actual output exceeds potential output, the output gap is positive and the economy has an expansionary gap, as shown by the blue bars. When actual output falls short of potential output, the output gap is negative and the economy suffers a recessionary gap, as shown by the red bars. Note that the economy need not be in recession for actual output to fall below potential output.

Source: Developed from estimates by the OECD Economic Outlook, 97 (May 2015), Annex Table 10. Figures for 2015 are OECD projections. OECD data can be found at http://www.oecd.org/home/.

an agreement that seems possible and that all would prefer, then they have failed to coordinate in some way. Recessionary gaps can thus be viewed as resulting from a **coordination failure**.

If employers and workers can increase output and employment by agreeing to lower nominal wages, why don't they? As we have already seen, some workers are operating under long-term contracts, so wages aren't very flexible, particularly in the downward direction. But if long-term contracts are a problem, why not negotiate shorter ones? First, negotiating

coordination failure

A situation in which workers and employers fail to achieve an outcome that all would prefer

contracts is costly and time consuming (for example, airline union contracts take an average of 1.3 years to negotiate). Longer contracts reduce the frequency, and thus reduce the average annual cost, of negotiations. Second, long-term contracts reduce the frequency of strikes, lockouts, and other labor disputes. Thus, both workers and employers gain from longer contracts, even though such contracts make wages more sticky and make recessionary gaps more likely to linger.

When demand is slack, why do employers lay off workers rather than cut nominal wages? Yale economist Truman Bewley interviewed over 300 managers, union officials, and employment recruiters and concluded that

continued

resistance to pay cuts comes, not from workers or unions, but from employers. Employers believe that pay cuts damage worker morale more than layoffs do. By lowering morale, pay cuts increase labor turnover and reduce productivity. In contrast, the damage from layoffs is brief and limited because laid off workers are soon gone and cannot disrupt the workplace, and remaining workers may be more grateful just to have jobs. What's more, even during severe recessions such as the Great Recession, about nine in ten workers still have jobs, so most workers have less incentive to support a wage cut to maintain employment.

Another reason workers may be reluctant to accept lower nominal wages is unemployment benefits. The incentive to accept a lower wage is reduced by the prospect of unemployment benefits. The greater these benefits and the longer they last, the less the pressure to accept a lower wage. For example, in the latter part of the 1920s, unemployment benefits nearly tripled in Great Britain and eligibility requirements were loosened. Despite record high unemployment during the Great Depression, money wages in Great Britain remained unchanged during the period. For some people, unemployment benefits had become a viable alternative to accepting a lower wage. Because of the high unemployment rates from the Great Recession, Congress extended benefits and some states added to that extension. In New York, for example, some unemployed workers were eligible for up to 99 weeks of benefits.

Sources: Truman F. Bewley, *Why Wages Don't Fall During a Recession* (Harvard University Press, 2000); Laurence Ball and David Romer, "Sticky Prices as Coordination Failure," *American Economic Review*, 81 (June 1991): 539–552; Daniel K. Benjamin and Levis A. Kochin, "Searching for an Explanation of Unemployment in Interwar Britain," *Journal of Political Economy*, 87 (June 1979): 441–478; and *Survey of Current Business*, 95 (June 2015).

To Review: When the actual price level differs from the expected price level, output in the short run departs from the economy's potential. In the long run, however, market forces shift the short-run aggregate supply curve until the economy once again produces its potential output. Thus, surprises about the price level change real GDP in the short run but not in the long run. Shifts of the aggregate demand curve change the price level but do not affect potential output, or long-run aggregate supply.

 **CHECKPOINT**

Why do shifts of the aggregate demand curve change the price level in the long run but not potential output?

10-4 Changes in Aggregate Supply

In this section, we consider factors other than changes in the expected price level that may affect aggregate supply. We begin by distinguishing between long-term trends in aggregate supply and **supply shocks**, which are unexpected events that affect aggregate supply, sometimes only temporarily.

10-4a What If Aggregate Supply Increases?

The economy's potential output is based on the willingness and ability of households to supply resources to firms, the level of technology and know-how, and the institutional underpinnings of the economic system. Any change in these factors could affect the economy's potential output. Changes in the economy's potential output over time were introduced in the earlier chapter that focused on U.S. productivity and growth. The supply of labor may change over time because of a change in the size, composition, or quality of the labor force or a change in preferences for labor versus leisure. For example, the U.S. labor force has more than doubled since 1948 as a result of population growth and a growing labor force participation rate, especially among women with children. At the same time, job training, education, and on-the-job experience increased the quality of labor. Increases in the quantity and the quality of the labor force have increased the economy's potential GDP, or long-run aggregate supply.

The quantity and quality of other resources also change over time. The capital stock—machines, buildings, and trucks—increases when gross investment exceeds capital depreciation. And the capital stock improves with technological breakthroughs. Even the quantity and quality of land can be increased—for example, by claiming land from the sea, as is done in the Netherlands and in Hong Kong, or by revitalizing soil that has lost its fertility. These increases in the quantity and quality of resources increase the economy's potential output.

Finally, institutional changes that define property rights more clearly or make contracts more enforceable, such as the introduction of clearer patent and copyright laws, will increase the incentives to undertake productive activity, thereby increasing potential output. *Changes in the labor force, in the quantity and quality of other resources, and in the institutional arrangements of the economic system tend to occur gradually.* Exhibit 6 depicts a gradual shift of the economy's potential output from $17.0 trillion to $17.5 trillion. The long-run aggregate supply curve shifts from *LRAS* out to *LRAS'*.

In contrast to the gradual, or long-run, changes that often occur in the supply of resources, *supply shocks* are unexpected events that change aggregate supply, sometimes only temporarily. **Beneficial supply shocks** increase aggregate supply; examples include (1) abundant harvests that increase the food supply, (2) discoveries of natural resources, such as oil in Alaska or the North Sea, (3) technological breakthroughs that allow firms to combine resources more efficiently, such as faster computers or the Internet, and (4) sudden changes in the economic system that promote more production, such as tax cuts that stimulate production incentives or stricter limits on frivolous product liability lawsuits.

Exhibit 7 shows the effect of a beneficial supply shock from a technological breakthrough. The beneficial supply shock shown here shifts the short-run and long-run aggregate supply curves rightward. Along the aggregate demand curve, *AD*, the equilibrium combination of price and output moves from point *a* to point *b*. *For a given aggregate demand curve, the happy outcome of a beneficial supply shock is an increase in output and a decrease in the price level.* The new equilibrium at point *b* is a short-run

Moodboard/Corbis

supply shocks
Unexpected events that affect aggregate supply, sometimes only temporarily

beneficial supply shocks
Unexpected events that increase aggregate supply, sometimes only temporarily

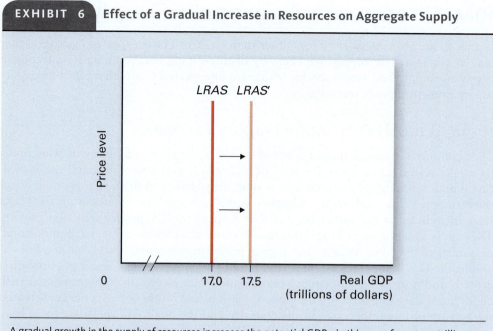

EXHIBIT 6 Effect of a Gradual Increase in Resources on Aggregate Supply

A gradual growth in the supply of resources increases the potential GDP—in this case, from $17.0 trillion to $17.5 trillion. The long-run aggregate supply curve shifts to the right.

and a long-run equilibrium in the sense that there is no tendency to move from that point as long as whatever caused the beneficial effect continues, and a technological discovery usually has a lasting effect. Likewise, substantial new oil discoveries usually benefit the economy for a long time. On the other hand, an unusually favorable growing season won't last. When a normal growing season returns, the short-run and long-run aggregate supply curves return to their original equilibrium position—back to point *a* in Exhibit 7.

10-4b What If Aggregate Supply Decreases?

adverse supply shocks
Unexpected events that reduce aggregate supply, sometimes only temporarily

Adverse supply shocks are sudden, unexpected events that reduce aggregate supply, sometimes only temporarily. For example, a drought could reduce the supply of a variety of resources, such as food, building materials, and water-powered electricity. An overthrow of a government could destabilize the economy. Terrorist attacks could shake the institutional underpinnings of the economy, as occurred in America, England, Spain, and the Middle East. Such attacks add to the cost of doing business—everything from airline screening to building security.

An adverse supply shock is depicted as a leftward shift of both the short-run and long-run aggregate supply curves, as shown in Exhibit 8, moving the equilibrium combination from point *a* to point *c* and reducing potential output from $17.0 trillion to $16.8 trillion. As mentioned earlier, the combination of reduced output and a higher price level is often referred to as stagflation. The United States encountered stagflation during the 1970s, when the economy was rocked by a series of adverse supply shocks, such as crop failures around the globe and the oil price hikes by OPEC in 1974 and again in 1979. If the effect of the adverse supply shock is temporary, such as a poor growing season, the aggregate supply curve returns to its original position once things return to normal. But some economists question an economy's ability to bounce back from a prolonged period of high unemployment, as discussed next.

10-4c Hysteresis and the Natural Rate of Unemployment

Between World War II and the mid-1970s, unemployment in Western Europe was low. From 1960 to 1974, for example, the unemployment rate in France never got as high as 4 percent. The worldwide recession of the mid-1970s, however, jacked up unemployment rates. But unemployment continued to climb in Europe long after the recession ended, topping 10 percent during the 1990s. In February 2015, the unemployment rate in the 19 countries of the eurozone averaged 11.3 percent, twice the rate in the United States.

Some observers claim that the natural rate of unemployment has increased in Europe, and they have borrowed a term from physics, **hysteresis** (pronounced *his-ter-eé-sis*), to argue that the natural rate of unemployment depends in part on the recent history of unemployment. *The longer the actual unemployment rate remains above what had been the natural rate, the more the natural rate itself increases.* For example, those unemployed can lose valuable job skills, such as an out-of-work computer programmer who loses touch with the latest developments. As weeks of unemployment stretch into months and years, the shock and stigma may diminish, so the work ethic weakens. What's more, some European countries offer generous unemployment benefits indefinitely, reducing the hardship of unemployment. On average, unemployment benefits in Western Europe replace 60 to 80 percent of lost pay versus about 50 percent in the United States. Some Europeans have collected unemployment benefits *for more than a decade*.

Another explanation for high unemployment in Europe is that legislation introduced there in the 1970s made it more difficult to lay off workers. In most European countries, job dismissals must be approved by worker councils, which consider such factors as the worker's health, marital status, and number of dependents.

hysteresis
The theory that the natural rate of unemployment depends in part on the recent history of unemployment; a long period of high unemployment can increase the natural rate of unemployment

EXHIBIT 7   Effects of a Beneficial Supply Shock on Aggregate Supply

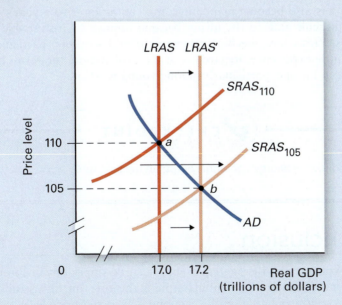

A beneficial supply shock that has a lasting effect, such as a breakthrough in technology, permanently shifts both the short-run and the long-run aggregate supply curves to the right. A beneficial supply shock lowers the price level and increases output, as reflected by the change in equilibrium from point *a* to point *b*. A temporary beneficial supply shock shifts the aggregate supply curves only temporarily.

EXHIBIT 8   **Effects of an Adverse Supply Shock on Aggregate Supply**

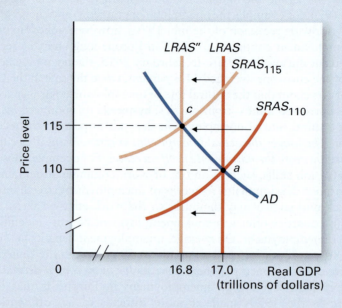

Given the aggregate demand curve, an adverse supply shock, such as a drought, shifts the short-run and long-run aggregate supply curves to the left, increasing the price level and reducing real GDP, a movement called stagflation. This change is shown by the move in equilibrium from point *a* to point *c*. If the shock is just temporary, the shift of the aggregate supply curves will be temporary.

Severance pay has also become mandatory and can amount to a year's pay or more. With layoffs difficult and costly, hiring became almost an irreversible decision for an employer, so firms have become reluctant to add workers, particularly untested workers with little experience. Regardless of the explanation, the result has been high unemployment in Europe, particularly among young workers.

**CHECKPOINT**

What can shift an economy's potential output in the long run?

10-5 Conclusion

This chapter explains why the aggregate supply curve slopes upward in the short run and is vertical at the economy's potential output in the long run. Firms and resource suppliers negotiate contracts based on the economy's expected price level, which depends on expectations about aggregate demand. Unexpected changes in the price level can move output in the short run away from its potential level. But if firms and resource suppliers fully adjust to price surprises, the economy in the long run moves toward its potential output. Potential output is the anchor for analyzing aggregate supply in the short run and long run.

Summary

1. Short-run aggregate supply is based on resource demand and supply decisions that reflect the expected price level. If the price level turns out as expected, the economy produces its potential output. If the price level exceeds expectations, short-run output exceeds the economy's potential, creating an expansionary gap. If the price level is below expectations, short-run output falls short of the economy's potential, creating a recessionary gap.

2. Output can exceed the economy's potential in the short run, but not in the long run. In the long run, higher nominal wages will be negotiated at the earliest opportunity. This increases the cost of production, shifting the short-run aggregate supply curve leftward along the aggregate demand curve until the economy produces its potential output.

3. If output in the short run is less than the economy's potential, and if wages and prices are flexible enough, lower nominal wages will reduce production costs in the long run. These lower costs shift the short-run aggregate supply curve rightward along the aggregate demand curve until the economy produces its potential output.

4. Evidence suggests that when output exceeds the economy's potential, nominal wages and the price level increase. But there is less evidence that nominal wages and the price level fall when output is below the economy's potential. Wages appear to be "sticky" in the downward direction. What usually closes a recessionary gap is an increase in aggregate demand.

5. The long-run aggregate supply curve, or the economy's potential output, depends on the amount and quality of resources available, the state of technology and know-how, and the rules of the game, such as patent laws and business practices, that shape production incentives. Increases in resource availability, improvements in technology and know-how, or institutional changes that provide more attractive production incentives increase aggregate supply and potential output.

6. Supply shocks are unexpected, often temporary, shifts of the aggregate supply curve. Beneficial supply shocks increase output, sometimes only temporarily. Adverse supply shocks reduce output and increase the price level, a combination called stagflation. Adverse supply shocks may be temporary.

Key Concepts

Nominal wage   214
Real wage   214
Potential output   214
Natural rate of unemployment   214
Short run   215
Short-run aggregate supply (SRAS) curve   217

Short-run equilibrium   218
Expansionary gap   218
Long run   219
Long-run equilibrium   220
Recessionary gap   220
Long-run aggregate supply (LRAS) curve   222

Coordination failure   225
Supply shocks   227
Beneficial supply shocks   227
Adverse supply shocks   228
Hysteresis   229

Questions for Review

1. **Short-Run Aggregate Supply**   In the short run, prices may rise faster than costs. This chapter discusses why this might happen. Suppose that labor and management agree to adjust wages continuously for any changes in the price level. How would such adjustments affect the slope of the aggregate supply curve?

2. **Potential Output**   Define the economy's potential output. What factors help determine potential output?

3. **Actual Price Level Higher than Expected**   Discuss some instances in your life when your actual production for short periods exceeded what you considered your potential, or normal, production. Why does this occur only for brief periods?

4. **Nominal and Real Wages**   Complete each of the following sentences:

    a. The _____ wage measures the wage rate in dollars of the year in question, while the _____ wage measures it in constant dollars.

    b. Wage agreements are based on the _____ price level and negotiated in _____ terms. Real wages are then determined by the _____ price level.

    c. The higher the actual price level, the _____ is the real wage for a given nominal wage.

    d. If nominal wages are growing at 2 percent per year while the annual inflation rate is 3 percent, then real wages change by _____.

5. **Recessionary Gaps**   After reviewing Exhibit 3 in this chapter, explain why recessionary gaps occur only in the short run and only when the actual price level is below what was expected.

6. **Short-Run Aggregate Supply**   In interpreting the short-run aggregate supply curve, what does the adjective *short-run* mean? Explain the role of labor contracts along the *SRAS* curve.

7. **Recessionary Gap**   What does a recessionary gap imply about the actual rate of unemployment relative to the natural rate? What does it imply about the actual price level relative to the expected price level? What must happen to real and nominal wages in order to close a recessionary gap?

8. **Expansionary Gap**   How does an economy that is experiencing an expansionary gap adjust in the long run?

9. **Case Study: U.S. Output Gaps and Wage Flexibility**   Unemployment is costly to employers, employees, and the economy as a whole. What are some explanations for the *coordination failures* that prevent workers and employers from reaching agreements?

10. **Long-Run Adjustment**   In the long run, why does an actual price level that exceeds the expected price level change nominal wages? Why do these changes eventually shift the short-run aggregate supply curve?

11. **Long-Run Aggregate Supply**   The long-run aggregate supply curve is vertical at the economy's potential output level. Why is the long-run aggregate supply curve located at this output rather than below or above potential output?

12. **Long-Run Aggregate Supply**   Determine whether each of the following, other things held constant, would lead to an increase, a decrease, or no change in long-run aggregate supply:
    a. An improvement in technology
    b. A permanent decrease in the size of the capital stock
    c. An increase in the actual price level
    d. An increase in the expected price level
    e. A permanent increase in the size of the labor force

13. **Changes in Aggregate Supply**   What are supply shocks? Distinguish between beneficial and adverse supply shocks. Do such shocks affect the short-run aggregate supply curve, the long-run aggregate supply curve, or both? What is the resulting impact on potential GDP?

Problems and Exercises

14. **Real Wages**   In Exhibit 2 in this chapter, how does the real wage rate at point *c* compare with the real wage rate at point *a*? How do nominal wage rates compare at those two points? Explain your answers.

15. **Natural Rate of Unemployment**   What is the relationship between potential output and the natural rate of unemployment?
    a. If the economy currently has a frictional unemployment rate of 2 percent, structural unemployment of 2 percent, seasonal unemployment of 0.5 percent, and cyclical unemployment of 2 percent, what is the natural rate of unemployment? Where is the economy operating relative to its potential GDP?
    b. What happens to the natural rate of unemployment and potential GDP if cyclical unemployment rises to 3 percent with other types of unemployment unchanged from part (a)?
    c. What happens to the natural rate of unemployment and potential GDP if structural unemployment falls to 1.5 percent with other types of unemployment unchanged from part (a)?

16. **Expansionary and Recessionary Gaps**   Answer the following questions on the basis of the following graph:

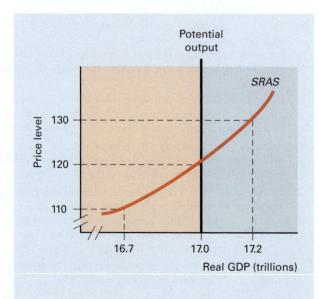

a. If the actual price level exceeds the expected price level reflected in long-term contracts, real GDP equals _____ and the actual price level equals _____ in the short run.
b. The situation described in part (a) results in a(n) _____ gap equal to _____.
c. If the actual price level is lower than the expected price level reflected in long-term contracts, real GDP equals _____ and the actual price level equals _____ in the short run.
d. The situation described in part (c) results in a(n) _____ gap equal to _____.
e. If the actual price level equals the expected price level reflected in long-term contracts, real GDP equals _____ and the actual price level equals _____ in the short run.
f. The situation described in part (e) results in a(n) _____ gap equal to _____.

17. **Long-Run Adjustment**   The ability of the economy to eliminate any imbalances between actual and potential output is sometimes called self-correction. Using an aggregate supply and aggregate demand diagram, show why this self-correction process involves only temporary periods of inflation or deflation.

18. **Changes in Aggregate Supply**   List three factors that can change the economy's potential output. What is the impact of shifts of the aggregate demand curve on potential output? Illustrate your answers with a diagram.

19. **Supply Shocks**   Give an example of an adverse supply shock and illustrate graphically. Now do the same for a beneficial supply shock.

20. **Hysteresis**   High unemployment rates in Europe remains a timely topic. Use any Web browser to search for the words "European unemployment." Simply by scanning the headlines, see how many possible explanations you can list. How do these explanations compare with those offered in this chapter?

Fiscal Policy

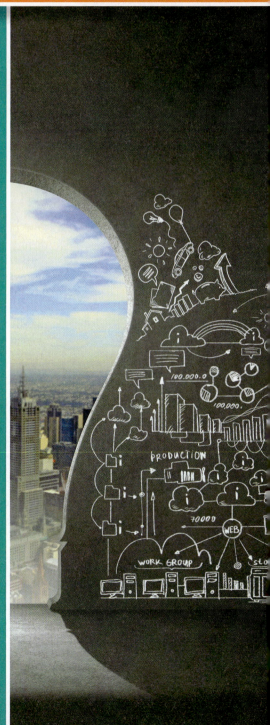

AP Images/Damian Dovarganes

- *How did the cash-for-clunkers program work out?*

- *What is the appropriate role of fiscal policy in the economy?*

- *Can fiscal policy reduce swings in the business cycle?*

- *Why did fiscal policy fall on hard times for a quarter century, and what brought it back to life?*

- *Does fiscal policy affect aggregate supply?*

Answers to these and other questions are addressed in this chapter, which examines the theory and practice of fiscal policy.

President Obama claimed on February 17, 2010, that "it is largely thanks to the Recovery Act that a second depression is no longer a possibility." The Japanese government cut taxes and increased spending to stimulate its troubled economy. These are examples of fiscal policy, which focuses on the effects of taxing and public spending on aggregate economic activity. In this chapter, we examine the role of fiscal policy in moving the economy to its potential output. We review U.S. fiscal policy and discuss limitations to its effectiveness. The Great Recession had a major impact on the economy. We'll consider the fiscal response to that calamity.

A more complex model of fiscal policy appears in the appendix to this chapter.

Topics discussed in this chapter include:

- Theory of fiscal policy
- Discretionary fiscal policy
- Automatic stabilizers
- Fiscal policy in practice
- Limits of fiscal policy
- Deficits, surpluses, then more deficits
- Fiscal policy response to the Great Recession
- Cash for clunkers

11-1 Theory of Fiscal Policy

Our macroeconomic model so far has viewed government as passive. But government purchases and transfer payments at all levels in the United States total more than $7.0 trillion a year, making government an important player in the economy. From highway construction to unemployment compensation to income taxes to federal deficits, fiscal policy affects the economy in myriad ways. We now move fiscal policy to center stage. As introduced in Chapter 3, *fiscal policy* refers to government purchases, transfer payments, taxes, and borrowing as they affect macroeconomic variables such as real GDP, employment, the price level, and economic growth. When economists study fiscal policy, they usually focus on the federal government, although governments at all levels affect the economy.

11-1a Fiscal Policy Tools

automatic stabilizers
Structural features of government spending and taxation that reduce fluctuations in disposable income, and thus consumption, over the business cycle

discretionary fiscal policy
The deliberate manipulation of government purchases, taxation, and transfer payments to promote macroeconomic goals, such as full employment, price stability, and economic growth

The tools of fiscal policy sort into two broad categories: automatic stabilizers and discretionary fiscal policy. **Automatic stabilizers** are revenue and spending programs in the federal budget that automatically adjust with the ups and downs of the economy to stabilize disposable income and, consequently, consumption and real GDP. For example, the federal income tax is an automatic stabilizer because (1) once adopted, it requires no congressional action to operate year after year, so it's *automatic*, and (2) it reduces the drop in disposable income during recessions and reduces the jump in disposable income during expansions, so it's a *stabilizer*, a smoother. **Discretionary fiscal policy**, on the other hand, requires the deliberate manipulation of government purchases, transfer payments, and taxes to promote macroeconomic goals like full employment, price stability, and economic growth. President Obama's 2009 stimulus plan, which was enacted by Congress, is an example of discretionary fiscal policy. Discretionary fiscal policy usually requires congressional approval. Some discretionary policies are temporary, such as one-time tax cuts or government spending increases to fight a recession. President Bush's 2001 and 2008 one-time tax rebates are examples. Let's next consider how, in theory, fiscal policy can be used to close a recessionary gap and an expansionary gap.

11-1b Discretionary Fiscal Policy to Close a Recessionary Gap

What if the economy produces less than its potential? Suppose the aggregate demand curve *AD* in Exhibit 1 intersects the aggregate supply curve at point *e″*, yielding the short-run output of $16.5 trillion and price level of 105. Output falls short of the economy's potential, opening up a recessionary gap of $0.5 trillion. Unemployment exceeds the natural rate. If markets adjusted naturally to high unemployment, the short-run aggregate supply curve would shift rightward in the long run to achieve equilibrium at the economy's potential output, point *e*. History suggests, however, that wages and other resource prices could be slow to respond to a recessionary gap.

Suppose policy makers believe that natural market forces will take too long to return the economy to potential output. They also believe that the appropriate increase

---

Discretionary Fiscal Policy to Close a Recessionary Gap

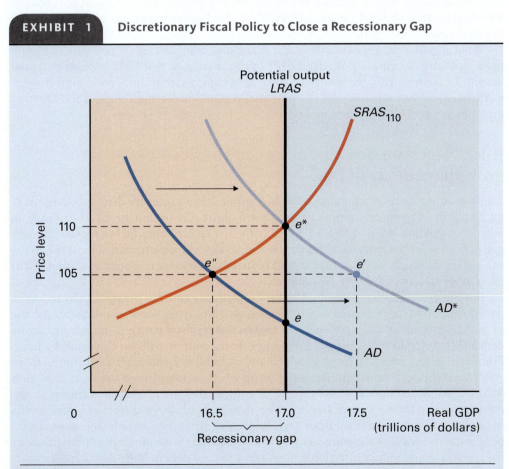

The aggregate demand curve *AD* and the short-run aggregate supply curve, *SRAS*$_{110}$, intersect at point *e″*. Output falls short of the economy's potential. The resulting recessionary gap could be closed by discretionary fiscal policy that increases aggregate demand by just the right amount. An increase in government purchases, a decrease in net taxes, or some combination could shift aggregate demand out to *AD**, moving the economy out to its potential output at *e**.

in government purchases, decrease in net taxes, or some combination of the two could increase aggregate demand just enough to return the economy to its potential output. A \$0.2 trillion increase in government purchases reflects an **expansionary fiscal policy** that increases aggregate demand, as shown in Exhibit 1 by the rightward shift from AD to AD^*. If the price level remained at 105, the additional spending would increase the quantity demanded from \$16.5 to \$17.5 trillion. This increase of \$1.0 trillion reflects the simple spending multiplier effect, given a constant price level.

At the original price level of 105, however, excess quantity demanded causes the price level to rise. As the price level rises, real GDP supplied increases, but real GDP demanded decreases along the new aggregate demand curve. The price level rises until quantity demanded equals quantity supplied. In Exhibit 1, the new aggregate demand curve intersects the aggregate supply curve at e^*, where the price level is 110, the one originally expected, and output equals potential GDP of \$17.0 trillion. Note that *an expansionary fiscal policy aims to close a recessionary gap*.

The intersection at point e^* is not only a short-run equilibrium but also a long-run equilibrium. If fiscal policy makers are accurate enough (or lucky enough), the appropriate fiscal stimulus can close the recessionary gap and foster a long-run equilibrium at potential GDP. But the increase in output results in a higher price level. What's more, if the federal budget was in balance before the fiscal stimulus, an increase in government spending creates a budget deficit. In fact, the federal government has run deficits in all but four years since 1960.

What if policy makers overshoot the mark and stimulate aggregate demand more than necessary to achieve potential GDP? In the short run, real GDP exceeds potential output. In the long run, the short-run aggregate supply curve shifts back until it intersects the aggregate demand curve at potential output, increasing the price level further but reducing real GDP to potential output.

11-1c Discretionary Fiscal Policy to Close an Expansionary Gap

Suppose output exceeds potential GDP. In Exhibit 2, the aggregate demand curve, AD', intersects the aggregate supply curve to yield short-run output of \$17.5 trillion, an amount exceeding the potential of \$17.0 trillion. The economy faces an expansionary gap of \$0.5 trillion. Ordinarily, this gap would be closed by a leftward shift of the short-run aggregate supply curve, which would return the economy to potential output but at a higher price level, as shown by point e''.

But the use of discretionary fiscal policy introduces another possibility. By reducing government purchases, increasing net taxes, or employing some combination of the two, the government can implement a **contractionary fiscal policy** to reduce aggregate demand. This could move the economy to potential output without the resulting inflation. If the policy succeeds, aggregate demand in Exhibit 2 shifts leftward from AD' to AD^*, establishing a new equilibrium at point e^*. Again, with just the right reduction in aggregate demand, output falls to \$17.0 trillion, the potential GDP. Closing an expansionary gap through fiscal policy rather than through natural market forces results in a lower price level, not a higher one. Increasing net taxes or reducing government purchases also reduces a government deficit or increases a surplus. So a contractionary fiscal policy could reduce inflation and reduce a federal deficit. Note that *a contractionary fiscal policy aims to close an expansionary gap*.

Such precisely calculated expansionary and contractionary fiscal policies are difficult to achieve. Their proper execution assumes that (1) potential output is accurately gauged, (2) the relevant spending multiplier can be predicted accurately, (3) aggregate

EXHIBIT 2 Discretionary Fiscal Policy to Close an Expansionary Gap

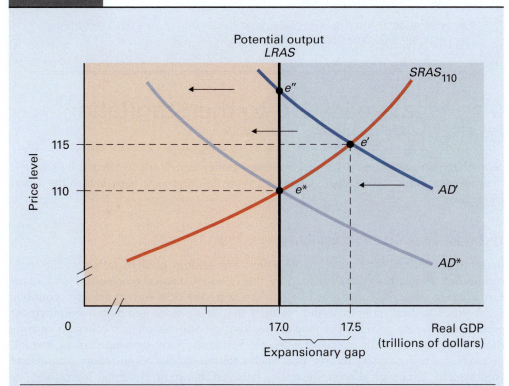

The aggregate demand curve *AD'* and the short-run aggregate supply curve, *SRAS*₁₁₀, intersect at point *e'*, resulting in an expansionary gap of $0.5 trillion. Discretionary fiscal policy aimed at reducing aggregate demand by just the right amount could close this gap without inflation. An increase in net taxes, a decrease in government purchases, or some combination could shift the aggregate demand curve back to *AD** and move the economy back to potential output at point *e**.

demand can be shifted by just the right amount, (4) various government entities can somehow coordinate their fiscal efforts, and (5) the shape of the short-run aggregate supply curve is known and remains unaffected by the fiscal policy itself.

11-1d The Multiplier and the Time Horizon

In the short run, the aggregate supply curve slopes upward, so a shift of aggregate demand changes both the price level and the output level. When aggregate supply gets in the act, we find that the simple multiplier overstates the amount by which output changes. The exact change of equilibrium output in the short run depends on the steepness of the aggregate supply curve, which in turn depends on how sharply production costs increase as output expands. *The steeper the short-run aggregate supply curve, the less impact a given shift of the aggregate demand curve has on real GDP and the more impact it has on the price level, so the smaller the spending multiplier.*

If the economy is already producing its potential, then in the long run, any change in fiscal policy aimed at stimulating aggregate demand increases the price level but does not affect output. Thus, *if the economy is already producing its potential, the spending multiplier in the long run is zero.*

CHECKPOINT

What discretionary fiscal policies could close a recessionary gap? What discretionary fiscal policies could close an expansionary gap?

11-2 Fiscal Policy Up to the Stagflation of the 1970s

Now that you have some idea of how fiscal policy can work in theory, let's take a look at fiscal policy in practice, beginning with the approach used before the Great Depression.

11-2a Before the Great Depression

classical economists
A group of 18th- and 19th-century economists who believed that economic downturns corrected themselves through natural market forces

Before the 1930s, discretionary fiscal policy was seldom used to influence the macroeconomy. Public policy was shaped by the views of **classical economists**, who advocated *laissez-faire*, the belief that free markets were the best way to achieve economic prosperity. Classical economists did not deny that depressions and high unemployment occurred from time to time, but they argued that the sources of such crises lay outside the market system, in the effects of wars, tax increases, poor growing seasons, natural disasters, changing tastes, and the like. Such external shocks could reduce output and employment, but classical economists also believed that natural market forces, such as changes in prices, wages, and interest rates, could correct these problems.

Simply put, classical economists argued that if the economy's price level was too high to sell all that was produced, prices would fall until the quantity supplied equaled the quantity demanded. If wages were too high to employ all who wanted to work, wages would fall until the quantity of labor supplied equaled the quantity demanded. And if the interest rate was too high to invest all that had been saved, interest rates would fall until the amount invested equaled the amount saved.

So the classical approach implied that natural market forces, through flexible prices, wages, and interest rates, would move the economy toward potential GDP. There appeared to be no need for government intervention. What's more, the government, like households, was expected to live within its means. The idea of government running a deficit year after year was considered immoral. Thus, before the onset of the Great Depression, most economists believed that discretionary fiscal policy could do more harm than good. Besides, the federal government itself was a bit player in the economy. At the onset of the Great Depression, for example, all U.S. federal outlays, which include both government purchases and transfer payments, were only about 3 percent relative to GDP (compared to about 22 percent today).

11-2b The Great Depression and World War II

Although classical economists acknowledged that capitalistic, market-oriented economies could experience high unemployment from time to time, the depth and duration of the Depression strained belief in the economy's ability to heal itself. The Great Depression was marked by four consecutive years of contraction during which unemployment reached 25 percent. Investment plunged 80 percent. Many factories sat idle. With vast unemployed resources, output and income fell well short of the economy's potential.

The stark contrast between the natural market adjustments predicted by classical economists and the years of high unemployment during the Great Depression represented a collision of theory and fact. In 1936, John Maynard Keynes, of Cambridge University in England, published *The General Theory of Employment, Interest, and Money,* a book that challenged the classical view and touched off what would later be called the Keynesian revolution. *Keynesian theory and policy were developed in response to the problem of high unemployment during the Great Depression.* Keynes's main quarrel with the classical economists was that prices and wages did not seem to be flexible enough to ensure the full employment of resources. According to Keynes, prices and wages were relatively inflexible in the downward direction—they were "sticky"— so natural market forces would not return the economy to full employment in a timely fashion. Keynes also believed business expectations could at times become so grim that even very low interest rates would not spur firms to invest all that consumers might save.

Three developments in the years following the Great Depression bolstered the use of discretionary fiscal policy in the United States. The first was the influence of Keynes's *General Theory,* in which he argued that natural forces would not necessarily close a recessionary gap. Keynes thought the economy could get stuck well below its potential, requiring the government to increase aggregate demand to boost output and employment. The second development was the impact of World War II on output and employment. The demands of war greatly increased production and erased cyclical unemployment during the war years, pulling the U.S. economy out of its depression. The third development, largely a consequence of the first two, was the passage of the **Employment Act of 1946**, which gave the federal government responsibility for promoting full employment and price stability.

Prior to the Great Depression, the dominant fiscal policy was a balanced budget. During 1929, the year the stock market crashed, and 1930, the first full year of the Great Depression, the federal budget yielded surpluses. Indeed, to reduce a deficit in 1932, federal tax rates were raised. In the wake of Keynes's *General Theory* and World War II, however, policy makers grew more receptive to the idea that fiscal policy could improve economic stability. The objective of fiscal policy was no longer to balance the budget, but instead to promote full employment with price stability even if budget deficits resulted.

Employment Act of 1946
Law that assigned to the federal government the responsibility for promoting full employment and price stability

11-2c Automatic Stabilizers

This chapter so far has focused mostly on discretionary fiscal policy—conscious decisions by public policy makers to change taxes and government spending to achieve the economy's potential output. Now let's get a clearer picture of automatic stabilizers. *Automatic stabilizers smooth out fluctuations in disposable income over the business cycle by stimulating aggregate demand during recessions and dampening aggregate demand during expansions.* Consider the federal income tax. The federal income tax system is progressive, meaning that the fraction of income paid in taxes increases as a taxpayer's income increases. During an economic expansion, employment and incomes rise, moving some taxpayers into higher tax brackets. As a result, taxes claim a growing fraction of income. This slows the growth in disposable income and, hence, slows the growth in consumption. Therefore, the progressive income tax relieves some of the inflationary pressure that might otherwise arise as output increases during an economic expansion. Conversely, when the economy is in recession, output declines, and employment and incomes fall, moving some people into lower tax brackets. As a result, taxes take a smaller bite out of income, so disposable income does not fall as much as GDP. Thus, the progressive income tax cushions declines in disposable income, in consumption, and in aggregate demand.

Another automatic stabilizer is unemployment insurance. During economic expansions, the system automatically increases the flow of unemployment insurance taxes from the income stream into the unemployment insurance fund, thereby moderating consumption and aggregate demand. During contractions, unemployment increases and the system reverses itself. Unemployment payments automatically flow from the insurance fund to the unemployed, increasing disposable income and propping up consumption and aggregate demand. Likewise, welfare payments automatically increase during hard times as more people become eligible. *Because of these automatic stabilizers, GDP fluctuates less than it otherwise would, and disposable income varies proportionately less than does GDP.* Because disposable income varies less than GDP does, consumption also fluctuates less than GDP does (as was shown in an earlier chapter's case study).

The progressive income tax, unemployment insurance, and welfare benefits were initially designed not so much as automatic stabilizers but as income redistribution programs. Their roles as automatic stabilizers were secondary effects of the legislation. Automatic stabilizers do not eliminate economic fluctuations, but they do reduce their magnitude. The stronger and more effective the automatic stabilizers are, the less need for discretionary fiscal policy. Because of the greater influence of automatic stabilizers, *the economy is more stable today than it was during the Great Depression and before.* As a measure of just how successful these automatic stabilizers have become in cushioning the impact of recessions, consider this: Since 1948, real GDP declined 10 years, but real consumption fell only four years—in 1974, 1980, 2008, and 2009. *Without much fanfare, automatic stabilizers have been quietly doing their work, keeping the economy on a more even keel.*

11-2d From the Golden Age to Stagflation

The 1960s were the Golden Age of fiscal policy. John F. Kennedy was the first president to propose a federal budget deficit to stimulate an economy experiencing a recessionary gap. Fiscal policy was also used on occasion to provide an extra kick to an expansion already under way, as in 1964, when Kennedy's successor, Lyndon B. Johnson, cut income tax rates to keep an expansion alive. *This tax cut, introduced to stimulate business investment, consumption, and employment, was perhaps the shining example of fiscal policy during the Golden Age.* The tax cut seemed to work wonders, increasing disposable income and consumption. The unemployment rate dropped under 5 percent for the first time in seven years, the inflation rate dipped under 2 percent, and the federal budget deficit in 1964 equaled only 0.9 percent of GDP (compared with an average of 3.4 percent between 1980 and 2015).

Discretionary fiscal policy is a demand-management policy; the objective is to increase or decrease aggregate demand to smooth economic fluctuations. But the 1970s brought a different problem—stagflation, the double trouble of higher inflation and higher unemployment resulting from a decrease in aggregate supply. The aggregate supply curve shifted left because of crop failures around the world, sharply higher OPEC-driven oil prices, and other adverse supply shocks. Demand-management policies are ill suited to cure stagflation because an increase of aggregate demand would increase inflation, whereas a decrease of aggregate demand would increase unemployment.

 **CHECKPOINT**

Summarize fiscal policy from the Great Depression to stagflation.

11-3 Limits on Fiscal Policy's Effectiveness

Other concerns besides stagflation also caused policy makers and economists to question the effectiveness of discretionary fiscal policy. These concerns include the difficulty of estimating the natural rate of unemployment, the time lags involved in implementing fiscal policy, the distinction between current income and permanent income, and the possible feedback effects of fiscal policy on aggregate supply. We consider each in turn.

11-3a Estimating the Natural Rate of Unemployment

As discussed in the previous chapter, the unemployment that occurs when the economy is producing its potential GDP is called the *natural rate of unemployment.* Before adopting discretionary policies, public officials must correctly estimate this natural rate. Suppose the economy is producing its potential output of $17.0 trillion, as in Exhibit 3, where the natural rate of unemployment is 5.0 percent. Also suppose that public officials mistakenly believe the natural rate to be 4.0 percent, and they attempt to reduce unemployment and increase real GDP through discretionary fiscal policy. As a result of their policy, the aggregate demand curve shifts to the right, from *AD* to *AD'*. In the short run, this stimulation of aggregate demand expands output to $17.2 trillion and reduces unemployment to 4.0 percent, so the policy appears successful. But stimulating

EXHIBIT 3 **When Discretionary Fiscal Policy Overshoots Potential Output**

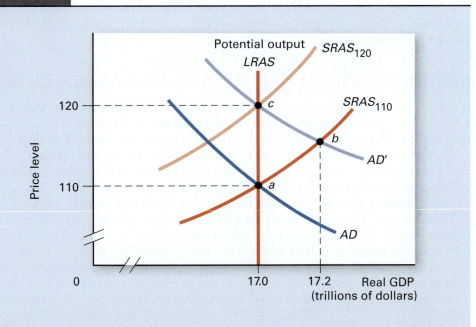

If public officials underestimate the natural rate of unemployment, they may attempt to stimulate aggregate demand even if the economy is already producing its potential output, as at point *a*. This expansionary policy yields a short-run equilibrium at point *b*, where the price level and output are higher and unemployment is lower, so the policy appears to succeed. But the resulting expansionary gap will, in the long run, reduce the short-run aggregate supply curve from $SRAS_{110}$ to $SRAS_{120}$, eventually reducing output to its potential level of $17.0 trillion while increasing the price level to 120. Thus, attempts to increase production beyond potential GDP lead only to inflation in the long run.

aggregate demand opens up an expansionary gap, which in the long run results in a leftward shift of the short-run aggregate supply curve. This reduction in aggregate supply pushes up prices and reduces real GDP to $17.0 trillion, the economy's potential. Thus, policy makers initially believe their plan worked, but pushing production beyond the economy's potential leads only to inflation in the long run.

Given the effects of fiscal policy, particularly in the short run, we should not be surprised that elected officials might try to use it to get reelected. Research suggests that public officials use fiscal policy to boost their reelection chances. This has created what some argue is a **political business cycle**, which results from the economic fluctuations that occur when discretionary policy is manipulated for political gain. During an election year, incumbent presidents use expansionary policies to stimulate the economy. For example, a study of 18 industrial economies over three decades found that incumbents boosted healthcare spending during election years.[1] There is also evidence that municipal officials, just before an election, spend more on those public goods most visible to the electorate, such as city parks.[2]

political business cycles
Economic fluctuations that occur when discretionary policy is manipulated for political gain

11-3b Lags in Fiscal Policy

The time required to approve and implement fiscal legislation may hamper its effectiveness and weaken discretionary fiscal policy as a tool of macroeconomic stabilization. Even if a fiscal prescription is appropriate for the economy when proposed, the months and sometimes years required to approve and implement legislation means the medicine could do more harm than good. The policy might kick in only after the economy has already turned itself around. Because a recession is not usually identified until at least six months after it begins, and because the 11 recessions since 1945 lasted only 11 months on average, discretionary fiscal policy allows little room for error (more about timing problems in a later chapter).

11-3c Discretionary Fiscal Policy and Permanent Income

It was once believed that discretionary fiscal policy could be turned on and off like a water faucet, stimulating or dampening the economy at the right time by just the right amount. Given the marginal propensity to consume, tax changes could increase or decrease disposable income to bring about desired change in consumption. A more recent view suggests that people base their consumption decisions not merely on changes in their current income but also on changes in their permanent income.

Permanent income is the income a person expects on average over the long term. Altering tax rates does not affect consumption much if people view the change as only temporary. For example, one-time tax rebates seem to have had little impact on consumption. The stimulative effects of the $117 billion tax-rebate program in early 2008 were disappointing. Surveys showed that only about 20 percent of households spent most of their rebate check. Other households saved most of it or paid down debt.[3] The *temporary* nature of the tax cuts meant that households faced only a small increase in

permanent income
Income that individuals expect to receive on average over the long term

---

1. Niklas Potrafke, "The Growth of Public Health Expenditures in OECD Countries: Do Government Ideology and Electoral Motives Matter?" *Journal of Health Economics*, 29 (December 2010): 797–810.
2. Linda Goncalves Veiga and Francisco Jose Veiga, "Political Business Cycles at the Municipal Level," *Public Choice*, 131 (April 2007): 45–64.
3. See Matthew D. Shapiro and Joel Slemrod, "Did the 2008 Tax Rebates Stimulate Spending?" *American Economic Review,* 99 (May 2009): 374–379; and Kanishka Misra and Paolo Surico, "Consumption, Income Changes, and Heterogeneity: Evidence from Two Fiscal Stimulus Programs," *American Economic Journal: Macroeconomics*, 6 (October 2014): 84–106.

their permanent income. Because permanent income changed little, consumption changed little. In short, *to the extent that consumers base spending decisions on their permanent income, attempts to fine-tune the economy with temporary tax changes are less effective.*

CHECKPOINT

Identify some reasons why discretionary fiscal policy may not work very well.

11-4 Fiscal Policy from 1980 to 2007

After examining fiscal policy up through the era of stagflation and considering limitations of fiscal policy, you are in a position to look at fiscal policy in recent decades.

11-4a Fiscal Policy During the 1980s

So far we have limited the discussion of fiscal policy to its effect on aggregate demand. Fiscal policy may also affect aggregate supply, although this is usually unintentional. For example, suppose the government increases unemployment benefits, paid for by higher taxes on earnings. If the marginal propensity to consume is the same for both groups, the increased spending by beneficiaries just offsets the reduced spending by workers. There would be no change in aggregate demand and thus no change in equilibrium real GDP, simply a redistribution of disposable income from the employed to the unemployed.

But could the program affect labor supply? Higher unemployment benefits reduce the opportunity cost of not working, so some job seekers may decide to search at a more leisurely pace. Meanwhile, higher tax rates reduce the opportunity cost of leisure, so some with jobs may decide to work fewer hours. In short, the supply of labor could decrease as a result of higher unemployment benefits funded by higher taxes on earnings. A decrease in the supply of labor would decrease aggregate supply, reducing the economy's potential GDP.

Both automatic stabilizers, such as unemployment insurance, welfare benefits, and the progressive income tax, and discretionary fiscal policies, such as legislated changes in tax rates, may affect individual incentives to work, spend, save, and invest, although these effects are usually unintended consequences. We should keep these secondary effects in mind when we evaluate fiscal policies. It was concern about the effects of taxes on the supply of labor that motivated the tax cuts approved in 1981, when President Reagan and Congress agreed on a 23 percent reduction in average income tax rates to increase aggregate supply. But government spending grew faster than tax revenue, causing higher budget deficits, which stimulated aggregate demand. The incentive effects of the tax cuts on aggregate supply and the stimulus effects of deficit spending on aggregate demand both contributed to the longest peacetime expansion to that point in the nation's history.

11-4b 1990 to 2007: From Deficits to Surpluses Back to Deficits

The large federal budget deficits of the 1980s and first half of the 1990s reduced the use of discretionary fiscal policy as a tool for economic stabilization. Because deficits were already high during economic expansions, it was hard to justify increasing deficits to stimulate the economy. For example, President Clinton proposed a modest stimulus package in early 1993 to help the recovery that was already under way. His opponents blocked the measure, arguing that it would increase the budget deficit. President George W. Bush's tax cuts during his first term were widely criticized by the opposition as budget-busting sources of a widening deficit.

Clinton did not get his way with his stimulus package, but in 1993, he did manage to substantially increase taxes on high-income households, a group that pays the lion's share of federal income taxes (the top 10 percent of earners pay about 70 percent of federal income taxes collected). The Republican Congress elected in 1994 imposed more discipline on federal spending as part of their plan to balance the budget. Meanwhile, the economy experienced a strong recovery fueled by growing consumer spending, rising business optimism based on technological innovation, market globalization, and the strongest stock market in history. The confluence of these events—higher taxes on the rich, more spending discipline, and a strengthening economy—changed the dynamic of the federal budget. Tax revenues gushed into Washington, growing an average of 8.3 percent per year between 1993 and 1998; meanwhile, federal outlays remained in check, growing only 3.2 percent per year. By 1998, that one-two punch knocked out the federal deficit, a deficit that only six years earlier reached a record at the time of $290 billion. The federal surplus grew from $69 billion in 1998 to $236 billion in 2000.

But in early 2001, the economy suffered a recession, so newly elected President George W. Bush pushed through an across-the-board $1.35 trillion, ten-year tax cut to "get the economy moving again." Then on September 11, 2001, 19 men in four hijacked airplanes ended thousands of lives and reduced the chances of a strong economic recovery. Although the recession lasted only eight months, the recovery was weak, and jobs did not start coming back until the second half of 2003, nearly two years after the recession officially ended. But, between 2003 and 2007, the economy added more than 8 million jobs. By late 2007, the economic expansion, which began in late 2001, had lasted six years, somewhat longer than average for expansions after World War II. The economy peaked in December 2007. The strengthening economy helped cut the federal deficit from $413 billion in 2004 to $161 billion in 2007. Then the economy fell apart.

 **CHECKPOINT**

Summarize fiscal policy during the 1980s and 1990s. When and why did the federal budget show a surplus?

11-5 Fiscal Policy During and After the Great Recession

After peaking in December 2007, the U.S. economy entered a recession, this time precipitated by declining home prices and rising foreclosure rates, as more borrowers failed to make their mortgage payments. The recession began quietly. Many economists doubted that one was even underway (the starting date of December 2007 would not be officially announced until a year later). But as a precaution, Congress and President Bush enacted a $168 billion plan in early 2008 to stimulate the softening economy. The centerpiece was a $117 billion one-time tax rebate of up to $600 for individual filers and up to $1,200 for joint filers. Probably because the tax cuts were temporary, the results were disappointing and the stimulation minimal. As noted already, surveys showed that most households saved the rebate or used it to pay down debt; the marginal propensity to consume from rebate money was estimated to be less than one-third.

After a quiet start, the recession gathered steam. Job losses jumped six-fold from an average of 31,000 a month during the first quarter of 2008 to an average of 191,000 a month in the second quarter. Then things got worse. In the third quarter, monthly job losses averaged 334,000.

11-5a The Financial Crisis

The problems of falling home prices and rising default rates that simmered throughout 2007 and the first half of 2008 reached a boiling point in September 2008 when Lehman Brothers, the nation's fourth-largest investment bank, with assets of over $600 billion and about 25,000 employees, filed for what became the largest bankruptcy in U.S. history. The financial crisis froze credit markets around the world. Nobody wanted to lend for fear that the borrower might go bankrupt.

Facing financial chaos, public policy makers were emboldened to take some extraordinary measures. The first of these was the Troubled Asset Relief Program, or TARP, passed in October 2008 and aimed at unfreezing financial flows by investing what ultimately totaled $426 billion in financial institutions and in two car makers (these investments became known derisively as "bailouts"). Nearly all that was eventually paid back with interest to the U.S. Treasury (the Treasury lost about $9 billion on its $80 billion investment in General Motors and Chrysler). TARP, to be discussed in a later chapter, helped calm credit markets, but the economy and the stock market continued to worsen. In the fourth quarter of 2008, real GDP fell 8.2 percent from the previous quarter (at an annualized rate), the largest drop in many decades, and job losses averaged 662,000 a month, or 21 times the average during the first three months of the year. The unemployment rate in 2008 climbed from 5.0 percent in January to 7.4 percent in December, at the time the highest in nearly two decades.

11-5b President Obama's Stimulus Package

With the economy bleeding jobs, policy makers had a sense of urgency if not panic. On February 17, 2009, newly-elected President Barack Obama signed the **American Recovery and Reinvestment Act**, a $787 billion package of tax benefits and spending programs aimed at stimulating aggregate demand. The president called the measure "the most sweeping economic recovery package in our history." He predicted the measure would "create or save three and a half million jobs over the next two years." The projected cost would later rise to $831 billion, or about $7,000 per U.S. household.

According to the White House Web site Recovery.gov, which was created to track the stimulus package and its consequences, 37 percent funded tax cuts, 28 percent funded entitlements (such as Medicaid), and 35 percent funded grants, contracts, and loans. Most of the tax cuts were one-time reductions for individuals. Grants, contracts, and loans included some "shovel-ready" infrastructure projects, such as bridges and roads, but these projects were slow to get underway and they represented just a small fraction of stimulus spending (only 4 percent of stimulus funds went to the Federal Highway Administration for road and bridge projects).

The stimulus package was all deficit spending. The rationale for deficit spending is that unemployed labor and idle capital will be put to work. And if the spending multiplier exceeds 1.0, a dollar of government spending should produce more than a dollar of new output and income. Thus, the effectiveness of any stimulus program depends

American Recovery and Reinvestment Act

At an estimated cost of $831 billion, the largest stimulus measure in U.S history; enacted in February 2009

on the size of the tax and spending multipliers. During the debate on the measure, one group of economists argued that the multipliers were less than 1.0 and another group, including the president's economists, argued they were greater than 1.0. Unfortunately, because of chronic deficits since the early 1980s, discretionary fiscal policies had not been used much, at least not explicitly, so few researchers had attempted to measure those effects, and not all those researchers tried to estimate multipliers.

Still, recent research suggests that *permanent* tax cuts had more of an impact on the economy than government spending increases, and of those studies that tried to estimate a government spending multiplier, the average was less than 1.0. For example, a recent study of more than 100 developing countries between 1970 and 2010 estimated a government spending multiplier of only 0.4.[4]

11-5c Fiscal Policy Since 2007

To gain some perspective on fiscal policy during and after the Great Recession, which began in December 2007, let's look at federal spending and federal deficits during the period. The height of each bar of Exhibit 4 shows nominal federal spending from 2007 through 2014. The blue portion of each bar shows the amount funded by federal revenue sources, such as taxes, charges, and the like. The red portion of each bar shows the amount that was borrowed—that is, deficit financing. For example, in 2007, $2,567 billion of federal spending came from federal revenue and $161 billion was borrowed.

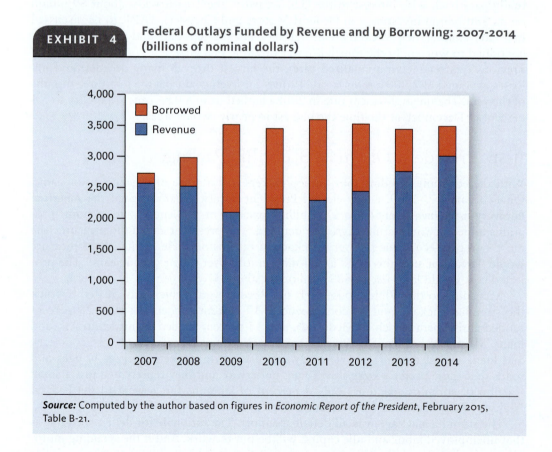

EXHIBIT 4   **Federal Outlays Funded by Revenue and by Borrowing: 2007-2014 (billions of nominal dollars)**

Source: Computed by the author based on figures in *Economic Report of the President*, February 2015, Table B-21.

[4.] Aart Kraay, "Government Spending Multipliers in Developing Countries: Evidence from Lending by Official Creditors," *American Economic Journal: Macroeconomics*, 6 (October 2014): 170–208.

Thus, 6 percent of spending that year was from borrowing. Real GDP in 2007 increased by 1.8 percent.

Federal spending rose 9.3 percent in 2008, the first full year of the Great Recession. Fifteen percent of federal spending was borrowed in 2008. Real GDP declined 0.3 percent, and 3.6 million jobs were lost. Because of the $831 billion stimulus program signed by President Obama in February 2009, federal spending in 2009 rose 17.8 percent. That's the fastest peacetime growth rate in federal spending since the Great Depression. Of the $3,518 billion spent in 2009, $1,413 had to be borrowed. You can see from Exhibit 4 that the federal deficit grew in 2009 because spending increased and revenue decreased. Alongside the stimulus plan in 2009, automatic stabilizers kicked in to boost spending and reduce revenue. As a result, 40 percent of spending in 2009 had to be borrowed, the highest share of deficit financing since World War II. Despite all the fiscal stimulus coming from a 17.8 percent increase in spending and a $1,413 billion deficit, real GDP in 2009 declined by 2.8 percent, and the economy lost 5.1 million jobs. Supporters of the stimulus program said the economy would have been much worse without the stimulus. For example, President Obama claimed that this stimulus package prevented another Great Depression.[5]

In 2010, 37 percent of federal spending was borrowed. Real GDP that year rose 2.5 percent, and 1.1 million jobs were added back, making 2010 the first full year of economic recovery. But four years of trillion-dollar deficits seemed to limit federal spending between 2009 and 2014. Notice in Exhibit 4 that after the jump in federal outlays in 2009, nominal federal spending remained relatively flat through 2014. In inflation-adjusted dollars, federal spending actually declined. The share of spending coming from borrowed funds fell, too, from 40 percent in 2009 to 14 percent in 2014. Thus, any fiscal stimulus offered by the federal budget declined between 2009 and 2014, both because real federal spending declined and because deficit spending as a share of total spending declined.

Economists will be debating for years the actual impact of fiscal policy during this period. After the 2.8 percent drop in 2009, real GDP growth averaged 2.2 percent a year between 2010 and 2014. By April 2014 the economy had added all the jobs lost during the Great Recession, and by April 2015 had added another 3 million, for a net job growth of 2.2 percent. Despite that performance, this was still one of the weakest economic recoveries on record (during a comparable period following the sharp recession of 1982, real GDP grew an average of 4.6 percent a year, and after quickly recovering jobs lost during the recession, the economy added 14 million more, for a net job growth of 15.3 percent).

Advocates of the stimulus package argue that the weak recovery showed just how bad off the economy was and just how much this fiscal stimulus was needed. Some said the federal government did not borrow enough or spend enough. Another group of economists believe that the fiscal stimulus was not very effective because the government spending multiplier was less than 1.0 and because the large deficits and accumulating debt created an uncertain business climate, a climate that put a damper on economic growth and job creation.

The stimulus measure was never very popular. During his State of the Union address early in the election year of 2012, President Obama did not mention it, nor did he bring it up much during his successful campaign for

5. Ross Covin, "Obama Stimulus Plan Halted Economic Freefall: White House," Reuters, 17 February 2010.

a second term that year. Regardless of the effect of these deficits on real GDP and employment, what we do know is that federal debt grew $6.7 trillion between 2008 and 2014. The first $6.7 trillion of federal debt took the nation more than 220 years to accumulate, as it did by the end of 2003. Implications of a growing federal debt will be discussed in the next chapter.

It is said that geologists learn more about the nature of the Earth's crust from one major upheaval, such as a huge earthquake or major volcanic eruption, than from a dozen lesser events. The recession of 2007–2009 traumatized the economy and the economics profession. Events will be dissected for years to develop a clearer understanding of how the economy works and what went wrong.

Congress and the president also adopted some more modest stimulus programs, such as tax incentives for home buyers and for car buyers. Let's look at the program to stimulate car sales.

CASE STUDY

PUBLIC POLICY

CASH FOR CLUNKERS   On June 24, 2009, President Obama signed into law the Consumer Assistance to Recycle and Save (CARS) Act, better known as the "cash-for-clunkers" program. The measure initially appropriated $1 billion to pay between $3,500 to $4,500 to each car buyer who traded a "clunker," or an older car with gas mileage of 18 miles per gallon or less, for a new one with better gas mileage. The clunker had to be "drivable," and registered and insured by the same person for at least a year prior to the sale (to prevent someone from buying a junk just to trade in).

Once car dealers began submitting paperwork for government reimbursement, it became clear the program would soon burn through the $1 billion appropriation. So Congress put $2 billion more into the pot and limited the program to a month (the $1 billion was originally expected to last four months). The 135 pages of government rules were constantly changing, and the Web site dealers used often crashed. The 2,000 people needed to process paperwork had trouble reimbursing dealers, so some dealers dropped out of the program.

Still, nearly 680,000 new vehicles were sold during the month of the program (to add some perspective, there were more than 230 million registered vehicles at the time in the United States). That spike in sales, some argue, was clear evidence of the program's success. For example, the Transportation Secretary claimed this "is the one stimulus program that seems to be working better

than just about any other program." And the program's Web site claimed it was "wildly successful." But evidence suggests that the overwhelming majority of those car sales would have occurred anyway during the last half of 2009. For example, according to analysis by the automotive site Edmunds.com, which tracks car sales, the net effect of the program was only 125,000 additional vehicle sales, implying a government cost of $24,000 per additional sale.

But even if the program was expensive on a per-vehicle basis, didn't the economy in general and car makers in particular need a boost? First, the $3 billion spent on the program was money the government didn't have;

Justin Sullivan/Getty Images News/Getty Images

continued

the outlays increased the federal deficit, already at record levels. Ultimately, to pay for the program, taxes must be raised or other government spending must be cut. Even at a low interest rate of, say, 3.0%, the federal government will spend an extra $90 million a year just to pay the interest on that additional debt. Second, at least some of the stimulus benefited other economies. Japanese manufacturers accounted for 41 percent of the program sales and the Big Three (General Motors, Ford, and Chrysler), 39 percent. Third, automakers already received $80 billion in bailout funds ($9 billion of that was not repaid). What about helping other sectors hit hard by the Great Recession such as furniture makers and the travel industry? Why not "cash for couches" or "cash for cruises"?

Proponents of cash for clunkers would point out that cars are a special case, because a second objective of the program was to clear the air by replacing clunkers with cars that would get maybe 10 more miles to the gallon. Christopher Knittel, now of MIT, estimated that the government could have gotten 10 times more carbon reduction by spending the $3 billion in the market for carbon offsets.

For most buyers, the clunker money served as the down payment on a new car, so more people could afford one, and didn't that stimulate the economy? From that stimulus effect must be subtracted the housing, furniture, clothes, vacation trips, and other items that those consumers wouldn't be buying in the future, because they faced additional monthly payments for car leases or car loans. Finally, by mandating the destruction of each trade-in vehicle (a disposal facility had to crush or shred each clunker with evidence of such supplied to the government), Congress removed up to 680,000 drivable cars from the used-car market, inevitably raising the prices of the used cars that low-income households tend to buy. The destruction also reduced the supply of salvageable used parts that are bought mostly by low-income drivers looking to keep their cars running. Cash for clunkers was never that popular with the public. Polls show that most Americans did not approve of the program.

Sources: Ryan Sandler, "Clunkers or Junkers? Adverse Selection in a Vehicle Retirement Program," *American Economic Journal: Economic Policy*, 4 (November 2012): 253–281; Brent Snavely, "Price Tag On Auto Bailout: $9.3B," *Arizona Republic*, 1 January 2015; Shanjun Li, Joshua Linn, and Elisheba Spiller, "Evaluating 'Cash-for-Clunkers': Program Effects on Auto Sales and the Environment," *Journal of Environmental Economics and Management*, 65 (March 2013): 165–193; Mark R. Jacobsen and Arthur A. van Bentham, "Vehicle Scrappage and Gasoline Policy," *American Economic Review*, 105 (March 2015): 1312–1338; Christopher R. Knittel, "The Implied Cost of Carbon Dioxide Under the Cash for Clunkers Program," Working Paper (31 August 2009), at http://www.econ.ucdavis.edu/faculty/knittel/papers/CfC_final_latest.pdf; and the federal government program's site at http://www.cars.gov/.

 **CHECKPOINT**

Summarize fiscal policy during and after the Great Recession. Contrast the opinions about the effectiveness of fiscal policy during this period?

11-6 Conclusion

This chapter discussed fiscal policy in theory and in practice. It also examined several factors that reduce the effectiveness of fiscal policy. In the short run, the aggregate supply curve slopes upward, so the impact on equilibrium output of any change in aggregate demand is blunted by a change in the price level. In the long run, aggregate supply is a vertical line, so if the economy is already producing at its potential, the spending multiplier is zero. To the extent that consumers respond primarily to changes in their permanent incomes, temporary changes in taxes affect consumption less, so the tax multiplier is smaller. Various lags in fiscal policy also limit its effectiveness. Discretionary fiscal policy is presented in greater detail in the Appendix.

Summary

1. The tools of fiscal policy are automatic stabilizers and discretionary fiscal measures. Automatic stabilizers, such as the federal income tax, once implemented, operate year after year without congressional action. Discretionary fiscal policy results from specific legislation about government spending, taxation, and transfers. If that legislation becomes permanent, then discretionary fiscal policies often become automatic stabilizers.

2. In theory, an expansionary fiscal policy can close a recessionary gap by increasing government purchases, reducing net taxes, or both. Because the short-run aggregate supply curve slopes upward, an increase in aggregate demand raises both output and the price level in the short run. In theory, a contractionary fiscal policy can close an expansionary gap by reducing government purchases, increasing net taxes, or both. Fiscal policy that reduces aggregate demand to close an expansionary gap reduces both output and the price level.

3. Fiscal policy focuses primarily on the demand side, not the supply side. The problems of the 1970s, however, resulted more from a decline of aggregate supply than from a decline of aggregate demand, so demand-side remedies seemed less effective.

4. After the "supply-side" tax cuts of the early 1980s, government spending grew faster than tax revenue, creating sizable budget deficits. The incentive effects of tax cuts on aggregate supply combined with the stimulative effects of deficit spending on aggregate demand, contributed to the longest peacetime expansion to that point in the nation's history. These large deficits discouraged additional discretionary fiscal policy as a way of stimulating aggregate demand further, but success in erasing deficits in the late 1990s spawned renewed interest in discretionary fiscal policy, as reflected by President Bush's tax cuts in the face of the 2001 recession.

5. Tax cuts and new spending increased deficits into 2004, but the economy added over 8 million jobs by 2007. The added output and income cut the federal deficit from about $400 billion in 2004 to about $160 billion in 2007.

6. After peaking in December 2007, the economy turned down, as consumers, firms, and financial markets were spooked by falling home prices and rising foreclosure rates. Job losses increased sharply after the financial crisis of September 2008. Government officials first tried to calm financial markets with TARP, then tried to stimulate the economy with the largest fiscal program in history. The economy lost 8.7 million jobs between December 2007 and December 2009. Those jobs returned by 2014, but economic growth during the recovery was still among the weakest on record.

Key Concepts

Automatic stabilizers   234

Discretionary fiscal policy   234

Expansionary fiscal policy   236

Contractionary fiscal policy   236

Classical economists   238

Employment Act of 1946   239

Political business cycles   242

Permanent income   242

American Recovery and Reinvestment Act   245

Questions for Review

1. **Fiscal Policy**   Define *fiscal policy*. Determine whether each of the following, other factors held constant, would, in the short run, lead to an increase, a decrease, or no change in the level of real GDP demanded:

    a. A decrease in government purchases
    b. An increase in net taxes
    c. A reduction in transfer payments
    d. A decrease in the marginal propensity to consume

2. **The Multiplier and the Time Horizon**   Explain how the steepness of the short-run aggregate supply curve affects the government's ability to use fiscal policy to change real GDP.

3. **Evolution of Fiscal Policy**   What did classical economists assume about the flexibility of prices, wages, and interest rates? What did this assumption imply about the self-correcting tendencies in an economy in recession? What disagreements did Keynes have with classical economists?

4. **Automatic Stabilizers**   Often during recessions, the number of young people who volunteer for military service increases. Could this rise be considered a type of automatic stabilizer? Why or why not?

5. **Permanent Income**   "If the federal government wants to stimulate consumption by means of a tax cut, it should employ a permanent tax cut. If the government wants to stimulate saving in the short run, it should employ a temporary tax cut." Evaluate this statement.

6. **Fiscal Policy**   Explain why effective discretionary fiscal policy requires information about each of the following:

    a. The slope of the short-run aggregate supply curve
    b. The natural rate of unemployment
    c. The size of the spending multiplier
    d. The speed with which self-correcting forces operate

7. **Automatic Stabilizers**   Distinguish between discretionary fiscal policy and automatic stabilizers. Provide examples of automatic stabilizers. What is the impact of automatic stabilizers on disposable income as the economy moves through the business cycle?

8. **Fiscal Policy Effectiveness**   Determine whether each of the following would make fiscal policy more effective or less effective:

   a. A decrease in the marginal propensity to consume
   b. Shorter lags in the effect of fiscal policy
   c. Consumers suddenly becoming more concerned about permanent income than about current income
   d. More accurate measurement of the natural rate of unemployment

9. **From Deficits to Surpluses to Deficits**   What effect did the financial crisis of 2008 have on the federal budget deficit?

10. **Fiscal Policy from 2007 to 2014**   Despite sizable deficits from 2010 to 2012, in what two ways was the fiscal stimulus of federal spending declining?

11. **Case Study: Cash for Clunkers**   Studies indicate that the "Cash-for-Clunkers" program only shifted sales from later to earlier in 2009. Assuming that this is true, what was the spending multiplier for the program?

Problems and Exercises

12. **Fiscal Policy with an Expansionary Gap**   Using the aggregate demand–aggregate supply model, illustrate an economy with an expansionary gap. If the government is to close the gap by changing government purchases, should it increase or decrease those purchases? In the long run, what happens to the level of real GDP as a result of government intervention? What happens to the price level? Illustrate this on an AD–AS diagram, assuming that the government changes its purchases by exactly the amount necessary to close the gap.

13. **Fiscal Policy During the Great Recession**   Using the aggregate demand–aggregate supply model, illustrate what President Obama was trying to accomplish with the $831 billion stimulus program. What were some costs and benefits of this program?

Demand-Side Effects of Government Purchases and Net Taxes

Using the income-expenditure framework developed earlier, in this appendix we initially focus on the demand side to consider the effect of changes in government purchases, transfer payments, and taxes on real GDP demanded. The short story is this: *At any given price level, an increase in government purchases or in transfer payments increases real GDP demanded, and an increase in net taxes decreases real GDP demanded, other things constant.* Next, we see how and why.

Changes in Government Purchases

Let's begin by looking at Exhibit 5, with real GDP demanded of $17.0 trillion, as reflected at point *a,* where the aggregate expenditure line crosses the 45-degree line. Here we assume that government purchases and net taxes equal $1.0 trillion each and do not vary with income—that is, they are independent of income. Because government purchases equal net taxes, the government budget is balanced.

Now suppose federal policy makers, believing that unemployment is too high, decide to stimulate aggregate demand by increasing government purchases $0.1 trillion, or by $100 billion. To consider the effect on aggregate demand, let's initially assume that nothing else changes, including the price level and net taxes. This additional spending shifts the aggregate expenditure line up by $0.1 trillion to $C + I + G' + (X - M)$. At real GDP of $17.0 trillion, spending now exceeds output, so production increases. This increase in production increases income, which in turn increases spending, and so it goes through the series of spending rounds.

The initial increase of $0.1 trillion in government purchases eventually increases real GDP demanded at the given price level from $17.0 trillion to $17.5 trillion, shown as point *b* in Exhibit 5. Because output demanded increases by $0.5 trillion as a result of an increase of $0.1 trillion in government purchases, the multiplier in our example is equal to 5 (assuming, as in earlier chapters, that the marginal propensity to consume is 0.8). *As long as consumption is the only spending component that varies with income, the multiplier for a change in government purchases, other things constant, equals* $1/(1 - MPC)$, or $1/(1 - 0.8)$ in our example. Thus, we can say that for a given price level, and assuming that only consumption varies with income,

$$\Delta \text{ Real GDP demanded} = \Delta G \times \frac{1}{1 - MPC}$$

where, again, the delta symbol (Δ) means "change in." This same multiplier appeared two chapters back, when we discussed shifts of the consumption function.

Changes in Net Taxes

A change in net taxes also affects real GDP demanded, but the effect is less direct. A *decrease* in net taxes, other things constant, *increases* disposable income at each level of real GDP, so consumption increases. In Exhibit 6, we begin again at equilibrium point *a,* with real GDP demanded equal to $17.0 trillion. To stimulate aggregate demand, suppose federal policy makers cut net taxes by $0.1 trillion, or by $100 billion, other things constant. We assume that net taxes do not vary with income. A $100 billion reduction in net taxes could result from a tax cut, an increase in transfer payments, or some combination of the two. The $100 billion decrease in net taxes increases disposable income by $100 billion at each level of real GDP. Because households now have more disposable income, they spend more and save more at each level of real GDP.

Because households save some of the tax cut, consumption increases in the first round of spending by less than the full tax cut. Specifically, *consumption spending*

| EXHIBIT 5 | **Effect of a \$0.1 Trillion Increase in Government Purchases on Aggregate Expenditure and Real GDP Demanded** |

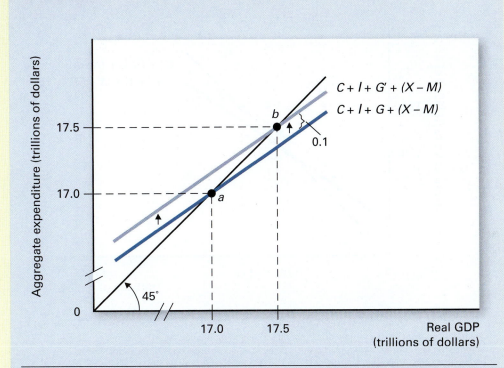

As a result of a \$0.1 trillion increase in government purchases, the aggregate expenditure line shifts up by \$0.1 trillion, increasing the level of real GDP demanded by \$0.5 trillion. This model assumes the price level remains unchanged.

at each level of real GDP rises by the decrease in net taxes multiplied by the marginal propensity to consume. In our example, consumption at each level of real GDP increases by \$100 billion times 0.8, or \$80 billion. Cutting net taxes by \$100 billion causes the aggregate expenditure line to shift up by \$80 billion, or \$0.08 trillion, at all levels of real GDP, as shown in Exhibit 6. This initial increase in spending triggers subsequent rounds of spending, following a now-familiar pattern in the income-expenditure cycle based on the marginal propensities to consume and to save. For example, the \$80 billion increase in consumption increases output and income by \$80 billion, which in the second round leads to \$64 billion in consumption and \$16 billion in saving, and so on through successive rounds. As a result, real GDP demanded eventually increases from \$17.0 trillion to \$17.4 trillion per year, or by \$400 billion.

The effect of a change in net taxes on real GDP demanded equals the resulting shift of the aggregate expenditure line times the simple spending multiplier. Thus, we can say that the effect of a change in net taxes is

$$\Delta \text{ Real GDP demanded} = (- MPC \times \Delta NT) \times \frac{1}{1 - MPC}$$

The simple spending multiplier is applied to the shift of the aggregate expenditure line that results from the change in net taxes. This equation can be rearranged as

$$\Delta \text{ Real GDP demanded} = \Delta NT \times \frac{-MPC}{1 - MPC}$$

where $-MPC/(1 - MPC)$ is the **simple tax multiplier**, which can be applied directly to the change in net taxes to yield the change in real GDP demanded at a given price level. This tax multiplier is called *simple* because, by assumption, only consumption varies with income (taxes do not vary with income). For example, with an MPC of 0.8, the simple tax multiplier equals -4. In our example, a *decrease* of \$0.1 trillion in net taxes results in an *increase* in real GDP demanded of \$0.4 trillion, assuming a given price level. As another example, an *increase* in net taxes

| EXHIBIT 6 | Effect of a $0.1 Trillion Decrease in Net Taxes on Aggregate Expenditure and Real GDP Demanded |

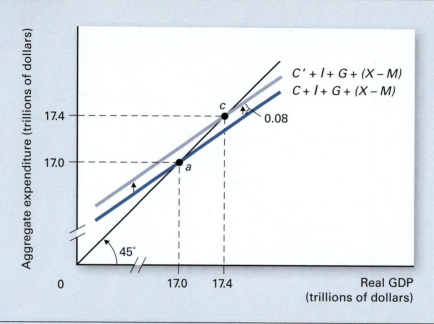

As a result of a decrease in net taxes of $0.1 trillion, or $100 billion, consumers, who are assumed to have a marginal propensity to consume of 0.8, spend $80 billion more and save $20 billion more at every level of real GDP. The consumption function shifts up by $80 billion, or $0.08 trillion, as does the aggregate expenditure line. An $80 billion increase of the aggregate expenditure line eventually increases real GDP demanded by $0.4 trillion. Keep in mind that the price level is assumed to remain constant during all this.

of $0.2 trillion would, other things constant, *decrease* real GDP demanded by $0.8 trillion.

Note two differences between the government purchase multiplier and the simple tax multiplier. First, the government purchase multiplier is positive, so an increase in government purchases leads to an increase in real GDP demanded. The simple tax multiplier is negative, so an increase in net taxes leads to a decrease in real GDP demanded. Second, the multiplier for a given change in government purchases is larger by 1 than the absolute value of the multiplier for an identical change in net taxes. In our example, the government purchase multiplier is 5, while the absolute value of the tax multiplier is 4. This holds because changes in government purchases affect aggregate spending directly—a $100 billion increase in government purchases increases spending in the first round by $100 billion. In contrast, a $100 billion decrease in net taxes increases consumption indirectly by way of a change in disposable income. Thus, each $100 billion decrease in net taxes increases disposable income by $100 billion, which, given an MPC of 0.8, increases consumption in the first round by $80 billion; people save the

other $20 billion. In short, at least in this simple model, an increase in government purchases has a greater impact on real GDP demanded than does an identical tax cut because some of the tax cut gets saved, so it leaks from the spending flow.

To Review: An increase in government purchases or a decrease in net taxes, other things constant, increases real GDP demanded. Although not shown, the combined effect of changes in government purchases and in net taxes is found by summing their individual effects.

Summary

The effect of an increase in government purchases on aggregate demand is the same as that of an increase in any other type of spending. Thus, the simple multiplier for a change in government purchases is $1/(1 - MPC)$. A decrease in net taxes (taxes minus transfer payments) affects consumption by increasing disposable income. A decrease in net taxes does not increase spending as much as would an identical increase in government purchases, because some of the tax cut is saved. The multiplier for a change in net taxes is $MPC/(1 - MPC)$.

Appendix Questions

1. **Changes in Government Purchases** Assume that government purchases decrease by $10 billion, with other factors held constant, including the price level. Calculate the change in the level of real GDP demanded for each of the following values of the MPC. Then, calculate the change if the government, instead of reducing its purchases, increased net taxes by $10 billion.

   a. 0.9
   b. 0.8
   c. 0.75
   d. 0.6

2. **Fiscal Multipliers** Explain the difference between the government purchases multiplier and the net tax multiplier. If the MPC falls, what happens to the net tax multiplier?

3. **Changes in Net Taxes** Using the income-expenditure model, graphically illustrate the impact of a $15 billion drop in government transfer payments on aggregate expenditure if the MPC equals 0.75. Explain why it has this impact. What is the impact on the level of real GDP demanded, assuming the price level remains unchanged?

4. **Fiscal Policy** This appendix shows how increased government purchases, with net taxes held constant, can eliminate a recessionary gap. How could a tax cut achieve the same result? Would the tax cut have to be larger than the increase in government purchases? Why or why not?

12 Federal Budgets and Public Policy

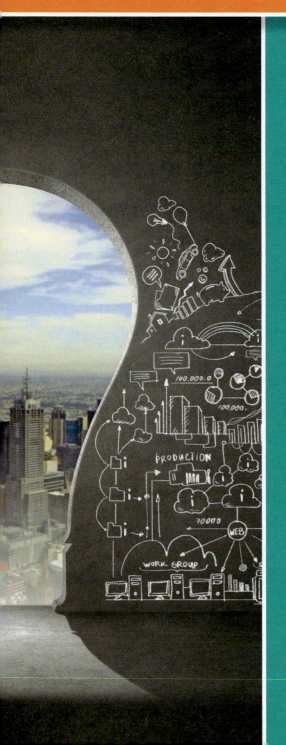

Jonathan Nourok/Photographer's Choice/Getty Images

- *How big is the U.S. federal budget, and where does the money go?*
- *Why is the federal budget process such a tangled web?*
- *In what sense is the federal budgeting process at odds with discretionary fiscal policy?*
- *How is a sluggish economy like an empty restaurant?*
- *Why has the federal budget been in deficit most years?*
- *What is the federal debt, and who owes it to whom?*
- *Can a nation run deficits year after year and decade after decade?*

Answers to these and other questions are examined in this chapter, which considers federal budgeting in theory and practice.

The word *budget* derives from the Old French word *bougette*, which means "little bag." The federal budget is now about $4,000,000,000,000—$4 trillion a year. That's big money! If this "little bag" held $100 bills, it would weigh 42,000 *tons*! These $100 bills could paper over a 24-lane highway stretching from northern Maine to California. A $4 trillion stack of $100 bills would tower 2,600 miles high. Here's another way to appreciate the size of the federal budget: If all 4,600 tons of gold stored in Fort Knox were sold at about $1,100 per ounce (the market price in mid-2015), the proceeds would fund the federal government for only about two weeks.

Government budgets have a tremendous impact on the economy. Government outlays at all levels amount to about 38 percent relative to GDP. Our focus in this chapter will be the federal budget, beginning with the budget process. We then look at federal deficits. We also examine the national debt and its impact on the economy. At some point, a giant federal debt could cripple the nation. Because you and your classmates will inherit liability for the federal debt, you may have a particular interest in this material.

Topics discussed in this chapter include:

- The federal budget process
- Rationale for deficit spending
- Impact of federal deficits
- Crowding out and crowding in
- The short-lived budget surplus
- Federal debt
- The sustainability of federal debt

12-1 The Federal Budget Process

The **federal budget** is a plan of outlays and revenues for a specified period, usually a year. Federal *outlays* include both government purchases and transfer payments. Exhibit 1 shows U.S. federal outlays by major category since 1960. As you can see, the share of outlays going to national defense dropped from over half in 1960 to only 15 percent in 2016. Social Security's share has grown every decade. Medicare, medical care for the elderly, was introduced in 1965 and has also grown sharply. In fact, Social Security and Medicare, programs aimed primarily at the elderly, combined for 38 percent of federal outlays in 2016. For the last two decades, welfare spending, which consists of cash and in-kind transfer payments, has remained relatively stable, and in 2016 accounted for 14 percent of federal outlays. And, thanks to record low interest rates, interest payments on federal debt were only 7 percent of federal outlays in 2016, down from 15 percent as recently as 1996. So 52 percent, or more than half the federal budget, redistributes income (Social Security, Medicare, and welfare); 15 percent goes for national defense; 7 percent services the federal debt; and the remaining 26 percent pays for everything else in the federal budget—from environmental protection to federal prisons to federal education aid. Note that the spike in "All Other Outlays" in 2009 was caused

federal budget
A plan for federal government outlays and revenues for a specified period, usually a year

EXHIBIT 1	Defense's Share of Federal Outlays Declined Since 1960 and Redistribution Increased

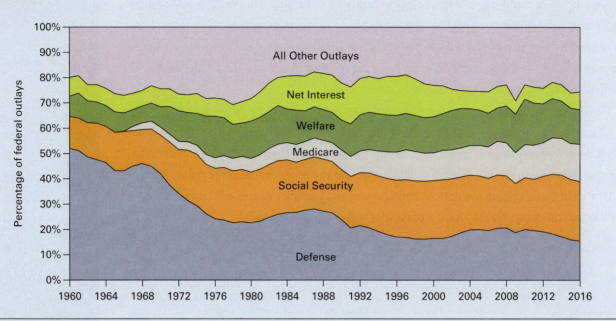

Source: Computed based on budget totals from *Economic Report of the President*, February 2015, Table B-21; and the Office of Management and Budget. For the most recent year, go to http://www.gpoaccess.gov/eop/. Percentage shares for 2015 and 2016 are estimates based on the president's budget.

by the $831 billion stimulus package passed early that year. Since the 1960s, the federal government has shifted its focus from national defense to income redistribution. Again, U.S. federal outlays in 2016 totaled about $4 trillion, or about $12,200 per capita.

12-1a Presidential and Congressional Roles

The president's budget proposal begins to take shape a year before it is submitted to Congress, with each agency preparing a budget request. In late January or early February, the president submits to Congress *The Budget of the United States Government,* a pile of books detailing spending and revenue proposals for the upcoming fiscal year, which begins October 1. At this stage, the president's budget is little more than detailed suggestions for congressional consideration. About the same time, the president's Council of Economic Advisers sends Congress the *Economic Report of the President,* which offers the president's take on the economy.

Budget committees in both the House and the Senate rework the president's budget until they agree on total outlays, spending by major category, and expected revenues. This agreement, called a **budget resolution**, guides spending and revenue decisions made by the many congressional committees and subcommittees. The budget cycle is supposed to end before October 1, the start of the new fiscal year. Before that date, Congress should have approved detailed plans for outlays along with revenue projections. Thus, the federal budget has a congressional gestation period of about nine months—though, as noted, the president's budget usually begins taking shape a year before it's submitted to Congress.

budget resolution

A congressional agreement about total outlays, spending by major category, and expected revenues; it guides spending and revenue decisions by the many congressional committees and subcommittees

The size and composition of the budget and the difference between outlays and revenues measure the budget's fiscal impact on the economy. *When outlays exceed revenues, the budget is in deficit. A deficit stimulates aggregate demand in the short run but increases the federal debt and reduces national saving, which in the long run could impede economic growth. Alternatively, when revenues exceed outlays, the federal budget is in surplus. A surplus dampens aggregate demand in the short run but reduces the federal debt and boosts domestic saving, which in the long run could promote economic growth.*

12-1b Problems With the Federal Budget Process

The federal budget process sounds good on paper, but it does not work that well in practice. Here are some problems.

Continuing Resolutions Instead of Budget Decisions

Congress often ignores the timetable for developing and approving a budget. Because deadlines are frequently missed, budgets typically run from year to year based on **continuing resolutions**, which are agreements to allow agencies, in the absence of an approved budget, to spend at the rate of the previous year's budget. Poorly conceived programs continue through sheer inertia; successful programs cannot expand. For example, beginning in 2009, the U.S. Senate failed to pass a budget for three years in a row. During that stretch, the federal government was funded by one continuing resolution after another, and all this was accompanied by huge budget deficits.

> **continuing resolutions**
> Budget agreements that allow agencies, in the absence of an approved budget, to spend at the rate of the previous year's budget

Lengthy Budget Process

You can imagine the difficulty of using the budget as a tool of discretionary fiscal policy when the budget process takes so long and relies on continuing resolutions. Given that the average recession since World War II has lasted only eleven months and that budget preparations begin more than a year and a half before the budget takes effect, planning discretionary fiscal measures to reduce economic fluctuations is difficult if not impossible. That's one reason why attempts to stimulate an ailing economy often seem so halfhearted; by the time Congress and the president agree on a fiscal remedy, the economy has usually recovered on its own.

> **entitlement programs**
> Guaranteed benefits for those who qualify for government transfer programs such as Social Security and Medicare

Uncontrollable Spending Categories

Congress has only limited control over much of the budget. *Most federal outlays are determined by existing laws.* For example, once Congress establishes eligibility criteria, **entitlement programs**, such as Social Security, Medicare, and Medicaid, take on lives of their own, with each annual appropriation simply reflecting the amount required to support the expected number of entitled beneficiaries. Healthcare reform introduced another major entitlement program, the cost of which has not yet been fully calculated. Congress has no say in such appropriations unless it chooses to change benefits or eligibility criteria. Most entitlement programs have such politically powerful constituencies that Congress is reluctant to mess with the structure.

Overly Detailed Budget

The federal budget is divided into thousands of accounts and subaccounts, which is why it fills volumes. To the extent that the budget is a way of making political payoffs, such micromanagement allows elected officials to reward friends and punish enemies with great precision. For example, a recent budget included $176,000 for the Reindeer Herders Association in Alaska, $400,000 for the Southside Sportsman Club in New York, and $5 million for an insect-rearing facility in Mississippi. By budgeting in such detail, Congress may lose sight of the big picture. When economic conditions change or when the demand for certain public goods shifts, the federal government cannot easily reallocate funds. Detailed budgeting is not only time consuming, it reduces the flexibility of discretionary fiscal policy and is subject to political abuse.

12-1c Possible Budget Reforms

Some reforms might improve the budget process. First, the annual budget could become a two-year budget, or *biennial budget*. As it is, Congress spends nearly all of the year working on the budget, and even then sometimes fails to pass one, as noted already. The executive branch is always dealing with three budgets: administering an approved budget, defending a proposed budget before congressional committees, and preparing the next budget for submission to Congress. With a two-year budget, Congress would not be continually involved with budget deliberations, and cabinet members could focus more on running their agencies (many states have adopted two-year budgets). A two-year budget, however, would require longer-term economic forecasts and would be less useful than a one-year budget as a tool of discretionary fiscal policy.

Another possible reform would be to simplify the budget document by concentrating only on major groupings and eliminating line items. Each agency head would receive a total budget, along with the discretion to allocate that budget in a manner consistent with the perceived demands for agency services. The drawback is that agency heads may have different priorities than those of elected representatives. On the plus side, elected officials would be less able to insert favorite pork-barrel projects into the budget.

CHECKPOINT

How have federal spending priorities changed since the 1960s?

12-2 Fiscal Impact of the Federal Budget

When government outlays—government purchases plus cash and in-kind transfer programs—exceed government revenue, the result is a *budget deficit*, a flow measure already introduced. Although the federal budget was in surplus from 1998 to 2001, before that it had been in deficit every year but one since 1960. After 2001 the budget slipped back into the red, where it remains. To place federal deficits in perspective, let's first examine the economic rationale for deficit financing.

12-2a The Rationale for Deficits

Deficit financing has been justified for outlays that increase the economy's productivity—capital outlays for investments such as highways, waterways, and dams. The cost of these capital projects should be borne in part by future taxpayers, who will also benefit from these investments. Thus, there is some justification for shifting some of the cost of capital projects to future taxpayers. State and local governments issue debt to fund capital projects, such as schools and infrastructure. But the federal government does not issue bonds to fund specific capital projects.

Before the Great Depression, federal deficits occurred primarily during wartime. Because wars often impose great hardship on the population, public officials have been understandably reluctant to tax citizens still more to finance war-related spending. Deficits during wars were largely self-correcting, however, because military spending dropped after a war, but tax revenue did not.

The Great Depression led John Maynard Keynes to argue that public spending should offset any drop in private spending. As you know by now, Keynes argued that a federal budget deficit would stimulate aggregate demand. As a result of the Great Depression, automatic stabilizers were also introduced, which increased public outlays during recessions and decreased them during expansions. Deficits increase during recessions because tax revenues decline while spending programs such as unemployment benefits and welfare increase. For example, between 2007 and 2009, corporate tax revenue fell 62 percent but welfare spending jumped 45 percent. An economic expansion reverses these flows. As the economy picks up, so do personal income and corporate profits, boosting tax revenue. Unemployment compensation and welfare spending decline. Thus, federal deficits usually fall during the recovery stage of the business cycle.

12-2b Budget Philosophies and Deficits

Several budget philosophies have emerged over the years. Prior to the Great Depression, fiscal policy focused on maintaining an **annually balanced budget**, except during wartime. Because tax revenues rise during expansions and fall during recessions, an annually balanced budget means that spending increases during expansions and declines during recessions. But such a pattern magnifies fluctuations in the business cycle, overheating the economy during expansions and increasing unemployment during recessions.

A second budget philosophy calls for a **cyclically balanced budget**, meaning that deficits during recessions are paid for by surpluses during expansions. Such a fiscal policy dampens swings in the business cycle without increasing the federal debt. Nearly all state governments have "rainy day" funds to build up budget surpluses during good times for use during hard times.

A third budget philosophy is **functional finance**, which says that policy makers should be concerned less with balancing the budget annually, or even over the business cycle, and more with ensuring that the economy produces its potential output. If the budgets needed to keep the economy producing its potential involve chronic deficits, so be it. Since the Great Depression, budgets in this country have seldom balanced. *Although budget deficits have been larger during recessions than during expansions, the federal budget has been in deficit in all but 14 years since 1929.* One major problem with functional finance is that chronic deficits accumulate into a federal debt that at some point could cripple an economy.

12-2c Federal Deficits Since the Birth of the Nation

Between 1789, when the U.S. Constitution was adopted, and 1929, the year the Great Depression started, the federal budget was in deficit 33 percent of the time, primarily during war years. After a war, government spending dropped more than government revenue. Thus, deficits arising during wars were largely self-correcting once the wars ended.

annually balanced budget
Budget philosophy prior to the Great Depression; aimed at matching annual revenues with outlays, except during times of war

cyclically balanced budget
A budget philosophy calling for budget deficits during recessions to be financed by budget surpluses during expansions

functional finance
A budget philosophy using fiscal policy to achieve the economy's potential GDP, rather than balancing budgets either annually or over the business cycle

Since the onset of the Great Depression, however, federal budgets have been in deficit in 84 percent of the years. Exhibit 2 shows federal deficits and surpluses as a percentage of GDP since 1929. Unmistakable are the huge deficits during World War II, which dwarf deficits in other years. Turning now to the last few decades, we see the relatively large deficits of the 1980s. These resulted from large tax cuts along with higher defense spending. Supply-side economists argued that tax cuts would stimulate enough economic activity to keep tax revenues from falling. Unspecified cuts in federal spending were supposed to erase a projected deficit, but Congress never made the promised cuts. In short, the president and Congress cut tax rates but not expenditures.

As the economy improved during the 1990s, the deficit decreased and then disappeared, turning into a surplus by 1998. But a recession in 2001, tax cuts, and higher federal spending turned surpluses into deficits. A weak recovery and the cost of fighting the war against terrorism worsened the deficits to 3.5 percent relative to GDP by 2003. But over the next four years, a stronger economy along with a rising stock market increased federal revenue enough to drop the deficit to about 1.2 percent relative to GDP in 2007.

Because of the global financial crisis and the Great Recession of 2007–2009, federal deficits relative to GDP swelled to levels not seen since World War II. The recession reduced revenues and expanded outlays, especially the $831 billion American Reinvestment and Recovery Act, more popularly known as the stimulus program. The 2009 deficit was $1.4 trillion, or 9.8 percent relative to GDP. Deficits topped $1 trillion each year through 2012. Relative to GDP, deficits were 8.6 percent in 2010, 8.4 percent in 2011, and 6.7 percent in 2012. Except for World War II, these were the largest deficits in the nation's history relative to GDP, even larger than during the Great Depression. From 2009 to 2012, about 36 cents of every dollar of federal spending had to be borrowed, much of it from foreigners. From 2013 to 2016, deficits relative

EXHIBIT   2   **Federal Deficits and Surpluses Relative to GDP Since the Great Depression**

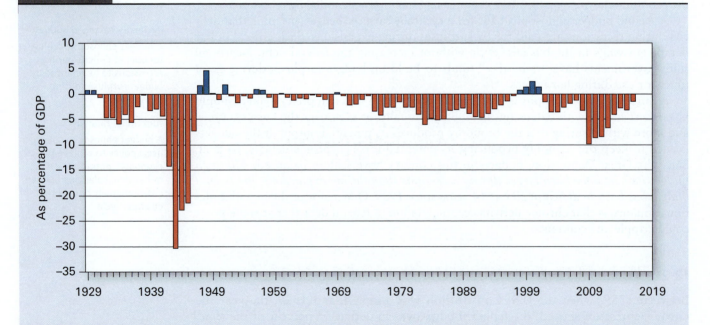

Source: Economic Report of the President, January 1964 and February 2015. Figures for 2015 and 2016 are projections based primarily on the president's budget and the author's estimates. For the latest data, go to http://www.gpoaccess.gov/eop/.

to GDP were 4.1 percent, 2.8 percent, 3.2 percent, and 2.5 percent, respectively. While moderate compared to 2009 to 2012 levels, these four years still added more than $2 trillion to the federal debt. President Obama's budget projections, which some called optimistic, add another $4.4 trillion to federal debt between 2017 and 2024.

That's a short history of federal deficits. Now let's consider why the federal budget has been in deficit so long.

12-2d Why Deficits Persist

As we have seen, recent deficits climbed as the global financial crisis spilled into the wider economy, decreasing tax revenues and increasing government outlays. But why has the budget been in deficit for all but 14 years since 1929? The most obvious answer is that, unlike budgeters in 49 states, federal officials are not required to balance the budget. But why deficits rather than balanced budgets or even surpluses? One widely accepted model of the public sector assumes that elected officials try to maximize their political support, including votes and campaign contributions. Voters like spending programs but hate paying taxes, so public spending wins support and taxes lose it. Candidates try to maximize their chances of getting elected and reelected by offering budgets long on benefits but short on taxes. Moreover, members of Congress push their favorite programs with little concern about the overall budget. For example, a senator from Mississippi was able to include $1.5 billion in a budget for an amphibious assault ship to be built in his hometown of Pascagoula. The Navy never even asked for the ship.

12-2e Deficits, Surpluses, Crowding Out, and Crowding In

What effect do federal deficits and surpluses have on interest rates? Recall that interest rates affect investment, a critical component of economic growth. What's more, year-to-year fluctuations in investment are a primary source of shifts in the aggregate demand curve. Let's look at the impact of government deficits and surpluses on investment.

Suppose the federal government increases spending without raising taxes, thereby increasing the budget deficit. How will this affect national saving, interest rates, and investment? An increase in the federal deficit reduces the supply of national saving, leading to higher interest rates. Higher interest rates discourage, or *crowd out*, some private investment, reducing the stimulating effect of the government's deficit. The extent of **crowding out** is a matter of debate. Some economists argue that although government deficits may displace some private-sector borrowing, expansionary fiscal policy results in a net increase in aggregate demand, leading to greater output and employment in the short run. Others believe that the crowding out is more extensive, so borrowing from the public in this way results in little or no net increase in aggregate demand and output.

Although crowding out is likely to occur to some degree, there is another possibility. If the economy is operating well below its potential, the additional fiscal stimulus provided by a higher government deficit could encourage some firms to invest more. Recall that an important determinant of investment is business expectations. Government stimulus of a weak economy could put a sunny face on the business outlook. As expectations grow more favorable, firms become more willing to invest. This ability of government deficits to stimulate private investment is sometimes called **crowding in**, to distinguish it from crowding out. Between 1993 and 2013, the Japanese government pursued deficit spending that averaged 6.5 percent relative to GDP as a way of getting that flat economy going, but with only limited success.

crowding out
The displacement of interest-sensitive private investment that occurs when higher government deficits drive up market interest rates

crowding in
The potential for government spending to stimulate private investment in an otherwise dead economy

Were you ever reluctant to patronize a restaurant because it was too crowded? You simply did not want to put up with the hassle and long wait and were thus "crowded out." Similarly, high government deficits may "crowd out" some investors by driving up interest rates. On the other hand, did you ever pass up an unfamiliar restaurant because the place seemed dead—it had no customers? Perhaps you wondered why? If you had seen just a few customers, you might have stopped in—you might have been willing to "crowd in." Similarly, businesses may be reluctant to invest in a seemingly lifeless economy. The economic stimulus resulting from deficit spending could encourage some investors to "crowd in."

12-2f The Twin Deficits

To finance the huge deficits, the U.S. Treasury must sell a lot of government IOUs. To get people to buy more of these Treasury securities, the government must offer higher interest rates, other things constant. So funding a higher deficit pushes up the market interest rates, other things constant. With U.S. interest rates higher, foreigners find Treasury securities more attractive. But to buy them, foreigners must first exchange their currencies for dollars. This greater demand for dollars causes the dollar to appreciate relative to foreign currencies. The rising value of the dollar makes foreign goods cheaper in the United States and U.S. goods more expensive abroad. Thus, U.S. imports increase and U.S. exports decrease, so the trade deficit increases.

Higher trade deficits mean that foreigners have dollars left over after they buy all the U.S. goods and services they want. With these accumulated dollars, foreigners buy U.S. assets, including U.S. government securities, and thereby help fund federal deficits. The increase in funds from abroad is both good news and bad news for the U.S. economy. The supply of foreign saving increases investment spending in the United States over what would have occurred in the absence of these funds. Ask people what they think of foreign investment in their town; they will likely say it's great. But foreign funds to some extent simply offset a decline in U.S. saving. Such a pattern could pose problems in the long run. The United States has surrendered a certain amount of control over its economy to foreign investors. And the return on foreign investments in the United States flows abroad. For example, a growing share of the federal government's debt is now owed to foreigners, as discussed later in the chapter.

America was once the world's leading creditor. Now it's the lead debtor nation, borrowing huge sums from abroad, helping in the process to fund federal deficits. Some critics blame U.S. fiscal policy as reflected in the large federal deficits for the switch from creditor to debtor nation. Japan and China are big buyers of U.S. Treasury securities. A debtor country becomes more beholden to those countries that supply credit.

12-2g A Short-Lived Budget Surplus Then More Deficits

Exhibit 3 summarizes the federal budget since 1970, showing outlays relative to GDP as the red line and revenues relative to GDP as the blue line. These percentages offer an overall look at the federal government's role in the economy. Between 1970 and 2016, federal outlays averaged 20.4 percent and revenues averaged 17.4 percent relative to GDP. When outlays exceed revenues, the federal budget is in deficit, measured each year by the vertical distance between the blue and red lines. Thus, on average, the federal budget has had a deficit of 3.0 percent relative to GDP between 1970 and 2016. The pink shading shows the annual deficit as a percent of GDP. In the early 1990s, federal outlays started to decline relative to GDP, while revenues increased. This shrank the deficit and, by 1998, created a surplus, as indicated by the blue shading. Specifically, the deficit in 1990, which amounted to 3.8 percent relative to GDP,

EXHIBIT 3	The Great Recession of 2007–2009 Cut Federal Revenues and Increased Federal Outlays, Resulting in Huge Deficits

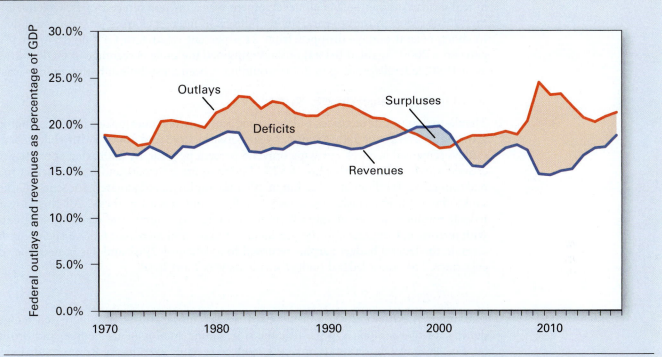

Source: Economic Report of the President, February 2015, Tables B-2 and B-21; and the Office of Management and Budget. Figures for 2015 and 2016 are projections based primarily on the president's budget. For the latest data, go to http://www.gpoaccess.gov/eop/.

became a surplus by 1998, which lasted through 2001. What turned a hefty deficit into a surplus, and why has the surplus turned back into an even bigger deficit?

Tax Increases

With concern about the deficits of the 1980s growing, Congress and President George H. W. Bush agreed in 1990 to a package of spending cuts and tax increases aimed at trimming budget deficits. Ironically, those tax increases not only may have cost President Bush reelection in 1992 (because they violated his 1988 election promise of "no new taxes"), but they also began the groundwork for erasing the budget deficit, for which President Bill Clinton was able to take credit. For his part, President Clinton increased taxes on high-income households in 1993, boosting the top marginal tax rate from 31 percent to 40 percent. The economy also enjoyed a vigorous recovery during the 1990s, fueled by rising worker productivity, growing consumer spending, globalization of markets, and a strong stock market. The combined effects of higher taxes on the rich and a strengthening economy raised federal revenue from 17.8 percent of GDP in 1990 to 20.1 percent in 2000. That may not seem like much of a difference, but it translated into an additional $240 billion in federal revenue in 2000.

Slower Growth in Federal Outlays

Because of spending discipline imposed by the 1990 legislation, growth in federal outlays slowed compared to the 1980s. What's more, the collapse of the Soviet Union reduced U.S. military commitments abroad. Between 1990 and 2000, the number of military personnel dropped by one-third and defense spending dropped 30 percent in real terms.

An additional impetus for slower spending growth came from Republicans, who attained congressional majority in 1994. Between 1994 and 2000, domestic spending grew little in real terms. Another beneficial development was a drop in interest rates, which fell to their lowest level in thirty years, saving billions in interest charges on the federal debt. In short, federal outlays dropped from 21.6 percent relative to GDP in 1990 to 17.4 percent in 2000. Again, if federal outlays remained the same percentage of GDP in 2000 as in 1990, federal spending in 2000 would have been $430 billion higher than it was.

A Reversal of Fortune in 2001

Thanks to the tax-rate increases and the strong economy, revenues gushed into Washington, growing an average of 8.4 percent per year between 1993 and 2000. Meanwhile, federal outlays remained in check, growing only 3.5 percent per year. By 2000, that combination created a federal budget surplus of $236 billion, quite a turnaround from a deficit that had topped $290 billion in 1992. But in 2001 unemployment increased, the stock market sank, and terrorists crashed jets into buildings and spread anthrax. All this slowed federal revenues and accelerated federal spending. To counter the recession and cope with terrorism, Congress and the president cut taxes and increased federal spending. As a result, the federal budget surplus returned to a deficit by 2002 and has been in the red ever since. The era of federal budget surpluses was short-lived.

Trillion-Dollar Deficits

The financial crisis of 2008 and the Great Recession of 2007–2009 increased budget deficits for two reasons. On the revenue side, falling employment, income, and profits cut tax receipts. Discretionary tax cuts reduced revenue even more. Revenues dropped from 17.7 percent relative to GDP in 2007 to only 14.6 percent in 2009. On the spending side, automatic stabilizers such as unemployment benefits and welfare payments increased federal outlays, as did discretionary spending such as bailouts and the $831 billion stimulus plan. Federal outlays jumped from 18.8 percent relative to GDP in 2007 to 24.4 percent in 2009. The federal deficit climbed from $161 billion in 2007 to $459 billion in 2008 to $1.4 trillion in 2009. Even after the recession ended, the federal deficit remained stub-bornly high, topping $1.0 trillion in 2010, 2011, and 2012.

Sequestration

Faced with large deficits and a growing debt far into the future, policy makers looked for ways to slow the growth of spending. In 2011 President Obama and Congressional leaders agreed that if their efforts to curb spending failed, automatic cuts would kick in. That alternative, called sequestration, seemed so crude and so broad that officials believed that just the threat of it would force them to adopt a more rational strategy. But guess what? Congress and the president couldn't agree on how to slow spending growth, so sequestration took hold. **Sequestration** refers to automatic cuts to certain categories of federal spending between 2012 and 2021 to slow spending growth by a total of $1.1 trillion. Some major programs such as Social Security, Medicaid, federal pensions, and veterans benefits were exempt. Defense spending was cut the most.

sequestration
Automatic cuts to certain categories of federal spending enacted in 2011 to reduce the growth of federal spending from 2012 to 2021

The cuts amounted to about $85 billion a year, or about 2.4 percent of the budget. That does not sound like much, but with some major programs exempt, other programs got hammered. Compared to pre-sequester spending levels, defense was cut by an average of 9 percent a year, for a total of $454 billion between 2012 and 2021. Nondefense spending programs that were not exempt were cut by 6.5 percent a year, for a total of $294 billion. In a separate action, Medicare was cut by 2 percent, or $170 billion. Because less would be borrowed as a result of sequestration, interest payments

| EXHIBIT 4 | Government Outlays as a Percentage of GDP in 1997 and 2016 |

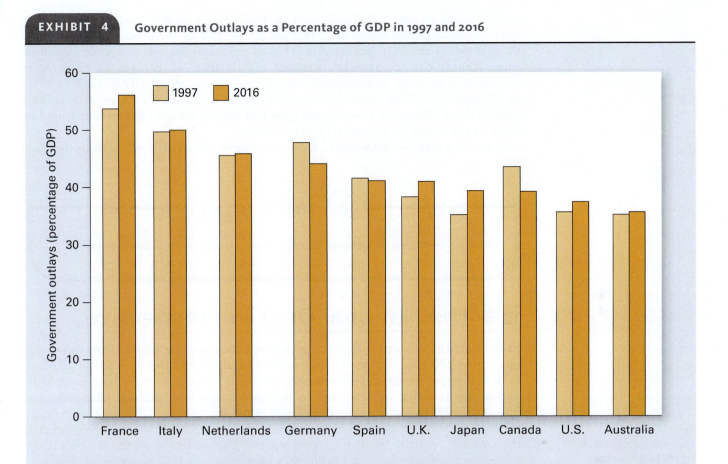

Government outlays relative to GDP increased in 7 of the 10 industrial economies between 1997 and 2016. The 10-country average increased slightly from 42 percent to 43 percent. In the United States, the percentage increased from 36 to 38.

Source: Developed from figures available in *OECD Economic Outlook*, 97 (May 2015), Annex Table 25. Figures for 2016 are projections.

on the debt would be cut by $170 billion. The sequester helped keep federal spending flat in 2012, 2013, and 2014 (see Exhibit 4 in the previous chapter).

Few liked the sequester, but alternative ways of cutting the growth in spending did not emerge. With defense spending particularly hard hit, policy makers looked for ways of getting around the sequester. In May 2015, Congress created a separate account not subject to the sequester to augment defense spending.[1] As a result of this breach of sequestration, the law may lose its effectiveness.

12-2h The Relative Size of the Public Sector

So far, we have focused on the federal budget, but a fuller picture includes state and local governments as well. For added context, we can look at government budgets over time compared to other major economies. Exhibit 4 shows government outlays at all levels relative to GDP in 10 industrial economies in 1997 and in 2016. Government outlays in the United States relative to GDP increased from 36 percent

[1] Nick Timoras, "U.S. Posts Biggest Monthly Surplus in Seven Years," *Wall Street Journal*, 13 May 2015.

in 1997 to 38 percent in 2016. Despite the increase, the United States is projected to have a smaller public sector in 2016 than all but one of the other listed countries. Outlays relative to GDP increased in seven of the major economies and decreased in three. The 10-country average increased slightly from 42 percent to 43 percent. Government grew the most in Japan, rising from 35 percent relative to GDP in 1997 to 39 percent in 2016. Two decades of trying to stimulate the Japanese economy swelled the public sector. Government spending shrank the most in Canada, dropping from 44 percent to 39 percent relative to GDP.

Let's now turn our attention to a consequence of federal deficits—a sizable federal debt.

CHECKPOINT

Why has the federal budget been in deficit most years since the Great Depression?

12-3 The National Debt in Perspective

Federal deficits add up. It took 39 presidents, six wars, the Great Depression, and more than 200 years for the federal debt to reach $1 trillion, as it did in 1981. It took only 5 presidents and 35 years for that debt to increase more than fivefold in real terms, as it did by 2016. The federal deficit is a flow variable measuring the amount by which outlays exceed revenues in a particular year. The federal debt, or the **national debt**, is a stock variable measuring the net accumulation of past deficits, the amount owed by the federal government. This section puts the national debt in perspective by looking at (1) changes over time, (2) U.S. government debt levels compared with those in other countries, (3) interest payments on the national debt, (4) who bears the burden of the national debt, and (5) what impact does the national debt have on the nation's future. Note that the national debt ignores the projected liabilities of Social Security, Medicare, and other healthcare entitlements or other federal retirement programs. If these liabilities were included, the national debt would more than triple.

national debt
The net accumulation of federal budget deficits

12-3a Measuring the National Debt

In talking about the national debt, we should distinguish between the gross debt and debt held by the public. The *gross debt* includes U.S. Treasury securities purchased by various federal agencies. Because the federal government owes this debt to itself, analysts often focus instead on *debt held by the public*, which includes U.S. Treasury securities held by households, firms, banks (including Federal Reserve Banks), and foreign entities. As of 2015, the gross federal debt stood at $18.6 trillion, and the debt held by the public stood at $13.5 trillion.

One way to measure debt over time is relative to the economy's production and income, or GDP (just as a bank might compare the size of a mortgage to a borrower's income). Exhibit 5 shows federal debt held by the public relative to GDP. The cost of World War II ballooned the debt from 44 percent relative to GDP in 1940 to 109 percent in 1946. After the war, the economy grew much faster than the debt, so by 1980, debt fell to only 26 percent relative to GDP. But high deficits in the 1980s and early 1990s nearly doubled debt to 49 percent relative to GDP by 1993. Budget surpluses

EXHIBIT 5	**Federal Debt Held by the Public as Percent of GDP Spiked Because of the Great Recession**

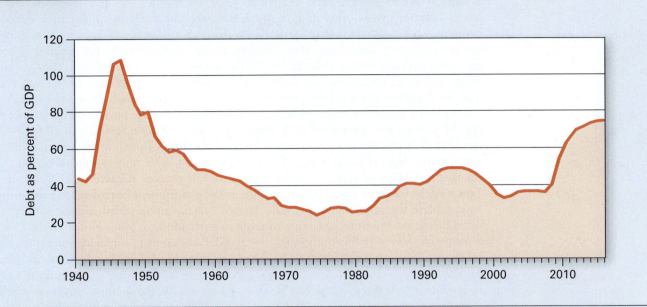

The huge cost of World War II rocketed federal debt from 44 percent of GDP in 1940 to over 100 percent by 1946. During the next few decades, GDP grew faster than federal debt so by 1980, federal debt had dropped to only 26 percent of GDP. But high deficits in recent years increased federal debt to 75 percent relative to GDP by 2016. That's double the percentage in 2007 and the highest since the early 1950s.

Sources: Figures for 2015 and 2016 are estimated based on the president's 2016 budget proposal. Computed by the author based on fiscal year figures from the *Economic Report of the President*, February 2013, Table 79; and *Economic Report of the President*, February 2015, Table B-22; plus updates from budget deliberations. For the latest data, go to http://www.gpoaccess.gov/eop/.

from 1998 to 2001 cut debt to 33 percent relative to GDP by 2001. A recession, a stock market slump, tax cuts, and higher federal spending increased debt to 37 percent relative to GDP in 2004, where it remained through 2007. Deficits from the 2007–2009 recession increased federal debt relative to GDP. Public debt was projected to climb to 75 percent relative to GDP by 2016. That's double the percentage in 2007 and the highest since the early 1950s, after World War II. For the next decade, the federal debt held by the public is projected by President Obama's budget assumptions to grow at about the same rate as GDP. If that turns out the be the case, then public debt as a percentage of GDP will remain at about 75 percent. Research suggests that once debt levels top 80 percent relative to GDP, lenders begin demanding higher interest payments, which could trigger still higher debt.[2]

But, again, this measure of the debt ignores the fact that the federal government is on the hook to pay Social Security and Medicare benefits that will create a big hole in the budget. Why are these other debts ignored? The U.S. Congress exempts itself from including the cost of promised retirement benefits in the budget. Yet firms as well as state and local governments include retirement commitments in their financial statements, as required by private accounting boards and by federal laws. As of 2015, the federal government should have $25 trillion set aside and earning interest to cover the Social Security retirement benefits of current workers beyond what payroll taxes would cover.

[2.] David Greenlaw et al. "Crunch Time: Fiscal Crises and the Role of Monetary Policy," NBER Working Paper No. 19297 (August 2013).

12-3b International Perspective on Public Debt

Exhibit 5 shows federal debt relative to GDP over time, but how does the United States compare with other major economies around the world? Because different economies have different fiscal structures—for example some rely more on a central government—we should consider the debt at all government levels. Exhibit 6 compares the net government debt in the United States relative to GDP with those of nine other industrial countries. *Net debt* includes outstanding liabilities of federal, state, and local governments minus government financial assets, such as loans to students and farmers, securities, cash on hand, and foreign exchange on reserve. Net debt for the 10 nations was projected to average 72 percent relative to GDP in 2016, below the United States figure of 86 percent (remember this is for all levels of government, not just the federal level). Australia was the lowest with only a 6 percent net debt relative to GDP, and Japan was the highest at 150 percent relative to GDP. Much of Japan's debt has been taken on since 2000 as the government borrowed to fund efforts to stimulate the ailing economy. The United States ranked third highest among the 10 industrialized nations, the same ranking as a decade ago. Thus, although the United States ranks low in public outlays relative to GDP, the country ranks high in public debt relative to GDP. That's because we have been running big deficits for decades, and really big ones lately. Net public debt has been increasing in many countries around the world to levels not seen since World War II. The average among the 30 most advanced economies more than doubled from 35 percent in 2000 to 72 percent in 2016. No question, governments on average have been taking on more debt, in part because of the Great Recession of 2007–2009.

12-3c Interest Payments on the National Debt

Purchasers of federal securities range from individuals who buy $25 U.S. savings bonds to institutions that buy $1 million Treasury securities. Because most Treasury securities

---

EXHIBIT 6   **Relative to GDP, U.S. Net Public Debt Is Above Average for Major Economies in 2016**

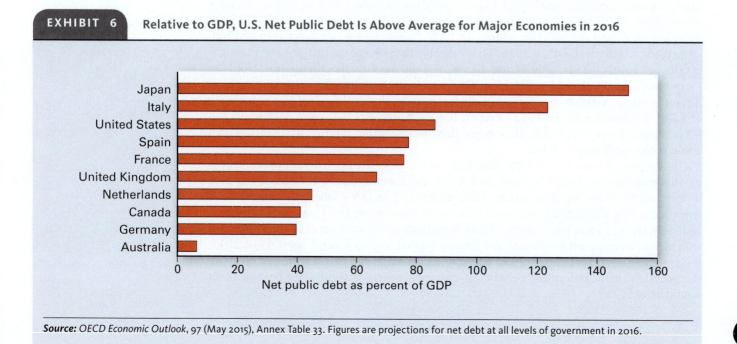

Source: *OECD Economic Outlook*, 97 (May 2015), Annex Table 33. Figures are projections for net debt at all levels of government in 2016.

are short term, nearly half the debt is refinanced every year. Based on a $13.5 trillion debt held by the public in 2015, a 1 percentage point increase in the nominal interest rate ultimately increases interest costs by $135 billion a year.

Exhibit 7 shows interest on the federal debt held by the public as a percent of federal outlays since 1960. After remaining relatively constant for two decades, interest payments climbed in the 1980s because growing deficits added to the debt and because of higher interest rates. Interest payments peaked at 15.4 percent of outlays in 1996, when the U.S. Treasury had to offer a 6.4 percent annual interest rate to sell 10-year bonds. Interest payments then began falling first because of budget surpluses and later because of lower interest rates. By 2015, interest payments were only 6.1 percent of outlays, because the interest rate on 10-year Treasury bonds dropped below 1.8 percent. Interest's share of federal outlays will climb as debt grows and as interest rates rise from historic lows of recent years. For example, if the average interest rate paid by the federal government in 2015 was 5.0 percent, instead of about 2.0 percent, annual interest payments on public debt of $13.5 trillion in 2016 would rise from 6.1 percent of federal outlays to 16.1 percent of federal outlays.

CHECKPOINT

What has happened to federal debt in recent decades, and how does the U.S. debt level compare with levels in other countries?

| EXHIBIT 7 | **Interest Payments on Federal Debt Held by the Public as Percent of Federal Outlays Peaked in 1996** |

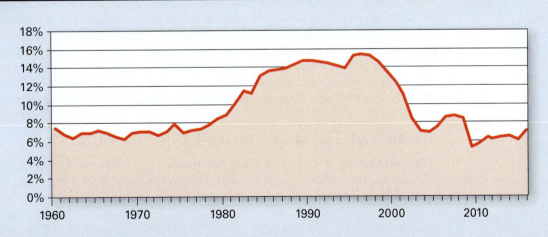

After remaining relatively constant during the 1960s and 1970s, interest payments as a share of federal outlays climbed during the 1980s and early 1990s because of growing deficits and higher interest rates. After peaking in 1996 at 15.4 percent of outlays, interest payments declined first because of budget surpluses and later because of record-low interest rates.

Source: Computed by the author based on figures found in the *Economic Report of the President*, February 2015. Figures for 2015 and 2016 are estimates based on the president's budget. For the latest figures, go to http://www.gpoaccess.gov/eop/.

12-4 Federal Debt and the Economy

In light of the giant deficits of recent years, a growing federal debt has become central to the debate about fiscal policy effectiveness. Let's consider some economic implications of high deficits and an accumulating debt.

12-4a Are Persistent Deficits Sustainable?

Given that deficits have been with us so long, we might ask: How long can the country run a deficit? The short answer is: As long as lenders are willing to finance that deficit at reasonable interest rates. And that depends on the confidence that lenders have about getting repaid. At some point, chronic deficits may accumulate into such a debt that lenders demand an extremely high interest rate or refuse to lend at all. As interest rates rise, debt service costs could eat up the budget.

U.S. government securities have been considered the safest in the world, and this has helped us finance our chronic deficits and rising debt. Ironically, the global financial crisis of 2008 encouraged investors around the globe to buy U.S. securities as they sought safety. This "flight to quality" drove down the interest rate the U.S. government had to pay, thus reducing the cost of servicing our debt. But that could change. Greece had little trouble borrowing until 2010, when the financial community decided the government debt there had become too high and therefore too risky.

Indebted countries such as Greece, Ireland, Spain, and Portugal all received rescue packages from international institutions, yet they continued to struggle, some with violent public protests against deficit-cutting remedies that reduced public spending and increased taxes. One sign of possible problems in the United States was the downgrading of the nation's credit risk by the chief credit-rating agency in 2011. For the first time in 70 years, debt issued by some U.S. "government entities" such as the Federal Farm Credit System and the Federal Deposit Insurance Corporation was judged to be more risky.[3]

Countries can continue to run deficits as long as the cost of servicing the resulting debt remains manageable. Suppose that debt service, which consists almost entirely of interest payments, remains at 10 percent or less of the federal budget. Something like that would appear to be sustainable (since 1960, U.S. debt service payments have averaged 9.8 percent of federal outlays). More generally, government could still run a deficit year after year, and the dollar amount of the deficit might even rise. As long as the economy is growing at least as fast as the debt service payments, those deficits should be manageable. But the trillion-dollar deficits experienced between 2009 and 2012 were not sustainable.

12-4b The Debt Ceiling and Debt Default

debt ceiling

A limit on the total amount of money the federal government can legally borrow

The **debt ceiling** is a limit on the total amount of money the federal government can legally borrow. About a century ago, Congress set the first debt ceiling and raised it whenever necessary, more than 80 times in all. The ceiling was largely a formality—until early 2011, that is, when the federal government faced sharply rising debt from giant deficits for years to come. In early 2011, the gross debt ceiling stood at $14.3 trillion. The federal government actually hit that ceiling in May of that year, but the U.S. Treasury was able to buy time by suspending payments to some retirement funds. At the time, the government was borrowing about 40 cents of each dollar spent, so without additional borrowing the Treasury would run out of money. The limit would be reached in early August.

[3.] Alan Zibel and Tess Stynes, "S&P Cuts U.S. Government Entities," *Wall Street Journal*, 8 August 2011.

If the debt ceiling had not been raised, the U.S. government would have missed some debt-service payments and would be in default. This would have triggered a cascade of troubles, not the least of which would be a sharply higher cost of borrowing or even an inability to borrow. Difficulty rolling over the more than $200 billion of debt that came due each month would cripple federal finances.

A default on what had been considered the securest investment in the world would also be catastrophic for world financial markets. Not only would the federal cost of borrowing increase sharply but also market interest rates would spike to reflect a riskier economy, so interest on everything from car loans to home loans would rise. Credit flows could dry up. Unemployment would jump as businesses cut jobs in the face of growing uncertainty.

Both Democrats and Republicans in Congress agreed in August 2011 that the debt ceiling should be raised. Before approving a higher debt ceiling, Republicans wanted to reduce future deficits by cutting spending. Democrats focused more on tax increases, especially on high-income households. In the end, the two sides came together enough to raise the debt ceiling and avert a fiscal crisis for a while.

12-4c Who Bears the Burden of the Debt?

Deficit spending is a way of billing future taxpayers for current spending. The national debt raises moral questions about the right of one generation to bequeath to the next generation the burden of its borrowing. To what extent do deficits and debt shift the burden to future generations? Let's examine two arguments about the burden of the federal debt.

We Owe It to Ourselves

It is often argued that the debt is not a burden to future generations because, although future generations must service the debt, those same generations receive the payments. It's true that if U.S. citizens forgo present consumption to buy bonds, they or their heirs will be repaid, so debt service payments stay in the country. Thus, future generations both service the debt and receive the payments. In that sense, the debt is not a burden on future generations. It's all in the family, so to speak.

Foreign Ownership of Debt

But the "we-owe-it-to-ourselves" argument does not apply to that portion of the national debt owed to foreigners. Foreigners who buy U.S. Treasury securities forgo present consumption and are paid back in the future. Foreign buyers reduce the amount of current consumption that Americans must sacrifice to finance a deficit. *A reliance on foreigners, however, increases the burden of the debt on future generations of Americans because future debt service payments no longer remain in the country.* Foreigners held nearly half of all federal debt held by the public in 2015, more than triple the share of two decades ago. So the burden of the debt on future generations of Americans has increased both absolutely and relatively.

Exhibit 8 shows the top ten foreign holders of U.S. Treasury securities in February 2015, when foreigners held a total of $6,163 billion of U.S. federal debt. China and Japan were tied for the lead with $1,224 billion each, or 20 percent each of foreign-held U.S. federal debt. Together, Asian countries (including some not shown) had more than half of foreign-held federal debt. Despite the growth in federal debt, U.S. Treasury securities are considered the safest in the world because they are backed by the U.S. government. Whenever there is trouble around the world, investors flock to U.S. Treasury securities in a "flight to quality." Some other countries have proven to be less trustworthy borrowers. Argentina, Mexico, and Russia, for example, all defaulted on some national debt.

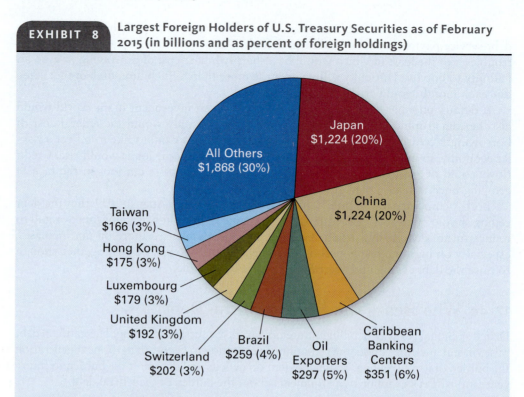

EXHIBIT 8 Largest Foreign Holders of U.S. Treasury Securities as of February 2015 (in billions and as percent of foreign holdings)

All Others
$1,868 (30%)

Japan
$1,224 (20%)

China
$1,224 (20%)

Taiwan
$166 (3%)

Hong Kong
$175 (3%)

Luxembourg
$179 (3%)

United Kingdom
$192 (3%)

Switzerland
$202 (3%)

Brazil
$259 (4%)

Oil
Exporters
$297 (5%)

Caribbean
Banking
Centers
$351 (6%)

Source: Developed by the author based on country totals from the U.S. Treasury Department at www. ustreas.gov/tic/mfh.txt. Caribbean banks include those in the Bahamas, Bermuda, the Cayman Islands, Panama, and the British Virgin Islands.

12-4d Crowding Out and Capital Formation

As we have seen, government borrowing can drive up interest rates, crowding out some private investment. The long-run effect of deficit spending depends on how the government spends the borrowed funds. If the funds are invested in better highways and a more educated workforce, this could enhance productivity in the long run. If, however, borrowed dollars go toward current expenditures such as more farm subsidies or higher retirement benefits, less capital formation results. With less investment today, there will be less capital in the future, thus hurting labor productivity and our future standard of living.

Ironically, despite the large federal deficits during the last few decades, public investments in roads, bridges, and airports—so-called *public capital*—declined, perhaps because a growing share of the federal budget goes toward income redistribution, especially for the elderly. On average the United States spent 3 percent of GDP building and maintaining the public infrastructure between 1950 and 1970. Since 1980 that share has averaged only 2 percent. Some argue that declining investment in the public infrastructure slows productivity growth. For example, the failure to invest sufficiently in airports and in the air traffic control system has led to congested air travel and flight delays, a problem compounded by the threat of terrorism. The $831 billion stimulus package approved in February 2009 was supposed to fund "shovel-ready" infrastructure improvements such as repairing crumbling roads and bridges. But surprisingly little went into such programs.

12-4e The National Debt and Economic Growth

Finally, what's the impact of the national debt on economic growth? Researchers have identified major public debt episodes in the advanced economies around the world since the early 1800s.[4] A major episode is one where the ratio of public debt to GDP exceeds 90 percent for at least five years in a row. Researchers found that the economy grows at least one percentage point less annually during these periods than during other periods. What's more, the growth slowdown can last a long time. Among the 26 episodes the researchers identified, 20 lasted more than a decade (five of the six shorter episodes were immediately after World Wars I and II). Across all 26 instances, the average duration of the slowdown was about 23 years. Thus the cumulative shortfall in output from a high national debt is potentially huge.

Perhaps most telling for the United States is that economic growth declines are significant even in the many episodes where debtor countries were able to secure continual access to capital markets at relatively low real interest rates. This suggests that the growth-reducing effects of high public debt are apparently not transmitted entirely through high real interest rates on that debt. Chairwoman of the Federal Reserve System, Janet Yellen, has noted that government officials need to "significantly improve their structural fiscal balance during good times so they have more space to provide stimulus when times turn bad."[5]

Government deficits of one generation can affect the standard of living of the next. Note again that our current measure of the national debt does not capture all burdens passed on to future generations. As mentioned earlier, if the unfunded liabilities of government retirement programs, especially Medicare, were included, this would more than triple the national debt. The following case study looks at how federal entitlement programs weigh on the federal budget.

Public Policy

REFORMING SOCIAL SECURITY AND MEDI-CARE Social Security is a federal redistribution program established during the Great Depression that collects payroll taxes from current workers and their employers to pay pensions to current retirees. More than 48 million beneficiaries averaged about $1,300 per month from the program in 2015. For two-thirds of beneficiaries, these checks account for more than half of their retirement income. Another 8 million receive disability benefits through Social Security. Social Security benefits increase each year to keep up with inflation as measured by the CPI. Medicare, established in 1965 to provide short-term medical care for the elderly, is an in-kind transfer program funded in part by payroll taxes on current workers and their employers (beneficiaries also pay premiums depending on their income). Medicare in 2015 helped pay medical expenses for more than 40 million Americans age 65 and older plus about 8 million other people with disabilities. Medicare costs averaged about $11,400 per beneficiary in 2015 and are growing faster than inflation. Social Security and Medicare are credited with helping reduce poverty among the elderly from about 35 percent in 1960 to under 10 percent most recently—a poverty rate below other age groups.

continued

[4.] Carmen M. Reinhart, Vincent R. Reinhart, and Kenneth S. Rogoff, "Public Debt Overhangs: Advanced Economy Episodes Since 1800," *Journal of Economic Perspectives*, 26 (Summer 2012): 69–86.

[5.] Jon Hilsenrath, "What the Big Economies Got Right, or Wrong, After Crisis," *Wall Street Journal*, 24 November 2014.

SilviaJansen/E+/Getty Images

Policy makers recognize the huge impact that 76 million baby boomers will have on such a pay-as-you-go program. Americans are living longer, fertility rates have declined, and healthcare costs are rising faster than inflation. According to the Social Security Administration, on average about 11,000 Americans are expected to turn 65 every day for the next 15 years. The 65-and-older population will nearly double by 2030 to 72 million people, or about 20 percent of the U.S. population.

In 1945, there were 42 workers per retiree. Today, there are only 2.8 workers per retiree. By 2030, only 2.1 workers will support each retiree. Based on current benefits levels, spending on Social Security and Medicare, now 8 percent relative to GDP and 38 percent of federal outlays, by 2030 will reach 14 percent relative to GDP and over 50 percent of federal outlays. The huge sucking sound will be the federal deficit arising mostly from Social Security and Medicare outlays. The Congressional Budget Office projects a 2030 federal deficit of 9 percent relative to GDP. All these numbers spell trouble ahead.

But you don't have to look into the future to find trouble. Because of the 2007–2009 recession, Social Security tax receipts declined as people lost jobs, and outlays increased as some of those out of work decided to retire early. As a result, in 2010 Social Security payouts exceeded pay-ins for the first time in history; payouts exceeded pay-ins by $50 billion, a number that could grow for decades. That wasn't supposed to happen until 2016, and it put more pressure on the entire federal budget. Prior to 2010, Social Security pay-ins exceeded payouts. The idea was that this surplus would accumulate over time, so there would be funds available when baby boomers started to retire. But Congress never saved any of the surplus; instead they raked it off, put IOUs in the Social Security Trust Fund, then spent it. That Trust Fund is simply a box of government IOUs. Nothing's there.

Medicare costs have also been taking off, growing an average of 7 percent per year for the last decade. Some people put off surgeries such as hip replacements until they become eligible for Medicare. Healthcare inflation costs run double the overall inflation rate in the economy. Payroll taxes that are supposed to pay for Medicare cover only half the annual cost of the program.

What to do, what to do? Possible reforms include increasing taxes, reducing benefits, raising the eligibility age, using a more accurate index to calculate the annual cost-of-living increase in benefits (meaning smaller annual increases), reducing benefits to wealthy retirees (they are already taxed on up to 85 percent of Social Security income and pay up to three times more for one part of Medicare), and slowing the growth of Medicare costs.

In summary, Social Security and Medicare helped reduce poverty among the elderly, but the programs grow more costly as the elderly population swells and as the flow of young people into the workforce slows. When Social Security was created in the 1930s, life expectancy was 60 years, so only a minority would ever reach 65 to get benefits. Now people live 20 years longer on average, and they collect benefits for most of those added years. Something has to give if these programs are to be available when you retire. President Obama and the Congress raised Medicare payroll taxes on high-income households, but these higher revenues are supposed to fund healthcare reform more generally, not Medicare in particular. Social Security and Medicare remain in big trouble. During the next decade the cost of Social Security is projected to grow by 77 percent and the cost of Medicare by 89 percent. Most elected officials are reluctant to address these problems because they fear upsetting senior citizens, a powerful voting bloc.

But there is some hope. As a way of reducing future deficits, a measure enacted in 2013 cut the growth of Medicare spending by 2 percent per year. This is projected to reduce the growth in spending by a total of $170 billion between 2014 and 2021. And healthcare reform has started to control the cost per Medicare beneficiary.

continued

Every dollar reduction in spending is a dollar reduction in federal debt and in the future cost of servicing that debt every year for what now looks like forever.

Sources: Gerald F. Seib, "Medicare and Social Security Costs? Out of Sight, Out of Mind," *Wall Street Journal*, 10 February 2015; William Reichenstein, "What Social Security Needs: Dependability," *Wall Street Journal*, 22 January 2015; Kevin S. Milligan, "How Is Economic Hardship Avoided by Those Retiring Before the Social Security Age?" *Journal of Pension Economics and Finance* (forthcoming); Atul Gawande, "Overkill: The Waste and the Danger of Unnecessary Care," *The New Yorker*, 11 May 2015; and Social Security and Medicare Boards of Trustees, "Status of the Social Security and Medicare Programs: A Summary of the 2015 Annual Reports," at http://www.ssa.gov/OACT/TRSUM/index.html.

CHECKPOINT

How could a giant federal debt have a negative impact on the economy?

12-5 Conclusion

John Maynard Keynes introduced the idea that federal deficit spending is an appropriate fiscal policy when private aggregate demand is insufficient to achieve potential output. The federal budget has not been the same since. Beginning in 1960, the federal budget was in deficit every year but one until 1998. And beginning in the early 1980s, large federal deficits dominated the fiscal policy debate. A major policy issue for the coming decade will be how to address high federal deficits and a growing debt. The difficulties that other nations faced in addressing their national debts suggest the kind of political challenge the United States could encounter.

Monetary policy is the regulation of the money supply by the Federal Reserve. The next few chapters introduce money and financial institutions, review monetary policy, and discuss the impact of monetary and fiscal policy on economic stability and growth. Once we bring money into the picture, we consider yet another reason why the simple spending multiplier is overstated.

Summary

1. The federal budget process suffers from a variety of problems, including overlapping committee jurisdictions, lengthy budget deliberations, budgeting by continuing resolutions, budgeting in too much detail, and a lack of control over most of the budget. Suggested improvements include instituting a biennial budget and budgeting in less detail.

2. Deficits increase during wars and severe recessions, but since 1960 deficits remained high during economic expansions.

3. To the extent that federal deficits crowd out private capital formation, this decline in private investment reduces the economy's ability to grow. This is one cost of deficit spending. Foreign holdings of debt also impose a burden on future generations because debt payments go to foreigners. Thus, the deficits of one generation of Americans can reduce the standard of living of the next.

4. After peaking at $290 billion in 1992, the federal deficit turned into a surplus by 1998 because of higher tax rates, reduced outlays, especially for defense, declining interest rates, and a strengthening economy fueled by growing labor productivity.

5. The recession of 2001 and terrorist attacks prompted tax cuts to "get the economy moving again." The recession of 2007–2009 cut federal revenue and spurred federal spending, both of which increased the deficit to $1.4 trillion in 2009 and at least $1 trillion in each of the next three years. The longer-term picture looks bleak as baby boomers begin retiring, prompting more spending for Social Security and Medicare.

6. Most recently the U.S. federal debt measured relative to GDP was above average for major industrial countries and was relatively high compared to U.S. historical levels stretching back decades. The Great Recession and policy responses to it rocketed the federal deficit above $1 trillion and sharply increased the national debt to a level that was not sustainable. To head off a fiscal crisis, policy makers held federal spending flat between 2009 and 2014.

Key Concepts

Questions for Review

1. **The Federal Budget Process** The federal budget passed by Congress and signed by the president shows the relationship between *budgeted* expenditures and *projected* revenues. Why does the budget require a forecast of the economy? Under what circumstances would actual government spending and tax revenue fail to match the budget as approved?

2. **The Federal Budget Process** In what sense is the executive branch of the U.S. government always dealing with three budgets?

3. **The Budget Process** In terms of the policy lags described in the previous chapter, discuss the following issues associated with the budget process:

   a. Continuing resolutions
   b. Uncontrollable budget items
   c. Overly detailed budget

4. **Budget Philosophies** Explain the differences among an annually balanced budget, a cyclically balanced budget, and functional finance. How does each affect economic fluctuations?

5. **Budget Philosophies** One alternative to balancing the budget annually or cyclically is to produce a government budget that would help the economy produce its potential output. Given the cyclical nature of government revenues and spending, how would the resulting budget deficit or surplus vary over the business cycle?

6. **Budget Philosophies** What are the possible short-term benefits and possible long-term costs of the functional finance approach to budgeting?

7. **Crowding Out**   Is it possible for U.S. federal budget deficits to crowd out investment spending in other countries? How could German or Japanese investment be hurt by large U.S. budget deficits?

8. **Crowding Out**   How might federal deficits crowd out private domestic investment? How could this crowding out affect future living standards?

9. **Interest on the Debt**   Why did interest payments on the national debt fall from 15.4 percent of the federal budget in 1996 to 6.1 percent in 2015? Why is this percentage expected to increase in the future?

10. **Burden of the Debt**   Suppose that budget deficits are financed mostly by foreigners. How does this create a potential burden on future generations of Americans?

11. **The Twin Deficits**   How is the U.S. budget deficit related to the foreign trade deficit?

12. **The Short-Lived Budget Surplus**   Why did the federal budget go from a deficit in 1992 to a surplus in 1998? Explain the factors that contributed to the turnaround.

13. **Case Study: Reforming Social Security and Medicare**   Why are the Social Security and Medicare programs headed for trouble? When did the trouble begin? What solutions have been proposed?

14. **Crowding Out and Capital Formation**   In earlier chapters, we've seen that the government can try to increase GDP in the short run by running a budget deficit. What are some long-term effects of deficit spending?

15. **Sustainability of Federal Debt**   Are large federal deficits and a growing federal debt sustainable? What can be learned from the experiences of other countries?

16. **The Private Sector**   Look at Exhibit 4. How have government outlays as a percent of GDP changed in the industrial countries depicted between 1997 and 2016? What explains the average trend in these economies?

Problems and Exercises

17. **The National Debt** Try the following exercises to better understand how the national debt is related to the government's budget deficit.

    a. Assume that the gross national debt initially is equal to $3 trillion and the federal government then runs a deficit of $300 billion:
       i. What is the new level of gross national debt?
       ii. If 100 percent of the deficit is financed by the sale of securities to federal agencies, what happens to the amount of debt held by the public? What happens to the level of gross debt?
       iii. If GDP increased by 5 percent in the same year that the deficit is run, what happens to gross debt as a percentage of GDP? What happens to the level of debt held by the public as a percentage of GDP?

    b. Now suppose that the gross national debt initially is equal to $2.5 trillion and the federal government then runs a deficit of $100 billion:

i. What is the new level of gross national debt?

ii. If 100 percent of this deficit is financed by the sale of securities to the public, what happens to the level of debt held by the public? What happens to the level of gross debt?

iii. If GDP increases by 6 percent in the same year as the deficit is run, what happens to gross debt as a percentage of GDP? What happens to the level of debt held by the public as a percentage of GDP?

18. **Public Outlays and Debt** In Exhibit 4, the United States ranks next to the lowest in 2016 among the 10 major economies shown for government outlays relative to GDP. But in Exhibit 6, the United States ranks third from the top in net government debt relative to GDP. How can U.S. public outlays be so relatively low yet U.S. net public debt be so relatively high?

13 Money and the Financial System

©igor Litvyak/Shutterstock.com

- *If Russia can't pay its bills, why don't officials there simply print more rubles (pictured above)?*

- *Why are you willing to exchange a piece of paper bearing Alexander Hamilton's portrait and the number 10 in each corner for a pepperoni pizza with extra cheese?*

- *Why do dimes and quarters have notched edges?*

- *What's the difference between the Fed and the Feds?*

- *Because money is banned in federal prisons, what do inmates use instead?*

- *Why was someone able to cash a check written on a clean but frayed pair of underpants?*

These and other questions are answered in this chapter, which introduces money and banking.

The word *money* comes from the name of the goddess (*Juno Moneta*) in whose temple Rome's money was coined. Money has come to symbolize all personal and business finance. You can read *Money* magazine and the "Money" section of *USA Today*, and visit Web sites such as www.moneyfactory.gov, site of the federal agency that prints money (a Google search for "money" returned about three billion hits). You can watch TV shows such as *Your Money, Mad Money, Fast Money*, and *Strictly Money*.

With money, you can articulate your preferences—after all, money talks. And when it talks, it says a lot, as in, "Put your money where your mouth is" and "Show me the money." Money is the grease that lubricates the wheels of market exchange (in fact, an old expression, "grease the palm," means to pay someone a tip or a bribe). Just as grease makes for an easier fit among gears, money reduces the friction—the transaction costs—of exchange. Too little leaves some parts creaking; too much gums up the works.

This chapter is obviously about money. We begin with the birth of money and trace its evolution in broad strokes from primitive economies to our own. Then we turn to developments in the United States, particularly the financial crisis of 2008, which is arguably the most important economic event since the Great Depression.

Topics discussed in this chapter include:

- Barter
- Functions of money
- Commodity money and fiat money
- The Federal Reserve System
- Depository institutions
- U.S. banking structure
- Subprime mortgages
- Mortgage-backed securities

13-1 The Birth of Money

In the beginning, there was no money. The earliest families were largely self-sufficient. Each produced all it consumed and consumed all it produced, so there was little need for exchange. Without exchange, there was no need for money. When specialization first emerged, as some people went hunting and others took up farming, hunters and farmers had to trade. Thus, the specialization of labor resulted in exchange, but the assortment of goods traded was limited enough that people could easily exchange their products directly for other products—a system called *barter*.

13-1a Barter and the Double Coincidence of Wants

Barter depends on a **double coincidence of wants**, which occurs when each trader is willing to exchange his or her product for something the other trader has to offer. If a

double coincidence of wants
Two traders are willing to exchange their products directly

hunter was willing to exchange hides for a farmer's corn, that was a coincidence. But if the farmer was also willing to exchange corn for the hunter's hides, that was a double coincidence—a *double coincidence of wants*. As long as specialization was limited, to, say, two or three goods, mutually beneficial trades were relatively easy to come by— that is, trade wasn't much of a coincidence. As specialization increased, however, finding the particular goods that each trader wanted became more difficult.

In a barter system, traders must not only discover a double coincidence of wants; they must also agree on an exchange rate. How many bushels of corn should the hunter get for a hide? If only two goods are traded, only one exchange rate needs to be worked out. As the variety of goods traded increases, however, exchange rates multiply. Specialization increased the transaction costs of barter. A huge difference in the values of the units to be exchanged also made barter difficult. For example, a hunter wanting to buy a home that exchanged for 1,000 hides would be hard-pressed finding a home seller needing that many. High transaction costs of barter gave birth to money.

13-1b The Earliest Money and Its Functions

Nobody actually recorded the emergence of money. We can only speculate about how it first came into use. Through experience with barter, traders may have found they could always find buyers for certain goods. If a trader could not find a good that he or she desired personally, some other good with a ready market could be accepted instead. So traders began to accept a certain good not for immediate consumption, but because that good could be easily traded later. For example, corn might have become acceptable because traders knew that it was always in demand. As one good became generally accepted in return for all other goods, that good began to function as **money**. *Any commodity that acquires a high degree of acceptability throughout an economy becomes money.* Money fulfills three important functions: a *medium of exchange*, a *unit of account*, and a *store of value*. Let's consider each.

Medium of Exchange

Separating the sale of one good from the purchase of another requires an item acceptable to all involved in the transactions. If a society, by luck or by design, can find a commodity that everyone accepts in exchange for whatever is sold, traders can save time, disappointment, and sheer aggravation. Suppose corn takes on this role, a role that clearly goes beyond its role as food. We then call corn a medium of exchange because it is accepted in exchange by all buyers and sellers, whether or not they want corn to eat. A **medium of exchange** is anything that is generally accepted in payment for goods and services. The person who accepts corn in exchange for some product believes corn can be traded later for whatever is desired.

In this example, corn is both a *commodity* and *money*, so we call it **commodity money**. The earliest money was commodity money. Gold and silver have been used as money for at least four thousand years. Cattle served as money, first for the Greeks, then for the Romans. In fact, the word *pecuniary* (meaning "of or relating to money") comes from the Latin word for cattle, *pecus*. Likewise, the word *fee* comes from the Old English word *feoh*, which also meant cattle. Roman soldiers received part of their pay in salt bricks; the salt portion was called the *salarium*, the origin of the word *salary*. Also used as money were wampum (strings of polished shells) and tobacco in colonial America, tea pressed into small cakes in Russia, rice in Japan, and palm dates in North Africa. Note that commodity money is a good, not a service; a service is intangible and cannot be held for later exchange.

money
Anything that is generally accepted in exchange for goods and services

medium of exchange
Anything that facilitates trade by being generally accepted by all parties in payment for goods or services

commodity money
Anything that serves both as money and as a commodity; money that has intrinsic value such as gold or silver coins

Unit of Account

A commodity such as corn that grows to be widely accepted becomes a **unit of account**, a standard on which prices are based. The price of hides or shoes or pots is measured in bushels of corn. Thus, corn serves not only as a medium of exchange; it also becomes a common denominator, a yardstick, for *measuring the value* of each product exchanged in the economy. Rather than having to determine exchange rates among all products, as required with a barter economy, people can price everything using a single measure, such as corn. For example, if a pair of shoes sells for 2 bushels of corn and a 5-gallon pot sells for 1 bushel of corn, then a pair of shoes has the same value in exchange as two 5-gallon pots.

unit of account
A common unit for measuring the value of each good or service

Store of Value

Because people do not want to buy something every time they sell something, the purchasing power acquired through a sale must somehow be preserved. Money serves as a **store of value** when it retains purchasing power over time. The better it preserves purchasing power, the better money serves as a store of value, and the more willing people are to accept it and hold it. Consider again the distinction between a stock and a flow. Recall that a *stock* is an amount measured at a particular point in time, such as the amount of food in your refrigerator or the amount of money you have with you right now. In contrast, a *flow* is an amount per unit of time, such as the calories you consume per day or the income you earn per week. *Money* is a stock and *income* is a flow. Don't confuse money with income. The role of money as a stock is best reflected by money's role as a store of value.

store of value
Anything that retains its purchasing power over time

13-1c Properties of the Ideal Money

The introduction of commodity money reduced the transaction costs of exchange compared with barter, but commodity money also involves some transaction costs. First, if the commodity money is perishable, as is corn, it must be properly stored or its quality deteriorates; even then, it won't maintain its quality for long. U.S. coins have a projected life of 30 years (a $1 note, 6 years). So the ideal money should be *durable*.

Second, if the commodity money is bulky, major purchases can become unwieldy. For example, truckloads of corn would be needed to purchase a home selling for 5,000 bushels of corn. So the ideal money should be *portable*, or easily carried. Dollar notes are easier to carry than dollar coins, which may explain why dollar coins never became popular in the United States, despite several attempts to introduce them.

Third, some commodity money was not easily divisible into smaller units. For example, when cattle served as money, any price involving a fraction of a cow posed an exchange problem. So the ideal money should be *divisible*.

Fourth, if commodity money like corn is valued equally in exchange, regardless of its quality, people will eat the best corn and trade away the rest. As a result, the quality remaining in circulation will decline, reducing its acceptability. To avoid this problem, the ideal money should be of *uniform quality*.

Fifth, commodity money often ties up otherwise valuable resources, so it has a higher opportunity cost than, say, paper money. For example, corn that is used for money cannot at the same time be used for corn on the cob, corn flour, popcorn, corn chips, corn oil, or biofuel. So the ideal money should have *a low opportunity cost*.

If the supply or demand for money fluctuates unpredictably, so will the economy's price level, and this is the final problem with commodity money. For example, if a bumper crop increases the supply of corn, more corn will be required to purchase other goods. This we call *inflation*. Likewise, any change in the demand for corn *as food*

EXHIBIT 1   **Six Properties of Ideal Money**

Quality	Rationale	Good Examples	Bad Examples
1. Durable	Money should not wear out quickly	Paper money; coins; sea shells	Strawberries; seafood
2. Portable	Money should be easy to carry, even relatively large sums	Diamonds; paper money	Lead bars; corn
3. Divisible	Market exchange is easier if denominations support a range of possible prices	Honey; paper money and coins	Cattle; diamonds
4. Uniform Quality	If money is not of uniform quality, people will hoard the best and spend the rest, reducing the quality in circulation	Salt bricks; paper money; coins	Diamonds
5. Low Opportunity Cost	The fewer resources tied up in creating money, the more available for other uses	Iron coins; paper money	Gold coins; diamonds; corn
6. Stable Value	People are more willing to accept and hold money if they believe it will keep its value over time	Anything whose supply can be limited by the issuing authority, such as paper money	Farm crops

from, say, the growing popularity of corn chips, would affect the exchange value of corn. Erratic fluctuations in the market for corn limit its usefulness as money, particularly as a unit of account and a store of value. So the ideal money *should maintain a relatively stable value over time*. Money supplied by a responsible issuing authority is likely to retain its value better over time than money whose supply depends on uncontrollable forces of nature such as good or bad growing seasons.

What all this boils down to is that the ideal money is durable, portable, divisible, of uniform quality, has a low opportunity cost, and is relatively stable in value. These qualities are reinforced in Exhibit 1, which also lists the rationale, good examples, and bad examples. Please spend a minute now reviewing the table. Now consider in the following case study how a commodity money emerged where currency was prohibited.

CASE STUDY

BRINGING THEORY TO LIFE

MACKEREL ECONOMICS IN FEDERAL PRISONS
The economist R. A. Radford spent several years in prisoner-of-war camps in Italy and Germany during World War II, and he wrote about his experience. Although economic activity was sharply limited, many features of a normal economy were found in the prison life he observed. For example, in the absence of any official currency behind bars, cigarettes came to serve all three roles of money: medium of exchange, unit of account, and store

of value. Cigarettes were of uniform quality, of limited supply (they came in rations from the International Red Cross), reasonably durable, and individually could support small transactions or, in packs, larger ones. Prices measured in cigarettes became fairly uniform and well known throughout a camp of up to 50,000 prisoners of many nationalities and languages.

Now fast-forward half a century to the U.S. federal prison system. Prisoners are not allowed to hold cash.

continued

Image Source/Jupiter Images

ironing, shoe shining, and cell cleaning), and to buy goods from other inmates (including special foods prepared with items from the commissary and illicit items such as home-brewed "prison hooch"). At those federal prisons where the commissary opens only one day a week, some prisoners fill the void by running mini-commissaries out of their lockers.

After wardens banned cans (because they could be refashioned into makeshift knives), the commodity money quickly shifted from cans of mackerel to plastic-and-foil pouches of mackerel. The mack is considered a good stand-in for the dollar because each pouch costs about $1 at the commissary, yet most prisoners, aside from weight-lifters seeking extra protein, would rather trade macks than eat them. The foil pouches fit in pockets, so they are portable. And the mack is durable; unopened, a foil packet is good for years.

Wardens try to discourage the mackerel economy by limiting the amount of food prisoners can stockpile. Those caught using macks as money can lose commissary privileges, can be reassigned to a less desirable cell, or can even spend time in the "hole." Still, market forces are so powerful that the mackerel economy survives in many federal prisons. Most state prisons have now banned smoking, and the mack has become the coin of the realm there too.

Whatever money sent by relatives or earned from prison jobs (at 40 cents an hour) goes into a prisoner's commissary account, which allows an inmate to buy items such as snacks and toiletries. In the absence of cash, to trade among themselves, federal prisoners also came to settle on cigarettes as their commodity money (despite official prohibitions against trade of any kind among inmates). Cigarettes served as the informal money until 2004, when smoking was banned in all federal prisons.

Once the ban took effect, the urge to trade created incentives to come up with some other commodity money. Prisoners tried other items sold at the commissary including postage stamps, cans of tuna, and Power Bars, but none of that seemed to catch on. Eventually prisoners settled on cans of mackerel, a bony, oily fish. So inmates informally use "macks"—as the commodity money came to be called—to settle gambling debts, to buy services from other inmates (such as haircuts,

Sources: R. A. Radford, "The Economic Organization of a P.O.W. Camp," *Economica*, 12 (November 1945): 189–201; Justin Scheck, "Mackerel Economics in Prisons Leads to Appreciation of the Oily Fillets," *Wall Street Journal*, 2 October 2008; and Ben Paynter, "Prison Economics," *Wired*, 31 January 2011, at http://www.wired.com/magazine/2011/01/st_prisoncurrencies/.

13-1d Coins

The division of commodity money into units was often natural, as in bushels of corn or heads of cattle. When rock salt was used as money, it was cut into uniform bricks. Because salt was usually of consistent quality, a trader had only to count the bricks to determine the amount of money. When silver and gold were used as money, both their quantity and quality were open to question. First, the amount had to be weighed, so transactions required scales. Second, because precious metals could be *debased* with cheaper metals, the quality of the metal had to be determined with each exchange. This was a nuisance.

This quantity and quality control problem was addressed by coining precious metals. *Coinage determined both the quantity and the quality of the metal.* Coins allowed payment by count rather than by weight. A flat surface on which this money was counted came to be called the *counter*, a term still used today. Initially, an image was stamped on only one side of a coin, leaving the other side blank. But people began shaving precious metal from the blank side. To prevent this, images were stamped on both sides. But another problem arose because bits of metal could still be clipped from the coin's edge. To prevent clipping, coins were bordered with a well-defined rim. If you have a dime or a quarter, notice the notches, or tiny serrations, on the edge. These serrations, throwbacks from the time when these coins were silver or gold, reduced the chances of "getting clipped."

token money
Money whose face value exceeds its cost of production

Token money is money whose face value exceeds its production cost. Some coins and all paper money now circulating in the United States are token money. For example, the 25-cent coin costs the U.S. Mint only about 12 cents to make. Minting 25-cent coins nets the U.S. Treasury hundreds of millions of dollars a year. But the penny and even the nickel now cost more to mint than they are worth in exchange.

CHECKPOINT

Identify three functions of money and six qualities of the ideal money.

13-2 Money and Banking

For thousands of years, commodity money facilitated market exchange. Money existed long before banks did. Now we explore how banking developed a special role in supplying a nation's money.

13-2a Early Banking

You have been around banks all your life, so you know more about them than you may think. But before we get to what you know, here's some background about how banking got started. The word *bank* comes from the Italian word *banca*, meaning "bench," which was a money changer's table. Banking spread from Italy to England, where London goldsmiths offered safekeeping for money and other valuables. The goldsmith gave depositors their money back on request, but because deposits by some tended to offset withdrawals by others, the amount of idle cash, or gold, in the vault changed little over time. Goldsmiths found that they could earn interest by lending from this pool of idle cash.

Goldsmiths offered depositors safekeeping, but visiting the goldsmith to get money to pay for each purchase became a nuisance. For example, a farmer might visit the goldsmith to withdraw enough money to buy a horse. The farmer would then pay the horse trader, who would promptly deposit the receipts with the goldsmith. Thus, money took a round-trip from goldsmith to farmer to horse trader and back to goldsmith. Because depositors soon grew tired of visiting the goldsmith every time they needed money, they began instructing the goldsmith to pay someone from their account. The payment amounted to moving gold from one stack (the farmer's) to another stack (the horse trader's). *These written instructions to the goldsmith were the first checks.* **Checks**

check
A written order instructing the bank to pay someone from an amount deposited

have since become official looking, but they need not be, as evidenced by the actions of a Montana man who paid a speeding fine with instructions written on clean but frayed underpants. The Western Federal Savings and Loan of Missoula honored the "check."

By combining the ideas of cash loans and checks, the goldsmith soon discovered how to make loans by check. Rather than lend idle cash, the goldsmith could simply create a checking balance for the borrower. *The goldsmith could extend a loan by creating an account against which the borrower could write checks. In this way gold-smiths, or banks, were able to create a medium of exchange, or to "create money."* This money, based only on an entry in the goldsmith's ledger, was accepted because of the public's confidence that these claims would be honored.

The total claims against the goldsmith consisted of claims by people who had deposited their money plus claims by borrowers for whom the goldsmith had created deposits. Because these claims exceeded the value of gold on reserve, this was the beginning of a **fractional reserve banking system**, a system in which bank reserves amounted to just a fraction of total deposits. The *reserve ratio* measured reserves as a percentage of total claims against the goldsmith, or total deposits. For example, if the goldsmith had reserves of $6,000 but deposits of $10,000, the reserve ratio would be 60 percent. The goldsmith was relying on the fact that not everyone would ask for their deposits at the same time.

fractional reserve banking system
Bank reserves amount to only a fraction of funds on deposit with the bank

13-2b Bank Notes and Fiat Money

Another way a bank could create money was by issuing bank notes. **Bank notes** were pieces of paper promising the bearer specific amounts of gold or silver when the notes were presented to the issuing bank for redemption. In London, goldsmith bankers introduced bank notes about the same time they introduced checks. *Whereas checks could be redeemed only if endorsed by the payee, notes could be redeemed by anyone who presented them.* Paper money was often "as good as gold," because the bearer could redeem it for gold. In fact, paper money was more convenient than gold because it was less bulky and more portable.

bank notes
Originally, pieces of paper promising a specific amount of gold or silver to anyone who presented them to issuing banks for redemption; today, Federal Reserve notes are mere paper money

The amount of paper money issued by a bank depended on that bank's estimate of the fraction of notes that would be redeemed. The higher the redemption rate, the fewer notes could be issued based on a given amount of reserves. Initially, these promises to pay were issued by private individuals or banks, but over time, governments took a larger role in printing and circulating notes. Once paper money became widely accepted, it was perhaps inevitable that governments would begin issuing **fiat money**, which derives its status as money from the power of the state, or by *fiat*. Fiat (pronounced "fee' at") money is money because the government says so. The word *fiat* is from Latin and means "so be it." Fiat money is not redeemable for anything other than more fiat money; it is not backed by something of intrinsic value. You can think of fiat money as mere paper money. It is acceptable not because it is intrinsically useful or valuable—as is corn or gold—but because the government says it's money. Fiat money is declared **legal tender** by the government, meaning that you are making a valid and legal offer when you pay with such money. *Gradually, people came to accept fiat money because they believed that others would accept it as well.* The currency issued in the United States and throughout most of the world is fiat money.

fiat money
Money not redeemable for any commodity; its status as money is conferred initially by government decree but eventually by common experience

legal tender
Currency that constitutes a valid and legal offer of payment

A well-regulated system of fiat money is more efficient for an economy than commodity money. Fiat money uses only paper and ink (a $1 note costs about 5 cents to make; a $100 note, about 12 cents),[1] but commodity money ties up something intrinsically valuable. Paper money makes up only part of the money supply. Modern money also includes checking accounts, which are electronic entries in bank computers.

13-2c The Value of Money

Money has grown increasingly more abstract—from a physical commodity, to a piece of paper representing a claim on a physical commodity, to a piece of paper of

[1.] "How Much Does It Cost to Produce Currency and Coins?" Board of Governors of the Federal Reserve System, at http://www.federalreserve.gov/faqs/currency_12771.htm.

no intrinsic value, to an electronic entry representing a claim on a piece of paper of no intrinsic value. So why does money have value? The commodity feature of early money bolstered confidence in its acceptability. Commodities such as corn, tobacco, and gold had value in use even if for some reason they became less acceptable in exchange. When paper money came into use, its acceptability was initially fostered by the promise to redeem it for gold or silver. But because most paper money throughout the world is now fiat money, there is no promise of redemption. So why can a piece of paper bearing the portrait of Alexander Hamilton and the number 10 in each corner be exchanged for a pizza or anything else selling for $10? *People accept these pieces of paper because, through experience, they believe that others will do the same.* The acceptability of money, which we now take for granted, is based on decades of experience with the stability of its value and with the willingness of others to accept it as payment. As we will soon see, when money's value becomes questionable, so does its acceptability.

The *purchasing power* of money is the rate at which it exchanges for goods and services. The higher the price level in the economy, the less can be purchased with each dollar, so the less each dollar is worth. The purchasing power of each dollar over time varies inversely with the economy's price level. As the price level increases, the purchasing power of money falls. To measure the purchasing power of the dollar in a particular year, you first compute the price index for that year and then divide 100 by that price index. For example, relative to the base period of 1982 through 1984, the consumer price index for 2015 was 238. The purchasing power of a dollar was therefore 100/238, or $0.42, measured in 1982–1984 dollars. Exhibit 2 shows the steady decline in the purchasing power of the dollar since 1960, when it was worth $3.38 in 1982–1984 dollars. Put another way, as measured by the CPI, the value of a dollar—that is, what it could buy—fell by 88 percent between 1960 and 2015.

EXHIBIT 2   **Purchasing Power of $1.00 Measured in 1982–1984 Constant Dollars**

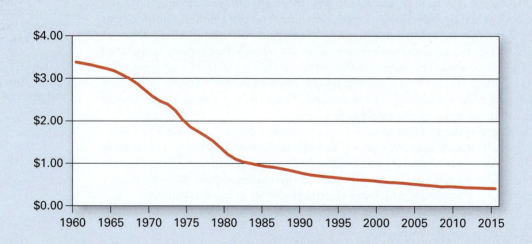

An increase in the price level over time reduces what $1.00 buys. Since 1960 the price level has risen every year except 2009, so the purchasing power of $1.00 (measured in 1982–1984 constant dollars) has fallen from $3.38 in 1960 to $0.42 in 2015.

Source: Developed using CPI figures from the U.S. Bureau of Labor Statistics. For the latest CPI, go to http://www.bls.gov/cpi/home.htm.

13-2d When Money Performs Poorly

One way to understand the functions of money is to look at instances where money did not perform well. In an earlier chapter, we examined hyperinflation in Zimbabwe. With prices growing by the hour, money no longer served as a reliable store of value, so workers couldn't wait to exchange their money for goods or for some "hard" currency—that is, a more stable currency. If inflation gets high enough, people no longer accept the nation's money and instead resort to some other means of exchange. On the other hand, if the supply of money dries up or if the price system is not allowed to function properly, barter may be the only alternative.

When the official currency fails to serve as a medium of exchange because of price controls or hyperinflation or when cash hoarding dries up money in circulation, some other means of exchange emerges. But this diverts more resources from production to exchange. A poorly functioning monetary system increases the transaction costs of exchange. *No machine increases the economy's productivity as much as properly functioning money.* Indeed, it seems hard to overstate the value of a reliable monetary system. This is why we pay so much attention to money and banking.

Let's turn now to the development of money and banking in the United States.

CHECKPOINT

What's a fractional reserve banking system?

13-3 Financial Institutions in the United States

You have already learned about the origin of modern banks: Goldsmiths lent money from deposits held for safekeeping. So you already have some idea of how banks work. Recall from the circular-flow model that household saving flows into financial markets, where it is lent to investors. Financial institutions, such as banks, mortgage companies, and finance companies, accumulate funds from savers and lend them to borrowers. Financial institutions, or **financial intermediaries**, earn a profit by "buying low and selling high"—that is, by paying a lower interest rate to savers than they charge borrowers.

13-3a Commercial Banks and Thrifts

A wide variety of financial intermediaries respond to the economy's demand for financial services. **Depository institutions**—such as commercial banks, savings banks, and credit unions—obtain funds primarily by accepting customer *deposits*. Depository institutions play a key role in providing the nation's money supply. Depository institutions can be classified broadly into commercial banks and thrift institutions.

Commercial banks are the oldest, largest, and most diversified of depository institutions. They are called **commercial banks** because historically they made loans primarily to *commercial* ventures, or businesses, rather than to households. Commercial banks hold most deposits in the United States. **Thrift institutions**, or **thrifts**, include savings banks and credit unions. Historically, savings banks specialized in making home mortgage loans. Credit unions, which are more numerous but smaller than savings banks,

financial intermediaries
Institutions such as banks, mortgage companies, and finance companies, that serve as go-betweens by borrowing from savers to lend to borrowers

depository institutions
Commercial banks and thrift institutions; financial institutions that accept deposits from the public

commercial banks
Depository institutions that historically made short-term loans, primarily to businesses

thrift institutions, or thrifts
Savings banks and credit unions; depository institutions that historically lent money to households

extend loans only to their "members" to finance homes or other major consumer purchases, such as new cars. For the most part, this chapter will ignore credit unions, which are numerous but small and specialized.

13-3b Birth of the Fed

Before 1863, banks in the United States were chartered by the states in which they operated, so they were called *state banks*. These banks, like the English goldsmiths, issued bank notes. Notes from thousands of different banks circulated and most were redeemable for gold. The National Banking Act of 1863 and later amendments created a new system of federally chartered banks called *national banks*. National banks were authorized to issue notes and were regulated by the Office of the Comptroller of the Currency, part of the U.S. Treasury. State bank notes were taxed out of existence, but state banks survived by creating checking accounts for borrowers. To this day, the United States has a *dual banking system* consisting of state banks and national banks.

During the 19th century, the economy experienced a number of panic "runs" on banks by depositors seeking to withdraw their money. A panic was usually set off by the failure of some prominent financial institution. Fearful customers besieged their banks. Borrowers wanted additional loans and extensions of credit, and depositors wanted their money back. *As many depositors tried to withdraw their money, they couldn't because each bank held only a fraction of its deposits as cash reserves.* To reduce such panics, Congress created the **Federal Reserve System** in 1913 as the central bank and monetary authority of the United States.

Nearly all industrialized countries had formed central banks by 1900—such as the Bundesbank in Germany, the Bank of Japan, and the Bank of England, which has been around since 1694. But the American public's suspicion of monopoly power led to the establishment of not one central bank but separate banks in each of 12 Federal Reserve districts around the country. The new banks were named after the cities in which they were located—the Federal Reserve banks of Boston, New York, Chicago, San Francisco, and so on, as shown in Exhibit 3 (which district are you in?). *Throughout most of its history, the United States had what is called a decentralized banking system. The Federal Reserve Act moved the country toward a system that was partly centralized and partly decentralized.* All national banks had to join the Federal Reserve System and thus were subject to new regulations issued by *the Fed*, as it came to be called (don't confuse *the Fed* with *the Feds*, shorthand for the FBI and other federal crime fighters). For state banks, membership was voluntary, and, to avoid the new regulations, most did not join.

13-3c Powers of the Federal Reserve System

The Federal Reserve was authorized to ensure sufficient money and credit in the banking system as needed to support a growing economy. The power to issue bank notes was taken away from national banks and turned over to Federal Reserve banks. (Take out a $1 note and notice what it says across the top: "FEDERAL RESERVE NOTE." On the front of a $1 note, the seal to the left of George Washington's portrait identifies which Federal Reserve bank issued the note.) The Federal Reserve was also granted other powers: *to buy and sell government securities, to extend loans to member banks, to clear checks in the banking system, and to require that member banks hold reserves equal to at least some specified fraction of their deposits.*

Federal Reserve banks do not deal with the public directly. Each may be thought of as a bankers' bank. Reserve banks hold deposits of member banks, just as depository

---

Federal Reserve System, or the Fed

The central bank and monetary authority of the United States

EXHIBIT 3   **The Twelve Federal Reserve Districts**

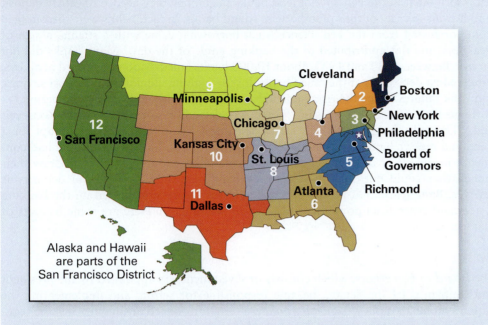

The map shows by color the area covered by each of the 12 Federal Reserve districts. Black dots note the locations of the Federal Reserve bank in each district. Identified with a white star is the Board of Governors headquarters in Washington, DC.

Sources: Federal Reserve Board Web site at http://www.federalreserve.gov/otherfrb.htm.

institutions hold deposits of the public, and they extend loans to member banks, just as depository institutions extend loans to the public. The name *reserve bank* comes from the responsibility to hold member bank *reserves* on deposit.

Reserves are funds that banks have on hand or on deposit with the Fed to promote banking safety, to facilitate interbank transfers of funds, to satisfy the cash demands of their customers, and to comply with Federal Reserve regulations. By holding bank reserves, a Reserve bank can clear a check written by a depositor at one bank and deposited at another bank, much like the goldsmith's moving of gold reserves from the farmer's account to the horse trader's account. Reserve banks are also authorized to lend to banks in need of reserves; the interest rate charged is called the *discount rate*.

A member bank is required to own stock in its district Federal Reserve bank, and this entitles the bank to a 6 percent annual dividend. Any additional profit earned by the Reserve banks is turned over to the U.S. Treasury. So, technically, the Reserve banks are owned by the member banks in the district, but in practice the Fed is a not-for-profit, independent agency of the federal government. When the Fed Chairman gets grilled, it's by Congress, not by member banks.

13-3d Banking Troubles During the Great Depression

From 1913 to 1929, both the Federal Reserve System and the national economy performed relatively well. But the stock market crash of 1929 was followed by the Great

reserves

Funds that banks use to satisfy the cash demands of their customers and the reserve requirements of the Fed; reserves consist of cash held by banks plus deposits at the Fed

Depression, creating a new set of problems for the Fed, such as bank runs caused by panicked depositors. The Fed, however, dropped the ball by failing to act as a lender of last resort—that is, the Fed did not lend banks the money they needed to satisfy deposit withdrawals in cases of runs on otherwise sound banks. In fact, banks were discouraged from borrowing from the Fed. Hence, such borrowing came with a stigma, a sign of weakness, and this contributed to the banking panic of the day.[2] Many banks did not survive. Between 1930 and 1933, about 10,000 banks failed—about one-third of all U.S. banks. Most depositors at the failed banks lost everything. Banking panics, lost savings, and bank failures fueled the rising unemployment and lost output during the period.[3]

In his first inaugural address in 1933, newly elected President Franklin D. Roosevelt said, "The only thing we have to fear is fear itself," a statement especially apt for a fractional reserve banking system. Most banks were sound as long as people had confidence in the safety of their deposits. But if many depositors tried to withdraw their money, they could not do so because each bank held only a fraction of deposits as reserves. Bank legislation passed during the Great Depression shored up the banking system and centralized power with the Fed in Washington. Here are some features of that legislation.

Board of Governors

The *Board of Governors*, which consists of seven members appointed by the president and confirmed by the Senate, became responsible for setting and implementing the nation's monetary policy. *Monetary policy,* a term introduced in Chapter 3, is the regulation of the economy's money supply and interest rates to promote macroeconomic objectives. The Board of Governors now oversees the 12 Reserve banks, making the system more centralized. Each governor serves a 14-year nonrenewable term, with one term expiring every even-numbered year. *The long tenure is designed to insulate board members from political pressure.* A new U.S. president can be sure of appointing only two members during a presidential term, so a new president could not change monetary policy that much. One governor is also appointed by the U.S. president to chair the Board for a four-year term, with no limit on reappointments.

Federal Open Market Committee

The **Federal Open Market Committee (FOMC)** makes decisions about the key tool of monetary policy, **open-market operations**—the Fed's buying and selling of government securities (tools of monetary policy are examined in the next chapter). The FOMC consists of the 7 board governors plus 5 of the 12 presidents of the Reserve banks; the chair of the Board of Governors heads the group. Because the New York Federal Reserve bank carries out open-market operations, that bank's president always sits on the FOMC. The structure of the Federal Reserve System is presented in Exhibit 4. The FOMC and, less significantly, the Federal Advisory Committee (which consists of a banker from each of the 12 Reserve bank districts) advise the board.

Regulating the Money Supply

Because reserves amount to just a fraction of deposits, the United States has a *fractional reserve* banking system, as already noted. The Federal Reserve System has a variety of tools to regulate the money supply, including *(1) conducting open-market*

Federal Open Market Committee (FOMC)

The 12-member group that makes decisions about open-market operations— purchases and sales of U.S. government securities by the Fed that affect the money supply and interest rates; consists of the 7 Board governors plus 5 of the 12 presidents of the Reserve banks

open-market operations

Purchases and sales of government securities by the Fed in an effort to influence the money supply and interest rates

---

[2.] Gary B. Gorton and Andrew Metrick, "The Federal Reserve and Panic Prevention: The Roles of Financial Regulation and Lender of Last Resort," *Journal of Economic Perspectives*, 27 (Fall 2013): 45–64.

[3.] Andrew J. Jalil, "A New History of Banking Panics in the United States, 1825–1929: Construction and Implications," *American Economic Journal: Macroeconomics* (forthcoming).

| EXHIBIT 4 | Organization Chart of the Federal Reserve System |

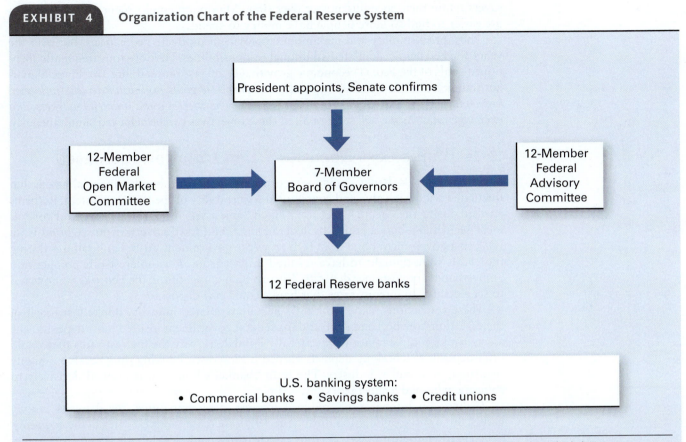

Members of the Board of Governors are appointed by the president and confirmed by the Senate. The 7 board members also belong to the 12-member Federal Open Market Committee, which advises the board. The Board of Governors controls the Reserve banks in each of the 12 districts, which in turn control the U.S. banking system.

operations—buying and selling U.S. government securities; (2) setting the discount rate—the interest rate charged by Reserve banks for loans to member banks; and (3) setting legal reserve requirements for member banks. We examine these long-standing tools in greater detail in the next two chapters and discuss some additional tools developed to deal with the financial crisis of 2008.

Deposit Insurance

Panic runs on banks stemmed from fears about the safety of bank deposits. The *Federal Deposit Insurance Corporation (FDIC)* was established in 1933 to insure the first $2,500 of each deposit account. Today the insurance ceiling is $250,000 per depositor per bank. Over 90 percent of all banks now purchase FDIC insurance, and deposits at FDIC-insured institutions totaled $10.6 trillion in 2015. Other insurance programs take care of the rest. *Deposit insurance, by calming fears about the safety of bank deposits, worked wonders to reduce bank runs.*

Goals of the Fed

The Fed's primary goals, its legal mandates, are price stability and maximum employment. Stable prices promote greater certainty, make economic planning easier, and help savers retain their spending power over time. Maximum employment means that jobs are easier to find so more people have money to spend.

Thus, price stability and maximum employment motivate Fed actions. But over the years, the Fed has accumulated additional responsibilities. Here are four frequently mentioned goals of the Fed: (1) economic growth, (2) interest rate stability, (3) financial market stability, and (4) exchange rate stability. *All these goals boil down to low inflation; high employment; economic growth; and stability in interest rates, financial markets, and exchange rates.* As we will see, not all of these objectives can be achieved simultaneously.

13-3e Banks Lost Deposits When Inflation Increased

Prior to the 1930s, banks could own corporate stocks and bonds, financial assets that fluctuated widely in value and contributed to instability of the banking system. Reforms enacted during the Great Depression limited bank assets primarily to loans and government securities—bonds issued by federal, state, and local governments. A *bond* is an IOU, so a government bond is an IOU from the government. Also, bank failures during the 1930s were thought to have resulted in part from fierce interest-rate competition among banks for customer deposits. To curb such competition, the Fed was empowered to set a ceiling on interest rates that banks could pay depositors.

These restrictions made banking a heavily regulated industry. Banks lost much of their freedom to wheel and deal, and the federal government insured most deposits. The assets banks could acquire were carefully limited, as were the interest rates they could offer depositors (checking deposits earned no interest). Banking thus became a highly regulated, even stuffy, industry. The term "banker's hours" was applied derisively to someone who had a short workday.

Ceilings on interest rates reduced interest-rate competition for deposits *among* banks. But a surge of inflation during the 1970s increased interest rates in the economy. When market interest rates rose above what banks could legally offer depositors, many withdrew their deposits and put them into higher-yielding alternatives. In 1972, Merrill Lynch, a major brokerage house, introduced an account combining a **money market mutual fund** with limited check-writing privileges. Money market mutual fund shares are claims on a portfolio, or collection, of short-term interest-earning assets. These mutual funds, as financial intermediaries, became stiff competition for bank deposits, especially checkable deposits, which at the time paid no interest at banks.

money market mutual fund
A collection of short-term interest-earning assets purchased with funds collected from many shareholders

13-3f Banking Deregulation

In response to the loss of deposits and other problems, Congress tried to ease regulations, giving banks greater discretion in their operations. For example, interest-rate ceilings for deposits were eliminated, and all depository institutions were allowed to offer money market deposit accounts. Such deposits jumped from only $8 billion in 1978 to $200 billion in 1982. Some states, like California and Texas, also deregulated state-chartered savings banks. The combination of deposit insurance, unregulated interest rates, and wider latitude in the kinds of assets that savings banks could purchase gave them a green light to compete for large deposits in national markets. Savings banks had been restricted to residential lending, but the 1982 legislation allowed them to make commercial loans. Once-staid financial institutions moved into the fast lane.

Banks could wheel and deal but with the benefit of deposit insurance. The combination of deregulation and deposit insurance encouraged some on the verge of failing to take bigger risks—to "bet the bank"—because their depositors would be protected by deposit insurance. This created a *moral hazard,* which in this case was the tendency of bankers to take unwarranted risks in making loans because deposits were insured. Banks that were virtually bankrupt—so-called zombie banks—were able to attract deposits because of deposit insurance. Zombie banks, by offering higher interest rates, also drew deposits away from healthier banks. Meanwhile, because deposits were insured, most depositors paid less attention to their banks' health. Thus, *deposit insurance, originally introduced during the Great Depression to prevent bank panics, caused depositors to become complacent about the safety of their deposits. Worse still, it caused those who ran troubled banks to take wild gambles to survive.*

13-3g Banks on the Ropes

Many of these gambles didn't pay off, particularly loans to real estate developers, and banks lost a ton of money. The insolvency and collapse of a growing number of banks prompted Congress in 1989 to approve what was then the largest financial bailout of any U.S. industry—a measure that would eventually cost about $180 billion in today's dollars. Taxpayers paid 80 percent of the total, and banks paid the remaining 20 percent through higher deposit insurance premiums. The money was spent to close down failing banks, pay off insured depositors, and find healthier banks to take over the deposit accounts. Exhibit 5 shows the number of bank failures in the United States by year since 1980. About 3,000 banks failed between the early 1980s and early 1990s, with 1989 the peak.

13-3h Banks Recover

As failed banks disappeared or merged with stronger banks, the industry got healthier. Bank profits grew fourfold during the 1990s. Although the number of commercial banks fell by half since the mid-1980s, the United States, with about 5,600

EXHIBIT 5   **U.S. Bank Failures Peaked in 1989**

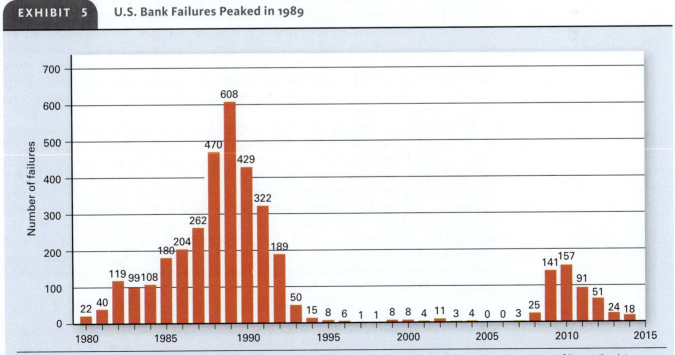

Source: Based on annual reports from the Federal Deposit Insurance Corporation. For the latest figures, go to http://www.fdic.gov/bank/individual/failed/banklist.html.

bank branches

A bank's additional offices that carry out banking operations

FDIC-insured commercial banks in early 2015, still had more than any other country. Other major economies have fewer than 1,000 commercial banks (Japan and Canada, for example, have fewer than 100 banks each, though most have many branches). The large number of U.S. banks reflects past restrictions on **bank branches**, which are additional offices that carry out banking operations. Again, Americans, fearing monopoly power, did not want any one bank to become too large or powerful. The combination of intrastate and interstate restrictions on branching spawned the many commercial banks that exist today, most of which are relatively small. For example, the bottom 98 percent of U.S. commercial banks in 2015 held just 20 percent of all deposits. Branching restrictions create inefficiencies, because banks cannot achieve optimal size and cannot easily diversify their portfolios of loans across different regions. Branching restrictions were one reason for bank failures during the Depression. Such restrictions meant a bank made loans primarily in one community—it had all its eggs in that basket. But researchers find that geographic expansion reduces bank risks.[4]

In recent years, federal legislation has lifted some restrictions on interstate branching and on the kinds of assets that banks can own. Two developments allowed banks to get around branching restrictions: bank holding companies and mergers. A **bank holding company** is a corporation that may own several different banks. The *Gramm-Leach-Bliley Act* of 1999 repealed some Depression-era restrictions on the kinds of assets a bank could own. A holding company can provide other services that banks are not authorized to offer, such as financial advising, leasing, insurance, credit cards, and securities trading. Thus, holding companies blossomed. About 90 percent of the nation's checking deposits are in banks owned by holding companies. But in the aftermath of the recent financial crises, policy makers restricted the kinds of assets a bank can own and trade, as you'll soon see.

bank holding company

A corporation that owns banks

Another important development that allowed banks to expand their geographical reach is *bank mergers,* which have spread the presence of some banks across the country. Banks are merging because they want more customers and expect the higher volume of transactions to reduce operating costs per customer. Nationwide banking is also seen as a way of avoiding the concentration of bad loans that sometimes occurs in one geographical area. The merger movement was initially fueled by a rising stock market and by federal legislation that facilitates consolidation of merged banks. More recently, some banks weakened by the financial crisis have been forced to merge with stronger banks to survive.

Bank holding companies and bank mergers have reduced the number of banks, but increased the number of branches. Exhibit 6 shows the number of commercial banks and bank branches in the United States since 1934. The number of banks, as indicated by "main offices," remained relatively constant between 1934 and 1982 but has since fallen by more than half as a result of failures, mergers, and holding companies. The number of bank branches increased steadily, however, more than doubling since 1982. So the number of branches per bank increased. In 1982, the average U.S. commercial bank had about three branches; by 2014, it had about 14 branches. But with the growth of online banking and cash-back with debit cards, banks now face less market pressure to increase the number of branches or even the number of ATMs.

---

[4] Martin Goetz, Luc Laeven, and Ross Levine, "Does the Geographic Expansion of Bank Assets Reduce Risk?" NBER Working Paper No. 20758 (December 2014).

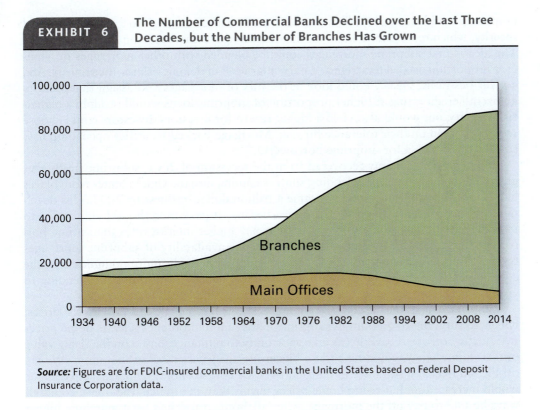

EXHIBIT 6 — The Number of Commercial Banks Declined over the Last Three Decades, but the Number of Branches Has Grown

Source: Figures are for FDIC-insured commercial banks in the United States based on Federal Deposit Insurance Corporation data.

CHECKPOINT

What is the Fed, what are its two mandated objectives, and what are some other goals?

13-4 Banking During and After the Great Recession of 2007–2009

The biggest financial development in recent years has been the introduction of the subprime mortgage, which contributed to the financial crisis of 2008 and the Great Recession. Here's what happened.

13-4a Subprime Mortgages and Mortgage-Backed Securities

Prior to 2000, only a credit-worthy, or *prime*, borrower could get a home mortgage. But new statistical techniques and better computers supposedly increased a lender's ability to assess the risk of a **subprime mortgage**, which is a mortgage for a borrower with a not-so-good credit rating. Any household with a credit history could be assigned a numerical credit score, and this score could be used to predict how likely that borrower would be to default on mortgage payments. Borrowers more likely to default would pay a higher interest rate to compensate the lender for their higher risk. Hundreds of

subprime mortgage
Mortgage for a borrower with a not-so-good credit rating

mortgage-backed security
A claim on payments made on the many mortgages bundled into this financial instrument

mortgages could then be bundled together based on credit scores into a **mortgage-backed security**, which represents a claim on the monthly payments made on those mortgages. The idea is that subprime mortgages could be blended with other mortgages in whatever proportion needed to arrive at a particular level of default risk for the security. And a securities-rating agency could look at the mix of mortgages and assign that security an overall credit rating. A higher proportion of subprime loans would result in a higher-risk security, but would also yield a higher return for investors. Investors could choose securities based on their tolerance for risk. Mortgage-backed securities opened up new sources of financing for subprime borrowers.

After the U.S economy recovered from the recession of 2001, subprime mortgages grew in popularity. Fueled by lending sources coming into the United States from places like China, the subprime market became a trillion dollar business by 2007. This development was considered good for America because it gave more households access to mortgage credit. Subprime borrowers might pay higher interest rates than prime borrowers, but at least they could get mortgages. The availability of subprime mortgages turned some renters into homeowners, a group presumably more committed to the community. Indeed, federal regulators pressured financial institutions into lending to groups that before the advent of subprime mortgages had been underserved.

Subprime loans increased the demand for housing, which raised housing prices, which, in turn, fueled a boom in subprime loans in a reinforcing cycle. As home prices rose, many borrowers saw this as an opportunity to refinance. Based on the rising value of their homes, they would take out a bigger mortgage, use most of that money to pay off the old one, and still have money left over. Of course, monthly mortgage payments would increase too, but rising home prices meant that, in a pinch, the house could always be sold to pay off the mortgage. After all, home prices had been marching higher for at least two decades. Mortgage-backed securities were considered a safe investment offering an attractive return. They were sold around the world. Banks and other financial institutions bought a lot of them. What could go wrong?

13-4b Bad Incentives Fueled the Financial Crisis of 2008

A subprime mortgage typically originated with a mortgage broker (two-thirds originated this way). The mortgage was then sold to an underwriter who bundled it with other mortgages and sold them as a mortgage-backed security to investors, the source of financing in the deal. Once the mortgage was originated, that mortgage broker earned a fee and soon lost interest in whether the borrower was good for the money. Research indicates that the riskier the loan, the higher the interest rate, and the more the broker made on that loan. Brokers had an incentive to encourage borrowers to apply for mortgages they could not afford, and some brokers falsified information on mortgage applications to make sure they would get approved. Some borrowers also exaggerated their income if there was no income verification (these became known as "liar's loans"). Making everything worse was the lax regulation of mortgage originators, who were not required to tell borrowers whether or not they could afford the loans. Some borrowers clearly could not afford to repay their loans. Research suggests that about a third of subprime loans should not have been made in the first place.[5]

Meanwhile, banks and other financial institutions were earning attractive fees creating and selling mortgage-backed securities. Underwriters of mortgage-backed securities usually had little incentive to make sure that those who bought the securities would

[5.] Sumit Agarwal et al. "Predatory Lending and the Subprime Crisis," *Journal of Financial Economics*, 113 (July 2014): 29–52.

ultimately get paid.[6] Worse yet, the credit-rating agencies that evaluated these securities also had a conflict of interest. They earned their fees by assessing the riskiness of these securities. But underwriters could shop around for the credit-rating agency that offered the highest rating. Thus, mortgage-backed securities tended to get better ratings than they deserved—that is, the securities were actually more risky than their credit ratings indicated.

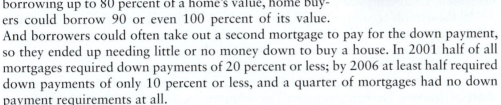

As housing prices rose and the profitability of converting mortgages into securities increased, underlying credit standards fell. Riskier borrowers could get mortgages with little trouble. The size of mortgages increased, as did the loan-to-value ratio, meaning that instead of borrowing up to 80 percent of a home's value, home buyers could borrow 90 or even 100 percent of its value. And borrowers could often take out a second mortgage to pay for the down payment, so they ended up needing little or no money down to buy a house. In 2001 half of all mortgages required down payments of 20 percent or less; by 2006 at least half required down payments of only 10 percent or less, and a quarter of mortgages had no down payment requirements at all.

Bundling hundreds of mortgages into a single mortgage-backed security made for a complicated investment, and this worsened the incentive problems. Yet as long as home prices were rising, everyone was happy—the borrower, the mortgage originator, the banker who underwrote and sold the mortgage-backed security, the credit-rater, and the investor who found the yield attractive. But housing prices reached a level that in retrospect was far out of whack with fundamentals of the housing market. After peaking in 2006, housing prices began to fall. Between 2006 and the middle of 2008, U.S. home prices plunged 22 percent on average. With housing prices tumbling, all the corners cut in the mortgage market soon became obvious. Many mortgages slipped "underwater," meaning that borrowers owed more than the house was worth. Such borrowers had an incentive to stop making payments. Many did, and defaults rose sharply, leading to millions of foreclosures.

Mortgage-backed securities quickly turned into "troubled assets." Because nobody wanted them, their value plummeted. Rising home foreclosures fed into the full-scale global financial panic in September 2008. The collapse of a major investment bank, Lehman Brothers, signaled that other financial institutions could soon follow. Nobody wanted to lend money they might not get back. Credit dried up. Panic spread to consumers, who cut consumption because of falling home prices, mounting job losses, and a collapsing stock market.

13-4c The Troubled Asset Relief Program, or TARP

Policy makers had not seen anything like this in their lifetimes. By early October 2008, a consensus had formed around a stopgap measure to help unfreeze credit markets and stabilize the banks. The **Troubled Asset Relief Program**, or **TARP**, authorized the U.S. Treasury to purchase up to $700 billion in mortgage-backed securities. The idea was to buy these illiquid, difficult-to-value, assets and get them off the banks' books. Treasury officials soon decided that TARP money would not be used to buy troubled assets but instead would be invested directly into financial institutions that were otherwise sound except for their troubled assets. The idea was to infuse new financial capital into these

Troubled Asset Relief Program, or TARP

Government program that invested in financial institutions and automakers to help stabilize these markets

---

6. See, for example, Benjamin J. Keys et al. "Did Securitization Lead to Lax Screening? Evidence from Subprime Loans," *Quarterly Journal of Economics*, 125 (February 2010): 307–362.

financial institutions to prevent more failures and to get banks lending again. The failure of Lehman Brothers was such a shock to financial markets that policy makers wanted to prevent other financial giants from collapsing. A trillion dollar institution such as AIG, with its financial ties to hundreds of other financial institutions, had become **too big to fail**—that is, its failure would have been such a disaster for the wider economy, that failure had to be prevented, even if it required a financial bailout.

TARP money was used to buy stakes in banks large and small (TARP money also bought government stakes in General Motors and Chrysler to keep the car makers operating). Once financial markets stabilized a bit and the stock market recovered some ground, the value of the Treasury's investment increased (ultimately, the Treasury would get its money back with interest from all except the automakers, where the loss amounted to about $9 billion). But housing prices continued to fall, homes continued to slip under water, and banks continued to suffer from mortgage defaults. Underwater loans were greatest in Nevada, Arizona, Florida, Michigan, and California.

All these troubles contributed to a spike in bank failures. As was shown in Exhibit 5, failures climbed from 25 in 2008 to 157 in 2010. By 2014, failures declined to just 18. Because of failures and mergers, the number of banks in the United States declined from about 18,000 in 1984 to about 6,500 in 2015. Eighty-seven percent were commercial banks, and 13 percent savings banks. Commercial banks account for the overwhelming share of deposits. The troubles created by subprime mortgages, mortgage-backed securities, and other financial problems prompted regulatory reform. That's discussed next.

13-4d The Dodd-Frank Act of 2010

In 2010, President Obama signed into law the most sweeping overhaul of financial regulations since the Great Depression. The **Dodd-Frank Wall Street Reform and Consumer Protection Act**, named for its sponsors in the Senate and House, took 18 months to develop and will take many years to implement. The legislation, which was 2,300 pages long, authorized 10 regulatory agencies to write and interpret hundreds of new rules governing financial markets.

Some provisions aim to remedy the incentive problems already discussed. To ensure that borrowers can repay a home loan, a mortgage originator must verify income, credit history, and job status. Mortgage originators cannot be paid more for funneling borrowers to riskier loans. To ensure that issuers of mortgage-backed securities are sensitive to the risk of these assets, issuers must retain at least 5 percent of the credit risk associated with the mortgages. And credit-rating agencies will be subject to new regulations.

For the first time, the law authorizes the Federal Reserve to regulate companies other than banks—such as insurance companies and investment firms—if they are engaged mostly in financial activities. The law imposes other regulations on banks, limiting their ability to trade on their own behalf and restricting their investments in hedge funds and private equity funds, which tend to be riskier.

The law establishes the *Financial Stability Oversight Council*, a super-regulator that monitors Wall Street's largest firms and other market participants to spot and respond to emerging systemic risks. The nine-member panel, led by the Treasury Department, includes regulators from other agencies. Regulators get new authority to seize and liquidate troubled financial firms if their failure would jeopardize the nation's financial stability (such as with AIG). The idea is that reducing systemic risk and maintaining financial stability become regulatory objectives. A new *Bureau of Consumer Financial Protection* has broad powers to write consumer-protection rules for banks and other firms that offer financial services.

Financial regulators get more funding, more information, and more power. Supporters say the law will reduce the likelihood of another financial crisis and will handle it better if one should occur. Others aren't so sure. Some economist argue that there are

too big to fail
A financial institution becomes so large and so interconnected with other financial institutions that its failure would be disastrous for the wider economy; its collapse must be prevented even if that requires a bailout

Dodd-Frank Wall Street Reform and Consumer Protection Act
Sweeping regulatory changes in 2010 aimed at preventing another financial crisis

many ways a firm can take risks, and banning one form of risk-taking just shifts traders to other kinds of risk. For example, at a high enough interest rate, a bank may be willing to lend to extremely risky borrowers. What other unintended consequences will the new regulations create? Will regulations stifle financial innovation? Will U.S. financial institutions lose business to foreign competitors? Will the availability of credit be impaired by increased uncertainty and costs? Will new financial products be developed that make the regulations irrelevant? Will credit flows get choked by regulatory bureaucracy and politics? More generally, how will capitalism change if government regulators can seize and liquidate any financial institution? It's said that the military is often planning for the previous war. Are regulators, the same ones who allowed all this to happen in the first place, gearing up to prevent the previous financial crisis?

There have been 17 financial crises in the United States since 1790. That's an average of one every 13 years. Researchers have traced how financial crises affected real per capita income. After examining one hundred such crises in 12 countries beginning in 1790, researchers concluded that it usually took years for per capita income to recover to its pre-crisis level. For example, six years after the onset of the recent financial crisis, only Germany and the United States (out of the 12 nations studied) had surpassed their 2007–2008 peaks of real per capita income.[7]

13-4e Top Banks in America and the World

The financial crisis of 2008 and the recession rattled the banking world. Let's take a look at the biggest banks in America and in the world. Exhibit 7 (a) shows the top 10 U.S. banks based on their U.S. assets at the end of 2014. Notice the wide range in size, with the top bank holding over eight times the assets as the bank ranked tenth. The top banks grew mostly through mergers and acquisitions. Because of the subprime mortgage and global financial crises of September 2008, some big banks that were in trouble had to be taken over by healthier banks. For example, Wachovia, in 2008 the nation's third largest bank, had to merge with Wells Fargo, then the nation's fourth largest. And Washington Mutual, at the time the sixth largest bank, was seized by the FDIC after a ten-day bank run during which depositors withdrew $16 billion, or about 10 percent of all deposits. The FDIC arranged for Washington Mutual to be acquired by JPMorgan Chase. You can see from panel (a) of Exhibit 7 that JPMorgan Chase most recently ranked first in assets among U.S. banks, and Wells Fargo ranked second.

How big are U.S. banks on the world stage? Not very. Only one U.S. bank ranked among the top 10 based on worldwide assets. As shown by Exhibit 7 (b), China is home to four of the world's five largest banks. France has two in the top 10. Thus, the United States has the second largest economy in the world (slightly below China's) but has only one bank among the top 10 in the world. This partly reflects America's lingering fear of big banks. Some U.S. banks may be considered "too big to fail," but all but JPMorgan Chase are still too small to rank among the world's top 10.

CHECKPOINT

What are subprime mortgages, and what role did they play in the financial crisis of 2008?

7. Carmen M. Reinhart and Kenneth S. Rogoff, "Recovery from Financial Crises: Evidence from 100 Episodes," *American Economic Review*, 104 (May 2014): 50–55.

EXHIBIT 7   **Top 10 Banks in America and in the World**

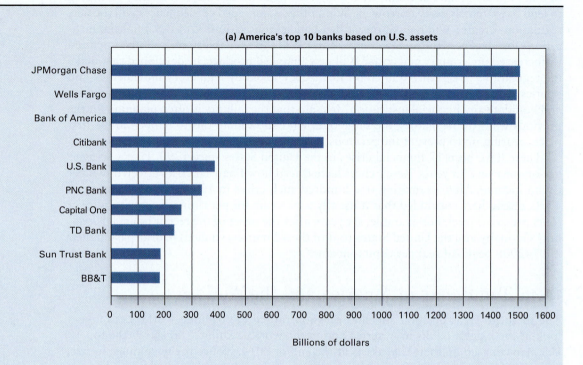

(a) America's top 10 banks based on U.S. assets

Billions of dollars

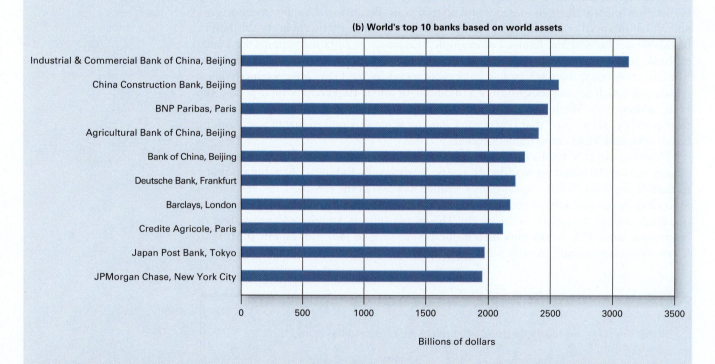

(b) World's top 10 banks based on world assets

Billions of dollars

Among America's top 10 banks (based on U.S. assets) in panel (a), size differs sharply, with the top bank about eight times larger than the tenth-ranked bank. Among the world's top 10 banks (based on worldwide assets) in panel (b), only one, JPMorgan Chase, is American.

(a) Source: As of year-end 2014 from the Federal Reserve Bank at http://www.federalreserve.gov/Releases/Lbr/current/default.htm.

(b) Source: "Top Banks in the World," Accuity, available at http://www.accuity.com/useful-links/bank-rankings/. Figures are for November 2014.

13-5 Conclusion

Money has grown increasingly more abstract over time, moving from commodity money to paper money that represented a claim on some commodity, such as gold, to paper money with no intrinsic value. As you will see, paper money constitutes only a fraction of the money supply. Modern money also consists of electronic entries in the banking system's computers. So money has changed from a physical commodity to an electronic entry. Money today does not so much change hands as change electronic accounts.

Summary

1. Barter was the first form of exchange. As specialization grew, it became more difficult to discover the double coincidence of wants that barter required. The time and inconvenience of barter led even simple economies to use money.

2. Anything that acquires a high degree of acceptability throughout an economy thereby becomes money. The first moneys were commodities, such as gold. Eventually, what changed hands were pieces of paper that could be redeemed for something of value, such as gold. As paper money became widely accepted, governments introduced fiat money—pieces of paper not officially redeemable for anything other than more pieces of paper. Nearly all currencies throughout the world today are fiat money. People accept fiat money because, through experience, they believe that other people will do so as well. The ideal money is durable, portable, divisible, of uniform quality, has a low opportunity cost, and is relatively stable in value.

3. The value of money depends on what it buys. If money fails to serve as a medium of exchange, traders find other means of exchange, such as barter. If a monetary system breaks down, more time must be devoted to exchange, leaving less time for production, so efficiency suffers. No machine increases an economy's productivity as much as a properly functioning money.

4. The Federal Reserve System, or the Fed, was established in 1913 to regulate the banking system and issue the nation's currency. After a third of the nation's banks failed during the Great Depression, the Fed's powers were increased and centralized. The primary powers of the Fed became (a) to conduct open-market operations (buying and selling U.S. government securities), (b) to set the discount rate (the interest rate the Fed charges borrowing banks), and (c) to establish reserve requirements (the share of deposits banks must hold in reserve).

5. Regulations introduced during the Great Depression turned banking into a closely regulated industry. Reforms in the 1980s gave banks more flexibility to compete for deposits with other kinds of financial intermediaries. Some banks used this flexibility to make risky loans, but these gambles often failed, causing bank failures. By the mid-1990s, U.S. banks were thriving once again. Mergers and holding companies create larger banks that span the nation. But U.S. banks are still not that large by world standards.

6. A decades-long rise in home prices, the growth of subprime mortgages, and the spread of mortgage-backed securities created the financial crisis of September 2008. Credit dried up. The government first tried to stabilize markets by investing in financial institutions. Later, the Dodd-Frank Act of 2010, the most sweeping reform of financial markets since the Great Depression, authorized regulators to write and interpret hundreds of new financial rules. Banks are back to being more tightly regulated about the kinds of assets they can own and trade.

Key Concepts

Double coincidence of wants 281

Money 282

Medium of exchange 282

Commodity money 282

Unit of account 283

Store of value 283

Token money 286

Check 286

Fractional reserve banking system 287

Bank notes 287

Fiat money 287

Legal tender 287

Financial intermediaries 289

Depository institutions 289

Commercial banks 289

Thrift institutions, or thrifts 289

Federal Reserve System, or the Fed 290

Reserves 291

Federal Open Market Committee (FOMC) 292

Open-market operations 292

Money market mutual fund 294

Bank branches 296

Bank holding company 296

Subprime mortgage 297

Mortgage-backed security 298

Troubled Asset Relief Program, or TARP 299

Too big to fail 300

Dodd-Frank Wall Street Reform and Consumer Protection Act 300

Questions for Review

1. **Barter** Define a double coincidence of wants and explain its role in a barter system.

2. **Money Versus Barter** "Without money, everything would be more expensive." Explain this statement.

3. **Functions of Money** What are the three important functions of money? Define each of them.

4. **Functions of Money** "If an economy had only two goods (both *nondurable*), there would be no need for money because exchange would always be between those two goods." What important function of money does this statement disregard?

5. **Characteristics of Money** Why is universal acceptability such an important characteristic of money? What other characteristics can you think of that might be important to market participants?

6. **Commodity Money** Why do you think rice was chosen to serve as money in medieval Japan? What would happen to the economy's price level if there was a particularly good rice harvest one year?

7. **Commodity Money** Early in U.S. history, tobacco was used as money. If you were a tobacco farmer and had two loads of tobacco that were of different qualities, which would you supply as money and which would you supply for smoking? Under what conditions would you use both types of tobacco for money?

Problems and Exercises

8. **Origins of Banking** Discuss the various ways in which London goldsmiths functioned as early banks.

9. **Types of Money** Complete each of the following sentences:
   a. A product that serves both as money and as a commodity is _____.
   b. Some coins and all paper money circulating in the United States have face values that exceed the value of the materials from which they are made. Therefore, they are forms of _____.
   c. If the government declares that creditors must accept a form of money as payment for debts, the money becomes _____.
   d. A common unit for measuring the value of every good or service in the economy is known as a(n) _____.

10. **Fiat Money** Most economists believe that the better fiat money serves as a store of value, the more acceptable it is. What does this statement mean? How could people lose faith in money?

11. **The Value of Money** When the value of money was based on its gold content, new discoveries of gold were frequently followed by periods of inflation. Explain.

12. **Case Study: Mackerel Economics in Federal Prisons** How well do pouches of mackerel satisfy each of the six properties of ideal money listed in Exhibit 1?

13. **Depository Institutions** What is a depository institution, and what types of depository institutions are found in the United States? How do they act as intermediaries between savers and borrowers? Why do they play this role?

14. **Federal Reserve System** What are the main powers and responsibilities of the Federal Reserve System?

15. **Bank Deregulation** Some economists argue that deregulating the interest rates that could be paid on deposits combined with deposit insurance led to the insolvency of many depository institutions. On what basis do they make such an argument?

16. **The Structure of U.S. Banking** Discuss the impact of bank mergers on the structure of American banking. Why do banks merge?

17. **Incentive Problems and the Financial Crisis of** 2008 What incentives motivated the behaviors that caused the financial crisis of 2008?

18. **Dodd-Frank Act** What are some goals of the Dodd-Frank legislation, and what are some possible unintended consequences of the measure?

Banking and the Money Supply

14

Matthias Kulka/Corbis

- *How is the Fed both literally and figuratively a money machine?*

- *How do banks create money?*

- *Why are banks called First Trust or Security National rather than Benny's Bank or Loans 'R' Us?*

- *Why are we so interested in banks, anyway?*

- *After all, isn't banking a business like any other, such as dry cleaning, auto washing, or home remodeling?*

- *Why not devote a chapter to the home-remodeling business?*

Answers to these and related questions are provided in this chapter, which examines banking and the money supply.

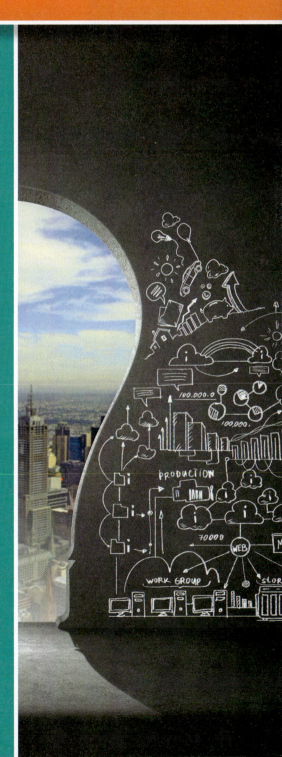

In this chapter, we take a closer look at the unique role banks play in the economy. Banks are special in macroeconomics because, like the London goldsmith, they can convert a borrower's IOU into money, one key to a healthy economy. Because regulatory reforms have eliminated many of the distinctions between commercial banks and thrift institutions, all depository institutions are usually referred to more simply as banks.

We begin by going over the definitions of money, from the narrow to the broad view. Then, we look at how banks work and how they create money. We also consider the Fed in more detail. As you will see, the Fed attempts to control the money supply directly by issuing currency and indirectly by regulating bank reserves.

Topics discussed in this chapter include:

- Money aggregates
- Checkable deposits
- Debit cards
- Bitcoin
- Balance sheets
- Money creation
- Money multiplier
- Tools of the Fed

14-1 Money Aggregates

When you think of money, what comes to mind is probably currency—dollar notes and coins. But as you learned in the last chapter, dollar notes and coins account for only part of the money supply. In this section, we consider two definitions of money.

14-1a Narrow Definition of Money: M1

Suppose you have some cash with you right now—dollar notes and coins. These are part of the money supply as narrowly defined. If you were to deposit this cash in your checking account, you could then write a check or use a debit card directing your bank to pay someone from your account. **Checkable deposits** are bank deposits that allow the account owner to draw down that account with a check or a debit card. Checkable deposits are included in the narrow definition of money. Banks hold a variety of checkable deposits. In recent years, financial institutions have developed other kinds of accounts that carry check-writing privileges but also earn interest.

Money aggregates are measures of the money supply defined by the Federal Reserve. The narrow definition, called **M1**, consists of currency (including coins) held by the nonbanking public, checkable deposits, and traveler's checks. Note that currency in bank vaults is not counted as part of the money supply because it is not being used as a medium of exchange—it's just sitting there out of circulation. But checkable deposits are money because their owners can write checks or use debit cards to tap them.

checkable deposits
Bank deposits that allow the account owner to write checks to third parties; debit cards can also access these deposits and transmit them electronically

money aggregates
Measures of the economy's money supply

M1
The narrow measure of the money supply, consisting of currency and coins held by the nonbanking public, checkable deposits, and traveler's checks

Checkable deposits are the liabilities of the issuing banks, which stand ready to convert them into cash. But unlike cash, checks are not legal tender, as signs that say " No Checks!" attest.

The currency circulating in the United States consists mostly of Federal Reserve notes, which are produced by the U.S. Bureau of Engraving and Printing and are issued by and are liabilities of the 12 Federal Reserve banks. Nearly one-third of the Fed's liabilities consist of Federal Reserve notes. The Fed spends about $600 million a year printing, storing, and distributing notes. Because Federal Reserve notes are redeemable for nothing other than more Federal Reserve notes, U.S. currency is *fiat money*. The other component of currency is coins, manufactured by the U.S. Mint, which sells these coins to Federal Reserve banks at face value. Like paper money, some U.S. coins are token money because the face value of the coins exceeds the cost of production (though the costs of minting the penny and the nickel now exceed their face values). The U.S. Mint, a division of the U.S. Treasury, reaps any profit from coin production (in 2014 this amounted to about $289 million, mostly from quarters).

About half of Federal Reserve notes are held abroad.[1] Some countries such as Panama, Ecuador, and El Salvador use U.S. dollars as their currency. In other countries, especially those that have experienced high inflation, U.S. dollars circulate alongside the local currency. In Vietnam, for example, some high-end restaurants list prices in U.S. dollars, not in dong, the national currency. Dollars circulating abroad are, in fact, a good deal for Americans because a $100 note that costs only about 12 cents to print can be "sold" to foreigners for $100 worth of goods and services. It's as if these countries were granting us an interest-free loan during the period the $100 note circulates abroad, usually years. But having our currency used around the world poses special problems when it comes to counterfeiting, as discussed in the following case study.

CASE STUDY

PUBLIC POLICY

FAKING IT   As just noted, about half of U.S. currency is held abroad, mostly as a safe, liquid, and portable store of value. The foreign demand for U.S. currency spiked immediately following the financial crisis of September 2008 as people sought the world's most trusted cash; some people around the world hoarded dollars.

One possible threat to the integrity of U.S. currency is the so-called supernote—a counterfeit $100 note of extremely high quality that began circulating around 1990; the suspected origin was North Korea. It was remarkable forgery, including sequential serial numbers and a polymer security thread that took Crane & Company, the supplier of paper for U.S. currency since 1879, years to develop. By perfectly matching the ferrous oxide inked in Benjamin Franklin's portrait, the supernote sometimes fools currency-scanning machines at the nation's 12 Federal Reserve banks.

Expert engravers produced the supernote, but technological improvements in copy machines, computers, and printers now allow even amateurs to make passable counterfeits. About half the fake notes found in a recent year were produced with computers, copiers, and printers, up from just 1 percent in 1995. On U.S. soil, the Secret Service seizes most counterfeit money before it circulates. But foreign counterfeiting poses a problem, because the Secret Service is primarily a domestic police force (few of its 2,000 agents work abroad). Most counterfeit money seized here is printed abroad, and seizures abroad have been growing.

continued

[1.] Ruth Judson, "Crisis and Calm: Demand for U.S. Currency at Home and Abroad," Board of Governors of the Federal Reserve System, International Finance Discussion Paper No. 1058 (November 2012), at http://www.federalreserve.gov/PubS/ifdp/2012/1058/ifdp1058.pdf.

© 2010 The Department of the Treasury

The $100 note was redesigned in 1996 for the first time since 1928. To help combat technological improvements in counterfeiting, the U.S. Treasury now redesigns U.S. currency every 7 to 15 years. New features include 3-D security images, a security thread, added color, and a bell that shifts inside a copper-colored inkwell. The $1 note is not popular with counterfeiters (why not?) and will not get a facelift. Vending machine owners also oppose any change in the $1 note (why?).

The $20 note is most popular among domestic counterfeiters, and the $100 note most popular among foreign counterfeiters. Colombia is the world's largest source of bogus American currency. Colombia borders on Ecuador, which converted to the U.S. dollar in 2000 and thus offers a ready outlet for counterfeits.

Most other countries that redesign their currency recall notes with the old design and impose a time limit on their validity. The United States has a policy of never recalling currency for fear that the world's hoarders of dollars might switch to other currencies, such as euros (remember, we want foreigners to keep hoarding their U.S. dollars). Over time, preference for the new design and the replacement of old, worn notes as they pass through the Fed will eventually eliminate old notes. But different designs of the same denomination will circulate side by side for some time, especially $100 notes. To give you some idea how long this could take, U.S. notes in denominations exceeding $100 were last printed in 1946, and the Fed began taking them out of circulation in 1969. Yet more than 100,000 notes of $1,000 or more are still hoarded by the public here and abroad and remain legal tender. Some still show up at Federal Reserve banks, where they are destroyed. Every U.S. note issued since 1861 remains legal tender today. That's one reason U.S. dollars are prized around the world. They all come with a lifetime money-back guarantee, so to speak.

Sources: Jo Craven McGinty, "Dollar Coin Loses Currency on Savings," *Wall Street Journal*, 3 April 2015; Jim Dwyer, "Awash in $100 Bills that Add Up to Zero," *New York Times*, 23 April 2010; "'Supernote' Investigation," U.S. Secret Service, 25 April 2006, at http://cryptome.org/supernote-nk.pdf; and "The Use and Counterfeiting of U.S. Currency Abroad, Part 3," *A Final Report to the Congress by the Secretary of the Treasury*, September 2006. The U.S. Treasury also has a Web site about new notes at www.newmoney.gov.

14-1b Broader Definition of Money: M2

Economists regard currency and checkable deposits as money because each serves as a medium of exchange, a unit of account, and a store of value. Some other financial assets perform the store-of-value function and can be converted into currency or to checkable deposits. Because these are so close to money, they are called near-monies and are included under a broader definition.

Savings deposits earn interest but have no specific maturity date. Banks often allow depositors to shift funds from savings accounts to checking accounts by phone, ATM card, or online, so distinctions between narrow and broad definitions of money have become blurred. **Time deposits** (also called *certificates of deposit*, or *CDs*) earn a fixed rate of interest if held for a specified period, ranging from several months to several years. Premature withdrawals are penalized by forfeiture of some interest. Neither savings deposits nor time deposits serve directly as media of exchange, so they are not included in M1, the narrow definition of money.

Money market mutual fund accounts, mentioned in the previous chapter, are another component of money when defined more broadly. But, because of restrictions on the minimum balance, on the number of checks that can be written per month, and on the minimum amount of each check, these popular accounts are not viewed as money as narrowly defined.

savings deposits

Bank deposits that earn interest but have no specific maturity date

time deposits

Bank deposits that earn a fixed interest rate if held for the specified period, which can range from several months to several years; also called certificates of deposit

Recall that M1 consists of currency (including coins) held by the nonbanking public, checkable deposits, and traveler's checks. **M2** includes M1 as well as savings deposits, small-denomination time deposits, money market mutual fund accounts, and other miscellaneous near-monies. Exhibit 1 shows the size and relative importance of each money aggregate. As you can see, compared to M1, M2 is nearly four times larger. Thus, the narrow definition of money is only a fraction of the broader aggregate. But distinctions between M1 and M2 become less meaningful as banks allow depositors to transfer funds from one account to another.

M2

A money aggregate consisting of M1 plus savings deposits, small-denomination time deposits, money market mutual funds, and other near-monies

14-1c Credit Cards and Debit Cards: What's the Difference?

You may be curious why the narrow definition includes funds accessed by debit cards but not funds accessed by credit cards. After all, most sellers accept credit cards as readily as they accept cash, checks, or debit cards (online sellers even prefer credit cards), and credit cards finance about 30 percent of all consumer purchases. Credit cards offer an easy way to get a loan from the card issuer. If you buy an airline ticket with a credit card, the card issuer lends you the money to pay for the ticket. You don't need money until you repay the credit card issuer. The credit card has not eliminated your use of money, merely delayed it.

EXHIBIT 1   Two Measures of the Money Supply (Week of May 4, 2015)

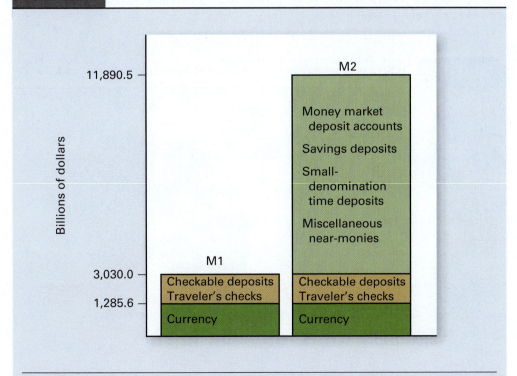

Source: Based on seasonally adjusted averages for the week from the Federal Reserve Board. For the latest data, go to http://www.federalreserve.gov/releases/h6/Current/.

On the other hand, when you use your debit card, you tap directly into your checking account to buy something and often to get cash back, paying with electronic money—part of M1. Debit cards get their name because they *debit*, or draw down, your checking account immediately. A **debit card**, also called a check card or bank card, is issued by a bank, sometimes jointly with Visa, MasterCard, or other major card issuers. Even though debit cards look like credit cards, and even may bear a name such as Visa, they are not credit cards.

Many people prefer debit cards to checks because no checkbook is required and payments are made directly and immediately. Transactions using debit cards and other electronic transfers now exceed payments by check. Debit cards usually require a personal identification number, or PIN, to use. In that regard, debit cards are safer than credit cards, which could be used more easily by a thief. But debit cards have some disadvantages. Whereas a debit card draws down your checking account immediately, credit cards provide a grace period between a purchase and required payment. And about half of credit card users prefer to borrow beyond the grace period—that is, to carry a balance from month to month. Also, because debit cards immediately reduce your checking account, you can't dispute a bill or withhold payment as you can after using a credit card and you can't stop payment as you can after writing a check. Still, debit cards, which came from nowhere a decade ago, are used by most households today.

How often have you heard a store clerk ask, "Will that be cash or charge?" Exhibit 2 shows how consumers chose to pay for their purchases in 2013 and how they are projected to pay in 2018. Based on the dollar volume of purchases, cash and checks will decline as a share of the total, while credit cards, debit cards, and electronic payments will increase. Cash and checks combined are projected to fall from 30 percent of all payments in 2013 to only 14 percent in 2018. The share of other types of payments combined is projected to increase from 70 percent in 2013 to 86 percent in 2018. Of course, credit-card balances are ultimately paid off with money.

debit card

Card that taps directly into a depositor's bank account to buy something and often to get cash back; also called a check card

---

EXHIBIT 2   U.S. Consumer Payments as a Share of Spending: 2013 and 2018

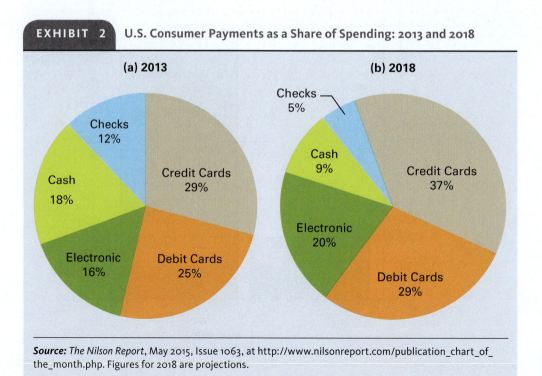

Source: The Nilson Report, May 2015, Issue 1063, at http://www.nilsonreport.com/publication_chart_of_the_month.php. Figures for 2018 are projections.

14-1d Is Bitcoin Money?

New forms of payments are being tried every day. For example, some people use smartphones as debit cards. Online payments are executed by systems such as Square, which operates like a credit card, and PayPal, which can be used like either a credit card or a debit card. These transactions are still settled in traditional currencies, such as U.S. dollars, through the banking system. But some new digital currencies, such as *bitcoin*, once they are initially purchased with traditional currencies, can fund some transactions without further reliance on traditional currencies or the banking system. A bitcoin user gets a digital wallet with a private key that serves as a password. With computers or mobile apps, users can send bitcoin to one another.

Bitcoin account holders need not use their real names, so they can buy or sell goods anonymously. This makes bitcoin attractive for drug dealings and other illegal activities, including ransoms.[2] But the safety of bitcoin is a question. A bitcoin account can be hacked, destroyed by a virus, or mistakenly deleted. For example, a British man in 2013 accidentally discarded a hard drive containing bitcoin worth $9 million at the time.[3] And in 2014, hackers stole $460 million in bitcoin from the world's largest bitcoin exchange, Mt. Gox, driving that exchange into bankruptcy.[4]

Is bitcoin really money? Since its inception, the dollar cost of one bitcoin has ranged from as low as six cents to as high as $971.45. Wide fluctuations relative to traditional currencies undermine bitcoin's functions as a unit of account and as a store of value. Bitcoin also lacks access to banking systems and deposit insurance. According to one economist who has studied the matter, bitcoin behaves more like a speculative investment than a currency.[5] And even as a speculative investment, bitcoin is more volatile than nearly any other asset one could find.

True, bitcoin is a medium of exchange as long as you can find others willing to accept this type of electronic payment. But it's not good as a unit of account or a store of value. So it's not so good as money. As of June 13, 2015, there were 14.3 million bitcoin in circulation throughout the world. Based on an exchange value of $231.33 per bitcoin on that date, the dollar value of bitcoin in circulation was $3.3 billion. By way of comparison, the supply of M1 at the time was about $3.0 trillion, or about 900 times greater. Bitcoin or another new currency could someday replace traditional currencies, but probably not soon.

 **CHECKPOINT**

Why is using a debit card like using cash, but using a credit card is not?

2. Nathaniel Popper, "For Ransom, Bitcoin Replaces the Bag of Bills," *New York Times*, 25 July 2015.

3. "Bitcoin Worth $9M Buried in Garbage Dump," *CNN Money*, 29 November 2013, at http://money.cnn.com/2013/11/29/news/bitcoin-haul-landfill/index.html.

4. Robert McMillan, "The Inside Story of Mt. Gox, Bitcoin's $460 Million Disaster," *Wired*, 3 March 2014, at http://www.wired.com/2014/03/bitcoin-exchange/.

5. David Yermack, "Is Bitcoin A Real Currency? An Economic Appraisal," in *Handbook of Digital Currency: Bitcoin, Innovation, Financial Instruments, and Big Data*, David Lee Kuo Chuen, ed. (Academic Press, 2015): 31-44.

14-2 How Banks Work

Banks attract deposits from savers to lend to borrowers, earning a profit on the difference between the interest paid depositors and the interest charged borrowers. Savers need a safe place for their money, and borrowers need credit; banks try to earn a profit by serving both groups. To inspire depositor confidence, a bank usually presents an image of trust and assurance with an impressive building, a big safe often visible from the lobby, and a name that sounds serious. Banks are more apt to be called Fidelity Trust, First National, or U.S. Bankcorp than Benny's Bank, Loans 'R' Us, or Loadsamoney. In contrast, *finance companies* are financial intermediaries that do not get their funds from depositors, so they can choose names aimed more at borrowers—names such as Household Finance, LendingTree, and The Money Store. Likewise, mortgage companies do not rely on depositors, so they pick names aimed at home buyers, names such as Lender's Depot, Quicken Loans, and Cheap Mortgages.

14-2a Banks are Financial Intermediaries

By bringing together both sides of the money market, banks serve as financial intermediaries, or as go-betweens. They gather various amounts from savers and repackage these funds into the amounts demanded by borrowers. Some savers need their money next week, some next year, some only after retirement. Likewise, borrowers need credit for different lengths of time. Banks, as intermediaries, offer desirable durations to both groups. In short, *banks reduce the transaction costs of channeling savings to creditworthy borrowers.* Here's how.

Coping with Asymmetric Information

Banks, as lenders, try to identify borrowers who are willing to pay interest and are able to repay their loans. But borrowers have more reliable information about their own credit history and financial plans than do lenders. Thus, in the market for loans, there is **asymmetric information**—an inequality in what's known by each party to the transaction. Asymmetric information is unequal information. This wouldn't be a problem if borrowers could be trusted to report relevant details to lenders. Some borrowers, however, have an incentive to suppress important information, such as other debts outstanding, a troubled financial history, or plans to use the borrowed money to fund a risky venture. Because of their experience and expertise in evaluating loan applicants, banks can better cope with asymmetric information than could an individual saver. Banks also know more about lending agreements than do individual savers. Thus, savers, rather than lending their money directly, are better off depositing their money in banks, and letting banks do the lending. *The economy is more efficient because banks develop expertise in evaluating creditworthiness, structuring loans, and enforcing loan contracts.*

asymmetric information
A situation in which one side of the market has more reliable information than the other side

Reducing Risk through Diversification

By developing a diversified portfolio of assets rather than lending funds to a single borrower, banks reduce the risk to each individual saver. A bank, in effect, lends a tiny fraction of each saver's deposits to each of its many borrowers. If one borrower fails to repay a loan, it hardly affects a large, diversified bank. Certainly such a default does not represent the personal disaster it would if one saver's entire nest egg had been loaned directly to that defaulting borrower.

Yet, as noted in the previous chapter, a bank can get into financial trouble if many borrowers fail to repay their loans. For example, when housing prices collapsed in 2007 and 2008, many borrowers owed the bank more than their homes were worth.

Some borrowers stopped making mortgage payments. These homes went into foreclosure and banks suffered heavy losses. The problem of these bad loans rippled through the economy and contributed to the global financial crisis of September 2008 and the Great Recession of 2007–2009, the worst downturn since the Great Depression.

14-2b Starting a Bank

We could consider the operation of any type of depository institution (commercial bank, savings bank, or credit union), but let's focus on commercial banks because they are the most important in terms of total assets. What's more, the operating principles also apply to other depository institutions. Suppose some business leaders in your hometown want to open a commercial bank called Home Bank. To obtain a *charter*, or the right to operate, they must apply to the state banking authority in the case of a state bank or to the U.S. Comptroller of the Currency in the case of a national bank. The chartering agency reviewing the application judges the quality of management, the need for another bank in the community, the proposed bank's funding, and the likely success of the bank. Note that a proposed restaurant would not be subject to such scrutiny, but a failed restaurant is not nearly as problematic for a community as a failed bank.

Suppose the founders plan to invest $500,000 in the bank, and they so indicate on their application for a national charter. If their application is approved, they incorporate, issuing themselves shares of stock—certificates of ownership. Thus, they exchange $500,000 for shares of stock in the bank. These shares are called the *owners' equity*, or the **net worth**, of the bank. Part of the $500,000, say $50,000, is used to buy shares in their district Federal Reserve bank. So Home Bank is now a member of the Federal Reserve System. With the remaining $450,000, the owners acquire and furnish the bank building.

To focus our discussion, we examine the bank's **balance sheet**, presented in Exhibit 3. As the name implies, a balance sheet shows a balance between the two sides of the bank's accounts. The left side lists the bank's assets. An **asset** is any physical property or financial claim owned by the bank. At this early stage, assets include the building and equipment owned by Home Bank plus its stock in the district Federal Reserve bank. The right side lists the bank's liabilities and net worth. A **liability** is an amount the bank owes. So far the bank owes nothing, so the right side includes only the net worth of $500,000. The two sides of the ledger must always be equal, or in *balance*, which is why it's called a *balance sheet*. So assets must equal liabilities plus net worth:

$$\text{Assets} = \text{Liabilities} + \text{Net worth}$$

The bank is now ready for business. Opening day is the bank's lucky day, because the first customer carries in a briefcase full of $100 notes and deposits $1,000,000 into a new checking account. In accepting this cash, the bank promises to repay the depositor that amount. The deposit therefore is an amount the bank owes—it's a liability of the

net worth
Assets minus liabilities; also called owners' equity

balance sheet
A financial statement at a given point in time showing assets on one side and liabilities plus net worth on the other side; because assets must equal liabilities plus net worth, the two sides of the statement must balance, hence the name

asset
Anything of value that is owned

liability
Anything that is owed to other people or institutions

EXHIBIT 3	Home Bank's Initial Balance Sheet

Assets		Liabilities and Net Worth	
Building and furniture	$450,000	Net worth	$500,000
Stock in district Fed	50,000		
Total	$500,000	Total	$500,000

EXHIBIT 4	Home Bank's Balance Sheet after $1,000,000 Deposit into Checking Account		

Assets		Liabilities and Net Worth	
Cash	$1,000,000	Checkable deposits	$1,000,000
Building and furniture	450,000	Net worth	500,000
Stock in district Fed	50,000		
Total	$1,500,000	Total	$1,500,000

bank. As a result of this deposit, the bank's assets increase by $1,000,000 in cash and its liabilities increase by $1,000,000 in checkable deposits. Exhibit 4 shows the effects of this transaction on Home Bank's balance sheet. The right side now shows two claims on the bank's assets: claims by the owners, called net worth, and claims by nonowners, called liabilities, which at this point consist of checkable deposits.

14-2c Reserve Accounts

required reserves

The dollar amount of reserves a bank is obligated by regulation to hold as cash in the bank's vault or on account at the Fed

required reserve ratio

The ratio of reserves to deposits that banks are obligated by regulation to hold

excess reserves

Bank reserves exceeding required reserves

Where do we go from here? As mentioned in the previous chapter, banks are required by the Fed to set aside, or to hold in reserve, a percentage of their checkable deposits. The dollar amount that must be held in reserve is called **required reserves**—checkable deposits multiplied by the required reserve ratio. The **required reserve ratio** dictates the minimum proportion of deposits the bank must hold in reserve. The current reserve requirement is 10 percent on checkable deposits (other types of deposits have no reserve requirement). All depository institutions are subject to the Fed's reserve requirements. Reserves are held either as cash in the bank's vault, which earns the bank no interest, or as deposits at the Fed, which earn a small rate of interest (most recently, one quarter of one percent, or 0.25 percent). Home Bank must therefore hold $100,000 as reserves, or 10 percent times $1,000,000.

Suppose Home Bank deposits $100,000 in a reserve account with its district Federal Reserve bank. Home Bank's reserves now consist of $100,000 in required reserves on deposit with the Fed and $900,000 in **excess reserves** held as cash in the vault. Home Bank earns no interest on cash in its vault. Excess reserves, however, can be used to make loans or to purchase interest-bearing assets, such as government bonds. By law, the bank's interest-bearing assets are limited primarily to loans and to government securities. (Note that if a bank is owned by a holding company, the holding company has broader latitude in the kinds of assets it can own.)

14-2d Liquidity Versus Profitability

Like the early goldsmiths, modern banks must be prepared to satisfy depositors' requests for funds. A bank loses reserves whenever a depositor withdraws cash, writes a check that gets deposited in another bank, or uses a debit card that ultimately shifts deposits to another bank. The bank must be in a position to satisfy all depositor demands, even if many ask for their money at the same time. Required reserves are not meant to be used to meet depositor requests for funds; therefore, banks often hold excess reserves or other assets, such as government bonds, that can be easily liquidated, or converted to cash, to satisfy any unexpected demand for cash. Banks may also want to hold excess reserves in case a valued customer needs immediate credit.

The bank manager must therefore structure the portfolio of assets with an eye toward liquidity but must not forget that survival also depends on profitability. **Liquidity** is the ease with which an asset can be converted into cash without a significant loss of value. *The objectives of liquidity and profitability are at odds.* For example, more liquid assets yield lower interest rates than less liquid assets do. The most liquid asset is cash in the bank's vault, but such reserves earn no interest.

At one extreme, suppose a bank is completely liquid, holding all its assets as cash in its vault. Such a bank would have no difficulty meeting depositors' demands for funds. This bank is playing it safe—too safe. The bank earns no interest and will fail. At the other extreme, suppose a bank uses all its excess reserves to acquire high-yielding but illiquid assets, such as long-term home loans. Such a bank runs into problems whenever withdrawals exceed new deposits. There is a trade-off between liquidity and profitability. The portfolio manager's task is to strike the right balance between liquidity, or safety, and profitability.

Because vault cash earns no interest, banks prefer to hold reserves at the Fed. Any bank short of required reserves at the end of the day can borrow from a bank that has excess reserves at the Fed. The **federal funds market** provides for day-to-day lending and borrowing among banks of excess reserves on account at the Fed. These funds usually do not leave the Fed—instead, they shift among accounts. For example, suppose that at the end of the business day, Home Bank has excess reserves of $100,000 on account with the Fed and wants to lend that amount to another bank that finished the day short $100,000 in required reserves. These two banks are brought together by a broker who specializes in the market for federal funds—that is, the market for reserves at the Fed. The interest rate paid on this loan is called the **federal funds rate**; this is the rate the Fed targets as a tool of monetary policy, but more on that later.

CHECKPOINT

Why is a bank in a better position to lend your savings than you are?

14-3 How Banks Create Money

Let's now discuss how the Fed, Home Bank, and the banking system as a whole can create fiat money. Excess reserves are the raw material the banking system uses to create money. Again, our discussion focuses on commercial banks because they are the largest and most important depository institutions, although thrifts operate the same way.

14-3a Creating Money through Excess Reserves

Suppose Home Bank has already used its $900,000 in excess reserves to make loans and buy government bonds and has no excess reserves left. In fact, let's assume there are no excess reserves in the banking system. With that as a point of departure, let's walk through the money creation process.

Round One

To start, suppose the Fed buys a $1,000 U.S. government bond from a securities dealer, with the transaction handled by the dealer's bank—Home Bank. The Fed pays the

liquidity
A measure of the ease with which an asset can be converted into money without a significant loss of value

federal funds market
A market for overnight lending and borrowing of reserves among banks; the interbank market for reserves on account at the Fed

federal funds rate
The interest rate charged in the federal funds market; the interest rate banks charge one another for overnight borrowing; the Fed's target interest rate

dealer by crediting Home Bank's reserve account with $1,000, so Home Bank can increase the dealer's checking account by $1,000. Where does the Fed get these reserves? It makes them up—creates them out of thin air, out of electronic ether! The securities dealer has exchanged one asset, a U.S. bond, for another asset, checkable deposits. A U.S. bond is not money, but checkable deposits are, so the money supply increases by $1,000 in this first round. Exhibit 5 shows changes in Home Bank's balance sheet as a result of the Fed's bond purchase. On the assets side, Home Bank's reserves at the Fed increase by $1,000. On the liabilities side, checkable deposits increase by $1,000. Of the dealer's $1,000 checkable deposit, Home Bank must set aside $100 in required reserves (based on a 10 percent required reserve ratio). The remaining $900 becomes excess reserves, which can fuel a further increase in the money supply.

Round Two

Suppose Home Bank is your regular bank, and you apply for a $900 loan to help pay student fees. Home Bank approves your loan and increases your checking account by $900. *Home Bank has converted your promise to repay, your IOU, into a $900 checkable deposit. Because checkable deposits are money, this action increases the money supply by $900.* The money supply has increased by a total of $1,900 to this point—the $1,000 increase in the securities dealer's checkable deposits and now the $900 increase in your checkable deposits. In the process, what had been $900 in Home Bank's excess reserves now back up its loan to you. As shown in Exhibit 6, Home Bank's loans increase by $900 on the assets side because your IOU becomes the bank's asset. On the bank's liabilities side, checkable deposits increase by $900 because the bank has increased your account by that amount. In short, Home Bank has created $900 in checkable deposits based on your promise to repay the loan.

When you write a $900 check for student fees, your college promptly deposits the check into its checking account at Merchants Trust, which increases the college's account by $900, and sends your check to the Fed. The Fed transfers $900 in reserves from Home Bank's account to Merchants Trust's account. The Fed then sends the check to Home Bank, which reduces your checkable deposits by $900. The Fed has thereby "cleared" your check by settling the claim that Merchants Trust had on Home Bank. Your $900 in checkable deposits at Home Bank has become your college's $900 in checkable deposits at Merchants Trust. The total increase in the money supply to this point is still $1,900.

EXHIBIT 5 **Changes in Home Bank's Balance Sheet after the Fed Buys a $1,000 Bond from Securities Dealer**

Assets		Liabilities and Net Worth	
Reserves at Fed	+$1,000	Checkable deposits	+$1,000

EXHIBIT 6 **Changes in Home Bank's Balance Sheet after Lending $900 to You**

Assets		Liabilities and Net Worth	
Loans	+$900	Checkable deposits	+$900

Round Three

But Merchants Trust now has $900 more in reserves on deposit with the Fed. After setting aside $90 as required reserves, or 10 percent of your college's checkable deposit increase, the bank has $810 in excess reserves. Suppose Merchants Trust lends this $810 to an English major starting a new business called "Note This," an online note-taking service for students in large classes. Exhibit 7 shows assets at Merchants Trust are up by $810 in loans, and liabilities are up by $810 in checkable deposits. At this point, checkable deposits in the banking system, and the money supply in the economy, are up by a total of $2,710 (= $1,000 + $900 + $810), all springing from the Fed's original $1,000 bond purchase.

The $810 loan is spent at the college bookstore, which deposits the check in its account at Fidelity Bank. Fidelity credits the bookstore's checkable deposits with $810 and sends the check to the Fed for clearance. The Fed reduces Merchants Bank's reserves by $810 and increases Fidelity's by the same. The Fed then sends the check to Merchants, which reduces the English major's checkable deposits by $810. So checkable deposits are down by $810 at Merchants and up by the same amount at Fidelity. Checkable deposits are still up by $2,710, as the $810 in checkable deposits has simply shifted from Merchants Trust to Fidelity Bank.

Round Four and Beyond

We could continue the process with Fidelity Bank setting aside $81 in required reserves and lending $729 in excess reserves, but you get some idea of money creation by now. Notice the pattern of deposits and loans. Each time a bank gets a fresh deposit, 10 percent goes to required reserves. The rest becomes excess reserves, which fuel new loans or other asset acquisitions. The borrower writes a check, which the recipient deposits in a checking account, thereby generating excess reserves to support still more loans. Because this example began with the Fed, the Fed can rightfully claim, "The buck starts here"—a slogan that appeared on a large plaque in the Federal Reserve chairman's office.

To Review: An individual bank can lend no more than its excess reserves. When the borrower spends those funds, reserves at one bank usually fall, but total reserves in the banking system do not. The recipient bank uses most of the new deposit to extend more loans, creating more checkable deposits. The potential expansion of checkable deposits in the banking system therefore equals some multiple of the initial increase in reserves. Note that our example assumes that banks do not allow excess reserves to sit idle, that borrowed funds do not idle in checking accounts, and that the public does not hold some of the newly created money as cash. If excess reserves remained just that or if borrowed funds idled in checking accounts, they would not fuel an expansion of the money supply.

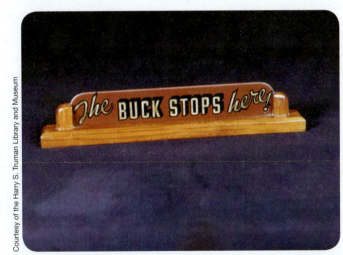

Courtesy of the Harry S. Truman Library and Museum

EXHIBIT 7	Changes in Merchants Trust's Balance Sheet after Lending $810 to English Major

Assets		Liabilities and Net Worth	
Loans	+$810	Checkable deposits	+$810

And if people chose to hold borrowed funds in cash rather than in checking accounts, that idle cash would not add to reserves in the banking system.

14-3b A Summary of the Rounds

Let's review the money creation process: *The initial and most important step is the Fed's injection of $1,000 in fresh reserves into the banking system.* By buying the bond from the securities dealer, the Fed immediately increased the money supply by $1,000. Home Bank set aside $100 as required reserves and lent you its $900 in excess reserves. You paid your college fees, and the $900 ended up in your college's checkable account. This fueled more money creation, as shown in a series of rounds of Exhibit 8. As you can see, during each round, the increase in checkable deposits (column 1) minus the increase in required reserves (column 2) equals the potential increase in loans (column 3). Checkable deposits in this example can potentially increase by as much as $10,000.

In our example, money creation results from the Fed's $1,000 bond purchase from the securities dealer, but excess reserves would also have increased if the Fed purchased a $1,000 bond from Home Bank, lent Home Bank $1,000, or freed up $1,000 in excess reserves by lowering the reserve requirement.

What if the Fed paid the securities dealer in cash? By exchanging Federal Reserve notes, which become part of the money supply in the hands of the public, for a U.S. bond, which is not part of the money supply, the Fed would have increased the money supply by $1,000. Once the securities dealer put this cash into a checking account—or spent the cash, so the money ended up in someone else's checking account—the banking system's money creation process would have been off and running.

14-3c Reserve Requirements and Money Expansion

The banking system as a whole eliminates excess reserves by expanding the money supply. With a 10 percent reserve requirement, the Fed's initial injection of $1,000 in fresh reserves could support up to $10,000 in new checkable deposits in the banking system as a whole, *assuming no bank holds excess reserves, borrowed funds don't sit idle, and people don't want to hold more cash.*

The multiple by which the money supply increases as a result of an increase in the banking system's reserves is called the **money multiplier**. The **simple money multiplier** equals the reciprocal of the required reserve ratio, or $1/r$, where r is the reserve ratio.

money multiplier
The multiple by which the money supply changes as a result of a change in fresh reserves in the banking system

simple money multiplier
The reciprocal of the required reserve ratio, or $1/r$; the maximum multiple of fresh reserves by which the money supply can increase

| EXHIBIT 8 | Summary of the Money Creation Resulting from the Fed's Purchase of $1,000 U.S. Government Bond |

Bank	(1) Increase in Checkable Deposits	(2) Increase in Required Reserves	(3) Increase in Loans $3 = (1) - (2)$
Round 1. Home Bank	$ 1,000	$ 100	$ 900
Round 2. Merchants Trust	900	90	810
Round 3. Fidelity Bank	810	81	729
All remaining rounds	7,290	729	6,561
Totals	$ 10,000	$ 1,000	$ 9,000

In our example, the reserve ratio was 10 percent, or 0.1, so the reciprocal is 1/0.1, which equals 10. The formula for the multiple expansion of money supply can be written as follows:

$$\text{Change in the money supply} = \text{Change in fresh reserves} \times 1/r$$

Again, the simple money multiplier assumes that banks hold no excess reserves, that borrowers do not let the funds sit idle, and that people do not want to hold more cash. The higher the reserve requirement, the greater the fraction of deposits that must be held as reserves, so the smaller the money multiplier. A reserve requirement of 20 percent instead of 10 percent would mean each bank must set aside twice as much in required reserves. The simple money multiplier in this case would be 1/0.2, which equals 5. The maximum possible increase in checkable deposits resulting from an initial $1,000 increase in fresh reserves would therefore be $1,000 × 5, or $5,000. *Excess reserves fuel the deposit expansion process, and a higher reserve requirement drains this fuel from the banking system, thereby reducing the amount of new money that can be created.*

On the other hand, with a reserve requirement of only 5 percent, banks would set aside less for required reserves, leaving more excess reserves available for loans. The simple money multiplier in that case would be 1/0.05, or 20. With $1,000 in fresh reserves and a 5 percent reserve requirement, the banking system could increase the money supply by a maximum of $1,000 × 20, which equals $20,000. Thus, the change in the required reserve ratio affects the banking system's ability to create money.

In summary, money creation usually begins with the Fed injecting new reserves into the banking system. An individual bank lends an amount no greater than its excess reserves. The borrower's spending ends up in someone else's checking account, fueling additional loans. *The fractional reserve requirement is the key to the multiple expansion of checkable deposits.* If each $1 deposit had to be backed by $1 in required reserves, the money multiplier would be reduced to 1, which is no multiplier at all.

14-3d Limitations on Money Expansion

Various leakages from the multiple expansion process reduce the size of the money multiplier, which is why 1/r is called the *simple* money multiplier. You could think of "simple" as meaning maximum. To repeat, our example assumes (1) that banks do not let excess reserves sit idle, (2) that borrowers do something with the money, and (3) that people do not choose to increase their cash holdings. How realistic are these assumptions? With regard to the first, banks have a profit incentive to make loans or buy some higher interest-bearing asset with excess reserves. Granted, banks earn some interest on reserves deposited with the Fed, but the rate is typically much less than could be earned on loans or on most other interest-bearing assets. The second assumption is also easy to defend. Why would people borrow money if they didn't need it for something? The third assumption is trickier. Cash may sometimes be preferable to checking accounts because cash is more versatile, so people may choose to hold some of the newly created money as cash. To the extent that people prefer to hold idle cash, this drains reserves from the banking system. With less excess reserves, banks are less able to make loans, reducing the money multiplier. Incidentally, for the money multiplier to operate, a particular bank need not use excess reserves in a specific way; it could use them to pay all its employees a Christmas bonus, for that matter. As long as the money ends up as checkable deposits in the banking system, away we go with the money expansion process.

14-3e Contraction of the Money Supply

We have already outlined the money creation process, so the story of how the Federal Reserve System can reduce bank reserves, thereby reducing the money supply, can be a brief one. Again, we begin by assuming there are no excess reserves in the system and the reserve requirement is 10 percent. Suppose the Fed *sells* a $1,000 U.S. bond to a securities dealer and gets paid with a check drawn on the security dealer's account at Home Bank. So the Fed gets paid by drawing down Home Bank's reserves at the Fed by $1,000. The Fed has thereby reduced the money supply by $1,000 in this first round.

Because the dealer's checking account was reduced by $1,000, Home Bank no longer needs to hold $100 in required reserves. But Home Bank is still short $900 in required reserves (remember, when we started, there were no excess reserves in the banking system). To replenish reserves, Home Bank must recall loans (ask for repayment before the due date), or sell some other asset. As the poet Robert Frost wryly observed, "A bank is a place where they lend you an umbrella in fair weather and ask for it back when it begins to rain." Suppose the bank calls in $900 loaned to a local business, and the loan is repaid with a check written against Merchants Bank. When the check clears, Home Bank's reserves are up by $900, just enough to satisfy its reserve requirement, but Merchants Bank's reserves and checkable deposits are down by $900. Checkable deposits are now down $1,900 as a result of the Fed's purchase of a $1,000 bond. Because there were no excess reserves at the outset, the loss of $900 in reserves leaves Merchants $810 short of its required level of reserves, forcing that bank to get more reserves.

And so it goes down the line. The Fed's sale of government bonds reduces bank reserves, forcing banks to recall loans or to somehow replenish reserves. This reduces checkable deposits each additional round. *The maximum possible effect is to reduce the money supply by the original reduction in bank reserves times the simple money multiplier, which again equals 1 divided by the reserve requirement, or 1/r.* In our example, the Fed's sale of $1,000 in U.S. bonds could reduce the money supply by as much as $10,000.

Now that you have some idea how fractional reserve banking works, we are in a position to summarize the Federal Reserve's role in the economy.

CHECKPOINT

How do banks create money?

14-4 The Fed's Tools of Monetary Control

As mentioned in the previous chapter, in its capacity as a bankers' bank, the Fed clears checks for, extends loans to, and holds deposits of banks. More than half of the narrow definition of money (M1) consists of checkable deposits. The Fed's control over checkable deposits works indirectly through its control over reserves in the banking system. You are already familiar with the Fed's three oldest tools for controlling reserves: (1) open-market operations, or the buying and selling of U.S. government bonds; (2) the discount rate, which is the interest rate the Fed charges for loans it makes to banks; and (3) the required reserve ratio, which is the minimum fraction of reserves that banks must hold against deposits. Let's examine each of these in more detail, then look at some other tools that emerged during the recent financial crisis.

14-4a Open-Market Operations and the Federal Funds Rate

The Fed carries out open-market operations whenever it buys or sells U.S. government bonds in the open market. The term "open market" here means that securities dealers compete to do business with the Fed based on price in an *open market*. Decisions about open-market operations are made by the Federal Open Market Committee, or FOMC, which meets every six weeks and during emergencies. To increase the money supply, the Fed directs the New York Fed to buy U.S. bonds. This is called an **open-market purchase**. To reduce the money supply, the New York Fed is directed to carry out an **open-market sale**. Open-market operations are relatively easy to carry out. They require no change in laws or regulations and can be executed in any amount—large or small—chosen by the Fed. Their simplicity and ease of use make them the tool of choice for the Fed.

Through open-market operations, the Fed influences bank reserves and the *federal funds rate*, which is the interest rate banks charge one another for borrowing excess reserves at the Fed, typically just for a day or two. Banks that need reserves can borrow excess reserves from other banks, paying the federal funds rate of interest. The federal funds rate serves as a good indicator of the "tightness" of monetary policy. For example, suppose the Fed buys U.S. bonds in the open market and thereby increases reserves in the banking system. As a result, more banks have excess reserves. Demand for excess reserves in the federal funds market falls and supply increases, so the federal funds rate—the interest rate for borrowing reserves in this market—declines. We can expect this lower federal funds rate to spread quickly to the economy at large. The excess reserves that have created the lower federal funds rate prompt banks to lower short-term interest rates in general, and this increases the quantity of loans demanded by the public.

open-market purchase
The purchase of U.S. government bonds by the Fed to increase the money supply

open-market sale
The sale of U.S. government bonds by the Fed to reduce the money supply

14-4b The Discount Rate

The second monetary policy tool available to the Fed is the **discount rate**, which is the interest rate the Fed charges for loans it makes to banks. Banks borrow from the Fed to satisfy their reserve requirements. A lower discount rate reduces the cost of borrowing, encouraging banks to borrow reserves from the Fed. The Fed usually does not encourage banks to borrow, but the Fed considers itself as the "lender of last resort," and a lender during a financial crisis, as occurred between 2007 and 2010 when some homeowners defaulted on their mortgages.

There are actually two discount rates. The *primary discount rate* is usually one percentage point above the federal funds rate. Thus, discount borrowing is less attractive than borrowing through the federal funds market. But during a financial crisis, the Fed could lower the primary discount rate to supply liquidity to the banking system as it did 12 times between August 2007 and December 2008, a response to the financial crisis. The Fed charges more interest on loans to banks considered less sound than to other banks. This *secondary discount rate* is usually about one-half a percentage point higher than the primary discount rate.

The Fed uses the discount rate more as a signal to financial markets about its monetary policy than as a tool for increasing or decreasing the money supply. The discount rate might also be thought of as an emergency tool for injecting liquidity into the banking system in the event of some financial crisis, such as the global credit crisis of 2008. Discount loans outstanding jumped from only $2 billion in August 2007, before the trouble started, to more than $130 billion in April 2009, when the economy was in a sharp recession. (Because of huge excess reserves held in the banking system, discount

discount rate
The interest rate the Fed charges banks that borrow reserves

loans have since nearly disappeared—only about $100 million in May 2015.) Banks would prefer to borrow reserves from other banks in the federal funds market rather than borrow reserves directly from the Fed.

14-4c   Reserve Requirements

The Fed also influences the money supply through reserve requirements, which are regulations regarding the minimum amount of reserves that banks must hold to back up deposits. Reserve requirements determine how much money the banking system can create with each dollar of fresh reserves. If the Fed increases the reserve requirement, then banks have less excess reserves to lend out. This reduces the banking system's ability to create money. On the other hand, a lower reserve requirement increases the banking system's ability to create money. Reserve requirements can be changed by a simple majority vote of the Board of Governors. But changes in the reserve requirement disrupt the banking system, so the Fed seldom makes such changes. As noted already, the current reserve requirement is 10 percent on checkable deposits and zero on other deposits; these have not changed in years. Some countries such as Australia, Canada, and the United Kingdom have no reserve requirement. Banks there still hold reserves to deal with everyday cash requirements and can borrow from their central banks (at relatively high rates) if necessary.

14-4d   Responding to Financial Crises

The Fed, through its regulation of financial markets, also tries to prevent major disruptions and financial panics. For example, during the uncertain days following the terrorist attacks of September 11, 2001, people used their ATM cards and debit cards to load up on cash. Some hoarded cash. To ensure the banking system had sufficient liquidity, the Fed bought all the government securities offered for sale, purchasing a record $150 billion worth in two days.[6] The Fed also eased some regulations to facilitate bank clearances, especially for banks struck during the attacks.

Likewise, when financial crises threatened in 1987, 1989, 1998, 2007, and 2008, the Fed worked to ensure the financial system had sufficient liquidity. For example, to calm fears during a rash of mortgage defaults in 2007 and 2008, the Fed lowered the discount rate from 6.25 percent to only 0.25 percent and encouraged banks to borrow from the Fed. To help banks improve their balance sheets, the Fed also began paying interest on bank reserves held at the Fed. To keep mortgage rates low, the Fed invested more than $1 trillion in mortgage-backed securities. And to help prevent the insurance giant AIG from collapsing, the Fed invested more than $90 billion in the company. As a general approach, Ben Bernanke, Fed chairman at the time, announced that the Fed would provide sufficient liquidity to reduce the harm of mortgage defaults on the overall economy. To prevent cash shortages during a crisis, the Fed stockpiles extra cash in bank vaults around the country and around the world.

14-4e   The Fed Is a Money Machine

One way to get a better idea of the Fed is to review its balance sheet, shown as Exhibit 9, with assets on the left and liabilities and net worth on the right. Because of the mortgage crisis and global financial meltdown of 2008, investors were reluctant to buy

[6] Anita Raghavan, Susan Pulliam, and Jeff Opdyke, "Banks and Regulators Drew Together to Calm Rattled Markets after Attack," *Wall Street Journal*, 18 October 2001.

EXHIBIT 9	Federal Reserve Bank Balance Sheet as of May 13, 2015 (Billions)

Assets		Liabilities and Net Worth	
U.S. Treasury securities	$2,460.3	Depository institution reserves	$2,643.8
Mortgage-backed securities	1,743.8	Federal Reserve notes outstanding	1,320.0
Other federal agency securities	35.9	U.S. Treasury balance	205.4
Foreign currencies	20.2	Other liabilities	274.5
Discount loans to depository institutions	0.1	Net worth	58.1
Bank buildings	2.2		
Other assets	239.3		
Total	$4,501.8	Total	$4,501.8

Source: Federal Reserve Bank at http://www.federalreserve.gov/releases/h41/Current/.

mortgage-backed securities. So the Fed stepped in and began buying them in late 2008. As of May 13, 2015, these securities still accounted for about 40 percent of the Fed's assets. U.S. government securities were about 55 percent of Fed assets (during normal times they might account for 90 percent of assets). These IOUs from the federal government result from open-market operations, and they earn the Fed interest. Other assets include foreign currencies, most of which the Fed acquired during the financial crisis as foreign central banks swapped their currencies for U.S. dollars. Note that nearly all the Fed's assets earn interest.

On the other side of the ledger, Federal Reserve notes outstanding account for about 30 percent of Fed liabilities. These notes—U.S. currency—are IOUs from the Fed and are therefore liabilities of the Fed, but the Fed pays no interest on these notes. Thus, nearly all the Fed's assets earn interest, whereas one of the Fed's primary liabilities—Federal Reserve notes—requires no interest payments by the Fed. The Fed does pay interest on reserves it holds on deposit, but that rate has been extremely low—again, just 0.25 percent since December 2008. *The Fed is therefore both literally and figuratively a money machine. It is literally a money machine because it supplies the economy with Federal Reserve notes; it is figuratively a money machine because most assets earn interest, but a main liability requires no interest payments.* The Fed also earns revenue from discount lending to banks and from other services it provides banks. After covering its operating costs, paying a small amount of interest on bank reserves at the Fed, and paying a 6 percent dividend to the member banks, the Fed turns over any remaining income to the federal government. In early 2015, the Fed sent the U.S. Treasury $97 billion, its 2014 operating surplus and a record amount.

On the right side of the ledger, you can see that depository institutions' reserves at the Fed totaled $2,643.8 billion (mostly excess reserves). This reflects a huge jump in recent years. One reason for the increase is that in late 2008, the Fed began paying a small amount of interest on bank reserves held by the Fed, as noted already. Also, because of the financial crisis, banks grew reluctant to make loans, preferring instead to let their reserves collect interest at the Fed. You can also see that the Fed held deposits of the U.S. Treasury, a reminder that the Fed is the federal government's banker.

14-5 Conclusion

Banks play a unique role in the economy because they can transform someone's IOU into a checkable deposit, and a checkable deposit is money. The banking system's ability to expand the money supply depends on the amount of excess reserves in that system. In our example, it was the purchase of a $1,000 U.S. bond that started the ball rolling. The Fed can also increase reserves by lowering the discount rate enough to stimulate bank borrowing from the Fed (although the Fed uses changes in the discount rate more to signal its policy than to alter the money supply). By reducing the required reserve ratio, the Fed not only instantly creates excess reserves in the banking system but also increases the money multiplier. In practice, the Fed rarely changes the reserve requirement because of the disruptive effect of such a change on the banking system. Finally, by purchasing long-term assets such as mortgage-backed securities, the Fed helped stabilize banks during and after the financial crisis, put reserves into the banking system, and lowered long-term interest rates to promote investment and help the housing market. In the next chapter, we consider how monetary policy affects the economy.

Summary

1. The money supply is narrowly defined as M1, which consists of currency held by the nonbanking public plus checkable deposits and traveler's checks. A broader money aggregate, M2, includes M1 plus savings deposits, small-denomination time deposits, money market mutual funds, and other miscellaneous near-monies.

2. Banks are unlike other financial intermediaries because they can turn a borrower's IOU into money—they can create money. Banks match the different desires of savers and borrowers. Banks also evaluate loan applications and try to diversify portfolios of assets to reduce the risk to any one saver.

3. In acquiring portfolios of assets, banks try to maximize profit while maintaining enough liquidity to satisfy depositors' requests for money. Assets that earn the bank more interest are usually less liquid.

4. Any single bank can expand the money supply by the amount of its excess reserves. For the banking system as a whole, however, the maximum expansion of the money supply equals a multiple of fresh bank reserves. The simple money multiplier is the reciprocal of the reserve ratio, or $1/r$. This multiplier is reduced to

the extent that (a) banks allow excess reserves to remain idle, (b) borrowers sit on their proceeds, and (c) the public withdraws cash from the banking system and holds it.

5. The key to changes in the money supply is the Fed's impact on excess reserves in the banking system. To increase excess reserves and thus increase the money supply, the Fed can buy U.S. government bonds, reduce the discount rate, or lower the reserve requirement. To reduce excess reserves and thus reduce the money supply, the Fed can sell U.S. government bonds, increase the discount rate, or increase the reserve requirement. By far the most important monetary tool for the Fed is open-market operations—buying or selling U.S. bonds.

6. The Fed was quite active during the financial crisis of 2008, pursuing several efforts to stabilize financial markets and unfreeze the flow of credit. Fed actions included extending discount loans to banks, offering interest on bank reserves at the Fed, helping AIG stay in business, and spending more than $1 trillion buying mortgage-backed securities and other long-term assets to stabilize banks and keep mortgage rates low.

Key Concepts

Checkable deposits 306	Net worth 313	Federal funds market 315
Money aggregates 306	Balance sheet 313	Federal funds rate 315
M1 306	Asset 313	Money multiplier 318
Savings deposits 308	Liability 313	Simple money multiplier 318
Time deposits 308	Required reserves 314	Open-market purchase 321
M2 309	Required reserve ratio 314	Open-market sale 321
Debit card 310	Excess reserves 314	Discount rate 321
Asymmetric information 312	Liquidity 315	

Questions for Review

1. **Money Aggregates**   What are the two measures of the money supply and how is each measure defined?

2. **Money Aggregates**   What portion of Federal Reserve notes circulate outside the United States? How does this affect the United States?

3. **Case Study: Faking It**   Why did the U.S. government consider it important to redesign the $100 note?

4. **Money Aggregates**   Determine whether each of the following is included in the M1 or M2 measures of the money supply:

    a. Currency held by the nonbanking public
    b. Available credit on credit cards held by the nonbanking public
    c. Savings deposits
    d. Large-denomination time deposits
    e. Money market mutual fund accounts

5. **Banks Are Financial Intermediaries**   In acting as financial intermediaries, what needs and desires of savers and borrowers must banks consider?

6. **Money Aggregates**   Suppose that $1,000 is moved from a savings account at a commercial bank to a checking account at the same bank. Which of the following statements are true and which are false?

    a. The amount of currency in circulation will fall.
    b. M1 will increase.
    c. M2 will increase.

7. **Bank Deposits**   Explain the differences among checkable deposits, savings deposits, and time deposits. Explain whether each of these deposits represents a bank asset or a bank liability.

8. **Reserve Accounts**   Explain why a reduction in the required reserve ratio cannot, at least initially, increase total reserves in the banking system. Is the same true of lowering the discount rate? What would happen if the Fed bought U.S. bonds from, or sold them to, the banking system?

9. **Liquidity Versus Profitability**   Why must a bank manager strike a balance between liquidity and profitability on the bank's balance sheet?

10. **Creating Money**   Often it is claimed that banks create money by making loans. How can commercial banks create money? Is the government the only institution that can legally create money?

11. **Fed Tools of Monetary Control**   What three tools can the Fed use to change the money supply? Which tool is used most frequently? What are three limitations on the money expansion process?

12. **Discount Rate**   What is the difference between the federal funds rate and the discount rate? What is the ultimate impact on the money supply of an increase in the discount rate?

13. **Federal Funds Market**   What is the federal funds market? How does it help banks strike a balance between liquidity and profitability?

14. **The Fed Is a Money Machine**   How is the Fed both literally and figuratively a money machine?

Problems and Exercises

15. **Monetary Aggregates**   Calculate M1 and M2 using the following information:

Large-denomination time deposits	$304 billion
Currency and coin held by the nonbanking public	$438 billion
Checkable deposits	$509 billion
Small-denomination time deposits	$198 billion
Traveler's checks	$18 billion
Savings deposits	$326 billion
Money market mutual fund accounts	$637 billion

16. **Money Creation**   Show how each of the following initially affects bank assets, liabilities, and reserves. Do not include the results of bank behavior resulting from the Fed's action. Assume a required reserve ratio of 0.05.

    a. The Fed purchases $10 million worth of U.S. government bonds from a securities trader who puts those funds in a checking account.
    b. The Fed loans $5 million to a bank.
    c. The Fed raises the required reserve ratio to 0.10.

17. **Money Creation** Show how each of the following would initially affect a bank's assets and liabilities.

    a. Someone makes a $10,000 deposit into a checking account.
    b. A bank makes a loan of $1,000 by establishing a checking account for $1,000.
    c. The loan described in part (b) is spent.
    d. A bank must write off a loan because the borrower defaults.

18. **Reserve Accounts** Suppose that a bank's customer deposits $4,000 in her checking account. The required reserve ratio is 0.25. What are the required reserves on this new deposit? What is the largest loan that the bank can make on the basis of the new deposit? If the bank chooses to hold reserves of $3,000 on the new deposit, what are the excess reserves on the deposit?

19. **Money Multiplier** Suppose that the Federal Reserve lowers the required reserve ratio from 0.10 to 0.05. How does this affect the simple money multiplier, assuming that excess reserves are held to zero and there are no currency leakages? What are the money multipliers for required reserve ratios of 0.15 and 0.20?

20. **Money Creation** Suppose Bank A, which faces a reserve requirement of 10 percent, receives a $1,000 checking deposit from a customer.

    a. Assuming that it wishes to hold no excess reserves, determine how much the bank should lend. Show these changes on Bank A's balance sheet.
    b. Assuming that the loan shown in Bank A's balance sheet is redeposited in Bank B, show the changes in Bank B's balance sheet if it lends out the maximum possible.
    c. Repeat this process for three additional banks: C, D, and E.
    d. Using the simple money multiplier, calculate the total change in the money supply resulting from the $1,000 initial deposit.
    e. Assume Banks A, B, C, D, and E each wish to hold 5 percent excess reserves. How would holding this level of excess reserves affect the total change in the money supply?

21. **Monetary Control** Suppose the money supply is currently $500 billion and the Fed wishes to increase it by $100 billion.

    a. Given a required reserve ratio of 0.25, what should it do?
    b. If it decided to change the money supply by changing the required reserve ratio, what change should it make?

Monetary Theory and Policy

15

Photodisc/Jupiter Images

- *Why do people maintain checking accounts and have cash in their pockets, purses, wallets, desk drawers, piggy banks, coffee cans—wherever?*

- *In other words, why do people hold money?*

- *How does the stock of money in the economy affect your ability to find a job, get a student loan, buy a car, or pay credit card bills?*

- *What have economic theory and the historical record taught us about the relationship between the amount of money in the economy and other macroeconomic variables?*

Answers to these and related questions are addressed in this chapter, which examines monetary theory and policy in the short run and in the long run.

The amount of money in the economy affects you in a variety of ways, but to understand these effects, we must dig a little deeper. So far, we have focused on how banks create money. But a more fundamental question is how money affects the economy, a topic called *monetary theory*. Monetary theory explores the effect of the money supply on the economy's price level, employment, and growth. The Fed's control over the money supply is called *monetary policy*. In the short run, changes in the money supply affect the economy by working through changes in the interest rate. In the long run, changes in the money supply affect the price level. Monetary policy affects the interest you pay on a car loan and the interest you earn on a bank account.

Topics discussed in this chapter include:

- Demand and supply of money
- Money in the short run
- Federal funds rate
- Money in the long run
- Velocity of money
- Monetary policy targets
- Stress test
- Quantitative easing

15-1 The Demand and Supply of Money

Let's begin by reviewing the important distinction between the *stock of money* and the *flow of income*. How much money do you have with you right now? That amount is a *stock*—an amount measured at a point in time. Income, in contrast, is a *flow*—an amount measured per period of time. Income is a measure of how much money you receive per period. Income has no meaning unless the period is specified. You would not know whether to be impressed that a friend earned $400 unless you knew whether this was per month, per week, per day, or per hour.

The **demand for money** is a relationship between the interest rate and how much money people choose to hold. Keep in mind that the quantity of money held is a stock measure. It may seem odd at first to be talking about the demand for money. You might think people would demand all the money they could get their hands on. But remember that money, the stock, is not the same as income, the flow. People express their demand for income by selling their labor and other resources. People express their demand for money by holding some of their wealth as money rather than holding other assets that earn more interest.

But we are getting ahead of ourselves. The question is: Why do people demand money? Why do people have money with them, stash money around the house, and have money in checking accounts? The most obvious reason people demand money is that money is a convenient medium of exchange. *People demand money to make purchases.*

demand for money

The relationship between the interest rate and how much money people choose to hold

15-1a The Demand for Money

Because barter represents an insignificant portion of exchange in the modern industrialized economy, households, firms, governments, and foreigners need money to conduct their daily transactions. Consumers need money to buy products, and firms need money to buy resources. *Money allows people to carry out economic transactions more easily and more efficiently*. With credit cards, the short-term loan delays the payment of money, but all accounts must eventually be settled with money.

The greater the value of transactions to be financed in a given period, the greater the demand for money. So the more active the economy is—that is, the more goods and services exchanged, reflected by real output—the more money demanded. Obviously an economy with a real GDP of $17 trillion needs more money than an economy half that size. Also, the higher the economy's price level, the greater the demand for money. The more things cost on average, the more money is needed to buy them. Shoppers in economies suffering from hyperinflation need mountains of cash.

You demand the money needed to fund your normal spending in the course of the day or week, and you may need money for unexpected expenditures. If you plan to buy lunch tomorrow, you will carry enough money to pay for it. But you may also want to be able to pay for other possible contingencies. For example, you could have car trouble or you could come across a sale on a favorite item. You can use checks, debit cards, or credit cards, for some of these unexpected purchases, but you still feel safer with some extra cash. You may have a little extra cash with you right now for who knows what. Even *you* don't know.

The demand for money is rooted in money's role as a medium of exchange. But as we have seen, money is more than a medium of exchange; it is also a store of value. People save for a new home, for college, for retirement. People can store their purchasing power as money or as some other financial assets, such as corporate and government bonds. When people buy bonds and other financial assets, they are lending their money and are paid interest for doing so.

The demand for any asset is based on the services it provides. The big advantage of money as a store of value is its liquidity: Money can be immediately exchanged for whatever is for sale. In contrast, other financial assets, such as corporate or government bonds, must first be *liquidated*, or exchanged for money, which can then be used to buy goods and services. Money, however, has one major disadvantage when compared to other financial assets. Money in the form of currency and traveler's checks earns no interest, and the rate earned on checkable deposits is well below that earned on other financial assets; in recent years that rate has been close to zero. So holding wealth as money means giving up some interest. For example, suppose a business could earn 3 percent more interest by holding financial assets other than money. The opportunity cost of holding $1 million as money rather than as some other financial asset would amount to $30,000 per year. *The interest forgone is the opportunity cost of holding money*.

15-1b Money Demand and Interest Rates

When the market interest rate is low, other things constant, the cost of holding money—the cost of maintaining liquidity—is low, so people hold more of their wealth in the form of money. Such was the case in 2015, when the interest paid on savings deposits and time deposits was close to zero. When the interest rate is high, the cost of holding money is high, so people hold less of their wealth in money and more in other financial assets that pay higher interest. Thus, *other things constant, the quantity of money demanded varies inversely with the market interest rate*.

The money demand curve D_m in Exhibit 1 shows the quantity of money people demand at alternative interest rates, other things constant. Both the quantity of money and the interest rate are in nominal terms. *The money demand curve slopes downward because the lower the interest rate, the lower the opportunity cost of holding money.* Movements along the curve reflect the effects of changes in the interest rate on the quantity of money demanded. Assumed constant along the curve are the price level and real GDP. If either increases, the demand for money increases, as reflected by a rightward shift of the money demand curve.

15-1c The Supply of Money and the Equilibrium Interest Rate

The supply of money—the stock of money available in the economy at a particular time—is determined primarily by the Fed through its control over currency and over excess reserves in the banking system. The supply of money S_m is depicted as a vertical line in Exhibit 2. *A vertical supply curve implies that the quantity of money supplied is independent of the interest rate.*

The intersection of the demand for money D_m with the supply of money S_m determines the equilibrium interest rate, i—the interest rate that equates the quantity of money demanded with the quantity supplied. At interest rates above the equilibrium level, the opportunity cost of holding money is higher, so the quantity of money people want to hold is less than the quantity supplied. At interest rates below the equilibrium level, the opportunity cost of holding money is lower, so the quantity of money people want to hold exceeds the quantity supplied.

If the Fed increases the money supply, the supply curve shifts to the right, as shown by the movement from S_m out to S'_m in Exhibit 2. At interest rate i, the quantity supplied now exceeds the quantity demanded. Because of the increased supply of money, people

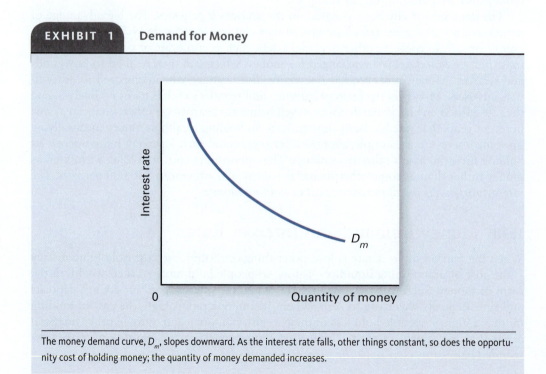

EXHIBIT 1   **Demand for Money**

The money demand curve, D_m, slopes downward. As the interest rate falls, other things constant, so does the opportunity cost of holding money; the quantity of money demanded increases.

EXHIBIT 2

EXHIBIT 2 **Effect of an Increase in the Money Supply**

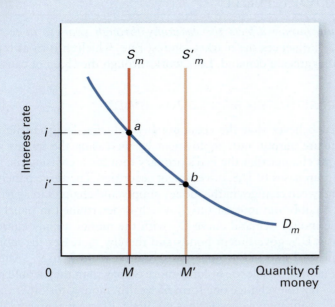

Because the money supply is determined by the Federal Reserve, it can be represented by a vertical line. At point *a*, the intersection of the money supply, S_m, and the money demand, D_m, determines the market interest rate, *i*. Following an increase in the money supply to S'_m, the quantity of money supplied exceeds the quantity demanded at the original interest rate, *i*. The new equilibrium occurs at point *b*.

are *able* to hold more money. But at interest rate *i* they are *unwilling* to hold that much. The opportunity cost of doing so is too high. Because people are now holding more of their wealth as money than they would like, they exchange some money for other financial assets, such as bonds. As the demand for bonds increases, bond sellers can pay less interest yet still attract enough buyers. The interest rate falls until the quantity of money demanded just equals the quantity supplied. With the decline in the interest rate to *i'* in Exhibit 2, the opportunity cost of holding money falls enough that the public is willing to hold the now-larger stock of money. Equilibrium moves from point *a* to point *b*. For *a given money demand curve, an increase in the money supply drives down the interest rate, and a decrease in the money supply drives up the interest rate.*

Now that you have some idea how money demand and money supply determine the market interest rate, you are ready to see how money fits into our model of the economy. Specifically, let's see how changes in the money supply affect aggregate demand and equilibrium output.

CHECKPOINT

Explain how the demand and supply of money determine the market interest rate.

15-2 Money and Aggregate Demand in the Short Run

In the short run, money affects the economy through changes in the interest rate. Monetary policy influences the market interest rate, which in turn affects investment, a component of aggregate demand. Let's work through the chain of causation.

15-2a Interest Rates and Investment

Suppose the Fed believes that the economy is producing less than its potential and decides to stimulate output and employment by increasing the money supply. Recall from the previous chapter that the Fed's primary tool for increasing the money supply is open-market purchases of U.S. government securities. The three panels of Exhibit 3 trace the links between changes in the money supply and changes in aggregate demand. We begin with equilibrium interest rate i, which is determined in panel (a) by the intersection of the money demand curve D_m with the money supply curve S_m. Suppose the Fed purchases U.S. government bonds and thereby increases the money supply, as shown by a rightward shift of the money supply curve from S_m to S'_m. After the increase in the supply of money, people are holding more money than they would prefer at interest rate i, so they try to exchange one form of wealth, money, for other financial assets. Exchanging dollars for financial assets has no direct effect on aggregate demand, but it does reduce the market interest rate. At the lower interest rate i', the quantity of money demanded equals the quantity supplied.

A decline in the interest rate to i', other things constant, reduces the opportunity cost of financing new plants and equipment, thereby making new investment more profitable. Likewise, a lower interest rate reduces the cost of financing a new house. So a

---

EXHIBIT   3   **Effects of an Increase in the Money Supply on Interest Rates, Investment, and Aggregate Demand**

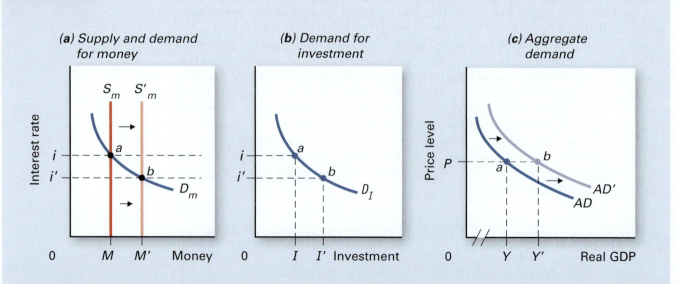

In panel (a), an increase in the money supply forces the interest rate down to i'. With the cost of borrowing lower, the amount invested increases from I to I', as shown in panel (b). This sets off the spending multiplier process, so the aggregate output demanded at price level P increases from Y to Y'. The increase is shown by the shift of the aggregate demand curve to the right in panel (c).

decline in the interest rate increases the quantity of investment demanded. Panel (b) shows the demand for investment D_I first introduced several chapters back. When the interest rate falls from i to i', the quantity of investment demanded increases from I to I'.

If the spending multiplier exceeds 1.0, this increase in investment could lead to a greater increase in aggregate demand, reflected in panel (c) by a rightward shift of the aggregate demand curve from AD to AD'. At the given price level P, real GDP increases from Y to Y'. The sequence of events can be summarized as follows:

$$M \uparrow \rightarrow i \downarrow \rightarrow I \uparrow \rightarrow AD \uparrow \rightarrow Y \uparrow$$

An increase in the money supply, M, reduces the interest rate, i. The lower interest rate stimulates investment, I, which increases aggregate demand from AD to AD'. At a given price level, real GDP demanded increases from Y to Y'. The entire sequence is also traced out in each panel by the movement from point a to point b.

Now let's consider the effect of a Fed-orchestrated *increase* in interest rates. In Exhibit 3 such a policy could be traced by moving from point b to point a in each panel, but we'll dispense with a blow-by-blow discussion of the graphs. Suppose the Federal Reserve decides to reduce the money supply to cool down an overheated economy. A decrease in the money supply would increase the interest rate. At the higher interest rate, businesses find it more costly to finance plants and equipment, and households find it more costly to finance new homes. Hence, a higher interest rate reduces the amount invested. The resulting decline in investment leads to a decline in aggregate demand.

As long as the interest rate is sensitive to changes in the money supply, and as long as investment is sensitive to changes in the interest rate, changes in the money supply affect investment. The extent to which a given change in investment affects aggregate demand depends on the size of the spending multiplier.

15-2b Adding the Short-Run Aggregate Supply Curve

Even after tracing the effect of a change in the money supply on aggregate demand, we still have only half the story. To determine the effects of monetary policy on the equilibrium real GDP in the economy, we need the supply side. An aggregate supply curve helps show how a given shift of the aggregate demand curve affects real GDP and the price level. In the short run, the aggregate supply curve slopes upward, so the quantity supplied increases only if the price level increases. *For a given shift of the aggregate demand curve, the steeper the short-run aggregate supply curve, the smaller the increase in real GDP and the larger the increase in the price level.*

Suppose the economy is producing at point a in Exhibit 4, where the aggregate demand curve AD intersects the short-run aggregate supply curve $SRAS_{110}$, yielding a short-run equilibrium output of $16.8 trillion and a price level of 105. As you can see, the actual price level of 105 is below the expected price level of 110, and the short-run equilibrium output of $16.8 trillion is below the economy's potential of $17.0 trillion, yielding a recessionary gap of $0.2 trillion.

At point a, real wages are higher than had been negotiated and many people are looking for jobs. The Fed can wait to see whether the economy recovers on its own. Market forces could cause employers and workers to renegotiate lower nominal wages. This would lower production costs, pushing the short-run aggregate supply curve rightward, thus closing the recessionary gap. But if Fed officials are impatient with natural market forces, they could try to close the gap using an expansionary monetary policy. For example, during 2007 and 2008, the Fed aggressively cut the federal funds rate from 5.25 percent to between 0 and 0.25 percent to stimulate aggregate demand. If the Fed lowers that rate by just the right amount, this stimulates investment, thus increasing

EXHIBIT 4   **Expansionary Monetary Policy to Close a Recessionary Gap**

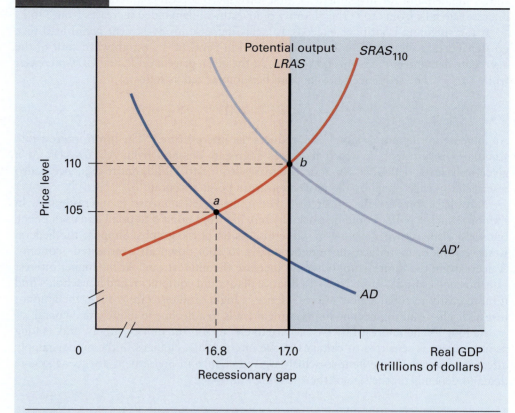

At point a, the economy is producing less than its potential in the short run, resulting in a recessionary gap of $0.2 trillion. If the Federal Reserve increases the money supply by just the right amount, the aggregate demand curve shifts rightward from *AD* to *AD'*. A short-run and long-run equilibrium is established at point *b*, with the price level at 110 and output at the potential level of $17.0 trillion.

the aggregate demand curve enough to achieve a new equilibrium at point *b*, where the economy produces its potential output. Given all the connections in the chain of causality between changes in the money supply and changes in equilibrium output, however, it would actually be quite remarkable for the Fed to execute monetary policy so precisely. If the Fed overshot the mark and stimulated aggregate demand too much, this would open up an expansionary gap, thus creating inflationary pressure in the economy.

To Review: As long as the money demand curve and the investment demand curve both slope downward, an increase in the money supply reduces the market interest rate, increasing investment and consequently increasing aggregate demand. And as long as the short-run aggregate supply curve slopes upward, the short-run effect of an increase in the money supply is an increase in both real output and the price level. But here is one final qualification: Lowering the interest rate may not always stimulate investment. Economic prospects may become so glum that lower interest rates may fail to achieve the desired increase in aggregate demand. In response to the recent financial crisis, for example, the Fed cut the federal funds rate to near zero by the end of 2008, but investment in 2009 still dropped sharply.

That's the theory of monetary policy in the short run. Let's next look at the federal funds rate in practice.

15-2c Recent History of the Federal Funds Rate

At 2:15 p.m. on December 16, 2008, immediately following a regular meeting, the Federal Open Market Committee (FOMC) announced that it would lower its target for the federal funds rate to between 0 and 0.25 percent, the tenth reduction in 15 months. As you know by now, the federal funds rate is the interest rate banks charge one another for overnight lending of reserves at the Fed. Because lowering the rate reduces the cost of covering any reserve shortfall, banks are more willing to lend to the public. To execute this monetary policy, the FOMC authorized the New York Fed to make open-market purchases to increase bank reserves until the federal funds rate fell to the target level.

For four decades, the Fed has reflected its monetary policy in this interest rate. (For a few years, the Fed targeted money aggregates, but more on that later.) There are many interest rates in the economy—for credit cards, new cars, mortgages, home equity loans, personal loans, business loans, and more. Why focus on such an obscure rate? First, by changing bank reserves through open-market operations, the Fed has a direct lever on the federal funds rate, so the Fed's grip on this rate is tighter than on any other market rate. Second, the federal funds rate serves as a benchmark for determining other short-term interest rates in the economy. For example, after the Fed announces a rate change, major banks around the country usually change by the same amount their prime interest rate—the interest rate banks charge their best corporate customers. The federal funds rate affects monetary and financial conditions, which in turn affect employment, aggregate output, and the price level. The Fed uses the federal funds rate to pursue its twin goals of price stability and maximum employment.

Exhibit 5 shows the federal funds rate since early 1999. As a lesson in monetary policy, let's walk through the Fed's rationale. In the summer of 1999, the FOMC became concerned that robust economic growth would trigger higher inflation. In a series of steps, the federal funds target was raised from 4.75 percent to 6.5 percent. The FOMC announced at the time that the moves "should markedly diminish the risk of rising inflation going forward." Some critics argued that the Fed's rate hikes contributed to the 2001 recession. In 2001, concerns about waning consumer confidence, weaker capital spending, and the 9/11 terrorist attacks prompted the FOMC to reverse course. Between the beginning of 2001 and mid-2003, the FOMC cut the rate from 6.5 percent to 1.0 percent, reflecting at the time the most concentrated monetary stimulus on record. The rate remained at 1.0 percent for a year. Some economists criticized the Fed for keeping rates too low too long. They charged that this "easy money" policy overstimulated the housing sector, encouraging some people to buy homes they couldn't afford. These home purchases, critics argued, inflated the bubble in housing prices and sowed the seeds for mortgage defaults that hit years later.

Anyway, after leaving the rate at 1.0 percent for a year, the FOMC began worrying again about inflationary pressure. Between June 2004 and June 2006, the target federal funds rate was increased from 1.0 percent to 5.25 percent in 17 steps. The FOMC then hit the pause button, leaving the rate at 5.25 percent for more than a year. This takes us up to September 2007, when troubles in the housing sector, a rising mortgage default rate, and a softening economy prompted the first in a series of federal funds rate cuts. After 10 cuts over 15 months, the target rate in December 2008 stood between 0 and 0.25 percent, the lowest in history. As you can see from Exhibit 5, the rate remained at a record low for years.

EXHIBIT 5   **Recent Ups and Downs in the Federal Funds Rate**

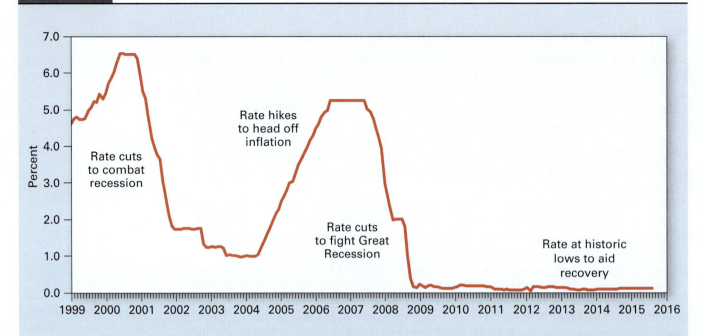

Since the early 1990s, the Fed has pursued monetary policy primarily through changes in the federal funds rate, the rate that banks charge one another for borrowing and lending excess reserves overnight.

Source: Based on monthly averages from the Federal Reserve System. Monthly averages are also available at http://www.thecommunitybanker.com/fedfundsrate-monthly.htm.

With the primary tool of monetary policy already at the bottom of its range, was the Fed out of ammunition in fighting the Great Recession? Another policy tool that the Fed relied upon more after 2008 is the way it communicates with the public, particularly its intentions about future policy. This drive for greater transparency is discussed in the following case study.

CASE STUDY

PUBLIC POLICY

GREATER FED TRANSPARENCY AS A POLICY TOOL   Decades ago, the Fed was a black box. Sure, the FOMC would meet regularly and, from time to time, release a cryptic statement about what they were up to. But the Fed's intentions were purposely vague. Fed statements and testimony were often designed to obscure more than to reveal. As former Fed Chairman Alan Greenspan noted

in his personal memoir, although earlier in his life he had learned "to write clearly in short, declarative sentences.... It was a skill [he] had to unlearn as chairman of the Fed." With so little concrete news coming from the Fed but with so much at stake, many large financial institutions employed economists as "Fed watchers" to help decipher the central bank's intentions.

continued

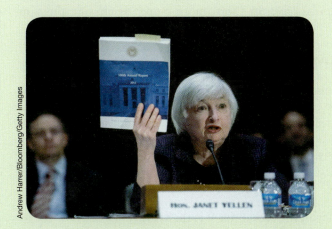

Andrew Harrer/Bloomberg/Getty Images

In the 1990s, the Fed began to signal its intentions more clearly. For example, in 1995 the FOMC started issuing a brief statement after each meeting noting its target for the federal funds rate. Since 2000, that post-meeting statement also indicated whether the group's "bias" in the future was to increase, decrease, or leave the rate unchanged. In 2005, the FOMC started providing Minutes three weeks after each meeting. In December 2008, after dropping the federal funds rate to record low levels, the Fed announced "the Committee anticipates that weak economic conditions are likely to warrant exceptionally low levels of the federal funds rate for some time." The Fed was saying that not only is the federal funds rate really low, but it will stay low for a long time.

In April 2011, then Fed Chairman Ben Bernanke began holding press conferences after half of the FOMC meetings.

This practice continued with Chairwoman Janet Yellen, who replaced Bernanke in 2014. These briefings are broadcast on C-SPAN, videotaped, and made available on the Fed's Web site. A transcript of each press conference is also available there. And in August 2011, the FOMC began projecting just how long it expected to keep its federal funds rate so low.

The Fed also communicates its intentions in other ways. The chairman testifies before Congress several times a year. All Fed governors and all district bank presidents give speeches and interviews many times a year. And several times a year, each Fed governor and district president offers a three-year forecast of inflation, unemployment, and real GDP. So there are abundant opportunities to learn what policy makers believe.

By generating such concrete news several times a year, FOMC meetings became widely followed media events, and allowed the Fed to reach a wider audience than just the financial markets. As Bernanke noted during a press briefing, "to the extent that we can communicate that rates will be lower for longer, that will ease financial conditions and be a way that we can affect the state of the economy."

Sources: Alan Greenspan, *The Age of Turbulence: Adventures in a New World* (Penguin Press, 2007), p. 43; Benjamin M. Friedman, "Has the Financial Crisis Permanently Changed the Practice of Monetary Policy? Has It Changed the Theory of Monetary Policy?" *The Manchester School*, 83 (September 2015): 5-19; "Transcript of Chairman Bernanke's Press Conference," various dates; and "Transcript of Chair Yellen's FOMC Press Conference," various dates. All transcripts, videos, FOMC Meeting Statements, and FOMC Meeting Minutes are available at http://www.federalreserve.gov/monetarypolicy/fomccalendars.htm.

 **CHECKPOINT**

Trace the steps between an increase in the money supply and an increase in equilibrium output.

15-3 Money and Aggregate Demand in the Long Run

When we looked at the impact of money on the economy in the short run, we found that money influences aggregate demand and equilibrium output through its effect on the interest rate. Here we look at the long-run effects of changes in the money supply on the economy. *The long-run view of money is more direct: if the central bank supplies more money to the economy, sooner or later people will spend more. But because the long-run aggregate supply curve is fixed at the economy's potential output, this greater spending simply increases the price level.* In short, more money is chasing the same output. Here are the details.

15-3a The Equation of Exchange

equation of exchange
The quantity of money, *M*, multiplied by its velocity, *V*, equals nominal GDP, which is the product of the price level, *P*, and real GDP, *Y*; or $M \times V = P \times Y$

Every transaction in the economy involves a two-way swap: The buyer exchanges money for goods and the seller exchanges goods for money. One way of expressing this relationship among key variables in the economy is the **equation of exchange**, first developed by classical economists. Although this equation can be arranged in different ways, depending on the emphasis, the basic version is

$$M \times V = P \times Y$$

velocity of money
The average number of times per year each dollar is used to purchase final goods and services

where *M* is the quantity of money in the economy; *V* is the **velocity of money**, or the average number of times per year each dollar is used to purchase final goods and services; *P* is the average price level; and *Y* is real GDP. The equation of exchange says that the quantity of money in circulation, *M*, multiplied by *V*, the number of times that money changes hands, equals the average price level, *P*, times real output, *Y*. The price level, *P*, times real output, *Y*, equals the economy's nominal income and output, or nominal GDP.

By rearranging the equation of exchange, we find that velocity equals nominal GDP divided by the money stock, or

$$V = \frac{P \times Y}{M}$$

For example, nominal GDP in 2015 was about $18.2 trillion, and the money stock as measured by M1 averaged about $3.0 trillion. The velocity of money indicates how often each dollar is used on average to pay for final goods and services during the year. So in 2015, velocity was $18.2 trillion divided by $3.0 trillion, or 6.1. Given GDP and the money supply, each dollar in circulation must have been spent 6.1 times on average to pay for final goods and services. There is no other way these market transactions could have occurred. The value of velocity is implied by the values of the other variables. Incidentally, velocity measures spending only on final goods and services—not on intermediate products, secondhand goods, financial assets, dollar transactions abroad, or illegal activity, even though such spending also occurs. So velocity underestimates how hard the money supply works during the year.

The equation of exchange says that total spending ($M \times V$) always equals total receipts ($P \times Y$), as was the case in our circular-flow analysis. As described so far, however, the equation of exchange is simply an *identity*—a relationship expressed in such a way that it is true by definition. Another example of an identity would be a relationship equating miles per gallon to the distance driven divided by the gasoline required.

15-3b The Quantity Theory of Money

quantity theory of money
If the velocity of money is stable, or at least predictable, changes in the money supply have predictable effects on nominal GDP

If velocity is relatively stable over time, or at least predictable, the equation of exchange turns from an identity into a theory—the quantity theory of money. The **quantity theory of money** states that if the velocity of money is stable, or at least predictable, then the equation of exchange can be used to predict the effects of changes in the money supply on *nominal* GDP, $P \times Y$. For example, if *M* increases by 5 percent and *V* remains constant, then $P \times Y$, or nominal GDP, must also increase by 5 percent. For a while, some economists believed they could use the equation of exchange to predict nominal output in the short run. Now, if at all, it's used primarily as a rough guide in the long run.

So an increase in the money supply results in more spending in the long run, meaning a higher nominal GDP. How is this increase in $P \times Y$ divided between changes in the price level and changes in real GDP? The answer does not lie in the quantity theory, for that theory is stated only in terms of nominal GDP. The answer lies in the shape of the aggregate supply curve.

The long-run aggregate supply curve is vertical at the economy's potential level of output. With real output, Y, fixed and the velocity of money, V, relatively stable, a change in the stock of money translates directly into a change in the price level. Exhibit 6 shows the effect of an increase in the money supply in the long run. An increase in the money supply causes a rightward shift of the aggregate demand curve, which increases the price level but leaves output unchanged at potential GDP. So the economy's potential output level is not affected by changes in the money supply. *In the long run, increases in the money supply, with velocity stable or at least not decreasing, result only in higher prices.* For example, an examination of 73 inflation periods across major economies since 1960 concludes that important triggers to inflation were expansionary monetary policies.[1]

To Review: If velocity is stable, or at least predictable, the quantity theory of money says that changes in the money supply will, in the long run, result in predictable effects on the economy's price level. Velocity's stability and predictability are key to the quantity theory of money. Let's consider some factors that might influence velocity.

EXHIBIT 6	In the Long Run, an Increase in the Money Supply Results in a Higher Price Level, or Inflation

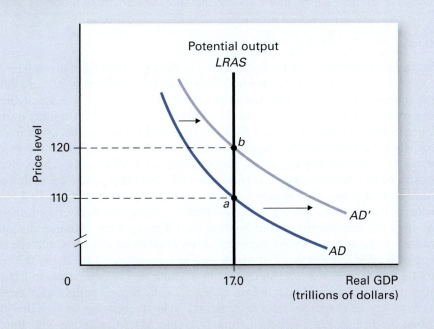

The quantity theory of money predicts that if velocity is stable, then an increase in the money supply in the long run results in a higher price level, or inflation. Because the long-run aggregate supply curve is fixed, increases in the money supply affect only the price level, not real output.

---

[1] John F. Boschen and Charles L. Weise, "What Starts Inflation: Evidence from the OECD Countries," *Journal of Money, Credit and Banking*, 35 (June 2003): 323–349.

15-3c What Determines the Velocity of Money?

Velocity depends in part on the customs and conventions of commerce. In colonial times, money could be tied up in transit for days as a courier on horseback carried a payment from a merchant in Boston to one in Baltimore. Today, the electronic transmission of funds occurs in an instant, so the same stock of money can move around much more quickly to finance many more transactions. *The velocity of money has also increased because of a variety of commercial innovations that facilitate exchange.* For example, a wider use of charge accounts and credit cards has reduced the need for shoppers to carry cash. Likewise, automatic teller machines have made cash more accessible at more times and in more places. What's more, debit cards are used at a growing number of retail outlets and consumers can get cash back on debit transactions, so people need less "walking-around" money.

Another factor affecting velocity depends on how stable money is as a store of value. *The better money serves as a store of value, the more money people hold, so the lower its velocity.* For example, the introduction of interest-bearing checking accounts made money a better store of value, so people were more willing to hold money in checking accounts. This financial innovation reduced velocity. On the other hand, when inflation increases, money turns out to be a poorer store of value. People become reluctant to hold money and try to exchange it for some asset that retains its value better. This reduction in people's willingness to hold money during periods of high inflation increases the velocity of money. During hyperinflations, workers usually get paid daily, boosting velocity even more. Thus, *velocity increases with a rise in the inflation rate, other things constant.* Money becomes a hot potato—nobody wants to hold it for long.

Again, the usefulness of the quantity theory in predicting changes in the price level in the long run hinges on how stable and predictable the velocity of money is over time.

15-3d How Stable Is Velocity?

Exhibit 7 graphs velocity since 1960, measured both as nominal GDP divided by M1 in panel (a) and as nominal GDP divided by M2 in panel (b). Between 1960 and 1980, M1 velocity increased steadily and in that sense could be considered at least predictable. M1 velocity bounced around during the 1980s. But in the early 1990s, more and more banks began offering money market funds that included limited check-writing privileges, or what is considered M2. Deposits shifted from M1 to M2, which increased the velocity of M1. Also, as already noted, more people used debit cards, which increased the velocity of M1 because people carried less cash (plus they could get cash back on debit-card transactions). M1 velocity increased from about 6.0 in 1993 to 10.5 in 2007. M1 velocity has dropped since the 2007–2009 recession. Because of extremely low interest rates, the opportunity cost of holding wealth in the form of money declined, so the quantity of money demanded increased. Also, because of anxiety about the economy, people hoarded more cash, all of which slowed velocity to 6.1 by 2015. M2 velocity appears slightly more stable, as you can see by comparing the two panels in Exhibit 7.

For a few years, the Fed focused on changes in the money supply as a target for monetary policy in the short run. Because M1 velocity became so unstable during the 1980s, the Fed in 1987 switched from targeting M1 to targeting M2. But when M2 velocity became volatile in the early 1990s, the Fed announced that money aggregates, including M2, would no longer be considered reliable guides for monetary policy in the short run. *Since 1993, the equation of exchange has been considered more of a rough guide linking changes in the money supply to inflation in the long run.*

What is the long-run relationship between increases in the money supply and inflation? Since the Federal Reserve System was established in 1913, the United States has

EXHIBIT 7 The Velocity of Money

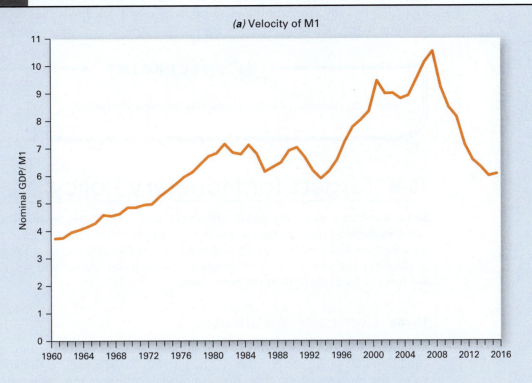

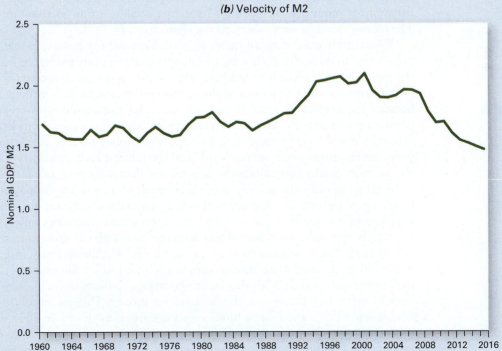

M1 velocity fluctuated so much during the 1980s that M1 growth was abandoned as a short-run policy target. M2 velocity appears more stable than M1 velocity, but both are now considered by the Fed as too unpredictable for short-run policy use.

Sources: *Economic Report of the President*, February 2015, and the Federal Reserve Board. Velocity in 2015 was estimated by the author based on nominal GDP and money supply projections as of May 2015.

suffered three episodes of high inflation, and each was preceded and accompanied by sharp increases in the money supply. These occurred from 1913 to 1920, 1939 to 1948, and 1967 to 1980. There is abundant evidence worldwide linking money growth with inflation in the long run.

CHECKPOINT

What's the relevance of velocity's stability on monetary policy?

15-4 Targets for Monetary Policy

In the short run, monetary policy affects the economy largely by influencing interest rates. In the long run, changes in the money supply affect the price level, though with an uncertain and variable lag. Should monetary authorities focus on the interest rates in the short run or the supply of money in the long run? As we will see, the Fed lacks the tools to focus on both at the same time.

15-4a Contrasting Policies

To demonstrate the effects of different policies, we begin with the money market in equilibrium at point e in Exhibit 8. The interest rate is i and the money stock is M, values the monetary authorities find appropriate. Suppose there is an increase in the demand for money in the economy, perhaps because of an increase in nominal GDP. The money demand curve shifts to the right, from D_m to D'_m.

When confronted with an increase in the demand for money, monetary authorities can choose to do nothing, thereby allowing the interest rate to rise, or they can increase the money supply enough to hold the interest rate constant. If monetary authorities do nothing, the quantity of money in the economy remains at M, but the interest rate rises because the greater demand for money increases the equilibrium combination from point e up to point e'. Alternatively, monetary authorities can try to keep the interest rate at its initial level by increasing the supply of money from S_m to S'_m. In terms of possible combinations of the money stock and the interest rate, monetary authorities must choose from points lying along the new money demand curve, D'_m.

A growing economy usually needs a growing money supply to pay for the increase in aggregate output. If monetary authorities maintain a constant growth in the money supply, and if velocity remains stable, the interest rate fluctuates unless the growth in the supply of money each period just happens to match the growth in the demand for money (as in the movement from e to e'' in Exhibit 8). Alternatively, monetary authorities could try to adjust the money supply each period by the amount needed to keep the interest rate stable. With this latter approach, changes in the money supply would have to offset any changes in the demand for money. This essentially is what the Fed does when it holds the federal funds target constant, as from late 2008 well into 2015.

Interest rate fluctuations could be harmful if they create undesirable fluctuations in investment. For interest rates to remain stable during economic expansions, the money supply would have to grow at the same rate as the demand for money. Likewise, for interest rates to remain stable during economic contractions, the money supply would have to shrink at the same rate as the demand for money. Hence, for monetary authorities to maintain the interest rate at some specified level, the money supply must increase

EXHIBIT 8 **Targeting Interest Rates Versus Targeting the Money Supply**

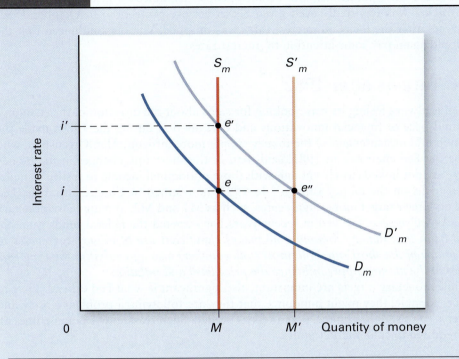

An increase in the price level or in real GDP, with velocity stable, shifts rightward the money demand curve from D_m to D'_m. If the Federal Reserve holds the money supply at S_m, the interest rate rises from i (at point e) to i' (at point e'). Alternatively, the Fed could try to hold the interest rate constant by increasing the money supply to S'_m. The Fed may choose any point along the money demand curve D'_m.

during economic expansions and decrease during contractions. But an increase in the money supply during an expansion would increase aggregate demand even more, and a decrease in the money supply during a contraction would reduce aggregate demand even more. *Such changes in the money supply would thus tend to worsen fluctuations in economic activity, thereby adding more instability to the economy.* With this in mind, let's review monetary policy over the years.

15-4b Targets before 1982

Between World War II and October 1979, the Fed attempted to stabilize interest rates. Stable interest rates were viewed as a prerequisite for an attractive investment environment and, thus, for a stable economy. Milton Friedman, a Nobel Prize winner, argued that this exclusive attention to interest rates made monetary policy a source of instability in the economy because changes in the money supply reinforced fluctuations in the economy. He argued that the Fed should pay less attention to interest rates and instead should focus on a steady and predictable growth in the money supply. The debate raged during the 1970s, and Friedman won some important converts. Amid growing concern about a rising inflation rate, the Fed, under a new chairman, Paul Volcker, announced in October 1979 that it would deemphasize interest rates and would instead target specific money aggregates. Not surprisingly, interest rates became much more volatile.

But many observers believe that a sharp reduction in money growth in the latter half of 1981 caused the recession of 1982. Inflation declined rapidly, but unemployment climbed to 10 percent. People were worried. As you might expect, the Fed was widely criticized. Farmers, politicians, and businesspeople denounced Volcker. Emotions ran high. Volcker was reportedly even given Secret Service protection. In October 1982, three years after the focus on interest rates was dropped, Volcker announced that the Fed would again pay some attention to interest rates.

15-4c Targets after 1982

The Fed is always feeling its way, looking for signs about the direction of the economy. The rapid pace of financial innovations and deregulation during the 1980s made the definition and measurement of the money supply more difficult. Alan Greenspan, who became the Fed chairman in 1987, said that, in the short run, changes in the money supply "are not linked closely enough with those of nominal income to justify a single-minded focus on the money supply."[2] In 1993, he testified in Congress that the Fed would no longer target money aggregates, such as M1 and M2, as a guide to monetary policy. As we've seen, the Fed in recent years has targeted the federal funds rate. *No central bank in a major economy now makes significant use of money aggregates to guide policy in the short run. Still, most policy makers also agree that in the long run, changes in the money supply influence the price level and inflation.*

While monetary targets are important, also significant is what Fed officials have to say. For example, they might announce that they are following a problem closely and are prepared to stabilize financial markets as needed. Such reassurance is sometimes all that's required to calm market jitters.

15-4d Other Fed Responses to the Financial Crisis

As we have seen, the Fed shapes monetary policy in a variety of other ways, as it did during and after the Great Recession of 2007–2009. To get a flavor of what the Fed has been up to, let's take a look at some of its responses.

Bailing Out AIG

In September 2008, as the global financial crisis was spreading, the Fed teamed up with the U.S. Treasury with a $182.5 billion package to rescue the insurance giant AIG from failure. At the time, the company was so interconnected with other financial entities that regulators believed they could not risk another bankruptcy, particularly after the panic created by the failure of Lehman Brothers. The Fed purchased some of AIG's troubled assets, taking them off AIG's balance sheet. The Fed and the Treasury also lent AIG enough money to keep the company running. AIG survived, and by June 2012 it had paid back the Fed with interest.

Some critics charged that AIG and some other large financial institutions should not have been bailed out because they helped cause the financial crisis. Chairman Bernanke said that the Fed tried to protect U.S. workers and consumers, groups that would have been hurt the most by a collapse of the financial system. He also noted that the Fed's investments that seemed like

[2.] Quoted in "Greenspan Asks That Fed Be Allowed to Pay Interest," *Wall Street Journal*, 11 March 1992.

bailouts actually paid off well enough that the Fed sent $80 billion in "profit" to the U.S. Treasury in 2010 and $77 billion in 2011, record amounts to that point and nearly double what was sent in 2009. We should also note that a share of AIG stock, which was selling for as much as $1,400 before the financial crisis, plunged to just $10 by early 2009, so shareholders lost nearly all their investment. Not much of a bailout for them.

Reducing the Risk of "Too Big to Fail"

Large financial institutions like AIG have financial dealings with thousands of other financial entities, so if one of these giants fails, as Lehman Brothers did in September 2008, that entails much collateral damage on the wider economy. With tougher supervisory oversight and greater capital requirements, the Fed and other regulators are trying to reduce the chances that a big financial institution will fail. For example, the Fed helped conduct a **stress test** of the 19 largest banks to determine which ones needed additional financial capital to weather a bad economy. Many banks had to raise billions more in capital.

The Dodd-Frank Act gave the Fed and the FDIC expanded oversight of large financial institutions, including for the first time those that are not depository institutions. Over the years, nonbank financial intermediaries such as mortgage companies, insurance companies, brokerage firms, money market mutual funds, and hedge funds came to represent a larger share of all lending in the economy, but because they did not rely on customer deposits, they had been out of the Fed's scope and control. The Dodd-Frank Act brought this so-called **shadow banking system** under the Fed's regulatory control.

Again, the objective of regulations is to reduce the probability that a large financial institution will collapse. But if one of these financial giants should get into serious trouble, the approach going forward is to let it fail through an orderly liquidation of the firm's assets. To that end, the Fed and the FDIC have set out rules for so-called *living wills*, which require each large financial institution, even one that appears in great shape, to prepare a blueprint for how it should be taken apart in the event of bankruptcy.

Quantitative Easing

The Fed typically changes the federal funds rate by buying or selling short-term government securities. But with that interest rate already at rock bottom by late 2008, the Fed was looking for other ways to help the economy. The Fed's answer was to buy long-term assets, such as government bonds and mortgage-backed securities. Doing so did not reduce short-term rates, which could not go lower, but it did bring down long-term rates, making investments more attractive. Purchasing mortgage-backed securities supported the mortgage and housing markets and helped stabilize financial markets more generally.

Through a variety of aggressive purchases since late 2008, the Fed added over $3 trillion in assets to its balance sheet. These asset purchases, called **quantitative easing**, directly lowered long-term interest rates, and indirectly raised bank reserves. Bank funds on deposit with the Fed increased by $2.5 trillion.

What are the risks of quantitative easing? The Fed could lose money on its purchases if these assets are sold back for less. Because the tool is unconventional and not well tested, nobody knows how much quantitative easing is too much. And too much money creation could trigger inflation, which is discussed next.

All these actions could be summed up as the *Fed trying to do whatever it takes to comply with its statutory mandate of price stability with maximum employment.* Fed officials did not want a repeat of the Great Depression, when they dropped the ball by not supplying the liquidity the financial system needed. As a result, some 10,000 banks failed during the Great Depression, versus fewer than 500 since the onset of the Great Recession.

stress test
Bank regulators assessed the soundness of large banks to determine which ones needed more financial capital to weather a bad economy

shadow banking system
Financial institutions, such as mortgage companies and brokerage firms, that do not rely on customer deposits to make loans

quantitative easing
Fed purchases of long-term assets to stabilize financial markets, reduce long-term interest rates, and improve the investment environment

15-4e What about Inflation?

At every press conference, the head of the Fed has reminded the public that the Fed's twin statutory mandates are price stability and maximum employment. In terms of price stability, the Fed seeks a target rate of 2 percent. Why not zero percent? According to the Fed, that would mean the economy at times would experience deflation—something the Fed wants to avoid. In terms of maximum employment, the Fed would like to see the minimum sustainable unemployment rate get down to a range between 5.0 percent and 5.2 percent. Why not lower? The Fed believes a rate much below that would tighten labor markets too much, risking higher inflation. (Each quarter, FOMC participants estimate the minimum sustainable unemployment rate, so that target changes over time.)

Because of asset purchases by the Fed, total assets on its balance sheet expanded from about $0.9 trillion in the summer of 2007, before the financial crisis, to about $4.5 trillion in the summer of 2015, with quantitative easing the reason for the jump. Some critics feared that buying all those assets would sooner or later lead to inflation. Why hasn't it, at least not as of 2015? Well, most of the funds that the Fed created to buy these assets ended up as idle bank reserves on account with the Fed. Remember that bank reserves are not part of the money supply. Banks were lending less because (1) the demand for loans was down, (2) lending standards had tightened with Dodd-Frank, (3) banks were now earning interest on their deposits at the Fed, reducing the opportunity cost of excess reserves, and (4) the financial crisis made banks more wary of lending. In the summer of 2015, banks had over $2.6 trillion on deposit with the Fed; this was up from just $13 billion in the summer of 2007, before the trouble started. Thus, between 2007 and 2015, bank reserves at the Fed increased 200-fold.

The money supply as measured by M1 did increase by 117 percent between 2007 and 2015, a period when real GDP grew by a total of only 11 percent. Doesn't that sound like a recipe for inflation? Not if the velocity of M1 slowed down considerably, which it did. The lower interest rate reduced the opportunity cost of holding cash, so people held more of it. And the uncertain economic times increased the demand for cash, with some people even hoarding it. All this slowed the velocity of M1, which fell from 10.5 in 2007 to 6.1 in 2015, a drop of 42 percent. The drop in velocity meant that the increase in the money supply did not increase nominal spending that much and thus did not result in much inflation. Between 2007 and 2015, the CPI increased an average of just 1.8 percent per year.

As noted earlier, the equation of exchange is an identity, meaning it is true by definition. Its usefulness as the quantity theory depends on velocity's stability or at least its predictability. Recent history shows that velocity has been neither stable nor predictable, so the quantity theory is of little use, particularly in the short run. Still, decades of research around the world suggest a link in the long run between sharp increases in the money supply and higher inflation.

Perhaps by the time you read this, the Fed will have begun to unwind long-term asset purchases made during and after the financial crisis. It will have to do so in a way that does not destabilize the economy. Remember that as the Fed sells these long term assets, this will reduce bank reserves in the system. If it sells its assets too quickly, the Fed must be mindful of the possibility of deflation, which is bad news and can be self-reinforcing. But as long as trillions of dollars sit in excess reserves at the Fed, inflation remains a risk. If banks start tapping their huge accumulation of excess reserves to make loans, the money supply will grow quickly. Unless velocity continues to drop, this growth in the money supply could trigger inflation. That's why Fed officials have made it clear that once the recovery picks up speed, they will begin selling assets to reduce bank reserves. But Fed officials have little experience with winding down assets of this magnitude.

15-4f International Considerations

As national economies grow more interdependent, the Fed has become more sensitive to the global implications of its action. What happens in the United States often affects markets overseas and vice versa. The Fed has tried to soothe troubled world markets in a variety of ways. When Mexico faced financial difficulties in 1982 and again in 1994, Fed officials helped arrange loans to prevent a financial crisis. A worldwide financial panic in the fall of 1998 because of defaults on Russian bonds prompted the Fed to lower the federal funds rate to supply more liquidity here and abroad. And a worldwide shortage of credit in 2007–2009 caused by mortgage defaults in the United States prompted the Fed to supply additional liquidity to the banking system to ensure the orderly functioning of financial markets.

Central banks around the world have also begun coordinating their activities, particularly during economic turmoil. For example, in October 2008, during the global financial crisis, six major central banks reduced interest rates in a joint effort to restore financial stability to world markets. Bernanke said he was in frequent contact with other central bankers, including Mario Draghi, head of the European Central Bank. (Incidentally, Draghi, like Bernanke, earned a Ph.D. in economics from MIT.) Although not the main focus of monetary policy, international considerations are of growing importance to the Fed, particularly because of recent fiscal instability in the eurozone.

CHECKPOINT

What specific policies did the Fed pursue during and after the Great Recession? What new monetary tools were developed to deal with the Great Recession?

15-5 Conclusion

This chapter has described two ways of viewing the effects of money on the economy's performance, but we should not overstate the differences. In the model that focuses on the short run, an increase in the money supply means that people are holding more money than they would like at the prevailing interest rate, so they exchange one form of wealth, money, for other financial assets, such as corporate or government bonds. This greater demand for other financial assets has no direct effect on aggregate demand, but it does reduce the interest rate, and thereby stimulates investment. The higher investment increases aggregate demand. The effect of this increase in demand on real output and the price level depends on the shape of the short-run aggregate supply curve.

In the model that focuses on the long run, changes in the money supply act more directly on the price level. If velocity is relatively stable or at least predictable, then a change in the money supply has a predictable effect on the price level in the long run. As long as velocity is not declining, an increase in the money supply means that people eventually spend more, increasing aggregate demand. But because long-run aggregate supply is fixed at the economy's potential output, increased aggregate demand leads simply to a higher price level, or to inflation, in the long run. Since 2007 the velocity of money has declined, so the increase in the money supply since then has not fueled much inflation, at least not as of 2015.

Summary

1. The opportunity cost of holding money is the higher interest forgone by not holding other financial assets instead. Along a given money demand curve, the quantity of money demanded relates inversely to the market interest rate, other things held constant. The demand for money curve shifts rightward as a result of an increase in the price level, an increase in real GDP, or an increase in both.

2. The Fed determines the supply of money, which is assumed to be independent of the interest rate. The intersection of the supply and demand curves for money determines the market interest rate. In the short run, an increase in the supply of money reduces the interest rate, which increases investment. This boosts aggregate demand, which increases real output and the price level.

3. The long-run approach focuses on the role of money through the equation of exchange, which states that the quantity of money, M, multiplied by velocity, V, the average number of times each dollar gets spent on final goods and services, equals the price level, P, multiplied by real output, Y. So $M \times V = P \times Y$. Because the aggregate supply curve in the long run is a vertical line at the economy's potential output, a change in the money supply affects the price level but not real output.

4. Between World War II and October 1979, the Fed tried to maintain stable interest rates as a way of promoting a stable investment environment. During the 1980s and early 1990s, the Fed paid more attention to growth in money aggregates, first M1 and then M2. But the velocity of M1 and M2 became so unstable that the Fed shifted focus back to interest rates, particularly the federal funds rate. To pursue its mandated goals of price stability and maximum employment, the Fed uses open-market operations to adjust the federal funds rate, raising the rate to prevent higher inflation and lowering the rate to stimulate employment.

5. As a result of the financial crisis of September 2008, the Fed broadened its scope of action to include offering interest on bank reserves at the Fed, bailing out a huge financial institution, investing more than $1 trillion in mortgage-backed securities to keep mortgage rates low, helping financial regulators perform stress tests on the nation's largest banks, introducing measures to help reduce the probability that a giant financial institution will fail, and reducing the impact of such a failure should one occur. The Fed's actions during the crisis suggest that it would try to do whatever was required to ensure the survival of the banking system and the economy.

Key Concepts

Demand for money   328

Equation of exchange   338

Velocity of money   338

Quantity theory of money   338

Stress test   345

Shadow banking system   345

Quantitative easing   345

Questions for Review

1. **Demand for Money**   Determine whether each of the following would lead to an increase, a decrease, or no change in the quantity of money people wish to hold. Also determine whether there is a shift of the money demand curve or a movement along a given money demand curve.

   a. A decrease in the price level
   b. An increase in real output
   c. An improvement in money's ability to act as a store of value
   d. An increase in the market interest rate

2. **Demand for Money**   If money is so versatile and can buy anything, why don't people demand all the money they can get their hands on?

3. **Monetary Policy**   What is the impact of a decrease in the required reserve ratio on aggregate demand?

4. **Federal Funds Rate**   Why has the Federal Reserve chosen to focus on the federal funds rate rather than some other interest rate as a tool of monetary policy?

5. **Case Study: Greater Fed Transparency as a Policy Tool**   In what sense has greater Fed transparency served as an additional policy tool, given that the federal funds rate could go no lower?

6. **Equation of Exchange**   Using the equation of exchange, show why fiscal policy alone cannot increase nominal GDP if the velocity of money is constant.

7. **Velocity of Money**   Determine whether each of the following would lead to an increase or a decrease in the velocity of money:

   a. Increasing the speed of funds transfers
   b. Decreased use of credit cards
   c. An increase in interest rates
   d. Increased customer use of debit cards at retailers

8. **Too Big to Fail**   How has the Fed tried to reduce the likelihood that a large financial institution will go bankrupt? In the event that one does fail, what document aims to minimize the impact on the wider economy?

9. **Supply of Money**   What does the shape of the money supply curve say about Fed policy? Describe the steps whereby an increase in the money supply leads to an increase in nominal output.

10. **How Stable Is Velocity?**   What factors have led to changes in the velocity of M1 and M2 during the past three decades?

11. **Money Supply Versus Interest Rate Targets** In recent years the Fed's policy focus has been the federal funds rate. How does the Fed raise or lower that rate, and how is that rate related to other interest rates in the economy such as the prime rate?

12. **Quantitative Easing** What's the difference between ordinary open-market purchases and quantitative easing?

Problems and Exercises

13. **Money and Aggregate Demand** Would each of the following increase, decrease, or have no impact on the ability of open-market operations to affect aggregate demand? Explain your answer.

    a. Investment demand becomes less sensitive to changes in the interest rate.
    b. The marginal propensity to consume rises.
    c. The money multiplier rises.
    d. Banks decide to hold additional excess reserves.
    e. The demand for money becomes more sensitive to changes in the interest rate.

14. **Monetary Policy and Aggregate Supply** Assume that the economy is initially in long-run equilibrium. Using an *AD–AS* diagram, illustrate and explain the short-run and long-run impacts of an increase in the money supply.

15. **Monetary Policy and an Expansionary Gap** Suppose the Fed wishes to use monetary policy to close an expansionary gap.

    a. Should the Fed increase or decrease the money supply?
    b. If the Fed uses open-market operations, should it buy or sell government securities?
    c. Determine whether each of the following increases, decreases, or remains unchanged in the short run: the market interest rate, the quantity of money demanded, investment spending, aggregate demand, potential output, the price level, and equilibrium real GDP.

16. **Equation of Exchange** Calculate the velocity of money if real GDP is 3,000 units, the average price level is $4 per unit, and the quantity of money in the economy is $1,500. What happens to velocity if the average price level drops to $3 per unit? What happens to velocity if the average price level remains at $4 per unit but the money supply rises to $2,000? What happens to velocity if the average price level falls to $2 per unit, the money supply is $2,000, and real GDP is 4,000 units?

17. **Quantity Theory of Money** What basic assumption about the velocity of money transforms the equation of exchange into the quantity theory of money? Also:

    a. According to the quantity theory, what will happen to nominal GDP if the money supply increases by 5 percent and velocity does not change?
    b. What will happen to nominal GDP if, instead, the money supply decreases by 8 percent and velocity does not change?
    c. What will happen to nominal GDP if, instead, the money supply increases by 5 percent and velocity decreases by 5 percent?
    d. What happens to the price level in the short run in each of these three situations?

18. **Money Supply Versus Interest Rate Targets** Assume that the economy's real GDP is growing.

    a. What will happen to money demand over time?
    b. If the Fed leaves the money supply unchanged, what will happen to the interest rate over time?
    c. If the Fed changes the money supply to match the change in money demand, what will happen to the interest rate over time?

    d. What would be the effect of the policy described in part (c) on the economy's stability over the business cycle?

19. **Expansionary Monetary Policy and Inflation** Between 2007 and 2015, assets on the Fed's balance sheet increased from $0.9 trillion to $4.5 trillion. Why didn't the resulting increase in bank reserves create higher inflation as of 2015?

16 Macro Policy Debate: Active or Passive?

Tom Hindman/west virgina press

- *Does the economy work fairly well on its own, or does it require active government intervention?*

- *Does government intervention do more harm than good?*

- *If people expect government to intervene when the economy falters, does this expectation affect people's behavior?*

- *Does this expectation affect government behavior?*

- *Is there a relationship between unemployment and inflation in the short run and in the long run?*

Answers to these and other questions are provided in this chapter, which discusses the appropriate role for government in economic stabilization.

You have studied both fiscal and monetary policy and are now in a position to consider the overall impact of public policy on the U.S. economy. This chapter distinguishes between two general approaches: the active approach and the passive approach. The active approach views the economy as relatively unstable and unable to recover from shocks when they occur. According to the active approach, economic fluctuations arise primarily from the private sector, particularly investment, and natural market forces may not help much or may be too slow once the economy gets off track. To move the economy to its potential output, the active approach calls for government intervention and discretionary policy.

The passive approach, on the other hand, views the economy as relatively stable and able to recover from shocks when they do occur. When the economy derails, natural market forces and automatic stabilizers nudge it back on track in a timely manner. According to the passive approach, not only is active discretionary policy unnecessary, but such activism may do more harm than good.

In this chapter, we consider the pros and cons of active intervention in the economy versus passive reliance on natural market forces and automatic stabilizers. We also examine the role that expectations play in stabilization policy. You will learn why unanticipated stabilization policies have more impact on employment and output than do anticipated ones. Finally, the chapter explores the trade-off between unemployment and inflation.

Topics discussed in this chapter include:

- Active versus passive approach
- Self-correcting mechanisms
- Problem of lags
- Rational expectations

- Policy rules and policy credibility
- The time-inconsistency problem
- Short-run and long-run Phillips curves
- Natural rate hypothesis

16-1 Active Policy Versus Passive Policy

According to the *active approach*, discretionary fiscal or monetary policy can reduce the costs of an unstable economy, such as from higher unemployment. According to the *passive approach*, discretionary policy may contribute to the instability of the economy and is therefore part of the problem, not part of the solution. The two approaches differ in their assumptions about the effectiveness of natural market forces compared with government intervention.

16-1a Closing a Recessionary Gap

Perhaps the best way to describe each approach is by examining a particular macroeconomic problem. Suppose the economy is in short-run equilibrium at point *a* in panel (a) of Exhibit 1, with real GDP at $16.8 trillion, which is below the economy's potential of $17.0 trillion. The recessionary gap of $0.2 trillion drives unemployment above its natural rate (the rate when the economy produces potential GDP). This gap could result from lower-than-expected aggregate demand. What should public officials do?

Passive Approach

Those who subscribe to the passive approach, as did their classical predecessors, have more faith in the *self-correcting forces* of the economy than do those who favor the active approach. In what sense is the economy self-correcting? According to the passive approach, wages and prices are flexible enough to adjust within a reasonable period to labor shortages or surpluses. High unemployment causes wages to fall, which reduces production costs, which in turn shifts the short-run aggregate supply curve rightward in panel (a) of Exhibit 1. (Money wages need not actually fall; money wage increases need only lag behind price increases, so that real wages fall. Or perhaps nonwage compensation is reduced, such as healthcare benefits.) The short-run aggregate supply curve, within a reasonable period, shifts from $SRAS_{110}$ to $SRAS_{100}$, moving the economy to its potential output at point *b*.

According to the passive approach, the economy is stable enough, gravitating in a reasonable time toward potential GDP. Automatic stabilizers also help move the economy toward potential GDP. Consequently, advocates of passive policy see little reason for discretionary policy. The passive approach is to let natural market forces and

---

EXHIBIT 1   **Closing a Recessionary Gap**

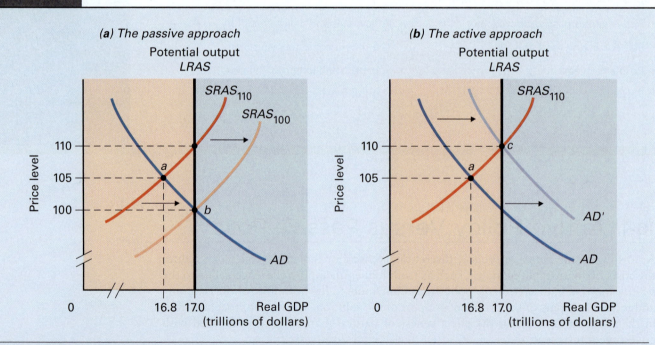

At point *a* in both panels, the economy is in short-run equilibrium, with unemployment exceeding its natural rate. According to the passive approach, shown in panel (a), high unemployment eventually causes wages to fall, reducing the cost of doing business. The decline in costs shifts the short-run aggregate supply curve rightward from $SRAS_{110}$ to $SRAS_{100}$, moving the economy to its potential output at point *b*. In panel (b), the government employs an active approach to shift the aggregate demand curve from *AD* to *AD'*. If the active policy works perfectly, the economy moves to its potential output at point *c*.

automatic stabilizers close the recessionary gap. So the prescription of passive policy is to do nothing beyond relying on the automatic stabilizers already built into taxes, transfers, and government purchases.

Active Approach

Advocates of an active approach, on the other hand, believe that prices and wages are not that flexible, particularly in the downward direction. They think that when adverse supply shocks or sagging demand push unemployment above its natural rate, market forces may be too slow to respond. The longer market forces take to reduce unemployment to the natural rate, the greater the output lost and the greater the economic and psychological cost to those unemployed. *Because advocates of an active policy associate a high cost with the passive approach, they favor an active stabilization policy to stimulate aggregate demand.*

Active Response to the Great Recession

A decision by public officials to intervene in the economy to achieve potential output—that is, a decision to use discretionary policy—reflects an active approach. In panel (b) of Exhibit 1, we begin at the same point *a* as in panel (a). At point *a*, short-run equilibrium output is below potential output, so the economy is experiencing a recessionary gap. Through discretionary monetary policy, discretionary fiscal policy, or some of both, as occurred in 2008 and 2009, active policy attempts to increase aggregate demand from *AD* to *AD'*, moving equilibrium from point *a* to point *c*, thus closing the recessionary gap.

During the Great Recession, policy makers tried to revive a troubled economy using both fiscal and monetary policy. President Barack Obama's $831 billion stimulus plan, the largest on record, was approved by Congress in February 2009 and was aimed at counteracting the sharp drop in output and employment triggered by the financial crisis. As noted in the previous chapter, the Fed had by that time already cut its target interest rate a record amount. This combination of fiscal and monetary policy was the most concentrated attempt to boost aggregate demand ever. One possible cost of using discretionary policy to stimulate aggregate demand is an increase in the price level, or inflation. But inflation has not been a problem in recent years. A larger cost of fiscal stimulus was an increase in the federal budget deficit, which rocketed from $459 billion in 2008 to $1.4 trillion in 2009. The deficit exceeded $1 trillion in each of the next three years.

16-1b Closing an Expansionary Gap

Let's consider the situation in which the short-run equilibrium output exceeds the economy's potential. Suppose the actual price level of 115 exceeds the expected price level of 110, resulting in an expansionary gap of $0.2 trillion, as shown in Exhibit 2. The passive approach argues that natural market forces prompt workers and firms to negotiate higher wages at their next opportunity. These higher nominal wages increase production costs, shifting the short-run supply curve leftward, from $SRAS_{110}$ to $SRAS_{120}$, as shown in panel (a). Consequently, the price level increases and output decreases to the economy's potential. So the natural adjustment process results in a higher price level, or inflation.

An active approach sees discretionary policy as a way to reach potential output without increasing the price level. Advocates of an active policy believe that if aggregate demand can be reduced from AD'' to AD', as shown in panel (b) of Exhibit 2, the equilibrium point will move down along the initial aggregate supply curve from *d* to *c*. *Whereas the passive approach relies on natural market forces and automatic stabilizers*

EXHIBIT 2   **Closing an Expansionary Gap**

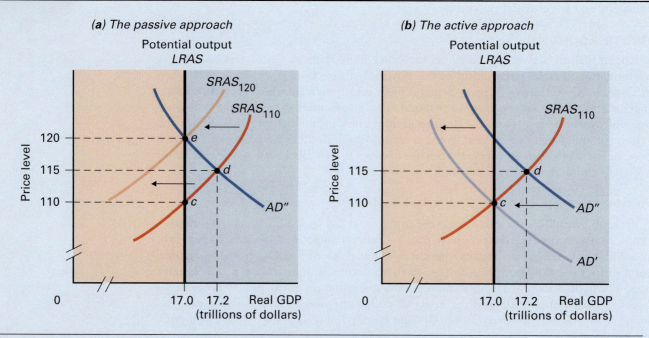

(a) The passive approach

(b) The active approach

At point *d* in both panels, the economy is in short-run equilibrium, producing $17.2 trillion, which exceeds the economy's potential output. Unemployment is below its natural rate. In the passive approach reflected in panel (a), the government makes no change in policy, so natural market forces eventually bring about a higher negotiated wage, increasing firm costs and shifting the short-run supply curve leftward to $SRAS_{120}$. The new equilibrium at point *e* results in a higher price level and lower output and employment. An active policy reduces aggregate demand, shifting the equilibrium combination in panel (b) from point *d* to point *c*, thus closing the expansionary gap without increasing the price level.

to close an expansionary gap through a decrease in the short-run aggregate supply curve, the active approach relies on just the right discretionary policy to close the gap through a decrease of the aggregate demand curve.

In the long run, the passive approach results in a higher price level and the active approach results in a lower price level. Thus, the correct discretionary policy can relieve the inflationary pressure associated with an expansionary gap. Whenever the Fed attempts to cool down an overheated economy by increasing its target interest rate, as it did in 17 steps between mid-2004 and mid-2006, it employs an active monetary policy to close an expansionary gap. The Fed tried to orchestrate a so-called *soft landing* to gently slow the rate of growth before that growth triggered unacceptably high inflation. We should note that heading off higher inflation is one thing, but policy makers are reluctant to take action that would actually reduce the price level—that is, create deflation. For example, in October 2014, the Bank of Japan announced a massive stimulus program to prevent deflation.[1] Once deflation takes hold, it can be self-reinforcing, as has been the case in Japan in recent years.

16-1c Problems With Active Policy

The timely adoption and implementation of an active policy is not easy. One problem is identifying the economy's potential output and the natural rate of unemployment.

[1.] Jacob M. Schlesinger, Eleanor Warnock, and Takashi Nakamichi, "Bank of Japan Announces Massive Stimulus Move," *Wall Street Journal*, 31 October 2014.

Suppose the natural rate of unemployment is 5 percent, but policy makers mistakenly believe it's 4 percent. As they pursue their elusive goal of 4 percent, they push aggregate output beyond its potential, fueling higher prices in the long run but with no permanent reduction in unemployment. Recall that when output exceeds the economy's potential, this opens up an expansionary gap, causing a leftward shift of the short-run aggregate supply curve until the economy returns to its potential output at a higher price level.

Even if policy makers can accurately estimate the economy's potential output and the natural rate of unemployment, formulating an effective policy requires detailed knowledge of current and future economic conditions. To craft an effective strategy, policy makers must first be able to forecast what aggregate demand and aggregate supply would be without active intervention. In other words, they must be able to predict what would happen with a passive approach. Second, they must have the tools needed to achieve the desired result relatively quickly. Third, they must be able to predict the effects of an active policy on the economy's key performance measures. Fourth, fiscal and monetary policy makers must work together, or at least not work at cross-purposes. Congress and the president pursue fiscal policy while the Fed pursues monetary policy; these groups usually fail to coordinate their efforts. If an active policy requires coordination, the policy may not work as desired. In early 1995, for example, Congress was considering an expansionary tax cut while the Fed was pursuing a contractionary monetary policy. Fifth, policy makers must be able to implement the appropriate policy, even when this involves short-term political costs. For example, during inflationary times, the optimal policy may call for a tax increase, a reduction in government spending, or a tighter monetary policy—steps that are unpopular because they could increase unemployment. Finally, policy makers must be able to deal with a variety of timing lags. As we see next, these lags complicate the execution of an active policy.

16-1d The Problem of Lags

So far, we have ignored the time required to implement policy. That is, we have assumed that the desired policy is selected and implemented instantaneously. We have also assumed that, once implemented, the policy works as advertised—again, in no time. Actually, there may be long, sometimes unpredictable, lags at several stages in the process. These lags reduce the effectiveness and increase the uncertainty of active policies.

Recognition Lag

First, is a **recognition lag**—the time it takes to identify a problem and determine how serious it is. For example, time is required to accumulate evidence that the economy is indeed performing below its potential. Even if initial data look troubling, many are usually revised later. For example, the government releases three estimates of quarterly GDP growth coming a month apart—an *advanced* estimate, a *preliminary* estimate, and a *final* estimate. What's more, these estimates are often revised years later. For example, in the third quarter of 2012, GDP growth estimates were revised all the way back to the first quarter of 2009. Therefore, policy makers sometimes wait for more proof before responding to what may turn out to be a false alarm. Because a recession is not identified as such until more than 6 months after it begins and because the average recession since 1945 has lasted only about 11 months, a typical recession is nearly over before officially recognized as a recession. What's more, the average lag between a recession's end and the official announcement that it has ended is about 15 months. So for a year or more after a recession ends, policy makers don't know for sure that it has ended. For example, the Great Recession ended in June 2009, but the announcement that the recession had ended did not come until September 2010.

recognition lag
The time needed to identify a macroeconomic problem and assess its seriousness

Decision-Making Lag

decision-making lag
The time needed to decide what to do once a macroeconomic problem has been identified

Even after enough evidence accumulates, policy makers often need time to decide what to do, so there is a **decision-making lag**. In the case of discretionary fiscal policy, Congress and the president must agree on an appropriate course of action. Fiscal policy usually takes months to develop and approve; it could take more than a year. On the other hand, the Fed can implement monetary policy more quickly and does not even have to wait for regular FOMC meetings. For example, as the economy weakened in 2008, the Fed announced interest rate cuts twice between regular meetings. So the decision-making lag is shorter for monetary policy than for fiscal policy.

Implementation Lag

implementation lag
The time needed to introduce a change in monetary or fiscal policy

Once a decision has been made, the new policy must be introduced, which usually involves an **implementation lag**. Again, monetary policy has the advantage: After a policy has been adopted, the Fed can immediately begin buying or selling bonds to influence bank reserves and thereby change the federal funds rate. The implementation lag is longer for fiscal policy. If tax rates change, new tax forms must be printed and distributed advising employers of changes in tax withholding. If government spending changes, the appropriate government agencies must get involved.

The implementation of fiscal policy can take more than a year. For example, in February 1983, the nation's unemployment rate reached 10.3 percent. The following month, Congress approved $9 billion to create what supporters claimed would be hundreds of thousands of new jobs. Fifteen months later, only $3.1 billion had been spent and only 35,000 new jobs had been created, according to a U.S. General Accounting Office study. By that time, the economy was already recovering on its own, lowering the unemployment rate from 10.3 percent to 7.1 percent and adding 6.2 million new jobs. So this public spending program was implemented only after the economy had bottomed out and began recovering. Likewise, in spring 1993, President Clinton proposed a $16 billion stimulus package to boost what appeared to be a sluggish recovery. The measure was defeated because it would have increased an already large federal deficit, yet the economy still added 5.6 million jobs over the next two years anyway. As a final example of an implementation lag, in early 2009, President Obama proposed what turned out to be an $831 billion program of tax cuts and spending increases to stimulate an economy reeling from the global financial crisis and the recession. Although Congress passed the measure relatively quickly, it took years to fully implement parts of the program. President Obama later acknowledged that many of the spending projects were not as "shovel-ready" as he had believed.

Effectiveness Lag

effectiveness lag
The time needed for changes in monetary or fiscal policy to affect the economy

Once a policy has been implemented, there is an **effectiveness lag** before the full impact of the policy registers on the economy. With monetary policy, the lag between a change in the federal funds rate and the change in aggregate demand and output can take from months to a year or more. Fiscal policy, once enacted, usually requires 3 to 6 months to take effect and between 9 and 18 months to register its full effect. Because of the effectiveness lag, the economy may turn around on its own before the policy registers its full impact. A fiscal stimulus may end up merely adding more inflationary pressure and more federal debt to a recovering economy.

Lags Obscure Active Policy

All these lags make active policy difficult to execute. The more variable the lags, the harder it is to predict when a particular policy will take hold and what the state of the economy will be at that time. To advocates of passive policy, these lags are reason enough to avoid active discretionary policy. *Advocates of a passive approach argue that an active stabilization policy imposes troubling fluctuations in the price level and real GDP because it often takes hold only after market forces have already returned the economy to its potential output level.*

Talk in the media about "jump-starting" the economy reflects the active approach, which views the economy as a sputtering engine that can be fixed by an expert mechanic. The passive approach views the economy as more like a supertanker on automatic pilot. The policy question then becomes whether to trust that automatic pilot (the self-correcting tendencies of the economy) or to try to override the mechanism with active discretionary policies.

16-1e A Review of Policy Perspectives

The active and passive approaches reflect different views about the stability and resiliency of the economy and the ability of Congress or the Fed to implement appropriate discretionary policies. As we have seen, advocates of an active approach think that the natural adjustments of wages and prices can be painfully slow, particularly when unemployment is high. Prolonged high unemployment means that much output must be sacrificed, and the unemployed must suffer personal hardship during the slow adjustment period. If high unemployment lasts a long time, labor skills may grow rusty, and some people may drop out of the labor force. Therefore, prolonged unemployment may cause the economy's potential GDP to fall and the natural rate of unemployment to rise.

Thus, active policy advocates see a high cost of not using discretionary policy. Despite the lags involved, they prefer action—through discretionary fiscal policy, discretionary monetary policy, or some combination of the two—to inaction. Passive policy advocates, on the other hand, believe that uncertain lags and ignorance about how the economy works undermine active policy. Rather than pursue a misguided activist policy, passivists prefer to rely more on the economy's natural ability to correct itself just using automatic stabilizers.

16-1f Active Policies, Passive Policies, and Presidential Politics

Consider the active and passive policies reflected in U.S. presidential politics. During the third quarter of 1990, after the longest peacetime economic expansion to that point of the 20th century, the U.S. economy slipped into a recession, triggered by Iraq's invasion of oil-rich Kuwait. Because of what at the time was considered a large federal deficit, policy makers were reluctant to pursue discretionary fiscal measures to revive the economy. That was left to the Fed. The recession lasted only eight months, but the unemployment rate continued to edge up in what was sarcastically called a "jobless recovery."

That sluggish recovery was the economic backdrop for the presidential election of 1992 between Republican President George H. W. Bush and Democratic challenger Bill Clinton. Because monetary policy did not seem to be providing enough of a kick, was more fiscal stimulus needed? With the federal budget deficit in 1992 already approaching $300 billion, a record amount to that point, would a higher deficit do more harm than good?[2]

Bush's biggest liabilities during the campaign were the slow recovery and high federal deficits; these were Clinton's biggest assets. Clinton argued that (1) Bush had

[2.] David Wessel, "Wanted: Fiscal Stimulus Without Higher Taxes," *Wall Street Journal*, 5 October 1992.

not done enough to revive the economy; (2) Bush could not be trusted because he broke a 1988 campaign pledge of "no new taxes" by signing a tax increase in 1990 to help cut federal deficits; and (3) Bush and his predecessor, Ronald Reagan, were responsible for the sizable federal deficits. Clinton promised to raise tax rates on the rich and cut them for the middle class. He also promised to create jobs through government spending programs that would "invest in America."

Bush tried to remind voters that the economy was growing again, so the recession was over. But that was a hard sell with unemployment averaging 7.6 percent during the six months leading up to the election (remember that the unemployment rate is a lagging indicator of economic activity). Clinton saw a stronger role for government, and Bush saw a stronger role for the private sector. Clinton's approach was more *active* and Bush's more *passive*. In the end, high unemployment rates during the campaign made people more willing to gamble on Clinton. Apparently, during troubled times, an active policy has more voter appeal than a passive one. Ironically, the economy at the time was stronger than described by the media and by challenger Clinton ("It's the economy, stupid" was Clinton's rallying cry). When the campaign dust settled, real GDP in the election year of 1992 grew by 3.6 percent. This would turn out to exceed the average annual growth rate of 3.3 percent during Clinton's first term. As a more recent comparison, not once between 2005 and 2015 did the U.S. economy grow as much as 3.6 percent a year.

George W. Bush was not about to make the same mistake as his father. Shortly after taking office in 2001, he proposed the first of three tax cuts to stimulate an economy in recession. This fiscal policy of tax cuts coincided with an aggressive monetary policy of federal funds rate cuts. This one-two punch was the greatest stimulus of aggregate demand to that point since World War II. Although the recession was over by the end of 2001, the unemployment rate continued to rise to a peak of 6.3 percent in June 2003 (again, the unemployment rate is a trailing economic indicator). Then, as if on cue, during the final 12 months before the election of 2004, the economy added 2 million jobs. Despite an unpopular war in Iraq, the additional jobs helped Bush get reelected.

The 2008 presidential election was like no other. President Bush was presiding over two unpopular wars and an economy sinking fast because of the financial crisis. But Bush was not on the ballot. Republican John McCain faced Democrat Barack Obama. Days after the financial crisis of September 2008, the two candidates issued a joint statement supporting TARP, the federal program to invest billions in ailing financial institutions and the most significant legislative action prior to the November election. So there was no policy difference between the two candidates on that big policy measure.

But the candidates differed on other issues. For example, McCain favored extending all the Bush tax cuts, which were set to expire. Obama said he would extend the Bush tax cuts only for those making less than $250,000 a year. Obama proposed broad health insurance mandates with more government regulations. McCain favored tax incentives to increase health coverage, saying he preferred "choices" to "mandates." Obama proposed creating millions of new jobs by investing in "green energy" programs. Not McCain. A presidential poll taken a month before the election found that those whose top concern was the economy preferred Obama over McCain by 2 to 1.[3] *When the economy is in trouble, voters seem to support a more active approach.* That's what they got with President Obama, whose active fiscal approach was joined by the most active monetary policy in history. Despite all that firepower, the recovery was modest through 2015. Supporters of the active approach argued that the tepid recovery was evidence of just how bad off things were to begin with. Critics of the active approach argued that the added taxes, public spending, and regulations created uncertainty about private enterprise and blunted incentives to work and to create jobs.

[3.] "Obama, McCain Lay Out Contrasts Before Undecided Voters," CNN, 8 October 2008.

What's the difference between active policy and passive policy? How do the two approaches differ in their assumptions about how well the economy works on its own?

16-2 The Role of Expectations

The effectiveness of a particular government policy depends in part on what people expect. As we saw in an earlier chapter, the short-run aggregate supply curve is drawn for a given expected price level reflected in long-term wage contracts. If workers and firms expect continued inflation, their wage agreements reflect these inflationary expectations. One approach in macroeconomics, called **rational expectations**, argues that people form expectations on the basis of all available information, including information about the probable future actions of policy makers. Thus, aggregate supply depends on what sort of macroeconomic course policy makers are expected to pursue. For example, if people were to observe policy makers using discretionary policy to stimulate aggregate demand every time output falls below potential, people would come to anticipate the effects of this policy on the price level and output. Robert Lucas, of the University of Chicago, won the 1995 Nobel Prize in Economics for his studies of rational expectations. We consider the role of expectations in the context of monetary policy, but fiscal policy would have a similar effect.

rational expectations
A school of thought that argues people form expectations based on all available information, including the likely future actions of government policy makers

16-2a Discretionary Policy and Inflation Expectations

Monetary authorities must testify before Congress regularly to offer an assessment of the economy. As noted in the previous chapter, the Fed also announces, after each meeting of the FOMC, any changes in its interest rate targets and the likely direction, or "bias," of future changes. The Fed head also holds a press conference after half the meetings to be more transparent about FOMC policy. And Fed officials often deliver speeches around the country. Those interested in the economy sift through all this material to discover the likely path of monetary policy.

Let's examine the relationship between Fed policy pronouncements, Fed actions, and equilibrium output. Suppose the economy is producing potential output so unemployment is at its natural rate. At the beginning of the year, firms and employees must negotiate wage agreements. While negotiations are under way, the Fed announces that throughout the year, monetary policy will aim at sustaining potential output while keeping the price level stable. This policy seems appropriate because unemployment is already at the natural rate. Workers and firms understand that the Fed's stable price policy appears optimal under the circumstances because an expansionary monetary policy would likely lead only to higher inflation in the long run. Until the year is under way and monetary policy is actually implemented, however, the public can't know for sure what the Fed will do.

As long as wage increases do not exceed the growth in labor productivity, the Fed's plan of a stable price level should work. Alternatively, workers could try to negotiate a higher wage growth, but that would ultimately lead to inflation. Suppose workers and firms believe the Fed's pronouncements and reach wage settlements based on a constant price level. If the Fed follows through as promised, the price level should turn out as expected. Output remains at the economy's potential, and unemployment remains at the natural rate. The situation is depicted in Exhibit 3. The short-run aggregate supply curve, $SRAS_{110}$, is based on wage contracts reflecting an expected price level of 110. If the Fed follows the announced course, the aggregate demand curve will be AD and equilibrium will be at point a, where the price level is as expected and the economy is producing $17.0 trillion, the potential output.

Suppose, however, that after workers and firms have agreed on nominal wages—that is, after the short-run aggregate supply curve has been determined—public officials become dissatisfied with the unemployment rate. Perhaps election-year concerns about unemployment, a false alarm about a recession, or overestimating potential output convince the Fed to act. An expansionary monetary policy increases the aggregate demand curve from AD, the level anticipated by firms and employees, to AD'. This unexpected policy stimulates output and employment in the short run to equilibrium point b. Output increases to $17.2 trillion, and the price level increases to 115. This temporary boost in output and reduction in unemployment may last long enough to help public officials get reelected.

So the price level is now higher than workers expected, and their agreed-on wage buys less in real terms than workers bargained for. At their earliest opportunity, workers will negotiate higher wages. These higher wage agreements will eventually cause the short-run aggregate supply curve in Exhibit 3 to shift leftward, intersecting AD' at point c, the economy's potential output (to reduce clutter, the shifted short-run aggregate supply curve is not shown). So output once again returns to the economy's potential GDP, but in the process the price level rises to 122.

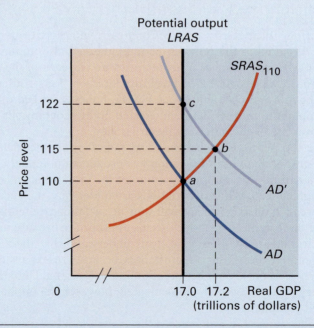

EXHIBIT 3   **Short-Run Effects of an Unexpected Expansionary Policy**

At point a, workers and firms expect a price level of 110; supply curve $SRAS_{110}$ reflects that expectation. But an unexpected expansionary policy shifts the aggregate demand curve out to AD'. Output in the short run (at point b) exceeds its potential. In the long run, costs increase, shifting $SRAS$ leftward until the economy produces its potential output at point c (the resulting supply curve is not shown). The short-run effect of an unexpected expansion is greater output, but the long-run effect is just a higher price level, or inflation.

Thus, the unexpected expansionary policy causes a short-run pop in output and employment. But in the long run, the increase in the aggregate demand curve yields only inflation. The **time-inconsistency problem** arises when policy makers have an incentive to announce one policy to shape expectations but then to pursue a different policy once those expectations have been formed and acted on.

16-2b Anticipating Policy

Suppose policy makers become alarmed by the high inflation. The next time around, the Fed once again announces a monetary policy aimed at producing potential output while keeping the price level stable at 122. Based on their previous experience, however, workers and firms have learned that the Fed is willing to accept higher inflation in exchange for a temporary boost in output. Workers may be fooled once by the Fed's actions, but they won't be fooled again. Thus, they and their employers take the Fed's announcement with a grain of salt. Workers, in particular, do not want to get caught again with their real wages down should the Fed implement a stimulative monetary policy. Workers and firms expect the Fed's actions will increase the price level. The bottom line is that workers and firms negotiate a high wage increase.

In effect, workers and firms are betting the Fed will pursue an expansionary policy regardless of pronouncements to the contrary. The short-run aggregate supply curve reflecting these higher wage agreements is depicted by $SRAS_{132}$ in Exhibit 4, where 132 is the expected price level. Note that AD' would result if the Fed followed its announced policy; that demand curve intersects the potential output line at point *c*, where the price

time-inconsistency problem
When policy makers have an incentive to announce one policy to influence expectations but then pursue a different policy once those expectations have been formed and acted on

EXHIBIT 4 **Short-Run Effects of a More Expansionary Policy Than Announced**

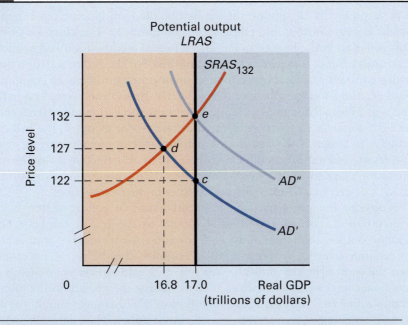

The Fed announces it plans to keep prices stable at 122. Workers and firms, however, expect monetary policy to be expansionary. The short-run aggregate supply curve, $SRAS_{132}$, reflects their expectations. If the Fed follows the announced stable-price policy, short-run output at point *d* is less than the economy's potential output of $17.0 trillion. To keep the economy at its potential, the Fed must stimulate aggregate demand as much as workers and firms expect (shown by point *e*), but this is inflationary.

level is 122. But *AD″* is the aggregate demand that workers and firms expect based on an expansionary monetary policy. They have agreed to wage settlements that will produce the economy's potential output if the Fed behaves as *expected*, not as *announced*. Thus, a price level of 132 is based on rational expectations. In effect, workers and firms expect the expansionary monetary policy to shift aggregate demand from *AD′* to *AD″*.

Monetary authorities must now decide whether to stick with their announced plan of a stable price level or follow a more expansionary monetary policy. If they pursue the constant-price-level policy, aggregate demand turns out to be *AD′* and short-run equilibrium occurs at point *d*. Short-run output falls below the economy's potential, resulting in unemployment exceeding the natural rate. If monetary authorities want to keep output at its potential, they have only one alternative—to match public expectations. Monetary authorities will likely pursue an expansionary monetary policy, an action that increases inflation and reinforces public skepticism of policy announcements. This expansionary policy results in an aggregate demand of *AD″*, leading to equilibrium at point *e*, where the price level is 132 and output equals the economy's potential.

Thus, workers and firms enter negotiations realizing that the Fed has an incentive to pursue an expansionary monetary policy. So workers and firms agree to higher wage increases, and the Fed follows with an expansionary policy, one that results in more inflation. Once workers and firms come to expect an expansionary monetary policy and the resulting inflation, such a policy does not spur even a temporary increase in output beyond the economy's potential. *Economists of the rational expectations school believe that if the economy is already producing its potential, an expansionary policy, if fully anticipated, has no effect on output or employment, not even in the short run. Only unanticipated expansionary policy can temporarily push output beyond its potential.*

16-2c Policy Credibility

If the economy is already producing its potential, an unexpected expansionary policy would increase output and employment temporarily. The costs, however, include not only inflation in the long term but also a loss of credibility in Fed pronouncements the next time around. Is there any way out of this? For the Fed to pursue a policy consistent with a constant price level, its announcements must somehow be *credible*, or believable. Workers and firms must believe that when the time comes to make a hard decision, the Fed will follow through as promised. Perhaps the Fed could offer some sort of guarantee to convince people it will stay the course—for example, the Fed chairman could promise to resign if the Fed does not follow the announced policy. Ironically, policy makers are often more credible and therefore more effective if they have some of their discretion taken away. In this case, a hard-and-fast rule could be substituted for a policy maker's discretion. We examine policy rules in the next section.

Consider the problems facing central banks in countries that have experienced hyperinflation. For an anti-inflation policy to succeed at the least possible cost in forgone output, the public must believe central bankers. How can central bankers in an economy ripped by hyperinflation establish credibility? Some economists believe that the most efficient anti-inflation policy is **cold turkey**: announcing and executing tough measures to stop inflation, such as halting the growth in the money supply. For example, in 1985, the annual rate of inflation in Bolivia was running at 20,000 percent when the new government announced a stern policy. The restrictive measures worked, and inflation was stopped within a month, with little loss in output. Around the world, credible anti-inflation policies have been successful.[4] However, drastic measures often

cold turkey

The announcement and execution of tough measures to reduce high inflation

---

[4] Thomas J. Sargent, "The Ends of Four Big Inflations," in *Inflation: Causes and Consequences*, Robert E. Hall, ed. (University of Chicago Press, 1982): 41–98.

involve costs. For example, some economists argue that the Fed's dramatic efforts to curb high U.S. inflation in the early 1980s triggered what was then the worst recession since the Great Depression. Some say that the Fed's pronouncements were simply not credible and therefore resulted in a recession.

Much depends on the Fed's time horizon. If policy makers take the long view, they will not risk their long-term policy effectiveness for a temporary reduction in unemployment. If Fed officials realize that their credibility is hard to develop but easy to undermine, they will be reluctant to pursue policies that ultimately just increase inflation. As then Fed Chairman Bernanke noted during his press briefing after an FMOC meeting,

> I guess the question is, does it make sense to actively seek a higher inflation rate in order to achieve a slightly [faster] reduction in the unemployment rate? The view of the Committee is that that would be very reckless. We have—we, the Federal Reserve, have spent 30 years building up credibility for low and stable inflation, which has proved extremely valuable in that we've been be able to take strong accommodative actions in the last four or five years to support the economy without leading to an unanchoring of inflation expectations or a destabilization of inflation. To risk that asset for what I think would be quite tentative and perhaps doubtful gains on the real side would be, I think, an unwise thing to do.[5]

Often Congress tries to pressure the Fed to stimulate the economy. By law, the Fed must "promote effectively the goals of maximum employment, stable prices, and moderate long-term interest rates." The law lets the Fed decide how best to do this. The Fed does not rely on congressional appropriations, so Congress can't threaten to withhold funds. Thus, although the U.S. president appoints the Board of Governors, and the Senate must approve these appointments, the Fed operates somewhat independently. Consider the link around the world between central bank independence and price stability in the following case study.

PUBLIC POLICY

CENTRAL BANK INDEPENDENCE AND PRICE STABILITY Some economists argue that the Fed would do better in the long run if it committed to the single goal of price stability rather than worry about achieving maximum employment as well. After all, most other central banks focus exclusively on price stability. But to focus on price stability, a central bank should be insulated from political influence, because price stability sometimes involves painful remedies. When the Fed was established, several features insulated it from politics, such as the 14-year terms with staggered appointments of Board members. Also, the Fed has its own income source (interest and capital gains earned from securities and fees earned from providing bank services), so it does not rely on Congress for a budget.

Does central bank independence affect performance? When central banks for 17 advanced industrial countries were ranked from least independent to most independent, inflation during the 15-year span examined turned out to be the lowest in countries with the most independent central banks and highest in countries with the least independent central banks. The least independent banks at the time were in Spain, New Zealand, Australia, and Italy. The most independent central banks were in Germany and Switzerland. Countries with the least independent central banks

continued

---

5. "Transcript of Chairman Bernanke's Press Conference," 25 April 2012, p. 8 at http://www.federalreserve .gov/monetarypolicy/fomccalendars.htm.

averaged four times higher inflation than countries with the most independent central banks. The U.S. central bank was considered relatively independent; U.S. inflation was double that of the most independent countries and half that of the least independent countries.

The trend around the world is toward greater central bank independence. For example, the Central Bank of New Zealand has adopted a monetary policy of inflation rate targeting, with price stability as the primary goal. Chile, Colombia, and Argentina—developing countries that suffered hyperinflation—have legislated more central bank independence. The agreement establishing a single European currency, the euro, identified price stability as the main objective of the European Central Bank. That bank has a policy of not reducing the interest rate if inflation exceeds 2.0 percent. In fact, the European Central Bank came under criticism before the recent financial crisis for not cutting interest rates even though a recession loomed and unemployment topped 8 percent. The Bank of England and Swiss National Bank also have an inflation target of no higher than 2.0 percent. Many central banks have adopted low inflation targets. The U.S. Federal Reserve's inflation target is 2.0 percent, and its target

in early 2015 for the minimum sustainable unemployment rate was a range of 5.0 percent to 5.2 percent.

Sources: Justin Lahart, "The Core of the Fed's Inflation Problem," *Wall Street Journal*, 22 May 2015; Jeffrey Sparshott, "Inflation Misses Fed's 2% Target for 36th Straight Month," *Wall Street Journal*, 1 June 2015; Alberto Alesina and Lawrence H. Summers, "Central Bank Independence and Macroeconomic Performance: Some Comparative Evidence," *Journal of Money, Credit and Banking*, 25 (May 1993): 151–162; and Stefano Eusepi and Bruce Preston, "Central Bank Communication and Expectations Stabilization," *American Economic Journal: Macroeconomics*, 2 (July 2010): 235–271. For online links to more than 160 central banks, including all those discussed in this case study, go to http://www.bis.org/cbanks.htm.

CHECKPOINT

How can expectations influence the effectiveness of discretionary policy?

16-3 Policy Rules Versus Discretion

Again, the active approach views the economy as unstable and in need of discretionary policy to cut cyclical unemployment when it arises. The passive approach views the economy as stable enough that discretionary policy is not only unnecessary but may actually worsen economic fluctuations. In place of discretionary policy, the passive approach often calls for predetermined rules to guide policy makers. In the context of fiscal policy, these rules take the form of automatic stabilizers, such as unemployment insurance, a progressive income tax, and transfer payments, all of which aim to dampen economic fluctuations. In the context of monetary policy, passive rules might be the decision to allow the money supply to grow at a predetermined rate, to maintain interest rates at some predetermined level, or to keep inflation below a certain rate. For example, as noted in the previous case study, the European Central Bank announced a rule that it would not lower its target interest rate if inflation exceeded 2.0 percent a year. Most central banks have committed to achieving low **inflation targets**, usually

inflation target
Commitment of central bankers to keep inflation at or below a certain rate for the next year or two

specifying a particular rate for the next year or two. Advocates of inflation targets say such targets encourage workers, firms, and investors to plan on a low and stable inflation rate. Opponents of inflation targets worry that the Fed would pay less attention to jobs and economic growth. In this section, we examine the arguments for policy rules versus discretion mostly in the context of monetary policy, the policy focus in recent decades.

16-3a Limitations on Discretion

The rationale for the passive approach rather than the use of active discretion arises from different views of how the economy works. One view holds that *the economy is so complex and economic aggregates interact in such obscure ways and with such varied lags that policy makers cannot possibly comprehend all that is going on well enough to pursue an active monetary or fiscal policy.* For example, if the Fed adopts a discretionary policy that is based on a misreading of the current economy or a faulty understanding of the lag structure, the Fed may be lowering the federal funds rate when a more appropriate course would be to leave the rate unchanged or even to raise it. As a case in point, during a meeting of the FOMC, one member lamented the difficulty of figuring out what was going on with the economy, noting, "As a lesson for the future, I'd like to remind us all that as recently as two meetings ago we couldn't see the strength that was unfolding in the second half [of the year].... It wasn't in our forecast; it wasn't in the other forecasts; and it wasn't in the anecdotal reports. We were standing right on top of it and we couldn't see it. That's just an important lesson to remember going forward."[6]

A comparison of economic forecasters and weather forecasters may shed light on the position of those who advocate the passive approach. Suppose you are in charge of the heating and cooling system at a major shopping mall. You realize that weather forecasts are unreliable, particularly in the early spring, when days can be warm or cold. Each day you must guess what the temperature will be and, based on that guess, decide whether to fire up the heater, turn on the air conditioner, or leave them both off. Because the mall is huge, you must start the system long before you know for sure what the weather will be. Once the system is turned on, it can't be turned off until much later in the day.

Suppose you guess the day will be cold, so you turn on the heat. If the day turns out to be cold, your policy is correct and the mall temperature will be just right. But if the day turns out to be warm, the heating system will make the mall unbearable. You would have been better off with nothing. In contrast, if you turn on the air conditioning system expecting a warm day but the day turns out to be cold, the mall will be freezing. The lesson is that if you are unable to predict the weather, you should use neither system. Similarly, if policy makers cannot predict the course of the economy, they should not try to fine-tune monetary or fiscal policy. Complicating the prediction problem is the fact that policy officials are not sure about the lags involved with discretionary policy. The situation is comparable to your not knowing how long the system actually takes to come on once you flip the switch.

This analogy applies only if the cost of doing nothing—using neither heat nor air conditioning—is relatively low. In the early spring, you can assume that there is little risk of weather so cold that water pipes freeze or so hot that walls sweat. A similar assumption in the passive view is that the economy is fairly stable and periods of prolonged unemployment are unlikely. In such an economy, the costs of *not*

---

[6] FOMC board member Thomas Melzer, in a transcript of the 22 December 1992 meeting of the Federal Open Market Committee, p. 14. Meeting transcripts are published after a five-year lag and are available at http://www.federalreserve.gov/monetarypolicy/fomc_historical.htm.

intervening are relatively low. In contrast, advocates of active policy believe that wide and prolonged swings in the economy (analogous to wide and prolonged swings in the outside temperature) make doing nothing risky.

16-3b Rules and Rational Expectations

Another group of economists also advocates the passive approach, but not because they believe the economy is too complex. Proponents of the rational expectations approach, discussed earlier, claim that people have a pretty good idea of how the economy works and what to expect from government policy makers. For example, people know enough about monetary policies pursued in the past to forecast, with reasonable accuracy, future policies and their effects on the economy. Some individual forecasts are too high and some too low, but on average, forecasts turn out to be about right. *To the extent that monetary policy is fully anticipated by workers and firms, it has no effect on the level of output; it affects only the price level.* Thus, only unexpected changes in policy can bring about short-run changes in output.

In the long run, changes in the money supply affect only inflation, not potential output, so followers of the rational expectations theory believe that the Fed should avoid discretionary monetary policy. Instead, the Fed should follow a predictable monetary rule. A monetary rule would reduce policy surprises and keep output near the natural rate. *Whereas some economists favor rules over discretion because of ignorance about the lag structure of the economy, rational expectations theorists advocate a predictable rule to avoid surprises, because surprises result in unnecessary departures from potential output.* For example, broad legislation to stimulate the economy, bail out the banks and automakers, and regulate financial institutions extensively were said to create uncertainty in the economy about what might be next. And this uncertainty discouraged some firms from hiring and kept some consumers from spending. Stanford economist John Taylor has argued that "we have plenty of evidence that rules-based monetary policies work and unpredictable discretionary policies don't."[7]

Despite support by some economists for explicit rules rather than discretion, central bankers have been reluctant to follow hard-and-fast rules about the course of future policy. Discretion has been used more than explicit rules since the early 1980s, though policy has become more predictable because the Fed now announces the probable trend of future target rate changes. As then Fed Chairman Paul Volcker argued more than three decades ago:

> The appeal of a simple rule is obvious. It would simplify our job at the Federal Reserve, make monetary policy easy to understand, and facilitate monitoring of our performance. And if the rule worked, it would reduce uncertainty....But unfortunately, I know of no rule that can be relied on with sufficient consistency in our complex and constantly evolving economy.[8]

Volcker's successor, Alan Greenspan, expressed similar sentiment:

> The Federal Reserve, should, some conclude, attempt to be more formal in its operations by tying its actions solely to the prescriptions of a formal policy rule. That any approach along these lines would lead to an improvement in economic performance, however, is highly doubtful.[9]

---

[7] John B. Taylor, "The Dangers of an Interventionist Fed," *Wall Street Journal*, 28 March 2012.

[8] Paul Volcker, before the Committee on Banking, Finance, and Urban Affairs, U.S. House of Representatives, August 1983.

[9] Alan Greenspan, "Monetary Policy Under Uncertainty," Remarks at a symposium sponsored by the Federal Reserve Bank of Kansas City, Jackson Hole, Wyoming, 29 August 2003, which can be found at http://www.federalreserve.gov/boarddocs/speeches/2003/20030829/default.htm.

Ben Bernanke, who succeeded Greenspan in 2006, viewed the matter mostly as a nonissue:

> [T]he argument that monetary policy should adhere mechanically to a strict rule, made by some economists in the past, has fallen out of favor in recent years. Today most monetary economists use the term "rule" more loosely to describe a general policy strategy, one that may include substantial scope for policymaker discretion and judgment.[10]

Nor did Janet Yellen, who succeeded Bernanke in 2014, want to have her hands tied by any rule:

> It would be a grave mistake for the Fed to commit to conduct monetary policy according to a mathematical rule....It is utterly necessary for us to provide more monetary-policy accommodation than those simple rules would have suggested.[11]

For the century of the Fed's existence, there has been an ongoing tension between rules and discretion. For example, the Fed had to learn how to slow the high inflation of the 1970s and early 1980s. The Fed experimented briefly with targeting the money supply, then targeting interest rates. More recently the Fed began targeting the inflation rate and has tried to influence long-term interest rates by purchasing mortgage backed securities. Thus, from time to time, Fed officials have used discretion to change the rules as circumstances changed, but once a new rule was adopted, such as inflation-rate targeting, that rule is followed until circumstances warrant a new rule.[12]

So far, we have looked at active stabilization policy, which focuses on shifts of the aggregate demand curve, and passive stabilization policy, which relies more on automatic stabilizers and natural shifts of the short-run aggregate supply curve. In the final section, we focus on an additional model, the Phillips curve, to shed more light on the relationship between aggregate demand and aggregate supply in the short and long runs.

CHECKPOINT

Why do some economists prefer that policy be shaped by predictable rules rather than by the discretion of policy makers?

16-4 The Phillips Curve

At one time, policy makers thought they faced a long-run trade-off between inflation and unemployment. This view was suggested by the research of New Zealand economist A. W. Phillips, who in 1958 published an article that examined the historical relation

---

[10.] Ben S. Bernanke, "The Logic of Monetary Policy," Remarks Before the National Economists Club, Washington, D.C., 2 December 2004, which can be found at http://www.federalreserve.gov/boarddocs/Speeches/2004/20041202/default.htm.

[11.] As quoted in Pedro Nicolaci da Costa and Ben Leubsdorf, "Yellen Balks at Proposal to Tie Rate to Formula," *Wall Street Journal*, 16 July 2014.

[12.] Benjamin M. Friedman, "Rules Versus Discretion at the Federal Reserve: On to the Second Century," *Journal of Macroeconomics*, 34 (September 2012): 608–615.

between inflation and unemployment in the United Kingdom.[13] Based on about 100 years of evidence, his data traced an inverse relationship between the unemployment rate and the rate of change in nominal wages (serving as a measure of inflation). This relationship implied that the opportunity cost of reducing unemployment was higher inflation, and the opportunity cost of reducing inflation was higher unemployment.

16-4a The Phillips Framework

The possible options with respect to unemployment and inflation are illustrated by the hypothetical **Phillips curve** in Exhibit 5. The unemployment rate is measured along the horizontal axis and the inflation rate along the vertical axis. Let's begin at point *a*, which depicts one possible combination of unemployment and inflation. Fiscal or monetary policy could be used to stimulate output and thereby reduce unemployment, moving the economy from point *a* to point *b*. Notice, however, that the reduction in unemployment comes at the cost of higher inflation. A reduction in unemployment with no change in inflation would be represented by point *c*. But as you can see, this alternative is not available.

Most policy makers of the 1960s came to believe that they faced a stable, long-run trade-off between unemployment and inflation. The Phillips curve was based on an era when inflation was low and the primary disturbances in the economy were shocks to aggregate demand. The effect of changes in aggregate demand can

EXHIBIT 5   **Hypothetical Phillips Curve**

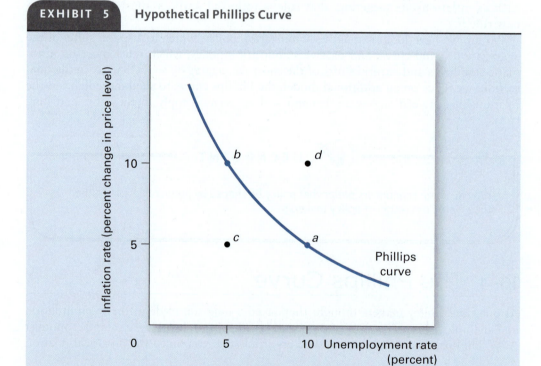

The Phillips curve shows an inverse relation between unemployment and inflation. Points *a* and *b* lie on the Phillips curve and represent alternative combinations of inflation and unemployment that are attainable as long as the curve itself does not shift. Points *c* and *d* are off the curve.

[13.] A. W. Phillips, "Relation between Unemployment and the Rate of Change in Money Wage Rates in the United Kingdom, 1861–1957," *Economica*, 25 (November 1958): 283–299.

be traced as movements along a given short-run aggregate supply curve. If aggregate demand increases, the price level rises but unemployment falls. If aggregate demand decreases, the price level falls but unemployment rises. With appropriate demand-management tools, policy makers believed they could choose any point along the Phillips curve. The 1970s proved this view wrong in two ways. First, some of the biggest disturbances were adverse *supply* shocks, such as those created by OPEC oil embargoes and worldwide crop failures. These shocks shifted the aggregate supply curve leftward. A reduction of the aggregate supply curve led to both higher inflation *and* higher unemployment. Stagflation was at odds with the Phillips curve. Second, economists learned that when short-run output exceeds potential, an expansionary gap opens. As this gap closes by a leftward shift of the short-run aggregate supply curve, greater inflation *and* higher unemployment result—again, an outcome inconsistent with a Phillips curve.

The increases in both inflation and unemployment caused by a decrease in aggregate supply can be represented by an outcome such as point *d* in Exhibit 5. By the end of the 1970s, increases in both inflation and unemployment suggested either that the Phillips curve had shifted outward or that it no longer described economic reality. The dilemma called for a reexamination of the Phillips curve, and this led to a distinction between the short-run Phillips curve and the long-run Phillips curve.

16-4b The Short-Run Phillips Curve

To discuss the underpinnings of the Phillips curve, we must return to the short-run aggregate supply curve. Suppose the price level this year is reflected by a price index of, say, 100, and that people expect prices to be about 3 percent higher next year. So the price level expected next year is 103. Workers and firms therefore negotiate wage contracts based on that expectation. As the short-run aggregate supply curve in Exhibit 6(a) indicates, if *AD* is the aggregate demand curve and the price level is 103, as expected, output equals the economy's potential, shown here to be $17.0 trillion. Recall that when the economy produces its potential, unemployment is at the natural rate.

The short-run relationship between inflation and unemployment is presented in Exhibit 6(b) under the assumption that people expect inflation to be 3 percent. Unemployment is measured along the horizontal axis and inflation along the vertical axis. Panel (a) shows that when inflation is 3 percent, the economy produces its potential. Unemployment is at the natural rate, assumed in panel (b) to be 5 percent. The combination of 3 percent inflation and 5 percent unemployment is reflected by point *a* in panel (b), which corresponds to point *a* in panel (a).

What if aggregate demand turns out to be greater than expected, as indicated by *AD′*? In the short run, the greater demand results in point *b*, with a price level of 105 and output of $17.1 trillion. Because the price level exceeds that reflected in wage contracts, inflation also exceeds expectations. Specifically, inflation turns out to be 5 percent, not 3 percent. Because output exceeds potential, unemployment falls below the natural rate to 4 percent. The new combination of unemployment and inflation is depicted by point *b* in panel (b), which corresponds to point *b* in panel (a).

What if aggregate demand turns out to be lower than expected, as indicated by *AD″*? In the short run, the lower demand results in point *c*, where the price level of 101 is less than expected and output of $16.9 trillion is below potential. Inflation of 1 percent is less than the expected 3 percent, and unemployment of 6 percent exceeds the natural rate. This combination is reflected by point *c* in panel (b), which corresponds to point *c* in panel (a).

Note that the short-run aggregate supply curve in panel (a) can be used to develop the inverse relationship between inflation and unemployment shown in panel (b), called

EXHIBIT 6   **Aggregate Supply Curves and Phillips Curves in the Short Run and Long Run**

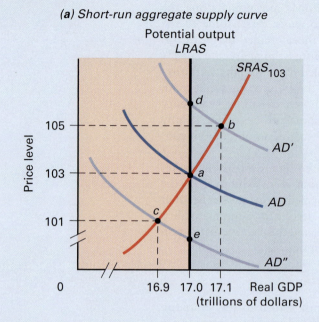

(a) Short-run aggregate supply curve

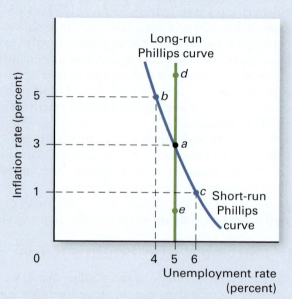

(b) Short-run and long-run Phillips curves

If people expect a price level of 103, which is 3 percent higher than the current level, and if *AD* turns out to be the aggregate demand curve, then the actual price level is 103 and output is at its potential. Point *a* in both panels represents this situation. Unemployment is the natural rate, assumed to be 5 percent in panel (b). If aggregate demand turns out to be greater than expected (*AD′* instead of *AD*), the economy in the short run is at point *b* in panel (a), where the price level of 105 exceeds expectations and output exceeds its potential. The resulting higher inflation and lower unemployment are shown as point *b* in panel (b). If aggregate demand turns out to be less than expected (*AD″* instead of *AD*), short-run equilibrium is at point *c* in panel (a), where the price level of 101 is lower than expected and output falls short of potential. Lower inflation and higher unemployment are shown as point *c* in panel (b). In panel (b), points *a*, *b*, and *c* trace a short-run Phillips curve. In the long run, the actual price level equals the expected price level. Output is at the potential level, $17.0 trillion, in panel (a). Unemployment is at the natural rate, 5 percent, in panel (b). Points *a*, *d*, and *e* depict long-run points in each panel. In panel (a) these points trace potential output, or long-run aggregate supply (*LRAS*). In panel (b), these points trace a long-run Phillips curve.

short-run Phillips curve

Based on an expected inflation rate, a curve that reflects an inverse relationship between the inflation rate and the unemployment rate

a **short-run Phillips curve**. This curve is created by the intersection of alternative aggregate demand curves along a given short-run aggregate supply curve. *The short-run Phillips curve is based on labor contracts that reflect a given expected price level, which implies a given expected rate of inflation.* The short-run Phillips curve in panel (b) is based on an expected inflation of 3 percent. If inflation turns out as expected, unemployment equals the natural rate. If inflation exceeds expectations, unemployment in the short run falls below the natural rate. If inflation is less than expected, unemployment in the short run exceeds the natural rate.

16-4c The Long-Run Phillips Curve

If inflation exceeds expectations, output exceeds the economy's potential in the short run but not in the long run. Labor shortages and shrinking real wages prompt higher wage agreements. The short-run aggregate supply curve shifts leftward until it passes through point *d* in panel (a) of Exhibit 6, returning the economy to its potential output.

The unexpectedly higher aggregate demand curve has no lasting effect on output or unemployment. Point *d* corresponds to a higher price level, and thus higher inflation. Closing the expansionary gap generates both higher unemployment and higher inflation, a combination depicted by point *d* in panel (b). Note that whereas points *a, b,* and *c* are on the same short-run Phillips curve, point *d* is not.

To trace the long-run effects of a lower-than-expected price level, let's return to point *c* in panel (a), where the actual price level is below the expected level, so output is below its potential. If workers and firms negotiate lower money wages (or if the growth in nominal wages trails inflation), the short-run aggregate supply curve could shift rightward until it passes through point *e*, where the economy returns once again to its potential output. Both inflation and unemployment fall, as reflected by point *e* in panel (b).

Note that points *a, d,* and *e* in panel (a) depict long-run equilibrium points; the expected price level equals the actual price level. At those same points in panel (b), expected inflation equals actual inflation, so unemployment equals the natural rate. We can connect points *a, d,* and *e* in the right panel to form the **long-run Phillips curve**. *When workers and employers adjust fully to any unexpected change in aggregate demand, the long-run Phillips curve is a vertical line drawn at the economy's natural rate of unemployment.* As long as prices and wages are flexible enough, the rate of unemployment, in the long run, is independent of the rate of inflation. *Thus, according to proponents of this type of analysis, policy makers cannot, in the long run, choose between unemployment and inflation. They can choose only among alternative rates of inflation.*

long-run Phillips curve
A vertical line drawn at the economy's natural rate of unemployment that traces equilibrium points that can occur when workers and employers have the time to adjust fully to any unexpected change in aggregate demand

16-4d The Natural Rate Hypothesis

The natural rate of unemployment occurs at the economy's potential output, discussed extensively already. An important idea that emerged from this reexamination of the Phillips curve is the **natural rate hypothesis**, which states that in the long run, the economy tends toward the natural rate of unemployment. This natural rate is largely independent of any *aggregate demand* stimulus provided by monetary or fiscal policy. Policy makers may be able to push output beyond its potential temporarily, but only if the policy surprises the public. The natural rate hypothesis implies that *the policy that results in low inflation is generally the optimal policy in the long run.* As noted earlier, the Fed believed that the natural rate of unemployment in 2015 was in the range of 5.0 percent to 5.2 percent. As noted already, each quarter those who participate in FOMC meetings estimate the natural rate, or minimum sustainable rate, of unemployment.

natural rate hypothesis
The natural rate of unemployment is largely independent of the stimulus provided by monetary or fiscal policy

16-4e Evidence of the Phillips Curve

What has been the actual relationship between unemployment and inflation in the United States? In Exhibit 7, each year since 1960 is represented by a point, with the unemployment rate measured along the horizontal axis and the inflation rate measured along the vertical axis. Superimposed on these points are short-run Phillips curves showing patterns of unemployment and inflation during what appears to be six distinct periods since 1960. Remember, each short-run Phillips curve is drawn for a given *expected inflation rate.* An increase in inflationary expectations shifts the short-run Phillips curve up and to the right, away from the origin.

The clearest trade-off between unemployment and inflation occurred between 1960 and 1969; the blue points for those years fit neatly along the blue curve. In the early part of the decade, inflation was low but unemployment relatively high; as the 1960s progressed, unemployment declined but inflation increased. Inflation during the decade averaged only 2.5 percent, and unemployment averaged 4.8 percent.

EXHIBIT 7   **Six Short-Run Phillips Curves Since 1960**

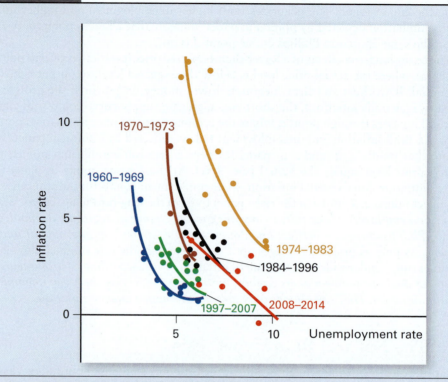

Each curve represents the U.S. unemployment-inflation combination for a given period, with colored points showing the years associated with each colored curve. Shifts of the short-run Phillips curve reflect changes in inflation expectations. Curves closer to the origin reflect lower expected inflation.

Source: Based on inflation and unemployment figures from the *Economic Report of the President*, February 2015, at http://www.whitehouse.gov/administration/eop/cea/economic-report-of-the-President and the U.S. Bureau of Labor Statistics at http://www.bls.gov/.

The short-run Phillips curve shifted away from the origin for the period from 1970 to 1973 (in maroon), when inflation and unemployment each climbed to an average of 5.2 percent. In 1974, sharp increases by OPEC in oil prices and crop failures around the world reduced aggregate supply, which sparked another outward shift of the Phillips curve. During the 1974–1983 period (in orange), inflation averaged 8.2 percent and unemployment 7.5 percent. After the Fed reduced inflationary expectations in the early 1980s, the short-run Phillips curve shifted inward. Average inflation for 1984–1996 (in black) fell to 3.7 percent and average unemployment fell to 6.1 percent. Data for 1997 to 2007 (in green) indicate a lower short-run Phillips curve, with average inflation of 2.5 percent and average unemployment of 5.0 percent. Finally, data for 2008 to 2014 (in red) suggest that the short-run Phillips curve may have shifted out, with inflation averaging 1.8 percent and unemployment averaging 7.9 percent. Thus, the Phillips curve shifted rightward between the 1960s and the early 1980s. Then the curve shifted back in stages between 1984 and 2007. But since 2008, the curve has shifted out again because of higher unemployment in the wake of the Great Recession. Also during the early years of the most recent period, higher energy prices boosted expectations for higher inflation.[14]

[14.] Olivier Coibion and Yuriy Gorodnichenko, "Is The Phillips Curve Alive and Well After All? Inflation Expectations and the Missing Disinflation," *American Economic Journal: Macroeconomics* (forthcoming). For more evidence on the Phillips curve, see Robert J. Gordon, "The Phillips Curve is Alive and Well: Inflation and the NAIRU During the Slow Recovery," NBER Working Paper No. 19390 (August 2013).

CHECKPOINT

Explain the shape of the short-run Phillips curve and the long-run Phillips curve.

16-5 Conclusion

This chapter examined the implications of active and passive policy. The important question is whether the economy is stable and self-correcting when it gets off track, or whether it is, instead, unstable and in need of active government intervention. Advocates of active policy believe that the Fed or Congress or both should reduce economic fluctuations by stimulating aggregate demand when output falls below its potential level and by dampening aggregate demand when output exceeds its potential level. Advocates of active policy argue that government attempts to reduce the ups and downs of the business cycle may not be perfect but are still better than nothing. Some activists also believe that a long stretch of high unemployment may be self-reinforcing, because some unemployed workers lose valuable job skills and grow to accept unemployment as a way of life, as may have happened in Europe.

Advocates of passive policy, on the other hand, believe that discretionary policy may worsen cyclical swings in the economy, leading to higher inflation in the long run with no permanent increase in potential output and no permanent reduction in the unemployment rate. Worse still, repeated efforts to stimulate the economy through fiscal policy have resulted in a huge federal debt, creating uncertainty and instability. Because of all this, this group of economists favors passive rules for monetary policy and automatic stabilizers for fiscal policy.

The active-passive debate in this chapter has focused primarily on monetary policy because discretionary fiscal policy has been hampered by large federal deficits that ballooned the national debt. But the Great Recession of 2007–2009 was so severe that most fiscal policy makers decided to worry later about deficits and debt.

Summary

1. Advocates of active policy view the private sector—particularly fluctuations in investment—as the primary source of economic instability in the economy. Activists argue that achieving potential output through natural market forces can be slow and painful, so the Fed or Congress or both should stimulate aggregate demand when actual output falls below potential.

2. Advocates of passive policy argue that the economy has enough natural resiliency to return to potential output within a reasonable period if upset by some shock. They point to the variable and uncertain lags associated with discretionary policy as reason enough to steer clear of active intervention.

3. The effect of particular government policies on the economy depends on what people come to expect. The theory of rational expectations holds that people form expectations based on all available information including past behavior by public officials. According to the rational expectations school, government policies are mostly anticipated by the public, and therefore have less effect than unexpected policies.

4. The passive approach suggests that the government should follow clear and predictable policies and avoid discretionary intervention to stimulate or dampen aggregate demand over the business cycle. Passive policies are reflected in automatic fiscal stabilizers and in explicit monetary rules, such as keeping inflation at or below a certain rate.

5. At one time, public officials thought they faced a stable trade-off between higher unemployment and higher inflation. More recent research suggests that if there is a trade-off, it exists only in the short run, not in the long run. Expansionary fiscal or monetary policies may stimulate output and employment in the short run. But if the economy was already at or near its potential output, these expansionary policies, in the long run, result only in more inflation. And federal deficits from expansionary fiscal policy can create a huge federal debt, which itself can create uncertainty and instability.

Key Concepts

Questions for Review

1. **Active Versus Passive Policy**   Contrast the active policy view of the behavior of wages and prices during a recessionary gap with the passive policy view.

2. **Active Policy**   Why do proponents of active policy recommend government intervention to close an expansionary gap?

3. **Active Versus Passive Policy**   According to advocates of passive policy, what variable naturally adjusts in the labor market, shifting the short-run aggregate supply curve to restore unemployment to the natural rate? Why does the active policy approach assume that the short-run aggregate supply curve shifts leftward more easily and quickly than it shifts rightward?

4. **Review of Policy Perspectives**   Why might an active policy approach be more politically popular than a passive approach, especially during a recession?

5. **The Role of Expectations**   Some economists argue that only unanticipated increases in the money supply can affect real GDP. Explain why this may be the case.

6. **Anticipating Monetary Policy**   In 1995, the Fed began announcing its interest rate targets immediately following each meeting of the FOMC. Prior to that, observers were left to draw inferences about Fed policy based on the results of that policy. What is the value of this greater openness?

7. **Policy Credibility**   What is policy credibility and how is it relevant to the problem of reducing high inflation? How is credibility related to the time-inconsistency problem?

8. **Case Study: Central Bank Independence and Price Stability**   One source of independence for the Fed is the term length for members of the Board of Governors. In the chapter before last, we learned that the Fed is a "money machine." Does this suggest another source of Fed independence from Congress?

9. **Rationale for Rules**   Some economists call for predetermined rules to guide the actions of government policy makers. What are two contrasting rationales that have been given for such rules?

10. **Rational Expectations**   Suppose that people in an election year believe that public officials are going to pursue expansionary policies to enhance their reelection prospects. How could such expectations put pressure on officials to pursue expansionary policies even if they hadn't planned to?

11. **Potential GNP**   Why is it hard for policy makers to decide whether the economy is operating at its potential output level? Why is this uncertainty a problem?

12. **Phillips Curves**   Describe the different policy trade-offs implied by the short-run Phillips curve and the long-run Phillips curve. What forces shift the long-run Phillips curve?

Problems and Exercises

13. **Active Versus Passive Policy**   Discuss the role that each of the following plays in the debate between the active and passive approaches:

    a. The speed of adjustment of the nominal wage
    b. The speed of adjustment of expectations about inflation
    c. The existence of lags in policy creation and implementation
    d. Variability in the natural rate of unemployment over time

14. **Problems with Active Policy**   Use an *AD–AS* diagram to illustrate and explain the short-run and long-run effects on the economy of the following situation: Both the natural rate of unemployment and the actual rate of unemployment are 5 percent. However, the government believes that the natural rate of unemployment is 6 percent and that the economy is overheating. Therefore, it introduces a policy to reduce aggregate demand.

15. **Policy Lags**   What lag in discretionary policy is described in each of the following statements? Why do long lags make discretionary policy less effective?

    a. The time from when the government determines that the economy is in recession until a tax cut is approved to reduce unemployment
    b. The time from when the money supply is increased until the resulting effect on the economy is felt
    c. The time from the start of a recession until the government identifies the existence and severity of the recession
    d. The time from when the Fed decides to reduce the money supply until the money supply actually declines

16. **Rational Expectations**   Using an *AD–AS* diagram, illustrate the short-run effects on prices, output, and employment of an increase in the money supply that is correctly anticipated by the public. Assume that the economy is initially at potential output.

17. **Long-Run Phillips Curve**   Suppose the economy is at point *d* on the long-run Phillips curve shown in Exhibit 6. If that inflation rate is unacceptably high, how can policy makers get the inflation rate down? Would rational expectations help or hinder their efforts?

Sheila Fitzgerald/Shutterstock.com

- *This morning you pulled on your Levi's jeans from Mexico, pulled over your Roots sweater from Canada, and laced up your Timberland boots from Thailand. After a breakfast that included bananas from Honduras and coffee from Brazil, you climbed into your Volvo from Sweden fueled by Venezuelan oil and headed for a lecture by a visiting professor from Hungary. If the United States is such a rich and productive country, why do we import so many goods and services?*

- *Why don't we produce everything ourselves?*

- *How can the U.S. economy grow if we import more goods and services?*

- *And why do some U.S. producers try to block imports?*

Answers to these and other questions are addressed in this chapter.

The world is a giant shopping mall, and Americans are big spenders. For example, the U.S. population is less than 5 percent of the world's population, but Americans buy 38 percent of the diamond jewelry sold around the world. Americans also buy Japanese cars, French wine, European vacations, Chinese products galore, and millions of other goods and services from around the globe. Foreigners buy U.S. products too—grain, aircraft, movies, software, higher education, trips to New York City, and millions of other goods and services. For example, California grows 80 percent of the world's almond supply.

In this chapter, we examine the gains from international trade and the effects of trade restrictions on the allocation of resources. The analysis is based on the familiar tools of demand and supply.

Topics discussed in this chapter include:

- Gains from trade
- Absolute and comparative advantage revisited
- Tariffs and quotas
- Cost of trade restrictions

- Free trade agreements
- World Trade Organization, or WTO
- Common market
- Arguments for trade restrictions

17-1 The Gains From Trade

A Virginia family that sits down to a dinner of Kansas prime rib, Idaho potatoes, and California string beans, with Georgia peach cobbler for dessert, is benefiting from interstate trade. You already understand why the residents of one state trade with those of another. Back in Chapter 2, you learned about the gains arising from specialization and trade. You may recall how you and your roommate could maximize output when you each specialized. The law of comparative advantage says that the individual with the lowest opportunity cost of producing a particular good should specialize in that good. Just as individuals benefit from specialization and trade, so do states and, indeed, nations. To reap the gains that arise from specialization, countries engage in international trade. *Each country specializes in making goods with the lowest opportunity cost.*

17-1a A Profile of Exports and Imports

Just as some states are more involved in interstate trade than others, some nations are more involved in international trade than others. For example, exports account for about one-quarter of the gross domestic product (GDP) in Canada and the United Kingdom; about one-third of GDP in Germany, Sweden, and Switzerland; and about half of GDP in the Netherlands. Despite the perception that Japan has a huge export sector, exports make up only about one-sixth of its GDP.

U.S. Exports

U.S. exports of goods and services amounted to $2.3 trillion in 2014, or 13 percent of GDP. The left panel of Exhibit 1 shows the composition by major category in 2014. The largest category is services, which accounted for 31 percent of U.S. exports. U.S. service exports include transportation, insurance, banking, education, consulting, and tourism. Capital goods ranked second, at 24 percent of the total, with aircraft the largest export industry (Boeing is the top U.S. exporter). Industrial supplies ranked third, at 22 percent of exports, with chemicals and plastics topping that list. Capital goods and industrial supplies help foreign producers make stuff and together accounted for nearly half of U.S. exports. Consumer goods (except food and autos, which appear separately) accounted for only 11 percent of exports (pharmaceuticals tops this group). Consumer goods also include entertainment products, such as movies and recorded music.

U.S. Imports

U.S. imports of goods and services totaled $2.8 trillion in 2014, or 16 percent relative to GDP. The right panel of Exhibit 1 shows the composition of U.S. imports. The biggest category, at 24 percent, is industrial supplies, with petroleum products accounting for most of that. Whereas consumer goods accounted for only 11 percent of U.S. exports, they were 22 percent of U.S. imports, with pharmaceuticals the largest item. Ranked third is capital goods, at 21 percent, with computers the largest item. Note that services, which accounted for 31 percent of U.S. exports, were only 17 percent of U.S. imports.

| EXHIBIT 1 | Composition of U.S. Exports and Imports in 2014 |

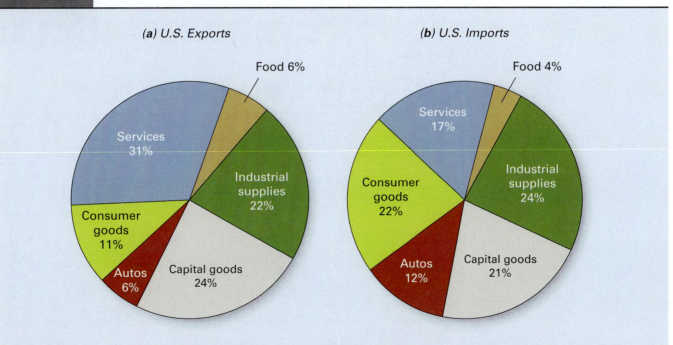

Sources: Based on federal government estimates of International Economic Accounts by the Bureau of Economic Analysis, U.S. Department of Commerce, at http://bea.gov/international/index.htm.

Trading Partners

World trade totaled about \$21 trillion in 2014, or 20 percent relative to world output of \$105 trillion that year. To give you some feel for America's trading partners, here were the top 10 destinations for U.S. exports of goods and services for 2014 in order of importance: Canada, Mexico, China, the United Kingdom, Japan, Germany, Brazil, South Korea, France, and India. The top 10 sources of U.S. imports in order of importance were China, Canada, Mexico, Japan, Germany, the United Kingdom, South Korea, France, India, and Saudi Arabia.

17-1b Production Possibilities without Trade

The rationale behind most international trade is obvious. For example, the United States produces little coffee because, aside from Hawaii, our climate is not suited to growing coffee beans. More revealing, however, are the gains from trade where the comparative advantage is not so obvious. Suppose that just two goods—food and clothing—are produced and consumed and that there are only two countries in the world—the United States, with a labor force of 100 million workers, and the mythical country of Izodia, with 200 million workers. The conclusions derived from this simple model have general relevance for international trade.

Exhibit 2 presents production possibilities tables for each country, based on the size of the labor force and the productivity of workers in each country. The exhibit assumes that each country has a given technology and that labor is efficiently employed. If no trade occurs between countries, Exhibit 2 also represents each country's *consumption possibilities* table. The production numbers imply that each worker in the United States can produce either 6 units of food or 3 units of clothing per day. If all 100 million U.S. workers produce food, they make 600 million units per day, as shown in column U_1 in panel (a). If all U.S. workers make clothing, they produce 300 million units per day, as shown in column U_6. The columns in between show some workers making food and some making clothing. Because a U.S. worker can produce either 6 units of food or 3 units of clothing, *the opportunity cost of 1 more unit of clothing is 2 units of food.*

EXHIBIT 2	Production Possibilities Schedules for the United States and Izodia

(a) The United States

Production Possibilities with
100 Million Workers (millions of units per day)

	U_1	U_2	U_3	U_4	U_5	U_6
Food	600	480	360	240	120	0
Clothing	0	60	120	180	240	300

(b) Izodia

Production Possibilities with
200 Million Workers (millions of units per day)

	I_1	I_2	I_3	I_4	I_5	I_6
Food	200	160	120	80	40	0
Clothing	0	80	160	240	320	400

Suppose Izodian workers are less educated, work with less capital, and farm less fertile soil than U.S. workers, so each Izodian worker can produce only 1 unit of food or 2 units of clothing per day. If all 200 million Izodian workers specialize in food, they can make 200 million units per day, as shown in column I_1 in panel (b) of Exhibit 2. If they all make clothing, total output is 400 million units per day, as shown in column I_6. Some intermediate production possibilities are also listed in the exhibit. Because an Izodian worker can produce either 1 unit of food or 2 units of clothing, *the opportunity cost of 1 more unit of clothing is ½ unit of food.*

We can convert the data in Exhibit 2 to a production possibilities frontier for each country, as shown in Exhibit 3. In each diagram, the amount of food produced is measured on the vertical axis and the amount of clothing on the horizontal axis. U.S. combinations are shown in the left panel by U_1, U_2, and so on. Izodian combinations are shown in the right panel by I_1, I_2, and so on. Because we assume for simplicity that resources are perfectly adaptable to the production of either good, each production possibilities curve is a straight line. The slope of this line differs between countries because the opportunity cost of production differs between countries. The slope equals the opportunity cost of clothing—the amount of food a country must give up to produce another unit of clothing. The U.S. slope is –2, and the Izodian slope is –½. The U.S. slope is steeper because its opportunity cost of producing clothing is greater.

Exhibit 3 illustrates possible combinations of food and clothing that residents of each country can produce and consume if all resources are efficiently employed and there is no trade between the two countries. **Autarky** is the situation of national self-sufficiency, in which there is no economic interaction with foreign producers or consumers. Suppose that U.S. producers maximize profit and U.S. consumers maximize utility with the combination of 240 million units of food and 180 million units of clothing—combination U_4. This is called the *autarky equilibrium.* Suppose also that

autarky

National self-sufficiency; no economic interaction with foreigners

| EXHIBIT 3 | **Production Possibilities Frontiers for the United States and Izodia Without Trade (millions of units per day)** |

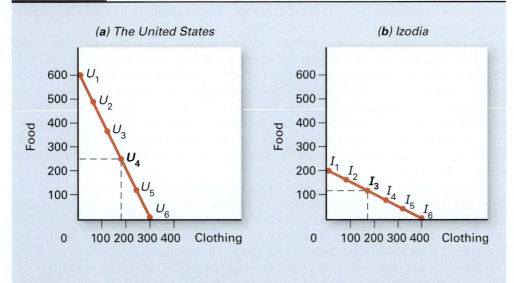

(a) The United States   *(b) Izodia*

Panel (a) shows the U.S. production possibilities frontier; its slope indicates that the opportunity cost of an additional unit of clothing is 2 units of food. Panel (b) shows production possibilities for Izodia; an additional unit of clothing costs ½ unit of food. Clothing has a lower opportunity cost in Izodia.

Izodians are in autarky equilibrium, identified as combination I_3, with 120 million units of food and 160 million units of clothing.

17-1c Consumption Possibilities Based on Comparative Advantage

In our example, each U.S. worker can produce more clothing and more food per day than can each Izodian worker, so Americans have an *absolute advantage* in the production of both goods. Recall from Chapter 2 that having an absolute advantage means being able to produce something using fewer resources than other producers require. Should the U.S. economy remain in autarky—that is, self-sufficient in both food and clothing—or could there be gains from specialization and trade?

As long as the opportunity cost of production differs between the two countries, there are gains from specialization and trade. *According to the law of comparative advantage, each country should specialize in producing the good with the lower opportunity cost.* The opportunity cost of producing 1 more unit of clothing is 2 units of food in the United States compared with ½ unit of food in Izodia. Because the opportunity cost of producing clothing is lower in Izodia, both countries will gain if Izodia specializes in clothing and exports some to the United States, and the United States specializes in food and exports some to Izodia.

terms of trade
How much of one good exchanges for a unit of another good

Before countries can trade, however, they must agree on how much of one good exchanges for another—that is, they must agree on the **terms of trade**. As long as Americans can get more than ½ a unit of clothing for each unit of food produced, and as long as Izodians can get more than ½ a unit of food for each unit of clothing produced, both countries will be better off specializing. After all, without trade Americans give up ½ unit of clothing to produce another unit of food, and Izodians give up ½ unit of food to produce another unit of clothing, so there would be no trade unless each country gets a better deal.

Suppose that market forces shape the terms of trade so that 1 unit of clothing exchanges for 1 unit of food. To produce another unit of clothing themselves, Americans would have to sacrifice 2 units of food. Likewise, to produce another unit of food themselves, Izodians would have to sacrifice 2 units of clothing.

Exhibit 4 shows that with 1 unit of food trading for 1 unit of clothing, Americans and Izodians can consume anywhere along their blue consumption possibilities frontiers. *The consumption possibilities frontier* shows a nation's possible combinations of goods available as a result of specialization and trade. (Note that the U.S. consumption possibilities curve does not extend to the right of 400 million units of clothing, because Izodia could produce no more than that.) The amount each country actually consumes depends on the relative preferences for food and clothing. Suppose Americans select combination U in panel (a) and Izodians select point I in panel (b).

Without trade, the United States produces and consumes 240 million units of food and 180 million units of clothing. With trade, Americans specialize to produce 600 million units of food; they eat 400 million units and exchange the rest for 200 million units of Izodian clothing. This consumption combination is reflected by point U. Through exchange, Americans increase their consumption of both food and clothing.

Without trade, Izodians produce and consume 120 million units of food and 160 million units of clothing. With trade, Izodians specialize to produce 400 million units of clothing; they wear 200 million and exchange the rest for 200 million units of U.S. food. This consumption combination is shown by point I. Through trade, Izodians, like Americans, are able to increase their consumption of both goods. How is this possible?

EXHIBIT 4	**Production (and Consumption) Possibilities Frontiers With Trade (millions of units per day)**

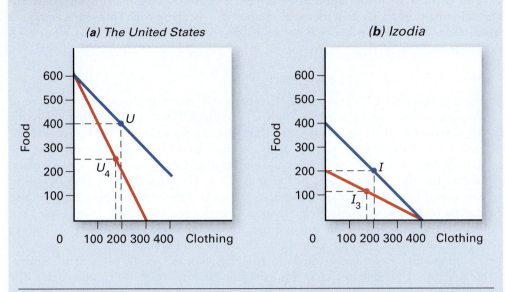

If Izodia and the United States can specialize and trade at the rate of 1 unit of clothing for 1 unit of food, both can benefit as shown by the blue lines. By trading with Izodia, the U.S. can produce only food and still consume combination U, which has more food and more clothing than U_4. Likewise, Izodia can attain preferred combination I by producing only clothing, then trading some clothing for U.S. food.

Because Americans are more efficient in the production of food and Izodians more efficient in the production of clothing, total output increases when each specializes. Without specialization and trade, world production is 360 million units of food and 340 million units of clothing. With specialization and trade, food increases to 600 million units and clothing to 400 million units. Thus, both countries increase consumption with trade. *Although the United States has an absolute advantage in both goods, differences in the opportunity cost of production between the two nations ensure that specialization and trade result in mutual gains.* Remember that comparative advantage, not absolute advantage, creates gains from specialization and trade. The only constraint on trade is that, for each good, *world production must equal world consumption.*

We simplified trade relations in our example to highlight the gains from specialization and trade. We assumed that each country would completely specialize in producing a particular good, that resources were equally adaptable to the production of either good, that the costs of transporting goods from one country to another were inconsequential, and that there were no problems in arriving at the terms of trade. The world is not that simple. For example, we don't expect a country to produce just one good. Regardless, there is broad evidence that specialization based on the law of comparative advantage still leads to gains from trade. For example, after examining the productivity of 17 crops on 1.6 million parcels of land in 55 countries around the world, researchers found strong evidence that international trade arises from comparative advantage.[1]

[1] Arnaud Costinot and Dave Donaldson, "Ricardo's Theory of Comparative Advantage: Old Idea, New Evidence," *American Economic Review*, 102 (May 2012): 453–458.

17-1d Reasons for International Specialization

Countries trade with one another—or, more precisely, people, firms, and governments in one country trade with those in another—because each side expects to gain from trade. How do we know what each country should produce and what each should trade?

Differences in Resource Endowments

Differences in resource endowments often create differences in the opportunity cost of production across countries. Some countries are blessed with an abundance of fertile land and favorable growing seasons. The United States, for example, has been called the "breadbasket of the world" because of its rich farmland ideal for growing wheat and corn. Coffee grows best in the climate and elevation of Colombia, Brazil, and Vietnam. Honduras has the ideal climate for bananas. Thus, the United States exports wheat and corn and imports coffee and bananas. Seasonal differences across countries also encourage trade. For example, in the winter, Americans import fruit from Chile, and Canadians travel to Florida for sun and fun. In the summer, Americans export fruit to Chile, and Americans travel to Canada for camping and hiking.

Resources are often concentrated in particular countries: crude oil in Saudi Arabia, fertile soil in the United States, copper ore in Chile, rough diamonds in South Africa. The United States grows abundant supplies of oil seeds such as soybeans and sunflowers, but does not yet extract enough crude oil to satisfy domestic demand. Thus, the United States exports oil seeds and imports crude oil. More generally, *countries export products they can produce more cheaply in return for products that are unavailable domestically or are cheaper elsewhere.*

Exhibit 5 shows, for 12 key resources, U.S. production as a percentage of U.S. consumption. If production falls short of consumption, this means the United States imports the difference. For example, because America grows coffee only in Hawaii, U.S. production is only 1 percent of U.S. consumption, so nearly all coffee is imported. The exhibit also shows that U.S. production falls short of U.S. consumption for crude oil and natural gas, and for metals such as zinc, copper, and aluminum. If U.S. production exceeds U.S. consumption, the United States exports the difference. For example, U.S.-grown cotton amounts to 502 percent of U.S. cotton consumption, so most U.S. grown cotton is exported. U.S. production also exceeds U.S. consumption for other crops, including wheat, oil seeds (soybeans, sunflower seeds, cottonseeds), and coarse grains (corn, barley, oats). In short, when it comes to basic resources, the United States is a net importer of crude oil and metals and a net exporter of coal and farm crops.

Economies of Scale

If production is subject to *economies of scale*—that is, if the long-run average cost of production falls as a firm expands its scale of operation—countries can gain from trade if each nation specializes. Such specialization allows firms in each nation to produce more of a particular good, which reduces average costs. For example, one country can make computer chips that are sold in many countries, and another country can make cars that are sold in many countries. The primary reason for establishing the single integrated market of the European Union was to offer producers there a large, open market of now more than 500 million consumers. Producers could thereby achieve economies of scale. Firms and countries producing at the lowest opportunity costs are most competitive in international markets. For example, most of the world's buttons and zippers come from the same Chinese city. Another Chinese city is the source of most of the world's socks.

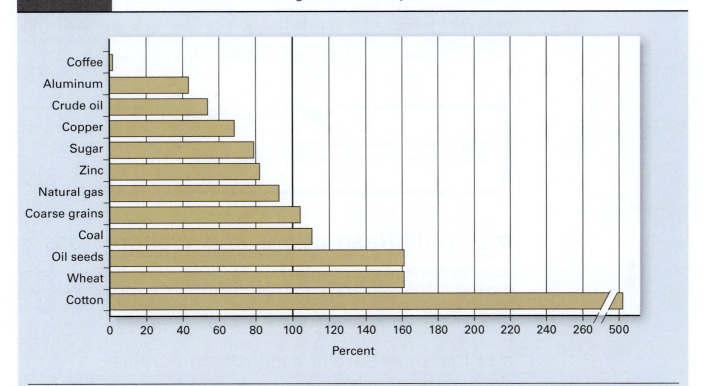

EXHIBIT 5   **U.S. Production as a Percentage of U.S. Consumption for Various Resources**

If U.S. production is less than 100 percent of U.S. consumption, then imports make up the difference. If U.S. production exceeds U.S. consumption, then the amount by which production exceeds 100 percent of consumption is exported.

Source: Based on annual figures selected from *The Economist Pocket World in Figures: 2015 Edition* (Profile Books, 2014).

Differences in Tastes

Even if all countries had identical resource endowments and combined those resources with equal efficiency, each country would still gain from trade as long as tastes differed across countries. Consumption patterns differ across countries and some of this results from differences in tastes. For example, the Czechs and Irish drink three times as much beer per capita as do the Swiss and Swedes. The French drink three times as much wine as do Australians. The Danes eat twice as much pork as do Americans. Americans eat twice as much chicken as do Hungarians. Americans like chicken, but not all of it. The United States is the world's leading exporter of chicken feet, and China is the world's leading importer (Tyson Foods alone ships about three billion chicken feet to China each year). Residents of West Africa prefer the dark bony meat of a chicken, such as backs and necks, so chicken farmers there sell these parts locally and ship chicken breasts abroad, where they are valued more.[2] Soft drinks are four times more popular in the United States than in Europe. The English like tea; Americans, coffee. Algeria has an ideal climate for growing grapes (vineyards there date back to Roman times). But Algeria's population is 99 percent Muslim, a religion that forbids alcohol consumption. Thus, Algeria exports wine.

[2] Drew Hinshaw, "As KFC Goes to Africa, It Lacks Only One Thing: Chickens," *Wall Street Journal*, 8 February 2013.

More Variety

Yet another reason for trade is to increase the *variety* of goods and services available. People prefer having a choice of products, and international trade helps broaden that choice.[3] International trade expands your selection of automobiles, computers, movies, clothing, drugs, wine, cheese, ethnic foods, and hundreds of other items.

CHECKPOINT

What are the gains from international trade, and why might countries still decide to trade even if no country has a comparative advantage?

17-2 Trade Restrictions and Welfare Loss

Despite the benefits of international trade, nearly all countries at one time or another erect trade barriers, which benefit some domestic producers but harm other domestic producers and all domestic consumers. In this section, we consider the effects of trade barriers and why they are imposed.

17-2a Consumer Surplus and Producer Surplus From Market Exchange

Before we explore the net effects of world trade on social welfare, let's develop a framework showing the benefits that consumers and producers get from market exchange. Consider the hypothetical market for apples shown in Exhibit 6. The height of the demand curve shows what consumers are willing and able to pay for each additional pound of apples. In effect, the height of the demand curve shows the *marginal benefit* consumers expect from each pound of apples. For example, the demand curve indicates that some consumers in this market are willing to pay $3.00 or more per pound for the first few pounds of apples. But every consumer gets to buy apples at the market-clearing price, which here is $1.00 per pound. Most consumers thus get a bonus, or a surplus, from market exchange.

The blue-shaded triangle below the demand curve and above the market price reflects the *consumer surplus* in this market, which is the difference between the most that consumers would pay for 60 pounds of apples per day and the actual amount they do pay. We all enjoy a consumer surplus from most products we buy.

Producers usually derive a similar surplus. The height of the supply curve shows what producers are willing and able to accept for each additional pound of apples. That is, the height of the supply curve shows the expected *marginal cost* from producing each additional pound. For example, the supply curve indicates that some producers face a marginal cost of $0.50 or less per pound for supplying the first few pounds. But every producer gets to sell apples for the market-clearing price of $1.00 per pound. The gold-shaded triangle above the supply curve and below the market price reflects the *producer surplus*, which is the difference between the actual amount that producers receive for 60 pounds and what they would accept to supply that amount.

[3.] Marc J. Melitz and Daniel Trefler, "Gains from Trade When Firms Matter," *Journal of Economic Perspectives*, 26 (Spring 2012): 91–118.

| EXHIBIT 6 | Consumer Surplus and Producer Surplus |

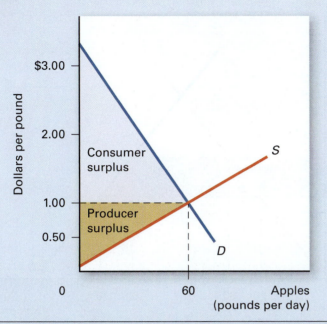

Consumer surplus, shown by the blue triangle, indicates the net benefits consumers reap from buying 60 pounds of apples at $1.00 per pound. Some consumers would have been willing to pay $3.00 or more per pound for the first few pounds. Consumer surplus measures the difference between the maximum sum of money consumers would pay for 60 pounds of apples and the actual sum they pay. Producer surplus, shown by the gold triangle, indicates the net benefits producers reap from selling 60 pounds at $1.00 per pound. Some producers would have supplied apples for $0.50 per pound or less. Producer surplus measures the difference between the actual sum of money producers receive for 60 pounds of apples and the minimum amount they would accept for this amount.

The point is that market exchange usually generates a surplus, or a bonus, for both consumers and producers. In the balance of this chapter, we look at the gains from international trade and how trade restrictions affect consumer and producer surplus.

17-2b Tariffs

A *tariff*, a term first introduced in Chapter 3, is a tax on imports. (Tariffs can apply to exports, too, but we will focus on import tariffs.) A tariff can be either *specific*, such as a tariff of $5 per barrel of oil, or *ad valorem*, such as 10 percent on the import price of jeans. Consider the effects of a specific tariff on a particular good. In Exhibit 7, *D* is the U.S. demand for sugar and *S* is the supply of sugar from U.S. growers (there are about 10,000 U.S. sugarcane growers). Suppose that the world price of sugar is $0.10 per pound. The **world price** is determined by the world supply and demand for a product. It is the price at which any supplier can sell output on the world market and at which any demander can purchase output on the world market.

With free trade, any U.S. consumers could buy any amount desired at the world price of $0.10 per pound, so the quantity demanded is 70 million pounds per month, of which U.S. producers supply 20 million pounds and importers supply 50 million pounds. Because U.S. buyers can purchase sugar at the world price, U.S. producers can't

world price

The price at which a good is traded on the world market; determined by the world demand and world supply for the good

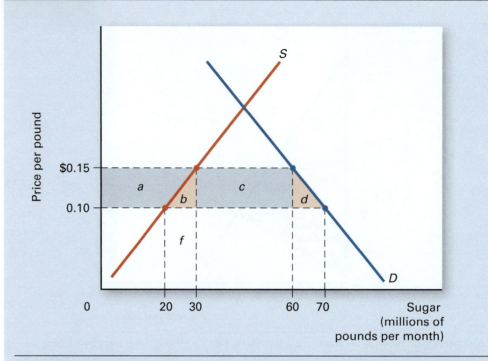

EXHIBIT 7   **Effect of a Tariff**

At a world price of $0.10 per pound, U.S. consumers demand 70 million pounds of sugar per month, and U.S. producers supply 20 million pounds per month; the difference is imported. After the imposition of a $0.05 per pound tariff, the U.S. price rises to $0.15 per pound. U.S. producers supply 30 million pounds, and U.S. consumers cut back to 60 million pounds. At the higher U.S. price, consumers are worse off; their loss of consumer surplus is the sum of areas *a*, *b*, *c*, and *d*. The net welfare loss to the U.S. economy consists of areas *b* and *d*.

charge more than that. Now suppose that a specific tariff of $0.05 is imposed on each pound of imported sugar, raising the U.S. price from $0.10 to $0.15 per pound. U.S. producers can therefore raise their own price to $0.15 per pound without losing business to imports. At the higher price, the quantity supplied by U.S. producers increases to 30 million pounds, but the quantity demanded by U.S. consumers declines to 60 million pounds. Because quantity demanded has declined and quantity supplied by U.S. producers has increased, U.S. imports fall from 50 million to 30 million pounds per month.

Because the U.S. price is higher after the tariff, U.S. consumers are worse off. Their loss in consumer surplus is identified in Exhibit 7 by the combination of the blue- and pink-shaded areas. Because both the U.S. price and the quantity supplied by U.S. producers have increased, their total revenue increases by the areas *a* plus *b* plus *f*. But only area *a* represents an increase in producer surplus. Revenue represented by the areas *b* plus *f* merely offsets the higher marginal cost U.S. producers face in expanding sugar output from 20 million to 30 million pounds per month. Area *b* represents part of the net welfare loss to the domestic economy because those 10 million pounds could have been imported for $0.10 per pound rather than produced domestically at a higher marginal cost.

Government revenue from the tariff is identified by area *c*, which equals the tariff of $0.05 per pound multiplied by the 30 million pounds imported, for tariff revenue of $1.5 million per month. Tariff revenue is a loss to consumers, but because the tariff goes to the government, it can be used to lower taxes or to increase public services, so it's not a loss to the U.S. economy. Area *d* shows a loss in consumer surplus because less sugar is consumed at the higher price. This loss is not redistributed to anyone else, so area *d* reflects part of the net welfare loss of the tariff. Therefore, areas *b* and *d* show the domestic economy's net welfare loss of the tariff; *the two triangles measure a loss in consumer surplus that is not offset by a gain to anyone in the domestic economy.*

In summary: Of the total loss in U.S. consumer surplus (areas *a*, *b*, *c*, and *d*) resulting from the tariff, area *a* goes to U.S producers, area *c* becomes government revenue, but areas *b* and *d* are net losses in domestic social welfare.

17-2c Import Quotas

An *import quota* is a legal limit on the amount of a commodity that can be imported. Quotas usually target imports from certain countries. For example, a quota may limit furniture from China or shoes from Brazil. To have an impact on the domestic market, a quota must be less than what would be imported with free trade. Consider a quota on the U.S. market for sugar. In panel (a) of Exhibit 8, *D* is the U.S. demand curve and *S* is the supply curve of U.S. sugar producers. Suppose again that the world price of sugar is $0.10 per pound. With free trade, that price would prevail in the U.S. market as well, and a total of 70 million pounds would be demanded per month. U.S. producers would supply 20 million pounds and importers, 50 million pounds.

EXHIBIT 8   **Effect of a Quota**

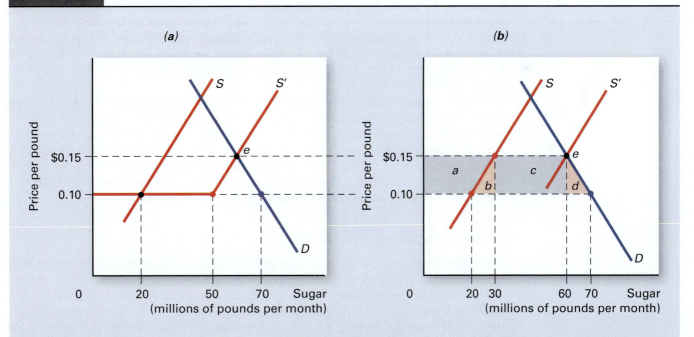

In panel (a), *D* is the U.S. demand curve and *S* is the supply curve of U.S. producers. If the government establishes a sugar quota of 30 million pounds per month, the supply curve combining U.S. production and imports becomes horizontal at the world price of $0.10 per pound and remains horizontal until the quantity supplied reaches 50 million pounds. For higher prices, the new supply curve equals the horizontal sum of the U.S. supply curve, *S*, plus the quota of 30 million pounds. The new U.S. price, $0.15 per pound, is determined by the intersection of the new supply curve, *S'*, with the U.S. demand curve, *D*. Panel (b) shows the welfare effect of the quota. As a result of the higher U.S. price, consumer surplus is cut by the shaded area. The blue-shaded areas illustrate the loss in consumer surplus that is captured by domestic producers and by those who are permitted to fulfill the quota, and the pink-shaded triangles illustrate the net welfare cost of the quota on the U.S. economy.

With a quota of 50 million pounds or more per month, the U.S. price would remain the same as the world price of $0.10 per pound, and the U.S. quantity would be 70 million pounds per month. In short, a quota of at least 50 million pounds would not raise the U.S. price above the world price because 50 million pounds were imported without a quota. A more stringent quota, however, would cut imports, which, as we'll see, would raise the U.S. price.

Suppose U.S. trade officials impose an import quota of 30 million pounds per month. As long as the U.S. price is at or above the world price of $0.10 per pound, foreign producers will supply 30 million pounds. So at prices at or above $0.10 per pound, the total supply of sugar to the U.S. market is found by adding 30 million pounds of imported sugar to the amount supplied by U.S. producers. U.S. and foreign producers would never sell in the U.S. market for less than $0.10 per pound because they can always get that price on the world market. Thus, the supply curve that sums domestic production and imports is horizontal at the world price of $0.10 per pound and remains so until the quantity supplied reaches 50 million pounds.

Again, for prices above $0.10 per pound, the new supply curve, S', adds horizontally the 30-million-pound quota to S, the supply curve of U.S. producers. The U.S. price is found where this new supply curve, S', intersects the domestic demand curve, which in Exhibit 8 occurs at point e. *By limiting imports, the quota raises the domestic price of sugar above the world price and reduces quantity below the free trade level.* (Note that to compare more easily the effects of tariffs and quotas, this quota is designed to yield the same equilibrium price and quantity as the tariff examined earlier.)

Panel (b) of Exhibit 8 shows the distribution and efficiency effects of the quota. As a result of the quota, U.S. consumer surplus declines by the combined blue and pink areas. Area a becomes U.S. producer surplus and thus involves no loss of U.S. welfare. Area c shows the increased economic profit to those permitted by the quota to sell Americans 30 million pounds for $0.15 per pound, or $0.05 above the world price. If foreign exporters rather than U.S. importers reap this profit, area c reflects a net loss in U.S. welfare.

Area b shows a welfare loss to the U.S. economy, because sugar could have been purchased abroad for $0.10 per pound, and the U.S. resources employed to increase sugar production could instead have been used more efficiently producing other goods. Area d is also a welfare loss because it reflects a reduction in consumer surplus with no offsetting gain to anyone. Thus, areas b and d in panel (b) of Exhibit 8 measure the minimum U.S. welfare loss from the quota. If the profit from quota rights (area c) accrues to foreign producers, this increases the U.S. welfare loss.

17-2d Quotas in Practice

The United States has granted quotas to specific countries. These countries, in turn, distribute these quota rights to their exporters through a variety of means. *By rewarding domestic and foreign producers with higher prices, the quota system creates two groups intent on securing and perpetuating these quotas.* Lobbyists for foreign producers work the halls of Congress, seeking the right to export to the United States. This strong support from producers, coupled with a lack of opposition from consumers (who remain rationally ignorant for the most part), has resulted in quotas that have lasted decades. For example, sugar quotas have been around more than 50 years. For the past three decades, U.S. sugar prices have ranged from 50 to 100 percent above the world price, costing American consumers billions.[4] Sugar growers, who account for only 1 percent

---

[4.] Burleigh Leonard, "U.S. Sugar Policy: Sweet Deal for a Few, Sour for Most," *Wall Street Journal*, 2 November 2014.

of U.S. farm sales, accounted for 17 percent of political contributions from agriculture.[5] Sugar growers even reversed a North American Free Trade Agreement provision that would have allowed tariff-free sugar from Mexico.

Some economists have argued that if quotas are to be used, the United States should auction them off to foreign producers, thereby capturing at least some of the difference between the world price and the U.S. price. Auctioning off quotas would not only increase federal revenue at a time when it's desperately needed, but an auction would reduce the profitability of getting quota rights, which would reduce pressure on Washington to perpetuate them. American consumers are not the only victims of sugar quotas. Thousands of poor farmers around the world miss out on an opportunity to earn a living by growing sugar cane for export to America.

17-2e Tariffs and Quotas Compared

Consider the similarities and differences between a tariff and a quota. Because both have identical effects on the price in our example, they both lead to the same change in quantity demanded. In both cases, U.S. consumers suffer the same loss of consumer surplus, and U.S. producers reap the same gain of producer surplus. The primary difference is that the revenue from the tariff goes to the U.S. government, whereas the revenue from the quota goes to whoever secures the right to sell foreign goods in the U.S. market. *If quota rights accrue to foreigners, then the domestic economy is worse off with a quota than with a tariff.* But even if quota rights go to domestic importers, quotas, like tariffs, still increase the domestic price, restrict quantity, and thereby reduce consumer surplus and economic welfare. Quotas and tariffs can also raise production costs. For example, U.S. candy manufacturers face higher production costs because of sugar quotas, making them less competitive on world markets. Finally, and most importantly, *quotas and tariffs encourage foreign governments to retaliate with quotas and tariffs of their own, thus shrinking U.S. export markets, so the welfare loss is greater than shown in Exhibits 7 and 8.*

17-2f Other Trade Restrictions

Besides tariffs and quotas, a variety of other measures limit free trade. A country may provide *export subsidies* to encourage exports and *low-interest loans* to foreign buyers. Some countries impose *domestic content requirements* specifying that a certain portion of a final good must be produced domestically. Other requirements masquerading as health, safety, or technical standards often discriminate against foreign goods. For example, Nigeria protects chicken growers by banning chicken imports (which is why KFCs there added fish to the menu). To gain access to Chinese markets, foreign producers must transfer their technological know-how to a Chinese partner, so it can be made available throughout China.[6] European countries once prohibited beef from hormone-fed cattle, a measure aimed at U.S. beef. Purity laws in Germany bar many non-German beers. Until the European Community adopted uniform standards, differing technical requirements forced manufacturers to offer as many as seven different versions of the same TV for that market. Sometimes exporters will voluntarily limit exports, as when Japanese automakers agreed to cut exports to the United States. The point is that *tariffs and quotas are only two of many devices used to restrict foreign trade.*

[5.] Michael Schroeder, "Sugar Growers Hold Up Push for Free Trade," *Wall Street Journal,* 3 February 2004.

[6.] Thomas J. Holmes, Ellen R. McGrattan, and Edward C. Prescott, "Quid Pro Quo: Technology Capital Transfers for Market Access in China," *Review of Economic Studies*, 82 (July 2015): 1154–1193.

Recent research on the cost of protectionism indicates that international trade barriers slow the introduction of new goods and better technologies. So, rather than simply raising domestic prices, trade restrictions slow economic progress.

CHECKPOINT

How do trade restrictions harm the economy, and why do they persist?

17-3 Efforts to Reduce Trade Barriers

bilateral agreement

Trade agreement between two countries

Although some groups in the economy have a special interest in restricting trade, the trend has been toward freer trade. In this section, we examine international efforts to lower trade barriers. A nation sometimes negotiates a trade agreement with another nation, in what is known as a **bilateral agreement**. For example, the United States has negotiated bilateral open-skies agreements to deregulate airline competition on international routes, agreements that have generated at least $4 billion a year in gains to travelers. And travelers would gain another $4 billion a year if agreements were reached with other countries where Americans travel frequently.[7]

17-3a Freer Trade by Multilateral Agreement

multilateral agreement

Trade agreement among more than two countries

General Agreement on Tariffs and Trade (GATT)

An international tariff-reduction treaty adopted in 1947 that resulted in a series of negotiated "rounds" aimed at freer trade

Mindful of how high tariffs cut world trade during the Great Depression, the United States, after World War II, invited its trading partners to negotiate lower tariffs and other trade barriers. A **multilateral agreement** is one reached among more than two countries. The result was the **General Agreement on Tariffs and Trade (GATT)**, an international trade treaty adopted in 1947 by 23 countries, including the United States. Each GATT member agreed to (1) reduce tariffs through multinational negotiations, (2) reduce import quotas, and (3) treat all members equally with respect to trade.

Trade barriers have been reduced through trade negotiations, or "trade rounds," under the auspices of GATT. Trade rounds offer a package approach rather than an issue-by-issue approach to trade negotiations. Concessions that are necessary but otherwise difficult to defend in domestic political terms can be made more acceptable in the context of a larger package that also contains politically and economically attractive benefits. Most early GATT trade rounds were aimed at reducing tariffs. The Kennedy Round in the mid-1960s included new provisions against **dumping**, which is selling a commodity abroad for less than is charged in the home market or less than the cost of production. The Tokyo Round of the 1970s was a more sweeping attempt to extend and improve the system.

dumping

Selling a product abroad for less than charged in the home market or for less than the cost of production

Uruguay Round

The final multilateral trade negotiation under GATT; this 1994 agreement cut tariffs, formed the World Trade Organization, and will eventually eliminate quotas

The most recently completed round was launched in Uruguay in September 1986 and ratified by 123 participating countries in 1994. The number of signing countries now exceeds 150. This so-called **Uruguay Round**, the most comprehensive of the eight postwar multilateral trade negotiations, included 550 pages of tariff reductions on 85 percent of world trade. As a result of the Uruguay Round, average tariffs fell from 6 percent to 4 percent of the value of imports (when GATT began in

---

[7.] Clifford Winston and Jia Yan, "Open Skies: Estimating Travelers' Benefits From Free Trade in Airline Service," *American Economic Journal: Economic Policy*, 7 (May 2015): 370–414.

1947, tariffs averaged 40 percent). The Uruguay Round also created the World Trade Organization to succeed GATT.

17-3b World Trade Organization

The **World Trade Organization (WTO)** now provides the legal and institutional foundation for world trade. Whereas GATT was a multilateral agreement with no institutional foundation, the WTO is a permanent institution in Geneva, Switzerland. A staff of about 600 economists and lawyers helps shape policy and resolves trade disputes among member countries. Whereas GATT involved only merchandise trade, the WTO also covers services and trade-related aspects of intellectual property, such as books, movies, and computer programs. The WTO will eventually phase out quotas, but tariffs will remain legal.

Whereas GATT relied on voluntary cooperation, the WTO settles disputes in a way that is faster, more automatic, and less susceptible to blockage than the GATT system was. The WTO resolved more trade disputes in its first decade than GATT did in nearly 50 years. Since 2000, developing countries have filed 60 percent of the disputes. But the WTO has also become a lightning rod for globalization tensions, as discussed in the following case study.

> **World Trade Organization (WTO)**
> The legal and institutional foundation of the multilateral trading system that succeeded GATT in 1995

CASE STUDY

BRINGING THEORY TO LIFE

DOHA ROUND AND ROUND The trade-barrier reductions from the Uruguay Round were projected to boost world income by more than $500 billion per year when fully implemented, or about $68 per person. In poor countries around the world, any additional income from reduced trade barriers could be a lifesaver.

But when WTO members met in Seattle in November 1999 to set an agenda and timetable for the next round of trade talks (later to become known as the Doha Round), all hell broke loose, as 50,000 protesters disrupted the city. Most were peaceful, but police made more than 500 arrests over three days, and property damage reached $3 million. T-shirts sold the week before the meeting dubbed the event the "Battle in Seattle," and so it was.

Organizers used their objections to free trade as a recruiting and fund-raising tool for a variety of interest groups, including labor unions, environmentalists, and farmers. Union members feared losing jobs overseas, environmentalists feared that producers would seek out countries with lax regulations, farmers in Japan, South Korea, Europe, and the United States feared foreign competition, and other groups feared technological developments such as hormone-fed beef and genetically modified food. The

Seattle protest remains by far the largest against free trade in the United States.

Protesters would probably be surprised to learn that WTO members are not of one mind about trade issues. For example, the United States and Europe usually push to protect worker rights around the world, but developing countries, including Mexico, Egypt, India, and Pakistan, object strenuously to focusing on worker rights. These poorer nations are concerned that the clothing, shoes, and textiles they make have not gained access to rich nations quickly enough. Many developing countries view attempts to impose labor and environmental standards as just the latest effort to block imports from poor countries. For example, workers in China rioted when U.S. companies operating there proposed shortening the work week. Chinese workers wanted a longer work week, believing they could earn more. And when India's Supreme Court tried to close some polluting factories, thousands of workers torched buses, threw stones, and blocked major roads, demanding the factories remain open.

Without international groups such as the WTO to provide a forum for discussing labor and environmental issues around the world, conditions in poor countries would likely

continued

AP Images/Imaginechina/Xu ruiping

a "sweatshop" and wanted it shut down. In part because of media pressure, Nike ended its contract with the factory.

After failing to get off the ground in Seattle, the round of talks was launched in 2001 in Doha, Qatar. In setting the agenda for the **Doha Round**, members agreed to improve market access around the world, phase out export subsidies, and substantially reduce distorting government subsidies in agriculture. Reaching agreement proved easier said than done. Headed by Brazil and India, a group of developing countries demanded stronger commitments to reduce agricultural subsidies in the United States, Europe, and Japan. But farmers

Doha Round

The multilateral trade negotiation round launched in 2001, but still unsettled as of 2015; the first trade round under the WTO

in these industrial economies wanted to keep their subsidies and protection from imports. For example, the average farm in Japan is about four acres, so farming there is inefficient and costly (rice in Japan is triple the world price). And developing countries such as Brazil and India are worried about cheaper imports from other developing countries such as China and Vietnam. Talks in Cancun in 2003, Hong Kong in 2005, and Geneva in 2006 and 2008 ended bitterly as the Doha Round went round and round. Talks in Nairobi, Kenya, in late 2015 represent the latest effort in the Doha Round.

But in the absence of a Doha agreement, some countries continue to reduce trade barriers through bilateral agreements. For example, the United States abolished tariffs on Korean automobiles and flat-screen TVs.

be worse. Working conditions in many poor countries have been slowly improving, thanks in part to trade opportunities along with pressure for labor rights from WTO and other international groups. For example, Cambodia is a poor country, but the highest wages in the country are earned by those working in the export sector. Take, for example, Deth, a young mother who sewed T-shirts and shorts at the June Textile factory in Cambodia, mostly for Nike. She worked from 6:15 a.m. to 2:15 p.m. with a half hour for lunch, extra pay for overtime, and double pay for working holidays. Though her pay was low by U.S. standards, it supported her family and was more than twice what judges and doctors average in Cambodia. Factories tend to hire young women, a group otherwise offered few job opportunities.

Factory jobs have provided women with status and social equality they never had. Researchers have also found that freer trade with Mexico has increased job opportunities there for women. Young women in Bangladesh who get garment jobs are more likely to enroll in school because those jobs reward literacy and numeracy; garment workers are also more likely to delay marriage and motherhood. Still, protest groups in rich countries called the June Textile factory

Sources: Kym Anderson, Gordon Rausser, and Johan Swinnen, "Political Economy of Public Policies: Insights from Distortions to Agricultural and Food Markets," *Journal of Economic Literature*, 51 (June 2013): 423–477; Rachel Heath and A. Mushfiq Mobarak, "Manufacturing Growth and the Lives of Bangladeshi Women," *Journal of Development Economics*, 115 (July 2015): 1–15; Ernesto Aguayo-Tellez et al. "Did Trade Liberalization Help Women? The Case of Mexico in the 1990s," *Research in Labor Economics* (forthcoming); Gina Chon, "Dropped Stitches," *Asiaweek*, 22 December 2000; and the Web site for the World Trade Organization Doha Round at http://www.wto.org/english/tratop_e/dda_e/dda_e.htm.

17-3c Common Markets

Some countries looked to the success of the U.S. economy, which is essentially a free trade zone across 50 states, and have tried to develop free trade zones of their own. The largest and best known is the European Union, which began in 1958 with a half dozen countries and by 2015 had expanded to 28 countries and over 500 million people. The idea was to create a barrier-free European market like the United States in which goods, services, people, and capital are free to flow to their highest-valued use. As of 2015, 19 members of the European Union had also adopted a common currency, the *euro*, which replaced national currencies in 2002. The European Union is an example of a **common market**, which consists of a group of countries with few or no trade restrictions with one another.

The United States, Canada, and Mexico introduced a free trade pact in 1994 called the North American Free Trade Agreement, or NAFTA. Through NAFTA, Mexico hopes to attract more U.S. investment by guaranteeing companies that locate there duty-free access to U.S. markets, which is where over two-thirds of Mexico's exports go. Mexico's 117 million people represent an attractive export market for U.S. producers, and Mexico's oil reserves could ease U.S. energy problems. The United States would also like to support Mexico's efforts to become more market oriented, as is reflected, for example, by Mexico's privatization of its phone system and banks. Creating job opportunities in Mexico also reduces pressure for Mexicans to cross the U.S. border illegally to find work. After more than a decade of NAFTA, agricultural exports to Mexico have doubled, as has overall trade among the three nations, but Americans still buy much more from Mexicans and Canadians than the other way around.

Free trade areas are springing up around the world. The United States signed a free trade agreement with five Central American countries and the Dominican Republic, called CAFTA-DR. Ten Latin American countries form Mercosur. And in 2015 the United States was negotiating the Trans-Pacific Partnership with 11 other nations in the Pacific, including China. Together, these countries represent up to 40 percent of world output. Elsewhere in the world, the Association of Southeast Asian Nations, or ASEAN, consists of 10 member countries. And South Africa and its four neighboring countries form the Southern African Customs Union. Regional trade agreements require an exception to WTO rules because bloc members can make special deals among themselves and thus discriminate against outsiders. Under WTO's requirements, any trade concession granted to one country must usually be granted to *all other* WTO members.

Incidentally, economic initiatives such as the European Union bind nations together economically so they are less likely to go to war against each other. War with countries that are trading partners would involve more economic loss than with other countries. That's yet another benefit of freer trade.

Still, economic integration is not a perfect solution, as evidenced by recent financial problems in the eurozone, which arose because unsustainable government deficits in some member countries such as Greece and Spain reduced confidence in the common currency. Member countries became much more vulnerable to the fiscal problems of other member countries.

common market
Group of countries that have few or no trade restrictions with one another

**CHECKPOINT**

Identify international efforts to reduce trade barriers.

17-4 Arguments for Trade Restrictions

Trade restrictions are often little more than handouts for the domestic industries they protect. Given the loss in social welfare that results from these restrictions, it would be more efficient simply to transfer money from domestic consumers to domestic producers. But such a bald payoff would be politically unpopular. Arguments for trade restrictions avoid mention of transfers to domestic producers and instead cite loftier goals. As we shall now see, none of these goals makes a strong case for restrictions, but some make a little more sense than others.

17-4a National Defense Argument

Some industries claim they need protection from import competition because their output is vital for national defense. Products such as strategic metals and military hardware are often insulated from foreign competition by trade restrictions. Thus, national defense considerations outweigh concerns about efficiency and equity. How valid is this argument? Trade restrictions may shelter the defense industry, but other means, such as government subsidies, might be more efficient. Or the government could stockpile basic military hardware so that maintaining an ongoing productive capacity would become less critical. Still, technological change could make certain weapons obsolete. Because most industries can play some role in national defense, instituting trade restrictions on this basis can get out of hand. For example, many decades ago U.S. wool producers secured trade protection at a time when some military uniforms were still made of wool.

The national defense argument has also been used to discourage foreign ownership of U.S. companies in some industries. For example, in 2005 a Chinese state-owned company was prevented from buying Unocal Oil. And in 2010, the Congressional Steel Caucus tried to block a Chinese attempt to buy a Mississippi steel plant, saying that such a deal "threatens American jobs and our national security."[8]

17-4b Infant Industry Argument

The infant industry argument was formulated as a rationale for protecting emerging domestic industries from foreign competition. In industries where a firm's average cost of production falls as output expands, new firms may need protection from imports until these firms grow enough to become competitive. Trade restrictions let new firms achieve the economies of scale necessary to compete with mature foreign producers.

But how do we identify industries that merit protection, and when do they become old enough to look after themselves? Protection often fosters inefficiencies. The immediate cost of such restrictions is the net welfare loss from higher domestic prices. These costs may become permanent if the industry never realizes the expected economies of scale and thus never becomes competitive. As with the national defense argument, policy makers should be careful in adopting trade restrictions based on the infant industry argument. Here again, temporary production subsidies may be more efficient than import restrictions.

17-4c Antidumping Argument

As we have noted already, *dumping* is selling a product abroad for less than in the home market or less than the cost of production. Exporters may be able to sell the good for less overseas because of export subsidies, or firms may simply find it profitable to sell for less in foreign markets where consumers are more sensitive to prices. But why shouldn't U.S. consumers pay as little as possible? If dumping is persistent, the increase in consumer surplus would more than offset losses to domestic producers. *There is no good reason why consumers should not be allowed to buy imports for a persistently lower price.*

An alternative form of dumping, termed *predatory dumping*, is the *temporary* sale abroad at prices below cost to eliminate competitors in that target market. Once the competition is gone, so the story goes, the exporting firm can raise the price in the foreign market. The trouble with this argument is that if dumpers try to take advantage

---

[8.] Yajun Zhang, "China Steel Group Accuses U.S. Lawmakers of Protectionism," *Wall Street Journal*, 5 July 2010.

of their monopoly position by sharply increasing the price, then other firms, either domestic or foreign, could enter the market and sell for less. There are few documented cases of predatory dumping.

Sometimes dumping may be *sporadic*, as firms occasionally try to unload excess inventories. Retailers hold periodic "sales" for the same reason. Sporadic dumping can be unsettling for domestic producers, but the economic impact is not a matter of great public concern. Regardless, all dumping is prohibited in the United States by the Trade Agreements Act of 1979, which calls for the imposition of tariffs when a good is sold for less in the United States than in its home market or less than the cost of production. In addition, WTO rules allow for offsetting tariffs when products are sold for "less than fair value" and when there is "material injury" to domestic producers. For example, U.S. producers of lumber and beer frequently accuse their Canadian counterparts of dumping.

17-4d Jobs and Income Argument

One rationale for trade restrictions that is commonly heard in the United States, and is voiced by WTO protesters, is that they protect U.S. jobs and wage levels. Using trade restrictions to protect domestic jobs is a strategy that dates back centuries. One problem with such a policy is that other countries usually retaliate by restricting *their* imports to save *their* jobs, so international trade is reduced, jobs are lost in export industries, and potential gains from trade fail to materialize. That happened big time during the Great Depression, as high tariffs choked trade and jobs.

Wages in other countries, especially developing countries, are often a fraction of wages in the United States. For example, including benefits, General Motors (GM) workers in Michigan earn about $50 per hour versus $7 for GM workers in Mexico, $4.50 in China, and $1 in India. (The minimum wage in China is less than $2 an hour and in Mexico and India is less than $1 an hour.) Looking simply at differences in wages, however, narrows the focus too much. Wages represent just one component of the total production cost and may not necessarily be the most important. Employers are interested in the labor cost per unit of output, which depends on both the wage and labor productivity. Wages are high in the United States partly because U.S. labor productivity remains the highest in the world. High productivity can be traced to better education and training and to the abundant computers, machines, and other physical capital that make workers more productive. U.S. workers also benefit greatly from better management and a relatively stable business climate.

But what about the lower wages in many developing countries? Low wages are often linked to workers' lack of education and training, to the meager physical capital available to each worker, and to a business climate that is less stable and hence less attractive for producers. For example, the total value of manufacturing output is about the same in the United States as in China, but Americans produce that output with only about 10 percent of the manufacturing workforce that's employed in China.[9] What's more, advances in technology are making differences in labor costs across countries less relevant. One example is, as noted earlier, that in the original iPad, manufacturing labor accounted for only $33 of its $499 retail price, and the final assembly in China accounted for just $8 of that $33.[10]

Karlheinz Schindler/picture-alliance/ ZB/Newscom

9. "Manufacturing and Innovation: Back to Making Stuff," *The Economist*, 21 April 2012.
10. "The Third Industrial Revolution," *The Economist*, 21 April 2012.

Once multinational firms build plants and provide technological know-how in developing countries, U.S. workers lose some of their competitive edge, and their relatively high wages could price some U.S. products out of the world market. This has already happened in the consumer electronics and toy industries. China makes 80 percent of the toys sold in the United States. Some U.S. toy sellers, such as the makers of Etch A Sketch, would no longer exist had they not outsourced manufacturing to China. Overall, competition from Chinese imports between 1999 and 2011 cost the U.S. economy about 2 million jobs, according to one estimate.[11]

Domestic producers do not like to compete with foreign producers whose costs are lower, so they often push for trade restrictions. Labor unions protested the Trans-Pacific Partnership on those grounds. According to one report, "Unions see the pact as one of the biggest threats to organized labor and the U.S. middle class since the North American Free Trade Agreement took effect in 1994."[12] But if restrictions negate any cost advantage a foreign producer might have, the law of comparative advantage becomes inoperative and domestic consumers are denied access to the lower-priced goods.

Over time, as labor productivity in developing countries increases, wage differentials among countries will narrow, much as they narrowed between the northern and southern United States during the last century. As technology and capital spread, U.S. workers, particularly unskilled workers, cannot expect to maintain wage levels that are far above comparable workers in other countries. So far, research and development has kept U.S. producers on the cutting edge of technological developments, but staying ahead in the technological race is a constant battle. As a sign of the times about how competition could squeeze down the wage gap across countries, the Volkswagen factory in Tennessee pays workers only about half of what GM pays in Michigan, yet many thousands applied for the 2,000 job openings.

17-4e Declining Industries Argument

Where an established domestic industry is in jeopardy of closing because of lower-priced imports, could there be a rationale for *temporary* import restrictions? After all, domestic producers employ many industry-specific resources—both specialized labor and specialized machines. This human and physical capital is worth less in its best alternative use. If the extinction of the domestic industry is forestalled through trade restrictions, specialized workers can retire voluntarily or can gradually pursue more promising careers. Specialized machines can be allowed to wear out naturally.

Thus, in the case of declining domestic industries, trade protection can help lessen shocks to the economy and can allow for an orderly transition to a new industrial mix. But the protection offered should not be so generous as to encourage continued investment in the industry. Protection should be of specific duration and should be phased out over that period.

The clothing industry is an example of a declining U.S. industry. The 22,000 U.S. jobs saved as a result of one trade restriction paid an average of less than $30,000 per year. But a Congressional Budget Office study estimated that the higher domestic clothing prices resulting from trade restrictions meant that U.S. consumers paid two to three times more than apparel workers earned. Trade restrictions in the U.S. clothing and textile industry started phasing out in 2005 under the Uruguay Round of trade agreements.

[11.] Daron Acemoglu et al. "Import Competition and the Great U.S. Employment Sag of the 2000s," NBER Working Paper No. 20395 (August 2014).

[12.] Melanie Trottman, "Unions Flex Muscle to Fight Pacific Trade Bill," *Wall Street Journal*, 10 June 2015.

Free trade may displace some U.S. jobs through imports, but it also creates U.S. jobs through exports. When Americans celebrate a ribbon-cutting ceremony for a new software company, nobody credits free trade for those jobs, but when a steel plant closes here, everyone talks about how those jobs went overseas. What's more, many foreign companies have built plants in the United States and employ U.S. workers. For example, a dozen foreign television manufacturers and all major Japanese automakers now operate plants in the United States.

The number employed in the United States has nearly doubled in the last four decades. To recognize this job growth is not to deny the problems facing workers displaced by imports. Some displaced workers, particularly those in steel and other unionized, blue-collar industries, are not likely to find jobs that pay nearly as well as the ones they lost. As with infant industries, however, the problems posed by declining industries need not require trade restrictions. To support the affected industry, the government could offer wage subsidies or special tax breaks that decline over time. The government has also funded programs to retrain affected workers for jobs that are in greater demand.

17-4f Problems With Trade Protection

Trade restrictions raise a number of problems in addition to those already mentioned. First, protecting one stage of production usually requires protecting downstream stages of production as well. Protecting the U.S. textile industry from foreign competition, for example, raised the cost of cloth to U.S. apparel makers, reducing *their* competitiveness. Thus, when the government protected domestic textile manufacturers, the domestic garment industry also needed protection. Second, the cost of protection includes not only the welfare loss from the higher domestic price but also the cost of the resources used by domestic producer groups to secure the favored protection. The cost of *rent seeking*—lobbying fees, propaganda, and legal actions—can sometimes equal or exceed the direct welfare loss from restrictions. The third problem with trade restrictions is the transaction costs of enforcing the myriad quotas, tariffs, and other trade restrictions. These often lead to smuggling and black markets. The fourth problem is that economies insulated from foreign competition become less innovative and less efficient. On the other hand, competing in the export market increases a firm's efficiency and productivity.[13] The final and biggest problem with imposing trade restrictions is that other countries usually retaliate, thus shrinking the gains from trade. Retaliation can set off still greater trade restrictions, leading to an outright trade war.

 **CHECKPOINT**

Identify five arguments often used to justify trade restriction. What are some unintended consequences of protecting certain industries from international competition?

---

13. David Atkin, Amit K. Khandelwal, and Adam Osman, "Exporting and Firm Performance: Evidence from a Randomized Trial," NBER Working Paper No. 20690 (November 2014); and Jan De Loecker, "Detecting Learning by Exporting," *American Economic Journal: Microeconomics*, 5 (August 2014): 1–21.

17-5 Conclusion

International trade arises from voluntary exchange among buyers and sellers pursuing their self-interest. Since 1950 world output has risen eightfold, while world trade has increased twentyfold. World trade offers many advantages to the trading countries: access to markets around the world, lower costs through economies of scale, a wider choice of products, the opportunity to utilize abundant resources, better access to information about markets and technology, improved quality honed by competitive pressure, reduced likelihood of war, and, most importantly, lower prices for consumers. Recent research suggests that access to a variety of higher quality goods may be one of the most significant gains from international trade, especially in developing countries such as India.[14] Comparative advantage, specialization, and trade allow people to use their scarce resources efficiently to satisfy their unlimited wants.

Despite the clear gains from free trade, restrictions on international trade date back centuries, and pressure on public officials to impose trade restrictions continues today. Domestic producers (and their resource suppliers) benefit from trade restrictions in their markets because they can charge domestic consumers more. Trade restrictions insulate domestic producers from the rigors of global competition, in the process stifling innovation and leaving protected industries vulnerable to technological change from abroad. With trade quotas, the winners also include those who have secured the right to import goods at the world prices and sell them at the domestic prices. Consumers, who must pay higher prices for protected goods, suffer from trade restrictions, as do the domestic producers who import resources. Other losers include U.S. exporters, who face higher trade barriers as their foreign counterparts retaliate with their own trade restrictions.

Producers have a laser-like focus on trade legislation, but consumers remain largely oblivious. Consumers purchase thousands of different goods and thus have no special interest in the effects of trade policy on any particular good. Congress tends to support the group that makes the most noise, so trade restrictions often persist, despite the clear and widespread gains from freer trade.

Summary

1. Even if a country has an absolute advantage in all goods, that country should specialize in producing the goods in which it has a comparative advantage. If each country specializes and trades according to the law of comparative advantage, all countries will benefit from greater consumption possibilities.

2. Import quotas benefit those with the right to buy goods at the world price and sell them at the higher domestic price. Both tariffs and quotas harm domestic consumers more than they help domestic producers, although tariffs at least yield government revenue, which can be used to fund public programs or to cut taxes.

3. Despite the gains from free trade, restrictions have been imposed for centuries. The General Agreement on Tariffs and Trade (GATT) was an international treaty ratified in 1947 to reduce trade barriers. Subsequent negotiations lowered tariffs and reduced trade restrictions. The Uruguay Round, ratified in 1994, lowered tariffs, created the World Trade Organization (WTO) as the successor to GATT, and will eventually phase out quotas. The Doha Round was launched in 2001, but failed to reach an agreement as of 2015.

4. Arguments used by producer groups to support trade restrictions include promoting national defense, nurturing infant industries, preventing foreign producers from dumping goods in domestic markets, protecting domestic jobs, and allowing declining industries time to wind down and exit the market.

5. Trade restrictions impose a variety of strains on the economy besides the higher costs to consumers. These include (1) the need to protect downstream stages of production as well, (2) expenditures made by favored domestic industries to seek and perpetuate trade protection, (3) costs incurred by the government to enforce trade restrictions, (4) the inefficiency and lack of innovation that result when an industry is insulated from foreign competition, and (5), most important, the trade restrictions imposed by other countries in retaliation.

[14.] Gloria Sheu, "Price, Quality, and Variety: Measuring the Gains from Trade in Differentiated Products," *American Economic Journal: Applied Economics*, 6 (October 2014): 66–89.

Key Concepts

Autarky   379

Terms of trade   380

World price   385

Bilateral agreement   390

Multilateral agreement   390

General Agreement on Tariffs and Trade (GATT)   390

Dumping   390

Uruguay Round   390

World Trade Organization (WTO)   391

Doha Round   392

Common market   393

Questions for Review

1. **Profile of Imports and Exports** What are the major U.S. exports and imports? How does international trade affect a country's consumption possibilities?

2. **Reasons for Trade**   What are the primary reasons for international trade?

3. **Gains from Trade**   Complete each of the following sentences:

   a. When a nation has no economic interaction with foreigners and produces everything it consumes, the nation is in a state of _____.

   b. According to the law of comparative advantage, each nation should specialize in producing the goods in which it has the lowest _____.

   c. The amount of one good that a nation can exchange for one unit of another good is known as the _____.

   d. Specializing according to comparative advantage and trading with other nations result in _____.

4. **Reasons for International Specialization** What determines which goods a country should produce and export?

5. **Tariffs**   High tariffs usually lead to black markets and smuggling. How is government revenue reduced by such activity?

Relate your answer to the graph in Exhibit 7 in this chapter. Does smuggling have any social benefits?

6. **Trade Restrictions**   Exhibits 7 and 8 show net losses to the economy of a country that imposes tariffs or quotas on imported sugar. What kinds of gains and losses would occur in the economies of countries that export sugar?

7. **The World Trade Organization** What is the World Trade Organization (WTO) and how does it help foster multilateral trade? (Check the WTO Web site at http://www.wto.org/.)

8. **Case Study: The Doha Round and Round**   What were the major sticking points holding up progress in the Doha Round?

9. **Arguments for Trade Restrictions** Explain the national defense, declining industries, and infant industry arguments for protecting a domestic industry from international competition.

10. **Arguments for Trade Restrictions** Firms hurt by lower-cost imports typically argue that restricting trade will save U.S. jobs. What's wrong with this argument? Are there ever any reasons to support such trade restrictions?

Problems and Exercises

11. **Comparative Advantage**   Suppose that each U.S. worker can produce 8 units of food or 2 units of clothing daily. In Fredonia, which has the same number of workers, each worker can produce 7 units of food or 1 unit of clothing daily. Why does the United States have an absolute advantage in both goods? Which country enjoys a comparative advantage in food? Why?

12. **Comparative Advantage**   The consumption possibilities frontiers shown in Exhibit 4 assume terms of trade of 1 unit of clothing for 1 unit of food. What would the consumption possibilities frontiers look like if the terms of trade were 1 unit of clothing for 2 units of food?

13. **Import Quotas**   How small must a quota be to have an impact? Using a demand-and-supply diagram, illustrate and explain the net welfare loss from imposing such a quota. Under what

circumstances would the net welfare loss from an import quota exceed the net welfare loss from an equivalent tariff (one that results in the same price and import level as the quota)?

14. **Trade Restrictions**   Suppose that the world price for steel is below the U.S. domestic price, but the government requires that all steel used in the United States be domestically produced.

   a. Use a diagram like the one in Exhibit 7 to show the gains and losses from such a policy.

   b. How could you estimate the net welfare loss (deadweight loss) from such a diagram?

   c. What response to such a policy would you expect from industries (like automobile producers) that use U.S. steel?

   d. What government revenues are generated by this policy?

RosalreneBetancourt 9 / Alamy

- *Why does a Big Mac cost four times more in Switzerland than in India?*

- *How can the United States export more than nearly any other country yet still have the world's highest trade deficit?*

- *Are high trade deficits a worry?*

- *What's the official "fudge factor" used in estimating the balance of payments?*

- *What's meant by a "strong dollar"?*

- *Why does a nation try to influence the exchange value of its currency?*

Answers to these and other questions are explored in this chapter, which focuses on international finance.

I f Starbucks wants to buy 1,000 espresso machines from the German manufacturer, Krups, it will be quoted a price in euros. Suppose the machines cost a total of €1 million (euros). How much is that in dollars? The dollar cost will depend on the exchange rate. When trade takes place across international borders, two currencies are usually involved. Supporting the flows of goods and services are flows of currencies that fund international transactions. The exchange rate between currencies—the price of one in terms of the other—is how the price of a product in one country translates into the price facing a buyer in another country. Cross-border trade therefore depends on the exchange rate.

Topics discussed in this chapter include:

- Balance of payments
- Trade deficits and surpluses
- Foreign exchange markets
- Arbitrageurs and speculators
- Purchasing power parity

- Flexible exchange rates
- Fixed exchange rates
- International monetary system
- Bretton Woods agreement
- Managed float

18-1 Balance of Payments

A country's gross domestic product, or GDP, measures the economy's income and output during a given period, usually quarterly and yearly. To account for dealings abroad, countries must also keep track of international transactions. A country's *balance of payments,* as introduced in Chapter 3, summarizes all economic transactions during a given period between residents of that country and residents of other countries. *Residents* include people, firms, organizations, and governments.

18-1a International Economic Transactions

The balance of payments measures economic transactions between a country and the rest of the world, whether these transactions involve goods and services, real and financial assets, or transfer payments. The balance of payments measures a *flow* of transactions during a particular period. Some transactions do not involve actual payments. For example, if *Time* magazine ships a new printing press to its Australian subsidiary, no payment is made, yet an economic transaction involving another country has occurred. Similarly, if CARE sends food to Africa or the Pentagon provides military assistance to the Middle East, these transactions must be captured in the balance of payments. So remember, although we speak of the *balance of payments,* a more descriptive phrase would be the *balance-of-economic transactions.*

Balance-of-payments accounts are maintained according to the principles of *double-entry bookkeeping*. Some entries are called *credits,* and others are called *debits*. As you will see, the balance of payments consists of several individual accounts. An individual account may not balance, but a deficit in one or more accounts must be offset by a net surplus in the other accounts. Because total credits must equal total debits, there is a *balance* of payments—hence, the name. During a given period, such as a year, the inflow of receipts from the rest of the world, which are entered as credits, must equal the outflow of payments to the rest of the world, which are entered as debits.

The first of two major categories in the balance of payments is the current account. The current account records *current* flows of funds into and out of the country, including imports and exports of goods and services, net income earned by U.S. residents from foreign assets, and net transfer payments from abroad. These are discussed in turn.

18-1b The Merchandise Trade Balance

The *merchandise trade balance,* a term introduced in Chapter 3, equals the value of merchandise exports minus the value of merchandise imports. The merchandise account reflects trade in goods, or tangible products (stuff you can put in a box), like French wine or U.S. computers, and is often referred to simply as the *trade balance*. Revenue from U.S. merchandise exports is a credit in the U.S. balance-of-payments account because U.S. residents get *paid* for the exported goods. Spending on U.S. merchandise imports is a debit in the balance-of-payments account because U.S. residents *pay* foreigners for imported goods.

If merchandise exports exceed merchandise imports, the trade balance is in *surplus*. If merchandise imports exceed merchandise exports, the trade balance is in *deficit*. The merchandise trade balance, which is reported monthly, influences foreign exchange markets, the stock market, and other financial markets. The trade balance depends on a variety of factors, including the relative strength and competitiveness of the domestic economy compared with other economies and the relative value of the domestic currency compared with other currencies. Strong economies with growing incomes tend to buy more of everything, including imports.

U.S. merchandise trade since 1960 is depicted in Exhibit 1, where exports, the blue line, and imports, the red line, are expressed as a percentage of GDP. During the 1960s, exports exceeded imports, and the resulting trade surpluses are shaded blue. Since 1976, imports have exceeded exports, and the resulting trade deficits are shaded pink. Trade deficits as a percentage of GDP increased from 1.3 percent in 1991 to a peak of 6.3 percent in 2006. The Great Recession of 2007–2009 slowed U.S. imports more than U.S. exports, so by 2009 the trade deficit relative to GDP fell to 3.6 percent, the lowest in more than a decade. Since then, merchandise imports increased slightly more than merchandise exports, so the U.S. trade deficit rose to $735.8 billion in 2014, or 4.2 percent relative to GDP that year.

Because per capita income in the United States ranks among the highest in the world, the United States imports more goods from each of the world's major economies than it exports to them. Exhibit 2 shows the U.S. merchandise trade deficit with major economies or regions of the world in 2014. The $343 billion trade deficit with China was by far the largest, more than double that of the combined 28 countries of the European Union. The Chinese spent $125 billion on U.S. goods in 2014, but sold $468 billion to Americans, or about $3,900 per U.S. household. So China sold America nearly four times more than it bought from America. Chances are, most of the utensils in your kitchen are from China; most toys are also Chinese made. China alone accounted for nearly half the U.S. merchandise trade deficit in 2014. The United States has a trade surplus with only a few major economies.

EXHIBIT 1 **U.S. Imports Have Topped Exports Since 1976, but Both Dropped During the Great Recession**

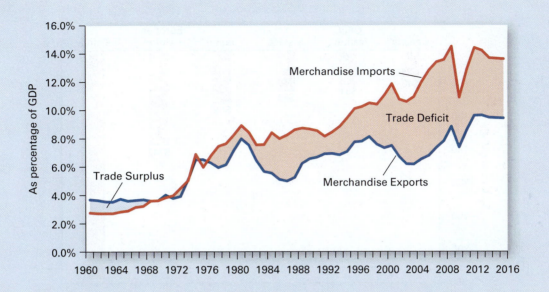

Note that since 1980, merchandise exports have remained in the range of about 5 percent to 10 percent of GDP. But merchandise imports have trended up from about 9 percent in 1980 to about 15 percent in 2008, before dropping off to 11 percent in 2009, the year following the financial crisis. Imports were back up to about 14 percent relative to GDP by 2011 and have remained there.

Source: Developed from merchandise trade data from the *Bureau of Economic Analysis*, U.S. Department of Commerce, at http://bea.gov/international/index.htm.

18-1c Balance on Goods and Services

The merchandise trade balance focuses on the flow of goods, but services are also traded internationally. *Services* are intangibles, such as transportation, insurance, banking, education, consulting, and tourism. Services are often called "invisibles" because they are not tangible. The value of U.S. service exports, as when an Irish tourist visits New York City, is listed as a credit in the U.S. balance-of-payments account because U.S. residents get paid for these services. The value of U.S. service imports, like computer programming outsourced to India, is listed as a debit in the balance-of-payments account because U.S. residents must pay for the imported services.

Because the United States exports more services than it imports, services have been in surplus for the last three decades. In 2014, the surplus in the services account totaled $231.1 billion. The **balance on goods and services** is the export value of goods and services minus the import value of goods and services, or *net exports*, a component of GDP. Because deficits in the merchandise trade account dominated surpluses in the services account, net exports of goods and services have been in deficit for decades. That deficit in 2014 totaled $504.7 billion.

18-1d Net Investment Income

U.S. residents earn investment income, such as interest and dividends, from foreign assets. This investment income flows to the United States and is a credit in the

balance on goods and services

The portion of a country's balance-of-payments account that measures the value of a country's exports of goods and services minus the value of its imports of goods and services

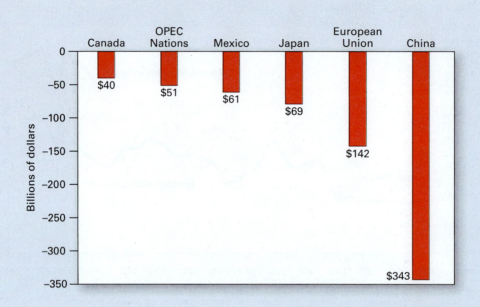

The United States imports more goods from each of the world's major economies than it exports to them. The largest U.S. trade deficit is with China, which sold nearly four times more to the United States in 2014 than it bought from the United States.

Source: Developed from export and import estimates are from the Bureau of Economic Analysis, U.S. Department of Commerce at http://bea.gov/international/index.htm.

balance-of-payments account. On the other side, foreigners earn investment income on their U.S. assets, and this payment flows out of the United States. This outflow is a debit in the balance-of-payments account. **Net investment income from abroad** is U.S. investment earnings from foreign assets minus foreigners' earnings from their U.S. assets. This figure bounces around from year to year between a positive and a negative number. In 2014, net investment income from foreign holdings totaled $217.9 billion.

net investment income from abroad

Investment earnings by U.S. residents from their foreign assets minus investment earnings by foreigners from their assets in the United States

18-1e Unilateral Transfers and the Current Account Balance

Unilateral transfers consist of government transfers to foreign residents, foreign aid, money workers send to families abroad, personal gifts to friends and relatives abroad, contributions of foreign charities, and the like. Money sent out of the country is a debit in the balance-of-payments account. For example, immigrants in the United States often send money to families back home. **Net unilateral transfers abroad** equal the unilateral transfers received from abroad by U.S. residents minus unilateral transfers sent abroad by U.S. residents. U.S. net unilateral transfers have been negative since World War II, except for 1991, when the U.S. government received sizable transfers from foreign governments to help pay their share of the Persian Gulf War. In 2014, net unilateral transfers were a negative $123.8 billion, with private transfers accounting for most of that (government grants and transfer payments made up the rest). Net unilateral transfers abroad averaged about $1,000 per U.S. household.

net unilateral transfers abroad

The unilateral transfers (gifts and grants) received from abroad by U.S. residents minus the unilateral transfers U.S. residents send abroad

The United States places few restrictions on money sent out of the country. Other countries, particularly developing countries, strictly limit the amount that may be sent abroad. More generally, many developing countries, such as China, restrict the convertibility of their currency into other currencies.

When we add net unilateral transfers to net exports of goods and services and net income from assets owned abroad, we get the **balance on current account**, which is reported quarterly. Thus, *the current account includes all international transactions in currently produced goods and services, net income from foreign assets, and net unilateral transfers*. It can be negative, reflecting a current account deficit; positive, reflecting a current account surplus; or zero. In 2014, the current account deficit was $410.6 billion.

18-1f The Financial Account

The current account records international transactions in goods, services, asset income, and unilateral transfers. The **financial account** records international purchases of assets, including financial assets, such as stocks, bonds, and bank balances, and real assets such as land, housing, factories, and other physical assets. For example, U.S. residents purchase foreign securities to earn a higher return and to diversify their investments. Money flows out when Americans buy foreign assets or build factories overseas. Money flows in when foreigners buy U.S. assets or build factories here. The international purchase or sale of assets is recorded in the financial account.

Between 1917 and 1982, the United States ran a financial account deficit, meaning that U.S. residents purchased more foreign assets than foreigners purchased U.S. assets. The net income from these foreign assets improved our current account balance. But in 1983, for the first time in 65 years, foreigners bought more U.S. assets than U.S. residents purchased abroad. Since 1983, foreigners have continued to buy more U.S. assets most years than the other way around, meaning there has usually been a surplus in the financial account. This is not as bad as it sounds, because foreign purchases of assets in the United States add to America's productive capacity and promote employment and labor productivity here. But any income from these assets flows to their foreign owners, not to Americans. Remember, the investment income from these assets shows up in the current account. Foreigners find America an attractive place to invest because U.S. capital markets are the deepest and most liquid in the world. In 2014, the financial account surplus was $141.6 billion.

18-1g Trade Deficits and Surpluses

Nations, like households, operate under a budget constraint. Spending cannot exceed income plus cash on hand and borrowed funds. We have distinguished between *current* transactions, which include exports, imports, asset income, and unilateral transfers, and *financial* transactions, which reflect net purchases of foreign real and financial assets. Any surplus or deficit in one account must be offset by deficits or surpluses in other balance-of-payments accounts.

Exhibit 3 presents the U.S. balance-of-payments statement for 2014. All transactions requiring payments from foreigners to U.S. residents are entered as credits, indicated by a plus sign (1), because they result in an inflow of funds from foreign residents to U.S. residents. All transactions requiring payments to foreigners from U.S. residents are entered as debits, indicated by a minus sign (–), because they result in an outflow of funds from U.S. residents to foreign residents. As you can see, a surplus in the financial account of $141.6 billion was more than offset by a current account deficit of $410.6 billion. A *statistical discrepancy* is required to balance the payments, and

balance on current account
The portion of the balance-of-payments account that measures a country's balance on goods and services, net investment income from abroad, plus net unilateral transfers abroad

financial account
The record of a country's international transactions involving purchases and sales of financial and real assets

EXHIBIT 3	U.S. Balance of Payments for 2014 (billions of dollars)

Current Account	
1. Merchandise exports	+1,635.1
2. Merchandise imports	−2,370.9
3. Merchandise trade balance (1 + 2)	−735.8
4. Service exports	+709.4
5. Service imports	−478.3
6. Goods and services balance (3 + 4 + 5)	−504.7
7. Net investment income from abroad	+217.9
8. Net unilateral transfers	−123.8
9. Current account balance (6 + 7 + 8)	−410.6
Financial Account	
10. Change in U.S.-owned assets abroad	−820.5
11. Change in foreign-owned assets in the United States	+962.1
12. Financial account balance (10 + 11)	+141.6
13. Statistical discrepancy	+269.0
TOTAL (9 + 12 + 13)	0.0

Source: Computed from estimates by the Bureau of Economic Analysis, U.S. Department of Commerce at http://bea.gov/international/index.htm.

that came to $269.0 billion in 2014. Think of the statistical discrepancy as the official "fudge factor" that (1) measures the error in the balance of payments and (2) satisfies the double-entry bookkeeping requirement that total debits must equal total credits. The statistical discrepancy was large in 2014, because the global financial crisis created unusual gyrations that continued to affect international accounts.

Foreign exchange is the currency of another country needed to carry out international transactions. A country runs a deficit in its current account when the amount of foreign exchange received from exports, from foreign assets, and from unilateral transfers falls short of the amount needed to pay for imports, pay foreign holders of U.S. assets, and make unilateral transfers. If the current account is in deficit, the necessary foreign exchange must come from a net inflow in the financial account. Such an inflow in the financial account could stem from borrowing from foreigners, selling domestic stocks and bonds to foreigners, selling a steel plant in Pittsburgh or a ski lodge in Aspen to foreigners, and so forth.

If a country runs a current account surplus, the foreign exchange received from exports, from foreign assets, and from unilateral transfers from abroad exceeds the amount needed to pay for imports, to pay foreign holders of U.S. assets, and to make unilateral transfers abroad. If the current account is in surplus, this excess foreign exchange results in a net outflow in the financial account through lending abroad, buying foreign stocks and bonds, buying a shoe plant in Italy or a villa on the French Riviera, and so forth.

When all transactions are considered, accounts must balance. The statistical discrepancy ensures that, in the aggregate, accounts sum to zero. A deficit in a particular account should not necessarily be viewed as a source of concern, nor should a surplus be a source of satisfaction. The deficit in the U.S. current account in recent years has usually been offset by a financial account surplus. As a result, foreigners have been acquiring more claims on U.S. assets.

CHECKPOINT

What are the major accounts in the balance of trade, and how do they balance out?

18-2 Foreign Exchange Rates and Markets

Now that you have some idea about international flows, we can take a closer look at the forces that determine the underlying value of the currencies involved. Let's begin by looking at exchange rates and the market for foreign exchange.

18-2a Foreign Exchange

Foreign exchange, recall, is foreign money needed to carry out international transactions. The **exchange rate** is the cost measured in one country's currency of one unit of another country's currency. Exchange rates are determined by the interaction of the households, firms, private financial institutions, governments, and central banks that buy and sell foreign exchange. The exchange rate fluctuates to equate the quantity of foreign exchange demanded with the quantity supplied. Typically, foreign exchange is made up of bank deposits denominated in the foreign currency. When foreign travel is involved, foreign exchange often consists of foreign paper money.

exchange rate
The cost measured in one country's currency of one unit of another country's currency

The foreign exchange market incorporates all the arrangements used to buy and sell foreign exchange. This market is not so much a physical place as a network of telephones and computers connecting financial centers all over the world. Perhaps you have seen pictures of foreign exchange traders in New York, Frankfurt, London, or Tokyo in front of computer screens amid a tangle of phone lines. The foreign exchange market is like an all-night diner—it never closes. A trading center is always open somewhere in the world.

We will consider the market for the euro in terms of the dollar. But first, a little more about the euro. For decades the nations of Western Europe tried to increase their economic cooperation and trade. These countries believed they would be more productive and more competitive with the United States if they acted less like many separate economies and more like the 50 United States, with a single set of trade regulations and a single currency. Imagine the hassle involved if each of the 50 states had its own currency.

In 2002, euro notes and coins entered circulation in the 12 European countries adopting the common currency. The big advantage of a common currency is that Europeans no longer have to change money every time they cross a border or trade with another country in the group. Again, the inspiration for this is the United States, arguably the most successful economy in world history.

So the euro is the common currency of the *eurozone,* as the now 19-country region is usually called. The cost, or exchange rate, of the euro in terms of the dollar is the number

Philip Lange/Shutterstock.com

currency depreciation

With respect to the dollar, an increase in the number of dollars needed to purchase one unit of foreign exchange in a flexible rate system

currency appreciation

With respect to the dollar, a decrease in the number of dollars needed to purchase one unit of foreign exchange in a flexible rate system

of dollars required to purchase one euro. An increase in the number of dollars needed to purchase a euro indicates weakening, or **depreciation**, of the dollar. A decrease in the number of dollars needed to purchase a euro indicates strengthening, or **appreciation**, of the dollar. Put another way, a decrease in the number of euros needed to purchase a dollar is a depreciation of the dollar, and an increase in the number of euros needed to purchase a dollar is an appreciation of the dollar.

Because the exchange rate is usually a market price, it is determined by demand and supply: The equilibrium price is the one that equates quantity demanded with quantity supplied. To simplify the analysis, suppose that the United States and the eurozone make up the entire world, so the demand and supply for euros in international finance is the demand and supply for foreign exchange from the U.S. perspective.

18-2b The Demand for Foreign Exchange

Whenever U.S. residents need euros, they must buy them in the foreign exchange market, which could include your local bank, paying for them with dollars. Exhibit 4 depicts a market for foreign exchange—in this case, euros. The horizontal axis shows the quantity of foreign exchange, measured here in billions of euros per day. The vertical axis shows the price per unit of foreign exchange, measured here in dollars per euro. The demand curve D for foreign exchange shows the inverse relationship between the dollar price of the euro and the quantity of euros demanded. Assumed constant along the demand curve are the incomes and preferences of U.S. consumers, expected inflation in the United States and in the eurozone, the euro price of goods in the eurozone, and interest rates in the United States and in the eurozone. U.S. residents have many

EXHIBIT 4   The Foreign Exchange Market

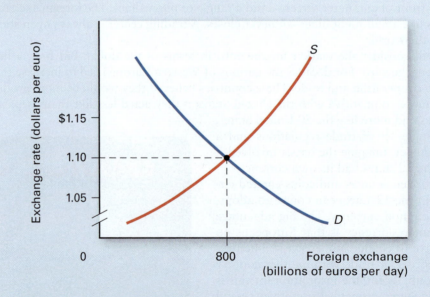

The fewer dollars needed to purchase one unit of foreign exchange, the lower the price of foreign goods and the greater the quantity of foreign goods demanded. Thus, the demand curve for foreign exchange slopes downward. An increase in the exchange rate makes U.S. products cheaper for foreigners. This implies an increase in the quantity of foreign exchange supplied. The supply curve of foreign exchange slopes upward.

reasons for demanding foreign exchange, but in the aggregate, the lower the dollar price of foreign exchange, other things constant, the greater the quantity of foreign exchange demanded.

A drop in the dollar price of foreign exchange, in this case the euro, means that fewer dollars are needed to purchase each euro, so the dollar prices of eurozone products (like German cars, Italian shoes, tickets to the Louvre, and eurozone securities) become cheaper. The cheaper it is to buy euros, the lower the dollar price of eurozone products to U.S. residents, so the greater the quantity of euros demanded by U.S. residents, other things constant. For example, a cheap enough euro might persuade you to tour Rome, climb the Austrian Alps, wander the museums of Paris, or crawl the pubs of Dublin.

18-2c The Supply of Foreign Exchange

The supply of foreign exchange is generated by the desire of foreign residents to acquire dollars—that is, to exchange euros for dollars. Eurozone residents want dollars to buy U.S. goods and services, acquire U.S. assets, make loans in dollars, or send dollars to their U.S. friends and relatives. Euros are supplied in the foreign exchange market to acquire the dollars people want. An increase in the dollar-per-euro exchange rate, other things constant, makes U.S. products cheaper for foreigners because foreign residents need fewer euros to get the same number of dollars. For example, suppose a Dell computer sells for $1,155. If the exchange rate is $1.05 per euro, that computer costs 1,100 euros; if the exchange rate is $1.10 per euro, it costs only 1,050 euros. The number of Dell computers demanded in the eurozone increases as the dollar-per-euro exchange rate increases, other things constant, so more euros will be supplied on the foreign exchange market to buy dollars.

The positive relationship between the dollar-per-euro exchange rate and the quantity of euros supplied on the foreign exchange market is expressed in Exhibit 4 by the upward-sloping supply curve for foreign exchange (again, euros in our example). The supply curve assumes that other things remain constant, including eurozone incomes and tastes, expectations about inflation in the eurozone and in the United States, and interest rates in the eurozone and in the United States.

18-2d The Foreign Exchange Rate

Exhibit 4 brings together the demand and supply for foreign exchange to determine the exchange rate. At a rate of $1.10 per euro, the quantity of euros demanded equals the quantity supplied—in our example, 800 billion euros per day. Once achieved, this equilibrium rate will hold until a change occurs in one of the factors that affect supply or demand. If the exchange rate is allowed to adjust freely, or to *float,* in response to market forces, the market will clear continually, as the quantities of foreign exchange demanded and supplied are equated.

What if the initial equilibrium is upset by a change in one of the underlying forces that affect demand or supply? For example, suppose higher U.S. incomes increase American demand for all normal goods, including those from the eurozone. This shifts the U.S. demand curve for foreign exchange to the right, as Americans buy more Italian marble, Dutch chocolate, German automobiles, Parisian vacations, and eurozone securities.

This increased demand for euros is shown in Exhibit 5 by a rightward shift of the demand curve for foreign exchange. The demand increase from D to D' leads to an increase in the exchange rate per euro from $1.10 to $1.12. Thus, the euro increases in value, or appreciates, while the dollar falls in value, or depreciates. An increase

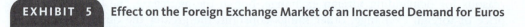

EXHIBIT 5   **Effect on the Foreign Exchange Market of an Increased Demand for Euros**

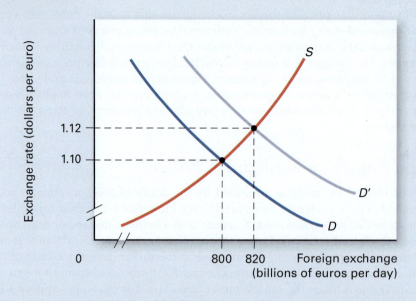

The intersection of the demand curve for foreign exchange, *D*, and the supply curve for foreign exchange, *S*, determines the exchange rate. At an exchange rate of $1.10 per euro, the quantity of euros demanded equals the quantity supplied. An increase in the demand for euros from *D* to *D'* increases the exchange rate from $1.10 to $1.12 per euro.

in U.S. income should not affect the euro supply curve, though it does increase the *quantity of euros supplied*. The higher exchange value of the euro prompts those in the eurozone to buy more American products and assets, which are now cheaper in terms of the euro.

To Review: Any increase in the demand for foreign exchange or any decrease in its supply, other things constant, increases the number of dollars required to purchase one unit of foreign exchange, which is a depreciation of the dollar. On the other hand, any decrease in the demand for foreign exchange or any increase in its supply, other things constant, reduces the number of dollars required to purchase one unit of foreign exchange, which is an appreciation of the dollar.

CHECKPOINT

Describe how the foreign exchange rate is determined. Use a diagram and explain the shapes of the curves.

18-3 Other Factors Influencing Foreign Exchange Markets

So far, the market for foreign exchange has been presented just like any other market: Demand and supply come together to determine the equilibrium exchange rate, or price of foreign exchange. Simple enough, but the market for foreign exchange is complicated by the types of actors in this market and by the types of regulations and restrictions involved. In this section, we look at how these other factors shape this market.

18-3a Arbitrageurs and Speculators

Exchange rates between two currencies are nearly identical at any given time in markets around the world. For example, the dollar price of a euro is usually the same in New York, Frankfurt, Tokyo, London, Zurich, Hong Kong, Istanbul, and other financial centers. **Arbitrageurs**—dealers who take advantage of tiny differences in exchange rates across markets by buying low and selling high—ensure this equality. For example, if one euro costs $1.09 in New York but $1.10 in Frankfurt, an arbitrageur could buy, say, $1,000,000 worth of euros in New York and at the same time sell them in Frankfurt for $1,009,174, thereby earning $9,174 minus the transaction costs of the trades.

Because an arbitrageur buys and sells simultaneously, little risk is involved. In our example, the arbitrageur increased the demand for euros in New York and increased the supply of euros in Frankfurt. These actions increased the dollar price of euros in New York and decreased it in Frankfurt, thereby squeezing down the difference in exchange rates. Note that arbitrage opportunities are short lived, most for just a fraction of a second. High-speed computers act on such opportunities instantly.[1] Exchange rates may still change because of market forces, but they tend to change in all markets simultaneously.

The demand and supply of foreign exchange arises from many sources—from importers and exporters, investors in foreign assets, central banks, tourists, arbitrageurs, and speculators. **Speculators** buy or sell foreign exchange in hopes of profiting by trading the currency at a more favorable exchange rate later. By taking risks, speculators aim to profit from market fluctuations—they try to buy low and sell high. In contrast, arbitrageurs take less risk, because they *simultaneously* buy currency in one market and sell it in another.

Finally, people in countries suffering from economic and political turmoil, such as occurred in Russia, Indonesia, the Philippines, and Zimbabwe, may buy *hard* currency as a hedge against the depreciation and instability of their own currencies. The dollar has long been accepted as an international medium of exchange. It is also the currency of choice in the world markets for oil and illegal drugs. But the euro eventually may challenge that dominance, in part because the largest euro denomination, the 500 euro note, is worth more than five times the largest U.S. denomination, the $100 note. So it would be about five times easier to smuggle euro notes than U.S. notes of equal value. Still, fiscal problems in some eurozone nations such as Greece and Spain have taken some of the shine off the euro.

18-3b Purchasing Power Parity

As long as trade across borders is unrestricted and as long as exchange rates are allowed to adjust freely, the **purchasing power parity (PPP) theory** predicts that the exchange rate between two currencies will adjust in the long run to equalize the cost across countries

arbitrageur
Someone who takes advantage of tiny differences in the exchange rate across markets by simultaneously purchasing currency in one market and selling it in another market

speculator
Someone who buys or sells foreign exchange in hopes of profiting from fluctuations in the exchange rate over time

purchasing power parity (PPP) theory
The idea that the exchange rate between two countries will adjust in the long run to equalize the cost of a basket of internationally traded goods

---

[1.] Takatoshi Ito et al. "Free Lunch: Arbitrage Opportunities in the Foreign Exchange Markets," NBER Working Paper No. 18541 (November 2012).

of an internationally traded basket of goods. *A given basket of internationally traded goods should therefore sell for about the same around the world (except for differences reflecting transportation costs and the like).* Suppose a basket of internationally traded goods that sells for $11,000 in the United States sells for €10,000 in the eurozone. According to the purchasing power parity theory, the equilibrium exchange rate should be $1.10 per euro. If this were not the case—if the exchange rate were, say, $1.05 per euro—then you could exchange $10,500 for €10,000, with which you buy the basket of commodities in the eurozone. You could then sell that basket of goods in the States for $11,000, yielding you a profit of $500 minus any transaction costs. Selling dollars and buying euros will also drive up the dollar price of euros.

The purchasing power parity theory is more of a long-run predictor than a day-to-day indicator of the relationship between changes in the price level and the exchange rate. For example, a country's currency generally appreciates when inflation is lower than that of other countries and depreciates when inflation is higher compared to other countries. Likewise, a country's currency generally appreciates when its real interest rates are higher than in other countries, because foreigners are more willing to buy and hold investments denominated in that high-interest currency. As a case in point, the dollar appreciated during the first half of the 1980s, when real U.S. interest rates were relatively high, and depreciated during 2002 to 2004, when real U.S. interest rates were relatively low.

Because of trade barriers, central bank intervention in exchange markets, and the fact that many products are not traded or are not comparable across countries, the purchasing power parity theory usually does not explain exchange rates at a particular point in time that well. For example, if you went shopping in Switzerland tomorrow, you would soon notice a dollar does not buy as much there as it does in the United States. The following case study considers the purchasing power parity theory based on the price of Big Macs around the globe.

BRINGING THEORY TO LIFE

THE BIG MAC INDEX As you have already learned, the PPP theory predicts that in the long run the exchange rate between two currencies should move toward equalizing the cost in each country of an identical basket of internationally traded goods. A lighthearted test of the theory has been developed by *The Economist* magazine, which compares prices around the world for a "market basket" consisting simply of one McDonald's Big Mac—a product that, though not internationally traded, is essentially the same in more than 100 countries. *The Economist* begins with the price of a Big Mac in the local currency and then converts that price into U.S. dollars based on the exchange rate prevailing at the time. A comparison of the dollar price of Big Macs across countries offers a crude test of the PPP theory, which predicts that prices should be roughly equal in the long run.

Exhibit 6 lists the dollar price of a Big Mac in January 2015, in 22 surveyed countries plus the eurozone average. By comparing the price of a Big Mac in the United States (shown as the green bar) with prices in other countries, we can derive a crude measure of whether particular currencies, relative to the dollar, are overvalued (red bars) or undervalued (blue bars). For example, because the price of a Big Mac in Switzerland, at $7.54, was 57 percent higher than the U.S. price of $4.79, the Swiss franc was the most overvalued currency relative to the dollar of the countries listed. But Big Macs were cheaper in most of the countries surveyed. The cheapest was in Russia, where $1.36 was 72 percent below the U.S. price. Hence, the Russian ruble at the time of the survey was the most undervalued currency relative to the dollar. (Simply put, in

continued

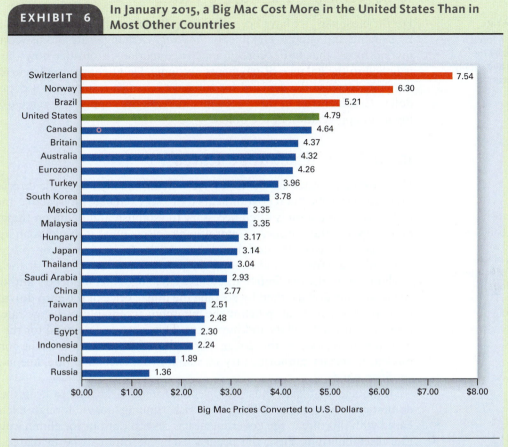

| EXHIBIT 6 | In January 2015, a Big Mac Cost More in the United States Than in Most Other Countries |

Switzerland 7.54
Norway 6.30
Brazil 5.21
United States 4.79
Canada 4.64
Britain 4.37
Australia 4.32
Eurozone 4.26
Turkey 3.96
South Korea 3.78
Mexico 3.35
Malaysia 3.35
Hungary 3.17
Japan 3.14
Thailand 3.04
Saudi Arabia 2.93
China 2.77
Taiwan 2.51
Poland 2.48
Egypt 2.30
Indonesia 2.24
India 1.89
Russia 1.36

$0.00 $1.00 $2.00 $3.00 $4.00 $5.00 $6.00 $7.00 $8.00

Big Mac Prices Converted to U.S. Dollars

Source: Based on a survey in "The Big Mac Index," *The Economist*, 22 January 2015. Local prices are converted into U.S. dollars using the prevailing exchange rate.

January 2015, a U.S. dollar went much further in Russia than in Switzerland.) The ruble was especially beaten down the month of the survey because the Russian economy was rocked by the collapse of oil prices (Russia is a major exporter of oil) and by international sanctions because of Russia's incursions into Ukraine.

Thus, Big Mac prices in January 2015 ranged from 57 percent above to 72 percent below the U.S. price. The price range lends little support to the PPP theory, but that theory relates only to traded goods. The Big Mac is not traded internationally. Part of the price of a Big Mac must cover rent, which can vary substantially across countries. Taxes and trade barriers, such as tariffs and quotas on beef, may also distort local prices. And wages differ across countries, with a McDonald's worker averaging about $9 an hour in the United States versus more like $4 an hour in Russia and only $1 an hour in India. So there are understandable reasons why Big Mac prices differ across countries. And price dispersion appears to have decreased more over time among those countries with stronger trade ties, a finding that is consistent with the theory of purchasing power parity.

Sources: "The Big Mac Index," *The Economist*, 22 January 2015; Mario J. Crucini and Hakan Yilmazkuday, "Understanding Long-Run Price Dispersion," *Journal of Monetary Economics*, 66 (September 2014): 226–240; Yukio Fukumoto, "International Price Dispersions of the Big Mac and Economic Integration," *Applied Economics Letters*, 18 (Issue 17, 2011):1633–1638; and the McDonald's Corporation international Web site at http://www.mcdonalds.com.

Patrik Stollarz/Bongarts/Getty Images

18-3c Flexible Exchange Rates

flexible exchange rate

Rate determined in foreign exchange markets by the forces of demand and supply without government intervention

For the most part, we have been discussing **flexible exchange rates**, which are determined by demand and supply. Flexible, or *floating,* exchange rates adjust continually to the myriad forces that buffet foreign exchange markets. Consider how the exchange rate is linked to the balance-of-payments accounts. Debit entries in the current or financial accounts increase the demand for foreign exchange, resulting in a depreciation of the dollar. Credit entries in these accounts increase the supply of foreign exchange, resulting in an appreciation of the dollar.

18-3d Fixed Exchange Rates

fixed exchange rate

Rate of exchange between currencies pegged within a narrow range and maintained by the central bank's ongoing purchases and sales of currencies

When exchange rates are flexible, governments usually have little direct role in foreign exchange markets. But if governments try to set exchange rates, active and ongoing central bank intervention is often necessary to establish and maintain these **fixed exchange rates**. Suppose the European Central Bank selects what it thinks is an appropriate rate of exchange between the dollar and the euro. It attempts to *fix,* or to *peg,* the exchange rate within a narrow band around the particular value selected. If the euro threatens to climb above the maximum acceptable exchange rate, monetary authorities must sell euros and buy dollars, thereby keeping the dollar price of the euro down. Conversely, if the euro threatens to drop below the minimum acceptable exchange rate, monetary authorities must sell dollars and buy euros. This increased demand for the euro will keep its value up relative to the dollar. Through such intervention in the foreign exchange market, monetary authorities try to stabilize the exchange rate, keeping it within the specified band.

currency devaluation

An increase in the official pegged price of foreign exchange in terms of the domestic currency

If monetary officials must keep selling foreign exchange to keep the value of their domestic currency from falling, they risk running out of foreign exchange reserves. Faced with this threat, the government has several options for eliminating the exchange rate disequilibrium. First, the pegged exchange rate can be increased, meaning that foreign currency costs more dollars. This is a **devaluation** of the dollar. (A decrease in the pegged exchange rate is called a **revaluation**.) Second, the government can reduce the domestic demand for foreign exchange directly by imposing restrictions on imports or on financial outflows. Many developing countries do this. Third, the government can adopt policies to slow the domestic economy, increase interest rates, or reduce inflation relative to that of the country's trading partners, thereby indirectly decreasing the demand for foreign exchange and increasing the supply of foreign exchange. Several Asian economies, such as South Korea and Indonesia, pursued such policies to stabilize their currencies. Finally, the government can allow the disequilibrium to persist and ration the available foreign reserves through some form of foreign exchange control.

currency revaluation

A reduction in the official pegged price of foreign exchange in terms of the domestic currency

This concludes our introduction to the theories of international finance. Let's examine international finance in practice.

CHECKPOINT

What is the purchasing power parity theory, and how well does the Big Mac index support it?

18-4 International Monetary System

From 1879 to 1914, the international monetary system operated under a **gold standard**, whereby the major currencies were convertible into gold at a fixed rate. For example, the U.S. dollar could be redeemed at the U.S. Treasury for one-twentieth of an ounce of gold. The British pound could be redeemed at the British Exchequer, or treasury, for one-fourth of an ounce of gold. Because each British pound could buy five times as much gold as each dollar, one British pound exchanged for $5.

The gold standard provided a predictable exchange rate, one that did not vary as long as currencies could be redeemed for gold at the official rate. But the money supply in each country was determined in part by the flow of gold among countries, so each country's monetary policy was influenced by the supply of gold. A balance-of-payments deficit resulted in a loss of gold, which theoretically caused a country's money supply to shrink. A balance-of-payments surplus resulted in an influx of gold, which theoretically caused a country's money supply to expand. The supply of money throughout the world also depended on the vagaries of gold discoveries. When gold production did not keep pace with the growth in economic activity, the price level dropped. When gold production exceeded the growth in economic activity, the price level rose. For example, gold discoveries in Alaska and South Africa in the late 1890s expanded the U.S. money supply, leading to inflation.

gold standard
An arrangement whereby the currencies of most countries were convertible into gold at a fixed rate

18-4a The Bretton Woods Agreement

During World War I, many countries could no longer convert their currencies into gold, and the gold standard eventually collapsed, disrupting international trade during the 1920s and 1930s. Once an Allied victory in World War II appeared certain, the Allies met in Bretton Woods, New Hampshire, in July 1944 to formulate a new international monetary system. Because the United States had a strong economy and was not ravaged by the war, the dollar was selected as the key reserve currency in the new international monetary system. All exchange rates were fixed in terms of the dollar, and the United States, which held most of the world's gold reserves, stood ready to convert foreign holdings of dollars into gold at a rate of $35 per ounce. Even though the rate that dollars could be exchanged for gold was fixed by the Bretton Woods agreement, *other* countries could adjust *their* exchange rates relative to the U.S. dollar if they found a chronic disequilibrium in their balance of payments—that is, if a country faced a large and persistent deficit or surplus. In short, America's promise to redeem foreign holdings of U.S. dollars for a fixed amount of gold anchored the international monetary system.

The Bretton Woods agreement also created the **International Monetary Fund (IMF)** to set rules for maintaining the international monetary system, to standardize financial reporting for international trade, and to make loans to countries with temporary balance-of-payments problems. The IMF lends a revolving fund of about $400 billion to economies in need of reserves. Headquartered in Washington, D.C., the IMF has about 190 member countries and a staff of 2,600 drawn from around the world (half the staff are economists).

International Monetary Fund (IMF)
An international organization that establishes rules for maintaining the international monetary system and makes loans to countries with temporary balance-of-payments problems

18-4b Demise of the Bretton Woods System

During the latter part of the 1960s, inflation increased in the United States more than in other countries. Because of U.S. inflation, the dollar had become *overvalued* at the official exchange rate, meaning that the gold value of the dollar exceeded the exchange value of the dollar. In 1971, U.S. merchandise imports exceeded merchandise exports for the first time since World War II. Foreigners exchanged dollars for gold. To stem this gold outflow, the

United States stopped exchanging gold for dollars, but this just made the dollar less attractive. In December 1971, the world's 10 richest countries met in Washington and devalued the dollar by 8 percent. They hoped this would put the dollar on firmer footing and would save the "dollar standard." With prices rising at different rates around the world, however, an international monetary system based on fixed exchange rates was doomed.

When the U.S. trade deficit tripled in 1972, it became clear that the dollar was still overvalued. In early 1973, the dollar was devalued another 10 percent, but this did not quiet foreign exchange markets. The dollar, for three decades the anchor of the international monetary system, suddenly looked vulnerable, and speculators began betting that the dollar would fall even more, so they sold dollars. Dollars were exchanged for German marks because the mark appeared to be the most stable currency. Bundesbank, Germany's central bank, tried to defend the dollar's official exchange rate by selling marks and buying dollars. Why didn't Germany want the mark to appreciate? Appreciation would make German goods more expensive abroad and foreign goods cheaper in Germany, thereby reducing German exports and increasing German imports. So the mark's appreciation would reduce German output and employment. But after selling $10 billion worth of marks to buy dollars, the Bundesbank gave up defending the dollar. As soon as the value of the dollar was allowed to float against the mark, the Bretton Woods system, already on shaky ground, collapsed.

18-4c The Current System: Managed Float

managed float system
An exchange rate system that combines features of freely floating rates with sporadic intervention by central banks

The Bretton Woods system has been replaced by a **managed float system**, which combines features of a freely floating exchange rate with sporadic intervention by central banks as a way of moderating exchange rate fluctuations among the world's major currencies. Most small countries, particularly developing countries, still peg their currencies to one of the major currencies (such as the U.S. dollar) or to a "basket" of major currencies. What's more, in developing countries, private international borrowing and lending are severely restricted; some governments allow residents to purchase foreign exchange only for certain purposes. In some countries, different exchange rates apply to different categories of transactions.

Critics of flexible exchange rates argue that they are inflationary, because they free monetary authorities to pursue expansionary policies; and flexible exchange rates have often been volatile. This volatility creates uncertainty and risk for importers and exporters, increasing the transaction costs of international trade. Furthermore, exchange rate volatility can lead to wrenching changes in the competitiveness of a country's export sector. These changes cause swings in employment, resulting in louder calls for import restrictions. For example, the exchange rate between the Japanese yen and the U.S. dollar has been relatively unstable, particularly because of international speculation.

Policy makers are always on the lookout for a system that will perform better than the current managed float system, with its fluctuating currency values. *Their ideal is a system that will foster international trade, lower inflation, and promote a more stable world economy.* International finance ministers have acknowledged that the world must find an international standard and establish greater exchange rate stability.

✅ CHECKPOINT

Trace the evolution of exchange rate regimes from the gold standard to the current system.

18-5 Conclusion

The United States is very much a part of the world economy, not only as one of the largest exporter nations but also as the largest importer nation. Although the dollar remains the unit of transaction in many international settlements—OPEC, for example, still prices crude oil in dollars—gyrations of exchange rates have made those involved in international finance wary of putting all their eggs in one basket. The international monetary system is now going through a difficult period as it gropes for a new source of stability more than four decades after the collapse of the Bretton Woods agreement.

Summary

1. The balance of payments reflects all economic transactions between one country and the rest of the world. The current account measures flows from (a) goods; (b) services, including consulting and tourism; (c) income from foreign assets; and (d) unilateral transfers, or public and private transfer payments to and from foreign residents. The financial account measures international transactions in real and financial assets.

2. Foreign exchange pays for transactions across international borders. In the absence of government intervention, the demand and supply of foreign exchange determines the market exchange rate. According to the theory of purchasing power parity (PPP), the exchange rate between two countries will adjust in the long run to equalize the cost of a basket of internationally traded goods.

3. Under a system of flexible, or floating, exchange rates, the value of the dollar relative to foreign exchange varies with market forces. An increase in the demand for foreign exchange or a decrease in its supply, other things constant, increases the value of foreign exchange relative to the dollar, which is a depreciation of the dollar. Conversely, a decrease in the demand for foreign exchange or an increase in its supply, other things constant, decreases the value of foreign exchange relative to the dollar, which is an appreciation of the dollar.

4. Under a system of fixed exchange rates, monetary authorities try to stabilize the exchange rate, keeping it between a specified ceiling and floor value. A country may try to hold down the value of its currency, so that exports will be cheaper to foreigners and imports will cost more to domestic consumers. One objective here is to increase domestic production and employment.

5. For much of the twentieth century, the international monetary system was based on fixed exchange rates. A managed float system has been in effect for the major currencies since the demise of the Bretton Woods system in the early 1970s. Although central banks often try to stabilize exchange rates, fluctuations in rates persist. These fluctuations usually reflect market forces, but they still raise the transaction costs of international trade and finance.

Key Concepts

Balance on goods and services   403
Net investment income from abroad   404
Net unilateral transfers abroad   404
Balance on current account   405
Financial account   405
Exchange rate   407

Currency depreciation   408
Currency appreciation   408
Arbitrageur   411
Speculator   411
Purchasing power parity (PPP) theory   411
Flexible exchange rate   414

Fixed exchange rate   414
Currency devaluation   414
Currency revaluation   414
Gold standard   415
International Monetary Fund (IMF)   415
Managed float system   416

Questions for Review

1. **Balance of Payments**   Suppose the United States ran a surplus in its balance on goods and services by exporting goods and services while importing nothing.

   a. How would such a surplus be offset elsewhere in the balance-of-payments accounts?

   b. If the level of U.S. production does not depend on the balance on goods and services, how would running this surplus affect our *current* standard of living?

   c. What is the relationship between total debits and total credits in the balance on goods and services?

d. When all international economic transactions are considered, what must be true about the sum of debits and credits?

e. What is the role of the statistical discrepancy?

2. **Foreign Exchange**   What is the difference between a depreciation of the dollar and a devaluation of the dollar?

3. **Arbitrageurs**   How do arbitrageurs help ensure that exchange rates are usually the same in markets around the world?

4. **Purchasing Power Parity**   According to the theory of purchasing power parity, what will happen to the value of the dollar (against foreign currencies) if the U.S. price level doubles and price levels in other countries remain constant? Why is the theory more suitable for analyzing events in the long run?

5. **Case Study: The Big Mac Index**   The Big Mac Index computed by *The Economist* magazine has consistently found the U.S. dollar to be undervalued against some currencies and overvalued against others. This finding seems to be at odds with the purchasing power parity theory. Explain why this index may not offer a fool-proof test of the theory.

6. **The Current System: Managed Float**   What is a managed float? What are the disadvantages of freely floating exchange rates that led countries to the managed float system?

7. **Merchandise Trade Balance**   Explain why a U.S. recession that occurs as the rest of the world is expanding will tend to reduce the U.S. trade deficit.

Problems and Exercises

8. **Balance of Payments**   The following are hypothetical data for the U.S. balance of payments. Use the data to calculate each of the following:

a. Merchandise trade balance
b. Balance on goods and services
c. Balance on current account
d. Financial account balance
e. Statistical discrepancy

	Billions of Dollars
Merchandise exports	350.0
Merchandise imports	2,425.0
Service exports	2,145.0
Service imports	170.0
Net income and net transfers	221.5
Outflow of U.S. capital	245.0
Inflow of foreign capital	100.0

9. **Balance of Payments**   Explain where in the U.S. balance of payments an entry would be recorded for each of the following:

a. A Hong Kong financier buys some U.S. corporate stock.
b. A U.S. tourist in Paris buys some perfume to take home.
c. A Japanese company sells machinery to a pineapple company in Hawaii.
d. U.S. farmers make a gift of food to starving children in Ethiopia.
e. The U.S. Treasury sells a bond to a Saudi Arabian prince.
f. A U.S. tourist flies to France on Air France.
g. A U.S. company sells insurance to a foreign firm.

10. **Determining the Exchange Rate**   Use these data to answer the following questions about the market for British pounds:

Pound Price (in $)	Quantity Demanded (of pounds)	Quantity Supplied (of pounds)
$4.00	50	100
3.00	75	75
2.00	100	50

a. Draw the demand and supply curves for pounds, and determine the equilibrium exchange rate (dollars per pound).
b. Suppose that the supply of pounds doubles. Draw the new supply curve.
c. What is the new equilibrium exchange rate?
d. Has the dollar appreciated or depreciated?
e. What happens to U.S. imports of British goods?

David Keith Jones/Images of Africa Photobank/Alamy

- *How might programs that send subsidized food and used clothing to poor countries have the unintended consequence of retarding economic development there?*

- *Why are some countries so poor while others are so rich?*

- *What determines the wealth of nations?*

- *Why do families in low-income countries have more children than those in higher-income countries?*

- *Why have abundant natural resources such as oil or diamonds turned out to be a curse for some countries?*

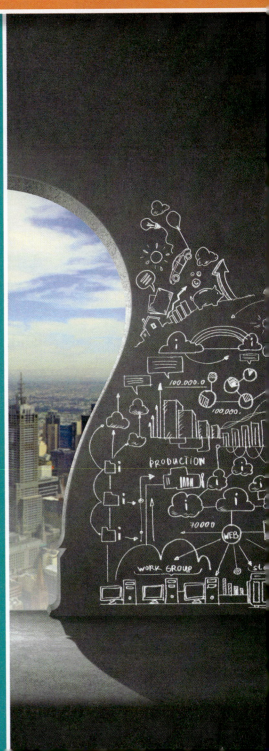

People around the world face the day under quite different circumstances. Even during a national recession, most Americans rise from a comfortable bed in a nice home, select the day's clothing from a wardrobe, choose from a variety of breakfast foods, and ride to school or to work in one of the family's personal automobiles. But some of the world's 7.4 billion people have little housing, clothing, or food. They have no automobile and no formal job. Their health is poor, as is their education. Many cannot read or write. The World Health Organization estimates that a billion people need eyeglasses but can't afford them.

In this chapter, we sort out rich nations from poor ones and try to explain the difference. We discuss sources of economic development, weigh the pros and cons of foreign aid, and see whether poorer countries are closing the income gap with richer ones.

Topics discussed in this chapter include:

- Developing countries
- The key to development
- Privatization
- The poorest billion

- Foreign trade and development
- Foreign aid and development
- Import substitution vs. export promotion
- Economic convergence

19-1 Worlds Apart

Differences in economic vitality among countries are huge. Countries are classified in a variety of ways based on their economic development. The yardstick most often used to compare living standards across nations is the amount an economy produces per capita, or *output per capita*. The World Bank, an economic development institution affiliated with the United Nations (UN), classifies economies based on income per capita. The measure begins with *gross national income (GNI)*, which is the market value of all goods and services produced by resources supplied by the countries' residents and firms, regardless of the location of the resources. For example, U.S. GNI includes profit earned by an American factory in Great Britain but excludes profits earned by a Japanese factory in Kentucky.

GNI measures both the value of output produced and the income that output generates. The World Bank estimates the GNI per capita, then adjusts figures across countries based on the purchasing power of that income in each country. Using this measure, the World Bank sorts countries around the world into three major groups: *high-income economies*, *middle-income economies*, and *low-income economies*.

Data on world population and world output are summarized in Exhibit 1. High-income economies in 2014 made up only 18 percent of the world's population, but accounted for 52 percent of world output. So high-income economies, *with less than*

EXHIBIT 1 Share of World Population and World Output From High-, Middle-, and Low-Income Economies as of 2014

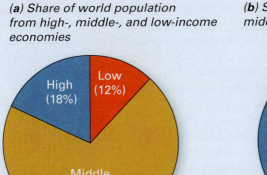
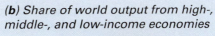
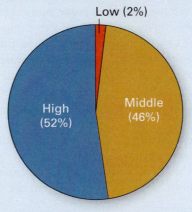

(a) Share of world population from high-, middle-, and low-income economies

High (18%)
Low (12%)
Middle (70%)

(b) Share of world output from high-, middle-, and low-income economies

Low (2%)
High (52%)
Middle (46%)

Source: Based on population and output estimated from the World Bank's *World Development Indicators: 2015,* Table 1. Find the World Bank at http://data.worldbank.org/products/wdi.

one-fifth of the world's population, produced more than half of the world's output. Middle-income economies made up 70 percent of the world's population, but accounted for 46 percent of world output. And low-income countries made up 12 percent of the world's population, but account for just 2 percent of world output.

19-1a Developing and Industrial Economies

The low- and middle-income economies are usually referred to as **developing countries**. Most high-income economies are also referred to as **industrial market countries**. So low- and middle-income economies, what are called developing countries, made up 82 percent of the world's population in 2014 but produced only 48 percent of the output. Compared to industrial market countries, developing countries usually have higher rates of illiteracy, higher unemployment, faster population growth, and exports consisting mostly of agricultural products and raw materials. Most developing countries are also known as *emerging market economies.*

On average, nearly half of the labor force in developing countries works in agriculture versus only about 3 percent in industrial market countries. Because farming methods are sometimes primitive in developing countries, farm productivity is low and some households barely subsist. For example, over half the labor force in India works in agriculture, but that sector accounts for less than one-fifth of the nation's output.[1] Industrial market countries, or *developed countries,* are primarily the economically advanced capitalist countries of Europe, North America, Australia, New Zealand, and Japan. They were the first to experience long-term economic growth during the 19th century.

developing countries
Low-income and middle-income economies; most are also known as emerging market economies

industrial market countries
Economically advanced capitalist countries of Europe, North America, Australia, New Zealand, and Japan; also known as developed countries and high-income economies

[1.] U.S. International Trade Commission, *Effect of Tariffs and Nontariff Measures on U.S. Agricultural Exports,* Investigation No. 332–504, USITC Publication 4107 (November 2009).

Exhibit 2 presents income per capita in 2014 for a sample of high-, middle-, and low-income economies. Because most countries in the sample have large populations, together they account for about 55 percent of the world's population. Countries are listed from top to bottom in descending order based on income per capita. Again, figures have been adjusted to reflect the actual purchasing power of the local currency in its respective economy. The bars in the chart are color-coded, with high-income economies in blue, middle-income economies in orange, low-income economies in red, and the world average in green. Per capita income in the United States, the exhibit's top-ranked country, was more than four times that of China, a middle-income economy. But per capita in China, in turn, was more than eight times that of Ethiopia and 18 times that of the Democratic Republic of the Congo, both poor African nations. Residents of China likely feel poor relative to Americans, but they appear well off compared to the poorest nations. U.S per capita income was 36 times that of Ethiopia, and 78 times that of the Congo, one of the poorest nations on Earth. Thus, there is a tremendous range of per capita income around the world. World per capita income in 2014 was $16,100, as shown by the green bar.

Exhibit 2 looks at income per capita, but neither income nor population is always measured accurately, especially in the poorest countries. Some economists have looked

---

EXHIBIT 2   **Per Capita Income for Selected Countries in 2014**

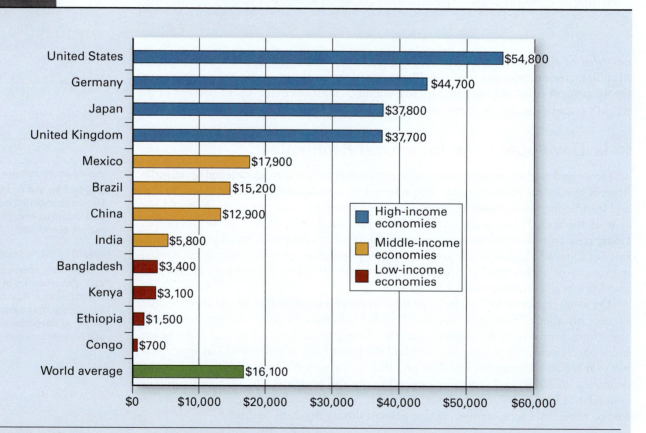

Source: Developed from estimates from the Central Intelligence Agency's *World Factbook: 2015,* at www.cia.gov/library/publications/the-world-factbook/index.html. Figures are based on the purchasing power of each country's currency.

for other ways of measuring an economy, such as how lit up a country is at night. The consumption of most goods and services at night requires light. As personal income rises, so does consumption and night lights, which can be measured from outer space by satellites. This night-light measure is useful, especially when income data are of poor quality, as with many African economies, or when income data are simply not available, as is the case with Somalia, Liberia, and North Korea.[2]

19-1b Health and Nutrition

Different stages of development among countries are reflected in a number of ways besides per capita income. For example, many people in developing countries suffer from poor health as a result of malnutrition and disease. HIV/AIDS is devastating some developing countries, particularly those in sub-Saharan Africa. In 2013, about 25 percent of people ages 15 to 49 in Swaziland, Botswana, and Lesotho had HIV/AIDS, compared with less than 1 percent in the United States.[3] The 20 countries with the highest incidence of HIV/AIDS were in Africa. Another health scourge in Africa is the tsetse fly. Harmful to humans and lethal to livestock, this fly has slowed the domestication of animals and use of plows, thus retarding economic development.[4] In sub-Saharan Africa, life expectancy at birth averaged 53 years versus 80 years in high-income economies, 69 years in middle-income economies, and 58 years in all low-income economies. Poor health has other bad consequences for the individual and the economy. For example, research shows that a higher rate of HIV/AIDS cuts the general level of education in the country. Even those not infected are less willing to invest in their own education.[5]

Malnutrition

Those in the poorest countries consume only half the calories of those in high-income countries. Even if an infant survives the first year, malnutrition can turn normal childhood diseases, such as measles, into life-threatening events. The World Health Organization cites malnutrition as the biggest single threat to the world's public health. Malnutrition is a primary or contributing factor in more than half of the deaths of children under the age of 5 in low-income countries. Diseases that are well controlled in the industrial countries—malaria, whooping cough, polio, dysentery, typhoid, and cholera—can become epidemics in poor countries. About a billion people on Earth don't have enough to eat.

Infant Mortality

Health differences among countries are reflected in the mortality rates of infants under one year of age. These rates are much greater in low-income countries than in high-income countries. Rates for our representative sample of high-, medium-, and low-income economies appear in Exhibit 3. Again, high-income economies are blue bars, middle-income are orange bars, low-income are red bars, and the world average is the green bar. Among the dozen countries shown, infant mortality was highest in the sub-Saharan African nation of the Congo. Rates for the four low-income economies in 2014 averaged 53.6 infant deaths per 1,000 live births. This was 13 times greater than the 4.1 rate for the four high-income economies. The world averaged 35.6 infant deaths per 1,000 live births. In 1990 the world average was double that, so health conditions have improved.

[2.] J. Vernon Henderson, Adam Storeygard, and David Weil, "Measuring Economic Growth from Outer Space," *American Economic Review*, 102 (April 2012): 994–1028.

[3.] *World Development Indicators: 2015*, World Bank, Table 3, at http://data.worldbank.org/products/wdi.

[4.] Marcella Alsan, "The Effects of the TseTse Fly on African Development," *American Economic Review*, 105 (January 2015): 382–410.

[5.] Jane G. Fortson, "Mortality Risk and Human Capital Investment: The Impact of HIV/AIDS in Sub-Saharan Africa," *Review of Economics and Statistics*, 93 (October 2011): 1–15.

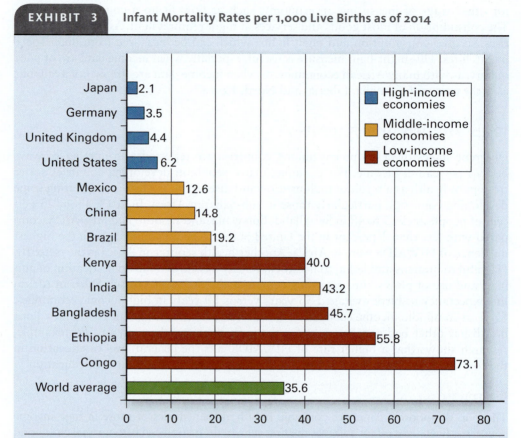

EXHIBIT 3 | **Infant Mortality Rates per 1,000 Live Births as of 2014**

Japan	2.1
Germany	3.5
United Kingdom	4.4
United States	6.2
Mexico	12.6
China	14.8
Brazil	19.2
Kenya	40.0
India	43.2
Bangladesh	45.7
Ethiopia	55.8
Congo	73.1
World average	35.6

Legend:
- High-income economies
- Middle-income economies
- Low-income economies

Source: Developed from estimates from the Central Intelligence Agency's *World Factbook: 2015,* at www.cia.gov/library/publications/the-world-factbook/index.

19-1c High Birth Rates

Developing countries are identified not only by their low incomes and high mortality rates but also by their high birth rates. In fact, the birth rate is one of the clearest ways of distinguishing between industrial and developing countries. Few low-income economies have a fertility rate below 2.2 births on average over a woman's lifetime, but no industrial market economy has a fertility rate above that level.

Exhibit 4 presents total fertility rates per woman for selected countries as of 2014. Ethiopia and the Congo, the two poorest nations on the list, each has among the world's highest fertility rates. For example, each woman in Ethiopia on average gave birth to 5.2 children during her lifetime. Note that the four low-income economies, shown as red bars, have the highest fertility rates. Historically, families tend to be larger in poor countries because children are viewed as a source of farm labor and as economic and social security as the parents age. Most developing countries have no pension or social security system for the aged. The higher child mortality rates in poorer countries also engender higher birth rates, as parents strive to ensure a sufficiently large family.

Sub-Saharan African nations are the poorest in the world and have the fastest-growing populations. Because of high fertility rates in the poorest countries, children under 15 years old make up nearly half the population there. In high-income countries, children make up less than one-fifth of the population. Italy, a high-income economy, became the

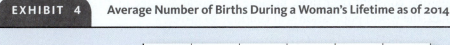

EXHIBIT 4 Average Number of Births During a Woman's Lifetime as of 2014

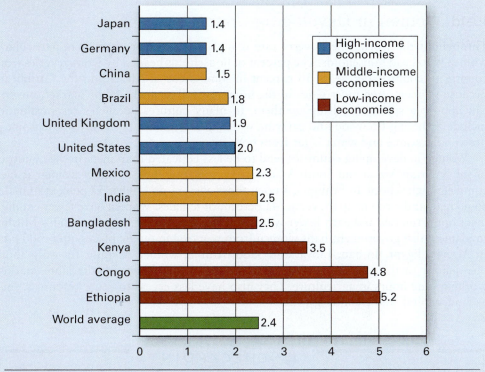

Source: Developed from estimates from the Central Intelligence Agency's *World Factbook: 2015,* at www.cia.gov/library/publications/the-world-factbook/index.html.

first country in history to have more people over the age of 65 than under the age of 15. Germany, Greece, Spain, Portugal, Japan, Hungary, Switzerland, and Canada have since followed. In the United States, 19.4 percent of the population in 2014 was under 15 years of age and 14.5 percent was 65 or older. An aging population poses fiscal problems, because these same countries typically offer generous health and pension benefits to the elderly.

Again, fertility rates are higher in developing economies than in industrial economies. The exceptions in Exhibit 4 are China and Brazil, middle-income countries with fertility rates lower than those of the United States and the United Kingdom. Fearing overpopulation, Chinese officials limit each family to one child. Brazil's fertility rate has declined due to greater urbanization, more women in the workforce, and wider availability of birth-control information.

In some developing countries, the population growth rate has exceeded the growth rate in total production, so the standard of living as measured by per capita output has declined. Still, even in the poorest of countries, attitudes about family size are changing. According to the United Nations, the birth rate during a typical woman's lifetime in a developing country has fallen from six children in 1965 to under three children today. Evidence from developing countries more generally indicates that when women have employment opportunities outside the home, fertility rates decline. And as women become better educated, they earn more and tend to have fewer children. Incidentally, after taking child mortality into account, a fertility rate of 2.1 would keep the population constant over time. Because the world average in 2014 was 2.4 births per woman, the world population will continue to grow.

19-1d Women in Developing Countries

Throughout the world, the poverty rate is higher for women than men, particularly women who head households. The percent of households headed by women varies from country to country, but nears 50 percent in some areas of Africa and the Caribbean. Because women often must work in the home as well as in the labor market, poverty can impose a special hardship on them. In many cultures, women's responsibilities include gathering firewood and carrying water, tasks that are especially burdensome if firewood is scarce and water is far from home.

Women in developing countries tend to be less educated than men. In the countries of sub-Saharan Africa and South Asia, for example, only half as many women as men complete high school. In Ethiopia, among those ages 15 and older, 57 percent of males could read and write in 2015, versus 41 percent of females. Women have fewer employment opportunities and earn lower wages than men do. For example, Sudan's Muslim fundamentalist government bans women from working in public places after 5:00 p.m. In Algeria, Egypt, Jordan, Libya, and Saudi Arabia, women account for only about one-quarter of the workforce. Women are often on the fringes of the labor market, working long hours in agriculture. They also have less access to other resources, such as land, capital, and technology.

CHECKPOINT

Besides income, identify ways that low-income economies differ from high-income economies.

19-2 Productivity: Key to Development

We have examined some signs of poverty in developing countries, but not why poor countries are poor. At the risk of appearing simplistic, we might say that poor countries are poor because they do not produce many goods and services. In this section, we examine why some developing countries experience such low productivity.

19-2a Low Labor Productivity

Labor productivity, measured in terms of output per worker, is by definition low in low-income countries. Why? Labor productivity depends on the quality of the labor and on the amount of capital, natural resources, and other inputs that combine with labor. For example, one certified public accountant with a computer and specialized software can sort out a company's finances more quickly and more accurately than can a thousand high school–educated file clerks with pencils and paper.

One way a nation raises its productivity is by investing more in human and physical capital. This investment must be financed by either domestic savings or foreign funds. Income per capita in the poorest countries is often too low to support much investment. In poor countries with unstable governments, the wealthy minority frequently invests in more stable foreign economies. This leaves less to invest domestically in either human or physical capital; without sufficient capital, workers remain less productive.

Another reason why wages are low in poor countries is that businesses are poorly run. For example, in many Indian manufacturing firms, equipment is not well maintained, employee theft is common because inventory is not well monitored, and workers are poorly trained and managed. A recent World Bank study found that offering simple management advice to Indian factories increased productivity by 20 percent.

19-2b Technology and Education

What exactly is the contribution of education to the process of economic development? Education helps people make better use of resources. If knowledge is lacking, other resources may not be used efficiently. For example, a country may be endowed with fertile land, but farmers may lack knowledge of irrigation and fertilization techniques. Or farmers may not have learned how to rotate crops to avoid soil depletion. In low-income countries, 39 percent of those 15 and older were illiterate during the period 2005 to 2009, compared to 17 percent in middle-income countries, and only 2 percent in high-income countries. Many children in developing countries drop out of school because their families can't afford it or would rather put the child to work. Child labor in developing countries obviously limits educational opportunities.

Education also makes people more receptive to new ideas and methods. Countries with the most advanced educational systems were also the first to develop. In the 20th century, the leader in schooling and economic development was the United States. In Latin America, Argentina was the most educationally advanced nation 100 years ago, and it is one of the most developed Latin American nations today. The growth of education in Japan during the 19th century contributed to a ready acceptance of technology and thus to Japan's remarkable economic growth in the 20th century.

Education is valued more in some countries than in others. For example, many teachers in Mexico are allowed to sell their tenured positions or even pass them on to their children.[6] And in India, about one-quarter of teachers in rural public schools were absent on any given day.[7]

19-2c Inefficient Use of Labor

Another feature of developing countries is that they use labor less efficiently than do industrial nations. Unemployment and underemployment reflect inefficient uses of labor. *Underemployment* occurs when skilled workers are employed in low-skill jobs or when people are working less than they would like—for example, a worker seeking full-time employment may find only a part-time job. *Unemployment* occurs when those willing and able to work can't find jobs.

Unemployment is measured primarily in urban areas, because in rural areas farm work is usually an outlet for labor even if many workers are underemployed there. The unemployment rate in developing nations on average is about 10 percent to 15 percent of the urban labor force. Unemployment among young workers—those aged 15 to 24—is typically twice that of older workers. In developing nations, about 30 percent of the combined urban and rural workforce is either unemployed or underemployed. In Zimbabwe, most people are unemployed; it's no surprise why Zimbabwe is so poor.

[6.] "Why Are Mexico's Teachers Wielding Axes?" *The Economist*, 28 April 2013.

[7.] Karthik Muralidharan et al. "The Fiscal Cost of Weak Governance: Evidence from Teacher Absences in India," NBER Working Paper No. 20299 (July 2014).

In some developing countries, the average farm is as small as two acres. Productivity is also low because few other inputs, such as capital and fertilizer, are used. *Although more than half the labor force in developing countries works in agriculture, only about one-third of output in these countries stems from agriculture.* In the United States, farmers account for only 2 percent of the labor force, but because of modern equipment one farmer can work hundreds or even thousands of acres (the average U.S. farm is about 500 acres). U.S. farmers, though only one-fiftieth of the labor force, grow enough to feed a nation and to lead the world in exports of grain, oil seeds, and cotton. The average value added per U.S. farm worker is about 75 times that of farm workers in low- and middle-income countries.

Low productivity obviously results in low income, but low income can, in turn, affect worker productivity. Low income means less saving and less saving means less investment in human and physical capital. Low income can also mean poor nutrition during the formative years, which can retard mental and physical development. These difficult beginnings may be aggravated by poor diet and insufficient health care in later life, making workers poorly suited for regular employment. Poverty can result in less saving, less education, less capital formation, a poor diet, and little health care—all of which can reduce a worker's productivity. Thus, *low income and low productivity may reinforce each other in a cycle of poverty.*

19-2d Natural Resources

Some countries are rich in natural resources. The difference is most striking when we compare countries with oil reserves and those without. The Middle East countries of Bahrain, Kuwait, Qatar, Saudi Arabia, and the United Arab Emirates are classified as high-income economies because they are lucky enough to be sitting atop huge oil reserves. But oil-rich countries are the exception. Many developing countries, such as Chad and Ethiopia, have little in the way of natural resources. Most developing countries without oil reserves are in trouble whenever oil prices rise. Since oil must be imported, higher oil prices drain oil-poor countries of precious foreign exchange.

Oil-rich countries also show us that an abundant supply of a natural resource is not in itself enough to create a modern industrial economy. On the other hand, Japan has one of the most developed economies in the world, yet has no oil reserves and little in the way of natural resources. Connecticut is consistently the most productive of the United States as measured by per capita income, but the state has few natural resources (its main natural resource is gravel). In fact, many researchers believe that reliance on resource wealth can be something of a curse for a nation, as you will read in the upcoming case study.

19-2e Financial Institutions

Another requirement for development is an adequate and trusted system of financial institutions. An important source of funds for investment is the savings of households and firms. People in some developing countries have little confidence in their currency because their governments finance a large fraction of public outlays by printing money. This practice results in high inflation and sometimes very high inflation, or hyperinflation, as has occurred recently in Zimbabwe, where annual inflation was just about incalculable. High and unpredictable inflation discourages saving and hurts development.

Developing countries have special problems because banks are often viewed with suspicion. At the first sign of trouble, many depositors withdraw their funds. Because banks cannot rely on a continuous supply of deposits, they cannot make loans for extended periods. If financial institutions fail to serve as intermediaries between savers and borrowers, the lack of funds for investment becomes an obstacle to growth. During the global financial crisis of 2008, banks in industrial market countries also suffered from depositors' sagging confidence. One measure of banking presence is the credit provided by banks as a percent of that nation's total output. This measure is more than five times greater in high-income countries than in low-income countries.

19-2f Capital Infrastructure

Production and exchange depend on a reliable infrastructure of transportation, communication, sanitation, and electricity. Roads, bridges, airports, harbors, and other transportation facilities are vital to commercial activity. Reliable mail service, telephone communications, Internet connections, clean water, and electricity are also essential for advanced production techniques. Imagine how difficult it would be to run even a personal computer if the supply of electricity and access to the Internet were unavailable or continually interrupted, as is often the case in many developing countries.

Some developing countries have serious deficiencies in their physical infrastructures. As just one measure, Exhibit 5 shows the number of mobile telephones per 100 people in 2013 for the 12 countries examined earlier. The high-income countries averaged about twice as many mobile phones per 100 people as the low-income countries. Brazil, the top rated in this category, had 135 mobile phones per 100 people. Bottom-ranked Ethiopia had just 27 mobile phones per 100 people. The world average was 93 mobile phones per 100 people. More Indians have access to mobile phones than to toilets (only

EXHIBIT 5 Mobile Phone Lines per 100 People for 2013

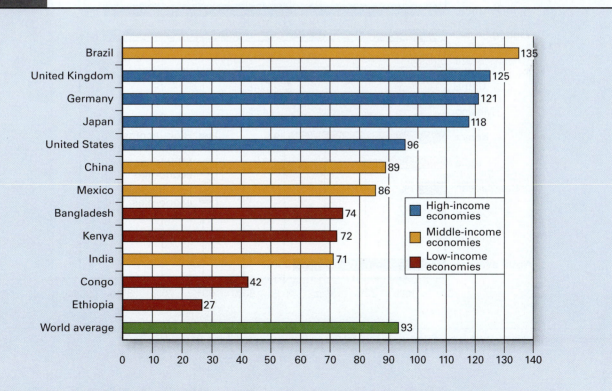

Source: The World Bank's *World Development Indicators: 2015*, Table 5, at http://data.worldbank.org/products/wdi.

about half the population has access to toilets). Incidentally, mobile phones in poor countries create opportunities to deliver education to those without access to schools. In an experiment in the African nation of Niger, those who took lessons on mobile phones tested quite well and retained what they learned.[8]

Phone lines help knit together an economy's communications network. Countries without reliable phone service have difficulty not only communicating but reaping the benefits of other technology advances, such as the Internet. Exhibit 6 shows Internet users as a percent of the population in 2013 for our sample of countries. There is an unmistakable digital divide between high-income and low-income economies. In the four high-income economies, an average 86 percent of the population used the Internet. In the four low-income economies, just 12 percent used the Internet on average. Even in India, which has a reputation as computer savvy, what with all the online support centers and software companies we read about, only 15 percent of the population were Internet users. Worldwide, 38 percent of the population used the Internet in 2013.

EXHIBIT 6   **Internet Users as Percent of Population for 2013**

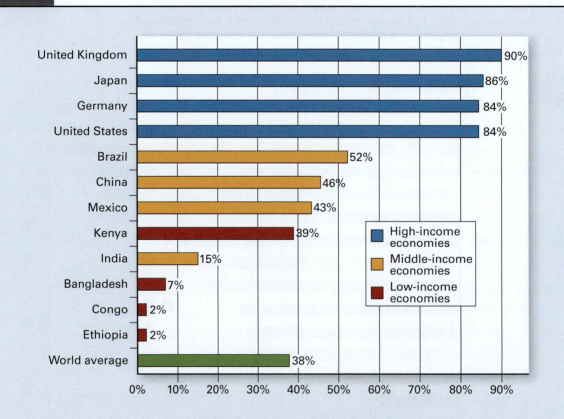

Source: The World Bank's *World Economic Indicators: 2015*, Table 4, at http://data.worldbank.org/products/wdi.

---

8. Jenny C. Aker, Christopher Ksoll, and Travis J. Lybbert, "Can Mobile Phones Improve Learning? Evidence from a Field Experiment in Niger," *American Economic Journal: Applied Economics*, 4 (October 2012): 94–120.

19-2g Entrepreneurship

An economy can have abundant supplies of labor, capital, and natural resources, but without entrepreneurship, the other resources will not necessarily be combined efficiently to produce goods and services. Unless a country has entrepreneurs who are able to bring together resources and take the risk of profit or loss, development may never get off the ground. Many developing countries were once under colonial rule, a system of government that offered the local population fewer opportunities to develop entrepreneurial skills. One sign of entrepreneurship is a willingness to become self-employed. Immigrants to the United States from developing countries are less likely to become self-employed here than are immigrants to the United States from industrial economies.[9]

One source of entrepreneurial experience for developing countries comes from McDonald's and other international franchises. For example, by providing management training, McDonald's stimulates entrepreneurship directly through its franchises and indirectly by showing competitors how a business is run. Such franchises also demonstrate to customers what they should come to expect in the way of service, cleanliness, quality, and the like.[10]

Franchise operators often face obstacles. For example, chickens from Ghana were not up to KFC's standards for quality, so franchise operators there tried to import chicken. But because Ghana's currency was relatively weak, imported chicken was too expensive. Thus, KFC is having a hard time operating n Ghana.[11]

Government officials sometimes decide that entrepreneurs are unable to generate the kind of economic growth the country needs. State enterprises are therefore created to do what government believes the free market cannot do. But state-owned enterprises may have objectives other than producing goods efficiently—objectives that could include providing jobs for friends and relatives of government officials. Also, with most state enterprises, there is little or no competition.

19-2h Rules of the Game

Finally, in addition to human capital, natural resources, financial institutions, capital infrastructure, and entrepreneurship, a successful economy needs reliable *rules of the game*. Perhaps the most elusive ingredients for development are the formal and informal institutions that promote production and exchange: the laws, customs, conventions, and other institutional elements that sustain an economy. A stable political environment with well-defined property rights is important. Little private-sector investment will occur if potential investors believe their capital might be appropriated by government, destroyed by civil unrest, blown up by terrorists, or stolen by thieves. For example, because of frequent ambushes and hijackings, many truckers have abandoned roads through Congo, South Sudan, and the Central African Republic, thereby reducing commercial opportunities for trade there.[12]

Under capitalism, the rules of the game include private ownership of most resources and the coordination of economic activity by the price signals generated by market

[9.] Ruth Uwaifo Oyelere and Willie Belton, "Coming to America: Does Having a Developed Home Country Matter for Self-Employment in the United States?" *American Economic Review,* 102 (May 2012): 538–542.

[10.] Adrian E. Tschoegl, "McDonald's—Much Maligned, But an Engine of Economic Development," *Global Economy Journal*, 7 (October 2007): 1–18.

[11.] Drew Hinshaw, "As KFC Goes to Africa, It Lacks Only One Thing: Chickens," *Wall Street Journal*, 8 February 2013.

[12.] Nicholas Bariyo, "Africa's Sugar Ambitions Turn Sour," *Wall Street Journal*, 20 October 2014.

forces. Market coordination answers the questions of what to produce, how to produce it, and for whom to produce it. Under socialism, the rules of the game include government ownership of most resources and the allocation of resources through central plans. For example, countries such as Cuba and North Korea carefully limit the private ownership of resources like land and capital. More generally, personal freedom is limited in centrally planned economies (for example, in North Korea, people need a government permit just to travel outside their own town).[13]

Although there is no universally accepted theory of economic development, around the world markets have been replacing central plans in many once-socialist countries. **Privatization** is the process of turning government enterprises into private enterprises in these transitional economies. Privatization is the opposite of *nationalization* (what the U.S. government did with airport security after 9/11, taking it away from airlines and federalizing it). For example, Russian privatization began in 1992 with the sale of municipally owned shops. Exhibit 7 presents, for 10 transitional economies, the gross domestic product (GDP) per capita in 2014 based on the purchasing power of the domestic currency. Notice the differences across these economies, with GDP per capita in the Czech Republic five times that of Vietnam.

privatization

The process of turning government enterprises into private enterprises

---

EXHIBIT   7   **GDP per Capita for Transitional Economies in 2014**

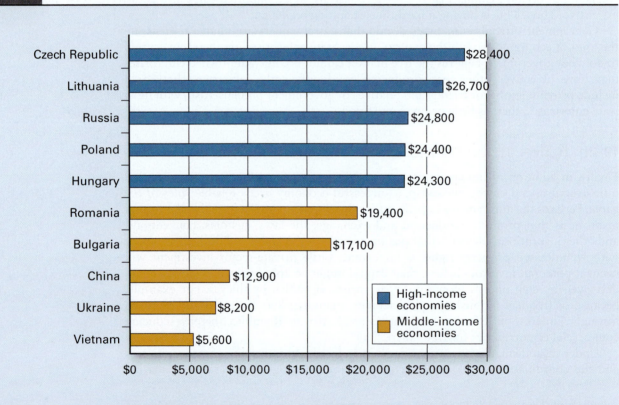

Source: Computed from estimates in the Central Intelligence Agency's *World Factbook: 2015*, at www.cia.gov/library/publications/the-world-factbook/index.html and the World Bank's *World Development Indicators: 2015*, at http://data.worldbank.org/products/wdi. Figures are based on the purchasing power of the local currency.

[13.] Peter Wonacott, "The Mystery of North Korean Fans," *Wall Street Journal*, 26 June 2010.

The Czech Republic, Lithuania, Russia, Poland, and Hungary, identified with blue bars, have joined the ranks of high-income economies. The other five are middle-income economies, and are identified with orange bars. Some of these transitional economies still reflect aspects of central planning. For example, banks in Vietnam are more likely to lend to businesses that are politically connected than to businesses that are the most profitable. Thus, the most profitable Vietnamese firms tend to avoid banks and rely instead on reinvested earnings and informal loans.[14]

But many once-communist economies are having a hard time with the transition to market economies. For example, manufacturers in Kazakhstan still have poor management practices. Such practices improve with greater privatization and more competition.[15]

Although it is common to sort countries into advanced industrial economies and developing economies, there are broad differences among developing economies, as discussed in the following case study, which looks at the billion people living in the poorest economies.

CASE STUDY

BRINGING THEORY TO LIFE

THE POOREST BILLION   Not long ago, the world was one-sixth rich and five-sixths poor. Now, thanks to impressive growth in places like China, the world is more like one-sixth rich, two-thirds not rich but improving, and one-sixth poor. Most developing economies are experiencing a rising standard of living. But that still leaves about a billion people trapped in economies that are not only extremely poor, but stagnant or getting worse. All told, about 45 countries fit into this poorest-billion category, including 30 countries in sub-Saharan Africa plus the likes of Cambodia, Haiti, Laos, Myanmar, North Korea, and Yemen.

Economist Paul Collier, of Oxford University in England, has examined what went wrong with these "trapped countries." Based on decades of research, he identifies some poverty traps. About 750 million people of the bottom billion have recently lived through, or are still in the midst of, a civil war. Such wars can drag on for years with economically disastrous consequences. For

example, the ethnic conflict in Burundi between the Hutus and the Tutsis lasted three decades, which helps explain why that country is among the poorest in the world. And war in the Congo over the last dozen years has killed more than five million people. Unfortunately, the poorer a country becomes, the more likely it is to succumb to civil war. And once a country goes through one civil war, more are likely. Researchers have found that Nigerians who were exposed to the civil war between birth and adolescence had a shorter adult stature, and this reduced their earnings and life expectancy. Ethnic conflict, or *civil war*, is Collier's first poverty trap.

But why, aside from poverty itself, are so many sub-Saharan countries mired in civil war? He finds that three factors heighten the risk of such conflicts: (1) a relatively high proportion of young, uneducated men with few job prospects (who, thus, have a low opportunity cost); (2) an imbalance between ethnic groups, with one tending to outnumber the rest; and (3) a supply of natural resources

continued

14. Edmund J. Malesky and Markus Taussig, "Where Is Credit Due? Legal Institutions, Connections, and the Efficiency of Bank Lending in Vietnam," *Journal of Law, Economics, & Organization*, 25 (October 2009): 535–578.

15. Nicholas Bloom, Helena Schweiger, and John Van Reenen, "The Land That Lean Manufacturing Forgot? Management Practices in Transition Countries," *Economics of Transition*, 20 (September 2012): 593–635.

Anadolu Agency/Getty Images

like diamonds or oil, which both creates an incentive to rebel and helps finance that rebellion. The presence of mineral wealth in an otherwise poor country can also undermine democracy itself. Government revenue from mineral sales reduces taxes, which dampens public debate about how taxes should be spent. For example, because of oil revenue, the Nigerian government relies less on taxes, so there is less pressure for government accountability, and hence fewer checks and balances on a corrupt government. Worse yet, a dictator becomes more entrenched after a natural resource windfall, such as the discovery of valuable minerals. Oil discoveries increase military spending in nondemocratic countries. Thus, *misuse of natural resource wealth* is Collier's second poverty trap. About 300 million of the poorest billion live in countries that have fallen into this trap.

This leads us to the third poverty trap: *a dysfunctional or corrupt government*. Government corruption is more prevalent in poor countries than in rich countries. Government officials who pursue self-glorification and self-enrichment do serious harm to the economy. Much of the public budget disappears through wasteful programs rife with graft and payoffs. For example, a recent survey that tracked government funds for rural health clinics in Chad found that less than 1 percent of the money reached the clinics. About 750 million of the poorest billion live in countries that pursue disastrous economic policies or where government corruption harms the economy.

Can these poorest billion be helped? It will take more than band concerts. Collier doubts that unconditional foreign aid makes much of a difference. He points to the ill effects of oil as an unconditional source of government revenue. International trade may help, but because these countries have difficulty competing with the likes of China or Vietnam, they may need special trade advantages.

Those who move from poor to rich countries usually benefit. For example, a Haitian with nine years of education could earn about eight times more in the United States than in Haiti. Is it any wonder that some risk their lives to migrate to America?

Another way the rest of the world could help is by requiring Western banks to report deposits by corrupt officials. The rest of the world could also assist these poor countries develop laws and regulations to ensure the transparent management of natural resources, to help detect fiscal fraud, and to promote a free press. But even with all that, what these countries need most, Collier argues, is about 10 years of peace—backed by an outside force if necessary, such as the UN. All that is a tall order, but the stakes are high for the billion people trapped and going nowhere in these poor nations.

Still, things may not be as grim as Collier claims. Even in sub-Saharan Africa, there is evidence of progress. Based on the ownership of durable goods, the quality of housing, the health and mortality of children, and the education of youths, sub-Saharan living standards have been growing at about 3.5 percent a year for the last two decades. That growth rate is triple the rate reflected in standard income data for these countries.

Sources: Paul Collier, *The Bottom Billion: Why the Poorest Countries Are Failing and What Can Be Done About It* (Oxford University Press, 2007); Paul Collier, *The Plundered Planet* (Oxford University Press, 2010); Antonio Cabrales and Esther Hauk, "The Quality of Political Institutions and the Curse of Natural Resources," *Economic Journal*, 121 (March 2011): 58–88; Richard Akresh et al., "War and Stature: Growing Up During the Nigerian Civil War," *American Economic Review*, 102 (May 2012): 273–277; Alwyn Young, "The African Growth Miracle," *Journal of Political Economy*, 120 (August 2012): 696–739; Aart Kraay and David McKenzie, "Do Poverty Traps Exist? Assessing the Evidence," *Journal of Economic Perspectives*, 28 (Summer 2014): 127–148; and Anca M. Cotet and Kevin K. Tsui,"Oil and Conflict: What Does the Country Evidence Really Show?" *American Economic Journal: Macroeconomics*, 5 (January 2013): 49–80.

19-2i Income Distribution Within Countries

Thus far the focus has been on income differences across countries, and these differences can be vast. But what about income differences within a country? Are poor countries uniformly poor or are there sizable income differences among that nation's population? One way to measure inequality across households is to look at the share of national income going to the poorest fifth of the population. As a point of reference, in the unlikely event that income in an economy were evenly distributed across all households, the poorest fifth would also receive exactly one-fifth, or 20 percent, of national income. More realistically, the poorest fifth receives less than 20 percent of the income, but how much less? Is the percent of income going to the poorest fifth higher for low-income countries than for high-income countries? In other words, is income more evenly distributed within poor countries than within rich countries? Not necessarily. Among our 12 nations, the poorest fifth of the population got an average of 7.7 percent of the income in the high-income countries, 5.8 percent in middle-income countries, and 7.2 percent in low-income countries. So, at least in this sample, income was less evenly distributed among middle-income countries than in high- or low-income countries.

CHECKPOINT

What factors help make workers in high-income economies more productive than workers in other economies?

19-3 International Trade and Development

Developing countries need to trade with developed countries to acquire the capital and technology that will increase labor productivity on the farm, in the factory, in the office, and in the home. To import capital and technology, developing countries must first acquire the funds, or foreign exchange, needed to pay for imports. Exports usually generate more than half of the annual flow of foreign exchange in developing countries. Foreign aid and private investment make up the rest.

19-3a Trade Problems for Developing Countries

Primary products, such as agricultural goods and other raw materials, make up the bulk of exports from developing countries, just as manufactured goods make up the bulk of exports from industrial countries. About half the merchandise exports from low-income countries consist of raw materials, compared to only 20 percent among high-income countries. A problem for developing countries is that the prices of primary products, such as coffee, cocoa, sugar, and rubber, fluctuate more widely than do the prices of finished goods, because crop yields fluctuate with the weather.

When developing countries experience trade deficits, they often try to restrict imports. Because imported food is critical to survival, developing countries are more likely to cut imports of capital goods—the very items needed to promote long-term growth and productivity. Thus, many developing countries cannot afford the modern machinery that will help workers there become more productive. Developing countries must also confront industrial countries' trade restrictions, such as tariffs and quotas, which often discriminate against primary products. For example, the United States strictly limits sugar imports and has done so for more than half a century. Such restrictions are one reason the Doha Round of trade agreements stalled.

19-3b Migration and the Brain Drain

Migration plays an important role in the economies of developing countries. A major source of foreign exchange in some countries is the money sent home by migrants who find jobs in industrial countries. Migrant workers around the world sent home about $440 billion in 2014, and that's expected to top $500 billion by 2016, according to the World Bank. For example, migrants from Mexico send home about a third of their U.S. earnings.[16] Thus migration provides a valuable safety valve for poor countries, and remittances can account for 10 percent of all income in poor countries.[17] There is evidence that migrant remittances help family members back home get more education or even start a business. But there is a downside. Often the best and the brightest professionals, such as doctors, nurses, and engineers, migrate to developed countries. For example, every year thousands of nurses migrate from countries such as Kenya and the Philippines to the United States, where half the world's nurses are employed. The financial attraction is powerful: A nurse in the Philippines would start there at less than $8,000 a year, compared with $36,000 in the United States.

So the upside of the brain drain for the poor country is the money sent home by overseas workers. What's more, recent research suggests some benefits to the country of origin when trained professionals move abroad. For example, some Indians who have migrated to the United States to work in computer technology have helped nurture India's software industry.[18] Still, a nation is usually hurt when its best and brightest leave for opportunities elsewhere. Some African countries are demanding compensation for the cost of educating the doctors and nurses who then move to high-income economies.

19-3c Import Substitution Versus Export Promotion

An economy's progress usually involves moving up the production chain from agriculture and raw material to manufacturing then to services. If a country is fortunate, this transformation occurs gradually through natural market forces. For example, in 1850 most U.S. jobs were in agriculture. Now most U.S. jobs are in the service sector. Sometimes governments try to speed up the evolution. Many developing countries, including Argentina and India, pursued a strategy called **import substitution**, whereby domestic manufacturers made products that until then had been imported. To insulate domestic manufacturers from foreign competition, the government imposed stiff tariffs and quotas. This development strategy became popular for several reasons. First, demand already existed for these products, so the "what to produce" question was easily answered. Second, import substitution provided infant industries a protected market. Finally, import substitution was popular with those who supplied resources to the favored domestic industries.

import substitution

A development strategy that emphasizes domestic manufacturing of products that up until then were imported

---

[16.] Dean Yang, "Migrant Remittances," *Journal of Economic Perspectives*, 25 (Summer 2011), p. 133.

[17.] Julian di Giovanni, Andrei Levchenko, and Francesc Ortega, "A Global View of Cross-Border Migration," *Journal of the European Economic Association*, 13 (February 2015): 168–202.

[18.] Frederic Docquier and Hillel Rapoport, "Globalization, Brain Drain, and Development," *Journal of Economic Literature*, 50 (September 2012): 681–730.

Like all trade protection, however, import substitution erased the gains from specialization and comparative advantage among countries. Often the developing country replaced low-cost foreign goods with high-cost domestic versions of those same goods. And domestic producers, shielded from foreign competition, often supplied inferior products and usually failed to become efficient. Worse still, other countries often retaliated with their own trade restrictions.

Critics of import substitution claim that export promotion is a surer path to economic development. **Export promotion** concentrates on producing for the export market. This development strategy begins with relatively simple products, such as textiles. As a developing country builds its technological and educational base—that is, as the developing economy learns by doing—producers can then make more complex products for export. Economists favor export promotion over import substitution because the emphasis is on comparative advantage and trade expansion rather than on trade restriction. Export promotion also forces producers to grow more efficient in order to compete on world markets. Research shows that facing global competition boosts domestic efficiency. What's more, export promotion requires less government intervention in the market than does import substitution.

Of the two approaches, export promotion has been more successful around the world. For example, the newly industrialized countries of East Asia have successfully pursued export promotion, while Argentina, India, and Peru have failed with their import-substitution approach. In 1965, the newly industrialized economies of Hong Kong, South Korea, Singapore, and Taiwan had an average income only 20 percent that of high-income countries. Now these four are themselves high-income countries. Most Latin American nations, which for decades had favored import substitution, are now pursuing free trade agreements with each other and with the United States. Even India is dismantling trade barriers, with an emphasis on importing high-technology capital goods. One slogan of Indian trade officials is "Microchips, yes! Potato chips, no!"

export promotion
A development strategy that concentrates on producing for the export market

19-3d Trade Liberalization and Special Interests

Although most people would benefit from freer international trade, some would be worse off. Consequently, governments in developing countries often have difficulty pursuing policies conducive to development. Often the gains from economic development are widespread, but the beneficiaries, such as consumers, do not recognize their potential gains. On the other hand, the losers tend to be concentrated, such as producers in an industry that had been sheltered from foreign competition, and they know quite well the source of their losses. So the government often lacks the political will and support to remove impediments to development, because the potential losers fight reforms that might harm their livelihood while the potential winners remain largely unaware of what's at stake. What's more, consumers have difficulty organizing even if they become aware of what's going on. A recent study by the World Bank suggests a strong link in Africa between governments that cater to special-interest groups and low rates of economic growth.

Nonetheless, many developing countries have been opening their borders to freer trade. People around the world have been exposed to information about the opportunities and products available on world markets. So consumers want the goods and firms want the technology and capital that are available abroad. Both groups want government to ease trade restrictions. Studies by the World Bank and others have underscored the successes of countries that have adopted trade liberalization policies.

CHECKPOINT

How could trade restrictions slow economic development in poorer countries?

19-4 Foreign Aid and Economic Development

We have already seen that because most poor countries do not generate enough savings to fund an adequate level of investment, these countries often rely on foreign financing. Private international borrowing and lending are heavily restricted by the governments of developing countries. Governments may allow residents to purchase foreign exchange only for certain purposes. In some developing countries, different exchange rates apply to different categories of transactions. Thus, the local currency is not easily convertible into other currencies. Some developing countries also require foreign investors to find a local partner who must be granted controlling interest. All these restrictions discourage foreign investment. In this section, we will look primarily at foreign aid and its link to economic development.

19-4a Foreign Aid

foreign aid

An international transfer made on especially favorable terms for the purpose of promoting economic development

Foreign aid is any international transfer made on especially favorable terms for the purposes of promoting economic development. Foreign aid includes grants, which need not be repaid, and loans extended on more favorable repayment terms than the recipient could normally secure. Such loans have lower interest rates, longer repayment periods, or grace periods during which repayments are reduced or even waived (similar to some student loans). Foreign aid can take the form of money, capital goods, technical assistance, food, and so forth.

Some foreign aid is granted by a specific country, such as the United States, to another specific country, such as the Philippines. Country-to-country aid is called *bilateral* assistance. Other foreign aid goes through international bodies such as the World Bank. Assistance provided by organizations that use funds from a number of countries is called *multilateral*. For example, the World Bank provides loans and grants to support activities that are viewed as prerequisites for development, such as health and education programs or basic development projects like dams, roads, and communications networks. And the International Monetary Fund extends loans to countries that have trouble with their balance of payments.

During the last four decades, the United States has provided the developing world with over $400 billion in aid. Most U.S. aid has been coordinated by the U.S. Agency for International Development (USAID), which is part of the U.S. Department of State. This agency focuses on health, education, and agriculture, providing both technical assistance and loans. USAID emphasizes long-range plans to meet the basic needs of the poor and to promote self-sufficiency. Foreign aid is a controversial, though relatively small, part of the federal budget. Since 1993, official U.S. aid has been less than 0.2 percent of U.S. GDP, compared to an average of 0.3 percent from 21 other industrialized nations.

19-4b Does Foreign Aid Promote Economic Development?

In general, foreign aid provides additional purchasing power and thus the possibility of increased investment, capital imports, and consumption. But it remains unclear whether foreign aid *supplements* domestic saving, thus increasing investment, or simply *substitutes* for domestic saving, thereby increasing consumption rather than investment. What is clear is that foreign aid often becomes a source of discretionary funds that benefit not the poor but their leaders. Historically, more than 90 percent of the funds distributed by USAID have gone to governments, whose leaders assume responsibility for distributing these funds. One goal of foreign aid seems to be to keep a friendly government in power.[19]

Much bilateral funding is tied to purchases of goods and services from the donor nation, and such programs can sometimes be counterproductive—they have unintended consequences. For example, in the 1950s, the United States began the Food for Peace program, which helped supply U.S. farm products abroad, but some recipient governments turned around and sold that food to finance poorly conceived projects. Worse yet, the availability of low-priced food from abroad drove down farm prices in the developing countries, hurting poor farmers there. The same holds for clothing. Used clothing donated to thrift shops and charitable organizations in industrialized countries typically winds up for sale in Africa, where the low price discourages local production of clothing.[20] Before used clothing swamped the continent, Africa had a textile industry, but no more. Textiles are often the first rung on the ladder to developing a broader manufacturing base.

Foreign aid may have temporarily raised the standard of living in some developing countries, but it has not necessarily increased their ability to become self-supporting at that higher standard of living. Many countries that receive aid are doing less of what they had done well. Their agricultural sectors have suffered. For example, though we should be careful when drawing conclusions about causality, per capita food production in Africa has fallen since 1960. Outside aid has often insulated public officials from their own incompetence and from the fundamental troubles of their own economies. There is also evidence that food aid increases the incidence and duration of civil conflicts in a country.[21] Most countries today that have achieved industrial status did so without foreign aid. Development success typically takes time and involves gradual movements toward freer markets.

In some cases, foreign aid has helped corrupt governments stay in power. Because of disappointment with the results of government aid, the trend is toward channeling funds through private nonprofit agencies such as CARE. More than half of foreign aid now flows through private channels. The privatization of foreign aid follows a larger trend toward privatization in transitional economies around the world.

19-4c Do Economies Converge?

If given enough time, will poor countries eventually catch up with rich ones? The **convergence** theory argues that developing countries can grow faster than advanced

convergence
A theory predicting that the standard of living in economies around the world will grow more similar over time, with poorer countries eventually catching up with richer ones

© Stephen Dorey/Alamy

19. Michael Faye and Paul Niehaus, "Political Aid Cycles," *American Economic Review*, 102 (December 2012): 3516–3530.
20. Garth Frazer, "Used-Clothing Donations and Apparel Production in Africa," *Economic Journal*, 118 (October 2008): 1764–1784.
21. Nathan Nunn and Nancy Qian, "US Food Aid and Civil Conflict," *American Economic Review*, 104 (June 2014): 1630–1666; and Benjamin Crost, Joseph Felter, and Patrick Johnston, "Aid Under Fire: Development Projects and Civil Conflicts," *American Economic Review*, 104 (June 2014): 1833–1856.

ones and should eventually close the gap. Here's why: It is easier to copy existing technology than to develop new technologies. Countries that are technologically backward can grow faster by adopting existing technology. But economies already using the latest technology must come up with a steady stream of breakthroughs to grow faster. For example, it's infinitely easier to buy a smartphone than to invent one.

Leading countries, such as the United States, find growth limited by the rate of creation of new knowledge and better technology. But follower countries can grow more quickly by, for example, adding computers where they previously had none. Until 1995, the United States, which made up about five percent of the world's population at the time, accounted for most of the world's computer purchases by households. But by 2000, most computers were bought by non-U.S. households.

What's the evidence on convergence? Between 1993 and 2012, growth in real GDP for developing countries averaged 5.4 percent per year, more than double the average for industrial countries.[22] National economies have been converging for decades, closing half the gap in the last 35 years. In 1990, 43 percent of the population in developing countries subsisted on less than $1 a day. By 2010, after adjusting for inflation, that share had fallen to 21 percent.[23] Some formerly poor countries have become high-income economies. As noted already, the newly industrialized Asian economies of Hong Kong, Singapore, South Korea, and Taiwan, by adopting the latest technology and investing in human resources, have closed the gap with the world leaders. These *Asian Tigers* have graduated from developing economies to industrial market economies. Some transitional economies have also become high-income economies. More generally, there does appear to be convergence in manufacturing productivity across a large group of developed and developing countries.[24] Even Africa has been doing better. Living standards in sub-Saharan Africa have been rising by an average of 3.5 percent per year over the last two decades.[25] Still, as discussed in the case study, as many as a billion people seem trapped in poor economies.

One reason per capita consumption has not grown faster in the poorest economies is that birth rates there are double those in richer countries, so poor economies must produce still more just to keep up with a growing population. Another reason why convergence is slow for the poorest parts of the world is the vast difference in the quality of human capital across countries. Whereas technology is indeed portable, the knowledge, skill, and training needed to take advantage of that technology are not. Common heritage seems to facilitate adoption of technology across nations. For example, some recent research finds that the closer the genetic distance between populations across nations—that is, the shorter the time since they shared common ancestors—the lower the barriers to technology adoption across nations.[26]

Countries with a high level of human capital can make up for other shortcomings. For example, much of the capital stock in Japan and Germany was destroyed during World War II. But the two countries retained enough of their well-educated and highly skilled labor force to rejoin elite industrial market economies in little more than a generation. But some countries, such as those in Africa, simply lack the human capital

[22] Anusha Chari and Peter Blair Henry, "Learning from Doers: Developing Country Lessons for Advanced Economic Growth," *American Economic Review*, 104 (May 2014): 260–265.

[23] Nicola Gennaioli et al. "Growth in Regions," *Journal of Economic Growth*, 19 (September 2014): 259–303.

[24] See Dani Rodrik, "Unconditional Convergence in Manufacturing," *Quarterly Journal of Economics*, 128 (February 2013): 165–204.

[25] Alwyn Young, "The African Growth Miracle," *Journal of Political Economy*, 120 (August 2012): 696–739.

[26] Enrico Spolaore and Romain Wacziarg, "How Deep Are the Roots of Economic Development?" *Journal of Economic Literature*, 51 (June 2013): 325–369.

needed to identify and absorb new technology. As noted already, such poor economies tend to have low education levels and low literacy rates. What's more, some countries lack the stable macroeconomic environment and the established institutions needed to nurture economic growth, such as reliable banks. Many developing countries have serious deficiencies in their infrastructures, lacking, for example, the steady source of electricity to power new technologies. In Northern Nigeria, near the Sahara, most villages have no electricity. Some of the poorest nations have been ravaged by civil war for years. And simply communicating can be challenging in some developing countries. Among Nigeria's 180 million population, for example, more than 500 languages are spoken by 250 distinct ethnic groups.

Even in the United States, with its common language, currency, and free flow of resources across state borders, large differences in productivity across states still remain. Researchers argue that little convergence has occurred among U.S. states since 1975.[27]

One final reason that convergence may take a long time is that the roots of economic development go back centuries. For example, researchers find that regions using the most advanced technologies in the year 1000 B.C. tended to remain the users of the most advanced technologies in 1500 A.D., and continue to do so today.[28]

 **CHECKPOINT**

What are some unintended consequences of foreign aid on economic development?

19-5 Conclusion

Because no single theory of economic development has become widely accepted, this chapter has been more descriptive than theoretical. We can readily identify the features that distinguish developing from industrial economies. Education is key to development, both because of its direct effect on productivity and because those who are more educated tend to be more receptive to new ideas. A physical infrastructure of transportation and communication systems and utilities is needed to link economic participants. And trusted financial institutions link savers and borrowers. A country needs entrepreneurs with the vision to move the economy forward. Finally, the most elusive ingredients are the laws, manners, customs and ways of doing business that nurture economic development. Economic history is largely a story of economies that have failed to produce a set of economic rules of the game that lead to sustained economic growth. However, some transitional economies and some newly emerging industrial countries in Asia show that economic development continues to be achievable.

[27] Chi-Young Choi and Xiaojun Wang, "Discontinuity of Output Convergence Within the United States: Why Has the Course Changed?" *Economic Inquiry*, 53 (January 2015): 49–71.

[28] Diego Comin, William Easterly, and Erick Gong, "Was the Wealth of Nations Determined in 1000 B.C.?" *American Economic Journal: Macroeconomics*, 2 (July 2010): 65–97.

Summary

1. Developing countries are distinguished by low output per capita, poor health and nutrition, high fertility rates, high infant mortality rates, poor education, and saving rates that are usually too low to finance sufficient investment in human and physical capital.

2. Worker productivity is low in developing countries because the stocks of human and physical capital are low, technological advances are not widely diffused throughout the economy, entrepreneurship is scarce, firms are poorly run, financial markets are not well developed, some talented professionals migrate to high-income countries, formal and informal institutions do not provide sufficient incentives for market activity, and governments may serve the interests of the group in power rather than the public interest.

3. The key to a rising standard of living is increased productivity. To foster productivity, developing nations must stimulate investment, support education and training programs, provide sufficient infrastructure, and foster supportive rules of the game.

4. Increases in productivity do not occur without prior saving, but low incomes in developing countries offer less opportunity to save. Even if some higher-income households in poor countries have the money to save, financial institutions are not well developed, and savings are often sent abroad, where there is a more stable investment climate.

5. Import substitution is a development strategy that emphasizes domestic production of goods that were imported. Export promotion concentrates on producing for the export market. Over the years, export promotion has been more successful than import substitution because it relies on specialization, comparative advantage, and competition.

6. Foreign aid has been a mixed blessing for most developing countries. In some cases, that aid has helped countries build the roads, bridges, schools, and other capital infrastructure necessary for development. In other cases, foreign aid has simply increased consumption and insulated government from painful but necessary economic reforms. Worse still, subsidized food and used clothing from abroad have undercut domestic production and economic development, particularly in Africa.

7. Convergence is a theory predicting that the standard of living around the world will grow more alike as poorer countries catch up with richer ones. Some Asian countries and some transitional economies that had been poor have caught up with the leaders, and many countries have moved up from the lower-income category, but some poor countries around the world have failed to close the gap.

Key Concepts

Questions for Review

1. **Developing Countries**   Why is agricultural productivity in developing countries usually so low?

2. **Worlds Apart**   Compare developing and industrial market economies on the basis of each of the following general economic characteristics, and relate the differences to the process of development:

   a. Diversity of the industrial base
   b. Infant mortality rates
   c. Educational level of the labor force

3. **Birth Rates**   Why is the birth rate in low-income countries higher than in high-income countries?

4. **Productivity and Development**   Among the problems that hinder growth in developing economies are poor infrastructure, lack of financial institutions and a sound money supply, a low saving rate, poor capital base, and lack of foreign exchange. Explain how these problems are interconnected.

5. **Privatization**   How has privatization contributed to productivity?

6. **Classification of Economies**   What are the arguments for using real per capita income to compare living standards between countries? What weakness does this measure have?

7. **Case Study: The Poorest Billion**   What three poverty traps help explain the plight of nations comprising the poorest billion people?

8. **Foreign Aid and Economic Development**   Foreign aid, if it is to be successful in enhancing economic development, must lead to a more productive economy. Describe some of the problems in achieving such an objective through foreign aid.

9. **International Trade and Development** From the perspective of citizens in a developing country, what are some of the benefits and drawbacks of international trade?

10. **Foreign Aid and Economic Development** It is widely recognized that foreign aid that promotes productivity in developing economies is superior to merely shipping consumer goods like food and clothing to these countries. Yet the latter is the approach frequently taken. Why do you think this is the case?

11. **Convergence** Explain the convergence theory. Under what circumstances is economic convergence less likely to occur?

Problems and Exercises

12. **Worlds Apart** Per capita income most recently was 78 times greater in the United States than in the Congo. Suppose income per capita grows an average of 3 percent per year in the United States and 6 percent per year in the Congo. Assuming such growth rates continue indefinitely into the future, how many years would it take before per capita income in the Congo exceeds that of the United States? (To simplify the math, suppose at the outset per capita income is $78,000 in the richer country and $1,000 in the poorer country.)

13. **Import Substitution Versus Export Promotion** Explain why domestic producers who supply a good that competes with imports would prefer an import-substitution approach to trade policy rather than an export-promotion approach. Which policy would domestic consumers prefer and why?

ability-to-pay tax principle Those with a greater ability to pay, such as those earning higher incomes or those owning more property, should pay more taxes

absolute advantage The ability to make something using fewer resources than other producers use

adverse supply shocks Unexpected events that reduce aggregate supply, sometimes only temporarily

aggregate demand The relationship between the economy's price level and aggregate output demanded, with other things constant

aggregate demand curve A curve representing the relationship between the economy's price level and real GDP demanded per period, with other things constant

aggregate expenditure Total spending on final goods and services in an economy during a given period, usually a year; the sum of consumption, investment, government purchases, and net exports

aggregate expenditure line A relationship tracing, for a given price level, spending at each level of income, or real GDP; the total of $C + I + G + (X - M)$ at each level of income, or real GDP

aggregate income All earnings of resource suppliers in an economy during a given period, usually a year

aggregate output A composite measure of all final goods and services produced in an economy during a given period; real GDP

aggregate supply curve A curve representing the relationship between the economy's price level and real GDP supplied per period, with other things constant

American Recovery and Reinvestment Act At an estimated cost of $831 billion, the largest stimulus measure in U.S history; enacted in February 2009

annually balanced budget Budget philosophy prior to the Great Depression; aimed at matching annual revenues with outlays, except during times of war

antitrust laws Prohibitions against price fixing and other anticompetitive practices

applied research Research that seeks answers to particular questions or to apply scientific discoveries to develop specific products

arbitrageurs Someone who takes advantage of tiny differences in the exchange rate across markets by simultaneously purchasing currency in one market and selling it in another market

asset Anything of value that is owned

association-is-causation fallacy The incorrect idea that if two variables are associated in time, one must necessarily cause the other

asymmetric information A situation in which one side of the market has more reliable information than the other side

autarky National self-sufficiency; no economic interaction with foreigners

automatic stabilizers Structural features of government spending and taxation that reduce fluctuations in disposable income, and thus consumption, over the business cycle

balance of payments A record of all economic transactions during a given period between residents of one country and residents of the rest of the world

balance on current account The portion of the balance-of-payments account that measures a country's balance on goods and services, net investment income from abroad, plus net unilateral transfers abroad

balance on goods and services The portion of a country's balance-of-payments account that measures the value of a country's exports of goods and services minus the value of its imports of goods and services

balance sheet A financial statement at a given point in time showing assets on one side and liabilities plus net worth on the other side; because assets must equal liabilities plus net worth, the two sides of the statement must balance, hence the name

bank branches A bank's additional offices that carry out banking operations

bank holding company A corporation that owns banks

bank notes Originally, pieces of paper promising a specific amount of gold or silver to anyone who presented them to issuing banks for redemption; today, Federal Reserve notes are mere paper money

barter The direct exchange of one product for another without using money

base year The year with which other years are compared when constructing an index; the index equals 100 in the base year

basic research The search for knowledge without regard to how that knowledge will be used

behavioral assumptions An assumption that describes the expected behavior of economic decision makers—what motivates them

beneficial supply shocks Unexpected events that increase aggregate supply, sometimes only temporarily

benefits-received tax principle Those who get more benefits from the government program funded by the tax should pay more of that tax

bilateral agreement Trade agreement between two countries

budget resolution A congressional agreement about total outlays, spending by major category, and expected revenues; it guides spending and revenue decisions by the many congressional committees and subcommittees

capital The buildings, equipment, and human skills used to produce goods and services

capital deepening An increase in the amount of capital per worker; one source of rising labor productivity

chain-weighted system An inflation measure that adjusts the weights from year to year in calculating a price index, thereby reducing the bias caused by a fixed-price weighting system

checkable deposits Bank deposits that allow the account owner to write checks to third parties; debit cards can also access these deposits and transmit them electronically

checks A written order instructing the bank to pay someone from an amount deposited

circular-flow model A diagram that traces the flow of resources, products, income, and revenue among economic decision makers

classical economists A group of 18th- and 19th-century economists who believed that economic downturns corrected themselves through natural market forces

coincident economic indicators Variables that reflect peaks and troughs in economic activity as they occur; examples include employment, personal income, and industrial production

COLA Cost-of-living adjustment; an increase in wages or transfer payments tied to increases in the price level

cold turkey The announcement and execution of tough measures to reduce high inflation

commercial banks Depository institutions that historically made short-term loans, primarily to businesses

commodity money Anything that serves both as money and as a commodity; money that has intrinsic value such as gold or silver coins

common market Group of countries that have few or no trade restrictions with one another

comparative advantage The ability to make something at a lower opportunity cost than other producers face

complements Goods, such as Pepsi and pizza, that relate in such a way that an increase in the price of one shifts the demand for the other leftward

consumer price index, or CPI A measure of inflation based on the cost of a fixed market basket of goods and services

consumption Household purchases of final goods and services, except for new residences, which count as investment

consumption function The relationship in the economy between consumption and income, other things constant

continuing resolutions Budget agreements that allow agencies, in the absence of an approved budget, to spend at the rate of the previous year's budget

contraction A period during which the economy declines as reflected by falling output, employment, income, and other aggregate measures

contractionary fiscal policy A decrease in government purchases, increase in net taxes, or some combination of the two aimed at reducing aggregate demand enough to return the economy to potential output without worsening inflation; fiscal policy used to close an expansionary gap

convergence A theory predicting that the standard of living in economies around the world will grow more similar over time, with poorer countries eventually catching up with richer ones

cooperative An organization consisting of people who pool their resources to buy and sell more efficiently than they could individually

coordination failure A situation in which workers and employers fail to achieve an outcome that all would prefer

corporation A legal entity owned by stockholders who share any profit but whose liability is limited to the value of their stock ownership

cost-push inflation A sustained rise in the price level caused by a leftward shift of the aggregate supply curve

crowding in The potential for government spending to stimulate private investment in an otherwise dead economy

crowding out The displacement of interest-sensitive private investment that occurs when higher government deficits drive up market interest rates

currency appreciation With respect to the dollar, a decrease in the number of dollars needed to purchase one unit of foreign exchange in a flexible rate system

currency depreciation With respect to the dollar, an increase in the number of dollars needed to purchase one unit of foreign exchange in a flexible rate system

cyclical unemployment Unemployment that fluctuates with the business cycle, increasing during recessions and decreasing during expansions

cyclically balanced budget A budget philosophy calling for budget deficits during recessions to be financed by budget surpluses during expansions

debit card Card that taps directly into a depositor's bank account to buy something and often to get cash back; also called a check card

debt ceiling A limit on the total amount of money the federal government can legally borrow

decision-making lag The time needed to decide what to do once a macroeconomic problem has been identified

deflation A sustained decrease in the price level

demand A relation between the price of a good and the quantity that consumers are willing and able to buy per period, other things constant

demand curve A curve showing the relation between the price of a good and the quantity consumers are willing and able to buy per period, other things constant

demand for money The relationship between the interest rate and how much money people choose to hold

demand-pull inflation A sustained rise in the price level caused by a rightward shift of the aggregate demand curve

demand-side economics Macroeconomic policy that focuses on shifting the aggregate demand curve as a way of promoting full employment and price stability

depository institutions Commercial banks and thrift institutions; financial institutions that accept deposits from the public

depreciation The value of capital stock used up to produce GDP or that becomes obsolete during the year

depression A severe and prolonged reduction in economic activity, as occurred during the 1930s

devaluation An increase in the official pegged price of foreign exchange in terms of the domestic currency

developing countries Countries with a lower living standard because of less human and physical capital per worker; low-income and middle-income economies; most are also known as emerging market economies

discount rate The interest rate the Fed charges banks that borrow reserves

discouraged workers Those who drop out of the labor force in frustration because they can't find work

discretionary fiscal policy The deliberate manipulation of government purchases, taxation, and transfer payments to promote macroeconomic goals, such as full employment, price stability, and economic growth

disequilibrium The condition that exists in a market when the plans of buyers do not match those of sellers; a temporary mismatch between quantity supplied and quantity demanded as the market seeks equilibrium

disinflation A reduction in the rate of inflation

disposable income, *DI* The income households have available to spend or to save after paying taxes and receiving transfer payments

division of labor Breaking down the production of a good into separate tasks

Dodd-Frank Wall Street Reform and Consumer Protection Act Sweeping regulatory changes in 2010 aimed at preventing another financial crisis

Doha Round The multilateral trade negotiation round launched in 2001, but still unsettled as of 2015; the first trade round under the WTO

double coincidence of wants Two traders are willing to exchange their products directly

double counting The mistake of including both the value of intermediate products and the value of final products in calculating gross domestic product; counting the same production more than once

dumping Selling a product abroad for less than charged in the home market or for less than the cost of production

economic fluctuations The rise and fall of economic activity relative to the long-term growth trend of the economy; also called business cycles

economic growth An increase in the economy's ability to produce goods and services; reflected by an outward shift of the economy's production possibilities frontier

economic model A simplification of reality used to make predictions about cause and effect in the real world

economic system The set of mechanisms and institutions that resolve the what, how, and for whom questions

economic theory A simplification of reality used to make predictions about cause and effect in the real world

economics The study of how people use their scarce resources to satisfy their unlimited wants

economy The structure of economic activity in a community, a region, a country, a group of countries, or the world

effectiveness lag The time needed for changes in monetary or fiscal policy to affect the economy

efficiency The condition that exists when there is no way resources can be reallocated to increase the production of one good without decreasing the production of another; getting the most from available resources

Employment Act of 1946 Law that assigned to the federal government the responsibility for promoting full employment and price stability

entitlement programs Guaranteed benefits for those who qualify for government transfer programs such as Social Security and Medicare

entrepreneur A profit-seeking decision maker who starts with an idea, organizes an enterprise to bring that idea to life, and assumes the risk of the operation

entrepreneurial ability The imagination required to develop a new product or process, the skill needed to organize production, and the willingness to take the risk of profit or loss

equation of exchange The quantity of money, M, multiplied by its velocity, V, equals nominal GDP, which is the product of the price level, P, and real GDP, Y; or $M \times V = P \times Y$

equilibrium The condition that exists in a market when the plans of buyers match those of sellers, so quantity demanded equals quantity supplied and the market clears

excess reserves Bank reserves exceeding required reserves

exchange rate The cost measured in one country's currency of one unit of another country's currency

expansion A period during which the economy grows as reflected by rising output, employment, income, and other aggregate measures

expansionary fiscal policy An increase in government purchases, decrease in net taxes, or some combination of the two aimed at increasing aggregate demand enough to reduce unemployment and return the economy to its potential output; fiscal policy used to close a recessionary gap

expansionary gap The amount by which actual output in the short run exceeds the economy's potential output

expenditure approach Calculating GDP by adding up spending on all final goods and services produced in the nation during the year

fallacy of composition The incorrect belief that what is true for the individual, or part, must necessarily be true for the group, or the whole

federal budget A plan for federal government outlays and revenues for a specified period, usually a year

federal budget deficit A flow variable measuring the amount by which federal government outlays exceed federal government revenues in a particular period, usually a year

federal debt A stock variable that measures the net accumulation of annual federal deficits

federal funds market A market for overnight lending and borrowing of reserves among banks; the interbank market for reserves on account at the Fed

federal funds rate The interest rate charged in the federal funds market; the interest rate banks charge one another for overnight borrowing; the Fed's target interest rate

Federal Open Market Committee (FOMC) The 12-member group that makes decisions about open-market operations—purchases and sales of U.S. government securities by the Fed that affect the money supply and interest rates; consists of the 7 Board governors plus 5 of the 12 presidents of the Reserve banks

Federal Reserve System The central bank and monetary authority of the United States

fiat money Money not redeemable for any commodity; its status as money is conferred initially by government decree but eventually by common experience

final goods and services Goods and services sold to final, or end, users

financial account The record of a country's international transactions involving purchases and sales of financial and real assets

financial intermediaries Institutions such as banks, mortgage companies, and finance companies, that serve as go-betweens by borrowing from savers to lend to borrowers

financial markets Banks and other financial institutions that facilitate the flow of funds from savers to borrowers

firms Economic units formed by profit-seeking entrepreneurs who employ resources to produce goods and services for sale

fiscal policy The use of government purchases, transfer payments, taxes, and borrowing to influence economy-wide variables such as inflation, employment, and economic growth

fixed exchange rates Rate of exchange between currencies pegged within a narrow range and maintained by the central bank's ongoing purchases and sales of currencies

flow variable A measure of something per period of time, such as your spending per week

foreign aid An international transfer made on especially favorable terms for the purpose of promoting economic development

foreign exchange Foreign money needed to carry out international transactions

fractional reserve banking system Bank reserves amount to only a fraction of funds on deposit with the bank

frictional unemployment Unemployment that occurs because job seekers and employers need time to find each other

full employment Employment level when there is no cyclical unemployment

functional finance A budget philosophy using fiscal policy to achieve the economy's potential GDP, rather than balancing budgets either annually or over the business cycle

GDP The market value of all final goods and services produced in the nation during a particular period, usually a year

GDP price index A comprehensive inflation measure of all goods and services included in the gross domestic product

General Agreement on Tariffs and Trade (GATT) An international tariff-reduction treaty adopted in 1947 that resulted in a series of negotiated "rounds" aimed at freer trade

gold standard An arrangement whereby the currencies of most countries were convertible into gold at a fixed rate

good A tangible product used to satisfy human wants

government purchases Spending for goods and services by all levels of government; government outlays minus transfer payments

gross domestic product, or GDP The market value of all final goods and services produced in the nation during a particular period, usually a year

gross world product The market value of all final goods and services produced in the world during a given period, usually a year

hyperinflation A very high rate of inflation

hypothesis A theory about how key variables relate

hysteresis The theory that the natural rate of unemployment depends in part on the recent history of unemployment; a long period of high unemployment can increase the natural rate of unemployment

implementation lag The time needed to introduce a change in monetary or fiscal policy

import substitution A development strategy that emphasizes domestic manufacturing of products that up until then were imported

income approach Calculating GDP by adding up all earnings from resources used to produce output in the nation during the year

income effect of a price change A fall in the price of a good increases consumers' real income, making consumers more able to purchase goods; for a normal good, the quantity demanded increases

income-expenditure model A relationship that shows how much people plan to spend at each income level; this model identifies, for a given price level, where the amount people plan to spend equals the amount produced in the economy

individual demand The relation between the price of a good and the quantity purchased per period by an individual consumer, other things constant

individual supply The relation between the price of a good and the quantity an individual producer is willing and able to sell per period, other things constant

industrial market countries Economically advanced capitalist countries of Western Europe, North America, Australia, New Zealand, and Japan, plus the newly industrialized Asian economies of Taiwan, South Korea, Hong Kong, and Singapore

industrial policy The view that government— using taxes, subsidies, and regulations—should nurture the industries and technologies of the future, thereby giving these domestic industries an advantage over foreign competition

Industrial Revolution Development of large-scale factory production that began in Great Britain around 1750 and spread to the rest of Europe, North America, and Australia

inferior good A good, such as used clothes, for which demand decreases, or shifts leftward, as consumer income rises

inflation An increase in the economy's average price level

inflation target Commitment of central bankers to keep inflation at or below a certain rate for the next year or two

Information Revolution Technological change spawned by the microchip and the Internet that enhanced the acquisition, analysis, and transmission of information

injection into the circular flow Any spending other than by households or any income other than from resource earnings; includes investment, government purchases, exports, and transfer payments

interest Payment to resource owners for the use of their capital; the dollar amount paid by borrowers to lenders

interest rate Interest per year as a percentage of the amount saved or borrowed

intermediate goods and services Goods and services purchased by firms for further reprocessing and resale

International Monetary Fund (IMF) An international organization that establishes rules for maintaining the international monetary system and makes loans to countries with temporary balance-of-payments problems

inventories Producers' stocks of finished and in-process goods

investment The purchase of new plants, new equipment, new software, new buildings, and new residences, plus net additions to inventories

labor The physical and mental human effort used to produce goods and services

labor force Those 16 years of age and older who are either working or looking for work

labor force participation rate The labor force as a percentage of the adult population

labor productivity Output per unit of labor; measured as real GDP divided by the hours of labor employed to produce that output

lagging economic indicators Variables that follow, or trail, changes in overall economic activity; examples include the interest rate, the unemployment rate, and the average duration of unemployment

law of comparative advantage The individual, firm, region, or country with the lowest opportunity cost of producing a particular good should specialize in that good

law of increasing opportunity cost To produce more of one good, a successively larger amount of the other good must be sacrificed

law of supply The amount of a good that producers are willing and able to sell per period is usually directly related to its price, other things constant

leading economic indicators Variables that predict, or *lead to*, a recession or recovery; examples include consumer confidence, stock market prices, business investment, and big-ticket purchases, such as automobiles and homes

leakages from the circular flow Any diversion of income from the domestic spending stream; includes saving, taxes, and imports

legal tender Currency that constitutes a valid and legal offer of payment

liability Anything that is owed to other people or institutions

life-cycle model of consumption and saving Young people borrow, middle agers pay off debt and save, and older people draw down their savings; on average, net savings over a lifetime is usually little or nothing

liquidity A measure of the ease with which an asset can be converted into money without a significant loss of value

long run In macroeconomics, a period during which wage contracts and resource price agreements can be renegotiated; there are no surprises about the economy's actual price level

long-run aggregate supply (LRAS) curve A vertical line at the economy's potential output; aggregate supply when there are no surprises about the price level and all resource contracts can be renegotiated

long-run equilibrium In macroeconomics, the price level and real GDP that occur when (1) the actual price level equals the expected price level, (2) real GDP supplied equals potential output, and (3) real GDP supplied equals real GDP demanded

long-run Phillips curve A vertical line drawn at the economy's natural rate of unemployment tracing equilibrium points that can occur when workers and employers have the time to adjust fully to any unexpected change in aggregate demand

long-term unemployed Those looking for work for 27 weeks or longer

M1 The narrow measure of the money supply, consisting of currency and coins held by the nonbanking public, checkable deposits, and traveler's checks

M2 A money aggregate consisting of M1 plus savings deposits, small-denomination time deposits, money market mutual funds, and other near-monies

macroeconomics The study of the economic behavior of entire economies, as measured, for example, by total production and employment

managed float system An exchange rate system that combines features of freely floating rates with sporadic intervention by central banks

marginal Incremental, additional, or extra; used to describe a change in an economic variable

marginal propensity to consume (MPC) The fraction of a change in income that is spent on consumption; the change in consumption divided by the change in income that caused it

marginal propensity to save (MPS) The fraction of a change in income that is saved; the change in saving divided by the change in income that caused it

marginal tax rate The percentage of each additional dollar of income that goes to the tax

market demand The relation between the price of a good and the quantity purchased per period by all consumers in the market, other things constant; sum of the individual demands in the market

market failure A condition that arises when the unregulated operation of markets yields socially undesirable results

market supply The relation between the price of a good and the quantity all producers in the market are willing and able to sell per period, other things constant

markets A set of arrangements by which buyers and sellers carry out exchange at mutually agreeable terms

medium of exchange Anything that facilitates trade by being generally accepted by all parties in payment for goods or services

mercantilism The incorrect theory that a nation's economic objective should be to accumulate precious metals in the public treasury; this theory prompted trade barriers, which cut imports, but other countries retaliated, reducing trade and the gains from specialization

merchandise trade balance The value during a given period of a country's exported goods minus the value of its imported goods

microeconomics The study of the economic behavior in particular markets, such as that for computers or for unskilled labor

mixed system An economic system characterized by the private ownership of some resources and the public ownership of other resources; some markets are regulated by government

monetary policy Regulation of the money supply to influence economy-wide variables such as inflation, employment, and economic growth

money Anything that is generally accepted in exchange for goods and services

money aggregates Measures of the economy's money supply

money income The number of dollars a person receives per period, such as $400 per week

money market mutual fund A collection of short-term interest-earning assets purchased with funds collected from many shareholders

money multiplier The multiple by which the money supply changes as a result of a change in fresh reserves in the banking system

monopoly A sole supplier of a product with no close substitutes

mortgage-backed security A claim on payments made on the many mortgages bundled into this financial instrument

movement along a demand curve A change in quantity demanded resulting from a change in the price of the good, other things constant

movement along a supply curve Change in quantity supplied resulting from a change in the price of the good, other things constant

MPC The fraction of a change in income that is spent on consumption; the change in consumption divided by the change in income that caused it

MPS The fraction of a change in income that is saved; the change in saving divided by the change in income that caused it

multilateral agreement Trade agreement among more than two countries

national debt The net accumulation of federal budget deficits

natural monopoly One firm that can supply the entire market at a lower per-unit cost than could two or more firms

natural rate hypothesis The natural rate of unemployment is largely independent of the stimulus provided by monetary or fiscal policy

natural rate of unemployment The unemployment rate when the economy produces its potential output

natural resources All gifts of nature used to produce goods and services; includes renewable and exhaustible resources

net domestic product Gross domestic product minus depreciation

net exports The value of a country's exports minus the value of its imports

net investment income from abroad Investment earnings by U.S. residents from their foreign assets minus investment earnings by foreigners from their assets in the United States

net taxes, NT Taxes minus transfer payments

net unilateral transfers abroad The unilateral transfers (gifts and grants) received from abroad by U.S. residents minus the unilateral transfers U.S. residents send abroad

net wealth The value of assets minus liabilities

net worth Assets minus liabilities; also called owners' equity

nominal GDP GDP based on prices prevailing at the time of production

nominal interest rate The interest rate expressed in dollars of current value (that is, not adjusted for inflation) as a percentage of the amount loaned; the interest rate specified on the loan agreement

nominal wage The wage measured in dollars of the year in question; the dollar amount on a paycheck

normal good A good, such as new clothes, for which demand increases, or shifts rightward, as consumer income rises

normative economic statement A statement that reflects an opinion, which cannot be proved or disproved by reference to the facts

not-for-profit organizations Groups that do not pursue profit as a goal; they engage in charitable, educational, humanitarian, cultural, professional, or other activities, often with a social purpose

open-market operations Purchases and sales of government securities by the Fed in an effort to influence the money supply and interest rates

open-market purchase The purchase of U.S. government bonds by the Fed to increase the money supply

open-market sale The sale of U.S. government bonds by the Fed to reduce the money supply

opportunity cost The value of the best alternative forgone when an item or activity is chosen

other-things-constant assumption The assumption, when focusing on the relation among key economic variables, that other variables remain unchanged; in Latin, *ceteris paribus*

partnership A firm with multiple owners who share the profits and bear unlimited liability for the firm's losses and debts

per-worker production function The relationship between the amount of capital per worker in the economy and average output per worker

permanent income Income that individuals expect to receive on average over the long term

Phillips curve A curve showing possible combinations of the inflation rate and the unemployment rate

physical capital Manufactured items used to produce goods and services; includes new plants and new equipment

political business cycle Economic fluctuations that occur when discretionary policy is manipulated for political gain

positive economic statement A statement that can be proved or disproved by reference to facts

potential output The economy's maximum sustainable output, given the supply of resources, technology and know-how, and rules of the game; the output level when there are no surprises about the price level

price ceiling A maximum legal price above which a product cannot be sold; to have an impact, a price ceiling must be set below the equilibrium price

price floor A minimum legal price below which a product cannot be sold; to have an impact, a price floor must be set above the equilibrium price

price index A number that shows the average price of products; changes in a price index over time show changes in the economy's average price level

price level A composite measure reflecting the prices of all goods and services in the economy relative to prices in a base year

private goods A good, such as pizza, that is both rival in consumption and exclusive

private property rights An owner's right to use, rent, or sell resources or property

privatization The process of turning government enterprises into private enterprises

product market A market in which a good or service is bought and sold

production A process that transforms resources into goods and services

production possibilities frontier, or PPF A curve showing alternative combinations of goods that can be produced when available resources are used efficiently; a boundary line between inefficient and unattainable combinations

productivity The ratio of a specific measure of output, such as real GDP, to a specific measure of input, such as labor; in this case productivity measures real GDP per hour of labor

profit Reward for entrepreneurial ability; sales revenue minus resource cost

progressive taxation The tax as a percentage of income increases as income increases

proportional taxation The tax as a percentage of income remains constant as income increases; also called a flat tax

public good A good that, once produced, is available for all to consume, regardless of who pays and who doesn't; such a good is nonrival and nonexclusive, such as a safer community

purchasing power parity (PPP) theory The idea that the exchange rate between two countries will adjust in the long run to equalize the cost of a basket of internationally traded goods

pure capitalism An economic system characterized by the private ownership of resources and the use of prices to coordinate economic activity in unregulated markets

pure command system An economic system characterized by the public ownership of resources and centralized planning

quantitative easing Fed purchases of long-term assets to stabilize financial markets, reduce long-term interest rates, and improve the investment environment

quantity demanded The amount of a good consumers are willing and able to buy per period at a particular price, as reflected by a point on a demand curve

quantity supplied The amount offered for sale per period at a particular price, as reflected by a point on a supply curve

quantity theory of money If the velocity of money is stable, or at least predictable, changes in the money supply have predictable effects on nominal GDP

quotas A legal limit on the quantity of a particular product that can be imported or exported

rational expectations A school of thought that argues people form expectations based on all available information, including the likely future actions of government policy makers

rational self-interest Each individual tries to maximize the expected benefit achieved with a given cost or to minimize the expected cost of achieving a given benefit

real GDP The economy's aggregate output measured in dollars of constant purchasing power

real GDP per capita Real GDP divided by the population; the best measure of an economy's standard of living

real gross domestic product The economy's aggregate output measured in dollars of constant purchasing power

real income Income measured by the goods and services it can buy; real income changes when the price changes

real interest rate The interest rate expressed in dollars of constant purchasing power as a percentage of the amount loaned; the nominal interest rate minus the inflation rate

real wage The wage measured in dollars of constant purchasing power; the wage measured in terms of the quantity of goods and services it buys

recession A period of decline in economic activity lasting more than a few months, as reflected by falling output, employment, income, and other aggregate measures

recessionary gap The amount by which actual output in the short run falls short of the economy's potential output

recognition lag The time needed to identify a macroeconomic problem and assess its seriousness

regressive taxation The tax as a percentage of income decreases as income increases

rent Payment to resource owners for the use of their natural resources

required reserve ratio The ratio of reserves to deposits that banks are obligated by regulation to hold

required reserves The dollar amount of reserves a bank is obligated by regulation to hold as cash in the bank's vault or on account at the Fed

reserves Funds that banks use to satisfy the cash demands of their customers and the reserve requirements of the Fed; reserves consist of cash held by banks plus deposits at the Fed

residential construction Building new homes or dwelling places

resource markets A market in which a resource is bought and sold

resources The inputs, or factors of production, used to produce the goods and services that people want; consist of labor, capital, natural resources, and entrepreneurial ability

revaluation A reduction in the official pegged price of foreign exchange in terms of the domestic currency

rules of the game The laws, customs, manners, conventions, and other institutional elements that determine transaction costs and thereby affect people's incentive to undertake production and exchange

savings deposits Bank deposits that earn interest but have no specific maturity date

scarcity Occurs when the amount people desire exceeds the amount available at a zero price

seasonal unemployment Unemployment caused by seasonal changes in the demand for certain kinds of labor

secondary effects Unintended consequences of economic actions that may develop slowly over time as people react to events

sequestration Automatic cuts to certain categories of federal spending enacted in 2011 to reduce the growth of federal spending from 2012 to 2021

service An activity, or intangible product, used to satisfy human wants

shadow banking system Financial institutions, such as mortgage companies and brokerage firms, that do not rely on customer deposits to make loans

shift of a demand curve Movement of a demand curve right or left resulting from a change in one of the determinants of demand other than the price of the good

shift of a supply curve Movement of a supply curve left or right resulting from a change in one of the determinants of supply other than the price of the good

short run In macroeconomics, a period during which some resource prices, especially those for labor, remain fixed by explicit or implicit agreements

short-run aggregate supply (SRAS) curve A curve that shows a direct relationship between the actual price level and real GDP supplied in the short run, other things constant, including the expected price level

short-run equilibrium In macroeconomics, the price level and real GDP that result when the aggregate demand curve intersects the short-run aggregate supply curve

short-run Phillips curve Based on an expected inflation rate, a curve that reflects an inverse relationship between the inflation rate and the unemployment rate

shortage At a given price, the amount by which quantity demanded exceeds quantity supplied; a shortage usually forces the price up

simple money multiplier The reciprocal of the required reserve ratio, or $1/r$; the maximum multiple of fresh reserves by which the money supply can increase

simple spending multiplier The ratio of a change in real GDP demanded to the initial change in spending that brought it about; the numerical value of the simple spending multiplier is $1/(1 - MPC)$; called "simple" because only consumption varies with income

social capital The shared values and trust that promote cooperation in the economy

sole proprietorship A firm with a single owner who has the right to all profits but who also bears unlimited liability for the firm's losses and debts

specialization of labor Focusing work effort on a particular product or a single task

speculators Someone who buys or sells foreign exchange in hopes of profiting from fluctuations in the exchange rate over time

stagflation A contraction, or stagnation, of a nation's output accompanied by inflation in the price level

stock variable A measure of something at a point in time, such as the amount of money you have with you right now

store of value Anything that retains its purchasing power over time

stress test Bank regulators assessed the soundness of large banks to determine which ones needed more financial capital to weather a bad economy

structural unemployment Unemployment because (1) the skills demanded by employers do not match those of the unemployed, or (2) the unemployed do not live where the jobs are

subprime mortgage Mortgage for a borrower with a not-so-good credit rating

substitutes Goods, such as tacos and pizza, that relate in such a way that an increase in the price of one shifts the demand for the other rightward

substitution effect of a price change When the price of a good falls, that good becomes cheaper compared to other goods, making consumers more willing to substitute that good for other goods

sunk cost A cost that has already been incurred, cannot be recovered, and thus is irrelevant for present and future economic decisions

supply A relation between the price of a good and the quantity that producers are willing and able to sell per period, other things constant

supply curve A curve showing the relation between price of a good and the quantity producers are willing and able to sell per period other things constant

supply shocks Unexpected events that affect aggregate supply, sometimes only temporarily

supply-side economics Macroeconomic policy that focuses on a rightward shift of the aggregate supply curve through tax cuts or other changes to increase production incentives

surplus At a given price, the amount by which quantity supplied exceeds quantity demanded; a surplus usually forces the price down

tariffs A tax on imports

tastes Consumer preferences; likes and dislikes in consumption; assumed to remain constant along a given demand curve

tax incidence The distribution of tax burden among taxpayers; who ultimately pays the tax

terms of trade How much of one good exchanges for a unit of another good

thrift institutions Savings banks and credit unions; depository institutions that historically lent money to households

time deposits Bank deposits that earn a fixed interest rate if held for the specified period, which can range from several months to several years; also called certificates of deposit

time-inconsistency problem When policy makers have an incentive to announce one policy to influence expectations but then pursue a different policy once those expectations have been formed and acted on

token money Money whose face value exceeds its cost of production

too big to fail A financial institution becomes so large and so interconnected with other financial institutions that its failure would be disastrous for the wider economy; its collapse must be prevented even if that requires a bailout

transaction costs The costs of time and information required to carry out market exchange

transfer payments Cash or in-kind benefits given to individuals by the government

Troubled Asset Relief Program, or TARP Government program that invested in financial institutions and automakers to help stabilize these markets

underemployment Workers are overqualified for their jobs or work fewer hours than they would prefer

underground economy Market activity that goes unreported either because it is illegal or because those involved want to evade taxes

unemployment benefits Cash transfers to those who lose their jobs and actively seek employment

unemployment rate The number unemployed as a percentage of the labor force

unit of account A common unit for measuring the value of each good or service

Uruguay Round The final multilateral trade negotiation under GATT; this 1994 agreement cut tariffs, formed the World Trade Organization, and will eventually eliminate quotas

utility The satisfaction received from consumption; sense of well-being

value added At each stage of production, the selling price of a product minus the cost of intermediate goods purchased from other firms

variable A measure, such as price or quantity, that can take on different values at different times

velocity of money The average number of times per year each dollar is used to purchase final goods and services

wages Payment to resource owners for their labor

world price The price at which a good is traded on the world market; determined by the world demand and world supply for the good

World Trade Organization (WTO) The legal and institutional foundation of the multilateral trading system that succeeded GATT in 1995